BASIC
Programming with the IBM PC®
Second Edition

Brooks/Cole Series in Computer Science

BASIC
Programming with the IBM PC®
Second Edition

Peter Mears
University of Louisville

Brooks/Cole Publishing Company
Pacific Grove, California

To the continuing memories of Dr. John Mead,
Distinguished Professor of Economics.

John is a fine professor and a very close friend. And at the
time of my writing this book, he is much alive and in good
health. Anyway, I know he's in good health, and I think he's
alive. But there again, it's so hard to tell with an economist.

Brooks/Cole Publishing Company
A Division of Wadsworth, Inc.

Printed in the United States of America

10 9 8 7 6 5 4 3 2

Library of Congress Cataloging in Publication Data

Mears, Peter, [date]
    Basic programming with the IBM PC/Peter Mears.—2nd ed.
        p. cm.
    Includes index.
    ISBN 0-534-12156-X
    1. IBM Personal Computer—Programming.   2. BASIC (Computer program
language) I. Title.
    QA76.8.I2594M428   1989
    005.265—dc20   89-30443
                                                                          CIP

Sponsoring Editor: Michael Sugarman
Editorial Assistant: Mary Ann Zuzow
Production Editor: Linda Loba
Manuscript Editor: Robert Burdette
Permissions Editor: Carline Haga
Interior Design: Roy Neuhaus
Interior Illustration: Carl Brown
Cover Design and Illustration: Roy Neuhaus
Art Coordinator: Lisa Torri
Typesetting: Bi-Comp, Inc.
Cover Printing: Phoenix Color Corporation
Printing and Binding: Arcata Graphics/Kingsport

PREFACE

Is it possible that somebody, somewhere, exists who has not heard about microcomputers? Unless they live on a remote island and are cut off from all human contact, I doubt it. Computers are becoming more and more commonplace and are constantly mentioned in the daily news. Yet despite this widespread exposure, many people do not know how to program a microcomputer. This is unfortunate.

This book can help you learn how to program the IBM Personal Computer (or IBM compatible computer). We will be using a form of the BASIC language called Microsoft BASIC which is an excellent language for beginners because it contains many easy-to-remember terms. This book is written simply, in a clear, concise style. Each chapter introduces key concepts in bold print, along with examples that demonstrate their application. In addition, programming suggestions are provided throughout the book to help you avoid troublesome points.

This book won't let you down. If you are willing to study the text and work through the problems at the end of the chapters, you will learn how to program in BASIC. Some concepts, such as DOS, are given an entire chapter, with each command demonstrated for reinforcement. A lot can be learned by simply making the programs shown in the book work to your satisfaction.

There are over 750 programming exercises and two dozen cases in this second edition. Programming exercises use a structured guidance technique: partial programs are given and the student must complete the programs to produce the required output. Then general instructions are given and the student is asked to write their own programs to produce the output shown. As the student progresses through the exercises, the prompts are selectively removed. This reduces the "where do I start?" anxiety that bothers many students, and the initial difficulty encountered in creating a computer program is thus minimized.

Mini-cases simulate projects that a programmer may be assigned in a real business environment. These cases are intended as the capstone to the learning that has occurred during the course, because they provide an opportunity to program a comprehensive project, using any of the techniques presented in the text.

In addition to presenting the concepts in an easy-to-absorb manner, this book contains a removable pocket guide. This convenient programming aid enables you to look up key BASIC statements at a glance. Last, but not least, is the companion diskette included with the book. This diskette contains extensive tutorials and data files. The tutorials reinforce key concepts in the book including tutorials on:

- How to use the keyboard
- Assigning values to variables
- BASIC and DOS commands
- Decision statements
- Repeating operations
- Using tables
- Sorting data

The data files on the companion diskette will be used to unleash the power of the computer so that the student does not have to spend hours keying in data. That is, the files provide the data so that students can concentrate on program development.

Then, after you learn the fundamentals of programming, comes the fun part. Let your imagination take over and use your own ideas to develop your own custom applications.

You will need the following:

- This book.
- Access to an IBM Personal Computer (or compatible) which should have at least 128K of memory.
- At least a single diskette drive (either single- or double-sided).
- A master disk containing MS DOS. The IBM DOS diskette can be used—version 2.X or above.
- If you have a dual-drive system or if a printer is available, so much the better, but it is not required.
- If the companion diskette is available, you will be able to run the educational tutorials and you will not have to key in data files. Many problems at the end of the chapters require this diskette.
- The companion diskette is not copy-protected. You are encouraged to make a backup copy and modify the programs for your own application. Refer to Appendix C for detailed instructions on copying this diskette and making it self-starting.
- Several blank diskettes will be needed to store your own programs. These diskettes can be used later for other applications if desired.

ACKNOWLEDGMENTS

Particular thanks are due to the following people who helped in developing this book:

Mr. Mike McCabe and Ms. Tomoko Able who developed many of the chapter problems.
Mr. Richard Hardesty and Mr. John Giles who developed several of the educational tutorials on the companion diskette.

Thanks also go to the reviewers of this book: Professor Robert Barrett, Indiana University-Purdue at Fort Wayne; Professor Robert Bergner, Rockford College, Rockford, Illinois; Dr. Raymond Fadous, University of Michigan-Flint; Professor Kathe Gardner, Lamar University, Beaumont, Texas; Professor Gary Locklair, Concordia College, Mequon, Wisconsin; Professor Josephine Muth, Cedar Grove, New Jersey; and Professor Ralph Szweda, Rochester, New York.

Finally, thanks are due to the fine editorial staff at Brooks/Cole: Mr. Mike Sugarman for his suggestions and Ms. Linda Loba for her attention to detail.

Peter Mears

CONTENTS

8 REFINING PROGRAMMING SKILLS 147

9 GETTING STARTED IN USING FILES 163

10 PROGRAM CONTROL STATEMENTS: BEGINNING 180

11 ADVANCED PROGRAM CONTROL 210

17 PUTTING IT ALL TOGETHER   373

18 SEQUENTIAL FILES   394

19 PROCESSING SEQUENTIAL FILES   412

GETTING STARTED

Upon completion of this chapter you should be able to

- Type the keyboard characters
- Understand the concept of a computer program
- Run a program stored on diskette

Programming is not difficult to learn if you remember that the computer cannot think and requires very precise instructions to perform its tasks. The computer's power arises from its ability to follow these instructions (called a program) correctly and rapidly.

A computer is an electronic device capable of performing operations (calculation, memory storage, and memory retrieval) very quickly. A *microcomputer* is fundamentally similar to its big brother, the *mainframe* computer, except that technical advances in electronics have reduced size and cost of the microcomputer. Of course, a microcomputer cannot perform all the functions of a large computer, such as handling airline reservations, but it is, nevertheless, a powerful device.

A program is a series of statements that tells the computer what to do. In writing a computer program, often called *coding*, the programmer combines letters, numbers, and special symbols into program statements, following the rules of a computer language. These program statements are grouped together to create a program. BASIC is a widely used programming language because so many of its terms are easy-to-remember English words.

As shown in Figure 1.1, a computer system consists of a keyboard, output display (monitor or printer), storage device (diskette or tape), and the central processing unit with memory.

The keyboard is the primary data entry device and will be discussed separately in the next section. The "brain" of the computer is the central processing unit, often called the CPU. The CPU is one or more electronic chips that control the computer's operations, including storing and retrieving data from memory.

The computer's memory is composed of several electronic chips that work extremely fast, performing operations in a millionth of a second. (It takes about one-thousandth of a second to wink your eye.) This tremendous speed gives the "micro" its power and usefulness. It can quickly perform those repetitive clerical tasks you always hated to do. However, the computer is electronic, so when it is turned off, anything in memory is erased (lost).

1

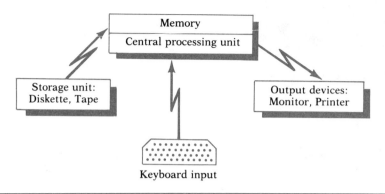

FIGURE 1.1   Components of a computer system

Programs or data to be used again should be stored on tape or diskette. Diskettes are a particularly convenient method of storage because they are easy to use and have a large storage capacity.

Microcomputer diskettes come in two major sizes: 5¼″ and 3½″. The 5¼″ diskette holds about 360,000 characters, which initially was considered to be a lot of data. As technology improved, diskette size was reduced and storage capacity increased. Typical storage capacity of a 3½″ diskette is 720,000 characters, although high-density devices are capable of storing and retrieving many times that amount.

A floppy disk is a reliable storage medium, provided that a few precautions are followed.

- Handle diskette with care. Bending may damage it.
- Store in its protective envelope when not in use.
- Handle the diskette from its plastic carrier; do not touch the inner diskette surface.
- Do not remove a diskette when the disk drive is running, as damage might occur to it. The small red in-use light appears when the drive is in operation, and a whirring sound also can be heard.
- Keep food, tobacco smoke, and drinks away from both diskette and computer. Spills and smoke can damage the equipment and the diskette.
- Keep diskette away from magnetic fields to avoid data loss.

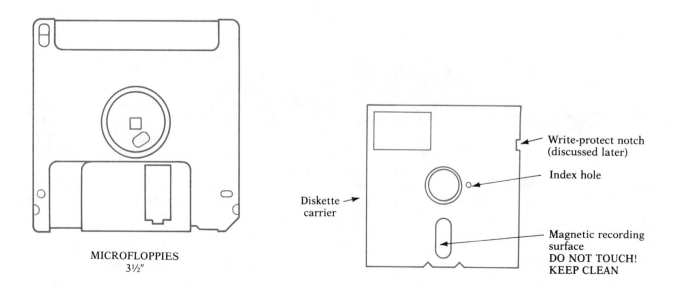

MICROFLOPPIES
3½″

Diskette carrier

Write-protect notch (discussed later)

Index hole

Magnetic recording surface
DO NOT TOUCH!
KEEP CLEAN

THE KEYBOARD

Program statements are typed into the microcomputer via a movable typewriter-like keyboard as shown in Figure 1.2. Although the computer's keyboard is similar to an electric typewriter's keyboard, there are a few differences, particularly the location of the Enter key. The Enter key is on the right-hand side of the keyboard next to the numeric keypad.

The Enter key, shown as ⏎ in Figure 1.2, is similar to the carriage return on a typewriter; when pressed, it causes the cursor (a dash) to return to the left edge of the screen. The cursor shows where the next character will appear. When a key is pressed, the computer simply displays what was typed and takes no action until the Enter key is pressed. It is often confusing to beginners that, if Enter is not pressed, the computer does nothing even though instructions are clearly displayed on the monitor. For example, if you type the BASIC command LOAD "ASSETS" (where ASSETS is the name of a program stored on diskette), no action is taken until you press Enter. Once you press Enter, the program called ASSETS is read and loaded into the computer's memory.

The Shift keys are the two keys near the bottom row of the keyboard that are pressed to obtain uppercase symbols. Using the keyboard diagram, locate the two Shift keys, shown as ⇧ .

Some keys have more than one symbol on them. When a key is pressed, the lowercase symbol appears on the screen unless the Caps Lock key is on or the Shift key is pressed. The upper symbol on these keys is obtained by holding a Shift key down with one finger and pressing the desired symbol with another finger.

The Caps Lock key and the Num Lock (Numeric Lock) key can be confusing. Once the Caps Lock key has been pressed, pressing other keys normally yields all uppercase letters. An exception occurs when the Shift key is pressed with the Caps Lock key on: letters change to lowercase! Likewise, pressing the Num Lock key normally permits numeric data to be entered via the numeric keypad on the right-hand side of the keyboard. However, the numeric keys return to their use as cursor control keys if the Shift key is held down. A few other keys may also be confusing. As shown

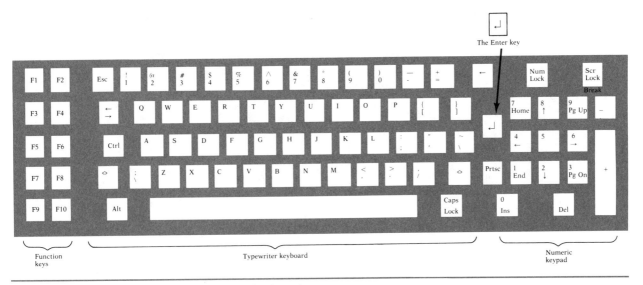

FIGURE 1.2 The IBM personal computer keyboard

in the keyboard diagram, the digits 0 through 9 (on the top row) are also on the numeric keypad. The top row can be used for numeric entry if the keypad is being used for cursor control.

Be careful when entering data, because the computer requires exact input. For example, if a program requires a digit, but a letter or special symbol is typed, an error will occur. Be careful not to type the letter O for the number 0 (zero), and do not use the letter l (small L) for the number 1. They might look the same to us, but the computer recognizes them as entirely different characters.

Unfortunately, mistakes will occur when typing. If the mistake is noticed before the Enter key is pressed, the Backspace key $\boxed{\leftarrow}$ can be used to move the cursor backward. As the cursor moves back (left on the screen), it deletes characters. You can type the desired characters and, when everything is correct, press the Enter key. Don't worry; typing errors cannot harm the computer.

> Remember, the computer requires exact input. Do not use letters when numbers are required. The letter l may look the same as the number 1, but the computer recognizes them as entirely different characters.

The Backspace key

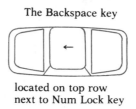

located on top row
next to Num Lock key

If a line has a hopeless number of errors, press the $\boxed{\text{Esc}}$ key. This is the Escape key; it deletes the entire line, which can then be retyped. The section on editing presents other error-correction techniques which are not needed as yet (see Chapter 8).

The Escape key

located on left of top row

> When learning how to use the computer, do not worry about making an error. Nothing can be typed on the keyboard that can damage the computer.

Again, remember that you cannot harm the computer while typing, so do not worry about making an error. Just use normal typing strokes. Press the keys with an easy, gentle typing pressure, just as you would on an electric typewriter. Do not jab or pound the keys. In BASIC, the Enter key must be pressed after typing a line to enter data into the computer's memory so that action can be taken.

STARTING THE SYSTEM

Starting the system consists of inserting the IBM-DOS diskette (the system diskette that came with the computer), turning on the computer, entering the date and time, and, finally, loading the appropriate programs.

    1. A typical IBM microcomputer, diskette drive, and monitor are shown in Figure 1.3. Begin the procedure of starting the system with the computer turned off.

    2. Raise the flap on the diskette drive and insert the IBM-DOS

FIGURE 1.3 IBM microcomputer. Right (top to bottom): keyboard, disk drive, monitor, printer. Left: IBM PC in use. (*Photos courtesy of Judy Blamer*)

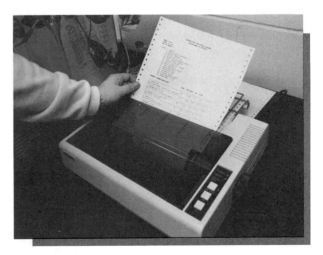

diskette with the label faceup. If a dual-drive system is used, insert the diskette in drive A, which is the drive on the left. The right-hand drive is drive B.

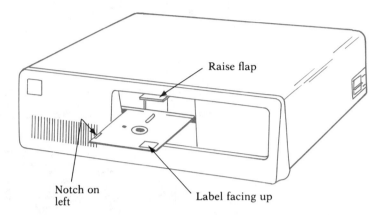

3. Close the flap on the diskette drive to secure the disk.

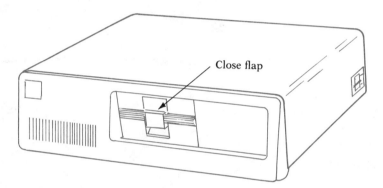

4. Turn the computer on. The switch is often located on the right-hand side of the console, toward the back.

The computer will hesitate a moment while checking memory and circuits. The fan will turn on, and the diskette drive will make a "grunting" sound as it comes on. Then a short beep can be heard after the computer completes its self-test of internal components.

5. Next, a request for the current date will appear. Type the current date in the form of 12/15/90 (for December 15, 1990). Then press the Enter key.

6. You will then be prompted for the current time. Type the time in the form of 9:30 (for 9:30 A.M.) or 14:30 (for 2:30 P.M.). Then press the Enter key. Steps 5 and 6 can be skipped by pressing Enter twice, but the time and date designation for the diskette files will be the time and date shown on the screen rather than the correct time and date.

7. The monitor will now display the prompt A>, which indicates that the Disk Operating System (DOS) has been loaded and that the current drive is A. DOS is the "traffic cop" of the system and is needed before a program can be executed.

Return the DOS diskette to its protective envelope. This completes the start-up procedure, often called "booting the system."

THE MENU SELECTION PROGRAM

Insert the companion diskette in drive A. Then, with the A> prompt displayed, type START and press the Enter key. A copy of a program called START.EXE stored on diskette will be retrieved, loaded into memory, and executed. If an error message appears, carefully retype the command. The screen will then appear as shown in Figure 1.4.

FIGURE 1.4 Introduction screen

You may wish to make the companion diskette self-loading by following the instructions in the Appendix. Once the necessary system files are transferred to the companion diskette, a shortcut can be taken by simply inserting the diskette and performing a system restart by pressing the Ctrl (Control), Alt (Alternate), and Del (Delete) keys at the same time. The screen will then appear as shown in Figure 1.4.

Now press any key, and the program selection menu will appear as shown in Figure 1.5. Many tutorials have several subprograms that can be run independently. This feature enables you to re-run either the entire tutorial or the subprogram for additional practice.

The program selection arrow is residing on the tutorial to introduce you to the IBM keyboard. You could press the space bar to select a differ-

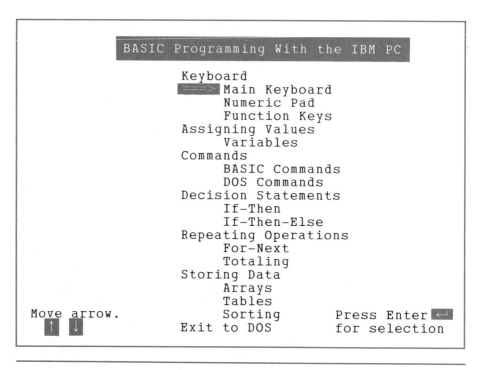

```
 ┌─────────────────────────────────────────────────────────────┐
 │        ▐ BASIC Programming With the IBM PC ▌                 │
 │                                                              │
 │                    Keyboard                                  │
 │              ▐===>▌ Main Keyboard                            │
 │                    Numeric Pad                               │
 │                    Function Keys                             │
 │              Assigning Values                                │
 │                    Variables                                 │
 │              Commands                                        │
 │                    BASIC Commands                            │
 │                    DOS Commands                              │
 │              Decision Statements                             │
 │                    If-Then                                   │
 │                    If-Then-Else                              │
 │              Repeating Operations                            │
 │                    For-Next                                  │
 │                    Totaling                                  │
 │              Storing Data                                    │
 │                    Arrays                                    │
 │                    Tables                                    │
 │  Move arrow.       Sorting         Press Enter ◄┘            │
 │   ▐↑▌ ▐↓▌    Exit to DOS           for selection            │
 └─────────────────────────────────────────────────────────────┘
```

FIGURE 1.5   Program selection menu

If there is a point you do not understand in one of the tutorials, then re-run the tutorial. You be the judge as to when you want to go to the next tutorial and when you want to quit.

ent tutorial, but, since this is the tutorial we want, press the Enter key. The program will be loaded from the diskette into memory and executed. The screen will then appear as shown in Figure 1.6.

Answer the questions as called for by the program. Re-run the keyboard tutorials until you feel comfortable with the topic presented. After completion of the keyboard tutorials, you be the judge as to whether you should run the remaining tutorials before or after reading a chapter. When you are through with the tutorials (or for that matter any diskette) return the diskette to its protective storage envelope.

Later on we will write our own programs in BASIC. This will be accomplished by loading the BASIC interpreter from the system diskette into memory by typing BASICA (for Advanced BASIC). However, for the moment let's just run the programs on diskette that will help us learn programming. These programs have been compiled (converted into machine language), so do not require that you load the BASIC interpreter into memory.

```
 ┌──────────────────────────────────────────────┐
 │                                              │
 │      BASIC Programming With the IBM PC       │
 │            ▐ Main Keyboard ▌                 │
 │                                              │
 │                   By                         │
 │               Peter Mears                    │
 │           (c) Copyright 1990                 │
 │                                              │
 │                                              │
 │  Press Enter                      ▐◄┘▌       │
 └──────────────────────────────────────────────┘
```

FIGURE 1.6   The keyboard program

SUMMARY

You have come a long way in this chapter. You have become familiar with the keyboard, learned how to start the system, and have learned how to execute a compiled program.

Nice going! We will direct our attention to writing our own BASIC programs in the next chapter.

The keyboarding programs stored on the diskette that is a companion to this book have a lot of built-in error-trapping routines. Deliberately make some errors in this controlled environment and observe what happens.

PROBLEMS

True/False. Problems 1–12.

1.1 Computers need precise instruction to perform tasks. T

1.2 A diskette can be used to store data for years after the computer is turned off. T

1.3 The Enter key is similar to the carriage return on a typewriter. T

1.4 A programmer writes general program instructions, and the computer figures out the specifics when the program is run. F

1.5 The letter O and the number 0 (zero) appear identical to the computer. F

1.6 The keyboard is the primary data entry device. T

1.7 DOS does not have to be in the computer if we are going to program in BASIC. F

1.8 Nothing typed via the keyboard will damage the computer.

1.9 The programs on the companion disk should not be run until one knows how to write programs. F

1.10 Pressing the Num Lock key changes the numeric pad so that it can be used for cursor control, or from cursor control back to being a numeric pad. T

1.11 The uppercase symbol on a key cannot be displayed without pressing the Shift key. T

1.12 The typist may type either the numeric 1 or the lowercase letter l as a shortcut when entering data. F

Other Problems. Problems 13–16 require the use of the DOS system master and the companion diskette.

1.13 Perform the following activities: (1) boot the system and (2) run the keyboarding programs on the companion diskette.

1.14 Boot the system with the DOS system master in drive A. When requested, enter the current date and time. Then remove the system master from drive A, and place the companion diskette in the drive. Type START and press Enter. What happened? What appeared on the screen?

1.15 With the program selection menu shown, Exit to DOS. With the A> prompt shown, type MAINKEY and press Enter. What happened? What appeared on the screen?

1.16 With the program selection menu shown, Exit to DOS. With the A> prompt shown, type NUMERIC and press Enter. What happened? What appeared on the screen?

Have you run the program on the numeric pad? Do it and observe the effect of the Num Lock (Numeric Lock) key. Particularly note what happens if it is not pressed when requested by the program.

PROGRAM DEVELOPMENT

Upon completion of this chapter you should be able to

- Follow the program development cycle
- Develop a top-down program design
- Develop a hierarchical chart
- Flowchart a problem
- Understand structured programming
- Develop variable names
- Assign values to variables by the direct assignment method
- Write a program

An orderly approach is needed in developing programs to assure that they are logical and easy to maintain. Notice the emphasis on the program development process, not just on writing a program. In fact, it is strongly suggested that you resist the urge to write code until you have analyzed the problem and developed a plan to solve it.

The program development process consists of the following six steps, each of which is discussed in this chapter:

1. Analyze the problem. The result should be a clear understanding of the problem.
2. Develop a hierarchical chart. This chart shows the logical modules needed to solve the problem.
3. Specify the detailed steps within a module. Either pseudocode or flowcharting can be used.
4. Code the program following structured programming guidelines.
5. Test and debug the program.
6. Train users and document the program.

The program development process is shown in Figure 2.1.

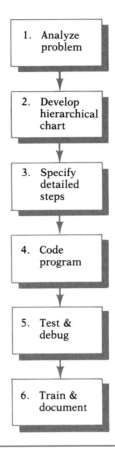

FIGURE 2.1 Program development process

STEP 1   ANALYZE THE PROBLEM

Many people are aware of the precise instructions needed to write a computer program. As a result, there is a tendency for the beginner to "jump into a problem" and immediately begin coding. The problem with this approach is that lack of planning results in poorly written programs that are difficult to understand and are prone to errors. At this point you are trying to develop an understanding of *what* is to be done. After you have gained a full understanding of what is needed, then your attention can be directed to *how* to do it, that is, to writing the program code.

The *top-down* approach to program design consists of beginning with the overall problem and breaking it down into simpler components. For example, suppose we wanted a program to print a paycheck. This program consists of three distinct components that perform a single function. These single-function components are called modules which, in this case, are:

Input the necessary data
Compute the employee's pay
Print the paycheck

That is, we start at the top (the overall problem) and work downward until we have broken the problem into a set of manageable modules. Again, please remember when using this top-down approach, think first, program later. The more time you spend on defining output and developing an overall solution, the easier the programming task will become.

One technique to encourage a logical, top-down program design is to draw the major modules in the form of boxes. Our payroll problem is shown in Figure 2.2.

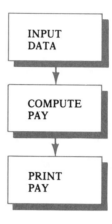

FIGURE 2.2   Top-down program design

STEP 2   DEVELOP A HIERARCHICAL CHART

After developing a top-down analysis, take a closer look at the modules. There are normally "hidden" hierarchical relationships within the problem. For example, what submodules are required within the module to compute pay? In order to calculate pay, data will be required from multiple sources. For example, hours worked may be entered via the keyboard, but hourly rate will more likely be input from a master file that also contains the employee's hourly rate and deductions such as health insurance. In addition, we will have to check a history file of what the employee has been paid to date to keep the IRS (Internal Revenue Service) happy.

A hierarchical chart of the input data module is shown in Figure 2.3. Each module can be quite complex and could be broken down again.

A complex process such as writing a payroll program becomes more manageable after dividing the problem into reasonably sized modules. The hierarchical chart shows the relationship between the main modules and the second-level modules. These second-level modules will become program subroutines.

Once a problem has been broken down into a logical set of hierarchically arranged modules, we have defined what should be done. Attention can then be directed to how to do it by identifying the specific program logic that will be required within each module.

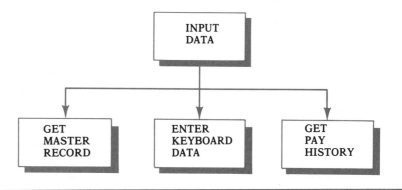

FIGURE 2.3   Top-down program hierarchical chart

STEP 3   SPECIFY THE DETAILED STEPS WITHIN A MODULE

There are two ways of defining the specific logic steps within a module. The first is to write out a brief description of the specific action to be taken in each module. Such descriptions are called *pseudocode* because they are not true programming code but are brief statements written in English.

The second way is to use *flowcharts*. Flowcharts graphically show the steps, in sequence, that are required to solve a problem. Given today's emphasis on top-down design and structured programming techniques, many programmers feel that flowcharts are not necessary. A flowchart is, in fact, a useful planning tool that graphically shows program logic.

When developing a flowchart, arrange the single modules required to solve a problem in the order that they will be performed. Connect each module with a line, including arrows, to show the direction of logic. Follow this flowchart when coding the program.

To prevent the flowchart from becoming too lengthy, complete PRINT statements are often not specified. When necessary, explanations are written to the right of the flowchart in legend-like format to explain variables or flowcharting steps.

The following are two of the symbols used when flowcharting:

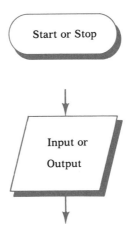

One example of an INPUT statement is

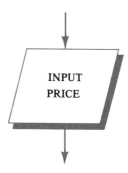

Descriptions may be enclosed inside a flowchart symbol:

Values are assigned to variables by using a rectangle:

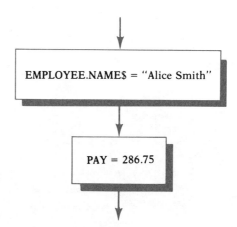

A decision is a comparison with a yes or a no answer to identify the desired paths of logic to be followed. Think of a train going down a track, where the track is a path of logic. This can be visualized as follows:

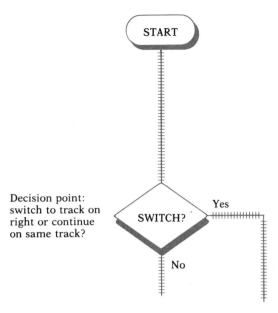

A decision point is a switch requiring a yes or no answer to this question: Do we switch tracks or continue on the same track? If the train switches to another track (another portion of the program), entirely different scenery (processing) may be encountered. Decision points are flowcharted using a diamond symbol and are programmed using an IF-THEN statement, which will be explained in Chapter 10.

When flowcharting decision points, the variable name used in the comparison is stated inside the diamond symbol. For example, if you want to decide if a sale is greater than 100, the comparison is flowcharted as shown below. (The symbol > means greater than.)

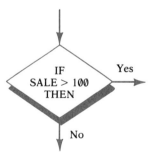

If SALE is greater than the value of 100, the logic track takes us to the right (where perhaps a bonus gift would be awarded). On the other hand, if SALE is not greater than 100, we follow the track of logic downward.

The symbols presented can be used to create a detailed flowchart that shows the steps required to solve a problem. For example, suppose a firm had a lengthy listing of its employees. This list contains each employee's name, age, sex, and income. Our problem is to read this list, identify the female employees who are between 20 and 35 years old, and print their names and incomes.

A flowchart to accomplish this is shown. The variable names are E.NAME$, AGE, SEX$, and INCOME. These variable names represent the employee's name, age, sex, and income. A complete explanation of the various steps in the flowchart is contained in Chapter 12.

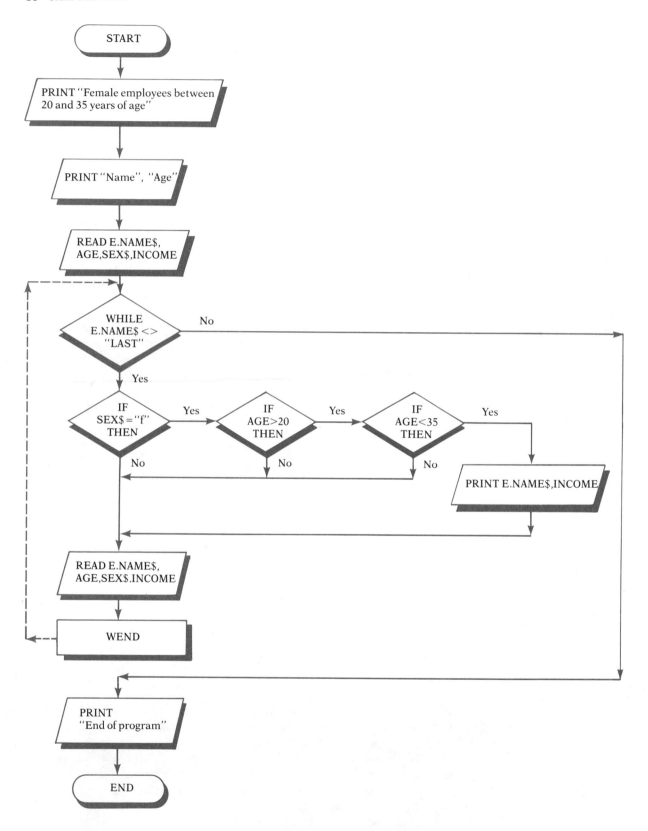

STEP 4   CODE THE PROGRAM FOLLOWING STRUCTURED PROGRAMMING GUIDELINES

A method of coding programs is needed so that the program code will be logical and easy to follow. This technique is called *structured programming*.

There should be only one entry point to, and one exit point from, each module. Following this rule permits each block of statements to be debugged separately, and it reduces errors.

The fundamental concept of structured programming is that any program can be written using only three major components:

1. Simple sequence, which is carrying out action in a statement-by-statement order;
2. Selection, which involves using a decision statement to select a path of logic; and
3. Loop control (repetition), which consists of carrying out action repeatedly.

The selection sequence consists of operations carried out one after the other. In the payroll example, you might encounter the following sequence of statements:

The selection (decision) statement permits either of two operations to be carried out. In our payroll example, suppose that overtime is paid if the hours worked are greater than 40. This would be shown as previously portrayed in the flowcharting example as

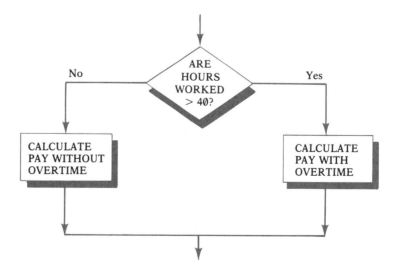

The looping statement permits an operation to be repeated as long as a certain condition exists. The WHILE and WEND statements are often used for this purpose as will be explained later. This can be shown as follows:

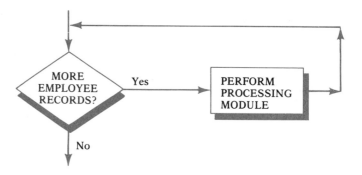

Confused? Please don't be; we are covering a lot of concepts before we "do the obvious" of coding a program. Structured programming can be viewed as a construction technique that begins when you decide what function a module is to perform. Ask yourself the questions

- What actions should the module take?
- In what order should these actions be executed?
- What are the decision points?
- How should repetition be controlled?

STEP 5   TEST AND DEBUG THE PROGRAM

When Pope said "to err is human," he must have tried to write a large program. The computer is very exact and even the most insignificantly misplaced decimal or comma or misspelled word can result in an error. Several techniques can be used to help detect errors (see Chapter 16), but errors will be minimized if the steps in the program development process are carefully followed.

STEP 6   TRAIN USERS AND DOCUMENT THE PROGRAM

No matter how well-written the program, the user must be instructed in running it. In addition, specific points likely to be encountered in operating the program should be written in the form of a procedure.

For example, if hours worked are to be entered into a payroll program, how should the values be entered? If an employee works four hours and ten minutes, is the value of $4\frac{1}{6}$ entered? I doubt it. But should one enter 4.1667, the decimal equivalent? Or is time rounded down to 4.1 hours? These and other points, such as how the program handles errors, must be considered and documented in order for the program to be usable.

WRITING A PROGRAM

Instructions are typed into the computer via the keyboard. When a program is run (executed), statements are processed one by one beginning at the lowest statement line number and progressing to the highest line number. The highest-numbered statement should contain the word END to signify the end of the program.

Remember, the BASIC interpreter must be loaded into the computer's memory before a BASIC program can be entered. If you are just starting the system, remember to load DOS, which serves as the traffic cop for the system. (This is automatically loaded when the computer is first started by using the DOS diskette.) Then BASIC (or the advanced BASICA) has to be loaded to allow your BASIC program statements to be interpreted by the computer.

BASIC is loaded into memory from a diskette containing the interpreter by typing BASICA while at the DOS level with the A> prompt displayed. The prompt will then change to a blinking dash (–) to indicate that you are at the BASIC level. A BASIC program such as the one shown in Figure 2.4 can then be typed into the computer. The statements are numbered in increments of 10 so that additional statements can easily be inserted at a later time.

```
10 REM Sample program
20 SALE = 100
30 PRINT SALE
40 END
```

FIGURE 2.4   Program to display a value

The program shown in Figure 2.4 is entered into the computer by typing each statement, line by line. The Enter key is pressed at the end of each line. Each program statement is accepted by the computer as it is typed, but no statement is executed until the RUN command (without a line number) is given.

The program is executed by typing in RUN and pressing the Enter key. The monitor will then appear as shown in Figure 2.5.

A program can be displayed by typing the command LIST and pressing the Enter key. This and other commands will be explained in greater detail in the chapters that follow.

```
10 REM Sample program
20 SALE = 100
30 PRINT SALE
40 END
RUN
 100
Ok
```

FIGURE 2.5   Executing the program to display a value

After the program shown in Figure 2.4 was entered, the following sequence of events occurred:

RUN ⟶ Entered by program operator

100
Ok ⟶ Computer responses

The first statement in a program should be a REM statement that tells what the program does. This will minimize confusion as programs are developed.

THE REM (REMARK) STATEMENT

Let's take a close look at this program to determine how it works. Statement 10 is a REM (remark) statement used to provide internal program documentation. REM statements are ignored when the RUN command is entered. However, when the program is listed, the entire program, including REM statements, is displayed. That is, REM statements are used only to remind the programmer why a program was written a certain way; the computer simply ignores REM statements during program execution.

ASSIGNING VALUES TO VARIABLES

The next statement encountered by the computer when the program is executed is statement 20 SALE = 100. This statement establishes a memory location in the computer for the variable called SALE, which is assigned the value of 100. That is, statement 20 creates the following variable name and stores the value of 100 in memory, visualized as follows:

SALE

```
┌─────────┐
│   100   │
└─────────┘
```

Statement 30 PRINT SALE is an instruction to the computer to display the value of the variable called SALE. This results in 100 being displayed as previously shown. Finally, statement 40 END signifies the end of the program and the computer responds with "Ok."

The output from the program shown in Figure 2.5 is not very descriptive. We need to label our program output so that others can understand what is happening. A more meaningful example will be discussed in a moment. Let's take a closer look at variable names.

Program logic is easier to understand if variable names are meaningful. For example, suppose we wrote 20 SALE = 100, as 20 S = 100. Either way is accepted by the computer; however, to humans the variable "S" is not meaningful because S is not as descriptive as the variable SALE. The extra effort spent in developing meaningful variable names pays off by making the program easy to understand.

Variable names should be descriptive whenever possible and may be up to 40 characters (letters, numbers, and symbols) in length. A variable name cannot be a BASIC reserved word, such as PRINT or RUN.

The first character in a variable name must be a letter. Letters, numbers, and the decimal point may be used, but blank spaces cannot be used in a variable name. Also, symbols should not be used in a name. Mathematical symbols such as + (plus), − (minus), / (divide), and * (multiply) are not accepted. In addition, although symbols such as $, %, !, and # may sometimes be used at the end of a variable name for special purposes, they have a special meaning which will be discussed later.

Let's take a look at typical variable names and their usages in frequently encountered BASIC statements. Some of the names which follow are illegal variable names. Illegal variable names simply are not accepted by the computer because they do not conform to BASIC syntax (rules of the language). Other variable names are legal, and that's fine, but what we want are legal variable names which are easy to understand and meaningful.

Confused? Please don't be. Simply make your variable names meaningful, and do not use blanks, symbols, or computer-reserved words. Let's "walk through" another program to determine how variable names are used to store and retrieve data. A program to calculate sales tax is shown in Figure 2.6. Take a look at the program before proceeding.

Variable Name/Usage	Comments
30 SALE = 12.75	This is the recommended usage of a variable name. The name is meaningful (assuming we are dealing with a sale) and easy-to-understand.
35 Sale = -25.2	This is legal. Variable names are automatically converted by the computer to uppercase (SALE). A name may be assigned to a negative value. Also, although we will number statements in units of 10, statement numbers can be any number.
70 85 = SALE	Illegal. The variable name must be on the left side of an assignment.
320 WEIGHT = 170#	Illegal. Symbols cannot be used in an assignment.
215 MY.WEIGHT = 165	Legal. A decimal may be used within a variable name.
120 MY WEIGHT = 175	Illegal. A blank space may not be used in a variable name.
27 RUN = 45	Illegal. RUN is a reserved word and may not be used as a variable name.
65 RETURN.GOODS.ALLOWANCE = 12	This is legal; however, too much typing is required. It would be better to rewrite the statement as 65 ALLOWANCE = 12 to reduce the chance of typing errors.
78 BIG.SALE = 345,000	Illegal. Symbols (the comma) cannot be used in an assignment.
63 Cars = -10.12	Legal. The variable name is automatically converted to uppercase. Negative values can be assigned to a variable name. However, this assignment should be avoided because it is difficult to envision why such a variable name would be negative.
92 UNITS = CARS	Legal. A variable can be assigned another variable. If CARS has previously been assigned the value of -10.12, then UNITS equals -10.12.
120 UNITS = CARS = 30	Illegal. Only one assignment can be made in an assignment statement (i.e., one and only one equal sign is permitted).

```
10 REM Calculating sales tax
20 TAXRATE = .05
30 SALE = 100
40 TAX = SALE * TAXRATE
50 PRINT "The sales tax is"
60 PRINT TAX
70 END
RUN
The sales tax is
 5
Ok
```

FIGURE 2.6 Program to calculate sales tax

Statement 10 is a REMark statement that tells us the purpose of the program: to calculate sales tax.

Statement 20 TAXRATE = .05 establishes a memory location in the computer for the variable called TAXRATE, which is assigned the value of .05. This direct assignment of the variable TAXRATE to the value .05 results in the following allocation in the computer's memory:

TAXRATE

| .05 |

Statement 30 SALE = 100 establishes a separate memory location in the computer for the variable called SALE, which is assigned the value of 100. This can be viewed as follows:

SALE

| 100 |

Statement 40 TAX = SALE * TAXRATE instructs the computer to look up the value stored in the memory location called SALE. Then it looks up the value stored in the memory location called TAXRATE. Finally, it multiplies the two values together (the * is the multiplication symbol) and stores the product in the location called TAX.

At this point in the program, three storage locations in memory (boxes), called TAX, SALE, and TAXRATE, have been established. These variables contain the following values:

TAX	SALE	TAXRATE
5	100	.05

> Don't be stingy in developing variable names. Use meaningful names so that the program is easy to understand.

Variable names are the means by which data is stored and retrieved. The process of looking up the value of a variable does not alter the stored value. The values of TAX, SALE, and TAXRATE will remain as shown unless a statement is written to specifically assign new values to the variables.

Statement 50 PRINT "The sales tax is" directs the computer to PRINT (display on the screen) whatever appears between the quotation marks. In this case, "The sales tax is" labels the output. This statement is not required for the computer's purposes, but rather to make the output easier to understand.

Statement 60 PRINT TAX instructs the computer to display the value of the variable TAX, which is 5. Last, statement 70 END signifies the last statement in the program.

> Statements should be numbered in increments of 10 so that additional statements can be added later without having to renumber the program. If desired, the command RENUM can be typed to automatically renumber a program in increments of 10.

Programs often require items that can change (vary) their values within the program, thus the term "variable." A direct assignment statement such as 20 TAX = 15 assigns the value 15 to the variable TAX. The value 15 is called a *numeric constant*, which is the value the computer will use in program execution. This results in a box-like assignment in memory that can be viewed as follows:

TAX

| 15 |

A variable can be assigned a mathematical expression such as RENT = 350 + 25, resulting in

RENT

375

Additionally, a variable can be assigned to the value of another variable in a mathematical expression, such as CHARGE = RENT + TAX. Using the previous value of TAX (15), this results in

CHARGE

390

Variables can be assigned different values, but the computer remembers only the last value of the variable. For example, suppose CHARGE is assigned the value of 450 by the statement CHARGE = 450. The former value of 390 is erased, resulting in

CHARGE

450

The values assigned to the program variables shown in Figure 2.6 can become confusing. For example, instead of using TAXRATE = .05, try the assignment statement TAXRATE = .055 and list the program. An exclamation point (!) appears that indicates the precision of the number (see Chapter 16). Program execution is not affected, so ignore the exclamation point.

We are using numeric variables in this chapter. Numeric variables can be assigned only a number or a variable containing a numeric quantity. Special symbols such as the dollar sign ($), the pound symbol (#), and the percent symbol (%) cannot be used in numerical assignments. That is, WAGES = $250.25 is illegal.

If the assignment expression becomes complex, it may help to read the equals symbol as "is replaced by." Thus the assignment CHARGE = 450 can be read as "the numeric value in CHARGE is replaced by 450." This helps to reinforce the point that a variable name is only a convenient means of storing and retrieving the value of a variable. Remember that this is the direct-assignment method. Additional methods of assigning values will be discussed later.

BASIC programs can be developed using the word LET before all assignment statements. The program shown in Figure 2.7 calculates sales

```
10 REM Calculating sales tax using LET
20 LET TAXRATE = .05
30 LET SALE = 100
40 LET TAX = SALE * TAXRATE
50 PRINT "The sales tax is"
60 PRINT TAX
70 END
RUN
The sales tax is
 5
Ok
```

FIGURE 2.7   Program to calculate sales tax using LET

tax in the same manner as the previous program shown in Figure 2.6. However, notice statements 20, 30, and 40:

```
20 LET TAXRATE = .05
30 LET SALE = 100
40 LET TAX = SALE * TAXRATE
```

The word LET is optional. It is used in this example to reinforce the point that BASIC statements are not mathematical equalities. We are simply "letting" a variable equal something so that the program can process the variable. Statement processing and program output is the same as the program shown in Figure 2.6.

DEBUGGING PROGRAMS

When Alexander Pope said "to err is human," he must have been thinking about students who are trying to develop programs. If you haven't already found out, you soon will: errors are a fact of life. The question is not what to do *if* an error is encountered, but what to do *when* an error is encountered.

Structured programming techniques will reduce but not eliminate errors. There are two major categories of errors: *syntax* errors and *logical* errors. Syntax errors are made by the programmer when using the BASIC language, such as misspelling PRINT, perhaps as PPRINT. The computer will catch these errors when the program is executed and prompt the user for a correction.

The other category of errors is called logical errors. These errors often cause the beginner the most problems. For example, if the TAXRATE shown in Figures 2.6 and 2.7 was assigned the value of 5 (instead of .05), the tax on a sale of $100 would be $500. The computer simply processes the data and would find nothing wrong with this. However, one could imagine the screams from the customer.

There are several techniques that can be used in debugging a program. If it's a syntax error, re-read the statement causing the error. If this doesn't help, re-read where similar statements were used in the book.

Logic errors can often be traced by pretending to be the computer. Take a 3″ × 5″ card or a folded sheet of paper. Place the card under the first statement in the program. Read the statement, and write down *exactly* what the computer does. Then move the card down and repeat one statement at a time for all statements in the program. This approach "forces" you to consider exactly what is being processed, and how it is logically being processed, one statement at a time.

Another approach is to read each statement out loud. Say each statement slowly, and think about what you are saying. Although this approach helps to focus your attention on the processing details, the approach can result in angry stares if done in a library.

Take a break: this enables you to take a fresh look at the problem at a later date. This is a useful technique that is difficult to follow if your program is due the next day. You will reduce pressures and minimize errors if you start a homework assignment well before it is due.

Ask a friend to look at your program, or better yet, explain the program, statement by statement, to a friend. (This is often called a program walk-through.) Unfortunately, we can lose a friend if we overdo this last step, so please resort to this only if all else fails. (Advanced debugging techniques are discussed in Chapter 17.)

This book pays particular attention to error detection and correction. True/False problems reinforce points discussed in the chapter. Debugging problems follow a structured guidance technique: Partial programs are given, and the student is asked to complete the program to produce the required output. As you progress through the problems, the prompts are selectively removed. This reduces the "where-do-I-start?" anxiety that bothers many students, and the initial difficulty encountered in creating a computer program is thus minimized.

Screen design problems are used throughout the book. These types of problems provide the solution (the program output) and ask the student to develop the program that produced the output. (More on this later.) Finally, after you are familiar with the concepts presented in the chapter, general problems are used to refine programming skills.

SUMMARY

In many respects, this is the most important chapter in the book. The key to program development is to resist the urge to code. Plan first, code later, for logical, well-developed programs.

If you haven't already done so, it would be a good idea to re-run the programs dealing with the keyboard that are on the companion diskette. Do you remember how we ran a program last time? Good. Start the system and load DOS into memory. This is accomplished by either booting on a DOS diskette or booting on the companion diskette if it has been made self-loading. If you boot on a DOS diskette, remove the diskette and insert the companion diskette. With A> shown, type START and press Enter.

The program selection menu will appear as shown in Figure 1.5.

The program selection pointer is residing on the first of the educational programs designed to show you how to use the IBM Personal Computer's keyboard. Now, re-run this and the other keyboarding programs. This time, deliberately make an error and observe how the computer reacts to errors made on the main keyboard, function keys, and the numeric pad. The latter can be particularly tricky if an error is made when switching from numeric entry to the program-editing mode. So, make your errors in this "controlled environment" where the computer will highlight what occurred and guide you to make the correct entry.

Please remember two things when you run these tutorials. First, you learn from your errors. Do not think of an error as an unforgivable, horrible mistake. An error is only something the computer cannot do. Errors permit us to learn about and understand the demands of the computer. After all, "to err is human."

Second, remember when running these tutorials that the computer is the most patient teacher you will ever have. If you do not understand a particular point, then re-run the tutorial. The Esc (Escape) key can be pressed to escape from any program and return to the menu selection screen whenever you like. Relax, set your own pace, and decide if you want to re-run a tutorial or to progress to the next.

If you wish to make the diskette self-loading, a shortcut can be taken. Simply restart the computer by pressing the following three keys at the same time: Ctrl (Control), Alt (Alternate), and Del (Delete). The screen will then appear as shown in Figure 1.4.

The tutorial called Variables is executed by pressing the space bar until the program selection pointer is at the program called Variables. The menu selection screen should appear as follows:

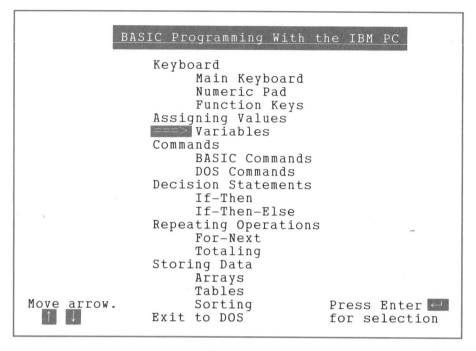

```
    BASIC Programming With the IBM PC

              Keyboard
                    Main Keyboard
                    Numeric Pad
                    Function Keys
              Assigning Values
         ===> Variables
              Commands
                    BASIC Commands
                    DOS Commands
              Decision Statements
                    If-Then
                    If-Then-Else
              Repeating Operations
                    For-Next
                    Totaling
              Storing Data
                    Arrays
                    Tables
    Move arrow.       Sorting        Press Enter ⏎
       ↑  ↓      Exit to DOS          for selection
```

Have you seen what happens when you press the Esc (Escape) key while running the tutorials? Why not? The computer is the most patient teacher you will ever have, so see for yourself what happens.

Now press the Enter key, and a copy of the program called Variables is retrieved from diskette, loaded into memory, and executed. The screen will appear as shown below.

```
    BASIC Programming With the IBM PC

                Variables

                  By
               Peter Mears
         (c) Copyright 1990
```

Enter data when requested by the program and observe how values are processed. This will give you a good idea of how a program handles data. After running the program, read the next chapter, which explains the various methods of displaying information.

Summary of terms

Name	Example	Purpose
END	50 END	Last program statement
PRINT	40 PRINT "The tax is"	Displays whatever is between quotation marks
PRINT	50 PRINT TAX	Displays the value of TAX
REM	10 REM Any comments	Use for internal program documentation. Appears only when program is listed.
RUN	RUN	Executes program in memory
=	20 SALE = 100	Assigns 100 to SALE
*	30 TAX = SALE * TAXRATE	Multiplies SALE times TAXRATE. Product assigned to TAX

PROBLEMS

True/False. Problems 1–9.

2.1 Variable names may have only letters in them. F

2.2 Variable names may not be nouns. F

2.3 Variable names may be easy-to-remember words like RUN and PRINT. F

2.4 The computer stores and retrieves the value of a variable. T

2.5 Variable names may be 40 characters long. T

*2.6 If a variable name is assigned twice in a program, only the current value is used. T

2.7 The PRINT statement may display the value of a variable or anything between quotation marks. T

2.8 The equal sign (=) assigns values to variables. T

2.9 Many different variable names may be used in a program. T

Program Completion—Beginning. Problems 10–20.
BASIC assignment statements are shown. Write the value of the variable in the indicated boxes.

SALE

2.10 `80 SALE = 15.95` ☐ 15.95

AMOUNT

2.11 `130 AMOUNT = 197.26` ☐ 197.26

TAXRATE

2.12 `90 TAXRATE = .15` ☐ .15

SUM

*2.13 `30 S = 27`
`40 SUM = S` ☐ 27

TOTAL

2.14 `150 TOTAL = AMOUNT + 10` ☐ 20

Hint: The value of the variable AMOUNT has 10 added and stored in TOTAL.

TAXRATE

2.15 `60 TAXRATE = .05`
`130 TAXRATE = .25` ☐ .05

Hint: A variable (a memory box) can only hold one value at a time. Before TAXRATE can be assigned a new value, the old value must be erased.

* The answer to this problem is in Appendix E.

SALE

2.16　10　SALE = 9.98
　　　20　PRINT SALE　　
　　　30　END

S

2.17　10　S = 14
　　　20　S = 15　　

GROSS.PAY　　　　　　　　　　DEDUCTIONS

2.18　10　GROSS.PAY = 480.70
　　　20　DEDUCTIONS = 180　　　　

PAY

　　　30　PAY = GROSS.PAY - DEDUCTIONS　　

　　　40　PRINT PAY
　　　50　END

ASSETS　　　　　　　　　　　LIABILITIES

2.19　10　ASSETS = 30000
　　　20　LIABILITIES = 25000　　　　

NET.WORTH

　　　30　NET.WORTH = ASSETS - LIABILITIES　　

　　　40　END

PRICE　　　　　LABOR

2.20　10　PRICE = 875
　　　20　LABOR = 525　　　　

MATERIAL　　　OVERHEAD

　　　30　MATERIAL = 150
　　　40　OVERHEAD = 25

GROSS

　　　50　GROSS = PRICE - LABOR - MATERIAL
　　　60　PRINT GROSS
　　　70　GROSS = GROSS - 50
　　　80　END

Hint: No instruction has been given to display GROSS, so only the computer knows the ending value. However, program execution is not affected.

Program Completion—Advanced. Problems 21–34.
Find and complete the necessary statements so that the output indicated will
be produced when the program is executed (run).

*2.21
```
10 REM Problem 2.21 starts tricky series
20 SALE = 100
30 PRINT Sale              ← What variable must go here?
40 END
RUN
 100
```

2.22
```
10 REM Problem 2.22
20 COST.OF.CAR = 12575
30 PRINT " The car costs"
40 PRINT Cost.of.Car       ← What variable must be here?
50 END
RUN
The car costs
 12575
```

2.23
```
10 REM Problem 2.23
20 STUDENT.NO = 298
30 PRINT "Student Number"  ← What must be here?
40 PRINT STUDENT.NO
50 END
RUN
The number of students is:
 298
```

2.24
```
10 REM Problem 2.24
20 COST = 19.95
30 Print "The Shirt Cost"  ← What variable must be here?
40 PRINT COST
50 END
RUN
The shirt costs
 19.95
```

2.25
```
10 REM Problem 2.25
20 WEIGHT = 255            ← What must be here?
30 PRINT "The weight in pounds is:"
40 PRINT WEIGHT
50 END
RUN
The weight in pounds is:
 255
```

2.26
```
10 REM Problem 2.26
20 EARNINGS = 97.55
30 Print Earnings          ← What variable must be here?
40 END
RUN
 97.55
```

2.27 Complete the program below to assign the value of 3921 to TUITION-
.COST. Then PRINT the value of TUITION.COST so that the output indicated will be produced when the program is executed (run).

```
10 REM Complete this program
20 TUITION.COST = 3921     ← What must be here?
30 PRINT Tuition.Cost      ← What must be here?
40 END
RUN
 3921
```

* The answer to this problem is in Appendix E.

2.28 Complete the following program to assign the value of 15950 to NEW.CAR. Then complete the PRINT statement so that program output will be labeled: "A nice new car costs:"

```
10 REM Complete this program
20 NEW.CAR = 15956          ← What must be here?
30 PRINT " A nice new Car Cost:"  ← What must be here?
40 PRINT NEW.CAR
50 END
RUN
A nice new car costs:
 15950
```

2.29
```
10 REM Problem 2.29
20 SALE = 37
30 COST = SALE - 5          ← What must be here?
40 PRINT "The item costs"
50 PRINT COST
60 END
RUN
The item costs
 32
```

2.30
```
10 REM Problem 2.30
20 TABLES = 259.95
30 CHAIRS = 49.25
40 PRINT tables             ← What variable must be here?
50 END
RUN
 259.95
```

2.31
```
10 REM Problem 2.31
20 DESK = 459.25
30 LAMP = 49.95
40 BENCH = 129.49
50 PRINT Lamp               ← What variable must be here?
60 END
RUN
 49.95
```

2.32
```
10 REM Problem 2.32
20 my.Cost = 26.45          ← What must be here?
30 PRINT "The cost of the gas is:"  ← What must be here?
40 PRINT MY.COST
50 END
RUN
The cost of the gas is:
 26.45
```

2.33
```
10 REM Problem 2.33
20 SHIRT = 13               ← What must be here?
30 PANTS = 32
40 SUM = SHIRT + PANTS
50 PRINT "The shirt and pants cost:"  ← What must be here?
60 PRINT SUM
70 END
RUN
The shirt and pants cost:
 45
```

2.34
```
10 REM Problem 2.34
20 SHOVEL = 9.95            ← What must be here?
30 PICK = 19.25
40 PRINT "The shovel costs:"
50 PRINT SHOVEL
60 Print " the pick cost:"  ← What must be here?
70 PRINT PICK
80 END
RUN
```

```
The shovel costs:
 9.95
The pick costs:
 19.25
```

Debugging Problems. Problems 35–57.
Problems 35–48 consist of single BASIC statements. Identify which of the statements are incorrect and write the correct statement. Note: Sometimes it will not be possible to rewrite the statement. In that case, clearly explain why the statement is incorrect.

*2.35   40 S = -12.25

2.36   50 SUM = 175 – 5.50

2.37   30 MYANSWER = ALICE + 2

2.38   60 MY.ANSWER = 22

2.39   10 ACTUAL.WEIGHT = 55 + 4#

2.40   70 TAX = .50

2.41   80 TAX + 4 = 5AMOUNT   *Amount5 = 4 + Tax*

2.42   90 PROFIT = SALES = EXPENSES

2.43   20 ACCOUNT = (55 – 5.7) + 2

2.44   DOLLAR = $2.25

2.45   10 20 = AGE

2.46   50 PRINT = 5

2.47   30 CORVETTE = MONEY

2.48   40 TOTAL PRICE = 13

The miniprograms shown in problems 49–57 contain errors. Some of the errors (program bugs) are easy to find; others will be difficult to detect. Find and correct the errors so the output shown will be produced when the program is executed (run).

*2.49
```
10 REM Carefully go over each statement
20 FIVE.PERCENT = 5%   .05
30 PRINT FIVE.PERCENT
40 END
RUN
 .05
```

2.50
```
10 REM It's easier to do it right the first time.
20 TOT SALES = 200
30 PRINT TOT SALES
40 END
RUN
 200
```

2.51
```
10 REM Can you find this error?
20 BIN.S = 125
30 PRINT "BIN.S"
40 END
RUN
 125
```

* The answer to this problem is in Appendix E.

2.52   10 REM Read this very carefully.
     20 ASSETS = -500   ← What must be changed here?
     30 PRINT ASSETS
     40 END
     RUN
      -500   ← Carefully look at the program
                                       statements!

2.53   10 REM To error is human but computers
     20 REM do not tolerate human errors!
     30 POUNDS.SOLD = #32.49
     40 REM PRINT POUNDS.SOLD
     50 END
     RUN
      32.49   ← What two errors must be corrected
                                         so this output is produced?

2.54   90 REM Isn't it easier to do it right
     100 REM the first time?
     110 PRINT "The sale is"
     120 PRINT SALE
     130 SALE = 200.25
     140 END
     RUN
      200.25   ← What must be corrected so this
                                       output is displayed?

2.55   10 REM It's easier to make errors
     20 REM than it is to find them.
     30 SALES = 20
     40 PRICE = $5.50
     50 REVENUE = SALES * PRICE
     60 PRINT REVENUE
     70 END
     RUN
      110   ← What must be corrected so this
                                       output is displayed?

*2.56   10 REM I hate program bugs.
     20 REM Can you find the error?
     30 SALES = 22.75
     40 REM Too many REMs are confusing.
     50 PRINT SALE
     60 REM You can carry a good thing too far!
     70 END
     RUN
      22.75   ← What must be corrected so this
                                       output is displayed?

2.57   10 REM It sure is easier to make an
     20 REM error than it is to find it!
     30 DOLLAR = $12.55
     40 PRINT "The total dollars spent was:"
     50 PRINT DOLLAR
     60 END
     RUN
      12.55   ← What must be corrected so this
                                       output is displayed?

* The answer to this problem is in Appendix E.

Screen Design Problems—Statement Development. Problems 58 and 59.
Write the necessary statements so that the output indicated will be produced
when the program is executed (run). XXX.XX indicates a value is to be printed.
In the next chapter PRINT USING will be discussed, so that output can be
obtained in dollars-and-cents format. For now, simply print the output.

2.58
```
10 REM Complete this program
20 BOOKS = 200
30 PRINT "          Enormous State University"
40 PRINT "              Book Store Bill"
50 Print "The cost of your books is:"
60 print Books
..
   200
```
{What statements must be here?}

```
┌─────────────────────────────────────┐
│                                      │
│      Enormous State University       │
│           Book Store Bill            │
│    The cost of your books is:        │
│       200                            │
│                                      │
└─────────────────────────────────────┘
```

2.59
```
10 REM Complete this program and calculate tax.
20 BOOKS = 200
30 PRINT "          Enormous State University"
40 PRINT "              Book Store Bill"
50 PRINT "The cost of your books is:
60 Print Books
70 print " The sales tax is:", 12
..
```
{What statements must be here?}

```
┌─────────────────────────────────────┐
│                                      │
│      Enormous State University       │
│           Book Store Bill            │
│    The cost of your books is:        │
│       200                            │
│    The sales tax is:                 │
│       12                             │
│                                      │
└─────────────────────────────────────┘
```

Screen Design Problems. Problems 60–64.
Develop a BASIC program, paying particular attention to the design of the
screen and the design of the printed output (when requested). General formats
are shown for your consideration which may be expanded on (improved) in
your program.

2.60 Display your name in this design where XXXX XXXXXXX is shown.
(Space output by including leading blank spaces inside the quotation.)

```
┌─────────────────────────────────────┐
│                                      │
│   -------------------------          │
│        XXXX XXXXXXX                   │
│        Computer wizard!              │
│   -------------------------          │
│                                      │
└─────────────────────────────────────┘
```

2.61 Display the following graph.

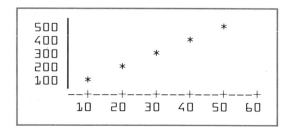

2.62 Ajax Building Contractors is constructing a small commercial building. They have agreed to construct the building for a fee of $12,245. They have the following major expenses:

Category	Cost
LABOR	8778
MATERIAL	2456
OVERHEAD	567

Develop a program to produce a management report according to the following format. Calculate and display the appropriate values where XX.XX is shown.

```
Ajax Building Contractors
Bus Stop Project
The total costs are:
   XXX.XX
The profit on the project is:
   XX.XX
```

Problems 63 and 64 require the following information:

The Itty-Bitty-Machines computer shop has the following computer-program disks for sale:

Category	Number
GAMES	41
UTILITIES	14
BUSINESS	25
SCIENTIFIC	6

2.63 Develop a program that utilizes variable names of each of the categories shown and assigns the number of disks to each category. Then print the variables according to the below format. Space your heading by including leading blank spaces within the quotation marks (i.e., `PRINT"     To-tal"` prints 4 leading blanks).

```
       Itty Bitty Machines
         Disks for Sale

Games: 41
Utilities: 14
Business: 25
Scientific: 6
```

2.64 Develop a program to produce a report according to the next format. Assign the number of disks to each category; XX indicates a total which is to be obtained by adding the indicated variables together.

```
            Itty Bitty Machines
              Disks for Sale
      Games and Utilities:
        XX
      Business and Scientific:
        XX
```

Other Problems. Problems 65–70.
Develop a BASIC program to solve each problem. Use a REM statement to identify the problem number, and clearly label all output.

2.65 Assign 435,000 to the variable SALES and display the variable.

2.66 Print the title of this book. Then, on the next line, print a row of dashes under the title.

*2.67 Calculate the weekly pay of an employee earning $3.55 per hour and working 35 hours per week.

2.68 Calculate pay using the variables HOURS, RATE, and PAY. Develop the necessary assignment statements to assign 34.45 to HOURS, 8.75 to RATE. A category called deductions is to be developed where $25 is deducted for the credit union. PRINT the PAY after deductions are taken out.

2.69 Assign your numeric age to the variable AGE and display the value.

2.70 Write a program that calculates the sales tax on a new $50,000 Corvette at a tax rate of 5%. Display the calculated tax.

* The answer to this problem is in Appendix E.

3 DISPLAYING INFORMATION

Upon completion of this chapter, you should be able to display the following on a monitor or a printer:

- Your name and address
- A letterhead, centered on a page
- Values for variables
- A sales report consisting of a column of numbers
- Numbers in dollars-and-cents format
- Reports in which values are intermixed with text

DISPLAYING INFORMATION

A PRINT statement is used to display anything between quotation marks. For example, the program shown in Figure 3.1 displays a person's name and address on a monitor after the RUN command is typed and the Enter key is pressed.

Now that we are becoming familiar with the BASIC language, programs will become longer as we attempt to accomplish more. A listing of the program is needed so that the program can be reviewed to verify that typing errors were corrected. This is accomplished by the LIST command, which displays the current program residing in memory. (Additional commands are discussed in the next chapter on managing information.)

As with any command, the LIST command is typed without a line number and the Enter key is pressed after typing the command. An example of the LIST command to display the program residing in memory is shown in Figure 3.2. Information between quotation marks is not changed when the program is listed, but notice that BASIC language words are all converted to uppercase characters when the program is listed.

Program output and listings are normally directed to the monitor but often a listing is needed on paper. This is particularly important for receipts and reports and in finding errors in lengthy programs. The statements used to direct output to an attached printer are LLIST and LPRINT. An example of using LLIST to obtain a printed copy of the program in memory is shown in Figure 3.3. (Turn the printer on before you use the LLIST command, to avoid an error message.)

The LPRINT statement is used to display output on a printer, as shown in Figure 3.4. The only difference between this example and the one shown in Figure 3.1, which directed output to a monitor, is that the command

The computer is a very patient teacher. A lot can be learned by making the programs shown in the figures work as intended.

```
1Ø REM     Printing information
2Ø PRINT "Mr. John Smith, Student"
3Ø PRINT "University of Micro Computers"
4Ø PRINT "College of Arts & Sciences"
5Ø PRINT "New York, NY  1ØØ1Ø"
6Ø END
RUN
Mr. John Smith, Student
University of Micro Computers
College of Arts & Sciences
New York, NY  1ØØ1Ø
Ok
```

FIGURE 3.1 Printing information between quotation marks

```
1Ø REM     Printing information
2Ø print  "Mr. John Smith, Student"
3Ø Print "University of Micro Computers"
4Ø print "College of Arts & Sciences"
5Ø PRINT "New York, NY  1ØØ1Ø"
6Øend
LIST
1Ø REM     Printing information
2Ø PRINT "Mr. John Smith, Student"
3Ø PRINT "University of Micro Computers"
4Ø PRINT "College of Arts & Sciences"
5Ø PRINT "New York, NY  1ØØ1Ø"
6Ø END
Ok
```

FIGURE 3.2 Displaying the program

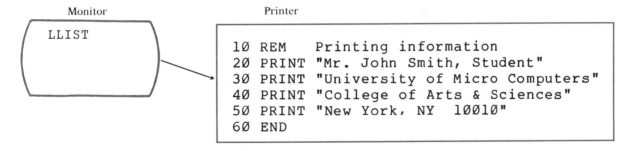

Monitor

LLIST

Printer

```
1Ø REM     Printing information
2Ø PRINT "Mr. John Smith, Student"
3Ø PRINT "University of Micro Computers"
4Ø PRINT "College of Arts & Sciences"
5Ø PRINT "New York, NY  1ØØ1Ø"
6Ø END
```

FIGURE 3.3 Obtaining a program listing

Do not confuse LLIST with LPRINT. LLIST is a command used to obtain a listing of the program statements. LPRINT is used as a statement to print the output of a program.

PRINT has been changed to LPRINT. When typed, the LLIST command appears on the monitor and not on the printout, although the program listing is on paper output. The RUN command also appears on the monitor and not on the printout, although program output is on paper. If program output is to be directed to both the monitor and to a printer, both PRINT and LPRINT statements must be used. An example of such an output is shown in Figure 3.5, where the monitor displays information of a more confidential nature than that contained on the printed output.

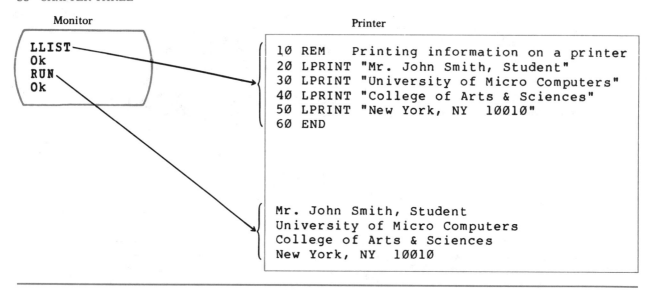

FIGURE 3.4 Obtaining a printed output

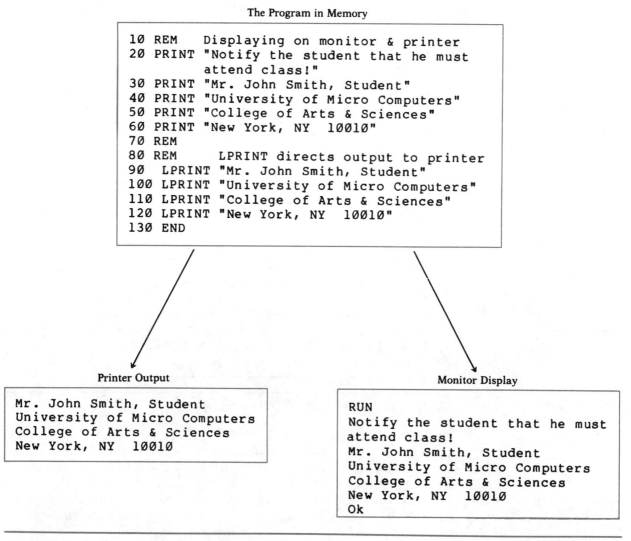

FIGURE 3.5 Dual monitor and printed output

USING THE TAB FUNCTION

A function is used like a variable in a statement to perform a specific, built-in service (function). In a moment, TAB will be used in a PRINT statement to direct program output to an exact position on a line. The normal display of information begins on the far left (first column) of the monitor or printed page. Program output is normally displayed on a monitor containing 24 lines of 80 columns of data as follows:

```
        1   2   3   4   5   6   7   ............80
  1  ┌─────────────────────────────────────────────┐
  2  │                                             │
  3  │                                             │
  4  │                                             │
  .  │                                             │
  .  │                                             │
  .  │                                             │
 24  └─────────────────────────────────────────────┘
```

The program shown below displays "Ajax Sales Corporation," beginning in the first column.

```
LIST
10 PRINT "Ajax Sales Corporation"
20 END
Ok
RUN
Ajax Sales Corporation
Ok
```

Some applications require output to be centered on a line, such as in printing a letterhead. This can be accomplished either by using blank spaces inside quotation marks or by using the TAB statement.

Inserting blank spaces inside quotation marks has the effect of moving the output to the right. For example, eight blanks are used to adjust the display in the output shown below.

```
LIST
10 PRINT "        Ajax Sales Corporation"
20 END
Ok
RUN
        Ajax Sales Corporation
Ok
```

The computer displayed the eight leading blanks and then displayed the characters resulting in Ajax Sales Corporation. Additional blanks can be inserted inside the quotation marks to move output farther to the right.

The blanks must be *inside* the quotation marks, as spaces outside the quotation marks do not affect program execution. For example, the following program has ten blanks inserted before the information in the quotation marks appears. Program output still begins in the first display column.

```
LIST
10 PRINT          "Ajax Sales Corporation"
20 END
Ok
RUN
Ajax Sales Corporation
Ok
```

If your patience holds out, sooner or later the letterhead can be centered using the technique of adding blanks inside the quotation marks. Instead of using this hit-or-miss approach, it is easier to use the TAB function for spacing output, as shown in Figure 3.6.

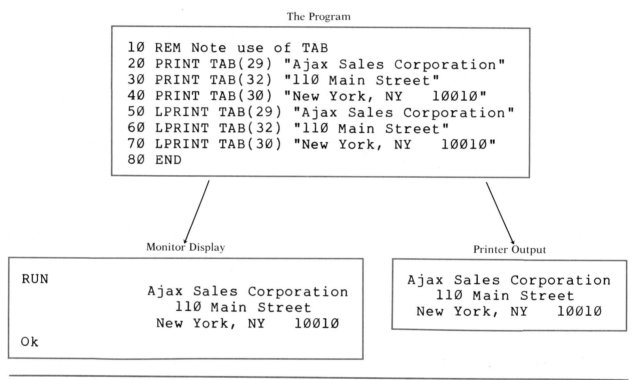

The Program

```
10 REM Note use of TAB
20 PRINT TAB(29) "Ajax Sales Corporation"
30 PRINT TAB(32) "110 Main Street"
40 PRINT TAB(30) "New York, NY   10010"
50 LPRINT TAB(29) "Ajax Sales Corporation"
60 LPRINT TAB(32) "110 Main Street"
70 LPRINT TAB(30) "New York, NY   10010"
80 END
```

Monitor Display

```
RUN
              Ajax Sales Corporation
                 110 Main Street
               New York, NY   10010

Ok
```

Printer Output

```
   Ajax Sales Corporation
      110 Main Street
    New York, NY   10010
```

FIGURE 3.6 Use of TAB function

The TAB function is used only within the PRINT and LPRINT statements. In Figure 3.6, statement `20 PRINT TAB(29) "Ajax Sales Corporation"` directs output to begin printing in the 29th column. Different TAB values are used to center each line of the letterhead.

Technically, TAB values can be from 1 through 255, but values are normally between 1 and 80 to format a line. If a TAB value greater than the current line width is used, the display will begin on the next line. When using TAB, do not space between the word TAB and the parenthesis or an error message will occur.

Multiple TAB functions can be used within the same PRINT or LPRINT statement to control output display further. An example is Figure 3.7, in which a printed letterhead contains the firm's phone number.

The TAB function can be used to produce a variety of different output. An example of using TAB to develop a class list is shown in Figure 3.8. Note statements 60 and 100, which are used to print dashes to highlight program output.

Individual program lines can be deleted by typing the statement number and pressing Enter. Change a line by retyping the statement using the same statement number. The last line typed will then be placed into memory.

```
10 REM Multiple TAB Statements
20 LPRINT TAB(29) "Ajax Sales Corporation"
30 LPRINT TAB(32) "110 Main Street" TAB(65) "Phone:"
40 LPRINT TAB(30) "New York, NY  10010" TAB(65) "202-555-1212"
50 END
                         Ajax Sales Corporation
                            110 Main Street                    Phone:
                         New York, NY  10010                   202-555-1212
```

FIGURE 3.7 Use of multiple TAB statements

```
10 REM Class list
20 PRINT TAB(10) "Introduction to Programming"
30 PRINT TAB(18) "Class List"
40 PRINT "Student" TAB(22) "Test" TAB(32) "Test" TAB(42) "Final"
50 PRINT "Name"    TAB(22) "#1"   TAB(32) "#2"   TAB(42) "Exam"
60 PRINT "----------------------------------------------"
70 PRINT "John Smith"  TAB(22) "89" TAB(32) "75" TAB(42) "88"
80 PRINT "Alice Jones" TAB(22) "72" TAB(32) "84" TAB(42) "93"
90 PRINT "Alfred E. Neuman" TAB(22) "98" TAB(32) "54"TAB(42) "37"
100 PRINT "----------------------------------------------"
110 END
RUN
            Introduction to Programming
                  Class List
Student              Test      Test      Final
Name                 #1        #2        Exam
-----------------------------------------------
John Smith           89        75        88
Alice Jones          72        84        93
Alfred E. Neuman     98        54        37
-----------------------------------------------
Ok
```

FIGURE 3.8 Using TAB to develop listings

DISPLAYING VALUES AND DESCRIPTIVE DATA

This chapter has been using the computer to display anything between the quotation marks. The real power of the computer is not just in its ability to control output display but in its ability to store, retrieve, and process variables rapidly.

When the program in Figure 3.9 is executed, values are stored in memory for variables called SELLING.PRICE, TAX.RATE, and SALE. This data is then retrieved and combined with information between quotation marks to create easy-to-read, understandable output.

When the program shown in Figure 3.9 is run, statements 20 and 30 establish memory storage locations for SELLING.PRICE and TAX.RATE. Statement 40 stores the product of SELLING.PRICE times TAX.RATE (the * symbol is multiplication) in the variable name called TAX. Statement 50 then stores the sum of the values of the variables SELLING.PRICE and TAX (the + symbol is addition) in the variable name SALE.

Spaces are used within a BASIC statement for ease of reading. Notice that, on lengthy programs, particular care has been paid to spacing variable names so the program is easy to read.

```
10 REM Displaying values and descriptive data
20 SELLING.PRICE = 110
30 TAX.RATE = .05
40 TAX  = SELLING.PRICE * TAX.RATE
50 SALE = SELLING.PRICE + TAX
60 PRINT "The selling price is $" SELLING.PRICE
70 PRINT "The sales tax is $" TAX
80 PRINT "Total sale including tax is $" SALE
90 END
RUN
The selling price is $ 110
The sales tax is $ 5.5
Total sale including tax is $ 115.5
Ok
```

FIGURE 3.9   Displaying the value of variables

The result is four variable names, with the following memory assignments:

SELLING.PRICE	TAX.RATE	TAX	SALE
110	.05	5.5	115.5

Statement `60 PRINT "The selling price is $" SELLING.PRICE` instructs the computer to display the statement between the quotation marks and then display the value of the variable SELLING.PRICE. This results in the following output:

```
The selling price is $ 110
```

Notice the space between the $ sign and the number. When numbers are printed, a leading space is automatically added. If the number is negative, a minus sign will appear in this space; since this number is positive, a blank space appears. In addition, a trailing space is automatically added.

Notice how information within the quotation marks makes the output easier to read. A detailed evaluation of statement 60 is as follows:

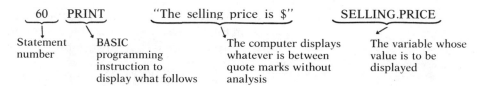

60	PRINT	"The selling price is $"	SELLING.PRICE
Statement number	BASIC programming instruction to display what follows	The computer displays whatever is between quote marks without analysis	The variable whose value is to be displayed

As with any BASIC statement, the computer processes statement 60 from left to right. The first word encountered is `PRINT`, which is an instruction to display whatever is specified in the rest of the statement, including whatever characters or symbols are between the quotation marks. In this case, `"The selling price is $"` is displayed on the monitor. Then a blank space is encountered between the trailing quotation mark and the variable name `SELLING.PRICE`.

Within a PRINT statement, the display position of each item is determined by the punctuation used to separate items. The following punctuation can be used:

1. A blank space or a semicolon between items in the PRINT statement causes the next value to be printed immediately after the last value.
2. A comma directs output to the next available PRINT zone. (More on this in a moment.)

Displaying information correctly is very important because errors are reduced when output is easy to read. Spacing is different for numeric variables than for string variables, such as names, which will be discussed later.

In the program shown in Figure 3.9, statements 60, 70, and 80 produce the following output:

```
The selling price is $ 110
The sales tax is $ 5.5
Total sale including tax is $ 115.5
Ok
```

In statements 60, 70, and 80, the gap between the dollar sign (which was inside the quotation marks) and the numeric values is created by the automatic spacing before and after numeric values. Also note that the trailing zeros in the decimal values have been dropped. We will soon overcome these problems with the PRINT USING statement.

In a PRINT statement the use of quotation marks allows any characters (except quotation marks) to be displayed, without special programming. Output can be formatted in whatever way improves readability. For example, statement 60 could just as easily have been written as

60 PRINT "The special sale price is only $"
SELLING.PRICE

Program execution would then result in the following display:

```
The special sale price is only $ 110
```

In some instances it might be desirable to display the value of a variable within a sentence. This can be accomplished as follows:

60 PRINT "The price of $" SELLING.PRICE
"is the lowest in town."

When executed, this statement would appear as shown below. Notice that a space is automatically left before and after the numeric variable SALE PRICE, resulting in an unwanted space between the $ and the value of 110. (This will be controlled by the PRINT USING statement to be discussed in a moment.)

The more time and care spent in developing a well-labeled program, the better the program. Frustration is minimized and errors are reduced if the program is easy to read.

```
The price of $ 110 is the lowest in town.
```

CONTROLLING OUTPUT DISPLAY WITH A SEMICOLON

The semicolon (;) is used to suppress the line feed in an output display. The computer assumed the existence of a semicolon when we were displaying the value of the variable SALE.PRICE along with the PRINT statement information. That is, a blank separating the variable name from the message is processed the same way as a semicolon in that the computer does not space to the next line.

The semicolon is particularly useful in keeping output on the same line when different PRINT statements are used. An example of this use is shown in Figure 3.10. Notice that the trailing semicolon in statements 70 and 90 resulted in the single line "We have an enrollment of 90 students this semester." Statement 60 PRINT displays a blank line to make the program output easy to read.

```
10 REM Using the semicolon to control output
20 NO.OF.STUDENTS = 90
30 TUITION       = 1250
40 INCOME = NO.OF.STUDENTS * TUITION
50 PRINT TAB(15) "Micro Mail Educational Firm"
60 PRINT
70 PRINT "We have an enrollment of";
80 PRINT NO.OF.STUDENTS;
90 PRINT "students this semster."
100 PRINT "Our tuition income is $";
110 PRINT INCOME
120 END
RUN
            Micro Mail Educational Firm

We have an enrollment of 90 students this semster.
Our tuition income is $ 112500
Ok
```

FIGURE 3.10 Using the semicolon

CONTROLLING OUTPUT DISPLAY WITH A COMMA

The display screen is divided into five zones of 14 characters each, plus a smaller sixth zone of 10 characters, for an 80-column display. The PRINT zones start at columns 1, 15, 29, 43, 57, and 71. A comma is used with a PRINT statement to direct output to the beginning of the next available print zone. If more characters are included in a PRINT statement than the zone can handle, the next zone (or zones) will be skipped. Also, if more zones are used than are available on one line of output, the display output will wrap around the screen and continue on the next line.

Commas can be thought of as pre-set tab stops and work just like a typewriter. The commas shown in Figure 3.11 are used to direct output to a PRINT zone so that numbers are in a column format. Notice that statement 60 PRINT displays a blank line to make program output easier to read.

Although there are six PRINT zones, the last zone is in columns 71–80 and is not a full 14 characters. We will avoid this problem by using the TAB statement to format output.

```
10 REM Note the comma for zone printing
20 ROOM = 287.95
30 PARKING = 8.2
40 FOOD = 57.4
50 ENTERTAINMENT = 25.75
60 PRINT
70 PRINT TAB(7) "Expenses"
80 PRINT ROOM, PARKING
90 PRINT FOOD, ENTERTAINMENT
100 END
RUN

      Expenses
 287.95          8.2
  57.4           25.75
Ok
```

FIGURE 3.11 Formatting output using PRINT zones

THE PRINT USING STATEMENT

Our primary use of the PRINT USING statement will be in printing values in dollars-and-cents format on the monitor. If desired, LPRINT USING can be utilized to format printer output. Let's first look at how these statements can be used to round values.

The general form of the PRINT USING statement is:

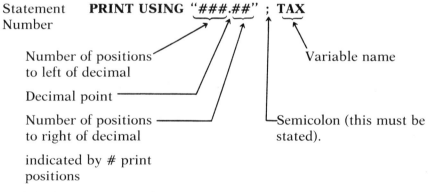

Statement Number
PRINT USING "###.##" ; TAX

Number of positions to left of decimal

Decimal point

Number of positions to right of decimal indicated by # print positions

Variable name

Semicolon (this must be stated).

The PRINT USING statement requires the semicolon. An error will occur without it.

Let's look at some partial program statements to demonstrate applications of the PRINT USING statement. For example, notice the output from the following program.

```
10 REM Note rounding
20 TAX = 14.857
30 PRINT "The tax is";
40 PRINT USING "###.##";TAX
50 END
RUN
The tax is 14.86
Ok
```

Although this output looks nice, it is tricky. The format specifies three spaces to the left of the decimal, as shown by three # (pound) symbols. The PRINT USING statement formats the output and spaces are not automatically inserted before and after numeric values. The space appears between "The tax is" and the value of 14.86 because of the extra (unused) print position. Also, notice that the decimal value was rounded to two print positions.

Look at the output from the next program, which has the same PRINT USING statement as before, but uses a larger numeric value. All three spaces to the left of the decimal are consumed by the value of TAX (114.857). Therefore, there is no blank space between "The tax is" and the number.

```
10 REM Note field size
20 TAX = 114.857
30 PRINT "The tax is";
40 PRINT USING "###.##";TAX
50 END
RUN
The tax is114.86
Ok
```

A percent sign (%) will be displayed if a number is printed that is larger than the allocated field size. In the example below, there are four places to the left of the decimal in TAX (1847.937), yet only three places have been allocated in the PRINT USING statement.

```
10 REM Field size is too big
20 TAX = 1847.937
30 PRINT "The tax is";
40 PRINT USING "###.##";TAX
50 END
RUN
The tax is%1847.94
Ok
```

There are two ways to display the dollar sign along with a number. First, the dollar sign can be displayed at a fixed position at the beginning of a field, with blank spaces up to the number. This is accomplished by placing a single dollar sign inside the PRINT USING format. An example is shown in Figure 3.12, in which statements have been numbered beginning with 100 to improve program readability. Notice that, although the same PRINT USING format processes different values, the dollar sign and decimal point are in alignment on the program output.

The second method uses a double dollar sign (called a floating dollar sign) inside the PRINT USING format. This allows the dollar sign to be displayed next to the number in a typical dollars-and-cents format as in Figure 3.13.

Notice the fancy spacing in some of the statements in Figure 3.14. A little extra time spent in developing a program pays off in that the program will be easy to understand.

A more detailed example of PRINT USING statements is shown in Figure 3.14. Notice the extra space in the sentence "The sales tax is $5.50." The space can be avoided by exercising greater care in selecting how many print positions (#) to use in the PRINT USING statement.

Another variation of the PRINT USING statement can be used to make it difficult to alter important documents such as paychecks by using two

```
100 REM  Note the dollar signs and decimals are in alignment
110 ROOM    = 287.95
120 PARKING = 8.2
130 FOOD    = 57.4
140 ENTERTAINMENT = 25.75
150 PRINT
160 PRINT "Expenses"
170 PRINT USING "$####.##";ROOM
180 PRINT USING "$####.##";PARKING
190 PRINT USING "$####.##";FOOD
200 PRINT USING "$####.##";ENTERTAINMENT
210 END
RUN

Expenses
$ 287.95
$   8.20
$  57.40
$  25.75
Ok
```

FIGURE 3.12 Using the dollar sign in a column format

```
10 REM Note floating $ sign
20 ROOM = 157.75
30 DISCOUNT = ROOM * .15
40 PRINT "The lodging bill is" ROOM
50 PRINT "Less a 15% discount of";
60 PRINT USING "$$###.##";DISCOUNT
70 END
RUN
The lodging bill is 157.75
Less a 15% discount of  $23.66
Ok
```

FIGURE 3.13 Typical dollars-and-cents format

asterisks before the dollar sign. The asterisks cause leading spaces in the numeric field to be filled with asterisks. An example of a check-protect feature is this program:

```
40 PAY = 176.347
50 PRINT USING "**$####.##";PAY
60 END
RUN
***$176.35
Ok
```

On large dollar values, a comma can be specified in the PRINT USING statement by placing it to the left of the decimal. A comma will then be printed in the number displayed in the appropriate position, as illus-

```
10  REM   Note extra space in output
20  SELLING.PRICE = 110
30  TAX.RATE       = .05
40  TAX  = SELLING.PRICE * TAX.RATE
50  SALE = SELLING.PRICE + TAX
60  REM
70   PRINT "The selling price is";
80   PRINT USING "$$###.##";SELLING.PRICE
90   PRINT "The sales tax is";
100 REM      The below PRINT USING field is too large
110 PRINT USING "$$##.##"; TAX
120 PRINT "Total sale including tax is ";
130 PRINT USING "$###.##"; SALE
140 END
RUN
The selling price is $110.00
The sales tax is  $5.50
Total sale including tax is $115.50
Ok
```

FIGURE 3.14   The PRINT USING statement

trated. Notice that a pound symbol (#) appears in statement 10 when the program is listed. This is due to the internal storage of the number. Program execution is not affected. (See Chapter 16 concerning double-precision numbers.)

```
10  pay = 10842.977
20  print using "$$######,.##";pay
30  pay = 842.9771
40  print using "$$######,.##";pay
LIST
10 PAY = 10842.977#
20 PRINT USING "$$######,.##";PAY
30 PAY = 842.9771
40 PRINT USING "$$######,.##";PAY
Ok
RUN
   $10,842.98
       $842.98
Ok
```

If you think that there are a lot of applications for the PRINT USING statement, you are right! Let's quickly review the major ones. The first is the "normal" usage in which the print positions in the PRINT USING statement exactly match the positions to be printed to the left of the decimal place. Note the extra blank inside the quotation mark as an aid in formatting output.

```
10 TEST = 123.456
20 PRINT "This is a demonstration ";
30 PRINT USING "###.##"; TEST
RUN
This is a demonstration 123.46
Ok
```

If the extra space is not included inside the quotation mark, the program and output would be as follows:

```
10 TEST = 123.456
20 PRINT "This is a demonstration";
30 PRINT USING "###.##"; TEST
RUN
This is a demonstration123.46
Ok
```

If desired, output can be spaced by placing an extra print position within the PRINT USING statement as follows:

```
10 TEST = 123.456
20 PRINT "This is a demonstration";
30 PRINT USING "####.##"; TEST
RUN
This is a demonstration 123.46
Ok
```

A double dollar sign ($$) specifies two more print positions, one of which is the dollar sign. This would be used as follows:

```
10 TEST = 123.456
20 PRINT "This is a demonstration";
30 PRINT USING "$$###.##"; TEST
RUN
This is a demonstration $123.46
Ok
```

However, if a number becomes large with the double dollar sign, the print position can be used up. The result appears as follows:

```
10 TEST = 1234.562
20 PRINT "This is a demonstration";
30 PRINT USING "$$###.##"; TEST
RUN
This is a demonstration$1234.56
Ok
```

Don't just read about the various features in BASIC. Enter some of the programs and run them. Then change a statement, re-run the program, and observe what happens.

The trick to understanding PRINT USING statements, as with other BASIC statements, is to start using them in your programs. You will then quickly understand how this statement can format output.

SUMMARY

PRINT statements are the means by which the computer displays information to users. A clear and accurate display of information increases the usefulness of the program and reduces user errors. It takes a lot of time to develop meaningful, professional output but it is time well spent.

As your programming skills increase, you will be able to write larger programs. The next chapter presents various techniques for saving, copying, and processing programs. These techniques save you from having to retype the program each time it is to be run.

Summary of terms

Name	Example	Purpose
LIST	`LIST`	Displays the program in memory on the monitor.
LLIST	`LLIST`	Displays the program in memory on an attached printer.
LPRINT	`90 LPRINT "Mr. John Smith, Buyer"`	Displays whatever is between quotation marks on the printer.
PRINT	`80 PRINT "Mr. John Smith, Buyer"`	Displays whatever is between quotation marks on the monitor.
TAB	`60 PRINT TAB(29) "Ajax Sales"`	Displays "Ajax Sales" beginning in the 29th column.
;	`70 PRINT "Ajax";` `80 PRINT " is best"`	A semicolon continues display on the same line. Result: `Ajax is best`
,	`230 PRINT ROOM, PARKING`	A comma directs display to the next print zone.
LPRINT USING		Displays output on a printer in the same format that PRINT USING displays output on a monitor.
PRINT USING	`30 PRINT "The tax is";` `40 PRINT USING "###.##";TAX`	# indicates the position of digits. Assume that TAX = 14.857; the value of TAX is displayed with three places to the left and two places to the right of the decimal. Values to right of the decimal are rounded.
Results in:		Result: `The tax is 14.86`
	`30 PRINT "The tax is";` `40 PRINT USING "$###.##"; TAX`	Blanks are used between the dollar sign and the number. Result: `The tax is$ 14.86`
	`30 PRINT "The tax is";` `40 PRINT USING "$$###.##";TAX`	The dollar sign appears next to the number. Result: `The tax is $14.86`

	`20 PAY = 176.347`
	`30 PRINT "Your pay is";`
	`40 PRINT USING "**$####.##";PAY`
		The asterisk fills up spaces before the dollar sign. Result:
		`Your pay is **$176.35`

	`20 PAY = 10842.972`
	`30 PRINT "Your pay is";`
	`40 PRINT USING "$$######,.##"`
		A comma is displayed in the appropriate position by placing it to the left of the decimal. Result:
		`Your pay is $10,842.97`

PROBLEMS

True/False. Problems 1–15.

3.1 The statement 30 PRINT "SALE" prints the value of the variable SALE. *F*

3.2 A PRINT statement displays whatever is between question marks. *F*

3.3 The command LLIST displays the program lines of the current program in memory on an attached printer. *T*

3.4 Commands are entered without line numbers. *T*

3.5 Commands can be entered only in uppercase letters. *F*

3.6 There are 80 columns across the screen. *T*

3.7 The letter *x* is used to multiply two variables together. *F*

3.8 A PRINT statement without anything following it displays a blank line. *T*

3.9 There are 22 lines down the screen.

3.10 TAB is used to move output down the designated number of lines. *F*

*3.11 30 PRINT TAB(20) "The sale is" is a valid BASIC statement. *F*

3.12 The PRINT USING statement can be used to format output. *T*

3.13 LPRINT is typed to get a printing of the current program in memory. *T*

3.14 The command LIST displays the program lines of the current program in memory on a monitor. *T*

3.15 65 PRINT TAB "The sale is" SALE is a valid BASIC statement. *F*

Identification of Program Output. Problems 16–27.
In Problems 16–19 assume that the following variables have the indicated values assigned in memory:

HATS	SWEATERS	SHIRTS.S	SHIRTS.M	SHOES
10	15	8	7	12

Write the specific output when the indicated partial program is executed.

3.16 60 PRINT "We have" SHIRTS.S "small shirts and";
70 PRINT SHIRTS.M "medium shirts."   *7 medium shirts*

3.17 120 TOTALSHIRTS = SHIRTS.S + SHIRTS.M
130 PRINT "Total number of shirts =" TOTALSHIRTS   *15*

3.18 80 PRINT "The number of shoes:" SWEATERS   *15*

Hint: Although the output is incorrectly labeled, the computer will "correctly" follow program instructions.

3.19 110 REM Partial program 3.19
120 PRINT "Clothing"
130 PRINT HATS, SWEATERS
140 PRINT SHIRTS.S, SHIRTS.M
150 PRINT, SHOES

* The answer to this problem is in Appendix E.

In Problems 20–27 write the exact output that would appear when the program is executed (run). Be careful to notice all spaces and the effect of the commas and semicolons.

3.20
```
10 REM Begin tricky problem 3.20
20 PRINT "Another day, another dollar?"
30 END
```
Another day, another dollar

*3.21
```
10 REM Problem 3.21
20 PRINT "Another day", "another dollar?"
30 END
```
Another day   another dollar

3.22
```
10 REM Problem 3.22
20 PRINT "Another day," "another dollar?"
30 PRINT END
```

3.23
```
10 REM Problem 3.23
20 PRINT "Another day" "another dollar?"
30 END
```

3.24
```
10 REM Problem 3.24
20 PRINT "Another day"; "another dollar?"
30 END
```

3.25
```
10 REM Problem 3.25
20 PRINT "Another day";
30 PRINT "another dollar?"
40 END
```

3.26
```
10 REM Problem 3.26. Note space inside quotes
20 PRINT "Another day ";
30 PRINT "another dollar!"
40 END
```

3.27
```
10 REM Problem 3.27
20 PRINT "Another day,";
30 PRINT " another dollar!!"
40 END
```

Program Completion—Beginning. Problems 28–31.
BASIC assignment statements are shown. Write the value of the variable in the indicated boxes.

*3.28
```
10 REM Problem 3.28
20 RATE = 4.35
30 HOURS = 10
40 PAY = RATE * HOURS
50 PRINT "The pay is"
60 PRINT PAY
70 END
RUN
```

RATE
4.35

HOURS
10

PAY
43.50

3.29
```
10 REM Problem 3.29
20 RATE = 4.35
30 HOURS = 10
40 PAY = RATE * HOURS
50 PRINT "The pay is";
60 PRINT USING "$$##.##";PAY
70 END
RUN
```

RATE
4.35

HOURS
10

PAY
$43.50

---

* The answer to this problem is in Appendix E.

RATE

HOURS

PAY

3.30
```
10 REM Problem 3.30
20 RATE = 3
30 HOURS = 3.33
40 PAY = RATE * HOURS
50 PRINT "Hours worked are";
60 PRINT USING "##.#"; HOURS
70 PRINT "At a pay of";
80 PRINT USING "$$#.##"; PAY;
90 PRINT ".  Thank you."
100 END
RUN
Hours worked are 3.33
At a pay of $ 9.99 .  Thank you.
```

(handwritten: RATE box = 3, HOURS box = 3.33, PAY box = 9.99)

3.31
```
10 REM Weird problem 3.31
20 UNITPRICE = 5.50
30 QTSOLD = 10
40 SALE = UNITPRICE * QTSOLD
50 PRINT
60 END
```
(handwritten: 55.00)

Hint: As humans we are looking for something when a program has been executed, but what will this program display when executed?

Program Completion—Advanced. Problems 32–40.
Find and complete the necessary statements so that the output indicated will be produced when the program is executed (run).

*3.32**
```
10 REM Problem 3.32
20 HOURS.WORKED = 50
30 PRINT "The hours worked are:  " Hours.worked    ← What variable name
40 END                                                 must be here?
RUN
The hours worked are: 50
```

3.33
```
10 REM Problem 3.33
20 Weight = 345.78                        ← What must be here?
30 PRINT "The weight is" WEIGHT
40 END
RUN
The weight is 345.78
```

3.34
```
10 REM Problem 3.34
20 Weight = 87                            ← What must be here?
30 PRINT "The weight is" WEIGHT "pounds"  ← What must be here?
40 END
RUN
The weight is 87 pounds
```

3.35
```
10 REM Problem 3.35
20 UNITS = 5
30 COST = 3
40 TOTAL = UNITS * Cost                   ← What must be here?
50 PRINT "You bought" UNITS ;             ← What must be here?
60 PRINT "The price is $" TOTAL
70 END
RUN
You bought 5 units.
The price is $ 15
```

* The answer to this problem is in Appendix E.

*3.36   10 REM Problem 3.36 uses TAB
        20 PRINT TAB(← What must be here?
        30 PRINT "Alfred E. Neuman"
        40 END
        RUN
                        Student Enrollment
        Alfred E. Neuman
        Ok

3.37   10 REM Problem 3.37 uses multiple TABS
        20 PRINT TAB(10) "Ajax Manufacturing Co."
        30 PRINT   ← What must be here?
        40 END
        RUN
                Ajax Manufacturing Co.
                Sales   Profit
        Ok

3.38   10 REM Problem 3.38
        20 PRINT TAB(7)   ← What must be here?
        30 PRINT   ← What must be here?
        40 END
        RUN
                Struggling Students University
        Dorm #   Room #
        Ok

3.39   10 REM Problem 3.39
        20 PRICE = 5.95
        30 QUANTITY = 5
        40 SALE = PRICE * QUANTITY
        50 PRINT "The total sale is"   ← What must be here?
        60 PRINT USING "$$##.##"; SALE   ← What must be here?
        70 PRINT ".   Thank you."
        80 END
        RUN
        The total sale is $29.75.   Thank you.

3.40   10 REM Problem 3.40
        20 TRUCK = 19595
        30 CAR = 9850
        40 PRINT TAB(← What must be here?
        50 PRINT "Trucks"   ← What must be here?
        60 PRINT TRUCK   ← What must be here?
        70 END
        RUN
                Happy Harry's Used Cars
        Trucks   Cars
         19595   9850
        Ok

Program Completion—PRINT USING. Problems 41–44.
Identify the PRINT USING statement that is required by the program so that the indicated output will be produced. Fill in the letter in the blank space provided.

---

* The answer to this problem is in Appendix E.

```
a.  PRINT USING "$####.##"; SOAP
b.  PRINT USING "$$.##"; SOAP
c.  PRINT USING "$###.##"; SOAP
d.  PRINT USING "$##.##"; SOAP
e.  PRINT USING "$###.##"; MEAT
f.  PRINT USING "$####.##"; MEAT
g.  PRINT USING "$###.##"; NAPKINS
h.  PRINT USING "$####.##"; NAPKINS
```

*3.41
```
60 REM Program 3.41
70 SOAP = .69
80 NAPKINS = 1.39
90 MEAT = 18.65
100                              _____
110                              _____
120                              _____
RUN
$    0.69
$    1.39
$   18.65
Ok
```

3.42
```
60 REM Program 3.42
70 SOAP = .69
80 NAPKINS = 1.39
90 MEAT = 18.65
100                              _____
110                              _____
120                              _____
RUN
$  0.69
$  1.39
$ 18.65
Ok
```

3.43
```
10 REM Program 3.43
20 SOAP = .69
30 PRINT "The soap costs";
40                               _____
RUN
The soap costs$0.69
Ok
```

3.44
```
10 REM Program 3.44 (Note extra space inside quote.)
20 REM (Same PRINT USING in previous problem.)
30 SOAP = .69
40 PRINT "The soap costs ";
50                               _____
RUN
The soap costs $0.69
Ok
```

Program Completion—Additional PRINT USING statements.
Problems 45–48.
Identify the PRINT USING statement that is required by the program so that the indicated output will be produced. Fill in the letter in the blank space provided.

* The answer to this problem is in Appendix E.

     a. `PRINT USING "####.##"; TAX`
     b. `PRINT USING "$$##.##"; TAX`
     c. `PRINT USING "$$###.##"; TAX`
     d. `PRINT USING "$$##.###"; TAX`
     e. `PRINT USING "$###.##"; TAX`
     f. `PRINT USING "$.##"; TAX`

*3.45
```
10 REM Problem 3.45
20 TAX = 45.955
30 PRINT "The tax is";
40                              _____
RUN
The tax is $45.955
Ok
```

3.46
```
10 REM Problem 3.46
20 TAX = 45.955
30 PRINT "The tax is";
40                              _____
RUN
The tax is $45.96
Ok
```

3.47
```
10 REM Problem 3.47
20 TAX = 145.955
30 PRINT "The tax is";
40                              _____
RUN
The tax is$145.96
Ok
```

3.48
```
10 REM Problem 3.48
20 TAX = 1145.955
30 PRINT "The tax is";
40                              _____
RUN
The tax is%$1145.96
Ok
```

Debugging Problems. Problems 49–73.
Problems 49–59 consist of single BASIC statements. Identify which of the statements are incorrect and write the correct statement.

*3.49   `12 PRODUCE = 50.45`

3.50   `23 OUR PRODUCE = 50.45`

3.51   `77 NEW.PRODUCT = - 243.45`

3.52   `35 OLD-PRODUCT = 122`

3.53   `44 print tab(10) "Hi there!"`

3.54   `59 PRINT TAB(50) "Ajax Grocery Store" TAB(60) "SALE!!"`

3.55   `76 PRINT TAB (22) "Be careful!"`

3.56   `92 DOLLAR.COST = $45.80`

3.57   `40 NEW = 22`

3.58   `77 THH.NEW.PRODUCT.COST = 24.95`

3.59   `12 TOTAL = SUM = ANS = 0`

* The answer to this problem is in Appendix E.

Debugging Problems—Miniprograms. Problems 60–70.
The miniprograms shown contain errors. Some of the errors (program bugs)
are easy to find, others will be difficult to detect. The programs were executed
and the screen appeared as shown. Find and correct the error so that a logical
output can be obtained when the program is executed.

*3.60   An attempt was made to print "Your tax bill is $11,618.94."

```
10 PRINT "Your tax bill is";
20 TAX = 11618.94
30 PRINT USING "$$#####,.##;TAX
RUN
Your tax bill is
Syntax error in 30
Ok
30 PRINT USING "$$#####,.##;TAX
```

3.61   An attempt was made to print "The grocery bill is $195.45."

```
82 GROCERY = 195.45
84 PRINT "The grocery bill is"
86 PRINT USING "$$###.##";GROCERY
RUN
The grocery bill is
 $195.45
Ok
```

An attempt was made to display the value of $235.75.

```
10 COST = 35.75
20 PRINT "The BIG COST is the $200 added to all fees"
30 PRINT USING "$$###.##";BIG.COSTS
40 BIG COSTS = COST + 200
RUN
The BIG COST is the $200 added to all fees
    $0.00
Ok
```

3.63   An attempt was made to print the value of the variable SALE under the
word "sale" in the print statement.

```
10 SALE = 25.75
20 PRINT "The extra big sale"
30 PRINT TAB (15) SALE
RUN
The extra big sale
Subscript out of range in 30
Ok
```

3.64   An attempt was made to print the remittance.

---

* The answer to this problem is in Appendix E.

```
10 REM Money sent is a REMITTANCE [REM]
20 GOODS = 10
30 REM = GOODS * 2
40 PRINT "The remittance is" REM
RUN
The remittance is
Syntax error in 40
Ok
40 PRINT "The remittance is" REM
_
```

3.65   An attempt was made to print the sales value of 22.45.

```
10 SALES = 22.45
20 PRINT "The sale is $" SALE
RUN
The sale is $ 0
Ok
```

3.66   An attempt was made to print the price.

```
10 PRICE = -99.95
20 PRINT USING "$$###.##" PRICE
RUN
Syntax error in 20
Ok
20 PRINT USING "$$###.##" PRICE
_
```

3.67   An attempt was made to print the cost.

```
10 COST = 2625.5
20 PRINT USING "$$##.##";COST
RUN
%$2625.50
Ok
```

3.68   An attempt was made to print:
"The bill for 12 shirts is $119.40," but an extra space appeared after "is."

```
10 TIES = 12
20 PRICE  = 9.95
30 TIE.BILL = PRICE * TIES
40 PRINT "The bill for" TIES "shirts is";
50 PRINT USING "$$####.##";TIE.BILL
RUN
The bill for 12 shirts is  $119.40
Ok
```

3.69   An attempt was made to print the total bill for shirts purchased for resale.

```
10 SHIRTS = 144
20 PRICE  = 29.95
30 SHIRT.BILL = PRICE * SHIRTS
40 REMARK                        SCREEN OUTPUT
50 PRINT "The bill for"  SHIRTS "shirts is";
60 PRINT USING "$$####,.##"; SHIRT.BILL
RUN
Syntax error in 40
Ok
40 REMARK                        SCREEN OUTPUT
_
```

3.70 An attempt was made to print the cost of the gallons of gas purchased using a dollar-and-cents format. (There are two bugs in this program.)

```
10 PRICE = 1.65
20 GALLONS = 10
30 COST = PRICE * GALLONS
40 PRINT USING  $$###0## ;COST
RUN
Syntax error in 40
Ok
40 PRINT USING  $$###0## ;COST
_
```

Debugging Problems. Problems 71–73.
Find and correct the error to produce the output shown when the program is executed.

3.71
```
20 REM Problem 3.71                Look closely and correct the error
30 PRICE = 5.95
40 QUANTITY = 5
50 SALE = PRICE * QUANTITY
60 PRINT TAB (8) "Ajax Sales"      ← What is the error?
70 PRINT "The total sale is";
80 PRINT USING "$$##.##"; SALE
90 END
RUN
        Ajax Sales
The total sale is $29.75
```

3.72
```
10 REM Problem 3.72
20 FEES = 133.95
30 STUDENTS = 22
40 TOTAL = FEES * STUDENTS
50 PRINT "The total fees of";
60 PRINT USING "$$##.##"; TOTAL    ← What is the error?
70 PRINT " is too low."
80 END
RUN
The total fees of $2946.90 is too low.
```

3.73
```
10 REM Problem 3.73
20 ROOM.COST = 695.95
30 PRINT "The semester dorm charge is";
40 PRINT USING "$$###.##", ROOM.COST   ← What is the error?
50 END
RUN
The semester dorm charge is $695.95
```

Screen Design Problems—Statement Development. Problems 74–76.
Write the necessary statements so that the output indicated will be produced when the program is executed.

3.74
```
10 REM You're on the honor roll!
20 PRINT TAB(16) "Dean's Honor Roll"
30 PRINT TAB(                           ← What must be here?
40 PRINT "Your Name" TAB(30) "Grade A+" ← Use your own name.
50 END
RUN
```

```
┌─────────────────────────────────────────────┐
│              Dean's Honor Roll               │
│         Outstanding Computer Students        │
│     Your Name                      Grade A+  │
└─────────────────────────────────────────────┘
```

*3.75
```
10 REM Problem 3.75
20 PRINT TAB(20) "Quick and Cheap Shop"
30 PRINT TAB(
40 PRINT
50 PRINT "Employee" TAB(15) "Social Security" TAB(40)
60 PRINT "Name"      TAB(15) "Number"
70 PRINT
80 PRINT "Mary Worth" TAB(15)
90 END
RUN
```

```
┌──────────────────────────────────────────────────┐
│              Quick and Cheap Shop                  │
│                Weekly Payroll                      │
│                                                    │
│   Employee        Social Security        Gross     │
│   Name            Number                 Pay       │
│                                                    │
│   Mary Worth      236-14-1856            $235.75   │
└──────────────────────────────────────────────────┘
```

3.76
```
10 REM Problem 3.76
20 PRINT TAB(10) "Tom's Used Car Sales"
30 PRINT TAB(
40 PRINT "Here a Lemon" TAB(
50 END
RUN
```

```
┌──────────────────────────────────────────────────┐
│              Tom's Used Car Sales                  │
│                Buy a Lemon-Cheap                   │
│   Here a Lemon                    There a Lemon    │
└──────────────────────────────────────────────────┘
```

Screen Design Problems. Problems 77–88.
Develop a BASIC program, paying particular attention to the design of the screen and the design of the printed output (when requested). General formats are shown for your consideration which may be expanded on (improved) in your program.

3.77 Write a program that displays the name and address of Jack's Auto Parts (below) on the monitor and printer. In addition, have a program display the following on the monitor:

---

* The answer to this problem is in Appendix E.

```
**Jack has the lowest prices in town**
              Jack's Auto Parts
              1450 S. Third St.
              New York, NY 00000
```

Problems 78 and 79 require the following information.

First National Bank of Flat Plains, Kansas, pays interest quarterly. At the end of the year a detailed statement of interest paid is sent to each account holder for reporting on their income tax.

Write a program to prepare the yearly interest statement according to the following format:

```
               First National Bank
               Flat Plains Kansas
               Interest Received
WINTER          $XX.XX
SPRING          $XX.XX
SUMMER          $XX.XX
FALL            $XX.XX

19XX Total:     $XXX.XX
Account:        239-21-7852
Account holder: Mr. Bob Jones
                194 S. Main St.
                St. Louis, MO 67510

All income must be reported to the I.R.S.
Form 1090 will not be sent.
```

3.78 First, develop the program to display the output on a printer. Bob received the following quarterly interest payments in 1989: winter $12.52, spring $5.25, summer $18.14, fall $6.55.

3.79 Next, develop the program to display the output on a monitor. Bob received the following quarterly interest payments in 1990: winter $25.00, spring $22.45, summer $19.50, fall $3.45.

Problems 80–82 require the following information.

Write a program to create and fill in a blank paycheck. Make the paycheck out to yourself for any amount. Print the amount with leading ****$ to prevent alterations according to the following format. (Don't try to cash the check.)

```
                      Slop Shops Inc.
                    PAYCHECK        Date  XX/XX/XX
          Pay to:_____  ****$X,XXX.XX
          Last National Bank
          Miami, FL 33037          _____
                                   Treasurer
```

3.80 Have the program display the paycheck on a monitor.

3.81 Have the program display the paycheck on a printer.

3.82 Have the program display the paycheck on both a monitor and on a printer.

Problems 83–85 require the following information.

Write a program to balance Tom Jones's checkbook. Display the output in the format shown.

```
┌─────────────────────────────────────┐
│                                     │
│              Tom Jones              │
│           October, 1990             │
│                                     │
│     Transaction        Amount       │
│     -----------        ------       │
│     BALANCE.FWD.       $500.73      │
│     Rent               $225.25      │
│     Electric Co.       $ 34.90      │
│     Campus Shop Co.    $ 90.00      │
│                        -------      │
│     BALANCE            $150.58      │
│                                     │
└─────────────────────────────────────┘
```

3.83   Have the program display the output on a monitor.

3.84   Have the program display the output on a printer.

3.85   Have the program display the output on both a monitor and on a printer.

3.86   Smith's Computer Store needs an inventory report containing the following information: (1) the list price of the computer; (2) current inventory (in units) of computers in stock; (3) the number of units (computers) sold; and (4) the gross sales.

Write a program to produce a printed inventory report according to this format:

```
┌─────────────────────────────────────────────┐
│                                             │
│           Smith's Computer Store            │
│          Monthly Inventory Report           │
│               January, 19XX                 │
│                                             │
│    List       Current      Units    Gross   │
│    Price      Inventory     Sold     Sales   │
│                                             │
│   $XXXX.XX    XX            XX      $XXXX.XX │
│                                             │
└─────────────────────────────────────────────┘
```

Use the following assignment statements in developing your program:

List Price = $5,129.95
Current Inventory = 16
Units Sold = 12

Problems 87 and 88 require the following information:

Consolidated Furniture Store needs a sales analysis report that calculates the mark-up for October. Mark-up in furniture sales is determined by the following formula:

```
MARK-UP = (SALE - COST.OF.GOODS) / SALE
```

The result is expressed in percentage form.

The sales analysis report is used to decide if prices should be changed. The report should include the sale amount, the cost of goods sold, and the calculated percent retail mark-up.

Write a program that will produce the report according to the following output:

```
┌─────────────────────────────────────────────────────┐
│            Consolidated Furniture Store              │
│               Sales Analysis Report                  │
│                 OCTOBER, 19XX                        │
│      SALE          COST OF GOODS      RETAIL % MARK-UP│
│      $X,XXX.XX      $XXX.XX           XX.X%           │
└─────────────────────────────────────────────────────┘
```

3.87 Prepare a sales analysis report using the following data.

> SALE = $1,652.97
> COST.OF.GOODS = $ 976.55

3.88 Prepare a sales analysis report for two items in stock. Use the following data.

First item in stock:

> SALE1 = $12,799.50
> COST.OF.GOODS1 = $7,650.95

Then change the variable assignments and re-run the report for the second item in stock.

Second item in stock:

> SALE2 = $550.75
> COST.OF.GOODS2 = $210.00

Other Problems. Problems 89–92.
Develop a BASIC program to solve each problem. Use a REM statement to identify the problem number, and clearly label all output.

3.89 Write a program to display "to," "get," and "her" on the same line to create one word. Use a different PRINT statement for each group of letters.

3.90 Develop a BASIC program to format a letterhead. This letterhead should consist of the company name, address, and phone number. (Use the name of any company.)

3.91 Write a program that centers and prints your name and address on the screen.

3.92 Mr. Tom Sawyer is a customer of Happy Smiles Wine and Cheese Shop. Mr. Sawyer has just purchased the following items for a Christmas party to be held by his firm, Fun Loving Important People (FLIP).

Item	
Wines	$456.49
Cheese	$125.50
Snacks	$35.95

We would love to obtain FLIP as a regular customer. Develop a program to print a professional, detailed bill to be sent to Mr. Sawyer.

4 USING COMMANDS TO MANAGE PROGRAMS

Upon completion of this chapter you should be able to

- Use key BASIC commands
- SAVE, LOAD, LIST, and RUN a file
- Name and KILL a file
- LOAD and RUN programs on the companion diskette

The discussion so far has focused on program statements to instruct the computer in processing data. We now turn our attention to managing these programs by the use of commands. Commands are different from programming statements because they process the program instead of processing data. The Enter key is still pressed after typing a command but statement line numbers are not normally used.

Commands are of two types: those that can be used while in the BASIC language and those that can be used at the DOS (disk operating system) level. Let's first master commands that can be used at the BASIC language level.

RUN

The computer will accept a command only when the cursor is displayed. Otherwise it is under control of a program. Press the keys Ctrl and Break to exit (break) the program and display the cursor.

The RUN command executes the current program in memory. Execution begins with the lowest numbered statement and progresses through the program until the END statement is reached. After the computer executes the command, the BASIC prompt Ok appears, to indicate that the computer is under the control of BASIC and waiting for another command.

LIST

The LIST command is used to display the program that is currently in memory. In Figure 4.1 the indicated program was in memory but it was not displayed until the LIST command was given. Notice the capitalized words. All BASIC instructions and variable names are translated into up-

```
1Ørem Using the LIST command
20 taxrate = .Ø5
3Ø sale = 1ØØ
4Ø Tax = sale * taxrate
5Ø print "The sales tax is"
6Ø print tax
7Øend
LIST
1Ø REM Using the LIST command
2Ø TAXRATE = .Ø5
3Ø SALE = 1ØØ
4Ø TAX = SALE * TAXRATE
5Ø PRINT "The sales tax is"
6Ø PRINT TAX
7Ø END
Ok
RUN
The sales tax is
  5
Ok
```

FIGURE 4.1 LISTing a program

percase except those between quotation marks or following a REM. The case you use does not affect program execution. Be careful with your use of spaces, however, because they are used to separate variable names and BASIC words.

CORRECTING ERRORS

Simple errors made in typing a program statement can be corrected by pressing the ⌐4⌐ or the backspace key and typing the correction. However, if you find numerous errors within a statement or if you find an error after pressing the Enter key, retype the whole statement, including the original statement number, or use the EDIT function (described later). When you type a duplicate statement number, the computer retains only the last statement in its memory.

In the program shown in Figure 4.1, statement 50, for example, could be changed by typing a revised statement at the end of the program, either before or after it was run or listed. For example, if 5Ø PRINT "The state sales tax is" were typed, statement 50 would become this latest revised statement. Additional statements could be added (notice the poor format) such as

```
65print "End of program"
68 print "Good by!"
```

A clear copy of the current program, including all changes, can then be obtained by the LIST command as shown in Figure 4.2. Notice how BASIC reserved words are changed to uppercase letters and a space is added after the statement number in statement 65.

If the number 4 appears when the left arrow key is pressed, the computer is in numeric mode. Press Num Lock once to convert the numeric pad to program edit mode.

```
LIST
10 REM Using the LIST command
20 TAXRATE = .05
30 SALE = 100
40 TAX = SALE * TAXRATE
50 PRINT "The sales tax is"
60 PRINT TAX
70 END
Ok
50 Print "The state sales tax is"
65print "End of program"
68 print "Good by!"
LIST
10 REM Using the LIST command
20 TAXRATE = .05
30 SALE = 100
40 TAX = SALE * TAXRATE
50 PRINT "The state sales tax is"
60 PRINT TAX
65 PRINT "End of program"
68 PRINT "Good by!"
70 END
Ok
```

FIGURE 4.2   Use of the LIST command

After proofreading to ensure that the desired changes have been entered, the program can be executed.

```
RUN
The state sales tax is
 5
End of program
Good by!
Ok
```

The RUN command can also be used to execute a program beginning with a specific statement number. For example, if the program shown in Figure 4.2 is in memory, the command RUN 68 results in "Good by!" being displayed.

When you are working on lengthy programs, it is often desirable to list a specific program statement that you have changed. Giving the command LIST, followed by typing a line number, and pressing the Enter key displays the line you typed. The command LIST 20 results in

```
20 TAXRATE = .05
```

A range of statements can be displayed by giving the LIST command followed by the beginning statement number, a hyphen, and then the ending statement number. For example, the command LIST 20-30 results in

```
20 TAXRATE = .05
30 SALE = 100
```

Programs can also be listed from a particular statement number to the end of the program by the command

LIST   Statement   _
        Number

Several uses of the LIST command are as follows:

```
LIST 40
40 TAX = SALE * TAXRATE
Ok
LIST 40-60
40 TAX = SALE * TAXRATE
50 PRINT "The state sales tax is"
60 PRINT TAX
Ok
LIST 40-
40 TAX = SALE * TAXRATE
50 PRINT "The state sales tax is"
60 PRINT TAX
65 PRINT "End of program"
68 PRINT "Good by!"
70 END
Ok
```

DELETE

Only the primary usage of BASIC terms is discussed. If you want to get fancy, try experimenting with different commands to see if they can be used as statements. For example, LIST can be used as a statement within a program to display the program automatically after it executes.

If a program is already in memory, an individual program statement can be deleted by entering the statement line number followed by the Enter key. The statement is assigned no information and is therefore eliminated (assigned nothing). A statement can also be erased by the command DELETE, for example: DELETE 65.

In the program shown in Figure 4.3, for example, statements 65 and 68 could have been deleted by entering each statement number followed by

```
LIST
10 REM Using the LIST command
20 TAXRATE = .05
30 SALE = 100
40 TAX = SALE * TAXRATE
50 PRINT "The state sales tax is"
60 PRINT TAX
65 PRINT "End of program"
68 PRINT "Good by!"
70 END
Ok
delete 65-68
Ok
LIST
10 REM Using the LIST command
20 TAXRATE = .05
30 SALE = 100
40 TAX = SALE * TAXRATE
50 PRINT "The state sales tax is"
60 PRINT TAX
70 END
Ok
```

FIGURE 4.3 Use of the DELETE command

pressing the Enter key. In Figure 4.3, the DELETE command was typed followed by the range of line numbers to be deleted: DELETE 65-68.

The uses of the BASIC commands DELETE and LIST are shown in Figure 4.3.

NEW

When a program is written, the computer does not anticipate the need for a clean space in memory. A program that is newly typed into memory will be combined with whatever currently exists in memory. This will result in a confused and often meaningless set of program instructions unless the NEW command is typed prior to entering the program.

Be careful when using the NEW command. The command will erase (destroy) any program from memory, even if it is a desirable program that you spent hours typing into memory.

A listing of the program shown in Figure 4.3 can be obtained as shown in Figure 4.4. When the NEW command is entered, the program is erased from memory. When the LIST command is reentered, nothing is displayed because the memory contents have been erased. Use of the NEW command does not affect program copies that have been stored on diskette.

> It is a good idea to use the command NEW before keying in your BASIC program. This clears the memory so that only the statements you enter will be present.

```
list
10 REM Using the LIST command
20 TAXRATE = .05
30 SALE = 100
40 TAX = SALE * TAXRATE
50 PRINT "The state sales tax is"
60 PRINT TAX
70 END
Ok
new
Ok
list
Ok
```

FIGURE 4.4 Use of the NEW command

CLS (CLEAR SCREEN TO BLANK)

The CLS command (which may also be used as a statement) clears the screen to black (blank screen) and returns the cursor to the upper left-hand position of the screen (called the home position). Use of CLS does not affect the current program in memory, which still may be listed and run.

Do not confuse CLS with the NEW command, which erases memory. CLS only clears the screen display and does not affect memory contents. (The screen may also be cleared by pressing the Ctrl and Home keys.)

For example, consider this short program:

> Although CLS is normally used as a command, it can also be used as a programming statement. This is a nice way to clear the screen before displaying program output.

```
10 CLS
20 END
RUN
```

```
Ok
_
```

FIGURE 4.5 Result of CLS

This program will produce a nearly blank screen as an output. As shown in Figure 4.5, only the word Ok appears. Because the screen turns to blank while the program is executing, the program does not appear on the screen, although it still resides in memory.

STOP (FREEZE) DISPLAY

Press Keys | Ctrl | Num Lock |

The groups of statements that make up a program control the computer. However, by using commands, you control the program that controls the computer.

The computer displays data at a rapid rate, which is often difficult to read. If you list a lengthy program, it will scroll up the screen before you can read it. You can stop output display temporarily by holding down the Ctrl key and then pressing the Num Lock key. When you want to resume the output display, press any key (such as the space bar). Stopping output temporarily is particularly useful when important information has to be recorded before the program places more data on the screen.

BREAKING THE PROGRAM

Press Keys | Ctrl | Break |

It is occasionally necessary to stop a program that is executing and to return to the BASIC language. This is accomplished by first pressing and holding the Ctrl key, then pressing the Break key. (The Break key is also the Scroll Lock key.) Pressing the Ctrl and Break keys at the same time while a program is executing stops (breaks) program execution. Program control remains at the BASIC level.

RESTARTING THE SYSTEM

If the computer system has to be restarted, it is quicker and easier to use three keystrokes than to turn the power switch off and back on. If the computer is turned off, several minutes will be required for the computer to reset itself and then to check its internal circuits.

Press and hold the following keys to quickly restart the computer:

Press Keys | Ctrl | Alt | Del |

Remember: when you restart the system everything in memory will be erased.

NAMING FILES

Anything stored on diskette is called a file. Let's develop an understanding of how programs can be stored and retrieved from diskette. For example, suppose we spend a lot of time creating a BASIC program. A name will have to be assigned to this program and the contents of memory saved under this name before leaving the BASIC level, or else everything will be lost.

Let's call the program "INVOICE." That is, "INVOICE" is the name by which the file, once saved, can later be retrieved. A file name should begin with a letter and can be up to eight characters long. The file name may include an optional three-character file extension separated from the name by a period. If this option is not used, BASIC assigns the extension .BAS to program files as an aid in identifying this as a BASIC file.

No spaces are permitted in file names. You cannot load a file that has a space in the name because the system will not "cross the space" to look for the rest of the name. The following are valid file names:

CLASS	SHIPPING
SHIPPING.INV	SHIPPING.01
PAYABLE	PAYABLE.001
PROGRAM1	PROG.1
AnyName	This is a valid name because all letters are automatically converted to capital letters.
FIG12-1	Preferred method if numbers are used. First, there is no blank space. Second, since a period is not used, the .BAS extension is added to show that a BASIC program has been saved.

The following are invalid file names:

FIG 12.1	This is not a valid file name and must be avoided. The program will not load correctly due to the blank space in the file name.
MY ONE	Again, no blanks are permitted.
RECEIVABLE	More than eight characters.
BIG.CAR.1	Only one file extension is allowed.
MY.CARS	Only a three-character extension is allowed in a file name.

When saving BASIC programs on diskette, a recommended procedure is to save them without specifying an extension. The BASIC language will then add the .BAS extension that permits programs to be quickly identified.

If you accidentally save a program with a space in the file name, the RENAME command at the DOS level (see next chapter) can be used. Rename the file to a correct name, which can then be loaded by BASIC.

THE FILES COMMAND

The command FILES typed at the BASIC level and followed by Enter displays a listing of the file names for the diskette files in the current drive. (Of course, this command should not be given unless there is a diskette in the drive.)

LOADING AND SAVING PROGRAMS

While at the BASIC level, the command LOAD "HELLO" loads a copy of the program named HELLO.BAS stored on diskette into memory. Once the program is loaded into memory, it can be executed (run) or modified as desired. Anything else residing in memory at the time the LOAD command is given will be lost. The process of loading a program does not alter the program stored on the diskette.

The SAVE command is used at the BASIC level to store the program currently in memory on a diskette. Assume that you are at the BASIC level and that the following program is currently in memory:

```
10  - - -
20  - - -
30  - - -
40  END
```
} Any program statements

The command to save a copy of this program on diskette under the name SALES is SAVE "SALES". This is accomplished by typing the command SAVE, followed by a space. Then type the beginning quotation mark and the word SALES. The ending quotation mark is optional. Finally, as with all commands, press Enter.

There are now two identical copies of the program. One program is in memory, and a second program is stored on diskette and is called SALES.BAS. (Remember: the .BAS extension is added automatically.) This can be viewed as follows:

Computer

Diskette
SALES.BAS

```
10  - - -
20  - - -
30  - - -
40  END
```

```
10  - - -
20  - - -
30  - - -
40  END
```

Suppose the program in memory is eliminated by typing the command NEW. Nothing now exists in the computer's memory, but the program on diskette called SALES.BAS is not altered.

Computer

Diskette
SALES.BAS

```
10  - - -
20  - - -
30  - - -
40  END
```

The command LOAD "SALES" tells the computer to retrieve a copy of the program called SALES.BAS storcd on diskette and load it into memory. Although the .BAS extension does not have to be specified, the quotation marks (at least the left one) must be specified. A space is not required between the command LOAD and the quotation mark, nor is the ending quotation mark required. However, a space and both quotes will be used in our examples.

Two copies of the program now exist. One is in memory and the other is contained on diskette under the name SALES.BAS. This can be viewed as shown on the next page.

Computer   Diskette
                           SALES.BAS

```
10  - - -          10  - - -
20  - - -          20  - - -
30  - - -          30  - - -
40  END            40  END
```

After you type the LOAD command, the program loaded into memory is executed. Instead of typing two separate commands such as LOAD "SALES", pressing Enter, and then typing RUN, a single more powerful command can be used. This is the RUN "program name" command.

The command RUN "SALES" has an implied load command. That is, the computer retrieves a copy of the program called SALES.BAS, loads it into memory, and then executes the program. You have a choice. Either type LOAD "SALES" and then type RUN or type the shortcut command RUN "SALES".

No matter which approach is used, there will be two copies of the program: the one stored on diskette and an electronic duplicate in the computer's memory. Now suppose we revise the program in memory by adding statement 15. If this revised program is saved on disk under the program name SALES, the former program called SALES.BAS is replaced by the modified program.

When developing programs, you may want to save the revised program in memory without destroying the original program stored on diskette, which may be needed for later reference. This is accomplished by giving the program currently in memory a new, unique name, by typing the BASIC command SAVE "SALES.01". The result is as follows:

                           Diskette
Computer   SALES.01   SALES.BAS

```
10  - - -        10  - - -          10  - - -
15  - - -        15  - - -          20  - - -
20  - - -        20  - - -          30  - - -
30  - - -        30  - - -          40  END
40  END          40  END
```

There are now three programs: the current program in memory, a duplicate called SALES.01 on diskette, and a third, older program on diskette under the name SALES.BAS.

If the command NEW is entered, the current program in memory is erased, leaving two diskette programs, SALES.BAS and SALES.01. That is, the BASIC command NEW results in

                           Diskette
Computer   SALES.01   SALES.BAS

```
                 10  - - -          10  - - -
                 15  - - -          20  - - -
                 20  - - -          30  - - -
                 30  - - -          40  END
                 40  END
```

The SALES.01 program could be executed by following the previous steps. Type LOAD "SALES.01" and press Enter to retrieve a copy from the diskette and load it into memory. This would result in

Diskette

Computer	SALES.01	SALES.BAS

```
  10  - - -        10  - - -        10  - - -
  15  - - -        15  - - -        20  - - -
  20  - - -        20  - - -        30  - - -
  30  - - -        30  - - -        40  END
  40  END          40  END
```

Suppose you wanted to change the name of the SALES.BAS file to the name INVOICE. This is accomplished by the NAME command, as follows:

```
NAME "SALES.BAS" AS "INVOICE.BAS"
```

The result of using the NAME command is shown below. Notice that, although the diskette name was changed, the computer's memory is not changed.

Diskette

Computer	SALES.01	INVOICE.BAS

```
  10  - - -        10  - - -        10  - - -
  15  - - -        15  - - -        20  - - -
  20  - - -        20  - - -        30  - - -
  30  - - -        30  - - -        40  END
  40  END          40  END
```

KILL (PROGRAM NAME)

Have you become confused about what a diskette contains? Then label the diskettes. Write the major program names on the label provided with the diskette and then put the label on the disk. In the next chapter, we will discuss how to get a list of your programs that can be taped on the diskette sleeve.

The BASIC command KILL followed by a program name will erase the program stored on a diskette. The file extension must be specified when using the KILL command, which is followed by pressing the Enter key. For example, the following command erases the program called INVOICE.BAS stored on a diskette:

```
KILL "INVOICE.BAS"
```

The KILL command eliminates the program and the diskette space can be used for other purposes. The BASIC command FILES will show that the program no longer exists. Although it is a good idea to eliminate useless programs, exercise caution to avoid destroying valuable programs.

NOW IT'S YOUR TURN

If you have not already done so, select the BASIC Commands tutorial on the companion disk. The screen will appear as shown below. BASIC commands will be easy to remember after you use them a few times.

```
BASIC Programming With the IBM PC

         BASIC Commands

              By
          Peter Mears
      (c) Copyright 1990
```

After you have run the BASIC Commands program, the menu selection program will again appear. There are two ways of leaving program control and going to the DOS level.The first is to press the down arrow until the pointer is next to the words "Exit to DOS," as shown below. Press the Enter key for the DOS level. Or if you prefer, simply press the Esc key and you will automatically exit to DOS.

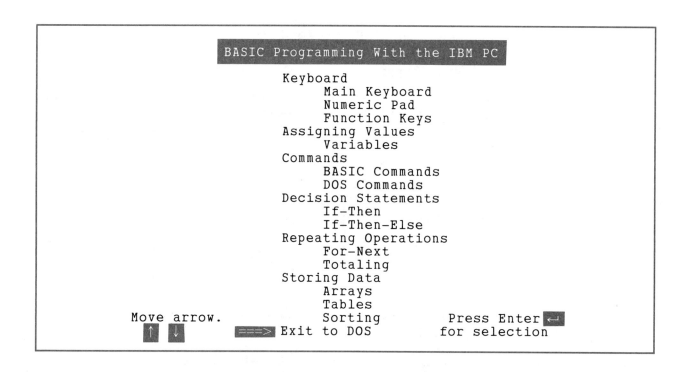

As we are going to process BASIC programs, load the BASIC interpreter by typing BASICA at the DOS level with a disk containing the interpreter in the drive.

When BASIC has been loaded, if you want the name of the files stored on the companion diskette, type the command FILES and press Enter. BASIC programs appear with the .BAS extension. Type RUN"FIG6-6" to execute the BASIC program saved on diskette as FIG6-6.BAS. Program output will appear as shown in Figure 6.6 in this text (see Chapter 6).

The programs on the companion disk that contain a .BAS extension can be executed when the BASIC interpreter is loaded. Programs indicated by .EXE are compiled and can be executed only at the DOS level.

SUMMARY

Program statements are used to process data. Commands are different in that they do not process data but assist the user in managing programs. Commands are typed without a statement line number. In the next chapter, attention is directed to using disk operating system (DOS) commands to control the diskette system.

Summary of terms

Name	Example	Purpose
CLS	CLS	Clears screen to blank.
DELETE	DELETE 50–90	Deletes (erases) statements 50 through 90 from memory.
LIST	LIST	Displays program in memory.
	LIST 40	Displays statement 40.
	LIST 40–	Displays statement 40 to end of program.
NEW	NEW	Erases memory. Used before typing a new program into memory.
FILES	FILES	Displays file names for diskette in current drive.
	FILES "B:"	Displays file names for diskette in drive B.
KILL	KILL "SALES.BAS"	Kills (erases) the program on diskette called SALES.BAS. The .BAS extension must be specified if it exists.
LOAD	LOAD "SALES"	Loads a copy of the program called SALES.BAS stored on diskette into memory.
	LOAD "SALES.01"	Loads a copy of the program called SALES.01 stored on diskette into memory.
	LOAD "B:SALES"	Loads a copy of the program called SALES.BAS from drive B diskette into memory.
NAME	NAME "OLD.BAS" AS "NEW.BAS"	This changes the name of the diskette file to NEW.BAS.
SAVE	SAVE "SALES"	Saves a copy of program in memory on diskette under the name of SALES.BAS.
	SAVE "SALES.01"	Saves a copy of program in memory on diskette under the name SALES.01.
	SAVE "B:SALES"	Saves a copy of program in memory onto the drive B diskette.

Special Keys

Keys	Purpose
[Ctrl] [Break]	Press both keys at the same time to "break" (stop) program execution.
[Ctrl] [Alt] [Del]	Press all three keys at the same time to restart the system.
[Ctrl] [Num Lock]	Press both keys at the same time to temporarily stop output display. Press any key to resume display.

PROBLEMS

True/False. Problems 1–8.

4.1 Commands need line numbers. F

4.2 PRINT and END are commands. F

4.3   RUN and LIST are commands.   T

4.4   Statements are executed in ascending order.   T

4.5   Numerous errors in one statement line can only be corrected by retyping the whole program.   F

4.6   LIST 100-200 displays the program lines from 100 to 200.   T

4.7   NEW 10 removes line 10 from memory.   F

4.8   CLS clears the screen.   T

Short-answer Problems. Problems 9–17.

4.9   What is a command?   *Processes the program*

4.10   What is the difference between a command and a BASIC statement?

4.11   What does the command LIST do?   *Statement Processes data*

4.12   What does the RUN command do?   *Runs program*

*4.13   What is the method for replacing a new for an old program statement without erasing the entire program and starting over?   *Retype statement using same #*

4.14   When typing a program statement, how can errors be corrected before the Enter key is pressed?   *Backspace*

4.15   How can a program be erased from the computer's memory?   *New*

4.16   How can a program residing in the computer's memory be displayed?   *Run*

4.17   What are the steps required to display a program stored on diskette?   *List*

Program Completion—Beginning. Problems 18–22.

BASIC assignment statements are shown. Write the value of the variable in the indicated boxes that would be assigned after the program is executed.

4.18
```
10 REM Ans to problem 18
20 ITEMS = 3
30 GROSS.PRICE = ITEMS *5.45
40 PRINT GROSS.PRICE
50 END
```

ITEMS   GROSS.PRICE

3   15.35

4.19
```
10 REM Ans to problem 19
20 ITEMS = 3
30 GROSS.PRICE = ITEMS *5.45
40 PRINT GROSS.PRICE
50 END
12 ITEMS = 2
```

ITEMS   GROSS.PRICE

4.20
```
10 REM Ans to problem 20
20 ITEMS = 3
30 GROSS.PRICE = ITEMS *5.45
40 PRINT GROSS.PRICE
```

* The answer to this problem is in Appendix E.

```
50 END
22 ITEMS = 2
```

ITEMS   GROSS.PRICE

[ ]   [ ]

4.21
```
10 REM Ans to problem 21
20 ITEMS = 3
30 GROSS.PRICE = ITEMS *5.45
40 PRINT GROSS.PRICE
50 END
DELETE 30
```

ITEMS   GROSS.PRICE

[3]   [ ]

4.22
```
10 REM Ans to problem 22
20 ITEMS = 3
30 GROSS.PRICE = ITEMS *5.45
40 PRINT GROSS.PRICE
50 END
DELETE 20
```

ITEMS   GROSS.PRICE

[ ]   [ ]

Debugging Problems—Commands. Problems 23–34.

These problems assume that the files shown are stored on a diskette in drive A. BASIC is loaded into memory. Incorrect commands were typed and the screen appeared as shown in the problems. Write the correct command that should have been typed.

ACCOUNT.BAS

```
10 REM Sale program
20 SALE = 20.45
30 PRINT SALE
40 END
```

PROB1.BAS

```
10 REM Sample program
20 ITEMS = 3
30 GROSS = ITEMS * 5.45
40 PRINT GROSS.PRICE
50 END
```

*4.23 An attempt was made to load the ACCOUNT file into memory.

```
LOAD ACCOUNT
Type mismatch
Ok
```

4.24 The ACCOUNT file was loaded into memory and displayed. An attempt was made to erase the screen.

* The answer to this problem is in Appendix E.

```
LIST
10 REM Sale program
20 SALE = 20.45
30 PRINT SALE
40 END
Ok
HOME
Syntax error
Ok
```

4.25 An attempt was made to display the file names stored on diskette.

```
FILE A
Syntax error
Ok
```

4.26 An attempt was made to save the contents of memory.

```
SAVE "SMITH"
Type mismatch
Ok
```

4.27 An attempt was made to erase the ACCOUNT program from diskette.

```
KILL "ACCOUNT"
Type mismatch
Ok
```

4.28 An attempt was made to rename the ACCOUNT file as ACCOUNT1.

```
RENAME "ACCOUNT.BAS AS ACCOUNT1.BAS"
Syntax error
Ok
```

4.29 An attempt was made to erase the PROB1 program from diskette.

```
ERASE "PROB1.BAS"
Syntax error
Ok
```

4.30 Nothing is in memory, and an attempt was made to display the contents of the ACCOUNT file stored on diskette. Several commands were given as shown on the screen. What should be typed?

```
DISPLAY ACCOUNT
Syntax error
Ok
LOAD "ACCOUNT"
Type mismatch
Ok
LOAD ACCOUNT LIST
Type mismatch
Ok
```

4.31 An attempt was made to exit to DOS.

```
START
Syntax error
Ok
EXIT
Syntax error
Ok
```

4.32 An attempt was made to load the ACCOUNT file into memory. (The ACCOUNT file does exist and is saved on diskette.)

```
LOAD" ACCOUNT.BAS
Path not found
Ok
LOAD" ACCOUNT
Path not found
Ok
```

4.33 An attempt was made to save the ACCOUNT file on a formatted diskette in drive B. The computer error message is incorrect. There are no files on the diskette in drive B.

```
10 REM Sale program
20 SALE = 20.45
30 PRINT SALE
40 END
SAVE"B: ACCOUNT
Too many files
Ok
```

4.34 An attempt was made to erase the last two lines in the PROB1.BAS program currently in memory.

```
NEW
Ok
```

Beginning Commands. Problems 35–42 use the following program, called DEMO, *stored on diskette:*

```
10 PRINT "BASIC"
20 PRINT "PROGRAMMING"
30 END
```

4.35 What is the command to display the program names saved on diskette? *List*

4.36 What is the command to load the program into the computer's memory? *Load*

4.37 What is a BASIC statement that will add the words "is fun" so that they *print* will appear on a separate line, under the word "Programming"?

4.38 What is the command to save the program revised in Problem 4.37 on diskette under the name DEMO1? *Save " Demo1"*

*4.39 After saving the revised program on diskette, how many programs exist, and where are they located? *2*

4.40 What is the command that allows you to see the names of all programs that have been saved on diskette? *Files*

4.41 What is the command to erase the program called DEMO on diskette? (Be sure to state the complete command.) *Kill*

4.42 What is the command to erase the current program in memory?

delete

Multiple commands and steps. Problems 43–52 use the following programs stored on diskette.

One program is called TEST, and the other is called CLOTHES.

TEST

```
10 - -
20 - -
30 - -
40 END
```

CLOTHES

```
10 - -
12 - -
20 END
```

4.43 Assume that the computer is off. What are the steps required to start up the computer so that a BASIC program can be written? I'll give you the first two steps: (1) insert the IBM DOS system diskette in drive A, and (2) turn on the computer.

*4.44 Assume that the system diskette is in the drive and that your disk contains the programs TEST and CLOTHES. What are the steps and commands necessary to load the program called CLOTHES into memory?

4.45 After the program called CLOTHES has been loaded into memory, how many copies are there of the BASIC programs, and where are the programs located?

4.46 What is the command to display statements 12 through 20? *List 12-20*

4.47 Suppose that statement 14 is added to the current program in memory. What is the command to revise the old program on diskette called CLOTHES so that it contains the new statement? *Save*

4.48 After revising the CLOTHES program on diskette, how many BASIC programs are there, and where are the programs located? *2*

4.49 What are the commands to clear the screen and then display a copy of the current program in memory? *cls List*

4.50 What is the command to erase the current program in memory? *delete*

4.51 What are the commands to display the TEST program? *List test*

4.52 What is the command to rename the TEST program to PROGRAM.OLD?

Name

Commands and steps on program in memory. Problems 53–60 use the following program, which has been typed into the computer and resides in memory:

```
10 Selling.price = 25
20 Quantity.sold = 3
30 Total = Sold.price * Quantity.sold
40print "Total sale is" Total
50end
30 Total = Selling.price * Quantity.sold
```

* The answer to this problem is in Appendix E.

4.53 What is the command to display the current program in memory? *List*

4.54 Write the program as it will actually appear when the LIST command is given.

4.55 What is the command to execute the program? *Run*

*__4.56__ What is the exact output that will appear when the program is executed?

4.57 What is the command to display statement lines 30 through 50? *List 30-50*

4.58 What are the two ways of erasing statement 30? *Delete 30 or 30(enter)*

4.59 What is the command for erasing statements 30 through 50? *delete 30-50*

4.60 Suppose that program statement 40 is retyped as follows:

```
40Print "The grand total is" Total     List 40
```

What is the command to display only statement line 40?

Additional commands on program in memory. Problems 61–65 use the following program, which has been typed into the computer and resides in memory.

```
10 Pay = 40 + 5
20Print PAY
30end
5 Rem Problems 61-65
```

4.61 What is the command to display the current program in memory? *List*

4.62 What is the command to save the program on disk under the name ADDITION? *Save "addition"*

4.63 What is the command to display the program names stored on diskette? *Files*

*__4.64__ Assume that the screen is cleared and that the LIST command is given. Write the program statements that will appear on the screen.

4.65 What is the command to erase the ADDITION program stored on diskette? *Kill "Addition"*

Commands affecting memory and diskette. Problems 66–72 use the following program, which has been typed into the computer and resides in memory:

```
10 NUMBER = 1
30 NUMBER = 2
50 PRINT NUMBER
40 NUMBER = 3
60end
30 number = 4
10rem Problems 66-72
```

4.66 What are the specific program statements that will be displayed when the program is listed?

4.67 What is the output when the program is run?

4.68 If the command DELETE 30–40 is entered and the program is executed, what is the output? *nothing*

4.69 What is the command to save the current program in memory on diskette under the name "OHBOY"? *Save "ohboy"*

4.70 After saving the program on diskette, how many copies of the program are there, and where are they located? *2 - 1 on disk 1 in memory*

* The answer to this problem is in Appendix E.

4.71 What is the command to save the current program in memory on a formatted disk in drive B as "OHBOY2"?

4.72 What is the command to delete the program previously saved as "OH-BOY" from diskette?

Other Problems. Problems 73–76.

Write a program to calculate and display the profit McDogs Hamburgers makes on a single $1.25 hamburger if the meat costs $.55, the bun costs $.15, the pickles cost $.04, and the onions, $.03.

4.73 Save the program under the name "PROFIT."

4.74 Load "PROFIT" and run it to see if it was correctly saved.

4.75 Modify the program to calculate and display the profit made if 155,000 hamburgers are sold. Save this modified program under "PROFIT.TOT."

4.76 Change the file name of PROFIT.TOT to PROFIT.HAM.

* The answer to this problem is in Appendix E.

USING THE DISK OPERATING SYSTEM

Upon completion of this chapter you should be able to

- Create your own program diskette
- Copy individual files
- Make a backup copy of a diskette
- Use selected DOS commands
- Copy the companion diskette

You will need

- The companion diskette
- At least one blank double-sided, double-density diskette. Two would be preferable. Later, you will be able to use these diskettes for other purposes if desired.
- The IBM DOS diskette (the system master diskette that came with the computer). DOS 2.X or higher can be used.

USING THE DISK OPERATING SYSTEM

Programs and data are stored on diskette in the form of diskette files. The BASIC language is not complete enough to manage these files, so an additional system is needed. This system is called the disk operating system and is contained on the DOS diskette.

When using the computer it is extremely important to remember whether you are at the BASIC level or the DOS (system) level. The computer prompt will show the current level. The prompt appears as a blinking dash at the BASIC level. When at the DOS level, the prompt appears as A> to indicate that the current diskette drive is A.

DOS is accessed while at the BASIC level by typing the command SYSTEM and pressing the Enter key. The prompt A> then appears. Be careful when changing to the DOS level, because any BASIC programs in memory will be lost. If the program you are developing has not been saved on diskette, save it before typing SYSTEM. While at the DOS level, you can return to BASIC by typing BASICA and pressing Enter. The dash prompt (—) will then appear.

DISPLAYING THE DISKETTE FILE NAMES

Programs and data are stored on diskette in the form of files. These files can be displayed while at DOS by the DIR command. When the command

It takes a little practice to get used to DOS, so why not practice? Make the commands work as intended so that you will understand how they are used.

DIR is typed and the Enter key pressed, the programs stored on the diskette in the current drive will be displayed along with their size, creation time, and creation date.

If there are many files on the diskette, the files will scroll off the screen too quickly to be read, so the command DIR /P is more useful. This command displays one screen of file names at a time. Any key can be pressed to resume the display. The DIR /W command can be entered instead to display the file names in a condensed format.

Let's try the DIR command. Insert the DOS diskette in the drive while in DOS; type DIR. The screen will appear as shown below if DOS 2.1 is used.

```
A>dir

  Volume in drive A has no label
  Directory of A:\

  COMMAND    COM    17792    10-20-83    12:00p
  ANSI       SYS     1664    10-20-83    12:00p
  FORMAT     COM     6912    10-20-83    12:00p
  CHKDSK     COM     6400    10-20-83    12:00p
  SYS        COM     1680    10-20-83    12:00p
  DISKCOPY   COM     2576    10-20-83    12:00p
  DISKCOMP   COM     2188    10-20-83    12:00p
  COMP       COM     2534    10-20-83    12:00p
  EDLIN      COM     4608    10-20-83    12:00p
  MODE       COM     3139    10-20-83    12:00p
  FDISK      COM     6369    10-20-83    12:00p
  BACKUP     COM     3687    10-20-83    12:00p
  RESTORE    COM     4003    10-20-83    12:00p
  PRINT      COM     4608    10-20-83    12:00p
  RECOVER    COM     2304    10-20-83    12:00p
  ASSIGN     COM      896    10-20-83    12:00p
  TREE       COM     1513    10-20-83    12:00p
  GRAPHICS   COM      789    10-20-83    12:00p
  SORT       EXE     1408    10-20-83    12:00p
  FIND       EXE     5888    10-20-83    12:00p
  MORE       COM      384    10-20-83    12:00p
  BASIC      COM    16256    10-20-83    12:00p
  BASICA     COM    26112    10-20-83    12:00p
```

There are two types of DOS commands: internal and external. Internal commands reside in the computer. They are typed after the DOS prompt and do not require use of the DOS system master diskette. External commands are different. They reside as files on the DOS system master diskette. The system master diskette must be inserted in the drive before external DOS commands can be used.

The following internal commands will be discussed in this chapter.

INTERNAL COMMANDS	
CLS	Clears screen
COPY	Copies a file
DATE	Displays DATE
DIR	Displays directory of files
ERASE	Erases file
RENAME	Renames file
TIME	Displays time
VER	Displays DOS version

Key external commands discussed in this chapter are as shown.

EXTERNAL COMMAND	
CHKDSK	Checks a diskette
DISKCOMP	Compares a diskette after DISKCOPY
DISKCOPY	Copies a diskette
FORMAT	Formats a diskette

Notice the screen previously produced with a DIR command. This system master diskette contains the files CHKDSK.COM, DISKCOMP.COM, DISKCOPY.COM, and FORMAT.COM. Again, when we want to use one of these external commands, the system master diskette must be in the drive.

The distinction between internal and external DOS commands will become clear in a moment. Let's take a close look at a few internal (built-in) commands.

CLEARING THE SCREEN

The command to clear the screen is CLS. This is the same as the BASIC CLS command. The cursor returns to the upper left-hand corner, and the DOS prompt A> appears. The screen would then appear as shown below after CLS is typed and the Enter key is pressed.

```
A>
```

IDENTIFYING THE DOS VERSION

It is important that you consistently use the same DOS version. The diskette is formatted differently for different major versions of DOS, which can present problems if DOS 1.X, 2.X, 3.X, 4.X, or other versions are used interchangeably. No harm is done by changing within the same general DOS, such as DOS 2.1 being swapped with DOS 2.2.

The current version of DOS loaded into the computer can be identified by typing VER and pressing the Enter key. The screen would then appear as shown below if DOS 2.1 is used.

```
A>VER

IBM Personal Computer DOS Version 2.1
```

DISPLAYING/CHANGING THE DATE OR TIME

The date and time entered into the system at system start-up can be displayed at DOS. For example, after the DOS prompt appears, type DATE, and the screen will appear as shown (based on a date of 12/15/90 entered on system start-up).

```
A>DATE

Current date is Sat 12-15-90
Enter new date: _
```

A new date can be entered, or just press the Enter key to leave the currently assigned value. In a similar manner, the TIME command could be entered to display the time, based on the time entered at system start-up.

CHANGING THE DEFAULT DRIVE

To simplify DOS commands, we will always work from drive A as the current (default) drive. Commands will be typed after the DOS prompt A> is shown.

A directory of drive B can be obtained by typing DIR B:.

The default drive can be changed, say to drive B, by typing the drive letter followed by a colon, as shown. All commands subsequently typed will then affect the default drive. An example of this is shown. Type A: to change back to drive A.

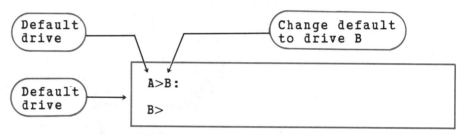

CREATING A DISKETTE FOR YOUR OWN PROGRAMS

Several activities will have to be performed to create a diskette to store your own programs. First, the diskette has to be formatted so that the computer can store data on it. Formatting is a process by which the computer electronically establishes a structure that permits data to be recorded. The formatting process destroys any data on the diskette, so do not format a diskette containing valuable data or programs.

Second, we will have to transfer the system files from the DOS diskette onto the program diskette during the formatting process. Finally we will have to transfer the BASIC file called the interpreter onto our diskette. The reason for the last two steps is that we want a diskette which can stand on its own. That is, we do not want to have to load the DOS system files and the BASIC interpreter file from another diskette each time we want to run a program on our program diskette.

The DOS system files are required by the computer to govern its internal operations. There are actually three system files that will have to be transferred. IBMBIO.COM, IBMDOS.COM:, and COMMAND.COM. The first two are hidden files and only the COMMAND.COM file will appear when the DIR command is given. These files cannot be transferred onto your diskette separately because space has not been allocated for them. They must be transferred during the formatting process by the DOS command FORMAT B:/S (or FORMAT A:/S for a single-drive system).

Follow the steps below for formatting a diskette. The DOS diskette should be in drive A. If the computer is not at the system level, type SYSTEM so that the A> prompt appears.

FORMATTING A DISKETTE

1. Insert the DOS diskette in drive A and a blank diskette in drive B as follows:

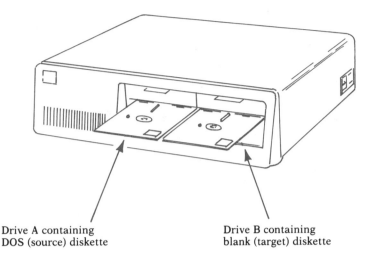

Drive A containing
DOS (source) diskette

Drive B containing
blank (target) diskette

Want to restart the system?
Then press the following
keys at the same time: Ctrl,
Alt, Del. This is quicker and
easier than turning the
power switch off and back
on again. However, a disk
containing the system files
must be in the drive.

2. Type FORMAT B:/S and press Enter. The screen will appear as
shown. If DOS 3.X is used, the last line reads "and strike ENTER when
ready."

```
A>FORMAT B:/S
Insert new diskette for drive B:
and strike any key when ready_
```

3. The process of formatting destroys any data that might be
stored on the diskette, so do not format a diskette containing valuable
data or programs. When you're to go ahead, press any key to format
the target diskette.

It will take about a minute for the computer to format the target
diskette. The three files just mentioned will be transferred during the
formatting process. After the process has been completed, the screen
will appear as follows for a double-density, double-sided diskette system (formatted using DOS 2.1). The number of bytes used and the
diskette space available will vary with different DOS versions.

```
A>FORMAT B:/S
Insert new diskette for drive B:
and strike any key when ready

Formatting...Format complete
System transferred

    362496 bytes total disk space
     40960 bytes used by system
    321536 bytes available on disk

Format another (Y/N)?
```

Be careful when you use system commands. If you want
to format on drive A, then
state drive A. That is, do not
get lazy and omit the drive
designator. As many owners
of the XT model are finding
out the hard way, it is all too
easy to format the built-in
hard disk accidentally by
omitting a drive designa-
tion. (It would be nice if
someone would build a
safety device to prevent this
from happening.)

4. The computer now wants to know if another diskette is to be
formatted. Type N (for No), and you have completed the process of
formatting a diskette which now contains the two hidden files and the
COMMAND.COM file.

5. The CHKDSK command can be used to verify the files on the
diskette in drive B. With the DOS diskette in drive A, type CHKDSK B:
and press Enter. The screen for a double-density, double-sided diskette

is shown below. The number of bytes used and the diskette space available will vary with different DOS versions. The total bytes free will vary with the size of the random access memory (RAM).

```
A>CHKDSK B:

    362496 bytes total disk space
     22528 bytes in 2 hidden files
     18432 bytes in 1 user files
    321536 bytes available on disk

    262144 bytes total memory
    237568 bytes free
A>
```

The command to format a diskette and transfer the hidden files using a single-drive system is FORMAT A:/S. The computer will prompt you when to remove the system diskette and insert the blank target diskette.

At this point, we have formatted a diskette so that it can accept file storage and retrieval. The screen would appear as shown below if DIR B: was typed.

```
A>DIR B:

 Volume in drive B has no label
 Directory of  B:\

COMMAND  COM     17792  10-20-83  12:00p
        1 File(s)     321536 bytes free

A>
```

A question that often arises is: Why doesn't the volume in drive B have a label? The message seems to be implying that we either did something wrong or, at a minimum, failed to do something. To prevent this volume label message from occurring each time a DIR or a CHKDSK is performed, you might wish to format your diskette using the /V option. You will then be given the opportunity to place your own volume name (label) on the diskette.

The command to format a disk, pass the system files, and permit the diskette to be labeled is FORMAT B:/S/V. After the command is typed and the Enter key is pressed, a prompt, "Insert new diskette for drive B: and strike any key when ready," appears.

After inserting the diskette to be formatted in drive B (you can reformat the previous diskette if desired), the diskette will be formatted, the system will be transferred, and you will be prompted to enter a volume label.

The screen would appear as shown after the label CLASS DISK is typed. In this case n (No) was typed to the prompt "Format another (Y/N)?"

```
A>FORMAT B:/S/V
Insert new diskette for drive B:
and strike any key when ready

Formatting...Format complete
System transferred

Volume label (11 characters, ENTER for none)? CLASS DISK


    362496 bytes total disk space
     40960 bytes used by system
    321536 bytes available on disk

Format another (Y/N)?n
A>
```

Now when DIR is typed on the drive, the volume label appears as shown. It makes you feel good, like a computer pro, doesn't it?

```
A>DIR B:

 Volume in drive B is CLASS DISK
 Directory of  B:\

COMMAND   COM    17792  10-20-83  12:00p
          1 File(s)     321536 bytes free

A>
```

THE COPY COMMAND

Once a diskette has been formatted, files can be copied onto it. The COPY command is a very powerful, frequently used command. When the COPY command is used to copy a file, the file is automatically loaded into memory. Then the file is saved on the same track, on both sides of the diskette. This reduces the moving around required by the drive when the file is later retrieved. Also, a file that is stored in multiple locations (sectors) on the source diskette is grouped together and then stored as a whole unit on the target diskette. Thus the copied file may be better than the original, in that it will load more quickly into the computer's memory.

The general form of the COPY command to copy a file from the current drive (we are assuming this is drive A) to drive B is

COPY FILENAME.EXT B:

Command ———————
File name including ———————
extension (if any)
Target drive containing
formatted disk

Let's demonstrate this command by copying the advanced language file called BASICA from the source (system) diskette onto the formatted diskette containing the three system files. Follow the steps that follow to copy the file from the source disk in drive A to the formatted target disk in drive B.

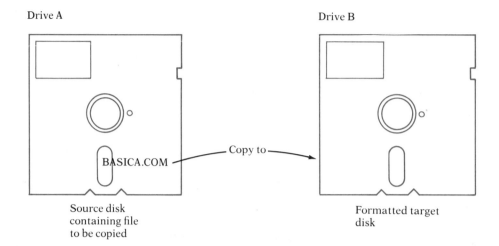

Drive A   Drive B

BASICA.COM — Copy to →

Source disk
containing file
to be copied

Formatted target
disk

1. Insert the source (system) disk in drive A and the target diskette in drive B. The COPY command does not normally require use of the system diskette; however, the BASIC file we want to copy is on this diskette.
2. Type COPY BASICA.COM B: and press Enter to copy the file onto the target diskette.
3. Type DIR B: to verify that a copy of the file is now on the target diskette in drive B.

Congratulations! You have now formatted your own diskette, transferred the system files, and copied the BASIC interpreter to your diskette. From now on, you can use your own diskette to boot the system and to save files.

ADDITIONAL USE OF THE COPY COMMAND

A program has been saved on the diskette that is a companion to this book, called FIG6-6.BAS. (A complete listing of this BASIC program is shown as Figure 6.6 in Chapter 6 of this book.) Remove the diskette that is currently in drive A, and insert the companion diskette in the drive. Drive B should have the formatted target diskette containing the BASIC interpreter file.

Type COPY FIG6-6.BAS B: to copy the file from your diskette in drive A to the target diskette in drive B. After copying, remove the companion diskette from drive A, and place the target diskette in drive A. We can now experiment with the target diskette by trying additional DOS commands.

The FIG6-6.BAS file can be visualized as follows:

FIG6-6.BAS

```
10 REM
20 - -
     •
190 END
```

Suppose we wanted to make a backup copy of the FIG6-6.BAS file and call the backup TEST.BAS. The general form of the COPY command to make a backup copy on the same diskette drive is

By copying in this manner, two identical copies exist on the same diskette. We can then experiment with one copy, with the comfort of knowing that a backup exists in the event damage occurs.

The command to copy our file and create a backup copy called TEST.BAS is COPY FIG6-6.BAS TEST.BAS. The effect of this command can be visualized as shown. TEST.BAS is a duplicate of FIG6-6.BAS on the same diskette.

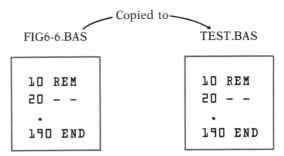

The most common form of the COPY command is to copy a file from a diskette in drive A to a formatted target diskette in drive B. The command to copy FIG6-6.BAS from drive A to drive B, using the same file name, is COPY FIG6-6.BAS B:.

Simple enough, right? However, if we want to copy a file from the diskette in drive A to a formatted diskette in drive B and change the file name at the same time, the command is

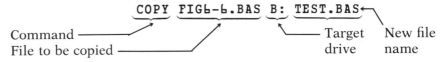

The use of this command can be visualized as shown.

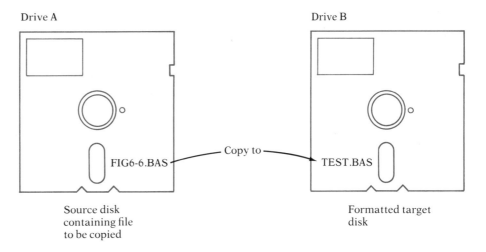

Suppose we wanted to rename our TEST.BAS file to AWFUL.BAS. This can be accomplished with the RENAME command. The general form of

the RENAME command is

The command to rename TEST.BAS to the new name AWFUL.BAS is RENAME TEST.BAS AWFUL.BAS. The effect of this command can be visualized as shown. Note that there are still two files on this diskette—the former FIG6-6.BAS and the "old" TEST.BAS, which is now called (i.e., has been renamed as) AWFUL.BAS.

FIG6-6.BAS   AWFUL.BAS

```
10 REM            10 REM
20 - -            20 - -
   •                 •
190 END           190 END
```

ERASING A FILE

An unwanted file can be removed from the diskette by the ERASE command. For security reasons, it is recommended that you transfer control to the disk drive containing the unwanted file. That is, if A> is shown and the file to be erased is in drive B, type B:, so that the default drive is B>. Then type DIR to confirm the existence of the file and its exact spelling, including file extension if any.

The command to erase a file (or DELETE) is

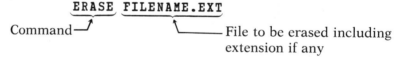

For example, the command to erase the file called AWFUL.BAS from the diskette is: ERASE AWFUL.BAS.

COPYING A DISKETTE

If you save the programs created while reading this book, your diskette will soon contain numerous programs. In fact, you will soon be developing a library of programs, some of which will be valuable.

Once a diskette contains valuable programs, it is a good idea to make a backup copy of the disk. Then you can work with the original diskette, knowing that there is another copy available in the event the program is damaged or destroyed. Programs are copied at the DOS level with A> shown. If you are in BASIC, type SYSTEM to return to the DOS level.

Individual programs can always be copied onto another diskette by following the procedure previously presented. That is, format a target diskette, then copy a file using the command COPY PROGRAM.BAS B:. If there are numerous programs to be copied, it is suggested that the command COPY *.* B: be used. This command has an advantage over the DISKCOPY command: as each file is loaded into memory and copied onto the diskette, fractured files are eliminated as each file is placed on the target diskette in a contiguous manner. Unnecessary skipping of sectors is avoided, and system performance will improve.

The DISKCOPY command can be used to make a copy of the entire disk. There are several differences between the DISKCOPY command and the COPY command. When using the DISKCOPY command, an unformatted target diskette can be used because the command will format while copying the original. DISKCOPY requires use of the system master because it is an external system command.

DISKCOPY versus COPY	
DISKCOPY	COPY
Requires system master	Built into computer
Automatically formats diskette	Needs a formatted diskette
Copies entire diskette	Copies only specified files

The steps to copy an entire diskette using the DISKCOPY command are as follows:

1. Insert the system diskette in drive A and close the flap on the drive.

2. If A> is not shown on screen, type SYSTEM and press Enter.

3. Type DISKCOPY A: B: and press Enter. (Use DISKCOPY A: for a single-drive system.) The screen will appear as shown below for a dual-drive system.

```
A>DISKCOPY A: B:
Insert source diskette in drive A:
Insert target diskette in drive B:
Strike any key when ready
```

4. Remove the system diskette and insert the source (original) diskette in drive A.

5. Insert a target diskette in drive B. Data on the target diskette will be destroyed (written over) in the copying process.

6. Press any key. It will take about a minute to make a copy of the source diskette.

7. After a copy is made, return both the original and the copy to their protective envelopes. Store the backup copy in a safe place.

Do you want to repeat the last DOS command? Press the function key F3, then press the Enter key. Try it!

The copying process for a single-drive system consists of inserting the system master and typing DISKCOPY A:. Remove the system diskette, insert the source diskette, and press any key. The computer will prompt you when to insert the target diskette. The source diskette may have to be reinserted several times during the copying process until its contents are copied onto the target diskette.

COMPARING SOURCE AND TARGET DISKETTES

After copying the contents of the source onto the target diskette, the question often arises: Is the copy OK? In other words, how do we know that the copy made is an exact electronic duplicate of the source diskette? Questions regarding the accuracy of the copying process can be answered using the DISKCOMP (disk compare) command.

After copying a diskette, follow the steps below when using the DISKCOMP command. The process begins with the system diskette in drive A. (The target diskette is still in drive B.) If the A> prompt is not shown, type SYSTEM to return to the DOS level.

1. Type DISKCOMP A: B: and press Enter. (Type DISKCOMP A: for a single-drive system.) The monitor will appear as shown below for a dual-drive system.

```
A>DISKCOMP A: B:
Insert first diskette in drive A:
Insert second diskette in drive B:
Strike any key when ready
```

2. Remove the system diskette and insert the source (original) diskette.

3. Press any key. When the comparison is completed, the words "Diskettes compare ok" will appear if the copy made is a duplicate of the original. The monitor will appear as shown below.

```
A>DISKCOMP A: B:
Insert first diskette in drive A:
Insert second diskette in drive B:
Strike any key when ready
Comparing 9 sectors per track, 2 side(s)
Diskettes compare ok
Compare more diskettes (Y/N)?
```

In the unlikely event that the comparison does not check out, recopy the diskette. If the comparison still does not check out, the target diskette is probably damaged and another one should be used.

LABELING THE PROGRAM DISKETTE

Each diskette contains a notch (cutout) on the upper right-hand side that permits the computer to copy onto the diskette. On valuable diskettes it is a good idea to cover this notch with the adhesive-backed tab that is supplied with the diskette. This prevents the computer from accidentally destroying programs by writing onto the diskette.

Write the words "Program Disk" on the label supplied with the diskette and then transfer the label to the disk. Do not use pencil or ball point or write directly onto the disk, as the pressure of the writing tip may damage the diskette.

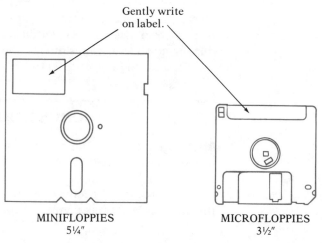

Gently write
on label.

MINIFLOPPIES
5¼"

MICROFLOPPIES
3½"

The notch on the 5¼″ diskette can be covered using the tab supplied by the manufacturer to protect the files from being accidentally erased. This file protection is activated on the 3½″ diskette by sliding the built-in tab up (the sliding tab is in the upper right-hand corner of the diskette).

PRINTING THE DISKETTE FILE NAMES

How often have you looked at a diskette and wondered what it contained? Or have you played the game: "I know I have that program on one of these diskettes"? Well, if you have, you know that it would be easier to find programs if a printed copy of the file names were taped on the paper sleeve that holds the diskette.

You can get a printout of the files stored on diskette from either the BASIC or DOS level. The steps required to obtain a printout while in BASIC are

The disk file names can be printed on paper. In BASIC, the following steps can be used: CLS, FILES, and then Shift and PrtSc (Print Screen). A printout at the DOS level can be made by pressing Ctrl and PrtSc to echo output to a printer. Then DIR output will be printed. The Ctrl and PrtSc combination is needed to return output to normal.

1. Turn off the status of the function keys that appears at the bottom of the screen by typing the command KEY OFF. The status can be redisplayed later by the command KEY ON.

2. Clear all data from the screen. This is accomplished by typing the command CLS (which stands for clear screen).

3. Now type the command FILES to display the diskette files.

4. Adjust the paper so that the top is even with the guide bar before turning on the printer. This ensures that the form feed is correct.

5. Turn on the printer. Press Shift and PrtSc (Print Screen) to print what is on the screen (the listing of the files).

6. Remove the paper, trim the excess, and tape the list on the protective diskette sleeve.

Although it is relatively easy to obtain a listing of the files at the BASIC level, there is one problem. The FILES command displays several file names on the same line, so the listing is difficult to read. The DOS command DIR displays one file name per line. The file listing obtained in this manner will be easier to read.

The steps required to obtain a printout of the files at the DOS level are

1. Begin at the DOS level with the A> prompt displayed. If you are not at this level, type SYSTEM and insert the desired diskette.

2. Adjust paper and turn on printer.

3. Press the Ctrl and PrtSc keys. Now everything that appears on the screen will also be printed.

4. Type DIR and press Enter to obtain a printed copy of the file names. Remember, DIR is a built-in system command, so the system diskette does not have to be in the drive when you use the command.

When the DIR command is typed, the file names will be printed, one name per line.

5. After printing, press the Ctrl and PrtSc keys to stop the printer from printing additional information.

6. Remove the page, cut off the excess paper, and tape the listing on the protective paper sleeve that holds the diskette. Do not allow the paper or the tape to come in contact with any of the cut-out areas on the diskette.

RESTARTING THE SYSTEM

Remove the DOS diskette and place our program diskette in drive A (the only drive on a single-drive system). Perform a system restart by pressing and holding down the following keys:

Ctrl	Alt	Del

The BASIC interpreter contained on diskette is an extension of the BASIC in ROM. It is possible to write limited BASIC programs without loading the BASIC interpreter from disk.

The prompt A> will appear, indicating you are at the system level. Type BASICA to load the advanced BASIC into memory. The dash prompt indicates that you are at the BASIC level ready to begin programming.

It is strongly suggested that you key in some of the programs in this book and then modify the programs for your own specialized applications. When the program executes correctly, save the revised program on your diskette for future use.

EXECUTING PROGRAMS

The BASIC interpreter is required to run BASIC programs because the computer does not execute program statements directly. The interpreter translates each statement, line by line, into the computer's machine language as the program is running. The interpreter checks for errors and then performs the requested function. The computer does not know exactly where in memory each line or each variable is located. If the program branches to a particular line (more on this later), the interpreter searches through every line in the program, starting with the first, until the desired line number is found.

The interpreter also creates a list of the variable names used in a program. Then, when a name is used again, perhaps to print the variable's value, this list is searched from the beginning until the variable is found. All this processing by the interpreter results in the BASIC language being relatively slow.

However, commercial programs called compilers are available to speed program execution. A compiler accepts a BASIC program and, when the compiler is executed, an object file is created containing the necessary machine code. All translation takes place during the initial compilation. Because the object file is in machine code, no translation occurs when the program is run, thus speeding up execution.

The programs compiled on the companion diskette are indicated by the .EXE extension. These programs are executed from DOS by simply typing the program name. The START program was executed in this manner and other .EXE programs can also be executed without using the program selection menu.

SUMMARY

Now that the fundamentals of disk management have been mastered, programs can be quickly stored and retrieved. The next chapter develops programming skills by presenting several techniques that can be used to assign values to variable names.

As your programming skills increase, you will have a tendency to increase the length and complexity of your programs. Develop the habit of saving these programs. Who knows what will happen in the future? They may become collectors' items.

Key DOS commands

Name	Example	Purpose
B:	B:	Changes the current drive to drive B. The prompt will appear as B>. Typing A: returns default to drive A.
BASICA	BASICA	Returns control from DOS level to advanced BASIC.
CHKDSK	CHKDSK	Displays space remaining on diskette in current drive.
	CHKDSK B:	Displays space remaining on drive B diskette.
COPY	COPY SALE.BAS	Copies the SALE.BAS file on a single-drive system from source onto target diskette. The file extension must be specified.
COPY SALE.BAS	ITEM.BAS	Makes a backup copy by copying SALE.BAS and creates a file called ITEM.BAS.
COPY SALE.BAS	B: ITEM.BAS	Copies the SALE.BAS file from the current drive to drive B as ITEM.BAS. The file extension must be specified.
	COPY *.* B:	Copies all files from current drive to drive B.
DIR	DIR	Displays files in current drive along with their size and creation time and date.
	DIR /P	Same as DIR, but stops after screen is full.
	DIR /W	Displays files in current drive in condensed format. (Same as FILES command in BASIC.)
DISKCOMP	DISKCOMP	Compares diskettes on a single-drive system to determine if a disk was correctly copied.
	DISKCOMP A: B:	Compares diskettes in drives A and B to determine if a disk was correctly copied.
DISKCOPY	DISKCOPY	Copies diskette on a single-drive system.
	DISKCOPY A: B:	Copies drive A diskette onto drive B diskette. Formatting is performed while copying.
ERASE	ERASE SALE.BAS	Erases (deletes) file from current drive. The file extension must be specified if it exists. (Same as KILL command in BASIC.)
FORMAT	FORMAT	Formats a diskette on a single-drive system. Any data on the diskette will be erased during formatting.
	FORMAT B:	Formats drive B diskette. Any data on diskette will be erased during formatting.
	FORMAT B:/S	Formats and transfers system files to drive B diskette.
FORMAT B:/S/V		Formats and transfers system files to drive B diskette. A volume label can be applied.
RENAME SALE.BAS	ITEMS.BAS	Renames the SALE.BAS file on current drive to the new file name ITEMS.BAS.

If you have not already done so, select the DOS Commands tutorial on the companion disk. The screen will appear as shown below. DOS commands are often difficult to remember, so please run this tutorial a couple of times. Then try the commands for yourself, and observe what happens.

```
BASIC Programming With the IBM PC
          DOS Commands
               By
          Peter Mears
        (c) Copyright 1990
```

PROBLEMS

True/False. Problems 1–21.

5.1 The command DIRECTORY displays the diskette files when the computer is at the DOS level.

*5.2 The command to copy the BASIC language from the system master in drive A to a formatted diskette in drive B is: COPY BASIC B:.

5.3 The command to format a diskette in drive B is FORMAT B.

5.4 The prompt B> indicates that the computer is at the DOS (system) level and that the current (default drive) is drive B.

5.5 You should label your diskette by writing on the label with black ballpoint pen, so the writing is easy to read.

5.6 The flashing prompt — indicates that the computer is at the BASIC level.

5.7 The command to leave BASIC and go to the DOS level is DOS.

5.8 The command to display the diskette files at the DOS level is FILES.

5.9 The command to format a diskette in drive B without passing the system files is FORMAT B:.

5.10 The command to check a diskette in drive B to determine if the diskette is formatted correctly and to identify if anything is wrong is CHKDSK.

5.11 The command to format a disk in drive B, pass the system files, and permit a volume label to be added is FORMAT B:/S/V.

5.12 The command to copy selected files from one diskette onto another is DISKCOPY A: B:.

5.13 After a diskette has been formatted using FORMAT B:, the command SYS B: can be used to transfer the system files to the formatted diskette.

5.14 The command DISKCOMP A: B: can be used to assure that the results of the DISKCOPY A: B: worked correctly (that is, the copy made is identical to the original diskette).

5.15 The command to change the current default drive A to drive B is simply to type B: after the prompt A>.

In problems 16–21, assume the current drive is A> and there is a file called FIGURE12.BAS on the disk in drive A. You are copying from drive A to a formatted diskette in drive B.

5.16 The command to copy the file to drive B is COPY FIGURE12.BAS.

* The answer to this problem is in Appendix E.

5.17   The command to copy the file to drive B under a new file name of TEST.BAS is COPY FIGURE12.BAS TEST.BAS B:.

5.18   The command to make a backup copy called XFIGURE.BAS on the same drive is COPY FIGURE12.BAS XFIGURE.BAS.

5.19   The command to remove the file is KILL "FIGURE12.BAS".

5.20   A command that can be given to see if the file was copied to drive B is DIR B:/P.

5.21   The command to change the name of the file to FIGUREXX.BAS is RENAME FIGUREXX.BAS.

Debugging Problems—Commands. Problems 22–27.
Incorrect commands were typed, and the screen appeared as shown in the problems. Write the correct command that should have been typed.

*5.22   An attempt was made to FORMAT a blank diskette in drive B, and the screen appeared as shown. What went wrong? What is about to happen?

```
A>FORMAT
Insert new diskette for drive A:
and strike any key when ready
```

5.23   A DIR was given on a recently formatted diskette in drive B, and the screen appeared as shown. What was the exact FORMAT command that must have been typed to create this diskette?

```
A>DIR B:

Volume in drive B is TEST_DISK
Directory of  B:\

COMMAND  COM   17792  10-20-83  12:00p
        1 File(s)    321536 bytes free
```

5.24   An attempt was made to copy the BASICA interpreter from the DOS system master in drive A to a formatted disk in drive B. What went wrong?

```
A>COPY BASICA.COM
File cannot be copied onto itself
        0 File(s) copied
```

5.25   What are the exact directory commands that could have been typed to result in the screen as shown?

```
Volume in drive B is TEST_DISK
Directory of B:\

COMMAND  COM   17792  10-20-83  12:00p
FIG6-6   BAS     359   1-01-80  12:29a
FIG8-5   BAS     640   1-01-80  12:01a
FIG13-8  BAS    1024   1-01-80  12:03a
        4 File(s)    318464 bytes free
```

* The answer to this problem is in Appendix E.

The screen shown in Problem 25 is needed to answer Problems 26 and 27.

5.26 An attempt was made to copy the FIG6-6 BASIC file on drive A to a formatted diskette in drive B. What went wrong? What command should have been typed?

```
A>COPY FIG 6-6.BAS B:
Invalid number of parameters
```

5.27 An attempt was made to make a backup of the FIG13-8 file on drive A by creating a SAMPLE.BAS file on the same drive. What went wrong? What command should have been typed?

```
A>COPY FIG13.6.BAS SAMPLE.BAS
FIG13.6.BAS File not found
        0 File(s) copied
```

In Problems 28–33 indicate which of the following commands are built into the computer and which commands require that the system master be in the diskette drive.

Command/example	Built into computer	Requires system master

5.28 `COPY SAM.BAS B:`
5.29 `COPY SAM.BAS PETE.BAS`
5.30 `FORMAT B:/S`
5.31 `CHKDSK B:`
5.32 `DIR B:/P`
5.33 `DISKCOMP A: B:`

Type the following program into the computer and save it on your program diskette under the name DEMO. This program will be used in Problems 34–43. The BASIC interpreter is loaded unless otherwise indicated.

```
10 SALE = 100
20 TAX.RATE = .05
30 TAX = SALE * TAX.RATE
40 PRINT "The tax is" TAX
45 PRINT "The sales tax is" TAX
50 END
```

5.34 Rename the program called DEMO to the new name SUM.
5.35 Restart the system using the Control key and two other keys. Then LOAD "SUM" into memory.
5.36 List all program lines to check the program for errors.
*__5.37__ Delete line 45.
5.38 Save the corrected program on your diskette under the name SUM.

* The answer to this problem is in Appendix E.

5.39 There are now _____ copies of the program. Where are the programs located?

5.40 What is the command to erase the program called SUM from memory?

*__5.41__ What is the command to go from the BASIC level to the DOS level?

5.42 What is the command to erase the diskette program called SUM at the DOS level?

5.43 What is the command to display the program names at the DOS level?

Problems 44–50 require the use of both the companion diskette and a formatted program diskette. While at the DOS level copy the programs named below from the companion diskette onto your formatted program diskette. What is the first line in each program?

*__5.44__ `FIG6-6.BAS`

5.45 `FIG13-8.BAS`

5.46 `FIG14-15.BAS`

5.47 `BUDGET.ASC`

5.48 `STOCKS.ASC`

5.49 `SUPPLIES.ASC`

5.50 `FIG15-10.BAS`

The following information will be used in Problems 51–68.
Assume the following files reside on the diskette in drive A and on the diskette in drive B as shown. The current default drive is A>.

Drive A disk files	Drive B disk files

`SAM.BAS`
`PAGEIT`
`ALICE.BAS`
	`POTTERY.BAS`

5.51 What is the command to display the files in drive A, including the file creation date?

5.52 What is the command to display the files in drive B, without changing the default drive? The file creation date should be included in the display.

5.53 What is the command to display the files in drive A without including the file creation date in the display?

5.54 What is the command to display the files in drive B without changing the default drive? The file creation date should not be included in the display.

5.55 What is the command to clear the screen?

5.56 What is the command to display the system date?

5.57 What is the command to copy the file ALICE.BAS to the diskette in drive B?

5.58 What single command can be given to copy all the files on drive A to the diskette in drive B?

5.59 What is the command to make a backup copy of SAM.BAS called JONES.BAS on drive A?

5.60 What is the single command to copy SAM.BAS to drive B and with the name of THOMAS.BAS?

* The answer to this problem is in Appendix H.

5.61 What is the command to kill the file SAM.BAS from drive A?

5.62 What is the command to kill the BASIC program file called ALLICE? (Be careful on this.)

5.63 What is the command to kill the file PAGEIT?

5.64 What is the command to change the name of the file ALICE.BAS to SUSAN.BAS?

5.65 What is the command to change the default drive to drive B?

5.66 With drive B as the default drive, what is the command to copy the file POTTERY.BAS to the disk in drive A?

Assume that the default drive is A and that the files are on disk as shown.

5.67 What are the exact steps and commands to copy the entire diskette in drive A onto the diskette in drive B? (The existing files on drive B will be destroyed in the process.)

5.68 What are the exact steps and commands to load the file called SAM.BAS into memory? (Carefully note the files currently on diskette before answering this question.)

A diskette that does not contain valuable programs or data will be needed for Problems 69–72.

5.69 Create your own program diskette by formatting and transferring the system files to the diskette. Use an original volume label.

5.70 Copy BASICA from the DOS diskette onto the newly created target diskette.

5.71 Copy the program called FIG6-6.BAS from the companion diskette onto your program diskette.

5.72 Load the BASIC interpreter, then load FIG6-6.BAS. Verify that this is the same program as shown in Chapter 6, Figure 6.6.

ASSIGNING VALUES TO PROGRAM VARIABLES

Upon completion of this chapter, you should be able to assign values in programs using

- Numeric and string variables
- Direct assignment statements
- READ and DATA statements
- INPUT statements

Variables are the means by which values are stored and retrieved. There are three methods for assigning values to variables. The first is the direct assignment method, by which either numeric values or character strings are assigned to variables. The second method is the **READ and DATA** statements, and the third is the INPUT statement.

THE DIRECT ASSIGNMENT METHOD

The direct assignment method is used to assign a value to a variable directly. Although this technique has been presented previously, let's go over it again. As can be seen in the program shown in Figure 6.1, numeric values are assigned directly to the variables called SHIRT and PANTS.

Statement **20 SHIRT = 50** and statement **30 PANTS = 45.5** assign numeric values to the indicated variables, resulting in the following memory assignments:

SHIRT	PANTS
50	45.5

Statement **40 CLOTHES = SHIRT + PANTS** retrieves values of the variables SHIRT and PANTS, adds the two together, and assigns the sum to CLOTHES. This results in the following memory assignments:

CLOTHES	SHIRT	PANTS
95.5	50	45.5

```
10 REM Directly assigning values to variables
20 SHIRT = 50
30 PANTS = 45.5
40 CLOTHES = SHIRT + PANTS
50 PRINT "The clothing bill is";
60 PRINT USING "$$##.##";CLOTHES
70 END
RUN
The clothing bill is $95.50
Ok
```

FIGURE 6.1 Direct assignment method

The value of the variable CLOTHES is then displayed as previously explained. We have been taking the long way around in explaining the direct assignment method in order to demonstrate how variables are assigned. The program shown in Figure 6.2 accomplishes the same objective as the previous program by statement **20 CLOTHES = 50 + 45.5**, where CLOTHES is set equal to the sum of 50 + 45.5. This could have been simplified even further by using **20 CLOTHES = 95.5** because the programmer could have totaled the values without the aid of the computer.

It is a lot easier to understand program logic if meaningful variable names are used. Spend a few minutes to develop logical variable names.

```
10 REM Simplifying assignments
20 CLOTHES = 50 + 45.5
30 PRINT "The clothing bill is";
40 PRINT USING "$$##.##";CLOTHES
50 END
RUN
The clothing bill is $95.50
Ok
```

FIGURE 6.2 Simplifying the direct assignment method

The programs shown in Figures 6.1 and 6.2 use the direct assignment method to assign numeric values to variables. In a similar manner, character strings can be used to assign letters and special characters to string variables.

String variables are variable names followed by a dollar sign. The dollar sign is a signal that letters, special characters, or a mixture of characters, such as a street address, will be assigned. Quotation marks surround data assigned to the string variable in the direct assignment method. We will refer to this grouping of data as a character string.

Special statements are required to process string variables, and they cannot be arithmetically processed as we have been doing with numeric values. When you stop to think about it, this is a logical constraint. Assume that a string variable contains your name. It does not make sense to add, subtract, multiply, or divide such an assignment. Any attempt to do so will result in an error.

An error will also occur if a numeric variable (a variable name without an ending dollar sign) is assigned a character string. Character strings can be assigned only to string variables.

String variables enhance BASIC programs and can be used to make the programs "conversational"

Figure 6.3 shows an example of the use of string variables. When executed, statement 20 assigns the value of 85 to SALE and statement 30

```
10 REM Assigning character strings
20 SALE = 85
30 SALE.ITEM$ = "Size 10 sports slacks"
40 PRINT "The price of " SALE.ITEM$
50 PRINT "is only";
60 PRINT USING "$$##.##";SALE
70 END
RUN
The price of Size 10 sports slacks
is only $85.00
Ok
```

Technically speaking, a program will execute without an END statement, but use of the statement is strongly recommended. END provides a good visual reference as to where the program ends.

FIGURE 6.3 Use of character strings

assigns the character string "Size 10 sports slacks" to the string variable SALE.ITEM$. This can be viewed as follows:

SALE   SALE.ITEM$

| |
| 85 |

| |
| Size 10 sports slacks |

Statement `40 PRINT "The price of " SALE.ITEM$` is executed from left to right, resulting in "The price of " being displayed. Then the value of the string variable SALE.ITEM$ is displayed: "Size 10 sports slacks."

Note the blank space inside the quotation marks surrounding "The price of." This is necessary because spaces are not automatically inserted around character strings. If the blank space were not enclosed inside the quotation marks, the output shown below would be produced.

```
The price ofSize 10 sports slacks
```

Statements 50 and 60 execute as explained previously and the program ends. As will be seen in the examples that follow, string variables are useful in making programs easier to read and understand. However, another method is available to assign values to variables, which is more flexible than the direct assignment method.

READ AND DATA STATEMENTS

NAME (or NAME$) is a BASIC reserved word and cannot be used. Hence variables that are assigned a person's name are often called CUSTOMER$ or EMPLOYEE$.

Variable names specified in the READ statement are assigned the values contained in DATA statements. This is a more efficient method of assigning values to variables, particularly if numerous variables are used.

The general form of the READ statement is

Statement	**READ**	First	Second	Any
Number		Variable,	Variable, . . .	Variable

DATA statements contain the values for variables specified in the READ statement. The general form of the DATA statement is

Statement	**DATA**	First	Second	Any
Number		Value,	Value, . . .	Value

The variables specified in the READ statement are assigned the values contained in the DATA statements. An example of READ and DATA statements appears in the program listing shown in Figure 6.4. String and numeric variables are intermixed to produce a customized bill. Program output is shown in Figure 6.5.

```
10 REM Assigning values with READ/DATA
20 READ CUSTOMER$, QT.BOUGHT
30 READ UNIT.PRICE, DESCRIPTION$
40 SALE = QT.BOUGHT * UNIT.PRICE
50 REM
60 PRINT "Dear " CUSTOMER$ ":"
70 PRINT
80 PRINT "Your purchase of" QT.BOUGHT "of our " DESCRIPTION$
90 PRINT"at a price of";
100 PRINT USING "$$##.##"; UNIT.PRICE;
110 PRINT" each was a wise investment decision."
120 PRINT "Please enclose the sum of" ;
130 PRINT USING "$$###.##"; SALE
140 PRINT
150 PRINT "Thank you for your business."
160 REM
170 DATA "Ms. Susan Citizen", 5
180 DATA 25.50, "Old Kentucky plates"
190 END
```

FIGURE 6.4 Programming READ and DATA statements

```
RUN
Dear Ms. Susan Citizen:

Your purchase of 5 of our Old Kentucky plates
at a price of $25.50 each was a wise investment decision.
Please enclose the sum of $127.50

Thank you for your business.
Ok
```

FIGURE 6.5 Program output

Values for variables specified in READ statements are contained in DATA statements. The computer uses an indirect method of assigning these values: An internal data list is first created for all items in all DATA statements; then—one by one—items are read from this internal data list.

When a program encounters a READ statement, data items are taken off the internal data list. With the DATA statements shown in Figure 6.4, the following would occur:

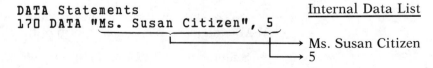

DATA Statements	Internal Data List
170 DATA "Ms. Susan Citizen", 5	Ms. Susan Citizen
	5

```
180 DATA 25.50, "Old Kentucky plates"
```
→ 25.50
→ Old Kentucky plates

The computer creates this internal data list, which is not apparent to (known by) the programmer. After the creation of the internal data list, a pointer points to the first element in the data list.

Now let's look closely at statement 20. The first portion of the statement (READ CUSTOMER$) assigns the data item "Ms. Susan Citizen" to the string variable CUSTOMER$, and the pointer moves to the next item in the data list. This can be viewed as follows:

Internal Data List

Ms. Susan Citizen
→ 5
25.50
Old Kentucky plates

Variable Assignment

CUSTOMER$
| Ms. Susan Citizen |

The second portion of statement **20 READ QT.BOUGHT** assigns a data value of 5 to the variable QT.BOUGHT, and the pointer moves to the next data list item. This can be viewed as follows:

Internal Data List

Ms. Susan Citizen
5
→ 25.50
Old Kentucky plates

Variable Assignment

CUSTOMER$
| Ms. Susan Citizen |

QT.BOUGHT
| 5 |

The order of items in the DATA statement is very important. A computer constructs an internal data list from all items in the DATA statements. If one value is omitted, all following program values will be read incorrectly.

Statement **30 READ UNIT.PRICE, DESCRIPTION$** assigns the value of 25.50 to the variable UNIT.PRICE. The pointer moves down the list, and the character string "Old Kentucky plates" is assigned to the string variable DESCRIPTION$. The pointer again moves down the list.

All values have now been assigned to variables, and the internal data list pointer is pointing at nothing. This can be viewed as follows:

Internal Data List

Ms. Susan Citizen
5
25.50
Old Kentucky plates
→

Variable Assignments

CUSTOMER$	QT.BOUGHT	UNIT.PRICE	DESCRIPTION$
Ms. Susan Citizen	5	25.50	Old Kentucky plates

If an attempt is made to READ additional values, an out-of-data message will occur unless the internal data list pointer is restored. The original set of values can be assigned to different variables by using the RESTORE statement. RESTORE resets the internal data list pointer to the first item in the data list.

The general form of the RESTORE statement is

Statement **RESTORE**
Number

In summary, when READ and DATA statements are used, an internal data list is automatically created. The data list elements are then assigned, one at a time, to the variables specified in the READ statements.

Several points should be noted. First, the order of variables in the READ statement must match the corresponding data elements, or an error will occur. Every variable in the READ statement must have a corresponding element of the correct type (numeric or string) in a DATA statement. You may have more than one data element per DATA statement, as long as the READ statement variable has a corresponding element of the correct type. Second, commas are used to separate variables in the READ statement and data elements in the DATA statement. Quotation marks do not have to be used around character strings in the DATA statement unless the string contains a comma, colon, or important leading or trailing blank space. DATA statements merely provide values for an internal data list; they are not themselves executed. They may be placed anywhere in the program, but they are often placed near the end of the program to simplify program maintenance.

THE INPUT STATEMENT

Consider the program shown in Figure 6.6, which uses READ and DATA statements to assign a customer name and sale amount to the appropriate variables. A customized sales bill is then produced. But what if you wanted to produce a bill for a different customer? You would have to modify the DATA statement for each customer. Another, more flexible method is needed to assign values to variables after the program is executed.

The program shown in Figure 6.6 has been saved on the companion diskette as FIG6-6. This can be loaded into memory by the command LOAD"FIG6-6".

```
10 REM Using READ/DATA to prepare bill
20 READ CUSTOMER$, SALE
30 TAX = SALE * .05
40 BILL = SALE + TAX
50 REM
60 PRINT "Dear " CUSTOMER$ ":"
70 PRINT "The price of the item purchased was";
80 PRINT USING "$$###.##";SALE
90 PRINT "The tax is";
100 PRINT USING "$$#.##"; TAX
110 PRINT "The total bill including tax is";
120 PRINT USING "$$###.##";BILL
130 REM
140 DATA "Alfred E. Neuman", 100
150 END
Ok
RUN
Dear Alfred E. Neuman:
The price of the item purchased was $100.00
The tax is $5.00
The total bill including tax is $105.00
Ok
```

FIGURE 6.6 The use of READ and DATA statements

The INPUT statement is a more flexible method for assigning values to variables because the data can be entered via the keyboard after the RUN command is given. The program no longer has to be modified to accommodate different values. When the program is executed, the program stops whenever an INPUT statement is reached and a "?" prompt is displayed to signal that the computer is awaiting an input. The input consists of values for the variables specified in the INPUT statement.

The general form of the INPUT statement is

INPUT statements are used when data changes frequently during program execution. READ and DATA statements are used for relatively permanent data, such as tax tables.

Statement Number	**INPUT**	First Variable,	Second Variable, . . .	Any Variable

An example of an INPUT statement is shown in the sequence of figures which follow, beginning with Figure 6.7. The screen would appear as shown after the program is typed and the RUN command is executed. Note that the program is asking the user to answer a question.

```
10 REM Use of an INPUT statement
20 PRINT "Press Enter after typing customer name."
30 INPUT CUSTOMER$
40 PRINT "Thank you " CUSTOMER$ ".  We appreciate your business."
50 END
RUN
Press Enter after typing customer name.          Program is waiting
?    ←                                           for data
```

FIGURE 6.7 Use of an INPUT statement

Statement 20 PRINT "Press Enter after typing customer name." is an instruction to the user and is not required by the program. If specific instructions are not included in the program, the user will often look at the ? prompt when the INPUT statement is reached and forget what is to be entered.

Statement 30 INPUT CUSTOMER$ has established a storage location in memory as follows:

CUSTOMER$

Although the program shown in Figure 6.7 has been executed, a value has not been assigned to the CUSTOMER$ variable specified in the INPUT statement. A ? prompt appears on the monitor to remind the user that the computer is awaiting a value. Assume that the name Alfred E. Neuman is typed and the Enter key is pressed. This results in the following memory assignment:

CUSTOMER$

Alfred E. Neuman

Quotation marks are not used when entering character strings via the INPUT statement. The monitor, including program output, would appear as shown in Figure 6.8 after typing the customer's name and pressing the Enter key.

```
10 REM Use of an INPUT statement
20 PRINT "Press Enter after typing customer name."
30 INPUT CUSTOMER$
40 PRINT "Thank you " CUSTOMER$ ".  We appreciate your business."
50 END
RUN
Press Enter after typing customer name.
? Alfred E. Neuman
Thank you Alfred E. Neuman.  We appreciate your business.
Ok
```

The ? prompt displayed by the INPUT statement is confusing unless a PRINT statement describes what is to be entered. Please spend the time necessary to label clearly all data to be entered by the operator.

FIGURE 6.8   Program output

A trailing semicolon can be used after the PRINT statement which labels the INPUT statement. This arranges the data in a more user-friendly format. An example of the use of a trailing semicolon is shown in Figure 6.9, the screen after typing the program and executing the RUN command. Note that the question mark appears along with the prompt "Customer name?"

```
10 REM Use of an INPUT with trailing semicolon
20 PRINT "Customer name";
30 INPUT CUSTOMER$
40 PRINT "Thank you " CUSTOMER$ ".  We appreciate your business."
50 END
RUN
Customer name?
```

FIGURE 6.9   Use of INPUT with a trailing semicolon

Type the customer's name, and press Enter. The monitor will then appear as shown in Figure 6.10.

```
10 REM Use of an INPUT with trailing semicolon
20 PRINT "Customer name";
30 INPUT CUSTOMER$
40 PRINT "Thank you " CUSTOMER$ ".  We appreciate your business."
50 END
RUN
Customer name? Alfred E. Neuman
Thank you Alfred E. Neuman.  We appreciate your business.
Ok
```

FIGURE 6.10   Program output

A more practical program using an INPUT statement is shown in Figure 6.11. Program output is shown in Figure 6.12 as it would appear on the monitor. (LPRINT could be substituted for PRINT to direct output to an attached printer.) This output is the same as that produced from the program shown in Figure 6.6, which used READ and DATA statements. However, notice how easy it is to re-run the program to produce a customized billing for Susan Citizen. Because of this flexibility, the INPUT statement is a commonly used programming statement.

```
10 REM Using INPUT statements
20 PRINT "Press Enter after typing requested data."
30 PRINT "Customer name";
40 INPUT CUSTOMER$
50 PRINT "Sale in dollar and cents";
60 INPUT SALE
70 TAX = SALE * .05
80 BILL = SALE + TAX
90 PRINT
100 PRINT "Dear " CUSTOMER$ ":"
110 PRINT "The price of the item purchased was";
120 PRINT USING "$$###.##";SALE
130 PRINT "The tax is";
140 PRINT USING "$$#.##"; TAX
150 PRINT "The total bill including tax is";
160 PRINT USING "$$###.##";BILL
170 END
```

FIGURE 6.11 Use of multiple INPUT statements

```
RUN
Press Enter after typing requested data.
Customer name? Alfred E. Neuman
Sale in dollar and cents? 100

Dear Alfred E. Neuman:
The price of the item purchased was $100.00
The tax is $5.00
The total bill including tax is $105.00
Ok
RUN
Press Enter after typing requested data.
Customer name? Susan Citizen
Sale in dollar and cents? 112.50

Dear Susan Citizen:
The price of the item purchased was $112.50
The tax is $5.62
The total bill including tax is $118.12
Ok
```

FIGURE 6.12 Program output

In the program shown in Figure 6.11, notice statements 20, 30, and 50. These statements are used to label the INPUT statements. It cannot be overemphasized that if specific instructions are not given, users will become confused, and data entry errors will increase. Not only will an incorrect entry result in incorrect output, but if string data is entered when the program expects numeric data, the error message "Redo from start" will appear.

This is a confusing error message—what it means is that the value for the variable must be reentered. However, users will often attempt to "redo" the data entry from the start of the program, resulting in a hopelessly confused mess. The data will be wrong and, compounding the problem, the program cannot progress unless a value is assigned to the variable(s) specified in the INPUT statement.

It is strongly recommended that all data to be entered be clearly and accurately labeled with a PRINT statement directly before the necessary INPUT statement. This will save a lot of confusion and will help reduce errors in data entry.

The program shown in Figure 6.4, using READ and DATA statements, has been revised to have data statements entered after RUN is typed as shown in Figure 6.13. Notice that statements 40 and 70 contain single variables but that statement 100 INPUT UNIT.PRICE, DESCRIPTION$ contains two variables on the same INPUT statement. This is acceptable, but users must remember that a comma is required to separate values typed into the computer.

```
10 REM    Multiple variables per INPUT statement
20 PRINT "Press Enter after typing data."
30 PRINT "Customer's name";
40 INPUT CUSTOMER$
50 REM
60 PRINT "How many items were purchased";
70 INPUT QT.BOUGHT
80 REM
90 PRINT "Unit price, description, separated by a comma";
100 INPUT UNIT.PRICE, DESCRIPTION$
110 REM
120 SALE = QT.BOUGHT * UNIT.PRICE
130 PRINT
140 PRINT "Dear " CUSTOMER$ ":"
150 PRINT
160 PRINT "Your purchase of" QT.BOUGHT "of our " DESCRIPTION$
170 PRINT "at a sale price of";
180 PRINT USING "$$##.##";UNIT.PRICE;
190 PRINT " each was a wise decision."
200 PRINT "Please enclose the sum of ";
210 PRINT USING "$$##.##";SALE
220 PRINT "Thank you for your business."
230 END
```

FIGURE 6.13 Multiple variables per INPUT statement

The output for this program is shown in Figure 6.14. In actual practice, LPRINT would be used instead of PRINT to obtain paper copy for this customer billing.

Be careful when using one INPUT statement to assign values to two variables. The user must remember to separate each variable assignment (data element) with a comma. If too many commas are used, an "extra ignored" message will appear. An even worse error can be caused by an

```
RUN
Press Enter after typing data.
Customer's name? Ms. Susan Citizen
How many items were purchased? 5
Unit price, description, separated by a comma? 25.50,plates

Dear Ms. Susan Citizen:

Your purchase of 5 of our plates
at a sale price of $25.50 each was a wise decision.
Please enclose the sum of $127.50
Thank you for your business.
Ok
```

FIGURE 6.14   Program output

attempt to assign string data to numeric variables. When this occurs, a "Redo from start" error message appears, which is very confusing to a user. For these reasons, it is often best to assign only one variable on an INPUT statement. (More of this topic in Chapter 19.)

Do you know what G.I.G.O. stands for? Garbage In, Garbage Out! A program is only as good as the data it processes, so carefully label all data to be entered.

SUMMARY

Either numeric or character strings can be assigned to variable names. These are the three methods of assigning values to variables:

1. Direct assignment statements are statements such as **AMOUNT = 400** or **EMPLOYEE$ = "John Q. Citizen"**, which are used when values do not change often.
2. READ and DATA statements assign values contained in DATA statements to the variables specified in READ statements. READ and DATA statements are used when numerous program assignments have to be made.
3. The INPUT statement assigns values during program execution. When using an INPUT statement, directions should be given on entering data. This will minimize confusion.

Quotation marks are not required when typing a character string into the computer. However, the same rules apply as in using DATA statements: embedded commas and leading or trailing blanks require quotation marks.

You should now be familiar with the three methods of assigning values to variables. The next chapter shows various methods of processing numeric and string values.

Now would be a good time to re-run the Variables tutorial on the companion disk. Select the program, and the screen will appear as shown below. Notice the use of the direct assignment method for assigning values to variables. Contrast this with READ-DATA and INPUT for the assignment of values. Then work the problems in this chapter for a good understanding of how values are assigned to program variables.

```
BASIC Programming With the IBM PC

        Variables

            By
        Peter Mears
    (c) Copyright 1990
```

Summary of terms

Name	Example	Purpose
$	EMPLOYEE$ = "John Citizen"	The dollar sign indicates a string variable.
READ	10 READ EMPLOYEE$, PAY	Variables in READ statement are assigned values contained in DATA statements.
DATA	90 DATA "John Citizen", 225	Contains values for variables specified in READ statement.
RESTORE	150 RESTORE	Resets internal pointer if DATA statements are to be re-read by additional READ statements.
INPUT	50 PRINT "Type name and press Enter" 60 INPUT EMPLOYEE$	Used to enter data during program execution. Instructions should be displayed on what is to be entered.

Use commas where needed. They separate variable names in INPUT and READ statements. In DATA statements, commas separate data elements.

PROBLEMS

True/False. Problems 1–8.

6.1 String variable names are followed by a $. ⊤

6.2 String variables may be arithmetically processed. F

6.3 READ statements contain variables that are assigned values from DATA statements. ⊤

6.4 DATA statements contain only numeric data. ⊤

6.5 String and numeric variables cannot be intermixed within a program.

6.6 If the DATA statements run out of data, then the data list pointer is automatically restarted at the beginning of the data list. ⊤

6.7 When using INPUT statements data must be typed in just before the program is run. F

6.8 Quotation marks are used when entering character strings via the INPUT statement.

Program Completion—Beginning. Problems 9–12.
BASIC assignment statements are shown. Write the value of the variable in the indicated boxes.

6.9
```
30 READ PRICE, QT, DISCOUNT
90 DATA 9.95, 2, .05
```

PRICE	QT	DISCOUNT
9.95	2	.05

6.10
```
20 READ L2, L4, L2
30 DATA 2, 4, 6
```

L2	L4
6	4

Hint: The computer remembers the last value assigned to a variable.

HOURS   RATE

6.11   `1O READ HOURS, RATE`
         `6O DATA 40, 5, 36`

HOURS box: 40   RATE box: 5

Hint: Excess data elements are ignored.

ITEM$ PRICE

6.12   `6O READ ITEM$, PRICE`
         `7O DATA "Typewriter", 895.95`

ITEM$ box: Typewriter   PRICE box: 895.95

Program Completion—Advanced. Problems 13–24.
Find and complete the necessary statements, so that the output indicated will
be produced when the program is executed.

*6.13   `1O REM Problem 6.13`
       `2O READ QUANTITY`
       `3O DATA` 55   ← What must be here?
       `4O PRINT "We sold" QUANTITY "units."`
       `5O END`
       `RUN`
       `We sold 55 units.`

6.14   `1O REM Problem 6.14`
       `2O PRINT "Type quantity sold and press Enter."`
       `3O INPUT QUANTITY`
       `4O PRINT "We sold" QUANTITY "units."`
       `5O END`
       `RUN`
       `Type quantity sold and press Enter.`
       `?` 33   ← What must be typed here?
       `We sold 33 units.`

6.15   `1O REM Problem 6.15`
       `2O PRINT "Quantity sold";`
       `3O INPUT QUANTITY`
       `4O PRINT "We sold" QUANTITY "units."`
       `5O END`
       `RUN`
       `Quantity sold?` 250   ← What must be typed here?
       `We sold 250 units.`

6.16   `1O REM Problem 6.16`
       `2O PRINT "Student name";`
       `3O INPUT STUDENT$`
       `4O PRINT "Course grade";`
       `5O INPUT GRADE$`
       `6O PRINT STUDENT$ " received a grade of " GRADE$`
       `7O END`
       `RUN`
       `Student name?` Tom Smith   ← What must be typed here?
       `Course grade?` B+   ← What must be typed here?
       `Tom Smith received a grade of B+`

6.17   `1O REM Problem 6.17`
       `2O PRINT "Number of items in inventory";`
       `3O INPUT UNITS`
       `4O PRINT "Item description";`
       `5O INPUT ITEM$`
       `6O PRINT "There are" UNITS ITEM$ " in inventory."`
       `7O END`
       `RUN`
       `Number of items in inventory?`   ← What must be typed here?
       `Item description?`   ← What must be typed here?
       `There are 5 toy dolls in inventory.`

* The answer to this problem is in Appendix E.

6.18
```
10 REM Problem 6.18
20 PRINT "Dollar value of sale";
30 INPUT SALE
40 TAX = SALE * .05
50 PRINT "- - - - - - - - - - - - - - - - - - - -"
60 PRINT "On a sale of";
70 PRINT USING "$$###.##"; SALE;
80 PRINT " the tax is";
90 PRINT USING "$$##.##";TAX
100 END
RUN
Dollar value of sale?                 ← What must be typed here?
- - - - - - - - - - - - - - - - - - -
On a sale of $200.00 the tax is $10.00
```

6.19
```
10 REM Problem 6.19
20 READ ITEM$, AMOUNT
30 DATA                    ← What must be here?
40 PRINT "There were" AMOUNT ITEM$ "."
50 END
RUN
There were 5 hammers.
```

6.20
```
10 REM Problem 6.20
20 READ MONTHS.DUE, MONTHLY.DUES
30 BILL = MONTHS.DUE * MONTHLY.DUES
40 PRINT "Your bill for" MONTHS.DUE "months dues is";
50 PRINT USING "$$###.##"; BILL
60 DATA                    ← What must be here?
70 END
RUN
Your bill for 3 months dues is $135.00
```

6.21
```
10 REM Problem 6.21
20 PRINT "Club activity and fees."
30 PRINT "Club activity";
40 INPUT ACTIVITY$
50 PRINT "Activity dues";
60 INPUT DUES
70 PRINT "Your bill for " ACTIVITY$ " is";
80 PRINT USING "$$##.##"; DUES
90 END
RUN
Club activity and fees.
Club activity?             ← What must be typed here?
Activity dues?             ← What must be typed here?
Your bill for tennis is $45.00
```

6.22
```
10 REM Problem 6.22 is tricky.
20 READ STUDENT1$, STUDENT2$
30 DATA                    ← What must be here?
40 DATA                    ← What must be here?
50 PRINT "Summary of Names"
60 PRINT STUDENT2$
70 PRINT STUDENT1$
80 END
RUN
Summary of Names
Tim Allison
John Jackson
```

The data below will be needed for Problems 23–36.

Item	Price	Quantity
Baseballs	2.25	35
Ping Pong	2.95	20
Nurf balls	1.95	30
Basketballs	34.95	5
Rubber balls	2.55	60

*6.23
```
10 REM Problem 6.23
20 READ ITEM$, PRICE,                    ← What must be here?
30 DATA "Baseballs", 2.25, 35
40 PRINT TAB(18) "Bouncing Ball Toy Store"
50 PRINT TAB(10) "Item" TAB(25) "Price"
   TAB(40) "Quantity"
60 PRINT TAB(10) ITEM$  TAB(25) PRICE
TAB(41) QUANTITY
70 END
RUN
```

```
              Bouncing Ball Toy Store
      Item              Price           Quantity
      Baseballs         2.25                 35
```

6.24
```
10 REM Problem 6.24
20 READ ITEM$, PRICE, QUANTITY
30 DATA                                  ← What must be here?
40 PRINT TAB(18) "Bouncing Ball Toy Store"
50 PRINT TAB(10) "Item" TAB(25) "Price"
   TAB(40) "Quantity"
60 PRINT TAB(10) ITEM$ TAB(25) PRICE TAB(40) QUANTITY
70 END
RUN
```

```
              Bouncing Ball Toy Store
      Item              Price           Quantity
      Basketballs       34.95                5
```

Program Output—Missing Statements. Problems 25–27.
Find and complete the necessary statements so that the output indicated will be produced when the program is executed. Carefully study these programs. No assistance is given to identify which statements are missing or incomplete.

*6.25
```
10 REM Problem 6.25
20 READ PRODUCT$, SALE
30 DATA 1.95, "Nurfballs"
40 PRINT TAB(17) "Bouncing Ball Toy Store"
50 PRINT TAB(20) "Item"     TAB(32) "Price"
60 PRINT TAB(20) PRODUCT$
70 END
RUN
```

```
        Bouncing Ball Toy Store
            Item         Price
            Nurfballs    1.95
```

* The answer to this problem is in Appendix E.

6.26
```
10 REM Problem 6.26
20 READ ITEM$, PRICE, QUANTITY
30 DATA "Ping-Pong", 2.95, 20
40 COST =
50 PRINT TAB(18) "Bouncing Ball Toy Store"
60 PRINT TAB(10) "Item" TAB(25) "Price"
   TAB(40) "Quantity"
70 PRINT TAB(10) ITEM$ TAB(25) PRICE
   TAB(41) QUANTITY
80 PRINT
90 PRINT TAB(10) "The total cost is:" TAB(30)
100 PRINT USING "$$##.##";
110 END
RUN
```

```
            Bouncing Ball Toy Store
   Item              Price           Quantity
   Ping-Pong         2.95                  20

   The total cost is:    $59.00
```

6.27
```
10 REM Problem 6.27
20 READ ITEM1$, PRICE1, QUANTITY1
30 READ ITEM2$, PRICE2, QUANTITY2
40 DATA
50 DATA
60 PRINT TAB(18) "Bouncing Ball Toy Store"
70 PRINT TAB(10) "Item"  TAB(25) "Price" TAB(40)
   "Quantity"
80 PRINT TAB(10) ITEM1$  TAB(25) PRICE1
   TAB(41) QUANTITY1
90 PRINT TAB(10) ITEM2$  TAB(25) PRICE2
   TAB(41) QUANTITY2
100 END
RUN
```

```
            Bouncing Ball Toy Store
   Item              Price           Quantity
   Softballs         4.95                   5
   Footballs        24.95                   6
```

Program Output—Identification. Problems 28–36.
Write the output that would appear when the program shown is executed.

*6.28
```
20 REM Problem 6.28
30 READ MILES, GAL1, GAL2
40 MPG = MILES / (GAL1 + GAL2)
50 PRINT "Miles/Gallon=" MPG
60 DATA 500, 10, 15
RUN
```

6.29
```
60 REM Problem 6.29
70 READ SCORE1, SCORE2, FINAL
80 GRADE = .2 * SCORE1 + .3 * SCORE2 + .5 * FINAL
90 PRINT "Course grade is" GRADE
100 DATA 80, 90, 100
RUN
```

* The answer to this problem is in Appendix E.

```
6.30   80 REM Problem 6.30
       90 READ THING$, PRICE
       100 TAX = PRICE * .05
       110 PRINT THING$ " Price =" PRICE " Tax =" TAX
       120 READ THING$, PRICE
       130 PRINT "Nice " THING$ " for a price of only" PRICE
       140 DATA "Shirt", 10, "Suit", 150
       RUN

6.31   10 REM Problem 6.31
       20 TAX = 37.748
       30 S$ = "$$###.##"
       40 PRINT "The sales tax is";
       50 PRINT USING S$;TAX
       60 END
       RUN

6.32   10 REM Problem 6.32 is tricky
       20 READ PRICE1, PRICE2, PRICE3, PRICE4
       30 P$ = "$$###.##"
       40 PRINT USING P$; PRICE1, PRICE4
       50 DATA 12.83, 150.84, 38.91, 12.08
       60 END

6.33   10 REM Problem 6.33
       20 READ QUANTITY1, QUANTITY2, QUANTITY3
       30 TOTAL = QUANTITY1 + QUANTITY2 + QUANTITY3
       40 PRINT "First total:" TOTAL
       50 RESTORE
       60 READ X1, X2, X3
       70 TOTAL = X1 + X3
       80 PRINT "Second total:" TOTAL
       90 DATA 4, 6, 10
       100 END

6.34   10 REM Problem 6.34
       20 READ APPLES, PEARS, PEACHES, CHERRIES
       30 TOTAL = APPLES + CHERRIES
       40 PRINT "First total:" TOTAL
       50 RESTORE
       60 READ PEARS, APPLES, CHERRIES, PEACHES
       70 TOTAL = APPLES + CHERRIES
       80 PRINT "Second total:" TOTAL
       90 DATA 10, 20, 30, 60
       100 END

6.35   10 REM Problem 6.35 - Tricky. Read carefully!
       20 READ APPLES, PEARS, PEACHES, CHERRIES
       30 TOTAL = APPLES + CHERRIES
       40 PRINT "First total:" TOTAL
       50 DATA 10, 20, 30, 60
       60 END

6.36   10 REM Problem 6.36 Another tricky problem.
       20 READ APPLES, PEARS
       30 TOTAL = APPLES + CHERRIES
       40 PRINT "First total:" TOTAL
       50 RESTORE
       60 READ PEARS, APPLES, CHERRIES, PEACHES
       70 TOTAL = APPLES + CHERRIES
       80 PRINT "Second total:" TOTAL
       90 DATA 10, 20, 30, 60
       100 END
```

Debugging Problems—Miniprograms. Problems 37–46.
The miniprograms shown contain errors. Some of the errors (program bugs)
are easy to find; others will be difficult to detect. The programs were executed

and the screen appeared as shown. Find and correct the error, so that a logical output can be obtained when the program is executed.

*6.37 An attempt was made to READ values for AGE and INCOME.

```
85 READ AGE, INCOME
90 3500, 21
Syntax error
Ok
```

6.38 An attempt was made to display the following message: "A Plumber earns 45000".

```
90 DATA 45×500, "Plumber"
92 READ INCOME, OCCUPATION$
94 PRINT "A " OCCUPATION$ " earns " INCOME
run
A 500 earns  45
Ok
```

6.39 An attempt was made to display the following message: "Tom Smith received a grade of A".

```
10 PRINT "Student name";
20 INPUT STUDENT$
30 PRINT "Enter course grade";
40 INPUT GRADE
50 PRINT STUDENT$ " received a grade of " GRADE
run
Student name? Tom Smith
Enter course grade? A
?Redo from start
?
```

6.40 An attempt was made to READ a person's name and age.

```
10 READ NAME$, AGE
20 PRINT NAME$, AGE
30 DATA "Tom Smith", 28
run
Syntax error in 10
Ok
10 READ NAME$, AGE
```

6.41 An attempt was made to READ and PRINT values for ITEM, PRICE, and QUANTITY.

```
10 READ  ITEM$, PRICE, QUANTITY
20 PRINT ITEM$, PRICE, QUANTITY
30 DATA "Toy tiger, 19.95, 2
run
Out of DATA in 10
Ok
```

* The answer to this problem is in Appendix E.

6.42   An attempt was made to display the message "The student's name is Thomas Citizen".

```
10 MY.NAME$ = Thomas Citizen
20 PRINT "The student's name is " MY.NAME$
run
Type mismatch in 10
Ok
```

6.43   An attempt was made to read an item (Toy jet plane) from a data list. Then the program was to ask the user to enter the price of the item. Finally, the item and price were to be displayed. Identify the specific cause of the error without changing the program. Then rewrite the program to accomplish the objective stated.

```
30 READ ITEM
40 PRINT "Price of item";
43 READ ITEM
45 DATA "Toy jet plane"
47 PRINT "Price of item";
49 INPUT PRICE
run
Syntax error in 45
Ok
45 DATA "Toy jet plane"
```

6.44   An attempt was made to enter the car name "Trans Am".

```
102 PRINT "Type the car name."
104 PRINT "Spell the name correctly";
106 INPUT CAR
run
Type the car name.
Spell the name correctly? Trans Am
?Redo from start
?
```

6.45   An attempt was made to assign pricing data to the variables shown.

```
36 READ STOCK.NO, DATA
38 DATA 1234, 22.2
40 PRINT "Stock Number", "Data"
42 PRINT STOCK.NO, DATA
run
Syntax error in 36
Ok
36 READ STOCK.NO, DATA
```

6.46 An attempt was made to enter the price of an item.

```
81 PRINT "This is a mark-up program based on cost"
83 PRINT "Enter cost";
85 INPUT COST
87 MARK.UP = COST * 1.65
89 PRINT "The selling price is" MARK.UP
run
This is a mark-up program based on cost
Enter cost? $9.95
?Redo from start
?
```

Screen Design Problems. Problems 47–60.

Develop a BASIC program, paying particular attention to the design of the screen and the design of the printed output (when requested). General formats are shown for your consideration, which may be expanded on (improved) in your program.

Problems 47–49 require the information below.

The Stockholder's Relations Department of Precious Metals Company has developed DATA statements that reflect the status of stock ownership for current stockholders. The company has recently announced that a per-share dividend of $1.65 will be distributed to all current shareholders.

For program testing purposes, stock ownership data for a few shareholders is given below. Use the variable name STOCKHOLDER$ in your program to indicate the stockholder's name. Use the variable name SHARES.OWNED in your program to indicate shares owned.

Will Free   35

Karen Francis 14

Brian Louis   15

*6.47 Using READ and DATA statements, develop a program to produce the output shown below.

```
      Precious Metals Company
       Stockholder Department
     Outstanding Shares Report

Will Free has 35 shares
Karen Francis has 14 shares
Brian Louis has 15 shares
```

6.48 Using READ and DATA statements, develop a program to produce the output shown below. Note that a total is required.

```
      Precious Metals Company
       Stockholder Department
     Outstanding Shares Report

Will Free has 35 shares
Karen Francis has 14 shares
Brian Louis has 15 shares

Total number of shares: 64
```

* The answer to this problem is in Appendix E.

6.49 Using INPUT statements, develop a program to produce the output shown in Problem 6.48.

6.50 Using READ and DATA statements, develop a program to produce the output shown below.

```
              Decision Management Associates
                    Employee Listing
Employee          Social Security        Home
Name              Number                 Address
- - - - - -       - - - - - - - -        - - - - - - -
Phil Ryan         632-51-1673            411 Thorpe Ave.
Bill Flint        167-45-1462            143 Elm St.
Mary Jones        236-14-1856            211 Main St.
```

6.51 Using INPUT statements, develop a program to produce the output shown in Problem 6.50 on a printer.

6.52 Using READ and DATA statements, develop a program to produce the output shown below. Gross Pay is computed by multiplying hours worked times hourly rate (ignore overtime).

Data needed:
Bill Flint worked 85 hours during the pay period at a rate of $5.00 per hour worked. Mary Jones worked 76 hours at a rate of $7.50 per hour and Phil Ryan worked 80 hours at a rate of $9.25 per hour.

```
           Decision Management Associates
                        Payroll
        Employee          Social Security      Gross
        Name              Number               Pay
        Bill Flint        167-45-1462          $425.00
        Mary Jones        236-14-1856          $570.00
        Phil Ryan         632-51-1673          $740.00
```

6.53 Using INPUT statements, develop a program to produce the output shown in Problem 6.52.

Problems 54 and 55 require a program to be developed to produce the output shown.

```
              Bouncing Ball Toy Store
                 Inventory Analysis
       - - - - - - - - - - - - - - - - - -
       Item            Price          Quantity
       Nurf balls      1.95           30
       Rubber balls    2.55           60
```

6.54 Using READ and DATA statements, develop a program to produce the output on a printer.

6.55 Using an INPUT statement, develop a program to accept your own items, price, and quantity. Use the output shown as a general guide in developing your own printed output.

6.56 Using READ and DATA statements, develop a program to produce the output shown below.

```
        Honest Al's Pre-owned Car Company
- - - - - - - - - - - - - - - - - - - - -
Type of             Year             Asking
car                 of car           price
- - - - - - - - - - - - - - - - - - - - -
LeMans              1978             1200
```

6.57 Using INPUT statements, develop a program to produce the output shown in Problem 6.56 on a printer.

6.58 Using READ and DATA statements, develop a program to produce the output shown below.

```
        Honest Al's Pre-owned Car Company
- - - - - - - - - - - - - - - - - - - - -
Type of             Year             Asking
car                 of car           price
- - - - - - - - - - - - - - - - - - - - -
LeMans              1978             1200
Pinto               1972             300
TransAm             1989             12500
```

6.59 Using INPUT statements, develop a program to produce the output shown in Problem 6.58 on *both* the monitor and a printer.

6.60 Write a program which displays the following on the screen:

Customer name and address

Credit Rating

Print the name and address, but not the credit rating, on a printer. Use READ and DATA statements to assign each line of the address and the credit status to string variables. The screen should appear as follows:

```
John Johnston
900 Bowman Ln.
Louisville, KY 40111

Credit: GOOD
```

Other Problems. Problems 61–64.
Develop a BASIC program to solve each problem. Use a REM statement to identify the problem number and clearly label all output.

6.61 Compound interest is computed by the formula

AMOUNT = PRINCIPAL $*$ (1 + INTEREST.RATE) $\wedge$ YEARS

AMOUNT is the sum to be received the stated YEARS in the future.
PRINCIPAL is the dollar amount invested.
INTEREST.RATE is the interest rate in decimal value.
YEARS is the number of years of the investment.

Develop a program using INPUT statements to enter values for PRINCI-PAL, INTEREST.RATE, and YEARS. Clearly label program input so that the user will be guided in data entry. Also, clearly label all program output so that it will be easy to read.

The program should be flexible enough to permit any **PRINCIPAL** to be invested at any **INTEREST.RATE**, for any number of **YEARS**. Use the program to compute the amount to be received in three years on a $100 principal at an interest rate of 12 percent.

Hint: If $100 was invested for one year at 12% interest this would be computed as follows:

$$\text{AMOUNT} = 100 * (1 + .12)^1$$
$$\text{AMOUNT} = 100 * (1.12)$$
$$\text{AMOUNT} = 112$$

6.62 Write a program to print a check. The program should permit any value to be entered for the following items:

Date	(Any date)
Pay to the order of	(Any person)
Amount of	(Any dollars and cents)
Dollars	(Spell out the amount)

6.63 Write a program to produce a printed inventory summary for Smith's Computer Store. Use the output shown as a guide when developing your program. Values for Brand, Price, No. Sold (i.e., quantity sold) are unknown at this time. Gross sale is the product of Price times No. Sold.

```
Smith's Computer Store
Monthly Inventory Report
January, 1991

Brand    Price    No. Sold    Gross Sale
```

6.64 Write a program to develop and display a trial balance sheet as shown below. The date and dollars are to be entered by the program user.

```
                    BARRETT'S USED CARS
                       TRIAL BALANCE
                         9/14/XX

ACCT    ACCOUNT NAME              DEBITS        CREDITS
                              5,000.00
100     Cash                    300.00
110     Accounts Receivable                     400.00
120     Accounts Payable                      4,900.00
130     Equity
        totals here →         $X,XXX.XX     $X,XXX.XX
```

7 PROCESSING DATA AND HIGHLIGHTING PROGRAM OUTPUT

Upon completion of this chapter you should be able to

- Perform arithmetic operations
- Use the computer in a calculator mode
- Process strings
- Use LOCATE and COLOR statements to highlight output
- Make a professional screen and report design

Whenever a value is multiplied (*), divided (/), added (+), subtracted (−), or raised to a power (the ^ symbol on the 6 key), we are processing arithmetic values. Arithmetic symbols may be combined with variable names or quantities in a virtually unlimited number of ways. For example[1]:

PROFIT = 20 + 4	This adds the values 20 and 4 and assigns the sum of 24 to PROFIT.
GROSSPROFIT = 4.5 + PROFIT	This adds the value 4.5 to PROFIT and assigns the sum to GROSSPROFIT. If PROFIT is 24, then adding 4.5 yields 28.5, which is assigned to the variable GROSSPROFIT.
NET = 44 − 3.5	The value of 44 has 3.5 subtracted from it, yielding 40.5, which is assigned to the variable NET.
COMMISSION = .25 * SALE	This calculates one-fourth of SALE. If SALE had the previous value of 24, then the product of .25 times 24 (which is 6) is assigned to COMMISSION.
COMMISSION = SALE * .25	Same as above.

[1] These examples are for demonstration only. In actual practice there would be no need to have the computer simply process two numeric values. Just calculate the answer yourself and save the computer the time.

AVGSALE = SALE / CUSTOMERS	This divides the value of the variable **SALE** by the value of **CUSTOMERS** and assigns the result to **AVGSALE**.
AVGCOM = COMMISSION / 2	This divides **COMMISSION** by 2. If the value of **COMMISSION** is 6, then 6/2 (which is 3) is assigned to **AVGCOM**.
EOQ = 4^.5	This raises 4 to the ½ power, which is the same as taking the square root of 4. This can also be written as EOQ = SQR(4). (SQR is the preferred method. This function will be described later.)

HIERARCHY OF OPERATIONS

Arithmetic statements are processed following a very exact order of priority. BASIC statements are scanned by the computer from left to right, which is the same way we read a sentence. Although the statement isn't actually scanned over and over, you can think of the result as though the computation and re-scanning occur like this:

First, all exponentiation (raising to a power) is performed.
Second, multiplication and division are performed.
Third, addition and subtraction are performed.

For example,

$$X = 5 + 3^2 - 24 / 2*2$$

is evaluated using the order of priority as follows:
First, exponentiation is performed, yielding

$$X = 5 + 9 - 24 / 2*2$$

Second, multiplication and division are performed. Statements are scanned from left to right, and the division is encountered before the multiplication symbol. This results in

$$X = 5 + 9 - 12 * 2$$

Multiplication results in

$$X = 5 + 9 - 24$$

Third, addition and subtraction are performed. The addition is encountered first, resulting in

$$X = 14 - 24$$

Then subtraction is performed to obtain the final answer of -10.

If the order of priority is not considered carefully, an incorrect answer may occur. If arithmetic statements become complex, parentheses should be used to direct the order of statement execution. For example, notice the equation used to calculate overtime pay for people working over 40 hours per week:

$$PAY = 40 * RATE + 1.5 * RATE * (HOURS - 40)$$

In this equation, the parentheses direct that 40 be subtracted from HOURS before multiplication by 1.5 and RATE. This gives the hours over 40 upon which the higher rate is applied. Without the parentheses, an incorrect answer would occur.

It does no harm to use too many parentheses: When in doubt, use them. But be sure to use a closing parenthesis for every opening one. For example, the overtime formula could have been written as

$$\text{PAY} = (40 * \text{RATE}) + (1.5 * \text{RATE} * (\text{HOURS} - 40))$$

However, this is overdoing it; the excessive use of parentheses causes confusion and is poor programming practice.

Confused on the arithmetic order of priority? Then use parentheses to direct the order of arithmetic computations.

THE CALCULATOR MODE

In the discussion of arithmetic statements, statements were presented without program line numbers. If these statements are to be included in a program, line numbers must be added. However, there is another way to process numeric values. The word PRINT without a line number places the computer in a calculator mode. The indicated computations will be performed and the results will be displayed.

For example, the program shown in Figure 7.1 solves the statement shown and displays the results. The same answer is obtained on the lower half of the figure by using the computer in a calculator mode.

An effective way to check program answers is to use the PRINT command to turn the computer into a calculator. Then spot-check answers to verify that the program is working as intended.

```
10 REM Using PRINT as a command
20 ANSWER = 5 +3^2 - 24/2 * 2
30 PRINT ANSWER
40 END
RUN
-10
Ok
print 5 + 3^2 - 24/2 * 2
-10
Ok
```

FIGURE 7.1 Arithmetic statements: Program versus calculator mode

The use of the PRINT statement as a command brings up an interesting point. Many of the reserved words used in this book have multiple usage. We will concentrate on the primary use of a reserved word. For example, when we talk about PRINT as a statement, we mean that it is used primarily as a programming statement. The inquisitive or technically inclined reader is urged to read the three-page technical definition of PRINT in the Personal Computer Hardware Reference Library BASIC Manual, available from IBM.

STRING VARIABLES

Until now our discussion has been centered on assigning and processing numeric values. Alphanumeric data (any alphabetic characters, numbers, or special symbols) were handled by PRINT statements, which displayed

"ANYTHING BETWEEN QUOTATION MARKS!" Another way to handle alphanumeric data is by use of string variables.

A string is a sequence of alphabetic, numeric, and/or special characters. Variable names used to store and retrieve strings are followed by a dollar sign. For example, HAT, SHIRT, and SWEATER are numeric variable names, while HAT$, SHIRT$, and SWEATER$ are string variable names that can be assigned alphanumeric data.

The distinction between numeric and string variable names is important for two reasons. First, numeric variables cannot be assigned alphanumeric data. Any attempt to do so will result in an error message. Second, although strings can be assigned either numeric or alphabetic data, string data cannot be multiplied, divided, or raised to a power. That is, multiplying "Jack" times "Tom" means nothing and will result in an error message.

Direct assignment statements can be used either to assign numeric data to a numeric variable or to assign a character string to string variables. A program using both numeric and string variables is shown in Figure 7.2. Statement **20 YEARS.EMPLOYED = 12** assigns the numeric value of 12 to the variable YEARS.EMPLOYED. Statement **30 EMPLOY-EE.NAME$ = "Ms. Alice Smith"** assigns the character string between the quotation marks to the string variable EMPLOYEE.NAME$.

Actually we were using string variables when a customer name was assigned to the variable CUSTOMER$ using an INPUT statement. Although digits may be used in a string variable, they are not in a form suitable for calculation by the computer.

```
10 REM Using string variables
20 YEARS.EMPLOYED = 12
30 EMPLOYEE.NAME$ = "Ms. Alice Smith"
40 PRINT "The employee, " EMPLOYEE.NAME$;
50 PRINT ", worked" YEARS.EMPLOYED "years."
60 END
RUN
The employee, Ms. Alice Smith, worked 12 years.
Ok
```

FIGURE 7.2   Using string variables

When the program is executed, statements 20 and 30 result in the following assignments of values to our variables:

YEARS.EMPLOYED	EMPLOYEE.NAME$
12	Ms. Alice Smith

Particular attention should be paid to the blank space inside the quotation marks shown in statement 40. Blank spaces are automatically inserted before and after displaying numeric data. However, as stated in the last chapter, blank spaces are not automatically inserted before and after displaying string variables. This is not a major problem, provided that you exercise caution when spacing the output statements.

String variables personalize program output and improve readability when intermixed with PRINT statements. In the example shown in Figure 7.3, note statement 40 where the strings FIRST.NAME$ and LAST.NAME$ are joined to obtain FULL.NAME$. A blank space, " ", is joined between the strings to give a space between the first and last names.

```
10 REM Using strings to produce form letters
20 FIRST.NAME$ = "Alice"
30 LAST.NAME$ = "Smith"
40 FULL.NAME$ = FIRST.NAME$ + " " + LAST.NAME$
50 PRINT "Dear " FULL.NAME$ ":"
60 PRINT
70 PRINT "Hi " FIRST.NAME$ ", we are glad you joined our health club."
80 PRINT "We have a special plan available for the entire "
           LAST.NAME$ " family."
90 PRINT "Please let us know if you want us to mail you the details."
100 PRINT
110 PRINT "RSVP " FULL.NAME$
120 END
RUN
Dear Alice Smith:

Hi Alice, we are glad you joined our health club.
We have a special plan available for the entire Smith family.
Please let us know if you want us to mail you the details.

RSVP Alice Smith
Ok
```

Be careful when selecting variable names. NAME (even with a $ sign) is a reserved word and cannot be used as a variable name.

FIGURE 7.3   Use of strings in form letters

PROCESSING STRINGS

Let's develop an understanding of how strings are manipulated by taking a closer look at the DATE$ and TIME$ strings. Values for these strings are entered when the system is started. The TIME$ statement returns an eight-character string of the form hh:mm:ss (hours:minutes:seconds).

For example, assume that the current time is 15 seconds past ten-thirty AM. TIME$ can then be used as follows:

```
10 PRINT TIME$
20 END
RUN
10:30:15
Ok
```

or simply

```
PRINT TIME$
10:30:15
Ok
```

The DATE$ statement can be used to return a ten-character string of the form mm-dd-yyyy (month-day-year). If the date December 15, 1990, (12-15-90) were entered when the system was booted up, then DATE$ could be used as follows:

```
10 PRINT DATE$
20 END
RUN
12-15-1990
Ok
```

or simply

```
PRINT DATE$
12-15-1990
Ok
```

BASIC provides a number of built-in functions that provide manipulation of numbers and strings. Think of a function as a ready-made, special-purpose program that we do not have to write. A function and its argument together form an expression.

Five major functions are used in manipulating string variables. These are the VAL function, which returns the numeric value of the string; the LEN function, which returns string length; and the RIGHT$, MID$, and LEFT$ functions, which return specific portions of a string. An example of each function will be shown, along with its use in a BASIC statement.

The VAL function returns the leading numeric value (numeric characters) of the specified string up to the first nonnumeric character. For example, suppose that the DATE$ function has been assigned the date 06-25-90. The statement PRINT VAL(DATE$) results in the value of 6 being displayed.

This function can be used to extract beginning portions of a string such as a street address. For example:

```
10    STREET.ADDRESS$ = "121 South Main Street"
20    PRINT VAL(STREET.ADDRESS$)
30    END
RUN
 121
Ok
```

Remember, the VAL function returns the numeric value up to the first nonnumeric character. For example:

```
10    STREET.ADDRESS$ = "South 121 Main Street"
20    PRINT VAL(STREET.ADDRESS$)
30    END
RUN
 0
Ok
```

The LEN function returns the length of the specified string variable. Unprintable characters and blank spaces are included in this count. For example, PRINT LEN (DATE$) returns the length of the DATE$ string, which is 10. (The date 06-15-90 is considered to be 06-15-1990; including the dashes, this is ten characters.)

In the string variable specified, the RIGHT$ function returns a string of length stated when counting from the right. For example, PRINT RIGHT$(DATE$,4) returns the four right characters in the DATE$ string, resulting in the year 1990 being displayed.

RIGHT$ (String   Number of
            Variable,   Characters from right)

In the string variable specified, the MID$ function returns a string of the number of characters specified, beginning with the character stated. For example, PRINT MID$(DATE$,4,2) returns a string beginning with the fourth character and including two characters to the right. This results in two characters being displayed.

> **MID$** (String   Beginning   Number of
>   Variable,   Character,   Characters)

The DATE$ function normally uses dashes to separate the month, day, and year. A program to produce the current date in the format of month/day/year, separated by / is shown in Figure 7.4. Note the use of the MID$ function to assign the / symbol in place of the - symbol so that a fancy format is achieved. MID$ can be used both as a function (appears on the right side of the assignment) and as a statement (appears on the left side of the assignment).

```
10 REM Using the MID$ function
20 TODAY.DATE$ = DATE$
30 MID$(TODAY.DATE$,3,1) = "/"
40 MID$(TODAY.DATE$,6,1) = "/"
50 PRINT "Fancy format:  " TODAY.DATE$
60 PRINT
70 PRINT "Normal format: " DATE$
80 END
RUN
Fancy format:  12/15/1990

Normal format: 12-15-1990
Ok
```

FIGURE 7.4   Using the MID$ function

In the string variable specified, the LEFT$ function returns a string of length stated when counting from the left. For example, PRINT LEFT$(DATE$,2) returns the two left characters in the DATE$ string, resulting in the month 12 being displayed.

> **LEFT$** (String   Number of
>   Variable,   Characters
>   from left)

The STRING$ function returns a string of repetitive characters. It may be used with the PRINT statement for drawing lines, among other things, and is of the following form:

> **PRINT STRING$** (Number of   Characters to
>   Characters,   be printed)

For example, PRINT STRING$(20, "-") displays a 20 character dashed line as follows: --------------------.

THE LOCATE STATEMENT

The cursor can be directed to begin placing characters at any position of the monitor. The IBM monochrome monitor can display up to 25 lines consisting of 80 columns of data. When the screen is cleared by the CLS statement, the cursor returns to its home location of first line, first column. Another way to return the cursor to this location is by use of the LOCATE statement. The general form of the LOCATE statement is

Statement	**LOCATE**	Line	Column
Number		Number,	Number

We will expand our use of these string processing functions when we learn more about BASIC. In Chapter 16 they will be used to check for data entry errors and in graphing student grades. In Chapter 17, they will be used in word processing applications.

The LOCATE statement is very handy and will be used many times in this book. The lower left-hand corner of the screen is considered to be the 24th row, 1st column because the 25th line is normally used to display the function key assignments. However, output can be displayed on the 25th line by using the following LOCATE statement. (First use the KEY OFF command to clear the line.)

```
60 LOCATE 25,1
70 PRINT "Display message on 25th line
         beginning in column 1."
```

THE COLOR FUNCTION

There are four major parameters that can be assigned to the COLOR statement that are useful in highlighting output on a monochrome monitor. These are

COLOR 7,0	This is the normal display of white (light green) characters on a black (dark grey) background. (Amber monitors are black on amber.)
COLOR 0,7	This is a reverse display of black characters on a white background.
COLOR 16,7	This produces flashing black characters on a white background. This is often distracting and caution should be exercised before using this statement.
COLOR 31,0	This produces flashing white characters on a black background. This is a nice way to highlight output.

When a COLOR statement is executed, the display mode specified is in effect for all subsequent output until another COLOR statement is specified. COLOR should be used sparingly to prevent overpowering the operator and it will be necessary to reset to the default value of COLOR 7,0 as soon as possible.

An example of a fancy output program is shown in Figure 7.5. Program output is shown in Figure 7.6. Notice that the output isn't the only thing that is fancy. The apostrophe (the single quote on the quotation key) was used for an abbreviated REM (remark) statement. This is a particularly useful way of adding internal program documentation where necessary to clarify program statements.

The LOCATE statement is useful in directing output (the cursor) to specific points on the screen. However, a printer cannot "jump around," so the statement cannot be used to control printed output.

The LEN statement and LOCATE statement can be used together with the TAB statement as an aid in centering program output. An example of this is shown in Figure 7.7 where a value of half the length of the string is computed.

```
10 REM COLOR 0,7 reverses -  COLOR 7,0 for normal
20 CLS                                    'Clears screen
30 PRINT
40 PRINT TAB(25) "Introducing"
50 COLOR 0,7                              'Reverses output
60 LOCATE 4,21                            'Moves to 4th line, 19th column
70 PRINT " BASIC Programming "
80 COLOR 7,0                              'Changes to normal output
90  PRINT TAB(16) STRING$(28,"-")         'Prints a line
100 PRINT TAB(18) "A lot can be learned by"
110 PRINT TAB(18) "making the figures work!"
120 PRINT TAB(16) STRING$(28,"-")
130 END
```

FIGURE 7.5   Highlighting program output

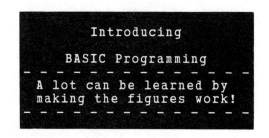

FIGURE 7.6   Program output

```
10 REM Demo of centering
20 PRINT "What is your name";
30 INPUT A$
40 X = .5 * LEN(A$)                    ' Compute half of length
50 PRINT TAB(40 - X) A$                ' Centering on a line
60 LOCATE 12, 40 - X                   ' Centering on screen
70 PRINT A$
80 END
```

FIGURE 7.7   Centering program output

```
RUN
What is your name? Sam Jackson
                                              Sam Jackson




Ok
                                              Sam Jackson
```

FIGURE 7.8   Program output

SCREEN AND REPORT DESIGN

The design of the data displayed on a monitor (screen) or on a printed report is partly a science, partly an art. There are no "hard and fast" rules, but one thing is certain. The more you know about the user, the better the design. An unskilled user will require many instructions, and all program output must be extensively labeled. Skilled users do not require this much hand-holding; they know what they are doing.

This would seem to suggest a "the more the better" approach in screen and report designs. That is, there is a tendency for beginners to provide too much data, in the belief that users can simply ignore what they don't need. As we will see in a moment, that's a mistake: too much data is annoying, confusing, and error-prone.

In reality, a screen or report design is the design of the user interface. User needs must come first, not the needs of the programmer. A good easy-to-understand design begins with pencil and paper. The design is first sketched on paper, so that full attention can be focused on the user's needs. Programming tends to "lock in" a design, and if you rush into programming, the interface "looks" and "feels" wrong. Users will not find the program friendly.

REPORT DESIGN

Let's first take a look at designing a printed report; then we'll look at screen designs. The examples in this book have stressed business applications, so that useful reports can be produced. It is hoped that we have been developing reports in an easy-to-read format, but we may have been overlooking a major point: management is often overloaded with data, and we may be producing something that will be ignored.

Mountains of data exist in many firms in the form of endless reports and page after page of computer printouts. It isn't that management doesn't want reports; it's just that they have to sort through a large amount of data to identify the facts that affect them.

In our enthusiasm to use the computer, more reports are generated. Even reports on reports are prepared, when no busy person could possibly read everything he or she currently receives. And then we wonder why many people dislike computers!

The computer should be used as a management tool that reduces, not increases, the amount of data. Programs should be developed to condense massive amounts of data into brief, manageable amounts of information that permit decisions to be made.

One of the keys to using the computer as a data-reduction tool is the use of arrays to store the results of internal program calculations. Consider the hand processing usually required after calculating and distributing paychecks: all too often someone is assigned the task of going through a payroll listing to identify the people who worked overtime.

A computer printout can easily be a hundred pages in length. Summarizing such output is a time-consuming, thankless task because the person preparing the report is caught in a "Catch-22." The computer is needed to provide the data to make a decision, yet so much data is provided that it is difficult to read it all and make a decision.

PRODUCING A REPORT

The microcomputer can be used to develop specialized reports that reduce data to manageable proportions. The term *data* is used to describe unorganized facts that are known about an item. A single data element (a fact) does not provide information that can be used for decision making because often there are too many data elements. These elements must be organized in a manner that will make them useful in making a decision.

For example, the name of a student enrolled in a course is a data element. If you are the registrar of a college or university trying to determine the number of students enrolled during a semester, a lengthy listing of thousands of students represents unorganized facts. The data must be organized into manageable portions before it is of any real use. This forces the registrar to manually process the data before the necessary information can be obtained.

Do you want to prepare a report for this person? If so, the data should be summarized in a way that quickly identifies the number of students enrolled during a particular term, perhaps by school.

THE REPORT FORMAT

The contents of a report will vary depending on the data available and the information required by the user. However, all reports contain three basic sections. The first is the report heading, consisting of the report title and column headings. The body of the report comes next, consisting of the detailed lines in the report. Then last, a summary (usually a total), that includes the date on which the report was prepared, concludes the report.

A typical report should have the format shown below:

```
              Micro University
        Student Enrollment by School

Title →

Column Heading →      School            Fall, 1991
Optional Underlining →

Detail                Arts & Sciences    2,346
Lines →               Business             730
                      Education            450
                      Engineering          576
                      Other                320

Summary →             Total Enrollment:  4,422

Date Prepared →       Prepared on:
                      10/15/91
```

Title → | Report Heading
Column Heading →
Optional Underlining →
Detail Lines → | Report Body
Summary → | Report Summary
Date Prepared →

SCREEN DESIGN

Screen design is different from report design for several reasons. First, screens can be separated into two types: screens used primarily for data entry and screens used primarily for data output. It is difficult for most people to read data on a screen; hence, errors become more numerous. An effective screen design will normally minimize the data presented. Other than holding the data presented to a minimum, the output data screen is virtually the same as the printed report design.

THE OUTPUT SCREEN

A general layout for an output screen is shown. This closely follows the report design previously shown.

General Layout for an Output Screen

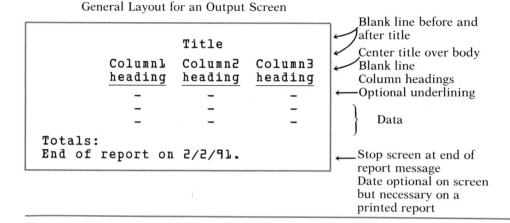

THE INPUT SCREEN

Data input screens are more difficult to design. The major point to remember is that you should not attempt to "fill" the screen. If the data isn't absolutely, positively necessary, it should not be on the screen. There should be just enough data on the screen so that the user knows what is to be done.

When the input screen is designed, do not be concerned with excessive blank spaces. A limited description draws attention to the specific task at hand and reduces data entry errors. A good approach is to begin the screen with a functional description that briefly tells the user the objective (function) being accomplished with the screen. Often when this is worded correctly, the input instructions can be condensed or even eliminated.

A general layout for an input screen is shown. The layout actually used should match the input document. Notice that since the lower half of the screen is not used, attention is focused on the specific question prompt.

General Layout for an Output Screen

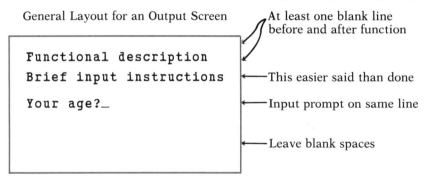

DESIGN PRINCIPLES

Here are a few principles to remember in screen and report design:

A design is the user's interface with the computer. The design process should begin with pencil and paper. This focuses attention on the user and does not lock in the design before we fully understand what is needed.

All screens and reports should be user friendly. A user-friendly design results in a program that can be used and understood without having to ask for assistance or having to guess what should be done.

KIS—Keep It Simple! A clean, uncluttered design is needed, with briefly labeled instructions. Plain English should be used, not computer jargon.

Minimize the use of sound, flashing messages, or inverse (highlighted) instructions. An overuse of attention-getters results in confusion. Use them sparingly, or not at all.

Always lay out the screen the way people read: from left to right, top to bottom. Don't jump around in your layout. Use a "different screen" if necessary.

Leave plenty of blank lines. It is harder to read data on a screen than on a printed page. Blank lines are needed so that attention can be focused on important items.

Creativity is OK, a busy screen is not. If you like to box instructions, LOCATE, or center data, then do so. Just keep your design uncluttered.

After the design is complete, program it, and then test the program out! Give the screen/report to a potential user. If the user has any question or doubt about what should be done or what something means, then revise, revise, revise! If something has to be explained to a potential user, then the report is not user friendly.

SUMMARY

This chapter began with a discussion of numeric values. Numeric values (numbers) can be arithmetically processed by raising to a power (^), multiplying (*), dividing (/), adding (+), and subtracting (−). A quick answer can be obtained by using the computer in a calculator mode. If arithmetic statements become complex, parentheses should be used to direct the order of statement execution. This minimizes errors that might otherwise occur in following the arithmetic order of priority.

The discussion of screen and report design began by stressing that a design should first be made on paper. Then, after several revisions, program the design. In addition, we want less data, not more. Screen data tends to overwhelm users, and there are often too many printed reports. Simple input screens should be developed to produce brief reports that meet users' needs.

Symbols	Examples	Action
*	20 PAY = RATE * HOURS	Multiply
/	40 AVG = TOTAL / NUMBER	Divide
+	80 PROFIT = COST + MARKUP	Add
−	30 NET = GROSS − RETURNS	Subtract
^	50 SQUARE = 2^2	Raise to a power
( )	40 OVERTIME = 1.5 * RATE * (HOURS −40)	Directs order of computations
'	40 '	Same as spelling out REM

By the way, congratulations! You have come a long way in learning BASIC. By now you should be able to

- modify the programs in this book
- write your own programs
- store programs
- assign values to variables
- process data
- understand the principles of screen and report design

Are you unsure or hesitant about any of these points? If so, take a break, then go back and re-read the appropriate chapter. Once you have learned the basics, we are ready to begin refining our programming skills.

Summary of terms

Name	Example	Purpose
COLOR	20 COLOR 1,0	Underlines.
	20 COLOR 7,0	Normal display of white characters on black background.
	20 COLOR 0,7	Reverse display of black characters on white background.
	20 COLOR 15,0	High Intensity
	20 COLOR 16,7	Flashing black characters on white background.
	20 COLOR 31,0	Flashing white characters on black background.
LOCATE	20 LOCATE 3,8	Locates cursor on the third line, eighth column to display output.
STRING$	PRINT STRING$(20,"_")	Prints character inside quote marks 20 times.
PRINT	PRINT .05 * 120	Places the computer in calculator mode.
TIME$	10 PRINT TIME$ or PRINT TIME$	Displays the time based on entry made when system was booted.
DATE$	10 PRINT DATE$ or PRINT DATE$	Displays the date based on entry made when system was booted.
STRING PROCESSING: Assume ADDRESS$ = "19 Main St."		
LEFT$	20 PRINT LEFT$(ADDRESS$,7)	Returns a seven-character string counting from the left, which is 19 Main.
LEN	20 PRINT LEN(ADDRESS$)	Returns the length of string specified, which is 11.
MID$	20 PRINT MID$(ADDRESS$,4,7)	Returns string beginning with fourth character, and including the next six characters. (Main St)
RIGHT$	20 PRINT RIGHT$(ADDRESS$,3)	Returns with three-character string counting from right, which is "St."
VAL	20 PRINT VAL(ADDRESS$)	Returns leading numeric characters, which is 19.

PROBLEMS

True/False. Problems 1–7.

7.1 The symbol / indicates division. T

7.2 The symbol ^ indicates raising to a power. T

7.3 The first order of priority includes adding and subtracting. F

7.4 String variables may be manipulated within a program to utilize desired portions of a string.

7.5 The computer performs operations inside parentheses before it performs operations outside them.

7.6 It is easier to understand program output if there is a lot of information on the screen.

7.7 All important data on the monitor should be highlighted by either flashing or by reverse video.

Debugging Problems—Miniprograms. Problems 8–14.
The miniprograms shown contain errors. The programs were executed and the screen appeared as shown. Find and correct the error(s) so that a logical output can be obtained when the program is executed.

*7.8 An attempt was made to print the date, but a 0 was displayed.

```
10 PRINT "Today's date" DATE$
run
Today's date 0
Ok
```

7.9 An attempt was made to print the time, but an error message was displayed.

```
10 PRINT "Current time:" TAB (40) TIME$
run
Current time:
Subscript out of range in 10
Ok
```

7.10 An attempt was made to display the first three characters in a string, but the screen appeared as shown.

```
10 NAME$ = "Sam Jones"
20 PRINT LEFT$(NAME$,3)
run
Syntax error in 10
Ok
10 NAME$ = "Sam Jones"
```

7.11 An attempt was made to LOCATE a message on the screen, but an error message occurred.

```
10 LOCATE 40,30
20 PRINT "Hi there"
run
Illegal function call in 10
Ok
```

* The answer to this problem is in Appendix E.

7.12   An attempt was made to display "Apt. #2" but only #2 was displayed.

```
10 TEST$ = "14 Broadway, Apt. #2"
20 PRINT RIGHT$(TEST$,3)
run
 #2
Ok
```

7.13   An attempt was made to display "train" but an error message occurred. (Study this program carefully.)

```
78 READ ITEM, QUANTITY, PRICE
80 DATA "Toy train", 3,872, 19.95
82 PRINT RIGHT$(ITEM$,5), PRICE
run
Syntax error in 80
Ok
80 DATA "Toy train", 3,872, 19.95
```

7.14   An attempt was made to display "Mac," but an error message occurred. Even after correcting for the error, only "Ma" appeared.

```
64 READ AMOUNT, TRUCK$
68 DATA 85972, "Big Mac Truck"
70 PRINT MID(TRUCK$,4,3)
run
Type mismatch in 70
Ok
```

Program Output. Problems 15–17.
BASIC *assignment statements are shown. Write the output that would appear when the partial programs are executed.*

CAR.DEALER$	MODEL.CAR$	QUANTITY	COST
Glendale Ford	Station Wagon	2	12500

*7.15   `70 PRINT "Our car dealer is " CAR.DEALER$`

7.16   `80 PRINT CAR.DEALER$ " has a " MODEL.CAR$ " for`
       `   sale."`

7.17   `80 TOTAL.COST = QUANTITY * COST`
       `90 SAVINGS    = TOTAL.COST * .1`
       `100 NET       = TOTAL.COST - SAVINGS`
       `110 PRINT "Buy" QUANTITY "Retail price is" TOTAL.COST`
       `120 PRINT "Discount of" SAVINGS "Your cost is only $"`
       `   NET`

* The answer to this problem is in Appendix E.

Program Output—Time. Problems 18–22.
Assume that the TIME$ string contains the value 11:30:15. Write the output that would appear when the partial program statements are executed.

*7.18   `80 PRINT "Current time is " TIME$`

7.19   `80 PRINT "The string length is" LEN(TIME$)`

7.20   `80 PRINT "The hour is " LEFT$(TIME$,2)`

7.21   `80 PRINT "The minute is " MID$(TIME$,4,2)`

7.22   `80 PRINT "The second is " RIGHT$(TIME$,2)`

Program Output—Date. Problems 23–25.
Assume that the DATE$ string contains the value 12:12:92. Complete the statement and write the output that would appear when the partial program statements are executed.

*7.23   `30 PRINT "The current month is:" _____ (DATE$`

7.24   `30 PRINT "This is the "_____ (DATE$ )" day of the month."`

7.25   `30 PRINT "The year is "_____ (DATE$`

Program Output—General. Problems 26–31.
Write the output that will appear when the programs shown are executed.

*7.26
```
10 REM Problem 7.26
20 K9 = 5 ^ 2 - (5 * 3)
30 PRINT K9
40 END
RUN
```

7.27
```
10 REM Problem 7.27
20 ANSWER = SQR(9)
30 PRINT "The answer is" ANSWER
40 END
RUN
```

7.28
```
10 REM Problem 7.28
20 COMMISSION.RATE = .05
30 SALE = 200
40 COMMISSION = COMMISSION.RATE * SALE
50 PRINT "The commission is" COMMISSION
60 END
RUN
```

7.29
```
10 REM Problem 7.29
20 P.O.COST = 10
30 CARRYINGCOST = 5
40 YEARLYDEMAND = 100
50 EOQ = SQR(2 * YEARLYDEMAND * P.O.COST /
   CARRYINGCOST)
60 PRINT "The Economic Order Quantity is" EOQ
70 END
RUN
```

7.30
```
10 REM Problem 7.30
20 B = 5
30 C = 10
40 A = B * C - 5
50 PRINT A
60 END
```

7.31
```
10 REM Problem 7.31
20 BIG.SALE = 20
30 DISCOUNT = 5
```

* The answer to this problem is in Appendix E.

```
40 PARTNERS = 2
50 ANSWER = BIG.SALE/PARTNERS - DISCOUNT
60 PRINT ANSWER
70 END
```

Program Development. Problems 32–43.
Using the formulas shown, develop short programs to accept input for the variables, and display the output. All values are to be entered via an INPUT statement. Be sure to label all program output. Test your answers using logical data.

7.32 $ANS = \dfrac{Y - Z}{2}$

7.38 $T = (I - C)^{-3}$

7.33 $Y = \sqrt{X}$

*7.39 $M = P \div \dfrac{(Q2 - Q1)}{R}$

7.34 $A = \dfrac{((X) + 4)}{Z}$

7.40 $Q = \sqrt{R} \times 3 \times \sqrt{S}$

7.35 $C = \dfrac{-A - B \times (X)}{X}$

7.41 $X = \dfrac{-B + \sqrt{B^2 - 4AC}}{2 \times A}$

7.36 $M = \dfrac{X1 + X2 + X3 + X4}{4}$

7.42 $X = \sqrt[3]{Z^2}$

7.37 $D = P - (P(R))$

7.43 $Y = A + B + X^2$

Debugging Problems. Problems 44–46.
The programs which follow contain errors. Find and correct the errors so the output shown will be produced when the program is executed.

7.44
```
10 READ TEST1, TEST2, TEST3, TEST4
20 AVG = TEST1 + TEST2 + TEST3 + TEST4 / 4
30 PRINT AVG
40 DATA 100, 100, 100, 100
50 END
RUN
 100
```

7.45
```
10 PRINT "Input your name."
20 INPUT YOUR.NAME$
30 PRINT YOUR.NAME$ " contains" VAL(YOUR.NAME$)
   "characters."
40 END
RUN
Input your name.
?_____
_____contains_____characters.
```

Hint: Carefully look at statement 30.

7.46
```
10 VARIABLE$ = "Wall Street Journal"
20 PRINT _____ (VARIABLE$,___)
30 PRINT _____ (VARIABLE$,___, ___)
40 PRINT _____ (VARIABLE$,___)
50 END
RUN
Wall
Street
Journal
```

Screen Design Problems. Problems 47–50.
Develop a BASIC program, paying particular attention to the design of the screen and the design of the printed output (when requested). General formats

* The answer to this problem is in Appendix E.

are shown for your consideration which may be expanded on (improved) in your program.

7.47 The Dearborne College Admissions Director sends out a letter to all graduating high school seniors who show an interest in Dearborne on their SAT information sheets. Write a program to create the following letter, using variables at the indicated _____ spaces (without the underlining). Design the monitor layout that will capture the necessary data.

Monitor

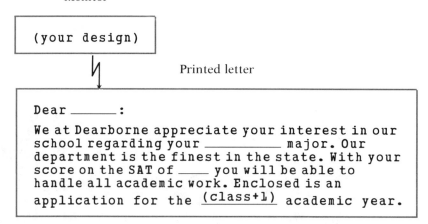

7.48 A local pet shop, Fins and Fur, wants a birthday greeting program. The user is to type the data indicated on the monitor; then a birthday message is printed for the pet owner. Use your imagination to come up with a creative birthday card.

Monitor

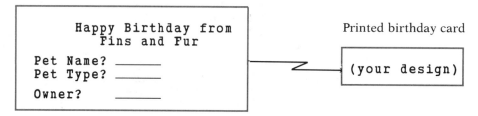

7.49 Tele-Marketing Corporation is developing a printed listing of customers who purchase at Big Flush Plumbing Supplies. Each customer will be given their choice of a free gift of a toilet-seat lid or a free plunger for completing data on a screen. They have requested that you design the screen so that the printed output shown will be produced.

Monitor

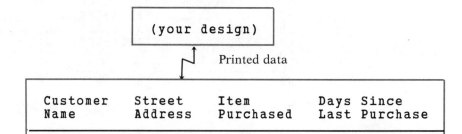

7.50 Jim delivers bagels and cheese to dorm students. He wants a program that will permit him to enter data into the computer at the time of the sale.

This will create a printout of all transactions for later analysis. The bagels cost Jim $.30 each. He sells them for $.50 each. Write a program to calculate the profit he makes on each customer. His first customer is Mr. Buck Smith who ordered five bagels.

Jim's Bagel Delivery				
Customer Name	Quantity Ordered	Selling Price	Cost of Sale	Profit on Sale
XXXXXXX	XX	$X.XX	$X.XX	$X.XX

Other problems. Problems 51–61.
Develop a BASIC program to solve each problem. Use a REM statement to identify the problem number and clearly label all output.

7.51   An Economic Order Quantity (EOQ) is often used in applications to determine the number of units to be ordered (purchased) at one time. This formula is

$$EOQ = \sqrt{\frac{2*C*B}{E}}$$

where

C = yearly consumption in units
B = purchase order cost in dollars per order
E = unit cost to stock an item per year

Write a program to solve the EOQ formula for any value of C, B, and E entered via the keyboard. Label all input. Use the following values of C, B, and E to check your work: 3,000 units, $50 for purchasing cost, $10 unit cost to stock.

*7.52   Based on existing road and traffic patterns, the manager of a new shopping center estimates that the drawing range for buyers is 4 miles. There are an average of 1100 people per square mile in this section of the city. Write a program to solve for:

A. The number of potential buyers. Hint: the area of a circle = πr^2 where $\pi = 3.1416$ and r is the radius of the circle.
B. Suppose that 15 percent of these potential buyers can be persuaded by an advertising campaign to become customers. Write a program to identify how many customers the shopping center can expect to have.

7.53   Miles per gallon of gasoline can be calculated by copying the odometer reading when the tank is full (MILEAGE1) and, when refilling, copying the odometer reading (MILEAGE2) and the gallons (GALLONS) of gas required to fill the tank to capacity. The formula for miles per gallon is

$$MPG = \frac{MILEAGE2 - MILEAGE1}{GALLONS}$$

Write a program using an INPUT statement to calculate miles per gallon for the following:

MILEAGE1	MILEAGE2	GALLONS
36,072.1	36,215.6	8.6

* The answer to this problem is in Appendix E.

Problems 54–59 are conversion programs. That is, they are designed to accept input in one unit, such as feet, and convert to another unit, such as miles. All programs are to make use of clearly labeled INPUT statements. All output is also to be clearly labeled.

*7.54   Determine the distance walked in feet if a hike of X miles is taken. Use a value of 2.3 to test your program. (There are 5,280 feet in a mile.)

7.55   Determine the cost per mile of driving a car if the car averages 21.2 miles per gallon of gasoline. This is based on a cost of X cents per gallon. Use a value of 1.45 to test your program.

7.56   For any three numbers X, Y, and Z, determine their sums and their average.

7.57   A tin can manufacturer makes specialty tin cans to customer order. The can is HEIGHT inches high and the diameter of the circular base is DIAMETER inches. The manufacturer charges $0.05 per square inch.

Develop an estimating program that will quote can cost based on the following formula:

```
AREA = (DIAMETER * 3.14) * HEIGHT
```

7.58   Semester grades are based on three tests and a final exam. Each test counts equally, but the final exam counts double (that is, the final exam counts twice as much as a single test).

Determine the semester average for a student whose grades are TEST1, TEST2, TEST3, and FINAL. Use values of 70, 65, 58, 89 to test your program.

7.59   Write a program to calculate the discount price of a computer that retails for $1850.00. Run the program three times, inputting 10%, 15%, and 37% discounts.

Problems 60 and 61 require the information below.

Mr. Mark Citizen is taking Statistics 101. Four tests are given, and an average grade is constructed as follows. Tests 1, 2, and 3 each count 20 percent of the total course grade. Test 4 is a final which counts 40 percent of the total grade. Develop a program to calculate and print the grade received in the course, based on the scores below. Label all scores.

Test 1   —   95
Test 2   —   84
Test 3   —   79
Test 4   —   92

7.60   Use READ and DATA statements to construct the course grade.

7.61   Use INPUT statements to construct the course grade. Label all input.

* The answer to this problem is in Appendix E.

8 REFINING PROGRAMMING SKILLS

Upon completion of this chapter you should be able to

- Use multiple statements per line
- Use the RENUM command
- Use the function keys
- Edit programs
- Play music

MULTIPLE STATEMENTS PER LINE

Program statements can be combined (grouped together) on a single line by using a colon to separate the statements. A maximum of 255 characters (counting the Enter key) can fit on a line, so several statements can technically be grouped together to compact programs drastically. However, when doing this, remember that extensive compacting makes programs difficult to read, understand, and modify.

If the REM statement is added at the beginning of a multiple statement line, nothing to the right of the REM is processed. However, a REM statement can be added at the end of the line, perhaps to clarify the statements. (As you know, an apostrophe can be used to indicate a REM statement.)

Avoid overdoing it when using multiple statements per line. The program can become difficult to understand and errors can be harder to detect.

The program shown previously in Figure 7.5 has been shortened by use of multiple statements per line, as shown in Figure 8.1. The same output display previously shown in Figure 7.6 will be produced when the program is executed.

USING THE RENUM COMMAND

Have you ever wondered how we get the statement numbers to appear in units of 10? There are two ways. First, the AUTO command can be used to automatically number statements in units of 10 when entering BASIC statements. This is activated by typing the command AUTO and pressing Enter.

The AUTO feature remains in effect until the Ctrl and Break keys are pressed. Frankly, this feature is often more trouble than it's worth, so its use is not stressed.

```
10 '      Use of multiple statements/line
20 CLS : PRINT : PRINT TAB(25) "Introducing" : LOCATE 4,21
30 COLOR 0,7    : PRINT " BASIC Programming " : COLOR 7,0
40 '
50 PRINT TAB(16) STRING$(28,"-")
60 PRINT TAB(18) "A lot can be learned by"
70 PRINT TAB(18) "making the figures work!"
80 PRINT TAB(16) STRING$(28,"-")
90 END
```

FIGURE 8.1   Using multiple statements per line

The easiest way of numbering statements is to type the statements in ascending order without worrying about units of 10. Then, by typing the command RENUM and pressing Enter, program statements are automatically renumbered in units of 10.

For example, the program shown in Figure 8.2 was typed into the computer. The command RENUM results in the program being renumbered to appear as shown when listed. Notice that the resulting program is the same as the one previously shown in Figure 8.1.

```
10 '      Type any line numbers, then use RENUM
12 CLS : PRINT : PRINT TAB(25) "Introducing" : LOCATE 4,21
30 COLOR 0,7    : PRINT " BASIC Programming " : COLOR 7,0
36 '
42 PRINT TAB(16) STRING$(28,"-")
44 PRINT TAB(18) "A lot can be learned by"
70 PRINT TAB(18) "making the figures work!"
72 PRINT TAB(16) STRING$(28,"-")
75 END
Ok
renum
Ok
list
10 '      Type any line numbers, then use RENUM
20 CLS : PRINT : PRINT TAB(25) "Introducing" : LOCATE 4,21
30 COLOR 0,7    : PRINT " BASIC Programming " : COLOR 7,0
40 '
50 PRINT TAB(16) STRING$(28,"-")
60 PRINT TAB(18) "A lot can be learned by"
70 PRINT TAB(18) "making the figures work!"
80 PRINT TAB(16) STRING$(28,"-")
90 END
Ok
```

FIGURE 8.2   Use of the RENUM command

The general form of the RENUM command is

RENUM   New   Old   Increment
            Number,   Number,

For example, suppose you wanted to renumber the program shown in Figure 8.2 so that the statement numbers begin with 9000 and are in increments of 20. The command to accomplish this is RENUM 9000,10,20.

The use of the RENUM command and the resulting output when the program is listed are shown in Figure 8.3. This use of RENUM permits creation of meaningful modules (program segments) when programs become longer.

```
9000 '       Type any line numbers, then use RENUM
9020 CLS : PRINT : PRINT TAB(25) "Introducing" : LOCATE 4,21
9040 COLOR 0,7    : PRINT " BASIC Programming " : COLOR 7,0
9060 '
9080 PRINT TAB(16) STRING$(28,"-")
9100 PRINT TAB(18) "A lot can be learned by"
9120 PRINT TAB(18) "making the figures work!"
9140 PRINT TAB(16) STRING$(28,"-")
9160 END
```

FIGURE 8.3   Expanded use of the RENUM command

THE FUNCTION KEYS

The function keys, often called the soft keys, are the ten keys labeled F1 through F10 on the left side of the keyboard. These keys activate built-in functions such as LIST, RUN, LOAD", and SAVE". The status of the function keys—that is, the character strings assigned to the function keys—is displayed on the 25th line.

The function key values can be displayed on the 25th line by the command KEY LIST, which can also be used as a statement. The function keys and their associated values are as follows (the ← arrow indicates that the Enter key is included with the function and does not have to be pressed):

F1 = LIST	F6 = ,"LPT1"←
F2 = RUN←	F7 = TRON←
F3 = LOAD"	F8 = TROFF←
F4 = SAVE"	F9 = KEY
F5 = CONT←	F10 = SCREEN 0,0,0←

The KEY OFF command (which can also be used as a statement) erases the function key display; however, the keys are still active. KEY ON redisplays the values, and pressing the appropriate key will activate the indicated function.

There are four function keys that are particularly useful when programming. These are the keys F1, F2, F3, and F4, which can be pressed to assist in listing, running, loading, and saving a program. To understand how these keys work, assume that a program called ASSETS is stored on diskette.

Press F3 and LOAD" will appear. Type the file name, for a total line of LOAD"ASSETS. Then press Enter, and a copy of the program called ASSETS stored on diskette will be loaded into memory.

Press F1 and the word LIST will appear. Press Enter and the program will be displayed.

Press F2 and the word RUN will appear; the program will then be executed. Changes can be made to the program and the revised program stored on diskette.

Press F4 and the word SAVE" will appear. Type the file name under which the program is to be saved, for a total line of SAVE"ASSETS. Press Enter and the program will be stored on diskette.

EDITING PROGRAMS

The IBM Personal Computer contains a very powerful program editor located on the numeric keypad. This editor is useful when changing any program statement but it is particularly useful when modifying programs containing several statements per line. Use of the editor permits changes to be incorporated without having to retype the entire line.

If the edit feature is not active, press the Num Lock key once to turn the numeric keypad into an editor. Frequently used editing keys are as follows:

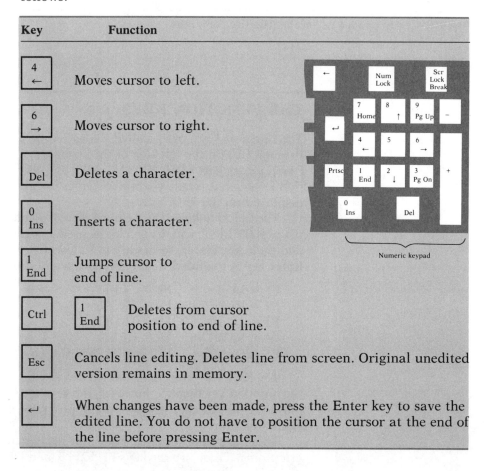

Key	Function
4 ←	Moves cursor to left.
6 →	Moves cursor to right.
Del	Deletes a character.
0 Ins	Inserts a character.
1 End	Jumps cursor to end of line.
Ctrl 1 End	Deletes from cursor position to end of line.
Esc	Cancels line editing. Deletes line from screen. Original unedited version remains in memory.
↵	When changes have been made, press the Enter key to save the edited line. You do not have to position the cursor at the end of the line before pressing Enter.

Numeric keypad

Let's use the program editor to practice making changes to a program. First, key in the program shown in Figure 8.4. Second, save the program on your program diskette, using the command SAVE"FIG8-4". As you remember, you can use the function key F4 to assist in saving this program. Pressing F4 yields SAVE", and you only have to type FIG8-4 and press Enter to save the program on diskette. Then erase the program in memory by typing NEW and pressing Enter.

```
10 REM Demo program for editing
20 CLS
30 LOCATE 6,24
40 PRINT "Introducing"
50 PRINT TAB(20) "BASIC Programming"
60 PRINT TAB(18) "A lot can be learned by"
70 PRINT TAB(18) "making the figures work!"
80 END
```

FIGURE 8.4   Editing a program

RUN produces

```
                  Introducing
                BASIC Programming
              A lot can be learned by
              making the figures work!
                    Ok
```

Let's load the program on diskette by pressing the F3 function key. This displays LOAD". Now complete the command line to obtain LOAD "FIG8-4". Then press Enter to load a copy of your program from diskette into memory. Press F1, then Enter, to list the program.

Let's change statement line 40 to read

40 PRINT "We want to introduce"

Line 40 is edited by typing EDIT 40 and pressing Enter. (A space is required between the word EDIT and the line number.) The monitor will then appear as follows, with the cursor positioned at the far left, ready to edit the line:

```
EDIT 40
40 PRINT "Introducing"
```

Press the ⑥→ key to move the cursor to the right, under the *I* in *Introducing*. Press the Ins (Insert) key, and the cursor will change to a flashing box. You are now in the insert mode, so type "We want to" followed by a space. The line being edited will appear as follows:

```
EDIT 40
40 PRINT "We want to Introducing"
```

Press the Ins key again to leave the insert mode. The cursor will return to its normal dashlike appearance. Type the small letter *i*. Then press the ⑥→ key to move the cursor to the right, under the second *i* in *introducing*. The line being edited will appear as follows:

```
EDIT 40
40 PRINT "We want to introducing"
```

There are several ways to edit the line. The way we will use is to press the ⎡Del⎤ key three times to delete the characters *ing*. This also closes up the ending quotation mark. Then press ⎡Ins⎤ and type *e*.

Now that the changes have been made, press Enter to save the edited line. When editing, it is not necessary to be at the end of the line before pressing Enter. The editing session can be cancelled by pressing the ⎡Esc⎤ key.

Now press the F2 key to run the program and display the revised output shown below.

The EDIT command, along with the program editor, makes it easy to revise programs. It is well worth your time to learn how to use the editing features.

```
            We want to introduce
         BASIC Programming
         A lot can be learned by
         making the figures work!
      Ok
```

Oops, we goofed! The line "We want to introduce" is not centered. Statement **30 LOCATE 6,24** must be changed to **LOCATE 6,19** to allow room for the longer line. However, this is not a problem because the editor can be used to make the changes quickly.

I'll write the first and last steps in using the program editor to center the line, then you write the remaining steps.

```
Step  1    EDIT 30
Step  2    _____
Step  3    _____
Step  4    _____
Step  5    Press F2 to run program.
```

After typing EDIT 30, the second step is to press the ⎡→⎤ key until the cursor appears under the number 2 in **LOCATE 6,24.** Then type 19 resulting in **LOCATE 6,19.** The fourth step is to press Enter.

Then press F2 to execute the program and obtain this output:

```
            We want to introduce
         BASIC Programming
         A lot can be learned by
         making the figures work!
      Ok
```

THE SOUND OF MUSIC

Advanced BASIC provides an interesting statement called PLAY that permits one to play music through the computer's built-in speaker. This is accomplished by specifying the PLAY statement (which can also be used as a command), followed by a character string signifying musical notes.

The musical notes of A, B, C, D, E, F, and G can be played when the following is executed: PLAY "A B C D E F G". The spaces within the string are ignored by the computer and are included here only to improve readability. Letters can be either uppercase or lowercase.

NOTES AND OCTAVES

The notes A through G can be played in any of seven octaves, numbered O0 (letter O, number 0) through O6 (letter O, number 6). The actual pitch at which each note sounds depends on the octave used.

To acquaint yourself better with computer music and how it works, try playing each of the following examples. First, imagine a piano keyboard as shown below. Note that the computer follows the normal music convention of beginning with C D E F G A B in octave 0 and progressing to octave 6 for a total of seven octaves. Also note the location of the black keys on the keyboard (more on this in a moment).

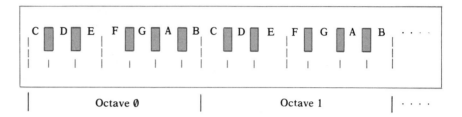

The following would play the note C in octave 2 through octave 5:

```
PLAY "O2C O3C O4C O5C"
```

The note C would be played back down several octaves by

```
PLAY "O5C O4C O3C O2C"
```

To play the notes up and down the octaves:

```
PLAY "O2C O3C O4C O5C O4C O3C O2C"
```

To play a scale, we begin in one octave and end in the next higher octave if we are moving up the keyboard. The following would play the C scale up and down for two octaves:

```
PLAY "O2 C D E F G A B O3 C D E F G A B O4 C"
PLAY "O3 B A G F E D C O2 B A G F E D C"
```

SHARPS AND FLATS

The black keys on the keyboard do not have names of their own, but will either raise or lower the pitch of a note a half step. For example, F sharp is written as F+ (the + indicates sharp) or F#. B flat is written as B− (the − indicates a flat).

Take a closer look at the keyboard. There are two pairs of white keys that do not have black keys between them. One pair is E and F, the other is B and C. To write a C flat, we would go down to the next lower key, and since there is no black key, we write B. The flat for F is E because again there is no black key between the F and E. A B sharp is written as C and an E sharp is F.

Let's try the G scale, which has an F sharp:

```
PLAY "O2 G A B O3 C D E F+ G"
```

Notice that, since the C major musical scale begins with C, we must switch octaves when C appears in midscale. That is, we started the G scale in octave 2, then at C we switched to octave 3.

Now let's get fancy. At this point, two things will become obvious. First, a lot of music can be played by using advanced BASIC. Second, the author is a programmer, not a musician, so please be patient if the "sound of music" sounds somewhat flat.

The A flat scale is harder to play because it is written with four flats: B, E, A, and D. Let's try an arpeggio up and down the keyboard in the key of A flat:

```
PLAY "01 A- 02 C E- A- 03 C E- A-"
PLAY "03 E- C 02 A- E- C 01 A-"
```

TIME VALUE

Each type of note has a specific time value, or length (L) of time that the note is held. The time value (number of beats) is indicated by a number following a note (letter).

The relationship between notes and L values is as follows:

Type of notes	Musical symbol	Beats	L value
Quarter note	♩	1	4
Half notes	♩	2	2
Dotted half notes	♩.	3	2.
Whole notes	𝅝	4	1

Explanation:
L value can be from 1 (a whole note) to a sixty-fourth note (64). The dot after an L value causes the note to be held for $1\frac{1}{2}$ beats in 4/4 time. This has the effect of multiplying the L value by $\frac{3}{2}$.

For example, all notes are quarter notes in the following:

```
PLAY "03 C4 D4 E4 C4 C4 D4 E4 C4"
```

Since all of the beats are the same (quarter notes), we can simplify the process by using L4 in the string as follows:

```
PLAY "03 L4 C D E C C D E C"
```

A tempo (T) must be assigned to our music to specify how many quarter notes are to be played per minute. Thus, T140 sets a tempo of 140 quarter notes a minute. The tempo can range from 32 to 255 quarter notes per minute. If T is not declared, a value of 120 is assumed. Try different tempos for each melody until the best one is found for your application.

Try the following tune, then speed up the tempo:

```
PLAY "T180 L4 03 E2 G2 02 C2 03 E2 E1 D1 F2"
```

Now for an all-time classic:

```
40 ' Swanee River
50 PLAY "T255 03 E1 D4 C4 E4 D4 C2"
60 PLAY "04 C2 03 A4 04 C2."
70 PLAY "03 G1 E2 C2 D1 E1 D4 C4 E4 D4 C2"
80 PLAY "04 C2 03 A4 04 C2."
90 PLAY "03 G2 E4 C4 D2 D2 C1"
```

There are five major ways of changing the way the notes are played:

MF Music Foreground. The computer waits until each note is played before continuing. BASIC programs are not executed during this time. MF is the default, or normal, state if nothing is declared.

MB Music Background. BASIC program statements will continue executing while up to 32 notes are played in the background at one

Do you want to try a "hot-rod" method of making program changes? Then use the cursor to move up to the desired line and make the change. The insert and delete keys can be used if desired. Just press Enter before leaving the line and the changes will be saved.

time. This permits interesting effects to be achieved while data is being displayed on the screen.

For example, the scale played in background is

30 PLAY "MB O3 C D E F G A B O4 C O3 B A G F E D C"

MN Music Normal. Each note plays $\frac{7}{8}$ of the time specified by L (length). This is the default setting of MN, ML, and MS (see below).

ML Music Legato. Each note plays the full period set by L.

MS Music Staccato. Each note plays $\frac{3}{4}$ of the time set by L.

A few selected classic tunes are shown in Figure 8.5. These can be incorporated into your programs where appropriate to add "a touch of class."

```
10 REM     Selected "Classic" tunes
20 PRINT "Tune from The Sorcerer"
30 PLAY "ML T255 O3 a O4 c8 O3 a O4 c8 O3 a O4c8"
40 PLAY "O3 e8 f+8 g+8"
50 PLAY "ML t255 O3 a O4 c8 O3 a O4 c8 O3 a O4c8"
60 PLAY "O3 e8 f+8 g+8"
70 PLAY "a2"
80 '
90  PRINT "Tune from Toccata"
100 PLAY "MN T 255 O3 a g a2 g f e d c+2 d2"
110 PLAY "O2 a g a2 e f c+ dl"
120 '
130 PRINT "Tune from The Horseman"
140 PLAY "MS T255 O3 e a eaO4 c O3 a O4 c e c f e c O3 a"
150 PLAY "b g+ O4 c O3 b g+ e a e O4 c O3 b2"
160 '
170 PRINT "Hail to the Chief"
180 PLAY "MN T175 O3 c f f g g O4 c2"
190 PLAY "O3 a8 f f8 a f d b-2 g e8 f"
200 END
```

FIGURE 8.5 Selected classic tunes

SUMMARY

The program shown in Figure 8.5 has been saved on the companion diskette as FIG8-5. This can be loaded into memory by the command LOAD"FIG8-5".

Now that you have refined your programming skills to a point where you're either playing tunes or at least "humming a few bars," you are ready for the next topic. We must start using files. I'm sure you can save your programs on diskette in the form of a file but how can your program analyze a lot of data without your having to retype the data statements? How can one group of data statements provide data for several different programs? These questions will be answered in the next chapter, when we start to use files.

Summary of terms

Name	Example	Purpose
AUTO	AUTO	Automatically numbers statements in units of 10. Stays active until Ctrl and Break keys are pressed.
EDIT	EDIT 20	Displays line 20 for editing.
KEY ON	KEY ON	Displays function keys at bottom of screen.
KEY OFF	KEY OFF	Erases function key display.
KEY LIST	KEY LIST	Lists all 10 function keys and their values on screen.
PLAY	PLAY "MB O3 C"	In music background, octave 3, the note of C is played.
Special keys		
F1	Press F1	Displays LIST. Then press Enter to list program.
F2	Press F2	Displays RUN and executes program without pressing Enter key.
F3	Press F3	Displays LOAD". Type in file name and press Enter to load a copy of the file into memory.
F4	Press F4	Displays SAVE". Type in file name and press Enter to save current program on diskette.
Special symbols		
:	20 TAX = .05 : SALE = 100	Permits multiple statements on one line.
'	20 TAX = .05 ' Sale tax rate	Is the same as REM.

PROBLEMS

True/False. Problems 1–13.

8.1   The " symbol can be used in place of a REM statement.

8.2   Assigning PRINT USING symbols to strings saves programming time and reduces errors.

The following are valid uses of the colon in program statements:

8.3   10 PRINT "I'm big" : PRINT "I'm strong."

8.4   10 PRINT "I'm big" : "and tall."

8.5   30 PRINT "Fancy spacing is nice if it" :
      PRINT "results in easy-to-read programs."

8.6   50 PRINT "There are several items: " "socks," "and shoes."

8.7   10 ' There are two ways: the right way and your way!

8.8   The EDIT command can be used to correct mistakes in programming statements.

8.9   Pressing F2 then Enter displays the program in memory on the screen.

8.10 40 EDIT is used to display line 40 for editing.

8.11 30 PLAY 'A B C D E F G' plays the notes A through G.

8.12 Pressing the function key F3 will display SAVE" for assistance in saving a program on diskette.

8.13 70 PRINT STRING$(15, "*") displays a line containing fifteen "*" symbols when executed. ⊤

Debugging Problems—Miniprograms. Problems 14–18.
The miniprograms shown contain errors. The programs were executed and the screen appeared as shown. Find and correct the error(s), so that a logical output can be obtained when the program is executed.

8.14 An attempt was made to play a tune and print a message, but the following error message appeared.

```
10 PLAY "MB 03 C"
20 PRINT "Now play it using the correct octave."
run
Illegal function call in 10
Ok
```

*8.15 An attempt was made to print a message, but the following error message appeared.

```
10 PRINT "Now is the time": "right now!"
run
Now is the time
Syntax error in 10
Ok
10 PRINT "Now is the time": "right now!"
```

8.16 An attempt was made to enter a person's name, but the following error message appeared.

```
10 PRINT "Enter your name";
20 INPUT NAME$ A$
30 LOCATE 4,10: PRINT NAME$
run
Enter your name? Sam Jackson
Syntax error in 20
Ok
20 INPUT NAME$
```

8.17 An attempt was made to enter a person's height, but the following error message appeared:

```
10 PRINT "Enter your height";
20 INPUT HEIGHT
30 LOCATE 7,20: PRINT HEIGHT
run
Enter your height? 6'2"
?Redo from start
?
```

* The answer to this problem is in Appendix E.

8.18 An attempt was made to highlight a student's name on the monitor, using the COLOR function. However, not only was the student's name highlighted but everything after the name was also highlighted.

```
10 PRINT "Customer name";
20 INPUT STUDENT$
30 LOCATE 11,10: PRINT STRING$(14,"*")
40 LOCATE 12,10: COLOR 0,7: PRINT STUDENT$
50 LOCATE 13,10: PRINT "Welcome to Programming"
55 LOCATE 14,10: PRINT STRING$(14,"*")
run
Customer name? Susie Sunshine

**************
Susie Sunshine
Welcome to Programming
**************
Ok
```

Program Output. Problems 19–28.
Write the output that will appear when the programs shown are executed.

8.19
```
10                        ' The REM symbol can be useful
20 SALE = 87.75     ' Sale is in dollars
30 PRINT "Sale = $";SALE
40 END
RUN
```

*8.20
```
19 'Use of the RENUM command
22 DOLLARS = 23.35
24 PRINT DOLLARS
25 END
RENUM
Ok
LIST
```

8.21
```
10 ' Don't get too tricky with REM's
20 ' SALE = 124.39
30 PRINT SALE
40 END
RUN
```

8.22
```
10 REM Multiple statements per line
20 SALE = 50 : TAX.RATE = .05
30 TAX = SALE * TAX.RATE
40 PRINT "Sale = $"; SALE
50 PRINT "Tax = $"; TAX
60 END
RUN
```

8.23
```
10 REM Problem 8.23
20 PRINT TAB(10) STRING$(15,"-")
30 PRINT TAB(10) "Summary"
40 PRINT TAB(10) STRING$(15,"-")
50 END
RUN
```

8.24
```
10 REM Problem 8.24
20 PRINT TAB(5) STRING$(15,"-") : PRINT TAB(5) STRING$(15,"-")
30 PRINT "This screen output is tricky" : CLS
40 PRINT TAB(5) STRING$(15,"*")
50 END
RUN
```

* The answer to this problem is in Appendix E.

8.25
```
10 REM The COLOR Function
20 PRINT "INPUT your name";         : INPUT YOUR.NAME$
30 COLOR 0,7 : PRINT YOUR.NAME$ : COLOR 7,0
40 END
RUN
```

*8.26
```
10 REM Programming Hints
20 '    Multiple statements per line
30 '    The single quote can be substituted for REM
40 ITEM$ = "shirts" : COST = 9.25
50 QUANTITY = 3 : TAX = .05
60 TOT = COST * QUANTITY * (1 + TAX)
70 PRINT QUANTITY SPC(1) ITEM$ "cost";
80 PRINT USING "$##.##"; TOT;
90 PRINT "including tax."
100 END
RUN
```

8.27
```
10 REM Problem 8.27
20 A = 22.5
30 'Wipe out : B = 100
40 PRINT A, B
50 END
RUN
```

8.28
```
10 'Note TAB
20 READ EMP.NAME$, SS.NUMBER$
30 PRINT EMP.NAME$ TAB(20) SS.NUMBER$
40 DATA Tim Clary, 223-88-4444
50 END
RUN
```

Screen Design Problems. Problems 29–33.
Develop a BASIC program, paying particular attention to the design of the screen and the design of the printed output (when requested). General formats are shown for your consideration; they may be expanded on (improved) in your program.

8.29   A local fast-food chain has a feature food item of the week. If this item is purchased, the customer's name is entered on the monitor, and a coupon is printed for the customer that is good for 20% off if an additional purchase is made on the same item within a month.

Monitor:

```
Date:               1/14/91
Featured item:      Garbage Pail Pizza        [1]
Price:              $9.95                      [2]

Customer name:      _____
```

Printed coupon:

```
(Your design)
```

Variables [1], [2] are contained on DATA statements and are to appear in the printed coupon along with the customer's name and the item's sale

---

* The answer to this problem is in Appendix E.

price. For example, if a customer purchases the "Garbage Pail Pizza," the cost would be $9.95 less a 20% discount of $1.99 = $7.96.

8.30 Green Grass Growing Group specializes in spraying yards for bugs, and as a bonus, fertilizer is added for green grass. They spray customers' yards three times a year. Develop a program to produce an output according to the format shown. Note that customer name, length, and width are inputs.

```
              Green Grass Growing Group
                 for Great Green Grass
      Customer name? NNNNNNNNN
      Length of lawn? XX
      Width of lawn? XX
      Cost of 1st spray:  $XX.XX Bug spray.
      Cost of 2nd spray:  $XX.XX Bug plus fertilizer.
      Cost of 3rd spray:  $XX.XX Bug, fertilizer & weed
      spray.

      Total cost for NNNNNNNNN is only $XXX.XX
```

Costs are computed as follows. First the area of the lawn is computed by multiplying length times width (in feet). The cost is then $.004 times this area for first spraying, $.005 for second spraying, and $.006 for third spraying.

8.31 Write a program to calculate John's commuting expenses from home to school. He carpools with 3 other students who share the cost equally. They travel 9 miles each way, which takes them 20 minutes. The car they use gets 15 m.p.g., and gas costs $1.15 per gallon.

Calculate the cost for John to carpool for one semester (75 weekdays). Compare that cost with the cost of riding the bus: $.50 each way for 75 days. Display the output in the form shown below.

```
              John's Commuting Expenses
       CAR                              BUS
       $XX.XX                           $XX.XX
```

*8.32 Sam's Gravel Co. sells gravel and sand. Write a program to print a customer receipt as shown below. The customer's name (CUSTOMER$), and tons purchased for each of the four grades indicated are entered using an INPUT statement. Sales tax is 5%.

The cost per ton is   GRADE1 = 10.45
                      GRADE2 = 11.74
                      GRADE3 = 19.98
                      GRADE4 = 31.95

The format of the program shown on the monitor is shown on the next page. Use the data indicated to check your work.

* The answer to this problem is in Appendix E.

```
              Sam's Gravel Co.

Customer's name? Thomas Edison
Enter the tons purchased for each grade.
Grade #1? 23
Grade #2? 323
Grade #3? 1
Grade #4? 12

------------------------------------
Bill for:        Thomas Edison
Subtotal         $XXXX.XX
Tax               $XXX.XX
Total            $XXXX.XX
```

8.33   Pat's Pretty House Painters specializes in house painting. Develop a program for Pat that will print out a customer quotation based on the user entry of the following:

- Customer Name
- Customer Address
- Number of Windows
- Length, width, and height of house (in feet)

Compute the costs as follows:

Windows at $30 per window
Trim at $0.20 LENGTH * WIDTH
Painting surface area of house: $0.04 per square foot

Print out a quotation in the following format:

```
     Pat's Pretty House Painters
Custom Quotation for:
<Customer Name>
<Customer Address>
Painting trim:             XXX.XX
Painting windows:          XXX.XX
Painting surface area:     XXX.XX
Total cost:              $X,XXX.XX

All work guaranteed for two years
```

Other problems. Problems 34–38.
Develop a BASIC program to solve each problem. Use a REM statement to identify the problem number, and clearly label all output.

8.34   Write a program that prints your name in the center of the screen in flashing black letters on a white background.

8.35   Develop a program that plays a tune of your choice. Have the program print what is to be played, play a portion of the tune in foreground, print what is to be played next, then play the remainder of the tune.

8.36   Develop a program to play "Twinkle, Twinkle, Little Star."

8.37   "Licking Good" is a large ice cream cake manufacturer specializing in ice cream cakes. The cakes are single-layer circular cakes that vary in height and diameter based on the customer order. This cake can be visualized as shown.

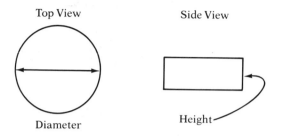

Top View   Side View

Diameter   Height

Customers telephone the firm for a price quotation for a cake of a specified diameter and height in inches. The price is computed based on the following formula:

$$\text{PRICE} = 1.75 * 3.14 * (\text{DIAMETER}/2)\char`^2 * \text{HEIGHT}$$

Develop a price quotation program using INPUT statements that will permit "Licking Good" to develop quick and accurate quotations.

8.38 A program is needed that will compute average and total weekly sales based on user entry of five sales. Use INPUT statements, and clearly label all input and output.

GETTING STARTED IN USING FILES

Upon completion of this chapter you should be able to

- Use ASCII Codes
- Save programs and data in ASCII format
- MERGE program files
- Use the TYPE command

To get started in using files, let's define our terms. The term *file* will be used to refer to anything stored on diskette. For example, we have been saving programs using the SAVE command, as in **SAVE "PROGRAM".** Although not apparent to the user, this command saves programs in compressed format to minimize diskette storage space. BASIC keywords such as PRINT are "tokenized," and numbers are stored in a minimum amount of bytes. Although this method of saving a program is useful, a program to be used by another program must be saved in a noncompressed, character-by-character form called ASCII format.

ASCII CODE

Suppose I gave you the following message:

. . . - - - . . .

Do you recognize the meaning of the dots and dashes? It's Morse code, the universal code that permits messages to be sent and received electrically. In this case, three dots mean S, three dashes mean O, and the trailing three dots mean S. The message is the universal distress signal SOS, which stands for save our ship.

This code was very important in sending messages before the telephone was invented. By various combinations of dots and dashes, all the numbers and letters of the alphabet can be represented. Once the sending and receiving operators are trained and the equipment is working correctly, messages can be sent and received quickly. Note that only the code is used, not the numbers and letters of the alphabet directly.

In a similar manner, the computer requires an internal code to process data, because it can send and receive only electrical pulses. All letters, special characters, and numbers must be converted to an internal numeric code. (The actual storage of all data by the computer is in terms of binary bits of 0 and 1. We are talking about the processing code, not the binary code.) This conversion to an internal code is entirely automatic, and the user is not aware that it is happening.

This internal code is called the American Standard Code for Information Interchange (ASCII, pronounced "ask key"). This is a widely used code for the representation of characters for computer processing. The whole ASCII character set is shown in Appendix C.

ASCII characters are associated with values from 0 through 255. If you want to see these values, consider the program shown in Figure 9.1. Any number between 0 and 255 can be entered and the corresponding character (our familiar numbers and letters) will be displayed. This is accomplished by the CHR$ function, which displays the character associated with an ASCII value.

```
10 REM  Displaying ASCII Codes
20 PRINT "Enter a number between 0 - 255";
30 INPUT N
40 PRINT "The ASCII value of" N "is " CHR$(N)
50 END
RUN
Enter a number between 0 - 255? 65
The ASCII value of 65 is A
Ok
RUN
Enter a number between 0 - 255? 97
The ASCII value of 97 is a
Ok
```

FIGURE 9.1 Program to display ASCII codes

Using the program shown in Figure 8.3 as an example, enter the number 83; the letter shown will be S. The letter O is obtained by entering the number 79. The ASCII code for SOS then becomes

Letter	ASCII code
S	83
O	79
S	83

The keyboard produces a binary code, which the computer converts to ASCII code. Thus the letters SOS are converted into the ASCII code 83, 79, and 83. One more conversion is required before the computer can actually do anything with the data. The numeric ASCII code has to be converted to binary form for processing by the computer. The electronic chips that make up the memory of the computer store data in one of two numeric states. A value of 1 is assigned to the state that exists when the circuit is on, and a value of 0 is assigned to the state that exists when the circuit is off. This smallest unit of computer storage is called a *bit* (binary digit).

USING ASCII CODES IN PROGRAMS

Remember, everything used by the computer is assigned an ASCII code. For example, there are different ASCII codes for uppercase and lowercase letters. The capital letter *A* has a code of 65 and the lowercase *a* has a code of 97.

The CHR$ statement can be used to gain access to the computer's character set. As you know, quotation marks are used in PRINT statements to indicate what will appear on the screen. The computer looks for the beginning and ending quotation marks to identify the data to be displayed. But what if you wanted to display a quotation mark itself? The symbol cannot be directly printed, because the computer uses it for a special purpose. One way around this problem is to utilize the value 34, which is the ASCII value assigned for a quotation mark. In Figure 9.2, for example, quotation marks are printed around the word "MANY" by the use of the statement CHR$(34). The computer then beeps twice. The first time, the sound is created by the BEEP statement; the second time, by CHR$(7), which is the same as BEEP. Program output is shown in Figure 9.3.

```
10 REM Using ASCII codes
20 CLS: LOCATE 5,5: BEEP
30 PRINT "There are " CHR$(34) "MANY" CHR$(34) " ASCII uses."
40 LOCATE 10,5
50 PRINT "Press Enter to continue";
60 INPUT A$
70 PRINT CHR$(7)
80 END
```

FIGURE 9.2 Program usages of ASCII codes

```
        There are "MANY" ASCII uses.



        Press Enter to continue?

Ok
```

FIGURE 9.3 Program output

ASCII codes can also be used in the STRING$ statement. For example, an ASCII code of 196 is a straight line. Using the STRING$ statement, a 20-character straight line could be obtained as follows:

PRINT STRING$(20,196)

ASCII codes can be used to create a box design by utilizing the following characters:

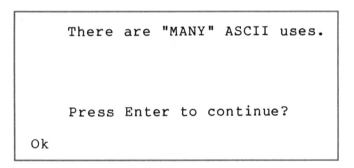

For example, the top line of a box could be printed by the following BASIC statement:

```
50 PRINT CHR$(218) STRING$(30,CHR$(196)) CHR$(191)
```

Left bracket ──────→

30 character line ──────────────────→

Right bracket

An example of a program that accepts a customer's name and then prints the name inside a box is shown in Figure 9.4. Program output is shown in Figure 9.5, where a customer's name, Al Jones, was entered. Note that program output is not centered within the box design.

```
10 REM   Use of ASCII characters for box design
20 PRINT "Customer name";
30 INPUT CUSTOMER$
40 CLS
50 LOCATE 10,20: PRINT CHR$(218) STRING$(30,CHR$(196)) CHR$(191)
60 LOCATE 11,20: PRINT CHR$(179) TAB(51)                CHR$(179)
70 LOCATE 12,20: PRINT CHR$(179) CUSTOMER$ TAB(51)      CHR$(179)
80 LOCATE 13,20: PRINT CHR$(179) TAB(51)                CHR$(179)
90 LOCATE 14,20: PRINT CHR$(192) STRING$(30,CHR$(196)) CHR$(217)
100 END
```

FIGURE 9.4   ASCII characters for a box design

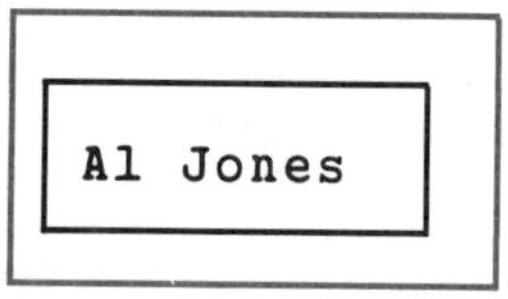

FIGURE 9.5   Program output

As long as we are going to the trouble of making our screens look "snappy" with boxes, let's center program output within the box design. A program to center the output is shown in Figure 9.6. Centering is based on the length of the CUSTOMER\$ string from the center of the box, which is approximately at the 35th position. Program output is shown in Figure 9.7.

```
10 REM    Output boxed and centered
20 PRINT "Customer name";
30 INPUT CUSTOMER$
40 X = 35 - (LEN(CUSTOMER$))/2
50 CLS
60 LOCATE 10,20:  PRINT CHR$(218) STRING$(30,CHR$(196)) CHR$(191)
70 LOCATE 11,20:  PRINT CHR$(179) TAB(51)                CHR$(179)
80 LOCATE 12,20:  PRINT CHR$(179)
90 LOCATE 12,X:   PRINT CUSTOMER$ TAB(51)                CHR$(179)
100 LOCATE 13,20: PRINT CHR$(179) TAB(51)                CHR$(179)
110 LOCATE 14,20: PRINT CHR$(192) STRING$(30,CHR$(196)) CHR$(217)
120 END
```

FIGURE 9.6   Centering program output

```
┌─────────────────┐
│  Al Jones       │
└─────────────────┘
```

FIGURE 9.7 Program output

USING ASCII CODES TO CONTROL PRINTER OUTPUT

Type size can be controlled on many dot matrix printers. Sizes are selected by entering LPRINT, followed by the appropriate CHR$ code. A few of the more useful codes are shown below. These codes will work only on an IBM-compatible dot matrix printer. You will have to experiment to identify the codes for your particular printer.

`LPRINT CHR$(12)`
Form feed for top of next page

`LPRINT CHR$(14);"Major Title"`
Produces a bold typeface useful in printing a report title.

`LPRINT CHR$(15);"Condensed print of 132 characters"`
Produces a small, condensed print size of 132 characters per line.

`LPRINT CHR$(18);"Return to normal print."`
Produces the normal output of 10 characters per inch.

`LPRINT CHR$(27);CHR$(69); "This is for emphasis."`
Produces a double-printed, extra-dark output.

`LPRINT CHR$(27);CHR$(70); "Cancels emphasis print."`

If the computer or printer is not behaving as you wish, shut it off. Although everything in memory will be lost, two good things will occur. First, it will show the machine that it is supposed to be a servant of mankind. Second, you will be able to approach the problem with a clear mind once you have had a break.

SAVING A PROGRAM IN ASCII FORMAT

When a program is to be used by another program, it must be saved in the character-by-character ASCII format. The command to save a program in ASCII format is **SAVE "PROGRAM",A**. For example, suppose the following program has been typed into the computer and is to be used by another program:

```
50 REM Second Program
60 PRINT "The total sale plus tax is $" TOTAL
70 DATA 100
80 END
```

The command **SAVE "PROGRAM2",A** saves the current program in memory in a diskette file called "PROGRAM2.BAS". The file is in ASCII format, a character-by-character representation of the program.

Programs stored in ASCII format can be

1. Processed by word processing programs for easy editing
2. Sent over phone lines to another computer
3. Merged with or chained to another program

Now we will focus our attention on merging programs that have been saved in ASCII format with programs currently in memory.

MERGING PROGRAMS

We want to retrieve a program stored in ASCII format from diskette and merge it with an existing program in memory. The LOAD command cannot be used for such purposes because that command automatically clears memory: LOAD would retrieve the desired program from diskette, but destroy the program currently residing in memory. Instead, the MERGE command is used. Memory is not cleared, and the current program in memory is combined (merged) with the program retrieved from diskette. Caution should be exercised in merging programs to ensure that line numbers do not overlap. If overlapping line numbers occur, the first line number will be replaced by the more recent line number from the program just retrieved from diskette.

For example, suppose that the following has been typed into the computer:

```
10 REM First program
20 READ SALE
30 TAX = SALE * .05
40 TOTAL = SALE + TAX
```

We can merge the current program residing in memory with the program previously saved in ASCII format called PROGRAM2. This combined program can then be listed, executed, and even saved under another program name. An example of this is shown in Figure 9.8.

```
10 REM First program
20 READ SALE
30 TAX = SALE * .05
40 TOTAL = SALE + TAX
MERGE "PROGRAM2"
Ok
LIST
10 REM First program
20 READ SALE
30 TAX = SALE * .05
40 TOTAL = SALE + TAX
50 REM Second Program
60 PRINT "The total sale plus tax is $" TOTAL
70 DATA 100
80 END
Ok
RUN
The total sale plus tax is $ 105
Ok
```

FIGURE 9.8 Using the MERGE command

Walk before you run. Beginners should load ASCII files into memory using the MERGE command. Then later on, experiment by "automatically" loading an ASCII file using the CHAIN MERGE statement.

THE CHAIN MERGE STATEMENT

The MERGE command merges the lines from an ASCII program file with the current program in memory. The CHAIN MERGE statement can be used to accomplish the same activity from within a program itself.

The general form of the CHAIN MERGE statement is

```
12 CHAIN MERGE "PROGRAM2", 20, ALL
```

Where

12 is the statement number

CHAIN MERGE reads in, merges, and executes the chained program. Variables are passed to the chained program from the current program in memory.

"PROGRAM2" is the name of the diskette program saved in ASCII format that is to be merged with the program in memory.

20 is the statement number where program execution is to begin.

ALL specifies that every variable in the current program is to be passed to the chained-to program.

To understand how the CHAIN MERGE statement can be used from within a program, assume that the following program has been written and is in memory:

```
10 REM First program
12 CHAIN MERGE "PROGRAM2",20,ALL
20 READ SALE
30 TAX = SALE * .05
40 TOTAL = SALE + TAX
```

When the program is executed, the statement in line 12 will chain merge the ASCII file PROGRAM2.BAS and begin execution at statement 20. An example of this is shown in Figure 9.9. Notice that when the first program is executed the output from the second program is produced. The contents of memory are then listed so that the effect of the CHAIN MERGE statement can be seen.

ASCII files are very useful. Before most communication packages can transfer a file over telephone lines to a remote computer, the file must be in ASCII format.

```
10 REM First program
12 CHAIN MERGE "PROGRAM2",20,ALL
20 READ SALE
30 TAX = SALE * .05
40 TOTAL = SALE + TAX
RUN
The total sale plus tax is $ 105
Ok
LIST
10 REM First program
12 CHAIN MERGE "PROGRAM2",20,ALL
20 READ SALE
30 TAX = SALE * .05
40 TOTAL = SALE + TAX
50 REM Second Program
60 PRINT "The total sale plus tax is $" TOTAL
70 DATA 100
80 END
Ok
```

FIGURE 9.9 Use of the CHAIN MERGE statement

THE TYPE COMMAND

TYPE is a DOS command that displays the contents of a specified file on the screen. Files saved in ASCII format appear in a readable format. Most other files are not readable, due to being saved in a compressed binary format.

Assume that the previously saved program called PROGRAM2 appears as **PROGRAM2.BAS**. To display the contents of this file, type the command **TYPE PROGRAM2.BAS** and press Enter. The file will then appear as shown below.

```
A>TYPE PROGRAM2.BAS
50 REM Second Program
60 PRINT "The total sale plus tax is $" TOTAL
70 DATA 100
80 END

A>
```

Do you want to see an example of a non-ASCII file that doesn't make any sense? Insert the DOS diskette and type the following command:

TYPE CHKDSK.COM

The command will result in a display similar to that shown in Figure 9.10. These are meaningless characters that do not correspond to any normal print characters.

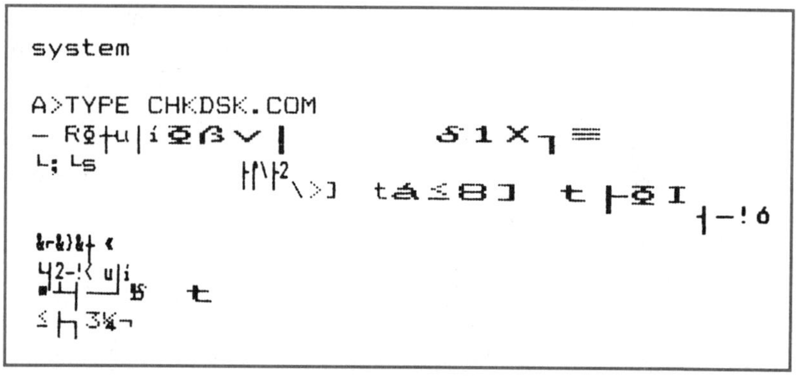

FIGURE 9.10   Display resulting from the command **TYPE CHKDSK.COM**

USING ASCII FILES IN PROGRAMS

The companion diskette contains several ASCII files. These will be used in the chapters that follow to provide data for the problems that appear at the end of the chapters. This will accomplish two objectives. First, it will save you the time and trouble of having to key in extensive data for solving problems. Second, by getting started in using ASCII files, you will find it easy to learn how to use the sequential and random-access files discussed in Chapters 18 through 21.

The ASCII files on the companion diskette are labeled with the extension .ASC. Let's retrieve some of these files. Insert the companion diskette and perform a system restart by pressing keys Ctrl–Alt–Del. With the menu selection program shown on the screen, exit to DOS and load BASIC.

Again, we are defining a file as an organized collection of data on diskette. In order to use the files, you must understand the structure of the data within them. This point is extremely important: If you do not understand the structure of its data, a file is meaningless.

Suppose we wanted to use the data in a file called EXAMPLE1.ASC, which is stored on the companion diskette. Unless you know that a program is contained in memory, it is a good idea to clear out the memory by using the command NEW. (Again, be careful when using this command, as anything in memory will be destroyed.)

Type NEW, press Enter. Then type MERGE"EXAMPLE1.ASC" to retrieve the file and load it into memory. Then type LIST and press Enter. This sequence of commands and the resulting display of the EXAMPLE1.ASC file are shown in Figure 9.11.

```
NEW
Ok
MERGE"EXAMPLE1.ASC"
Ok
LIST
9000 DATA Susan Smith, 35.5, 5.25
Ok
```

The disk directory does not indicate that a file is either protected or stored in ASCII format. We will use the .ASC extension to indicate that a file is saved in ASCII format.

FIGURE 9.11 Retrieving an ASCII file

Does this file really mean anything to you? I doubt it because the structure of the data is unknown. Before using a file, we have to know the organization of the data within it. Any attempt to use a file without understanding how the data is organized within it will lead to disaster!

In this case, the data is organized as follows:

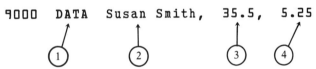

Where

1. This indicates that a program using a READ statement will be assigned the DATA elements that follow. A high-numbered statement will be used for statements stored in ASCII files so that the statements will not interfere when merged with the program in memory.
2. This is the first data element, which in this case is the employee name. The variable name in the program that will be assigned this value is called E.NAME$.
3. This is the hours worked in the pay period. The variable name in the program that will be assigned this value is called HOURS.WORKED.
4. This is the employee's hourly rate. The variable name in the program that will be assigned this value is called HOURLY.RATE.

We should have some idea of the data available and what we want to program before writing the program. If not, spend a few minutes and try to flowchart the program. This will clarify steps needed in processing the data and will result in a logical and efficient program.

A BASIC program to read and display values for E.NAME$, HOURS.WORKED, and HOURLY.RATE is shown in Figure 9.12. After the program is written, the ASCII file EXAMPLE1.ASC is merged, the program is listed (for the convenience of the reader), and executed.

```
10 REM Using an ASCII file
20 READ E.NAME$, HOURS.WORKED, HOURLY.RATE
30 PRINT "Employee name:  " E.NAME$
40 PRINT "Hours worked in pay period: " HOURS.WORKED
50 PRINT "Hourly rate is $" HOURLY.RATE "per hour."
MERGE"EXAMPLE1.ASC"
Ok
LIST
10 REM Using an ASCII file
20 READ E.NAME$, HOURS.WORKED, HOURLY.RATE
30 PRINT "Employee name:  " E.NAME$
40 PRINT "Hours worked in pay period: " HOURS.WORKED
50 PRINT "Hourly rate is $" HOURLY.RATE "per hour."
9000 DATA Susan Smith, 35.5, 5.25
Ok
RUN
Employee name:  Susan Smith
Hours worked in pay period:  35.5
Hourly rate is $ 5.25 per hour.
Ok
```

FIGURE 9.12 Program to process an ASCII file

ASCII data files are more trouble than they are worth when they only contain a single DATA statement. Don't worry—we will soon expand the examples to include processing multiple data elements. However, let's take a closer look at the importance of understanding the arrangement of data within the file before attempting to use the file.

Suppose that a firm has a large budget for office supplies, which may be broken down by department. The budget is further categorized by major category of supplies:

| Department number | Types of supplies | | | | |
	Pens	Tape	Staples	Paper	Typewriters
–	–	–	–	–	–
–	–	–	–	–	–
–	–	–	–	–	–

The budget, complete with dollar amounts by department numbers, would appear as follows:

	Pens	Tape	Staples	Paper	Typewriters
Dept #1	370	100	110	870	400
Dept #2	1170	100	100	1000	400
Dept #3	450	100	0	1000	550
Dept #4	300	300	300	1100	600
Dept #5	100	100	100	1000	1100
Dept #6	2100	500	400	2300	500
Dept #7	2100	500	400	2300	500
Dept #8	3350	850	1450	4700	2600
Dept #9	150	100	400	540	200
Dept #10	150	100	100	1000	400
Dept #11	200	200	300	4600	2200
Dept #12	400	400	350	1800	1500
Dept #13	1100	200	200	750	1100

This data, containing the departmental dollar budget by type of supply, is stored on the companion diskette under the file name BUDGET .ASC. Insert the disk, exit to DOS, and load BASIC. Press Enter after typing the following commands: NEW, CLS, MERGE "BUDGET.ASC", and LIST. The monitor will appear as shown in Figure 9.13.

```
9000 DATA  370,  100,  110,  870,  400
9010 DATA 1170,  100,  100, 1000,  400
9020 DATA  450,  100,    0, 1000,  550
9030 DATA  300,  300,  300, 1100,  600
9040 DATA  100,  100,  100, 1000, 1100
9050 DATA 2100,  500,  400, 2300,  500
9060 DATA 2100,  500,  400, 2300,  500
9070 DATA 3350,  850, 1450, 4700, 2600
9080 DATA  150,  100,  400,  540,  200
9090 DATA  150,  100,  100, 1000,  400
9100 DATA  200,  200,  300, 4600, 2200
9110 DATA  400,  400,  350, 1800, 1500
9120 DATA 1100,  200,  200,  750, 1100
9900 DATA -999,    0,    0,    0,    0
```

FIGURE 9.13 The BUDGET.ASC file

Can you read and understand the data? The file contains the budget by department and by type of supply item but the data does not contain labels. An intelligent use of this file requires an understanding of the organization of the data. In this case, the budget for the first department (Dept #1) for pens, tape, staples, paper, and typewriters is 370, 100, 110, 870, and 400; for the second department, 1170, 100, 100, 1000, and 400; and so forth.

The last line in the file `9900 DATA -999, 0, 0, 0, 0` is used as an end-of-file marker. Notice that it is not part of the departmental budget information. We will be using this last line later to signify that all data in the file has been processed.

SUMMARY

This chapter has been based on one fundamental premise: The best way to understand files is to begin using them. There are several exercises at the end of each chapter using the data stored in ASCII files. When completing these problems, spend a few minutes visualizing how the data is stored. Get a "feel" for the data and how it can be used. If you are willing to do that, you will soon be able to process files and adapt them to your own applications.

PROBLEMS

True/False. Problems 1–8.

9.1 BASIC programs are normally stored in a compressed binary format.

9.2 ASCII files are useful for merging with BASIC programs.

9.3 A BASIC program saved on diskette is not a file.

9.4 ASCII files only store numerical data.

9.5 If the line numbers in a data file are the same line numbers used in a program, then the computer automatically renumbers the line numbers in the data file when it is merged with the program.

9.6 A PRINT statement cannot directly print quotation marks.

9.7 The LOAD command is used to combine an ASCII file with the current memory contents.

9.8 Programs are saved in ASCII format by the command `SAVE"PROGRAM",ASC` where `PROGRAM` is the file name.

Debugging Problems—Incorrect Commands. Problems 9 and 10.
Identify why the following BASIC commands produced the error messages shown. Write the correct BASIC command.

*9.9 There is an ASCII file on the diskette in drive A (the current default drive) called PRODUCTS.ASC. When an attempt was made to type the contents of the file, the screen appeared as shown.

```
TYPE PRODUCTS.ASC
Syntax error
Ok
TYPE "PRODUCTS.ASC"
Syntax error
Ok
```

9.10 An attempt was made to merge the INCOME.ASC file into memory, and the screen appeared as shown.

```
MERGE INCOME.ASC
Type mismatch
Ok
```

* The answer to this problem is in Appendix E.

Program Output. Problems 11–16.
The program shown below accepts an INPUT value from 1 to 255 and prints
the corresponding ASCII character. Use this program as a guide, and write the
program output in the underlined area provided.

```
10 REM Display ASCII character
20 PRINT "Enter a number between 1 - 255" ; : INPUT N
30 PRINT "The ASCII character " CHR$(N) " has the value" N
```

*9.11

```
RUN
Enter a number between 1 - 255? 228
The ASCII character _____ has the value 228
Ok
```

9.12

```
RUN
Enter a number between 1 - 255? 80
The ASCII character _____ has the value 80
Ok
```

9.13

```
RUN
Enter a number between 1 - 255? 112
The ASCII character _____ has the value 112
Ok
```

9.14   Be careful on this problem. What is entered that has the numeric value 7?

```
RUN
Enter a number between 1 - 255? 7
The ASCII character _____ has the value 7
Ok
```

9.15

```
RUN
Enter a number between 1 - 255? 45
The ASCII character _____ has the value 45
Ok
```

9.16

```
RUN
Enter a number between 1 - 255? 95
The ASCII character _____ has the value 95
Ok
```

* The answer to this problem is in Appendix E.

Program Output. Problems 17–24.
The ASCII files on the companion diskette will be needed to answer Problems 17–24. Write a program to read the file, and display the first line of data in the requested ASCII file. Format the output as shown below.

*9.17   BUZZWORD.ASC

Language	Type	Jargon
--	--	--

9.18   INCOME.ASC

Name	Age	Sex	Income
--	--	--	--

9.19   PRODUCTS.ASC

Product I.D.	Description	Cost	Retail price	Begin inven.	Qt. sold	Location code
--	--	--	--	--	--	--

9.20   STOCKNAM.ASC

Ticker symbol	Company name	Business and markets
--	--	--

9.21   STOCKS.ASC

Ticker symbol	1990 High	1990 Low	1989 High	1989 Low	Last sale	Earnings per share
--	--	--	--	--	--	--

9.22   BUDGET.ASC

Pens	Tape	Staples	Paper	Typewriters
--	--	--	--	--

9.23   WAGES.ASC

Employee name	Hours worked	Hourly rate	Age
--	--	--	--

* The answer to this problem is in Appendix E.

9.24   SUPPLIES.ASC

Product number	Location code	Quantity	Price	Description
– –	– –	– –	– –	– –

Screen Design Problems. Problems 25–29.
Develop a BASIC program, paying particular attention to the design of the screen and the design of the printed output (when requested). General formats are shown for your consideration; they may be expanded on (improved) in your program.

*9.25   This program requires use of the SUPPLIES.ASC file on the companion diskette. (See Problem 9.24 for a description of the file.)

Develop a program to display the first record in the file in the format shown.

Monitor

```
        Big Bubba Supply Company
      Description    Quantity    Price
      ──────────    ────────    ─────
        XX            XX        $XX.XX
```

9.26   This program requires the use of the WAGES.ASC file on the companion diskette. (See Problem 9.23 for a description of the file.)

Develop a program to display the first record in the file in the format shown.

Monitor

```
      Better Built Tennis Company
           Employee Listing
      Name                   Age
      ──────                 ───
      – –                    – –
      Report completed on mm/dd/yy.
```

9.27   Develop a program to produce the monitor and printed bill using the format shown as a guide. (If your printer does not accept these ASCII codes, display the bill on the monitor.)

Monitor

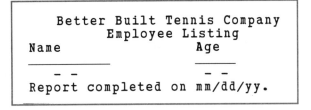

```
      Customer name?  Tom Jackson
      Address? 171 South Main Street
      City?  Atlanta
      State/Zip? GA 30333

      Item?  Books
      Weight?  45
```

* The answer to this problem is in Appendix E.

Bill

```
                Customer Invoice

             ┌─────────────────────────┐
             │       Tom Jackson       │
             │  171 South Main Street  │ ◄────
             │    Atlanta, GA 30333    │
             └─────────────────────────┘

The books delivered weighed 45 pounds.
At a delivery rate of $20 plus $2.10 per pound,
please send $XXX.XX.

Thank you.
```

Note:

Centered output

Box design

9.28 Develop a program to produce a box for a report heading including report title and date.

```
┌─────────────────────────────────┐
│        Ajax Monthly Sales       │
│   Report prepared on 12/15/90   │
└─────────────────────────────────┘
```

9.29 Modify the program in Problem 9.28 to produce a report for recording data. This report consists of two blank lines for recording data as shown below.

```
┌─────────────────────────────────┐
│        Ajax Monthly Sales       │
│   Report prepared on 12/15/90   │
├─────────────────────────────────┤
│                                 │
├─────────────────────────────────┤
│                                 │
└─────────────────────────────────┘
```

Other Problems. Problems 30–33.
Key in the following program, and merge the program with the WAGES.ASC file on the companion diskette. Then use the program and data to solve Problems 30–33.

```
10 REM Problems 9.30 - 9.33
20 READ EMPLOYEE$, HOURS, WAGE, AGE
30 PAY = WAGE * HOURS
40 PRINT EMPLOYEE$ TAB(20);
50 PRINT USING "$$####.##"; PAY
60 END
MERGE "WAGES.ASC"
```

9.30 Write the output that will occur when the program is executed.

9.31 Suppose that the following commands are typed:

```
DELETE 9000-9080
RUN
```

Write the output that will occur when the revised program is executed.

9.32 After deleting lines 9000 through 9080 in the ASCII file, add the following lines to the program:

```
35 COLOR 0,7: PRINT "Employee:" : COLOR 7,0
```

Then write the output that will occur when the revised program is executed.

9.33 Modify the program to calculate and print a paycheck for the first employee in the file.

10 PROGRAM CONTROL STATEMENTS: BEGINNING

Upon completion of this chapter, you should be able to program decisions by using

- GOTO statements
- IF-THEN statements
- WHILE and WEND statements

When a program is executed, the computer processes each statement in the program, one at a time, beginning with the lowest-numbered statement and progressing upward through the program. GOTO and IF-THEN statements can be used to alter this statement-by-statement order by transferring control to any statement desired.

THE GOTO STATEMENT

To develop an understanding of the flow of logic in a computer program, let's take a look at a train going down a track. The train begins at the starting point and moves forward from one station (statement) to another until it reaches the end of the line. This could be viewed as follows:

Soon after the train starts, station (statement) 10 is reached, and an activity occurs (the program displays "You're at station 10"). After completion of the activity at statement 10, the train moves onward to station 20, where another activity is performed (the program displays "You're at station 20"). Then the train moves on to station 30 for another activity (the program displays "You're at station 30"). Finally, the end of the line is reached, and the computer displays "Ok," meaning that the program has been executed.

But what if it is necessary for the train to run the route again? Is there a way to repeat the process automatically? Yes, there is. The train can be switched up to station 10 to run the route again.

In programming, this type of switching is performed by a GOTO statement, which can be visualized as shown on the next page.

A GOTO statement switches program execution to a statement (station) other than an immediately following statement. The general form of a GOTO statement is

| Statement number | **GOTO** | Statement number |

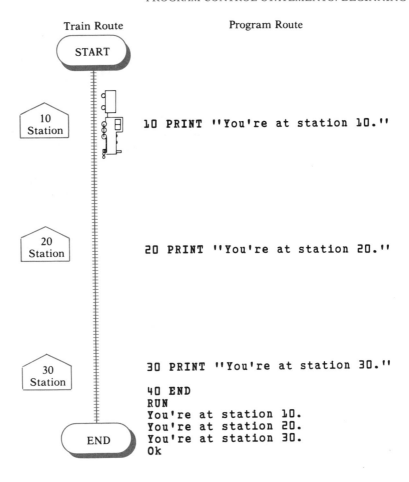

A GOTO statement switches the program route (flow) to any statement in the program. All other statements are ignored during the switch and execution begins with the indicated statement number.

Be careful when using a GOTO statement because an unending loop of logic may be created if control is passed *up* in a program. Take a close look at our train route: There is no way for the train (or program) to stop running. The train will move endlessly between the stations in the loop.

Although it is true that the Ctrl and Scroll Lock keys can be pressed to break (terminate) a program that is caught in an endless loop of logic, this is not a good method for ending a program. For one thing, it breaks the program, so statements outside the loop remain unexecuted. In a moment, we will see how IF-THEN statements are usually used with GOTO statements to prevent an endless loop of logic from occurring. But before we do, let's look at another example of using a GOTO statement to switch statement (station) execution. If a GOTO switch were used on the train track to avoid stations 20 and 30, the train would proceed as in the second following chart.

Once a GOTO switch has been placed on the track, it permanently redirects the train to the station indicated, whenever the train reaches the switch: There are no if's, and's, or but's with a GOTO switch.

This is actually no way to run a railroad nor is it good form for programming, because there is no way to reach stations (statements) 20 and 30. (And if the stations were not needed, they should not have been included on the route.)

Train Route

Program Route

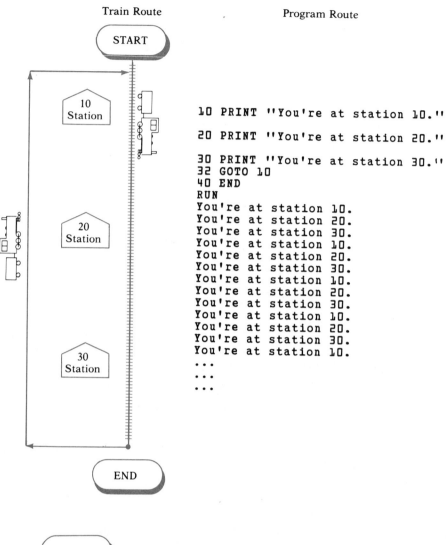

```
10 PRINT "You're at station 10."

20 PRINT "You're at station 20."

30 PRINT "You're at station 30."
32 GOTO 10
40 END
RUN
You're at station 10.
You're at station 20.
You're at station 30.
You're at station 10.
You're at station 20.
You're at station 30.
You're at station 10.
You're at station 20.
You're at station 30.
You're at station 10.
You're at station 20.
You're at station 30.
You're at station 10.
...
...
...
```

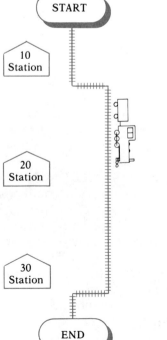

```
10 PRINT "You're at station 10."

12 GOTO 40

20 PRINT "You're at station 20."

30 PRINT "You're at station 30."

40 END
RUN
You're at station 10.
Ok
```

The GOTO statement is a single-purpose switch called an *unconditional branch*. We will often need a more intelligent switch, called a *conditional branch*, that can make a decision as to whether or not control should be switched to another path.

THE IF-THEN STATEMENT

Let's take another look at our train starting out and going down the track. Suppose that at station 10 the train is assigned 75 boxcars. And suppose that the next station on the main track is station 30, which is a small station that cannot handle over 24 boxcars. The train must then be directed to station 50, which is a larger station designed to handle a large number of boxcars.

How do we make the switch? If a GOTO statement is used, then all trains will be switched every time, even trains with only a dozen boxcars. Obviously, the GOTO switch is not the correct switch to be used at this point.

The IF-THEN statement would be a more useful switch here, because it can change the flow to different stations on the basis of stated conditions. This intelligent switch performs a comparison and uses the results of the comparison to make any necessary change in station assignment.

This can be viewed as follows:

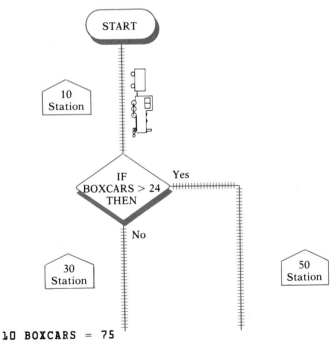

```
10 BOXCARS = 75

20 IF BOXCARS > 24 THEN 50

30 PRINT "Small station 30 has" BOXCARS "boxcars."

50 PRINT "Large station 50 has" BOXCARS "boxcars."
```

In this case, suppose that the train has 75 boxcars. The **IF-THEN** switch checks to determine if there are greater than 24 boxcars. (The > symbol means *greater than*.) Since the train has more than 24 boxcars, control switches to station 50. This can be viewed as follows:

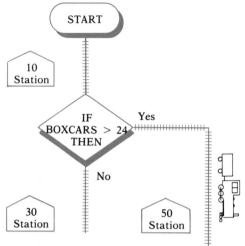

```
10 BOXCARS = 75
20 IF BOXCARS > 24 THEN 50
30 PRINT "Small station 30 has" BOXCARS "boxcars."
50 PRINT "Large station 50 has" BOXCARS "boxcars."
RUN
Large station 50 has 75 boxcars.
Ok
```

But now what? After processing at station 50, two tracks are not needed. Let's complete the track layout by returning the train to the main route. Now the train can proceed to station 60 and then to the end of the line.

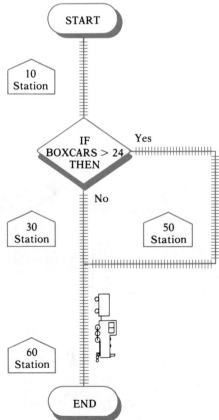

Now let's use the same logic to develop a flowchart. The stations become statements, which display the number of boxcars so that we can see what is happening. This flowchart is shown in Figure 10.1.

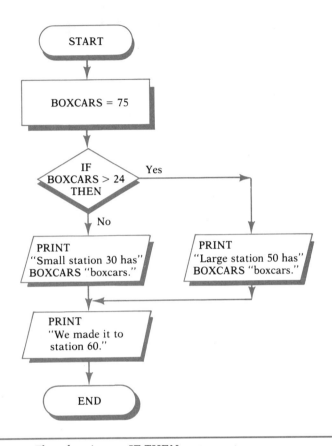

FIGURE 10.1 Flowcharting an IF-THEN statement

Notice the statement IF BOXCARS > 24 THEN. If the answer to the condition expressed is Yes (that is, the value of BOXCARS is greater than 24), then logic switches to the statement indicated: `PRINT "Large station 50 has" BOXCARS "boxcars."` Then control proceeds to statement 60, which is `PRINT "We made it to station 60."`

However, if the answer to the condition expressed in the IF-THEN statement is No (that is, the value of BOXCARS is not greater than 24), the switch is not activated. The statement `PRINT "Small station 30 has" BOXCARS "boxcars."` is reached automatically. Then control proceeds to statement 60.

Three steps are required to develop a program from a flowchart:

1. Number the statements on the flowchart to correspond to program statement numbers.
2. Code the program. When coding leave room for a GOTO statement, which may be needed to prevent statements from being reached on both the No and Yes condition (more on this in a moment).
3. Add any necessary GOTO statements to the program.

Let's take the steps one at a time and convert this example into a computer program. First, numbering the flowchart results in

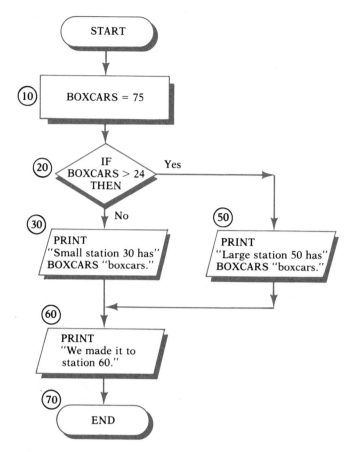

Then coding the program, using the flowchart as a guide, yields

```
10 BOXCARS = 75
20 IF BOXCARS > 24 THEN 50
30 PRINT "Small station 30 has" BOXCARS "boxcars."

50 PRINT "Large station 50 has" BOXCARS "boxcars."
60 PRINT "We made it to station 60."
70 END
```

A GOTO statement is needed here to prevent both conditions from being printed.

Finally, adding any necessary GOTO statements results in the desired BASIC program:

```
10 BOXCARS = 75
20 IF BOXCARS > 24 THEN 50
30 PRINT "Small station 30 has" BOXCARS "boxcars."
40 GOTO 60
50 PRINT "Large station 50 has" BOXCARS "boxcars."
60 PRINT "We made it to station 60."
70 END
RUN
Large station 50 has 75 boxcars.
We made it to station 60.
Ok
```

Another way of viewing an **IF-THEN** comparison is in terms of a true/false test. If the answer to the comparison is true (yes), then control passes to the right.

In summary, an **IF-THEN** statement is a decision statement that makes a comparison. If the answer to the comparison is Yes, then control passes to the indicated statement number. If the answer is No, then control continues to the next statement in the line.

The general form of the IF-THEN statement is

Statement **IF** Variable Relationship Item being **THEN** BASIC
number   name   symbol   compared to   statement

The following relationship symbols are used in an IF-THEN comparison:

Symbol	Relationship
=	Equal to
>	Greater than
<	Less than
>=	Greater than or equal to
<=	Less than or equal to
<>	Not equal to

Figure 10.2 presents a flowchart to calculate sales commission. The commission rate is normally 1% of monthly car sales but, if sales exceed $10,000 for the month, the commission rate is 2% of sales. The program accompanying this flowchart is shown in Figure 10.3.

The statement IF CARSALE > 10000 will be true (Yes) for some values of CARSALE and false (No) for other values. In this case, since CARSALE is 12500, the statement IF CARSALE > 10000 is true, so control passes to statement 70. On the other hand, if the answer to a comparison is No, control passes down to the following statement line—in this case, statement **6Ɖ GOTO 8Ɖ**. The GOTO statement is needed to prevent the computer from "accidentally" assigning the wrong value to COMRATE.

Exercise caution when programming to ensure that control passes to the desired statement only on the Yes condition. This often requires the addition of a GOTO statement in the program that is not specifically shown on a flowchart. Otherwise the wrong statement may be executed.

For example, separate paths of logic are not correctly maintained in the program below:

```
50 IF CARSALE > 10000 THEN 70

70 COMRATE = .02
80 COMMISSION = CARSALE * COMRATE
```

Add **6Ɖ GOTO 8Ɖ** here to prevent control from passing to statement 70 on the No condition

Values for variables used in the IF-THEN comparison can be assigned by either the direct assignment method, by READ-DATA statements, or by an INPUT statement. An example of a decision statement using an INPUT statement is shown in Figure 10.4. The semicolon in statement 30 permits values to be typed in next to the message "Enter monthly car sales".

Program looping enables specific program statements to perform numerous computations without re-running the program. A GOTO statement can be used to jump control up in a program, thus creating a loop. Two methods will be shown to prevent the loop from continuing endlessly, by checking for an end-of-data (trailer value) code. The first method uses a GOTO statement with an IF-THEN statement to check for the end-of-data code. The second method uses the WHILE and WEND statements to create a loop of logic. The latter is the preferred method.

If you find yourself trapped in an endless loop of logic, press the keys Ctrl and Break to exit (break) the program.

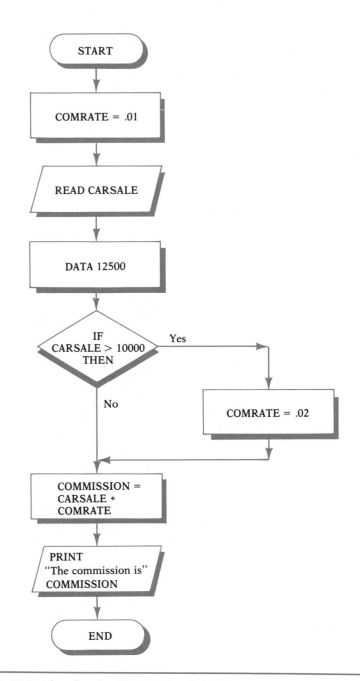

FIGURE 10.2 Flowcharting IF-THEN and GOTO statements

```
10 REM Note use of IF-THEN statement
20 COMRATE = .01
30 READ CARSALE
40 DATA 12500
50 IF CARSALE > 10000 THEN 70
60 GOTO 80
70 COMRATE = .02
80 COMMISSION = CARSALE * COMRATE
90 PRINT "The commission is";
100 PRINT USING "$$###.##"; COMMISSION
110 END
RUN
The commission is $250.00
Ok
```

We will expand our use of the IF-THEN statements in the next chapter. For now, concentrate on the use of IF-THEN to alter the sequence of statement execution.

FIGURE 10.3 Programming IF-THEN and GOTO statements

```
10 REM Using INPUT with IF-THEN
20 COMRATE = .01
30 PRINT "Enter monthly car sales"; : INPUT CARSALE
40 IF CARSALE > 10000 THEN 60
50 GOTO 70
60 COMRATE = .02
70 COMMISSION = CARSALE * COMRATE
80 PRINT "The commission is";
90 PRINT USING "$$###.##"; COMMISSION
100 END
RUN
Enter monthly car sales? 5000
The commission is  $50.00
Ok
RUN
Enter monthly car sales? 12000
The commission is $240.00
Ok
```

FIGURE 10.4   Using an INPUT with an IF-THEN statement

Notice the use of the trailing semicolon in statement 30, Figure 10.4. The INPUT statement displays the ? prompt next to the PRINT instructions. This results in an easy-to-read format for data entry.

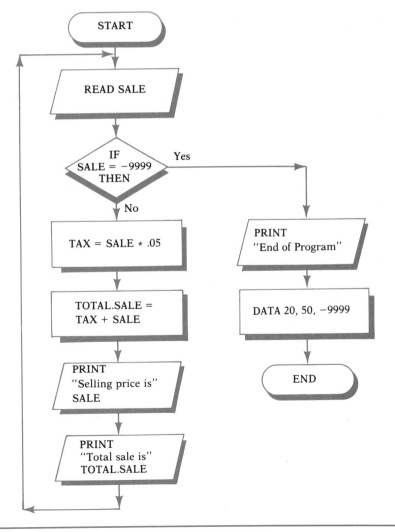

When reading values from DATA statements, the FOR-NEXT loop must match the number of values read. If the READ statement(s) request more values than are in the DATA statement(s), then an out-of-data error message will occur.

FIGURE 10.5   Flowchart using a trailer value to end program

The "fancy spacing" in Figure 10.6 is used to improve program readability. This was accomplished by first typing the program and by then using the cursor to adjust spacing. In the edit mode, press the up arrow and move the cursor to the desired line. Then move to the desired position and insert or delete. Press Enter while on the changed line and the line will be saved.

A flowchart using an end-of-data code is shown in Figure 10.5. In this case, the end-of-data code is the trailer value of −9999, which directs control to a statement outside the loop. Without this trailer value, there would not be a logical way to terminate the loop. An out-of-data error message would occur when the READ statement ran out of data.

The program accompanying the flowchart is shown in Figure 10.6. Notice that the statement to check for the trailer value immediately follows the READ SALE statement. IF SALE = −9999, this data is not to be processed, so control passes to end the program.

The PRINT USING and string assignment statements are not shown in the flowchart so that attention can be directed to the flow of logic. However, notice the use of S$ and SS$ in the program shown in Figure 10.6.

```
10  REM Note trailer value
20  S$  = "$$#.##"                    ' PRINT USING strings
30  SS$ = "$$##.##"
40                                    ' Begin loop
50  READ SALE
60  IF SALE = -9999 THEN 180
70      TAX = SALE * .05
80      TOTAL.SALE = TAX + SALE
90      PRINT "Selling price is";
100     PRINT USING SS$; SALE;
110     PRINT " plus tax of";
120     PRINT USING S$;  TAX;
130     PRINT "."
140     PRINT "Total sale is";
150     PRINT USING SS$; TOTAL.SALE
160 GOTO 50
170                                   ' End loop
180 PRINT "End of program"
190 DATA 20, 50, -9999
200 END
```

FIGURE 10.6 Program using a trailer value to end program

```
RUN
Selling price is $20.00 plus tax of $1.00.
Total sale is $21.00
Selling price is $50.00 plus tax of $2.50.
Total sale is $52.50
End of program
Ok
```

FIGURE 10.7 Program output

The small PRINT USING string is assigned to S$ and the larger string is assigned to SS$ to simplify programming.

Program output is shown in Figure 10.7. Notice how extensive use of PRINT USING results in an easy-to-read program output.

THE WHILE AND WEND STATEMENTS

The WHILE and WEND statements are used to execute a series of statements in a loop as long as a given condition is true. The general form of the WHILE statement, along with its corresponding WEND statement, is

Statement number	**WHILE**	(expression)
-	- -	
-	- -	(statements
-	- -	within the
-	- -	loop)
-	- -	
-	**WEND**	
-	- -	(any statement)

The WEND statement simply transfers control back up to the WHILE statement. This occurs as long as the expression in the WHILE statement is true. If it is not true, control is transferred to the statement following the WEND statement.

Using the previous trailer value of −9999 to signify the end-of-data, a partial flowchart of the WHILE and WEND statements is shown in Figure 10.8.

In this partial flowchart, a value for SALE is read from a DATA statement. The WHILE is encountered and, since SALE is <> −9999 (the condition is true), processing continues. TAX and TOTAL.SALE are computed and values are displayed. SALE is again read from a DATA statement. The WEND is encountered, which transfers control back to the WHILE statement. Since the statement is still true (SALE is again <> −9999), the loop continues.

Then a SALE value of −9999 is read from a DATA statement. The WEND again transfers control back up to the WHILE statement. This time the statement is not true, so control is transferred to the statement following WEND and the "End of Program" message is displayed.

A program using the WHILE and WEND statements is shown in Figure 10.9. Program output is the same as previously shown in Figure 10.7.

The WHILE and corresponding WEND statements are used to execute a series of statements in a loop as long as a given condition is true. The expression is considered true as long as it is not zero. Once it is not true, execution resumes with the statement following WEND.

An example of using a WHILE-WEND loop that executes statements until a zero is encountered is shown in Figure 10.10. Notice that the program is similar to the program previously shown in Figure 10.9.

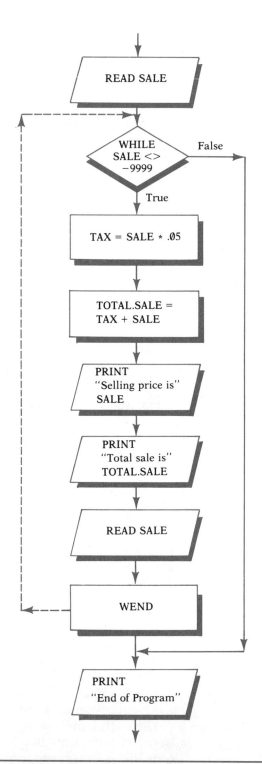

FIGURE 10.8 The WHILE and WEND statements

```
10 REM WHILE and WEND statements
20 S$  = "$$#.##"                    ' PRINT USING strings
30 SS$ = "$$##.##"
40 READ  SALE                        ' Read initial SALE value
50                                   ' Begin loop
60 WHILE SALE <> -9999
70      TAX = SALE * .05
80      TOTAL.SALE = TAX + SALE
90      PRINT "Selling price is";
100     PRINT USING SS$; SALE;
110     PRINT " plus tax of";
120     PRINT USING S$;  TAX;
130     PRINT "."
140     PRINT "Total sale is";
150     PRINT USING SS$; TOTAL.SALE
160 READ SALE
170 WEND
180                                      ' End loop
190 DATA 20, 50, -9999
200 PRINT "End of program"
210 END
```

FIGURE 10.9 Program using WHILE and WEND

```
10 REM Looping WHILE true
20 S$ = "$$#.##"                     ' Sets up PRINT USING strings
30 SS$ = "$$##.##"
40 READ  SALE                        ' Read initial SALE value
50                                   ' Begin loop
60 WHILE SALE                        ' Loops WHILE sale true (ie not zero)
70      TAX = SALE * .05
80      TOTAL.SALE = TAX + SALE
90      PRINT "Selling price is";
100     PRINT USING SS$; SALE;
110     PRINT " plus tax of";
120     PRINT USING S$;  TAX;
130     PRINT "."
140     PRINT "Total sale is";
150     PRINT USING SS$; TOTAL.SALE
160 READ SALE
170 WEND
180                                  ' End loop
190 DATA 20, 50, 0
200 PRINT "End of program"
210 END
```

FIGURE 10.10 A WHILE and WEND loop

SUMMARY

In this chapter, we have highlighted the use of an IF-THEN statement as an intelligent switch to transfer control to a specified statement. In addition, the WHILE and WEND statements were used to loop in a program until an end-of-data (trailer) value was encountered.

Notice that the use of WHILE and WEND eliminated the need for a GOTO statement and resulted in a "smoother," more straightforward flow of logic. As long as (WHILE) the end-of-data was not encountered, the statements within the loop were executed. When the end-of-data was encountered, control was transferred to the statement following the WEND.

IF-THEN statements are decision statements that can change the sequence of statement execution. If the answer to the comparison is Yes, the THEN clause is executed. The key to understanding programming lies in the ability to use the IF-THEN statement. In the next chapter, attention will be directed to using this statement in a more extended form.

If you have not already done so, select the IF-THEN tutorial on the companion diskette as shown below. Then run the program. Notice how control is transferred to the indicated statements on the basis of values you enter into the program.

```
BASIC Programming With the IBM PC

              IF-THEN

                 By
             Peter Mears
        (c) Copyright 1990
```

Summary of terms

Name	Example	Purpose
GOTO	80 GOTO 20	Transfers (jumps) control to specified statement number.
IF-THEN	50 IF AGE > 21 THEN 90	A decision statement that transfers control to statement 90 if the answer to the comparison is Yes.
WHILE	50 WHILE SALE <> −999	Loops between this and WEND as long as expression is satisfied.
WEND	90 WEND	Marks outer range of WHILE-WEND loop.
Symbols		
= (Equal to)	60 IF PAY = 200 THEN 80 70 GOTO 90 80 PRINT "The value" PAY "equals $200" 90 - -	
> (Greater than)	60 IF PAY > 890 THEN 80 70 GOTO 90 80 PRINT "The value" PAY "is greater than $890" 90 - -	
< (Less than)	60 IF PAY < 350 THEN 80 70 GOTO 90 80 PRINT "The value" PAY "is less than $350" 90 - -	

(table continued)

Summary of terms (continued)

Name	Example	Purpose
>= (Greater than or equal to)	60 IF PAY >= 600 THEN 80 70 GOTO 90 80 PRINT "The value" PAY "is > or = $600" 90 --	
<= (Less than or equal to)	60 IF PAY <= 500 THEN 80 70 GOTO 90 80 PRINT "The value" PAY "is < or = $500" 90 --	
<> (Not equal to)	60 IF PAY <> 450 THEN 80 70 GOTO 90 80 PRINT "The value" PAY "is not equal to $450" 90 --	

Do you want to see how long it takes to execute a WHILE-WEND loop? Then try this program with loops of different sizes.

```
10 REM Demo program
20 TIME$ = "0"
30 WHILE X < 3000
40        X = X + 1
50 WEND
60 PRINT TIME$
70 END
```

PROBLEMS

True/False. Problems 1–10.

10.1 GOTO statements need RETURN statements following them. F

10.2 An IF-THEN statement switches control to a different line only if specific requirements are met. T

10.3 GOTO and IF-THEN statements cannot be used together in the same program. F

10.4 You should draw a flowchart only after you have written the program, since flowcharts are so confusing. F

10.5 The symbols <> mean exactly equal to. F

10.6 The symbols => mean go to the right. F

10.7 The symbols <= mean go to the left. F

10.8 Every WHILE statement needs a corresponding WEND statement. T

10.9 IF-THEN statements compare the values of two variables. T

10.10 When you use a loop to read more than one line of data, you may not have more than 999 lines of data.

Debugging Problems—Miniprograms. Problems 11–13.
The miniprograms shown contain errors. The programs were executed and the screen appeared as shown. Find and correct the error(s), so that a logical output can be obtained when the program is executed.

*10.11 A sale value of 45 was entered. Although this is less than 50, the high sale message was printed.

```
10 PRINT "Enter sale";: INPUT SALE
20 IF SALE > 50 THEN 30 40
30 PRINT "The high sale is" SALE
40 END
run
Enter sale? 45
The high sale is 45
Ok
```

* The answer to this problem is in Appendix E.

10.12 An attempt was made to print values for SALE and TAX, yet the values of 40 and 2 appeared until the Control and Break keys were pressed.

```
10  READ SALE
20  WHILE SALE <> 99
30     TAX = .05 * SALE
40     PRINT SALE, TAX
50  WEND
60  DATA 40, 50, 99
run
   40                  2
   40                  2
   40                  2
   40                  2
   40                  2
   40                  2

^C
Break in 40
Ok
```

10.13 An attempt was made to print the amount of purchase (AMOUNT) and the markup (MARKUP) for DATA values of 40 and 50.

```
10  READ AMOUNT
20  WHILE AMOUNT <> -99
30     MARKUP = AMOUNT * 1.5
40     PRINT AMOUNT, MARKUP
50     READ AMOUNT
60  WEND
70  DATA 40, 50, 99
run
   40                  60
   50                  75
   99                  148.5
Out of DATA in 50
Ok
```

Program Output. Problems 14 and 15.
Write the first three lines of output that will appear when the programs shown are executed.

10.14
```
10  REM This is a bad condition
20  PRINT "Parrot"
30  GOTO 20
40  END
RUN
```

10.15
```
10  REM Problem 10.15
20  PRINT "Parrot";
30  GOTO 10
40  END
RUN
```

Program Output. Problems 16–26.
Write the output that will appear when the programs shown are executed.

*10.16
```
10  REM Problem 10.16
20  READ STOCK.NUMBER, PRICE
30  IF STOCK.NUMBER = 9999 THEN 130
```

* The answer to this problem is in Appendix E.

```
40 IF PRICE >= 20 THEN 20
50 PRINT "Stock #" STOCK.NUMBER "is less than 20"
60 GOTO 20
70 DATA 7751, 24.15
80 DATA 2193, 17.19
90 DATA 3900, 26.35
100 DATA 5671, 22.39
110 DATA 2314, 12.06
120 DATA 9999, 99.99
130 PRINT "End of program"
140 END
```

10.17
```
10 REM Problem 10.17
20 READ STOCK.NUMBER, PRICE
30 IF STOCK.NUMBER = 999 THEN 80
40 PRINT "Stock #" STOCK.NUMBER
50 GOTO 20
60 DATA 3900, 26.35
70 DATA 5671, 22.39
80 PRINT "End of program"
90 END
```

10.18
```
10 REM Problem 10.18
20 READ STOCK.NUMBER, PRICE
30 IF PRICE > 25.55 THEN 120
40 PRINT "Stock #" STOCK.NUMBER
50 GOTO 20
60 DATA 7751, 24.15
70 DATA 2193, 17.19
80 DATA 3900, 26.35
90 DATA 5671, 22.39
100 DATA 2314, 12.06
110 DATA 9999, 99.99
120 PRINT "End of program"
130 END
```

10.19
```
10 REM Problem 10.19 displays stocks
20 READ STOCK.NUMBER, PRICE
30 WHILE STOCK.NUMBER <> 9999
40    PRINT "Stock #" STOCK.NUMBER
50    READ STOCK.NUMBER, PRICE
60 WEND
70 PRINT "End of program"
80 DATA 7751, 24.15
90 DATA 2193, 17.19
100 DATA 3900, 26.35
110 DATA 9999, 99.99
120 END
```

10.20
```
10 REM Problem 10.20
20 READ STOCK.NUMBER, PRICE
30 WHILE STOCK.NUMBER <> 9999
40    IF PRICE > 22 THEN 60
50    PRINT "Stock #" STOCK.NUMBER
60    READ STOCK.NUMBER, PRICE
70 WEND
80 PRINT "End of program"
90 DATA 7751, 24.15
100 DATA 2193, 17.19
110 DATA 3900, 26.35
120 DATA 5671, 22.39
130 DATA 2314, 12.06
140 DATA 9999, 99.99
150 END
```

10.21
```
10 PRINT "What is your age";
20 INPUT AGE
30 IF AGE = 18 THEN PRINT "High insurance risk!"
40 END
RUN
What is your age? ←——————— (What must be entered here to
High insurance risk!              produce the indicated output?)
Ok
```

10.22
```
10 QUANTITY = 100
20 IF QUANTITY = 100 THEN 40
30 PRINT "Quantity sold =" QUANTITY : GOTO 50
40 PRINT "Exactly" QUANTITY "were sold."
50 END
RUN
```

10.23
```
10 PRINT "Enter sale amount ";
20 INPUT SALE
30 IF SALE > 200 THEN PRINT "Bonus stamps"
40 PRINT "Thanks for your business."
50 END
RUN
Enter sale amount?_____ (What range of sales values
Thanks for your business.     can be entered here to
Ok                            produce the indicated output?)
```

*10.24
```
10 PRINT "Sale", "Tax", "Total Sale"
20 READ SALE
30 IF SALE = -999 THEN 80
40 TAX = .05 * SALE : TOTAL = SALE + TAX
50 PRINT SALE, TAX, TOTAL
60 GOTO 20
70 DATA 100, 200, 300, -999
80 END
RUN
```

10.25
```
10 PRINT "Employees with over 5 years service"
20 READ EMPLOYEE$, YEARS
30 IF EMPLOYEE$ = "END" THEN 100
40 IF YEARS > 5 THEN PRINT EMPLOYEE$
50 GOTO 20
60 DATA John Jones, 4
70 DATA Ann Smith, 8
80 DATA Tom Mix, 12
90 DATA END, 0
100 END
RUN
```

10.26
```
10 REM Note use of WHILE-WEND loop
20 PRINT "Employees with over 5 years service"
30 READ EMPLOYEE$, YEARS
40 WHILE YEARS
50 IF YEARS > 5 THEN PRINT EMPLOYEE$
60 READ EMPLOYEE, YEARS
70 WEND
80 DATA John Jones, 4
90 DATA Ann Smith, 8
100 DATA Tom Mix, 12
110 DATA   0,        0
120 END
RUN
```

* The answer to this problem is in Appendix E.

Developing a Program from a Flowchart. Problems 27–37.
Develop a short BASIC program using the flowchart as a guide. Problems 27 and 28 are to be executed three times. First execute the program using the following DATA statement: DATA 18875,18. Then change the DATA statement to DATA 32750,47 and re-execute the program. Finally, change the DATA statement to DATA 26750,19 and re-execute the program.

*10.27

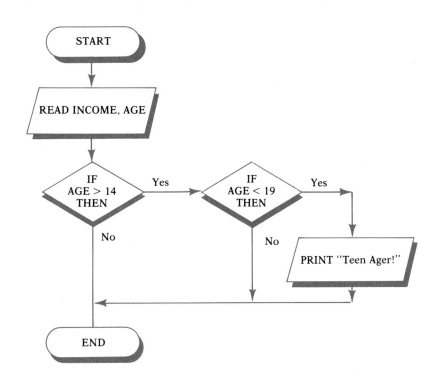

10.28

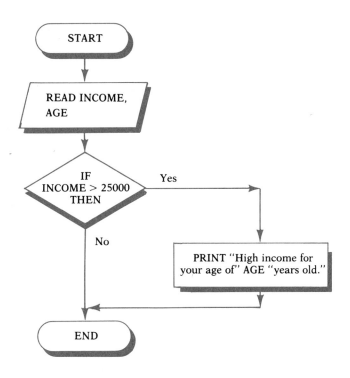

* The answer to this problem is in Appendix E.

10.29

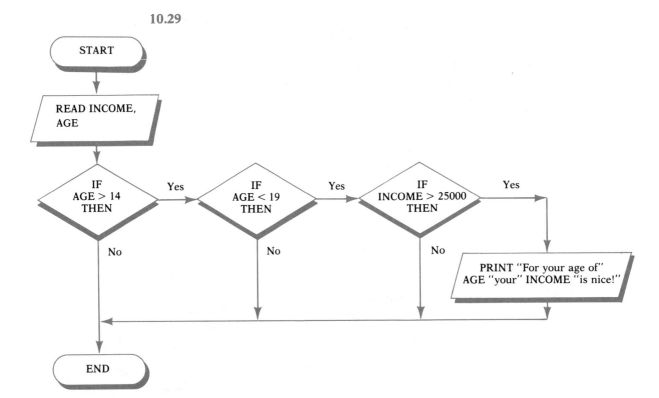

Develop a short BASIC program for Problems 30 and 31. Run the programs using values of 10, then 100, and finally 120 to check your answers.

10.30

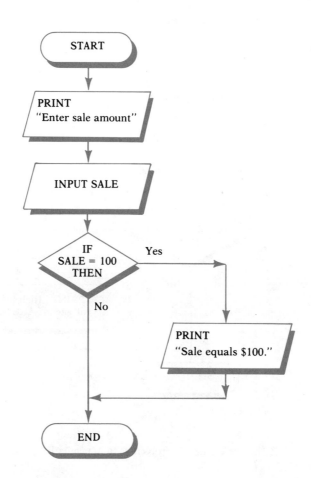

10.31

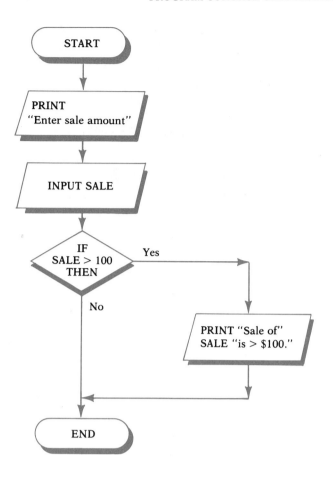

Use ASCII file "INCOME.ASC" for Problems 32–34. The data in this file are organized as follows:

Name	Age	Sex	Income
--	--	-	--

*10.32 This flowchart reads the first DATA statement, and if the employee is over 32 years old, then the data is displayed. Develop a program to analyze the first DATA statement as shown in the flowchart.

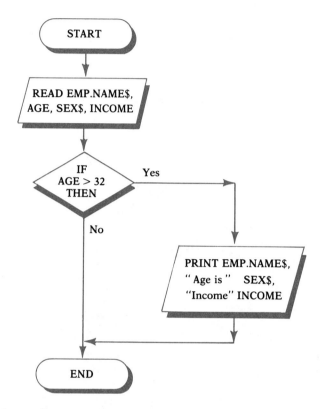

* The answer to this problem is in Appendix E.

10.33 This is a summary report to identify and display employees over 32 years of age. Develop a program to read and analyze all the DATA statements in the ASCII file.

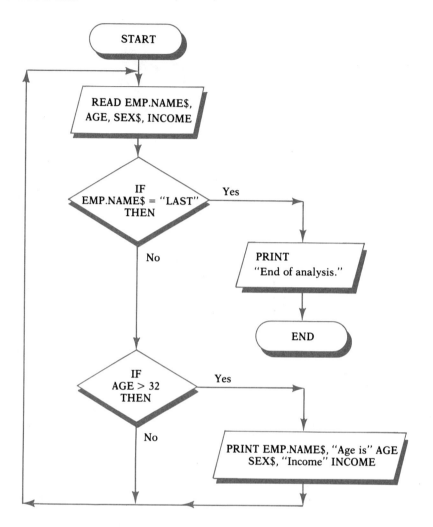

10.34 This flowchart identifies and displays employees over 21 and less than 40 years of age. Develop a program to read and analyze the DATA statements in the ASCII file.

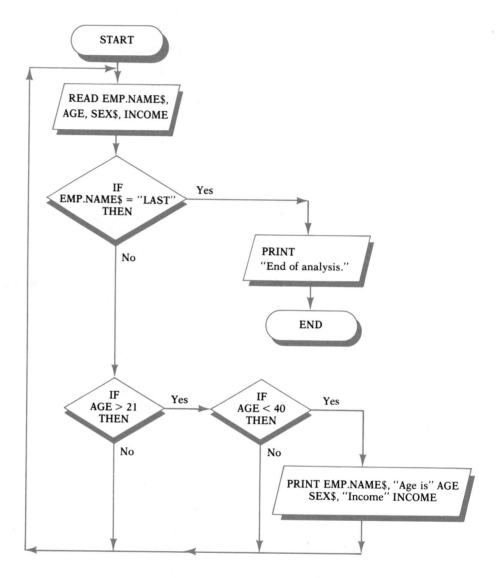

10.35 The flowchart below calculates cumulative interest earned for the year desired. YEAR, PRINCIPAL, and INTEREST.RATE are contained in a DATA statement as follows: **DATA 5, 10, .10**. Develop a BASIC program to calculate the principal and interest earned for each of five years.

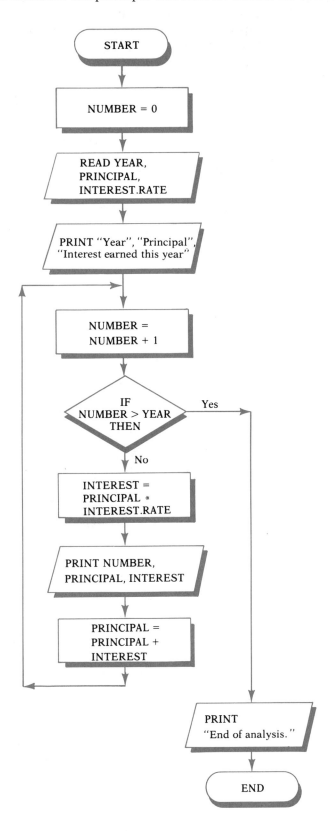

10.36 Modify the flowchart shown in Problem 10.35 to permit the year, principal, and interest rate to be entered via the keyboard after the program is executed. Develop a PRINT statement to guide the operator in entering the data.

10.37 An Economic Order Quantity (EOQ) is used to determine the number of items to order at one time. The EOQ formula requires values for the following variables:

D The demand in units per year
C The cost to store an item per year in dollars and cents
P The cost of placing a purchase order

Using the following flowchart as a guide, write a program to calculate E (the Economic Order Quantity) for all items in the inventory control system. Use a value of 9999 to signify the last item, and display the messages indicated for the different values of E. Use the following DATA statements to test your program:

```
900 DATA 125, 4, 20
910 DATA 8000, 2.5, 45
920 DATA 4500, 3, 15
930 DATA 9999, 0, 0
```

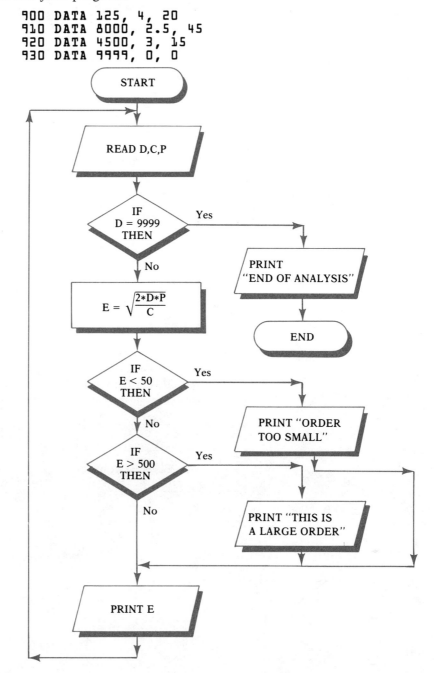

Screen Design Problems. Problems 38–40.
Develop a BASIC program, paying particular attention to the design of the screen and the design of the printed output (when requested). General formats are shown for your consideration; they may be expanded on (improved) in your program.

10.38 The ASCII file on the companion diskette called STOCKNAM.ASC will be needed to solve this problem. The format of the file is shown below.

```
Ticker        Company       Business
Symbol        Name          and Markets
  --            --             --
```

The Bent-Elbow Investment Club needs a record retrieval program. They want to be able to enter the first three characters of a company name. The program should then search the data file and display ticker symbol, full company name, and business and markets that match the entry.

Monitor output only

```
Bent-Elbow Investment Club

Company Name [END to end program]?

Ticker        Company       Business
Symbol        Name          and Markets
_____        _____        _____
  --            -             -
  --            -             -
  --            -             -
```

*10.39 The ASCII file on the companion diskette called PRODUCTS.ASC will be needed to answer this problem. The format of this ASCII file is as shown. [1], [2], [etc.] are for reference and are not included in the file.

Product I.D.	Description	Cost	Retail Price	Begin Inven.	Qt. Sold	Location Code
XXX	XXXXXXXXXXXXX [1]	$XXX.XX	$XXX.XX [2]	XX [3]	XX	X

Ajax Wholesale Company needs a program that prints the description [1], retail price [2], and beginning inventory [3] for all items in inventory that exceed a target retail price. This program will be used by the Marketing Department to determine inventory levels at various prices.

The monitor should be designed as follows:

```
Ajax Inventory Analysis Program

Target Price: _____
```

---

* Note: A similar but more complex version of this problem is in Chapter 11, Problem 11.37. The answer to problem 11.37 is in Appendix E.

Printed Program Output:

```
┌─────────────────────────────────────────────────┐
│ Ajax Inventory Analysis Program                  │
│ Items with a retail price over $XX.XX            │  ←The target price
│                                                  │
│ Description   Retail    Beginning                │
│ of product    price     inventory                │
│ ─────────────────────────────────────            │
│    - -             -              -              │
│    - -             -              -              │
│    - -             -              -              │
│                                                  │
│    - -             -              -              │
│ Report completed on mm/dd/yy.                    │
└─────────────────────────────────────────────────┘
```

10.40   The Top 40 Record, Tape, and Video Company is offering bonus coupons based on the total amount purchased. These coupons are used toward additional purchases made during a six-month period.

Amount of purchase	Bonus coupon
$20 or less	None
$20 but less than $50	15% of purchase
$50 but less than $100	20% of purchase
$100 and more	25% of purchase

After the total amount of purchase is entered into the cash register, the customer pays his bill (after deducting for any bonus coupons presented). The customer's name is then entered into the computer, and a bonus coupon is calculated. A typical output screen is shown.

```
┌──────────────────────────────────────────────────────────┐
│      Top 40 R.T.V. Company - Bonus Program               │
│      Customer name  END ends program? Tom Jackson        │
│      Amount of purchase? 34.50                           │
│                                                          │
│ ------------------------------------------------------   │
│ Bonus coupon of  $5.17                                   │
│ To:  Tom Jackson for your purchase of $34.50             │
│ ------------------------------------------------------   │
│                                                          │
│      Top 40 R.T.V. Company - Bonus Program               │
│      Customer name  END ends program? Alice Smith        │
│      Amount of purchase? 67.75                           │
│                                                          │
│ ------------------------------------------------------   │
│ Bonus coupon of $13.55                                   │
│ To:  Alice Smith for your purchase of $67.75             │
│ ------------------------------------------------------   │
│                                                          │
│      Top 40 R.T.V. Company - Bonus Program               │
│      Customer name  END ends program? END                │
│ End of program                                           │
│ Ok                                                       │
└──────────────────────────────────────────────────────────┘
```

Other Problems. Problems 41–44.
Develop a BASIC program to solve each problem. Use a REM statement to identify the problem number, and clearly label all output.

10.41 Develop a program to input sales (SALES) and to calculate the sales commission (SALES.COM) according to the following:

a) If the sale is less than 400, then the commission is 1%.
b) Otherwise the commission is 3% of sale.

Use the WHILE-WEND loop and input a value of 9999 to end the program.

10.42 This problem requires the use of the ASCII file on the companion diskette called BUZZWORD.ASC. This file is organized as follows:

Language	Type	Jargon
--	--	--

Develop a program that permits the user to enter the language desired (LAN.DESIRED$). Then read the file using the variables shown. If LAN.DESIRED = LANGUAGE$, then print the type and jargon. (Note that type and jargon are arbitrary and are not to be taken seriously.) Use a WHILE-WEND loop in your program.

10.43 Develop a program to read the below DATA statements on prices of new cars. Have the program identify and print the highest price and the lowest price. Hint: initially assign HIGH.PRICE to a low value and LOW.PRICE to a high value. Then make your comparisons and any necessary reassignments.

```
9000 DATA 12675,  8788, 15988,  7995
9010 DATA 14141, 27245,  6995, 13450
```

10.44 George Washington Nurseries maintains information on the products sold on READ/DATA statements. A sample of seven of these is shown below (999 is the last DATA statement).

Product number	Price	Quantity
200	15.95	5
205	132.00	4
210	140.55	10
211	35.00	6
220	52.00	8
350	17.95	7
422	5.95	22
999	0.00	00

Develop a flowchart and program to input the product number desired and display the price and quantity available. If an incorrect number is entered, then print the message "Product not found".

ADVANCED PROGRAM CONTROL

IF-THEN statements are powerful and useful programming statements. This chapter offers additional techniques to control the sequence of statement execution. Upon completion of this chapter you should be able to

- Use extended IF-THEN statements
- Use IF-THEN-ELSE statements
- Develop a small information-retrieval system (data-base)

EXTENDED IF-THEN STATEMENTS

The last chapter concentrated on using IF-THEN statements as an intelligent switch to transfer control of statement execution. The IF-THEN statement can be used in a more powerful form by including a BASIC statement to the right of the THEN clause. If the comparison is true, the statement to the right of the word THEN is executed. If the comparison fails, the statement is not executed.

An example of executing multiple statements to the right of the comparison (if the comparison is true) is shown in Figure 11.1. Notice that if the value of TEST is greater than 5 (that is, if the comparison is true), the statements to the right of the comparison are executed. If the comparison is not true, the statements are not executed.

The use of the IF-THEN statement in this extended format can simplify programming. For example,

> A BASIC statement can contain up to 255 characters, but the screen can display only 80 characters. Thus the statement can be continued on the next line. This results in the unusual spacing shown in Figure 11.1, statement 30.

```
60 IF PAY = 200 THEN 80
70 GOTO 90
80 PRINT "The value" PAY "equals $200"
90 - -
```

can be simplified to

```
60 IF PAY = 200 THEN PRINT "The value" PAY "equals
      $200"
```

Likewise,

```
60 IF PAY > 890 THEN 80
70 GOTO 90
80 PRINT "The value" PAY "is greater than $890"
90 - -
```

```
10 REM Execute to right if true
20 PRINT "Enter test value ";
30 INPUT TEST
40 IF TEST > 5 THEN PRINT "Value of" TEST "is > 5" :
      PRINT "The comparison is true!"
50 PRINT "End of program"
60 END
RUN
Enter test value ? 4
End of program
Ok
RUN
Enter test value ? 8
Value of 8 is > 5
The comparison is true!
End of program
Ok
```

FIGURE 11.1 Execution of IF-THEN statement

can be simplified to

```
60 IF PAY > 890 THEN PRINT "The value" PAY
      "is greater than $890"
```

```
60 IF PAY < 350 THEN 80
70 GOTO 90
80 PRINT "The value" PAY "is less than $350"
90 - -
```

can be simplified to

```
60 IF PAY < 350 THEN PRINT "The value" PAY
      "is less than $350"
```

```
60 IF PAY >= 600 THEN 80
70 GOTO 90
80 PRINT "The value" PAY "is > or = $600"
90 - -
```

can be simplified to

```
60 IF PAY >= 600 THEN PRINT "The value" PAY
      "is > or = $600"
```

```
60 IF PAY <= 500 THEN 80
70 GOTO 90
80 PRINT "The value" PAY "is < or = $500"
90 - -
```

can be simplified to

```
60 IF PAY <= 500 THEN PRINT "The value" PAY
      "is < or = $500"
```

```
60 IF PAY <> 450 THEN 80
70 GOTO 90
80 PRINT "The value" PAY "is not equal to $450"
90 - -
```

can be simplified to

```
60 IF PAY <> 450 THEN PRINT "The value" PAY
      "is not equal to $450"
```

```
10  REM   Note IF-THEN extension
20  COMRATE = .01
30  READ CARSALE
40  DATA 12500
50  IF CARSALE > 10000 THEN COMRATE = .02
60  COMMISSION = CARSALE *  COMRATE
70  PRINT "The commission is";
80  PRINT USING "$$###.##"; COMMISSION
90  END
RUN
The commission is $250.00
Ok
```

FIGURE 11.2   Using extended IF-THEN statements

The extended IF-THEN statement can include any BASIC statement to the right of the THEN clause, including an assignment statement. The program shown in Figure 11.2 uses our previous program on commission rates as an example. Notice statement **50 IF CARSALE > 10000 THEN COMRATE = .02**. This statement assigns the value of .02 (2%) to COM-RATE without transferring control to another statement. This is a preferred method of programming because it simplifies program logic and makes program maintenance easier.

When using meaningful variable names, be careful of reserved words. For example, NAME$ is a reserved word.

THE IF-THEN-ELSE STATEMENT

Notice Figure 11.3, statement 20. The trailing semicolon places the question mark next to the data displayed by the PRINT statement. This makes the output easier to read.

In an IF-THEN-ELSE comparison, if the result of the comparison is Yes (that is, if it is true), the THEN clause is executed. If the result of the comparison is No (that is, if it fails), the ELSE clause is executed. An example is shown in Figure 11.3. Notice the position of the word ELSE. The space bar was used to position ELSE on the second line in the IF-

```
10  REM Executes statements following ELSE
20  PRINT "Enter test value";
30  INPUT TEST
40  IF TEST > 5 THEN PRINT "Value of" TEST "is > 5."
                ELSE PRINT "Value of" TEST "is <= 5."
50  PRINT "End of program"
60  END
RUN
Enter test value? 8
Value of 8 is > 5.
End of program
Ok
RUN
Enter test value? 3
Value of 3 is <= 5.
End of program
Ok
```

FIGURE 11.3   Execution of IF-THEN-ELSE statement

```
10 REM   Note IF-THEN-ELSE statement
20 READ CARSALE
30 DATA 12500
40 IF CARSALE > 10000 THEN COMRATE = .02 ELSE COMRATE = .01
50 COMMISSION = CARSALE *  COMRATE
60 PRINT "The commission is";
70 PRINT USING "$$###.##"; COMMISSION
80 END
RUN
The commission is $250.00
Ok
```

FIGURE 11.4 Using IF-THEN-ELSE statement

THEN statement. It is easier to read lengthy statements if time is spent carefully to space key words within a statement.

The IF-THEN-ELSE statement can be used to make assignments based on varying conditions. For example, the program shown in Figure 11.4 is a shortened version of our commission program. The key to understanding this program is statement **40 IF CARSALE > 10000 THEN COMRATE = .02 ELSE COMRATE = .01**.

If the result of the IF test is Yes, the THEN clause is executed. That is, if CARSALE is greater than 10000, the variable COMRATE is assigned the value of .02. If the result of the IF test is No (CARSALE is not greater than 10000), the ELSE clause is executed. The ELSE clause assigns the variable COMRATE the value of .01.

After completion of the IF-THEN-ELSE statement, control passes to the statement following the IF-THEN-ELSE statement (assuming that neither the THEN nor the ELSE clause transfers control to a different statement).

Values for variables used in the IF-THEN comparison can be assigned by either the direct assignment method, by READ/DATA statements, or by an INPUT statement. An example of a decision statement using an INPUT statement is shown in Figure 11.5. The semicolon in statement 20 permits a value to be typed in next to the message "Enter monthly car sales."

> IF-THEN-ELSE statements are an excellent means of programming decision statements. The statements reflect the way we think and are easy to read and understand.

```
10 REM Using INPUT with IF-THEN-ELSE
20 PRINT "Enter monthly car sales";
30 INPUT CARSALE
40 IF CARSALE > 10000 THEN COMRATE = .02 ELSE COMRATE = .01
50 COMMISSION = CARSALE *  COMRATE
60 PRINT "The commission is";
70 PRINT USING "$$###.##"; COMMISSION
80 END
RUN
Enter monthly car sales? 10000
The commission is $100.00
Ok
RUN
Enter monthly car sales? 20000
The commission is $400.00
Ok
```

FIGURE 11.5 Using an INPUT with an IF-THEN statement

MORE IF-THEN COMPARISONS

Two other useful IF-THEN comparisons are the OR and the AND comparisons. The general form of the AND condition is

IF (condition)   **AND** (condition)   **THEN** --

The general form of the OR condition is

IF (condition)   **OR** (condition)   **THEN** --

For example, the flowchart shown in Figure 11.6 displays the incomes and ages of people from 21 through 35 years of age. AGE and INCOME are

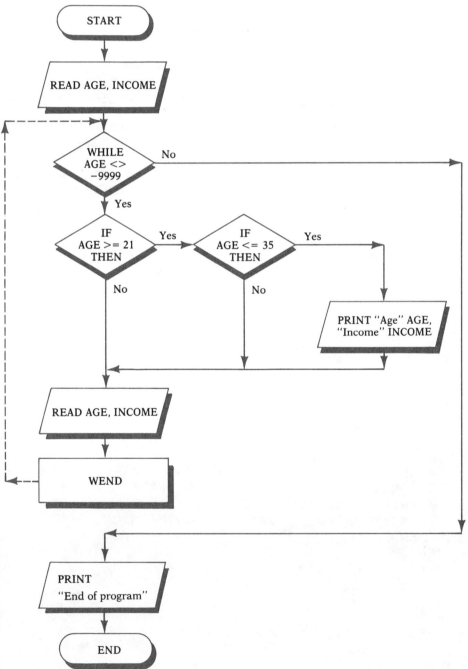

When using trailer values, each variable in either a READ or INPUT statement must be assigned a value. For example, suppose the statement READ HOURS, RATE uses a value of −999 for HOURS as an end-of-file marker. Then the last DATA statement must contain data −999, 0, so that a value can be read for both HOURS and RATE.

FIGURE 11.6   Flowcharting an IF-THEN-AND condition

read from the DATA statement WHILE AGE <> −9999 (the trailer value). If this value is not present, THEN control passes to the following statement. This is a multiple IF-THEN statement where each portion of the statement is tested, and both portions have to be true for the THEN clause to be executed. For example, if AGE >= 21 and AGE <= 35, then the PRINT statement is executed. If either or both conditions are not true, control passes to statement 50.

The program accompanying the flowchart is shown in Figure 11.7. Notice how the multiple IF-THEN comparison in statement 40 streamlines the program flow of logic. Also notice that the fancy spacing results in a program that is easy to read and maintain.

```
10 REM   Note IF-AND-THEN
20 READ AGE, INCOME
30 WHILE AGE <> -9999                    ' Begin WHILE-WEND loop
40      IF AGE >=21 AND AGE <=35 THEN PRINT
           "Age =" AGE, "Income =" INCOME
50         READ AGE, INCOME
60 WEND                                   ' End WHILE-WEND loop
70 DATA   20,      65500
80 DATA   28,      28975
90 DATA   34,      17800
100 DATA 56,      38500
110 DATA -9999, 0
120 PRINT "End of program."
130 END
RUN
Age = 28       Income = 28975
Age = 34       Income = 17800
End of program.
Ok
```

FIGURE 11.7 Programming an IF-THEN-AND statement

In the program shown in Figure 11.7, the following statements could be inserted to select the highest INCOME out of a series of values:

```
12 HIGH = 0
52 IF INCOME > HIGH
   THEN HIGH =
   INCOME
```

That is, the value of the variable HIGH would contain the highest value. Similar logic could be used to identify the lowest value.

In an IF-THEN-OR statement, if either one or the other comparison is true, the THEN clause is executed. For example, suppose that AGE and INCOME are read from a DATA statement. Also suppose that we wanted to display the age and income of those people who are either 20 or 34 years of age. The IF-THEN-OR test would be this: `IF AGE = 20 OR AGE = 34 THEN PRINT INCOME`.

That is, if either AGE is 20 (that is, the first test is true) or if AGE is 34 (that is, the second test is true) then age and income are displayed. A flowchart of the IF-THEN-OR comparison is shown in Figure 11.8. The program accompanying the flowchart is shown in Figure 11.9.

USE OF IF-THEN TO COMPARE STRINGS

IF-THEN statements can be used to compare string data. The process is relatively straightforward and it is very useful. We will center attention on using strings in IF-THEN comparisons to make programs conversational and easier to use. In addition, string comparisons will be extensively utilized in the small data-base examples that will follow in a moment.

The program shown in Figure 11.10 checks for a user named Mike. If this condition is found, Mike is reminded that a good night's sleep is

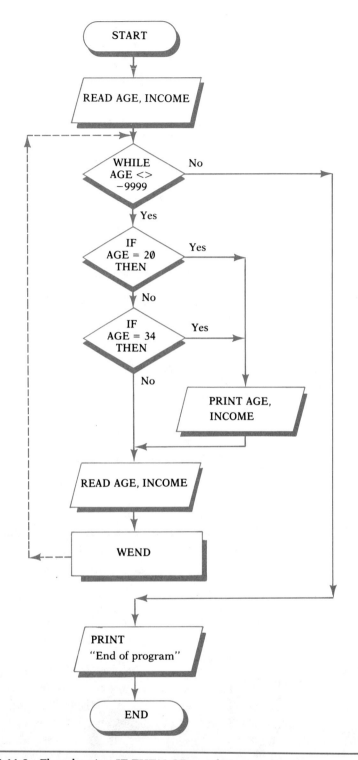

FIGURE 11.8 Flowcharting IF-THEN-OR conditions

```
10 REM   Note IF - OR - THEN
20 READ AGE, INCOME
30 WHILE AGE <> -9999
40     IF AGE =20 OR AGE = 34 THEN PRINT
       "Age =" AGE "Income =" INCOME
50     READ AGE, INCOME
60 WEND
70 DATA 20,   65554
80 DATA 28,   28976
90 DATA 34,   17800
100 DATA 56,   38500
110 DATA -9999, 0
120 PRINT "End of program."
130 END
RUN
Age = 20 Income = 65554
Age = 34 Income = 17800
End of program.
Ok
```

The INKEY$ statement retrieves a single value from the keyboard. The following statements can be placed where needed in the program to freeze the screen and permit reading the display:

100 PRINT "Press any key to continue.";
110 A$ = INKEY$: IF A$ = "" THEN 110

FIGURE 11.9 Programming an IF-THEN-OR statement

needed to reduce data entry errors. Notice statement **110 "Do you want instructions Y/N."** The IF-THEN tests for both the uppercase and lowercase **y** for a Yes response. If either **Y** or **y** is encountered, instructions are provided. If not, and the response was not **N** or **n**, an error message is displayed.

```
10 REM IF-THEN using strings
20 CLS
30                                    ' Log in procedure
40 PRINT "Enter first name";
50 INPUT N$
60                                    ' Personal message
70 IF N$ = "Mike" THEN 80 ELSE 100
80 BEEP : PRINT "I hope you had 8 hrs. sleep!"
90                                    ' Normal user
100 PRINT "Have a nice day " N$
110 PRINT "Do you want instructions Y/N? ";
120                                    ' Single keystroke
130 ANS$ = INPUT$(1)
140 PRINT ANS$
150 IF ANS$ = "Y" OR ANS$ = "y" THEN 170 ELSE 200
160                                    ' Detailed instructions
170 PRINT "Read page 50 in the manual."
180 GOTO 220
190                                    ' Y/N check
200 IF ANS$ = "N" OR ANS$ = "n"  THEN 220 ELSE 210
210 BEEP : PRINT "Only answer Y or N!"  : GOTO 110
220 REM    Program continues
```

FIGURE 11.10 Using IF-THEN on string data

Program output for entry of a first name, Pete, is shown below.

```
Enter first name ? Pete
Have a nice day Pete
Do you want instructions Y(Yes) N(No)? y
Read page 50 in the procedures manual.
Ok
```

Output from the same program for an entry of a first name of Mike is shown below. Notice how string variables can make program output more conversational.

```
Enter first name? Mike
I hope you had 8 hrs. sleep!
Have a nice day Mike
Do you want instructions Y/N? n
Ok
```

INPUT$(N) is a function that can be used to retrieve a single character from the keyboard. It is often easier to use than INKEY$. For example:

```
100 PRINT "Press any
key to continue.";
110 A$ = INPUT$(1)
```

NESTED WHILE-WEND LOOPS

WHILE-WEND loops may be nested. When doing this, each WEND will match the most recent WHILE. Although the nested statements do not have to be indented as shown below, indenting them makes the program easier to read.

Statement Number	BASIC Statement		
-	**WHILE** (expression)		
-		**WHILE** (expression)	
-		- -	
-		- -	(statements
-		- -	within the
-		- -	nested loop)
-		**WEND**	
-	**WEND**		
-	- -	(any statement)	

INPUT statements are useful in making programs conversational. Questions can be asked that require Yes or No answers to direct program execution.

Let's demonstrate the use of nested WHILE-WEND loops by considering a small information-retrieval system. This system locates and displays a specific item out of a group of items; in our example, the cost and location of a toy in inventory based on the entry (inquiry) of a desired item.

One way to accomplish this is to enter a product (PRODUCT$) and then read an item (ITEM$) from data statements. Then, if PRODUCT$ = ITEM$, have the desired information displayed. The trick to this approach is to use RESTORE to bring back the data list so that it can be again compared without encountering an out-of-data error message.

A partial flowchart to accomplish this is shown in Figure 11.11.

The problem with the partial flowchart shown in Figure 11.11 is that the program doesn't loop back and ask for another entry. A complete flowchart to accomplish this is shown in Figure 11.12.

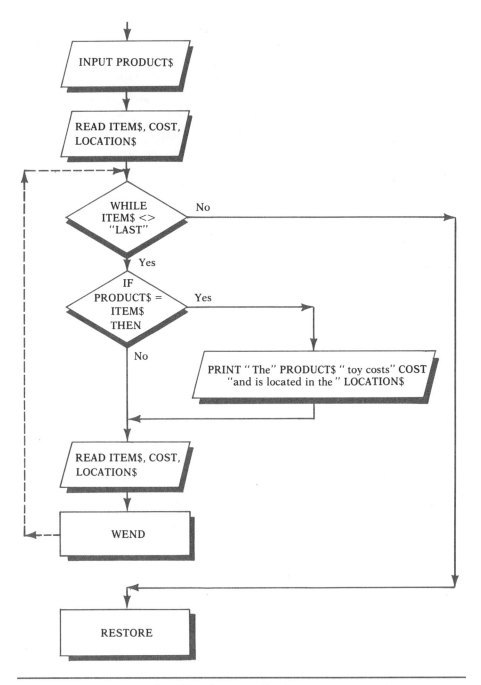

FIGURE 11.11 Partial flowchart for a small information-retrieval program

Remember, an internal data list is constructed for all DATA statement elements. RESTORE resets the pointer to the first element in the data list so the same data can be re-read.

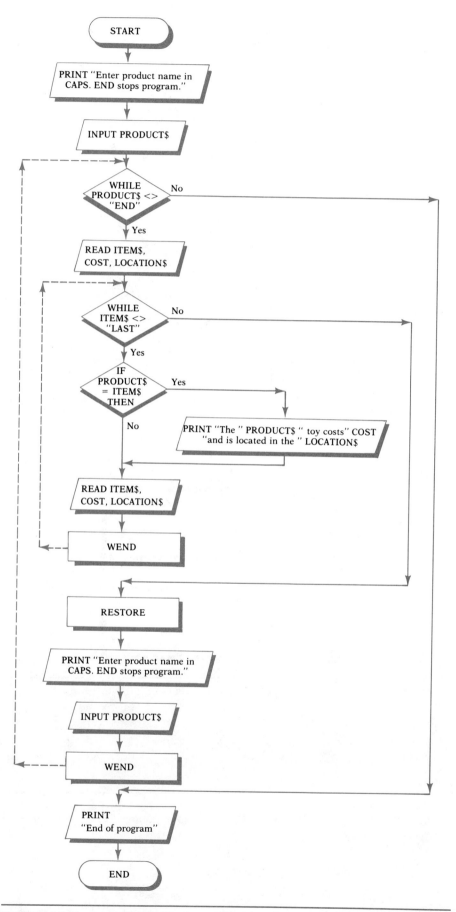

FIGURE 11.12 A small information-retrieval program

SUMMARY

IF-THEN statements are very useful programming statements, but you should exercise caution when using IF-THEN statements in programs that have multiple statements per line. If the comparison is true, then the clause to the right is executed. Otherwise the clause is not executed. That is, multiple statements on the line to the right of the comparison are executed only if the comparison is true.

If you have not already done so, select the IF-THEN-ELSE tutorial on the companion diskette as shown below. Then run the program. Enter your own data when requested. Notice how the value of a variable is compared in an IF-THEN statement to determine if a switch should be made in the program flow of logic.

The next chapter applies decision statements to problems requiring counting and totaling.

```
BASIC Programming With the IBM PC
          IF-THEN-ELSE
              By
          Peter Mears
       (c) Copyright 1990
```

Summary of terms

Name	Example	Purpose
IF-THEN-ELSE	50 IF AGE > 21 THEN PRINT "Age greater than 21" ELSE PRINT "Age not greater than 21."	A decision statement that executes the statement to the right of THEN if the comparison is true. If it is not true, the ELSE condition is executed.
IF-AND-THEN	50 IF AGE > 21 AND PAY = 200 THEN PRINT "Age greater than 21 and pay equals 200."	A decision statement. If both the first and second comparisons are true, the statement to the right of THEN is executed.
IF-OR-THEN	50 IF AGE = 21 or AGE = 22 THEN PRINT "It's either 21 or 22."	

PROBLEMS

True/False. Problems 1–6

11.1   A line number is the only thing that may follow the word THEN in an IF-THEN statement.

11.2   The symbols <> mean exactly equal to.

11.3   IF-THEN statements are conditional statements.

11.4   The ELSE clause in an IF-THEN statement is only executed when the THEN clause is not.

11.5   Values for variables in IF-THEN statements may only be entered via READ/DATA statements.

11.6   An IF-THEN statement can contain a maximum of one AND condition.

Debugging Problems, Miniprograms. Problems 7–11.
The miniprograms shown contain errors. The programs were executed and the screen appeared as shown. Find and correct the error(s), so that a logical output can be obtained when the program is executed.

11.7 An attempt was made to print the COST of the "Toy" items, but the screen appeared as shown.

```
10 READ ITEM$, COST
20 WHILE ITEM$ <> -999 End
30    IF ITEM$ = "Toy" THEN PRINT "Cost is" COST
40    READ ITEM$, COST
50 WEND
60 DATA "Boat", 4775
70 DATA "Toy", 19.95
80 DATA -999, 0
RUN
Type mismatch in 20
Ok
```

*11.8 An attempt was made to print the weight and sex of people who weighed more than 100 but less than 150 pounds. (The weight was increased by 10% to compensate for a tendency for people to underestimate their actual weight.) When the program was executed, nothing occurred—no output, nothing. After a minute, Control-break was pressed, resulting in the screen as shown. Technical note: Sometimes the message would be "Break in 30," or "Break in 40." After a couple of minutes the word "Overflow" appeared. Then to make matters worse, after that problem was solved, a syntax error occurred.

```
10 READ WEIGHT, SEX$
20 WHILE WEIGHT <> 999
30    WEIGHT = WEIGHT * 1.1
40    IF WEIGHT > 100 AND WEIGHT < 150 THEN PRINT SEX$, WEIGHT
50 WEND
60 DATA 175, "Male"        42 Read weight, sex$
70 DATA 140, "Female"
80 DATA 999, "end"
run
^C
Break in 20
Ok
```

11.9 An attempt was made to print the cars that cost over $1000 but less than $3000. The screen then appeared as shown. After correcting for the syntax error, a student asked if the WHILE COST loop of <> 0 has to match the value in the DATA statement of 000.

* The answer to this problem is in Appendix E.

```
10 REM Carefully study all of these programs
20 READ COST, CAR$
30 WHILE COST <> 0
40     WEIGHT = WEIGHT * 1.1
50     IF COST > 1000 AND < 3000 THEN PRINT CAR$, COST
60 READ COST, CAR$
70 WEND
80 DATA 999, "85 Escort"
90 DATA 2500,"86 Honda"
100 DATA 000, "end"
Ok
run
Syntax error in 50
Ok
50     IF COST > 1000 AND < 3000 THEN PRINT CAR$, COST
```

11.10 An attempt was made to print the names of the 21- and 25-year-old employees. The screen appeared as shown. After correcting the syntax error in all statements, there is still a serious error in logic that resulted in no program output.

```
10 READ NAME$, AGE
20 WHILE AGE <>  -999
30    IF AGE = 21 AND AGE = 25 THEN PRINT NAME$, Age
40    READ NAME$, AGE
50 WEND
60 DATA "Tom Jackson", 25
70 DATA "Alice Citizen", 19
80 DATA 00, -999
run
Syntax error in 10
Ok
10 READ NAME$, AGE
```

11.11 An attempt was made to print the students who received a grade over 90. After correcting for the syntax errors identified (the corrections were made but are not shown) an out-of-data message appeared when the program was executed.

```
10 READ STUDENT$, GRADE
20 WHILE STUDENT$ <> "end"
30    IF GRADE > 90 THEN PRINT "A- " STUDENT$
40    READ STUDENT$, GRADE
50 WEND
60 DATA "Susie Smith" 70
70 DATA "Alice Hunt"  91
80 DATA " end", 00
run
Syntax error in 60
Ok
60 DATA "Susie Smith", 70
run
Syntax error in 70
Ok
70 DATA "Alice Hunt", 91
run
A- Alice Hunt
Out of DATA in 40
Ok
```

What correction should be made?

Program Output. Problems 12–17.
Write the output that would appear when the programs shown are executed.

11.12
```
10 REM Program to highlight bonus stamps
20 PRINT "Enter sale amount ";
30 INPUT SALE
40 IF SALE > 200 THEN PRINT "Bonus stamps"
50 PRINT "Thanks for your business."
60 END
RUN
```
Enter sale amount?_____ (What range of sales values can be
Thanks for your business.   entered here to produce the indi-
                                      cated output?)

*11.13
```
10 REM Program to calculate sales tax
20 PRINT "Sale", "Tax", "Total Sale"
30 READ SALE
40 WHILE SALE <> -999
50 TAX = .05 * SALE
60 TOTAL = SALE + TAX
70 PRINT SALE, TAX, TOTAL
80 READ SALE
90 WEND
100 DATA 100, 200, 300, -999
110 END
RUN
```

11.14
```
10 REM Program to display employees with over 5 years
20 PRINT "Employees with over 5 years service"
30 READ EMPLOYEE$, YEARS
40 WHILE EMPLOYEE$ <> "END"
50 IF YEARS > 5 THEN PRINT EMPLOYEE$ " has over 5
   years."
60 READ EMPLOYEE$, YEARS
70 WEND
80 PRINT "End of analysis"
90 DATA John Jones, 4
100 DATA Ann Smith, 8
110 DATA Tom Mix, 12
120 DATA END, 0
130 END
RUN
```

11.15
```
10 REM Car insurance
20 PRINT "Enter your age";
30 INPUT AGE
40 IF AGE < 25 THEN INSUR = 450 ELSE INSUR = 200
50 PRINT "Your car insurance will cost";
60 PRINT USING "$$###.##";INSUR
70 END
RUN
```
Enter your age?_____ What range of values can be entered for age
                               that will produce the indicated output?
Your car insurance will cost $450.00
Ok

Problems 16 and 17 contain the following program variable names:

PERSON$—The name of the salesperson.
SALES—The number of sales made in a two-week period.
COMMISSION—The salesperson's commission.
PROFIT—Profit on the sales made.

11.16
```
10 REM Problem 11.16
20 REM Bonus analysis
30 READ PERSON$, SALES, COMMISSION, PROFIT
40 '
50 WHILE PERSON$ <> "END IT"
```

* The answer to this problem is in Appendix E.

```
60     IF SALES >= 10 OR PROFIT > 15000 THEN
          PRINT PERSON$ " receives a bonus!"
70     READ PERSON$, SALES, COMMISSION, PROFIT
80 WEND
90 '
100  PRINT "End of program."
9000 DATA Marsha Riggs,      9, .08, 16000
9010 DATA Bill Jefferson,    7, .05, 10000
9020 DATA George Mamilton,  12, .09, 14000
9030 DATA END IT,            0,  0,     0
9040 END
```

11.17
```
10 REM Problem 11-17
20 REM Sales & profit analysis
30 READ PERSON$, SALES, COMMISSION, PROFIT
40 '
50 WHILE PERSON$ <> "END IT"
60     IF SALES >= 9 AND PROFIT > 14000 THEN
          PRINT PERSON$ " receives a bonus!"
70     READ PERSON$, SALES, COMMISSION, PROFIT
80 WEND
90 '
100  PRINT "End of program."
9000 DATA Marsha Riggs,      9, .08, 16000
9010 DATA Bill Jefferson,    7, .05, 10000
9020 DATA George Mamilton,  12, .09, 14000
9030 DATA END IT,            0,  0,     0
9040 END
```

*Developing (partial) Miniprograms from a Flowchart. Problems 18–24.
Using the flowcharts shown as a guide, develop a partial BASIC program for
each problem.*

Begin your partial program with statement 200 REM Problem #. For
example, the program required in Problem 11.16 would begin as follows:
200 REM Problem 11.16.

11.18

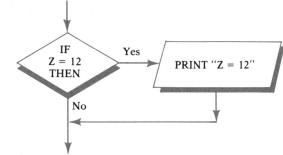

*11.19

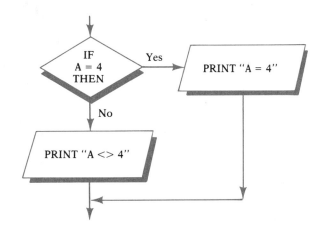

* The answer to this problem is in Appendix E.

11.20

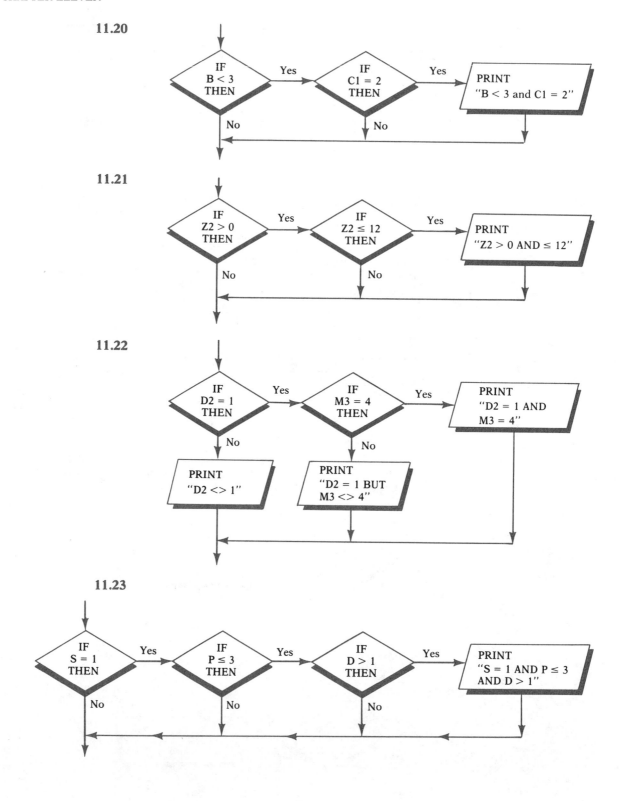

11.21

11.22

11.23

11.24

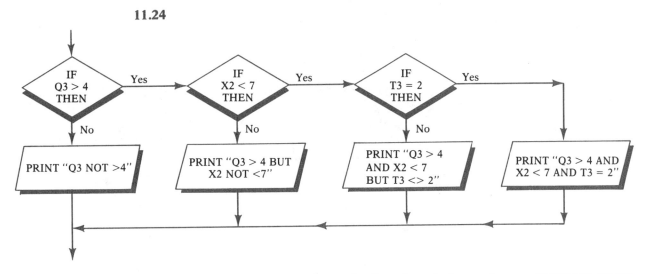

*11.25 Develop a program from the flowchart below using an IF-THEN-ELSE statement. Test your program by executing it, first with a value of 80, then with a value of 110.

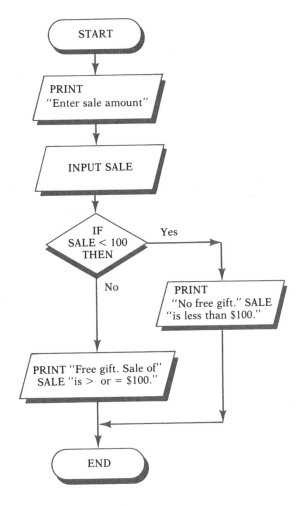

* The answer to this problem is in Appendix E.

11.26 Develop a program from the flowchart below. Test your program by executing it first with a value of 10, then with a value of 110.

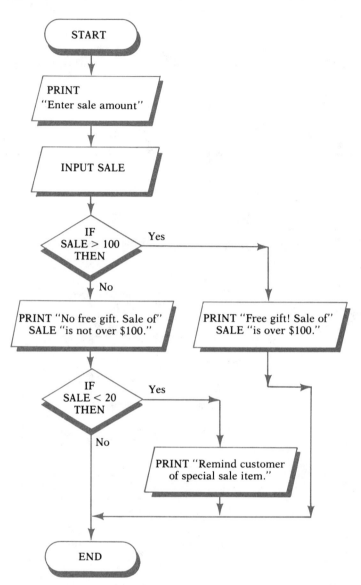

11.27 Develop a flowchart and program to calculate and display sales commissions. Input SALE via the keyboard. If SALE is over $1000, then COMMISSION.RATE is 3% of SALE, else COMMISSION.RATE is 2% of SALE. Display values with PRINT USING statements.

11.28 Using the following flowchart as a guide, develop a program that tests a DATA statement (in this case only one statement) to determine if a desired item is in stock. Run the program using different INPUT values for PRODUCT$ to check your work.

Use the following DATA statement:

```
DATA Airplane, 19.95
```

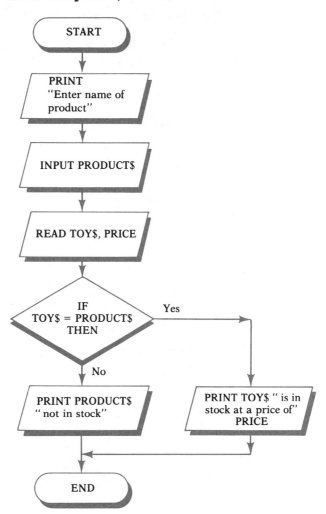

Problems 29–32 require the use of the ASCII file "INCOME. ASC" on the companion diskette. The data in this file is organized as follows:

Name	Age	Sex	Income
--	--	-	--

*11.29 Using the following flowchart as a guide, develop a program that reads the first DATA statement in the ASCII file. If AGE is over 21, then "Over 21" is printed, otherwise, "21 or under" is printed. (We will later expand this to read more than one DATA statement.)

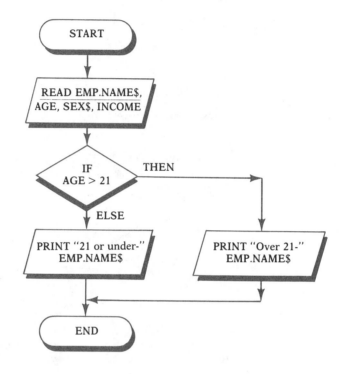

* The answer to this problem is in Appendix E.

11.30 Using the following flowchart as a guide, develop a program that reads and analyzes the data in the ASCII file until "LAST" is encountered.

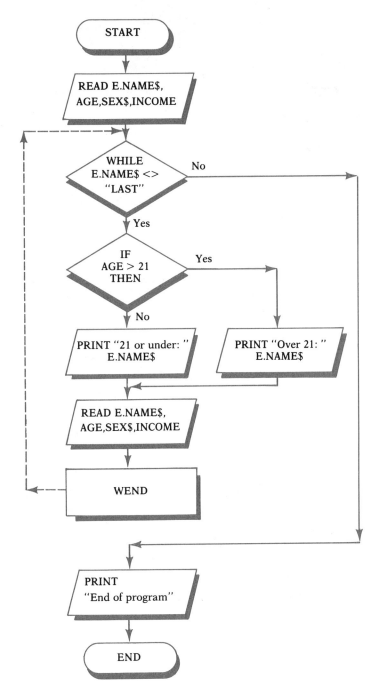

11.31 Using the following flowchart as a guide, develop a program that reads and analyzes the data in the ASCII file until "LAST" is encountered. This logic is used to identify female employees (code "f") greater than 20 and less than 35 years old.

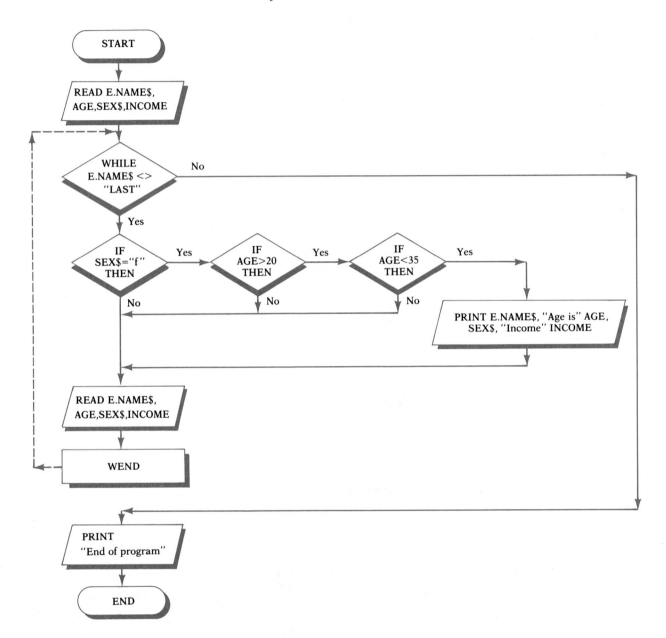

11.32 Using the flowchart below as a guide, develop a program that reads and analyzes the data in the ASCII file until "LAST" is encountered. This logic is used to identify female employees having an AGE greater than 21 and less than 32 with INCOME less than $20,000.

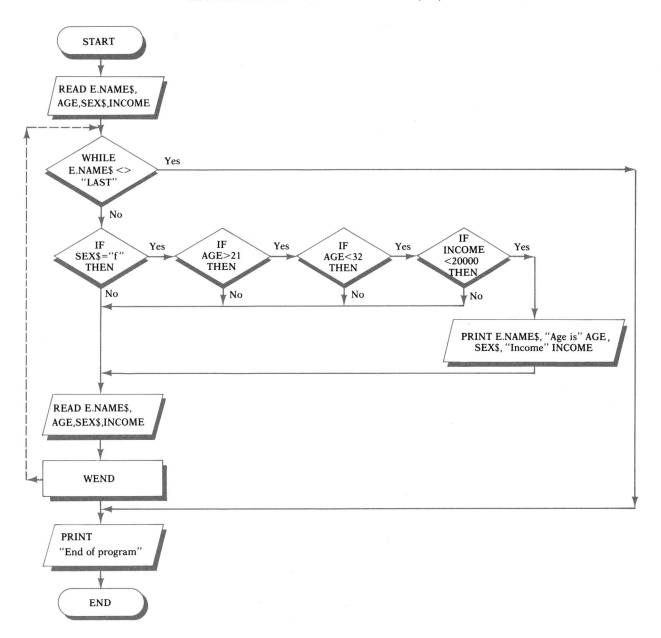

11.33 Using the following flowchart as a guide, Develop a program to enter a desired name via the keyboard. Call this variable NAME.WANT$. Then read the DATA statements in the "WAGES.ASC" file using variables called E.NAME$, HR.WORKED, HR.RATE, and AGE. IF NAME.WANT$ = E.NAME$, then the name and age are displayed.

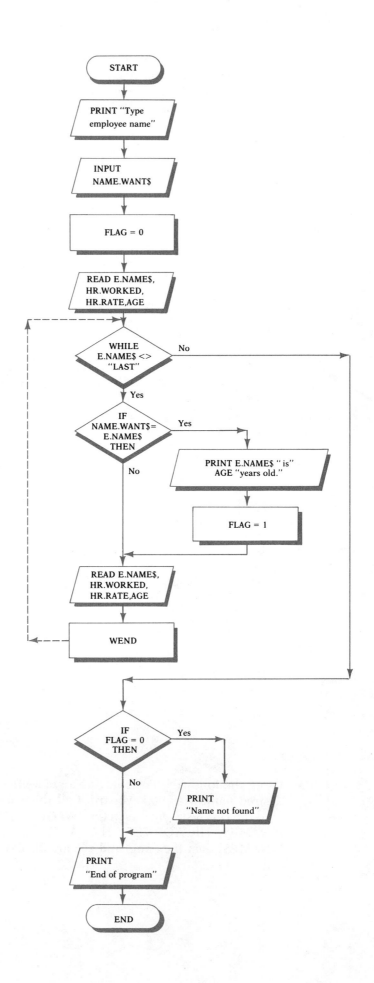

Screen Design Problems. Problems 34–41.
Develop a BASIC program, paying particular attention to the design of the screen and the design of the printed output (when requested). General formats are shown for your consideration; they may be expanded on (improved) in your program.

11.34   The ASCII file on the companion diskette called SUPPLIES.ASC will be needed to answer this problem. The format of this ASCII file is as shown.

```
Product    Location   Quantity   Price   Description
number     code
  --         --          --        --        --
```

Top Draw Office Supplies Company needs a monthly report created for its products in inventory. Develop a BASIC program to create a report using the following format:

```
-------------------------------------------------
            Top Drawer Office Supplies
            Items priced over $250
Description                 Unit  Quantity Potential
of item                     price in stock sales
-------------------------------------------------
Disks-10 SS SD              $4.95  225     $1,113.75
Disks-10 DS DD              $7.95  135     $1,073.25
Paper-8/11 Continuous       $25.95 114     $2,958.30
Paper-143/8 Continuous      $35.50  26       $923.00
Desk - Economy              $139.95 12     $1,679.40
Desk - Standard             $569.95 10     $5,699.50
 - - - Partial program output - - -
*** End of report created on mm/dd/yy ***
-------------------------------------------------
```

Note: Potential sales are calculated as unit price times the quantity in stock.

11.35   Metro Accountants, Inc., requires a program to produce a report showing the current ratio (current assets divided by current liabilities) for selected firms. Assign either good, fair, or poor to each ratio based on the following standard:

Good   Current ratio greater than 2.4
Fair   Current ratio from 2.4 through 1.95
Poor   Current ratio less than 1.95

The current assets and current liabilities for each firm are shown below. The report should be formatted as shown.

		Metro Accountants, Inc. Current Ratio Report MM/DD/YY		
Firm	Current assets	Current liabilities	Current ratio	Assessment
XXX	$XXXXX	$XXXXX	XX	XXX

Use the following data to produce the report:

	Firm	Current assets	Current liabilities
900 DATA	ABC Co. ,	50200,	2050
910 DATA	Firmware ,	45000,	20000
920 DATA	Zeke Hardware ,	100000,	60000
930 DATA	Dual Hydra ,	70000,	50000
940 DATA	Metro Pet Shop,	80000,	13876
950 DATA	END ,	0,	0

Use the following variable names:

FIRM$ = Firm name

ASSETS = Current assets

LIABILITIES = Current liabilities

11.36 Ms. Monroe is an income tax practitioner who operates a service that prepares income tax forms. Her fees for preparing the form are based on the following criteria:

Form Fees:

The base fee for a short form is $75.
The base fee for a long form is $250.

Income levels and charges:

Less than $10,000/year—base fee for short form.
$10,000 but less than $25,000/year—short-form fee + $100.
$25,000 but less than $35,000/year—base fee for long form.
$35,000/year and more—base fee for long form + $200.

Print a summary report in the format shown.

```
┌─────────────────────────────────────┐
│        Ms. Monroe's Tax Service      │
│              Fee Report              │
│  ----------------------------------  │
│  Customer       Customer      Fee    │
│  name           income        charged│
│  ----------------------------------  │
│  Bill                                │
│  Whayne         $14,872       $175   │
│       - -       $XX,XXX       $XXX   │
│       - -       $XX,XXX       $XXX   │
│       - -       $XX,XXX       $XXX   │
│       - -       $XX,XXX       $XXX   │
│  ----------------------------------  │
│  Prepared on: mm/dd/yy               │
└─────────────────────────────────────┘
```

Use the following data in developing the output:

CUSTOMER$	INCOME
Bill Whayne	$14872
Mary Citizen	$ 9950
Sue Smith	$27837
Zeke Jones	$21750
Sam Jackson	$42175

The ASCII file on the companion diskette called "PRODUCTS.ASC" will be needed to answer Problems 37–41. The format of this ASCII is as shown. [1], [2], [etc.] are for reference and are not included in the file.

Product I.D.	Description	Cost	Retail Price	Begin Inven.	Qt. Sold	Location Code
XXX	XXXXXXXXXXXXX [1]	$XXX.XX	$XXX.XX [2]	XX [3]	XX	X

*11.37 Ajax Wholesale Company needs a program that prints the description[1], retail price[2], and beginning inventory[3] for all items in inventory that exceed a target retail price. This program will be used by the Marketing Department to determine inventory levels at various prices.

An example of the monitor input/output is shown where several items were found that exceeded the user-entered target price. If no items were found, then print "Items not found greater than a target price of $XX.XX." (Notice the flowchart in Problem 33 on how this can be accomplished.)

```
        Ajax Inventory Analysis Program

     Target price   -99 stops search? 300

Description                 Retail        Beginning
of product                  price         inventory
------------------------------------------------------
Compe 27in mens 12 sp I     $315.75       2
Compe 27in mens 12 sp II    $375.15       0
Pro Fit Fitness Center      $358.87       5

*** End of report ***
Printed output Y/N?
```

Target price
←entered by user

} Obtained from data search

Printed output format if requested.

```
        Ajax Inventory Analysis Program
      Items with a retail price over $300.00
------------------------------------------------------
Description                 Retail        Beginning
of product                  price         inventory
------------------------------------------------------
Compe 27in mens 12 sp I     $315.75       2
Compe 27in mens 12 sp II    $375.15       0
Pro Fit Fitness Center      $358.87       5

*** Report completed on 01-01-1990 ***
```

←The target price

11.38 Revise the logic and output shown in Problem 37 to permit the user to enter a product description via the keyboard. Then search the file, and if the first three characters of the entered description match the DATA description, display the output. After the search is completed, give the user the option of obtaining a printed output.

* The answer to this problem is in Appendix E.

Test your program by entering a product description of "Professional." The screen should appear as shown. Develop your own format for the printed report.

```
              Product Retrieval Program

Product description END stops search? Professional

Description                      Retail      Beginning
of product                       price       inventory
------------------------------------------------------
Pro Fit Exercycle                $149.89     40
Pro Fit Fitness Center           $358.87      5
Pro Fit 110 lb. Wt Set            $33.58     35
Pro Fit Incl Wt Bench             $59.90     20
Pro Fit Blue Gym Bag #1           $11.95     85
Pro Fit Blue Gym Bag #2           $15.95     70
Pro Fit Blue Rq Bag  #3           $17.95     50
Pro Fit Alum. Rq bl Racq          $25.95     30
Pro Fit Blue Rq bl                 $2.95     95
*** End of report ***

Printed output Y/N?
```

11.39   Develop a stockroom-analysis program that searches the PRODUCTS.ASC file to identify the products on a particular aisle (i.e., rack of shelves within the stockroom). The program is to permit user entry of an aisle number as can be seen in the screen shown.

```
              Aisle Analysis Program

This program identifies the products on a
specified stockroom aisle at Ajax Corporation.

Enter aisle number. -99 stops search? 6

Description                      Retail      Aisle
of product                       price       number
------------------------------------------------------
Winslow Wood Tennis Rq           $49.95       6
Winslow Pro Tennis Rq            $54.98       6
Winslow Graphite Tennis Rq       $84.95       6
Winslow Tennis bl                 $2.95       6
Winslow Two-Tone Tennis bl        $3.75       6
*** End of report ***

Printed output Y/N?
```

If a printed output is requested, this output should be of the format shown. Test your program by requesting a stockroom search of aisle number 6.

```
          Aisle Analysis Program
          Aisle number:  6
     --------------------------------------------
     Description                    Retail    Aisle
     of product                     price     number
     --------------------------------------------
     Winslow Wood Tennis Rq         $49.95    6
     Winslow Pro Tennis Rq          $54.98    6
     Winslow Graphite Tennis Rq     $84.95    6
     Winslow Tennis bl              $2.95     6
     Winslow Two-Tone Tennis bl     $3.75     6

     *** Report completed on 01-01-1991 ***
```

Printed output format if requested.

```
     Analysis of Stockroom Aisle # XX

     Description        Retail      Aisle
     of product         price       number
     _____           _____      _____
       - -                -            -
       - -                -            -
       - -                -            -

     Report completed on mm/dd/yy.
```

11.40 Ajax Wholesale company needs a program that identifies the highest and lowest quantity sold for all items that exceed a target retail price. An example of the monitor input/output is shown where several items were found that exceeded the user-entered target price. (Develop only the monitor display; a printed output is not desired.) If no items are found, then print "Items not found greater than a target price of $XX.XX."

```
           Ajax Price/Quantity Sold Program

          Target price [0 stops search]? 250

     Description                    Retail    Quantity
     of product                     price     sold
     --------------------------------------------
     Kwinn 27in mens 10sp Racer     $287.89   1
     Compe 27in mens 12 sp I        $315.75   1
     Compe 27in mens 12 sp II       $375.15   0
     AFP Dual Action Rowcycle       $269.97   12
     Pro Fit Fitness Center         $358.87   2

     Lowest quantity sold:  0
     Highest quantity sold: 12
     *** End of report.  Press any key to continue. ***
```

11.41 A mark-up analysis program is needed that will identify profitable items in the PRODUCTS.ASC file. Mark-up (MARK.UP) is calculated as follows:

$$\text{MARK.UP} = \frac{\text{RETAIL} - \text{COST}}{\text{COST}}$$

Where
MARK.UP is a decimal value (i.e., 125% is 1.25; 30% is .30)
RETAIL   is the Retail Price (the selling price)
COST   is the Cost (what we paid for the item)

A user is to enter a target mark-up (TARGET.MARK) in decimal value. A MARK.UP is calculated for each item in inventory, and when the MARK.UP exceeds the TARGET.MARK, the record is printed. Check your work on a value of .75 as shown below:

```
                    Ajax Product Mark-Up Analysis

              Product description   -99 stops search.
              Enter target mark-up in decimal value.

              Your target mark-up? .75

Description                         Cost          Retail        Mark-up
of item                            of item        price         (decimal)
------------------------------------------------------------------------
Kwinn 13in tricycle (Tyke)         $12.83         $25.95        1.02
Kwinn 20in girls #2                $33.20         $94.99        1.86
Kwinn 27in mens 10sp Racer         $155.50        $287.89       0.85
Kwinn 24in moto-cr (Thund)         $57.60         $129.90       1.26
Kwinn 24in BMX (Duster)            $46.36         $109.83       1.37
Kwinn Bicycle Pump                 $2.26          $3.99         0.77
Pro Fit Blue Gym Bag #1            $5.50          $11.95        1.17
------------------------------------------------------------------------
*** End of report ***
Press any key to continue.
```

Other Problems. Problems 42–49.
Develop a BASIC program to solve each problem. Use a REM statement to identify the problem number, and clearly label all output.

Use the ASCII file "STOCKS.ASC" for Problems 42–44. The data in this file are organized as follows:

Ticker symbol	1989 High	1989 Low	1990 High	1990 Low	Last sale	Earnings per share
--	--	--	--	--	--	--

11.42 Write a program to print out the ticker symbol of all stocks having a low in 1990 that was lower than the stock's 1989 low price.

11.43 Write a program to display the ticker symbol of all stocks having the following criteria: earnings per share greater than $2.50 and a 1990 price swing over $75.00 per share.

Note: Price swing is computed by subtracting a stock's high price from its low price for the year.

11.44 Develop a program to analyze stock based on the following entries:

Target earnings/share—the user wants stocks that equal or exceed this amount.
Target cost—the user wants stocks that have a last sale of this amount or less.

Print the ticker symbols, earnings per share, and last sale value of all stocks that meet these conditions.

11.45   Using the flowchart shown in Problem 33 as a guide, develop a small information-retrieval program. Use the following DATA statements to test your program.

```
9000 DATA GUN,              5.95, 2nd floor
9010 DATA TRUCK,           11.95, 1st floor
9020 DATA DOLLS,           19.95, 3rd floor
9030 DATA DOLL HOUSE,      45.90, 3rd floor
9040 DATA BASEBALL,         4.95, 1st floor
9050 DATA GUN,            229.95, Sporting Dept
9060 DATA LAST,             0, 0
```

The ASCII file on the companion diskette called "WAGES.ASC" will be needed to answer Problems 46–49. The format of this ASCII file is as shown. A BASIC program is needed that searches the DATA statements based on user-entered data. Then, if the appropriate statement is found, print out the variables specified.

Employee name	Hours worked	Hourly rate	Age
- -	- -	- -	--

11.46   Develop a program based on a user-entered hourly rate. Print out all employees who make precisely that hourly rate.

11.47   Develop a program based on a user-entered hourly rate. Print out all employees who make within 10% of the specified hourly rate.

11.48   Develop a flowchart and program based on a user-entered gross pay. Have the program calculate the employee's pay (include time and one-half for all hours over 40 hours worked). Print out the employees' names and their gross pay for all gross pay that exceeds the user-entered gross pay.

11.49   Develop a program that calculates pay for an employee, based on the first three letters of the employee's first name. Check your work by entering the first name of "Martin." (There are several employees whose names begin with "Mar.")

REPEATING OPERATIONS

Upon completion of this chapter you should be able to

- Use program statement to count
- Develop totals
- Use FOR-NEXT statements

The objective of a business report is to assist the reader in making a decision by presenting timely, condensed information on key activities. Business reports are not designed to be read for pleasure: They are blunt and to the point. Unless the reader is familiar with the activity discussed, the report will be of little value.

A useful report contains information on important activities. For example, if a sales report is prepared for a top official, such as the vice president in charge of sales, more information than a single sales total is probably needed. Perhaps the important control point for this firm is at the department level. If so, sales by department should be developed and then totaled to obtain overall sales. We will use the concepts of counting and totaling to demonstrate how to program repetitive operations.

COUNTING

Subtotals and totals are a useful way to analyze data, but before using these techniques we will have to understand the concept of using an *accumulator* for counting. Once this is mastered, we will be able to total values.

The programs shown in Figure 12.1 count from 1 to 4 by using a loop of logic. The first program uses GOTO and IF-THEN statements to create a loop. The second program uses a WHILE-WEND loop. In both programs, control is transferred outside the loop when the value of the TOTAL variable exceeds 4.

The programs shown in Figure 12.1 use a variable called TOTAL as an accumulator, which stores values while the total is developed. Let's go through the program using the GOTO and IF-THEN loop step by step to develop an understanding of how a program counts. Initially we will develop a total by counting in units of 1, but later we will use other values.

Statement 10 is a REM statement and is not executed. Statement **20** **TOTAL = 1** assigns the value 1 to the variable called TOTAL. This is neces-

```
10 REM Using GOTO & IF-THEN
20 TOTAL = 1
30 IF TOTAL > 4 THEN 70
40 PRINT "Number" TOTAL
50 TOTAL = TOTAL + 1
60 GOTO 30
70 PRINT "Program ends." TOTAL "exceeds 4."
80 END
RUN
Number 1
Number 2
Number 3
Number 4
Program ends. 5 exceeds 4.
Ok
```

```
10 REM Using WHILE & WEND
20 TOTAL = 1
30 WHILE TOTAL <= 4
40      PRINT "Number" TOTAL
50      TOTAL = TOTAL + 1
60 WEND
70 PRINT "Program ends. TOTAL is:" TOTAL
80 END
RUN
Number 1
Number 2
Number 3
Number 4
Program ends. TOTAL is: 5
Ok
```

FIGURE 12.1   Loop of logic using GOTO, IF-THEN, and WHILE-WEND

sary so that we begin counting (totaling) from 1. At this point in the program, there is only one variable contained in memory, with the following assignment:

TOTAL

1

Statement **30 IF TOTAL > 4 THEN 70** transfers control to statement 70 when the value of TOTAL exceeds 4. Statement **40 PRINT "Number" TOTAL** is used to label the program output.

Let's take a close look at statement **50 TOTAL = TOTAL + 1**. The expression to the right of the equal sign (TOTAL + 1) executes first. The stored value of the variable TOTAL (which is 1) is retrieved, and 1 is added, yielding a sum of 2. Statement 50 thus reduces to TOTAL = 2, which results in the value 2 being assigned to TOTAL. The variable called TOTAL in memory now contains the following assignment:

TOTAL

```
┌─────┐
│  2  │
└─────┘
```

Statement **ᴸᴼ GOTO ᴈᴼ** transfers control to statement 30. Statement **ᴈᴼ IF TOTAL > 4 THEN 7ᴼ** retrieves the stored value of TOTAL (which is 2) and checks to determine if 2 is greater than 4. It is not, so control passes to statement **4ᴼ PRINT "Number" TOTAL** which displays the value of TOTAL.

Statement **5ᴼ TOTAL = TOTAL + ᴸ** again retrieves the stored value of the variable TOTAL (which is now 2), adds 1, and stores the sum 3 in TOTAL. The variable called TOTAL now contains

TOTAL

```
┌─────┐
│  3  │
└─────┘
```

Notice how TOTAL is accumulating by adding the value 1 each time the statement is executed. The other statements work as previously explained until statement **5ᴼ TOTAL = TOTAL + ᴸ** is reached again. The value stored in TOTAL (which is now 3) is retrieved, 1 is added, and the sum 4 is assigned to TOTAL. The variable called TOTAL now contains

TOTAL

```
┌─────┐
│  4  │
└─────┘
```

Statements are processed until statement **5ᴼ TOTAL = TOTAL + ᴸ** is reached again. The value stored in TOTAL (which is 4) is retrieved, 1 is added, and the sum 5 is assigned to TOTAL, resulting in

TOTAL

```
┌─────┐
│  5  │
└─────┘
```

When statement **3ᴼ IF TOTAL > 4 THEN 7ᴼ** is reached this time, TOTAL (which is 5) exceeds 4, so control is transferred to statement 70. A message is displayed, and the program ends. There is nothing significant about the variable name TOTAL; any variable name could be used instead. The important thing is to notice how the value contained in TOTAL is accumulated (totaled) until the desired value is exceeded.

Although accumulating this way is a useful concept, counting by 1's has a very limited application. A more general approach is needed to develop a total for any column of numbers.

An accumulator is a statement containing the same variable on both sides of the equal sign. The statement TOTAL = TOTAL + 1 permits the value of TOTAL + 1 to be stored back into TOTAL. This accumulates (sums) values and will be used in developing report totals.

TOTALING

A program to read a value from a DATA statement and accumulate value in a variable called TOTAL.VALUE is shown in Figure 12.2. A total is developed for four values and then displayed.

There are two accumulators in the program shown in Figure 12.2. The variable called TOTAL counts from 1 to 4, as previously explained, and TOTAL.VALUE is used to accumulate the DATA statement values. Because

```
10 REM Note the two accumulators
20 TOTAL = Ø : TOTAL.VALUE =Ø
30 TOTAL = TOTAL + 1
40 IF TOTAL > 4 THEN 80
50 READ VALUE
60 TOTAL.VALUE = TOTAL.VALUE + VALUE
70 GOTO 30
80 PRINT "The total of the values is" TOTAL.VALUE
90 DATA 20,10,1.5,5
100 END
RUN
The total of the values is 36.5
Ok
```

FIGURE 12.2 Developing a TOTAL

double accumulators are often used in business programs, let's go through this program step by step to develop an understanding of how values are accumulated.

Statement 10 is a REM statement and is not executed. Statement 20 assigns the value 0 to the two variables to be used as accumulators, resulting in

TOTAL	TOTAL.VALUE
0	0

Statement **30 TOTAL = TOTAL + 1** adds 1 to the value of TOTAL (which is 0) and stores the sum of 1 in TOTAL. Statement 40 checks to determine if TOTAL is greater than 4 (if it is not, control passes to statement **50 READ VALUE**). VALUE is assigned the first data element.

At this point in the program, three variables have been established, with these assignments:

TOTAL	TOTAL.VALUE	VALUE
1	0	20

Statement **60 TOTAL.VALUE = TOTAL.VALUE + VALUE** retrieves the value of the variable TOTAL.VALUE (which is 0), adds the value of the variable VALUE (which is 20), and stores the sum in TOTAL.VALUE. This results in the following:

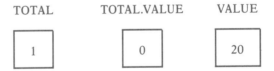

TOTAL	TOTAL.VALUE	VALUE
1	20	20

Statement **70 GOTO 30** passes control to statement **30 TOTAL = TO-TAL + 1**. The value of TOTAL (which is 1) is retrieved, the value 1 is added, and the sum 2 is stored in TOTAL. Statement 40 checks to determine if TOTAL is greater than 4 (it is not), and control passes to statement **50 READ VALUE**. VALUE is assigned the next data element.

At this point in the program, three variables have been established, with the following assignments:

TOTAL	TOTAL.VALUE	VALUE
2	20	10

Statement **60 TOTAL.VALUE = TOTAL.VALUE + VALUE** again retrieves the value of TOTAL.VALUE (which is 20), adds the value of the variable VALUE (which is 10), and stores the sum in TOTAL.VALUE. This results in the following:

TOTAL	TOTAL.VALUE	VALUE
2	30	10

Notice how the variable TOTAL.VALUE is accumulating the values of the variable VALUE. The program progresses through the statements as previously explained. TOTAL is incremented (increased) by 1, and another value for the variable VALUE is read from the DATA statement. This results in the following assignments:

TOTAL	TOTAL.VALUE	VALUE
3	30	1.5

Statement **60 TOTAL.VALUE = TOTAL.VALUE + VALUE** again retrieves the value of TOTAL.VALUE (which is 30), adds the value of the variable VALUE (which is 1.5), and stores the sum in TOTAL.VALUE. This results in the following assignments:

TOTAL	TOTAL.VALUE	VALUE
3	31.5	1.5

Then TOTAL is incremented by 1, another value for the variable VALUE is read (5), and that value is added to TOTAL.VALUE to obtain the final sum: 36.5. Notice how the two accumulators develop totals by storing values of the variables. Negative values could be totaled in the same manner.

```
10 REM Note -999 for end of data
20 TOTAL.VALUE = 0
30 READ VALUE
40 IF VALUE = -999 THEN 70
50 TOTAL.VALUE = TOTAL.VALUE + VALUE
60 GOTO 30
70 PRINT "The total of the values is" TOTAL.VALUE
80 DATA 20, 10, 1.5, 5, -999
90 END
RUN
The total of the values is 36.5
Ok
```

It is simple enough to use a WHILE and WEND loop to streamline the logic shown in Figure 12.3. However, such an approach will result in a more difficult program when developing the subtotals and grand totals shown in Figure 12.4.

FIGURE 12.3 Use of trailer value in totaling

A more flexible program, which totals any number of values, is shown in Figure 12.3. Note that the ending value of −999 is a trailer value, which signifies the end of data. The accumulator TOTAL.VALUE works as previously explained.

There are many applications where subtotals, as well as totals, are needed. The program shown in Figure 12.4 develops a subtotal in the accumulator called SUB.TOTAL. When the value of −999 is detected, the current value of SUB.TOTAL is displayed. Notice how SUB.TOTAL is then accumulated in the variable called GRAND.TOTAL, which is displayed when the trailing value of −9999 is detected. Both trailer values are required to display the last SUB.TOTAL and, finally, the GRAND.TOTAL.

The process of accumulating values in developing a total repeated the same totaling statement several times. Instead of using the open-ended loop created by the GOTO and IF-THEN statements, we could use other BASIC statements that repeat a loop a specific number of times. These are the FOR and NEXT statements.

```
10  REM  -999 for SUB.TOTAL.   -9999 for GRAND.TOTAL
20  GRAND.TOTAL = 0
30  SUB.TOTAL   = 0
40  READ VALUE
50  IF VALUE =  -999   THEN   90
60  IF VALUE = -9999   THEN 120
70  SUB.TOTAL = SUB.TOTAL + VALUE
80  GOTO 40
90  PRINT "The subtotal is"        SUB.TOTAL
100 GRAND.TOTAL = GRAND.TOTAL + SUB.TOTAL
110 GOTO 30
120 PRINT "The grand total is" GRAND.TOTAL
130 DATA 20, 10, 1.5, 5, -999, 30, 5, -999, -9999
140 END
RUN
The subtotal is 36.5
The subtotal is 35
The grand total is 71.5
Ok
```

The ! symbol will appear if a number such as 99999 is used. This indicates the precision of the number, which will be discussed in Chapter 16. Ignore it for the time being.

FIGURE 12.4 Developing subtotals and grand totals

THE FOR AND NEXT STATEMENTS

The FOR statement begins a loop of logic that will be executed a specific number of times. The corresponding NEXT statement identifies the range of the loop.

The general form of the FOR statement is

Statement number	**FOR**	Any numeric variable	=	Beginning number or variable	**TO**	Ending number or variable	**STEP**	Desired value

The general form of the corresponding NEXT statement is

Statement number	**NEXT**	Variable in FOR statement

Most programming applications count in units of 1, beginning with the number 1 and progressing upward until the ending number or variable containing the ending number is reached. Thus, a more common form of the FOR statement is

| Statement number | **FOR** | Any variable | **= 1 TO** | Ending number |

The general form of the corresponding NEXT statement is the same as before. The use of FOR and NEXT statements can simplify programming by reducing the number of statements required to execute a loop of logic a specific number of times.

As can be seen in the flowchart and program shown in Figure 12.5, a loop is created, which executes four times. Statement `10 X = 1 TO 4` begins the loop, and statement `30 NEXT X` identifies the outer range of the loop. Since statement `20 PRINT X` is trapped inside the loop, the statement is executed four times. After the fourth time, the loop is completed, and control passes to the statement following the NEXT statement. This is statement `40 END`, which ends the program.

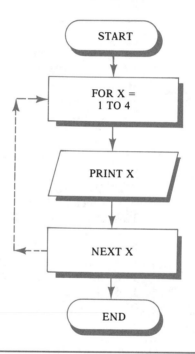

FIGURE 12.5 The FOR and NEXT statements

Two points should be kept in mind when using FOR and NEXT statements. First, every FOR must have a corresponding NEXT statement. The NEXT statement indicates the range of the loop and increments the variable in the FOR statement. Second, although control can be transferred out of a loop, reentry into a FOR-NEXT loop should come only from the FOR statement. This will ensure that the correct counting sequence is maintained.

For example, the programs shown in Figure 12.6 using the FOR-NEXT statements are similar to the one shown in Figure 12.5 except that TOTAL is used in place of the variable X. Now look at the program in the lower portion of Figure 12.6. Statements 20 and 30 are equivalent to `FOR X = 1 TO 4`. Statements 50 and 60 are equivalent to `NEXT X`.

Notice that the variable called TOTAL in the FOR statement increases each time through the loop. This is called *indexing*, and it is an important feature of the FOR-NEXT loop. The loop ends when TOTAL has the value of 5, which exceeds the upper limit stated in the FOR statement.

```
10 REM FOR-NEXT loop
20 FOR TOTAL = 1 TO 4
30     PRINT "Number" TOTAL
40 NEXT TOTAL
50 PRINT "Loop ends because" TOTAL "exceeds 4."
60 END
RUN
Number 1
Number 2
Number 3
Number 4
Loop ends because 5 exceeds 4.
Ok
```

```
10 REM GOTO & IF-THEN loop
20 TOTAL = 1
30 IF TOTAL > 4 THEN 70
40     PRINT "Number" TOTAL
50 TOTAL = TOTAL + 1
60 GOTO 30
70 PRINT "Program ends." TOTAL "exceeds 4."
80 END
RUN
Number 1
Number 2
Number 3
Number 4
Program ends. 5 exceeds 4.
Ok
```

FIGURE 12.6 Loop of logic using FOR and NEXT statements

The FOR and corresponding NEXT statements function as an automatic counter. Statement **20 FOR TOTAL = 1 TO 4** assigns the value of 1 to the variable TOTAL. Statement **40 NEXT TOTAL** increments TOTAL by one and transfers control to statement 20. If the value of TOTAL exceeds the upper range of the FOR loop, control automatically passes to the statement following the NEXT statement.

Technically, FOR and NEXT statements do not have to be used when programming, because a counter can be established in other ways, and GOTO and IF-THEN statements or a WHILE-WEND loop can then be used to obtain the same results. However, FOR and NEXT statements greatly simplify programming when a specific number of steps have to be performed.

We have been using the STEP portion of the FOR-NEXT loop in the default mode, stepping by 1. You can get elaborate with this feature, and it is possible to step by decimal values, either plus or minus. An example of "fancy stepping" is shown in Figure 12.7. We begin with the "two step" (counting by two's), then go to the half step. Finally, we perform a lively little number by stepping backward.

```
10  REM Using STEP
20  PRINT "The two step."
30  FOR FOOTWORK = 1 TO 12 STEP 2
40      PRINT FOOTWORK,
50  NEXT FOOTWORK
60  PRINT
70  PRINT "The half step."
80  FOR FOOTWORK = 1 TO 3 STEP .5
90      PRINT FOOTWORK,
100 NEXT FOOTWORK
110 PRINT
120 PRINT "The back step."
130 FOR FOOTWORK = 3 TO 1 STEP -.5
140     PRINT FOOTWORK,
150 NEXT FOOTWORK
160 PRINT
170 END

RUN
The two step.
 1              3              5              7              9
 11
The half step.
 1              1.5            2              2.5            3

The back step.
 3              2.5            2              1.5            1

Ok
```

FIGURE 12.7 Fancy stepping

We will be using the default of STEP 1 in the examples that follow. The flowchart shown in Figure 12.8 utilizes FOR and NEXT statements to establish a loop, which is used to total six values. The FOR and NEXT statements are shown inside of rectangular boxes with a dotted line connecting the middle of the NEXT box to the middle of the FOR box. The midpoints are connected, because, if control passes outside the FOR-NEXT loop, an accurate count cannot be kept.

The accumulator called TOTAL is initially set equal to 0. This is done so that we begin adding from a known value. Then the value of the variable K in the FOR statement is assigned the value 1. The value of the variable NUMBER is read from a DATA statement and accumulated in the variable called TOTAL. The NEXT K statement increments the variable K until the upper range of 6 is exceeded. Control then passes to the following statement, where the value of TOTAL is displayed.

The program accompanying this flowchart is shown in Figure 12.9. The READ statement inside the FOR-NEXT loop results in the assignment of each of the six data values to the variable called NUMBER. One value is assigned each time through the loop.

Remember, the variable name TOTAL is just a name: it is a variable name that permits the computer to store and retrieve values. The same results would be obtained if the variable name TWINKLE.TWINKLE were used in place of TOTAL.

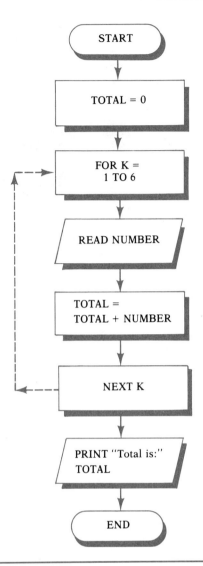

FIGURE 12.8   Flowchart using FOR and NEXT statements to read and total values

```
10 REM READ-DATA inside of FOR-NEXT loop
20 TOTAL = Ø
30 FOR K = 1 TO 6
40     READ NUMBER
50     TOTAL = TOTAL + NUMBER
60 NEXT K
70 PRINT "Total is:" TOTAL
80 DATA 2, 4, 4, 5, 5, 1
90 END
RUN
Total is: 21
Ok
```

FIGURE 12.9   Program using FOR and NEXT statements to read and total values

Do you want to see a potentially nasty quirk? If so, enter the following program. When entering the program, type statement 30 as **30 Y = .10**. Then list and run the program. Of course, since statement 20 assigns X = .1, then X must equal Y. But, unfortunately, not with BASICA.

```
10 REM Retype line 30 as: 30 Y = .10 then RUN
20 X = .1
30 Y = 9.999999E-02
40 IF X < > Y THEN 60
50 PRINT "BASICA is bug-free" : GOTO 70
60 PRINT "BASICA has an annoying bug"
70 END
```

The flowchart shown in Figure 12.10 uses an INPUT statement inside a loop created by FOR and NEXT statements. Values for the variable NUMBER are entered via the keyboard after the program is executed.

As can be seen in Figure 12.11, which is the program accompanying the flowchart, the semicolon in statement **40 PRINT "Type number";**

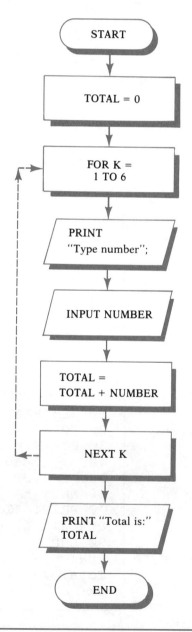

FIGURE 12.10 Flowchart using FOR and NEXT statements to input and total values

```
10 REM INPUT inside of FOR-NEXT loop
20 TOTAL = 0
30 FOR K = 1 TO 6
40     PRINT "Type number";
50     INPUT NUMBER
60     TOTAL = TOTAL + NUMBER
70 NEXT K
80 PRINT "Total is:   " TOTAL
90 END
RUN
Type number? 2
Type number? 4
Type number? 4
Type number? 5
Type number? 5
Type number? 1
Total is:    21
Ok
```

FIGURE 12.11 Program using FOR and NEXT statements to input and total values

stops the line feed so that the data are typed on the same line as the "?" prompt. Values to be totaled are typed, and the Enter key is pressed. After six times through the loop, control passes to the statement following the NEXT statement, and the total is printed.

If a variable is substituted for a beginning or ending number in the FOR statement, the statement will execute according to the value of the variable. For example, the flowchart previously shown in Figure 12.10 using an INPUT statement inside a FOR-NEXT loop has been changed. The revised flowchart is shown in Figure 12.12. The value of the variable NTIMES is used as the upper limit in the FOR statement. As a guide in entering data, the current value of the variable specified in the FOR statement is displayed by the statement `PRINT "Enter data value #" I`.

A program using a variable to vary the number of loops created by the FOR and NEXT statements is shown in Figure 12.13. This type of loop permits any number of items to be totaled. Note how the current value of the variable called I specified in the FOR statement is displayed by using statement 60 as an aid in data entry. This ability of the FOR-NEXT statement to keep track of data is called *indexing* and will be used frequently in the following chapters.

Beginning and ending values can be entered for the FOR-NEXT loop. An example of this is shown in Figure 12.14 where starting and ending values are entered. Symbols are then shown on the screen that are assigned to the ASCII code.

The use of loops within loops is called *nesting*. An example of nested FOR-NEXT loops is shown in Figure 12.15. The inside loop, the COLUMN loop, executes four times each time that the ROW loop (the outside loop) is executed.

Indenting within a FOR-NEXT loop, particularly a nested loop, makes the program easier to understand. It also assists in detecting errors.

The logic loops created by the FOR and NEXT statements shown in Figure 12.15 begin with statement `20 FOR ROW = 1 TO 3` and its corresponding statement `70 NEXT ROW`, which signify the range of the loop. Statement 20 alerts the computer that three passes through the loop will be required.

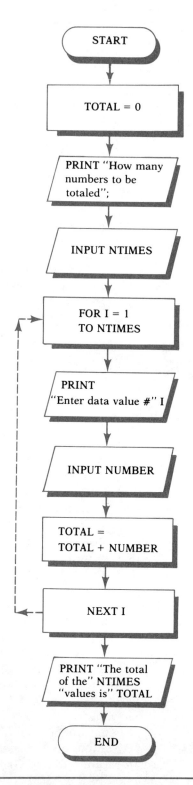

FIGURE 12.12 Varying the FOR-NEXT loop

```
10 REM Varying the FOR-NEXT loops
20 TOTAL = 0
30 PRINT "How many numbers will be totaled";
40 INPUT NTIMES
50 FOR I = 1 TO NTIMES
60     PRINT "Enter value #" I;
70     INPUT NUMBER
80     TOTAL = TOTAL + NUMBER
90 NEXT I
100 PRINT "Total of" NTIMES "values is" TOTAL
110 END
RUN
How many numbers will be totaled? 6
Enter value # 1 ? 2
Enter value # 2 ? 4
Enter value # 3 ? 4
Enter value # 4 ? 5
Enter value # 5 ? 5
Enter value # 6 ? 1
Total of 6 values is 21
Ok
```

FIGURE 12.13   Program to vary the FOR-NEXT loop

```
10 REM Beginning and ending loop values
20 PRINT "Starting value";: INPUT START.VALUE
30 PRINT "Ending value  ";: INPUT END.VALUE
40 FOR I = START.VALUE TO END.VALUE
50     PRINT "Value of" I "Yields symbol of " CHR$(I)
60 NEXT I
70 END
RUN
Starting value? 41
Ending value  ? 45
Value of 41 Yields symbol of )
Value of 42 Yields symbol of *
Value of 43 Yields symbol of +
Value of 44 Yields symbol of ,
Value of 45 Yields symbol of -
Ok
```

FIGURE 12.14   Varying beginning and ending values for the FOR-NEXT loop

```
10 REM Nested FOR-NEXT loops
20 FOR ROW = 1 TO 3
30      FOR COLUMN = 1 TO 4
40           PRINT ROW; COLUMN "     ";
50      NEXT COLUMN
60      PRINT
70 NEXT ROW
80 END
RUN
  1  1      1  2      1  3      1  4
  2  1      2  2      2  3      2  4
  3  1      3  2      3  3      3  4
Ok
```

FIGURE 12.15 Nested FOR-NEXT loops

Notice statements 30, 40, 50, and 60, which have been indented so that the statements within the loop are visually highlighted. Indenting was achieved by pressing the Tab key, ⇄ , after typing the statement number.

Also notice statement **60 PRINT**, which is needed to override the effect of the trailing semicolon in statement 40. The semicolon suppresses the line feed; hence, the printed numbers (1 1, 1 2, 1 3, 1 4, and so on) are displayed next to one another. The PRINT statement is needed so that the next series of numbers will be on a separate line.

When entry is made into the inner loop, statement **30 FOR COLUMN = 1 TO 4** and the corresponding statement **50 NEXT COLUMN**, this inner loop executes four times before the range of the outer loop is reached. In total, the inside loop will execute 12 times. Using FOR and NEXT statements to increment variables such as ROW and COLUMN will be useful in storing and retrieving data from memory.

SUMMARY

Numbers are totaled by the use of an accumulator. An accumulator is a statement with the same variable name on both sides of the equal sign, such as **30 TOTAL.VALUE = TOTAL.VALUE + VALUE**. VALUE is added to TOTAL.VALUE, and this sum is assigned back into TOTAL.VALUE. By using this technique, totals and subtotals can be developed as needed.

There are two tutorials on the companion diskette dealing with repeating operations. These are the FOR-NEXT tutorial and the tutorial on GOTO and Totaling. Select the FOR-NEXT tutorial as shown below. When requested, enter various beginning and ending values for the FOR-NEXT loop and observe what occurs.

```
BASIC Programming With the IBM PC

          FOR-NEXT

              By
          Peter Mears
       (c) Copyright 1990
```

After completing the FOR-NEXT tutorial, select the tutorial on GOTO and Totaling as shown below. This tutorial demonstrates branching and totaling of values. To observe how totals are developed, enter your own values when requested.

```
BASIC Programming With the IBM PC

            TOTALING

                By
            Peter Mears
        (c) Copyright 1990
```

In addition to the tutorials, there are two programs on the companion diskette that are used to demonstrate looping speed. The first of these is called "SPEED.BAS" and is shown below. The second program called "SPEED.EXE" uses the same BASIC code, except that it has been compiled. Run both of these programs, and notice how quickly the compiled version is executed.

```
10 REM Speed test
20 PRINT "Number of loops for speed test";
30 INPUT LOOPS
40 TIME$    = "0"
50 TOTAL    = 0
60 SLOWDOWN = 0
70 TOTAL    = TOTAL + 1
80 SLOWDOWN = TOTAL + 2
90 IF TOTAL < LOOPS THEN 70
100 BEEP
110 PRINT "Completed" TOTAL "loops in " TIME$ " seconds."
120 END
RUN
Number of loop for speed test? 7000
Completed 7000 loops in 00:01:03 seconds.
Ok
```

Summary of terms

Name	Example	Purpose
FOR	10 FOR ROW = 1 TO 5	Executes statements between FOR and NEXT five times.
NEXT	80 NEXT ROW	Shows range of loop and increments value in FOR statement.

PROBLEMS

True/False. Problems 1–6.

12.1   When using the computer as a counter, only the variable name TOTAL may be used. _False_

12.2   FOR-NEXT loops can act as counters. _True_

12.3   An accumulator is a variable in a loop that equals itself plus a quantity (or another variable). *true*

12.4   Every FOR statement must have a corresponding NEXT statement. *true*

12.5   A FOR-NEXT loop may only repeat operations 100 times.

12.6   Nested FOR-NEXT loops are loops within loops. *true*

Debugging Programs. Problems 7–10.
The following miniprograms contain one or more errors. Find and correct the error. Carefully study the corrected program in order to catch all errors that might occur.

*12.7   An attempt was made to print the value of INDEX, which should have been from 1 to 10. The screen appeared as shown.

```
10 FOR INDEX = 1 TO 10
20     PRINT "Value of index is:" ; INDEX
30 NEXT Index
run
NEXT without FOR in 30
Ok
```

12.8   An attempt was made to print the values of ROW and COLUMN in a nested FOR and NEXT loop.

```
10 FOR ROW = 1 TO 3
20 FOR COLUMN = 1 TO 5
30 PRINT ROW, COLUMN
40 NEXT ROW
50 NEXT COLUMN
run
NEXT without FOR in 50
Ok
```

12.9   An attempt was made to print the values of TOP and SIDE as follows:

```
1 1    1 2    1 3
2 1    2 2    2 3
```

The screen appeared as shown.

```
10 FOR TOP = 1 TO 2
20     FOR SIDE = 1 TO 3
30         PRINT TOP; SIDE
40     NEXT SIDE
50 NEXT TOP
run
 1   1
 1   2
 1   3
 2   1
 2   2
 2   3
Ok
```

12.10   An attempt was made to total six DATA statement values. A value of 20 was displayed, not the correct value of 24.

* The answer to this problem is in Appendix E.

```
    S Total = 0
10 FOR LOOP = 1 TO 6
20     TOTAL = TOTAL + VALUE
30     READ VALUE
40 NEXT LOOP
50 PRINT TOTAL
60 DATA 4, 4, 4, 4, 4, 4
run
 20
Ok
```

Program Output. Problems 11–15.
Write the output that would appear when the programs shown are executed.

12.11
```
10 FOR CLASS = 1 TO 3
20     FOR STUDENT = 1 TO 5
30         PRINT CLASS; STUDENT;
40     NEXT STUDENT
50     PRINT
60 NEXT CLASS
```

12.12
```
10 FOR ROW = 1 TO 3
20 PRINT "Row number" ROW
30 NEXT ROW
```

12.13
```
50 FOR NUMBER = 1 TO 4
60 PRINT "Record #" NUMBER
70 NEXT NUMBER
```

12.14
```
30 PRINT "Column #"
40 FOR COLUMN = 1 TO 5
50 PRINT COLUMN " " ;
60 NEXT COLUMN
```

12.15
```
30 SUM = 0
40 FOR I = 1 TO 4
50 READ VALUE
60 SUM = SUM + VALUE
70 NEXT I
80 PRINT "The total is" SUM
90 DATA 4, 1, -2, 3
```

Screen Design Problems. Problems 16–26.
Develop a BASIC program, paying particular attention to the design of the screen and the design of the printed output (when requested). General formats are shown for your consideration; they may be expanded on (improved) in your program.

12.16   A grade analysis program is needed that checks for DATA statement values and computes the number of students (shown as ##) in each grade category. The result of the analysis is then shown in the following format:

```
                Grade Analysis
    Grade         Range         Number of students
      A          90 - 100              ##
      B          80 - 89               ##
      C          70 - 79               ##
      D          60 - 69               ##
      F          Below 60              ##
```

Use the following DATA statement values to check your work:

```
9000 DATA 50, 90, 91, 89, 74, 55, 68, 81, 22, 86
```

12.17   A candidate for the office of city mayor has conducted a pre-election poll of several voters. Each voter polled was assigned a number from 1 to 3 as follows:

1—Will vote for the candidate.
2—Will not vote for the candidate.
3—Undecided.

Develop a program to tally the results of this poll and to display the results in the following format:

```
      Honest John for Mayor
      -------------------------
      For:           6
      Against:       3
      Undecided:     2
      Total:        11
      -------------------------
```

Use the following DATA statement values to check your work:

```
9000 DATA 1, 2, 2, 3, 1, 1, 1, 3, 1, 1, 2
```

12.18   Management at Unified Corporation needs a program to evaluate stock performance. The report must show the name of each stock in their portfolio, the number of shares, purchase price/share, total investment, and profit/loss of each stock. In addition, the report must show a total cost, total value, and total profit/loss for all stocks.

Write a program to generate an output according to the format shown below. Note the box design around the output shown on the screen.

```
                  UNIFIED CORPORATION
                     Stock Report
                        DATE
Stock    Number      Total      Current
Name    of Shares  Investment  Mkt. Value  Profit/Loss
XXXX       XXX     $X,XXX.XX   $X,XXX.XX   $X,XXX.XX
 .          .          .           .           .
 .          .          .           .           .
 .          .          .           .           .
XXXX       XXX     $X,XXX.XX   $X,XXX.XX   $X,XXX.XX
         TOTALS    $X,XXX.XX   $X,XXX.XX   $X,XXX.XX
```

Use the following data in developing the output.

Stock name	Number of shares	Original purchase price/share	Current price/share
Alcoa	40	130.00	138.75
Disney	20	75.00	125.75
Dow Chem	100	38.65	28.65
IBM	80	43.41	42.45
Monsanto	45	83.75	38.70
Texaco	60	62.50	93.47

*12.19 Jim delivers bagels and cream cheese to dorm students. The bagels cost Jim $.30 each. He sells them for $.50 each. Develop a program to keep track of his deliveries. Use the DATA statements listed below to obtain the following output.

```
                        Jim's Bagel Delivery
------------------------------------------------------------------
Customer          Qt.     Selling    Production    Jim's
name              sold    price      cost          profit
------------------------------------------------------------------
Buck Smith         5      $2.50      $1.50         $1.00
Bill Blaze         2      $1.00      $0.60         $0.40
Fred Herman        1      $0.50      $0.30         $0.20
John Johnson       2      $1.00      $0.60         $0.40
------------------------------------------------------------------
Totals:           10      $5.00      $3.00         $2.00
```

```
9000 DATA Buck Smith  ,  5,  Bill Blaze,     2
9010 DATA Fred Herman ,  1,  John Johnson,   2
9020 DATA LAST        ,  0
9030 END
```

12.20 Burkel Company needs a program to produce a mileage report showing the dollar allowance for mileage owed to their salespeople. At the end of each month, the salespeople must turn in their beginning and their ending mileage. If they did not travel during the month, they report the same number for the beginning and ending mileage. Each salesperson receives a $.30 per mile allowance. Develop a program to produce a report, including totals, according to the below format. (Note the use of the double lines for scoring.)

```
                     BURKEL COMPANY
                     MILEAGE REPORT
                       mm/dd/yy
Salesperson     Beginning     Ending      Total      Cash
Name            Mileage       Mileage     Miles      Allowance
================================================================
Sue Jenkins     13,000        13,600       600       $180.00
Bill Holten     XX,XXX        XX,XXX       XXX       $XXX.XX
Ted Snowded     XX,XXX        XX,XXX       XXX       $XXX.XX
Pat Altomore    XX,XXX        XX,XXX      X,XXX      $XXX.XX
================================================================
Total mileage is:      X,XXX
Total allowance is:    $XXX.XX
```

Use the following data in developing the output for the program.

Salesperson	Beginning mileage	Ending mileage
Sue Jenkins	13000	13600
Bill Holten	15600	16100
Ted Snowded	12100	12900
Pat Altomore	15666	16700

12.21 JJ's Liquor Store needs a monthly sales report, containing gross sales, sales tax, city tax, net sales, and totals, for its five major products: bourbon, vodka, Scotch, beer, and wine. The sales tax equals gross sales times

* The answer to this problem is in Appendix E.

10%; city tax equals gross sales times 5%; and net sales equals gross sales minus the sum of sales tax and city tax.

Develop a program to produce the report in the following format, using the data shown:

```
                    JJ's LIQUOR STORE
                   MONTHLY SALES REPORT
                        mm/dd/yy

PRODUCT      GROSS SALES      SALES TAX      CITY TAX      NET SALES
-----------------------------------------------------------------------
Bourbon      $1,200.00        $120.00        $60.00        $1,020.00
Vodka          $750.00         $XX.XX         $XX.XX         $XXX.XX
Scotch         $500.00         $XX.XX         $XX.XX         $XXX.XX
Beer         $1,100.00         $XXX.XX        $XX.XX         $XXX.XX
Wine           $800.00         $XX.XX         $XX.XX         $XXX.XX
-----------------------------------------------------------------------
Totals       $X,XXX.XX        $XXX.XX        $XXX.XX        $X,XXX.XX
```

12.22 Fun Boat cruises to Dynasty Island cost $250 per person. Fun Boat travel agents earn a 15% commission on their Dynasty Island sales. If an agent books more than 10 people on one cruise, he or she earns a bonus of $25 per person on those extra sales. Write a program to display output according to the following format and data:

```
                            Fun Boat
                       Commission Report
                          mm/dd/yy
-------------------------------------------------------------------------------
Sales        Book-    Total                                      Sales plus
People       ings     Sales        Commission      Bonus         Commissions
-------------------------------------------------------------------------------
B. Smith      12      $3000.00     $450.00         $50.00        $3,500.00
T. Hooker     11      $XXXX.XX     $XXX.XX         $XX.XX        $X,XXX.XX
S. Ewing       2       $XXX.XX      $XX.XX          $X.XX          $XXX.XX
S. Yomsuki    10      $XXXX.XX     $XXX.XX          $X.XX        $X,XXX.XX
-------------------------------------------------------------------------------
Total sales plus commissions:                                   $XX,XXX.XX
```

12.23 Develop a BASIC program that prints a banner based on user-supplied phrases. The program is to display the banner on the screen, and then give the user the option of printing the banner.

An example of the banner program is shown. The user entered the data "Go Falcons!", "Go!", and then entered "6" to repeat the short phrase six times. A printed output was requested, consisting of two banners.

Screen:

```
                         Create a Banner Program
------------------------------------------------------------
Type main phrase.  Type s to stop program.
Your phrase ? Go Falcons!

Second short phrase ? Go!
Number of repeats on short phrase ? 6

Go Falcons!
Go!  Go!  Go!  Go!  Go!  Go!
Printed output Y/N ? y
How many banners? 2
```

Printed output: Note the use of the bordering "*" symbol which automatically varies in length, depending on the phrase to be printed.

```
********************************
  Go Falcons!
  Go!   Go!   Go!   Go!   Go!   Go!
********************************

********************************
  Go Falcons!
  Go!   Go!   Go!   Go!   Go!   Go!
********************************
```

The ASCII file on the companion diskette called "PRODUCTS.ASC" will be needed to answer Problems 24 and 25. The format of this ASCII is as shown.

Product I.D.	Description	Cost	Retail Price	Begin Inven.	Qt. Sold	Location Code
XXX	XXXXXXXXXXXXX	$XXX.XX	$XXX.XX	XX	XX	X

12.24 Develop a sales-analysis program that searches the PRODUCTS.ASC file based on user entry of a target quantity sold (call it TARGET.SOLD). If the TARGET.SOLD is within 10% of the QT.SOLD, then display the description of the product, quantity sold, and the retail price. Check your work with a target quantity of 22.

```
     Ajax Sales Analysis Program

     Target quantity? 22
--------------------------------------
Description                Retail    Quantity
of Product                 Price     Sold
--------------------------------------
Pro Fit Exercycle          149.89    22
Pro Fit 110 lb. Wt Set      33.58    20
AFP Brown Rq Bag            17.79    23
--------------------------------------
Number of items found within 10% of 22 :   3
```

The general format of the printed output is shown below.

```
     Ajax Sales Analysis Program
--------------------------------------
Description                Retail    Quantity
of Product                 Price     Sold
--------------------------------------
```

12.25 A price-analysis program is needed that searches the PRODUCTS.ASC file based on a user entry of a target price. If the retail price of the item is within 10% of the target price, the item is displayed. An example of the screen based on a user-entered target price of $100 is shown.

```
                    Price Analysis Program

         Analyzes retail prices within 10% of target price.

         Target price [0 stops search]? 100

         ------------------------------------------------------
         Description                      Retail     Quantity
         of product                       price      sold
         ------------------------------------------------------
         Kwinn 20in boys (Slingray)       $99.08       15
         Kwinn 20in girls #2              $94.99       16
         Kwinn 24in BMX (Duster)          $109.83      18
         Kwinn Exer Bicycle               $109.95      25
         AFP Pro Compet. Tennis Rq        $99.89        1
         Retail price analysis range:  $90.00 to $110.00
         Average price: $102.75
         Highest price: $109.95
```

12.26 Expand the screen shown in Problem 25, so that a printed output can be produced. An example of the printed output based on a user-entered target price of $100 is shown.

```
                  Retail Price Analysis Program
         Price analysis range:  $90.00 to $110.00
         ------------------------------------------------------
         Description                      Retail     Quantity
         of product                       price      sold
         ------------------------------------------------------
         Kwinn 20in boys (Slingray)       $99.08       15
         Kwinn 20in girls #2              $94.99       16
         Kwinn 24in BMX (Duster)          $109.83      18
         Kwinn Exer Bicycle               $109.95      25
         AFP Pro Compet. Tennis Rq        $99.89        1
         ------------------------------------------------------
         Average price: $102.75 based on a sample size of 5
         Highest price: $109.95
         *** Report completed on 12-01-1990 ***
```

12.27 The following flowchart is of a program designed to sharpen your arithmetic skills. Program the flowchart shown on the next page.

Other Problems. Problems 28–35.
Develop a BASIC program to solve each problem. Use a REM statement to identify the problem number, and clearly label all output.

12.28 Change the flowchart in Problem 27 to test for multiplication skills. Then program the revised flowchart.

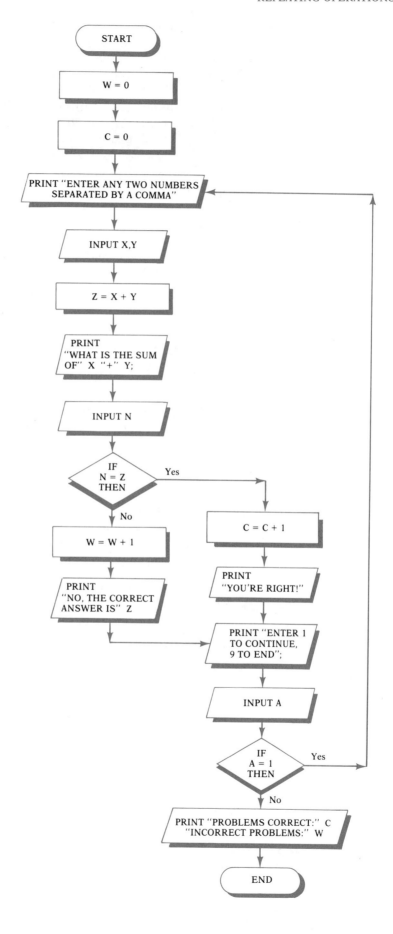

12.29 A program is needed to help grade-school students learn the multiplication tables 2 through 12. After the initial greeting, the computer should request what number they want to practice. Call this number NUMBER. The program should then request the answer to 2 * NUMBER, 3 * NUMBER, up to 12 * NUMBER. Two attempts should be permitted to obtain the correct answer. If the answer is still not correct, then give them the correct answer. After the multiplication table is completed, the students should be allowed to stop or to select another multiplication table.

12.30 The following represents the beginning salaries for musicians with a local orchestra. Develop a program to compute the mean and standard deviation (σ) using the formula shown. Values are to be read from DATA statements.

12470, 14500, 15100, 12800, 13000, 14000, 13500

Xi = Individual salary
AVG = Sum of salaries/Number of salaries in sample (N)

$$\sigma = \sqrt{\frac{\Sigma(Xi - AVG)^2}{N^2}}$$

12.31 Develop a flowchart and a program that prints a receipt for a customer of Sandy's Sporting Goods. Have the program search the ASCII file "PRODUCTS.ASC" for the item(s) each customer buys, subtotal the products' prices, calculate 6% sales tax, and calculate the total amount of the purchase. The receipt should also contain the customer's last name and how the purchase was paid for (cash, check, or credit card).

Check your work by using the following inputs for product identification: 019KW and 055AP. See Problem 24 for a description of the PRODUCTS.ASC file.

12.32 A program is needed that will analyze sales data. The program should be capable of totaling any number of sales that will be entered via the keyboard. Use a value of −999 to signify the end of the data. The following totals should be displayed:

A) Total of all sales
B) Total of small sales (sales under $50.00)
C) Total of large sales (sales over $100.00)

Use values of 24.95, 175, 132, 45, 55, and 200 to check your work.

The DATA statements shown below are used in Problems 33 and 34. The statements contain data obtained from student records consisting of the student name (S.NAME$), the CLASS (1 = freshman; 2 = sophomore; 3 = junior; 4 = senior), and the HOURS of credit completed.

```
9900 DATA John Dunlop   , 2,  40
9910 DATA Susan Smith    , 1,  28
9920 DATA John Jackson   , 2,  55
9930 DATA Pete Mears     , 4, 135
9940 DATA Alice Citizen, 2,  32
9950 DATA Mary Worth     , 2,  56
9960 DATA Susan Citizen, 3,  88
9970 DATA Alfred Neuman, 1,  15
9980 DATA LAST           , 0,   0
```

*12.33 Write a program to display the sophomores (code 2). Develop and display a total of the sophomores. The last DATA statement contains a trailer value of −999 to end the program.

* The answer to this problem is in Appendix E.

12.34 Write a program to display the freshmen (code 1). Develop and display the average of hours of credit these freshmen completed.

12.35 Develop a program to analyze stock earnings per share for the stocks in the ASCII file called "STOCKS.ASC". This file is organized as follows:

Ticker symbol	1989		1990		Last sale	Earnings per share
	High	Low	High	Low		
--	--	--	--	--	--	--

The user is to enter a target earning via the keyboard. If the target earning is within 10% of the earnings per share then:

1. Print the ticker symbol, last sale price, and earnings per share.
2. Calculate the number of stocks (different ticker symbols) within this category.
3. Calculate and print the average sale price for all stocks within the category.

Use a target earning of $4.00 to check your work.

ARRAYS

Upon completion of this chapter you should be able to

- Understand dimension statements and arrays
- Store and retrieve array data
- Prepare meaningful summary reports

As stated earlier, a variable name identifies a memory location for the storage and retrieval of values. If multiple values are retained in memory, then multiple variable names are needed. Instead of continuing the process of using a single variable to contain a single value, it is often more efficient to store values in an array format that permits storage of multiple values under a single variable name.

A single-dimension array can be thought of as a file cabinet arrangement of data in which each file drawer can store a value. Such an array permits orderly storage and retrieval of data. For example, suppose that four sales were made during a day, as follows:

```
SALE1    9.95
SALE2    3.90
SALE3    1.98
SALE4    1.00
```

Each sale could be given a distinct variable name, such as SALE1, SALE2, SALE3, and SALE4. Then direct assignment statements could be used as before to assign the indicated values:

SALE1	SALE2	SALE3	SALE4
9.95	3.90	1.98	1.00

The variable names can then be processed as previously discussed. For example, the following statement would display the value of the first sale (SALE1) and the value of the second sale (SALE2): `20 PRINT SALE1, SALE2`.

Instead of treating these four values as individual, unrelated data elements, the values can be stored in an array format. An array is a grouping of related values under the same variable name.

A dimension (DIM) statement is used to alert the computer that data will be stored in memory in an array format. The statement specifies the array name and the number of storage locations in memory that will be required for the array.

The dimension statement to reserve four locations in memory for an array called SALE is **10 DIM SALE(4)**. This statement contains the following instructions to the computer:

10	**DIM**	**SALE**	**(4)**
Statement number	Reserve storage locations in memory	Variable name of array	Number of storage locations

When a program containing statement 10 is executed, a file cabinet arrangement called SALE, consisting of four file drawers (storage locations), is created. As shown in Figure 13.1, the DIM statement has reserved a file cabinet location in memory consisting of only four storage locations. Other statements will be required to assign values to these storage locations.

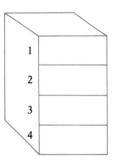

FIGURE 13.1 The array called SALE

The four storage locations in the SALE array are SALE(1), SALE(2), SALE(3), and SALE(4). Each array element location is distinct. That is, SALE(1) means the first storage location in the SALE array, which is completely different from SALE(2), the second storage location. Each array element location is separate and is addressed by a subscripted value.

Subscripted variables are of the form

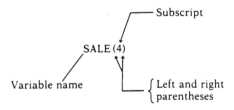

A program to store values in the SALE array is shown in Figure 13.2. Notice that each array element location is specified with a subscripted variable.

Let's take a closer look at the program shown in Figure 13.2. When executed, statement **20 DIM SALE(4)** establishes an array called SALE in memory consisting of four storage locations. Statement **30 READ SALE(1), SALE(2), SALE(3), SALE(4)** assigns values contained in the DATA statement to the specific locations in the SALE array. For example, the first part of statement **30 READ SALE(1)** assigns the first value in the DATA statement, 9.95, to the first location in the SALE array. At this

```
10 REM  Assigning array values
20 DIM  SALE(4)
30 READ SALE(1), SALE(2), SALE(3), SALE(4)
40 PRINT "Values in the SALE array are"
50 PRINT SALE(1), SALE(2), SALE(3), SALE(4)
60 DATA 9.95, 3.90, 1.98, 1.00
70 END
RUN
Values in the SALE array are
 9.95           3.9            1.98            1
Ok
```

Place the DIM statement early in the program, perhaps under the REM statement. This will simplify program modification.

FIGURE 13.2   Assigning values to arrays using READ and DATA statements

beginning point in the program, the following single assignment has been made:

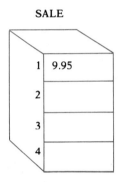

The remainder of statement 30 is executed, assigning values contained in the DATA statements to the remaining array locations. Study the program shown in Figure 13.2 and write the array assignments in the following SALE array:

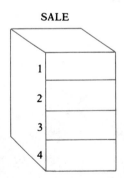

When assignment of values to the SALE array is completed, the array contains the values 9.95, 3.90, 1.98, and 1.00. Did you get the same answers? I hope so; now let's take another look at subscripted variables. When using subscripted variables it is important to remember that the subscripted variable SALE(3) is the value in the third location of the SALE array. The variable SALE3 (no parentheses) is a completely different variable and is not stored or processed in the same way.

For example, assume that the variable SALE3 has been assigned the value of 146.78. The difference between SALE(3), which is the third location in the SALE array, and SALE3, which is a separate variable, is illustrated in Figure 13.3.

The program

```
10   DIM SALE(4)
20   SALE(3) = 1.98
30   SALE3 = 146.78
40   END
RUN
Ok
```

results in the following memory assignments:

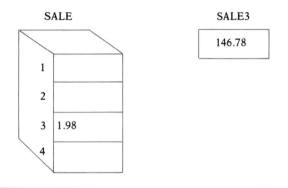

FIGURE 13.3 Location of different values

It is easier to use an INPUT statement if small amounts of data are to be entered after program execution. For example, the program shown in Figure 13.4 can be used to enter four values via the keyboard into an array called SALE. The values are then displayed.

```
10 REM INPUT array values
20 DIM SALE(4)
30 S$ = "$$###.##"                                    ' PRINT USING string
40 PRINT "Enter 1st value";: INPUT SALE(1)            ' User entered values
50 PRINT "Enter 2nd value";: INPUT SALE(2)
60 PRINT "Enter 3rd value";: INPUT SALE(3)
70 PRINT "Enter 4th value";: INPUT SALE(4)
80 PRINT
90 PRINT TAB(10) "Summary of sales"
100 PRINT USING S$; SALE(1), SALE(2), SALE(3), SALE(4)
110 END
RUN
Enter 1st value? 10.25
Enter 2nd value? 8.99
Enter 3rd value? 2.49
Enter 4th value? 17.65

          Summary of sales
   $10.25     $8.99     $2.49    $17.65
Ok
```

FIGURE 13.4 Assigning values to arrays using an INPUT statement

Study the program listing and output shown in Figure 13.4. Using this information as a guide, write the values assigned to the sales array in the space below. The values entered into the array created by the program shown in Figure 13.4 are as follows: 10.25, 8.99, 2.49, and 17.65.

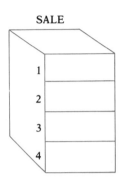

SALE

In Figure 13.5 the DATA statements begin in line 9000. This was accomplished by renumbering a portion of the program with the command:

RENUM New statement number
Old statement number

For example, if the program had lines 130 through 170, these could be changed to the lines shown by the command: **RENUM 9000, 130**. See Chapter 16 for a complete explanation of the RENUM command.

Alphanumeric data (strings) can also be stored in array format. For example, the program shown in Figure 13.5 reads alphanumeric data values into three arrays: E.NAME$ (employee name), HOURS.WORKED, and HOURLY.RATE. Values in the third array location are then displayed.

When the program shown in Figure 13.5 is executed, arrays are established in memory for variables called E.NAME$, HOURS.WORKED, and HOURLY.RATE. Study the program; then complete the array assignments shown in Figure 13.6. Refer to Figure 13.12 to check your work.

The programs used so far to assign values to array locations are useful for only a limited amount of data. It is just too difficult to type each subscripted variable to store and retrieve large quantities of data. A more flexible approach is shown in Figure 13.7, in which FOR-NEXT statements are used to index specific array locations. In this example a summary report displays the employee's name and hours worked.

```
10 REM    Note use of strings
20 '                                      Reserve storage
30 DIM   E.NAME$(4), HOURS.WORKED(4), HOURLY.RATE(4)
40 '                                    Assign values
50 READ E.NAME$(1), HOURS.WORKED(1), HOURLY.RATE(1)
60 READ E.NAME$(2), HOURS.WORKED(2), HOURLY.RATE(2)
70 READ E.NAME$(3), HOURS.WORKED(3), HOURLY.RATE(3)
80 READ E.NAME$(4), HOURS.WORKED(4), HOURLY.RATE(4)
90 '                                   Display values
100 PRINT "The data stored in the third array locations:"
110 PRINT E.NAME$(3), HOURS.WORKED(3), HOURLY.RATE(3)
120 '
9000 DATA "John Citizen"   , 45, 5.75
9010 DATA "Susie Snowflake", 40, 7.25
9020 DATA "Jack Smith"     , 52, 7.10
9030 DATA "Alice Smith"    , 30, 6.50
9040 END
RUN
The data stored in the third array locations:
Jack Smith      52              7.1
Ok
```

FIGURE 13.5 Numeric and alphanumeric arrays

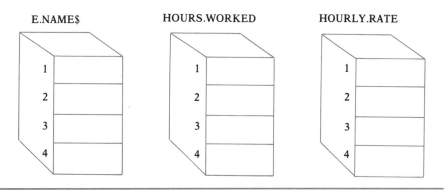

FIGURE 13.6 Array assignments

```
10 REM Note use of FOR-NEXT
20 '                                    Reserve storage
30 DIM E.NAME$(4), H.WORK(4), H.RATE(4)
40 '                                    Assign values
50 FOR I = 1 TO 4
60     READ E.NAME$(I), H.WORK(I), H.RATE(I)
70 NEXT I
80 '                                    Print heading
90 PRINT STRING$(37,"-")
100 PRINT TAB(4) "Summary Report of Hours Worked"
110 PRINT TAB(5) "Name" TAB(25) "Hours"
120 PRINT STRING$(37,"-")
130 '                                   Print data
140 FOR I = 1 TO 4
150     PRINT TAB(5) E.NAME$(I) TAB(25) H.WORK(I)
160 NEXT I
170 PRINT STRING$(37,"-")
180 '
9000 DATA "John Citizen"    , 45, 5.75
9010 DATA "Susie Snowflake", 40, 7.25
9020 DATA "Jack Smith"      , 52, 7.10
9030 DATA "Alice Smith"     , 30, 6.50
9040 END
RUN
-------------------------------------
    Summary Report of Hours Worked
    Name                  Hours
-------------------------------------
    John Citizen          45
    Susie Snowflake       40
    Jack Smith            52
    Alice Smith           30
-------------------------------------
Ok
```

FIGURE 13.7 Using FOR-NEXT to index array locations

PROCESSING ARRAY VARIABLES

Although several programming statements are required to store data in memory using an array, the data, once stored, can be arithmetically processed, used in IF-THEN statements, and displayed with PRINT (including PRINT USING) statements. In fact, array variables are processed the same as other variables, provided the specific subscripted variable is stated.

The program shown in Figure 13.8 processes array variables. In this example, PAY is calculated for a group of four employees. If H.WORK (hours worked) exceeds 40 hours per week, then overtime hours are paid at $1\frac{1}{2}$ times the normal hourly rate. Program output is shown in Figure 13.9.

DEVELOPING SUMMARY REPORTS

The program shown in Figure 13.8 has been saved on the companion diskette as FIG13-8. This can be loaded into memory by the command LOAD "FIG13-8".

The microcomputer provides us with an excellent opportunity to write programs that will produce specialized reports. One way to prepare meaningful summaries is to store data and/or program calculations in arrays for later processing. Then, after the major program activity (such as computing paychecks) has been executed, specialized summary reports can be prepared.

```
10 REM Processing array variables                 FIG13-8
20 '                                              Reserve storage
30 DIM E.NAME$(4), H.WORK(4), H.RATE(4), PAY(4)
40 S$ = "$$###.##"                            ' Print string
50 '                                              Assign values
60 FOR I = 1 TO 4
70     READ E.NAME$(I), H.WORK(I), H.RATE(I)
80 NEXT I
90 '                                              Print heading
100 PRINT STRING$(37,"-")
110 PRINT TAB(12) "Payroll Analysis"
120 PRINT "Employee Name" TAB(31) "Pay"
130 PRINT STRING$(37,"-")
140 '                                             Calculate pay
150 FOR I = 1 TO 4
160     IF H.WORK(I) > 40  THEN PAY(I) = H.RATE(I) * 40 + 1.5 * H.RATE(I) *
          (H.WORK(I) - 40) ELSE PAY(I) = H.WORK(I) * H.RATE(I)
170     PRINT E.NAME$(I) TAB(30);
180     PRINT USING S$; PAY(I)
190 NEXT I
200 PRINT STRING$(37,"-")
210 '
9000 DATA "John Citizen"    , 45, 5.75
9010 DATA "Susie Snowflake", 40, 7.25
9020 DATA "Jack Smith"      , 52, 7.10
9030 DATA "Alice Smith"     , 30, 6.50
9040 END
```

FIGURE 13.8 Processing array variables

```
------------------------------------------
              Payroll Analysis
Employee Name                       Pay
------------------------------------------

John Citizen                     $273.13
Susie Snowflake                  $290.00
Jack Smith                       $411.80
Alice Smith                      $195.00
------------------------------------------
```

FIGURE 13.9   Processing array variables—program output

The program shown in Figure 13.8 will be used to demonstrate this point. For example, suppose a summary report was needed for people paid more than $275 during a pay period. Since pay is calculated within the program, a summary report can be prepared by saving the calculated values in an array for later processing. Then, after the checks are printed, an IF-THEN statement can be used to identify and print the pay greater than $275.

The program shown in Figure 13.10 uses this technique to store internal calculations. Program output is shown in Figure 13.11.

Summary reports are often called *management by exception*. That is, the reports permit management to save time by just looking at the exception instead of having to review lengthy reports.

```
10 REM Storing program calculations
20 DIM E.NAME$(4), H.WORK(4), H.RATE(4), PAY(4)
30 S$ = "$$###.##"                           ' Print string
40 '                                          Read into arrays
50 FOR I = 1 TO 4
60     READ E.NAME$(I), H.WORK(I), H.RATE(I)
70 NEXT I
80 PRINT STRING$(37,"-")
90 PRINT TAB(12) "Payroll Analysis"
100 PRINT "Employee Name" TAB(31) "Pay"
110 PRINT STRING$(37,"-")
120 '                                         Calculate pay
130 FOR I = 1 TO 4
140     IF H.WORK(I) > 40  THEN PAY(I) = H.RATE(I) * 40 + 1.5 * H.RATE(I) *
            (H.WORK(I) - 40) ELSE PAY(I) = H.WORK(I) * H.RATE(I)
150     PRINT E.NAME$(I) TAB(30);
160     PRINT USING S$; PAY(I)
170 NEXT I
180 PRINT
190 PRINT TAB(5) "Summary of paychecks over $275"
200 PRINT
210 '                                         Summary report
220 FOR I = 1 TO 4
230     IF PAY(I) > 275 THEN PRINT E.NAME$(I) TAB(30);:
            PRINT USING S$; PAY(I)
240 NEXT I
250 PRINT STRING$(37,"-")
260 '
9000 DATA "John Citizen"    , 45, 5.75
9010 DATA "Susie Snowflake", 40, 7.25
9020 DATA "Jack Smith"      , 52, 7.10
9030 DATA "Alice Smith"     , 30, 6.50
9040 END
```

FIGURE 13.10   Summary report based on internal program calculations

```
------------------------------------------
                 Payroll Analysis
       Employee Name                 Pay
------------------------------------------

       John Citizen               $273.13
       Susie Snowflake            $290.00
       Jack Smith                 $411.80
       Alice Smith                $195.00

         Summary of paychecks over $275

       Susie Snowflake            $290.00
       Jack Smith                 $411.80
------------------------------------------
```

You can get tricky with DIM statements. Technically, if an array variable name is used that has not been dimensioned, it can have a subscript up to 10. Also, you can use the 0 location, such as SALE(0); hence the array is always one larger than the declared dimension. These features tend to cause confusion, so their use is not recommended.

FIGURE 13.11 Internal calculations—program output

TOTALING ARRAY VALUES

Totaling can be performed as discussed previously, but caution must be exercised to specify the exact array location used. Assume that the arrays shown in Figure 13.12 exist in memory and contain the indicated assignments. The array HOURS.WORKED will be used to demonstrate how array values can be totaled.

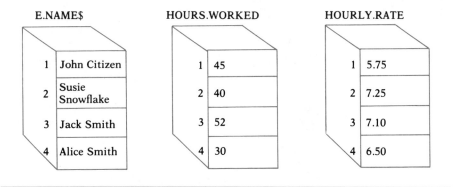

FIGURE 13.12 Assigned array values

The following partial program totals values in the four locations of the HOURS.WORKED array.

```
100 TOTAL = HOURS.WORKED(1) + HOURS.WORKED(2) +
            HOURS.WORKED(3) + HOURS.WORKED(4)
110 PRINT "The total hours worked are" TOTAL
```

The partial program retrieves the value of the HOURS.WORKED array in the first, second, third, and fourth locations, adds them together, and stores the sum in TOTAL. Although this method might appear easy for totaling, it is difficult to type the numerous subscripted variables that would be necessary to total a large array. Besides, this consumes large amounts of memory, and the computer's memory may not be big enough if a large array is to be totaled.

A more efficient means of totaling is to use a FOR-NEXT loop to index the array locations and then store the values in an accumulator. This can be accomplished as follows:

```
100 TOTAL = 0
110 FOR I = 1 TO 4
120     TOTAL = TOTAL + HOURS.WORKED(I)
130 NEXT I
140 PRINT "The total hours worked are" TOTAL
```

Let's carefully evaluate the statements in this partial program. Statement `100 TOTAL = 0` establishes a variable in memory called TOTAL and assigns it the value of 0. Statement `110 FOR I = 1 TO 4` assigns the value 1 to I and stores it in memory. At this point, variables TOTAL and I have the following memory assignments:

TOTAL   I

| 0 | | 1 |

Statement `120 TOTAL = TOTAL + HOURS.WORKED(I)` retrieves the value of HOURS.WORKED(1), which is 45 (see the HOURS.WORKED array in Figure 13.12). This is added to the value of TOTAL (which is 0), and the sum of 45 is stored back into TOTAL. Statement `130 NEXT I` increments the value of I. The following assignments now exist in memory:

TOTAL   I

| 45 | | 2 |

Statement 120 then retrieves the value of HOURS.WORKED(2), which is 40, and adds it to TOTAL (45). The sum of 85 is stored back into TOTAL. Statement `130 NEXT I` increments the value of I. The following assignments now exist in memory:

TOTAL   I

| 85 | | 3 |

Statement 120 then retrieves the value of HOURS.WORKED(3), which is 52, and adds it to TOTAL (85). The sum of 137 is stored back into TOTAL. Statement `130 NEXT I` increments the value of I. The following assignments now exist in memory:

TOTAL   I

| 137 | | 4 |

Finally, statement 120 retrieves the value of HOURS.WORKED(4), which is 30, adds it to TOTAL (137), and stores the final sum of 167 in TOTAL. This sum is then displayed in statement 140. Notice how totals greatly increase the usefulness of a report.

SUMMARY

An array is an orderly arrangement of data in memory under a single variable name. An array can be thought of as a file cabinet in which each cabinet drawer stores a value for later use.

Summary of terms

Name	Example	Purpose
DIM	10 DIM HOURS(20)	Reserves storage in memory for 20 numeric values
	10 DIM EMP.NAME$(20)	Reserves storage in memory for 20 string values

Dimension statements are used to reserve memory storage and to alert the computer that an array is going to be used. If the computer's memory size is large enough, thousands of values may be stored in array format. Array values are processed the same way as other variables, but the specific array location must be stated whenever the variable is used.

The storage of data in memory for subsequent processing is an important concept. There are three tutorials on the companion diskette dealing with this topic. These are the tutorials on arrays, sorting, and tables.

Select the tutorial on arrays as shown below. This tutorial will assist you in developing an understanding of how data is stored and can be accessed. Attention will next be directed to techniques for sorting array data.

```
BASIC Programming With the IBM PC

        Arrays

           By
       Peter Mears
   (c) Copyright 1990
```

PROBLEMS

True/False (Problems 1–6)

13.1 An array can be used to store different values under the same variable name. _true_

13.2 The DIM statement reserves memory space for an array. _true_

13.3 Values cannot be assigned to arrays using an INPUT statement. _false_

13.4 Numeric data may not be used in a string array. _False_

13.5 Data may be assigned to an array using a READ statement within a FOR-NEXT loop. _true_

13.6 DIMension statements are usually placed at the end of a program. _False_

Debugging Programs. Problems 7–11.
The following miniprograms contain one or more errors. Find and correct the error. Carefully study the corrected program in order to catch all errors that might occur.

13.7 An attempt was made to read five values into the SALE array and then print the array.

```
10 DIM SALE(4)
20 FOR I = 1 TO 5
30     READ SALE(I)
40 NEXT I
50 FOR I = 1 TO 5
60     PRINT SALE(I)
70 NEXT I
80 DATA 10, -2.25, -45, 34, 76
run
Subscript out of range in 30
Ok
```

*13.8 An attempt was made to read values into the CLOTHES$, PRICE, and QUANTITY arrays; then if the quantity was greater than 4, print the CLOTHES$ and QUANTITY. The screen appeared as shown.

```
10 DIM CLOTHES$(4), PRICE(4), QUANTITY(4)
20 FOR I = 1 TO 4
30     IF QUANTITY(I) > 4 THEN PRINT CLOTHES$(1), QUANTITY(1)
40 NEXT I
50 DATA "Shirt", 24.95, 5          25 Read clothes$(4) price(4) Quantity
60 DATA "Blouse", 14.95, 2
70 DATA "Socks", 1.95, 28
80 DATA "Pants", 39.95, 7
run
Ok
```

Note: This program contains several bugs.

13.9 An attempt was made to assign values to the SALE and ITEM$ array. The screen appeared as shown.

```
10 DIM SALE(600), ITEM$(600)
20 FOR I = 1 TO 5
30     READ SALE(I), ITEM$(I)
40 NEXT I
50 FOR I = 1 TO 5
60     PRINT SALE(I), ITEM$(I)
70 NEXT I
80 DATA 19.95, 39.95, .49, 6.49, 7.50
90 DATA "Truck", "Doll", "Ball", "Kite", "Paints"
run
Syntax error in 90
Ok
90 DATA "Truck", "Doll", "Ball", "Kite", "Paints"
```

13.10 An attempt was made to assign student names and grades to an array; then if the grade was over 70, print their names and grades. The screen appeared as shown.

* The answer to this problem is in Appendix E.

```
10 DIM NAME$(4), GRADE(4)
         3              3
20 FOR I = 1 TO 4 3
30    READ NAME$(I), GRADE(I)
40 NEXT I
50 FOR I = 1 TO 4 3
60    IF GRADE(I) > 70 THEN PRINT NAME$(I), HOURS(I)
70 NEXT I
80 DATA "Davis", 89
90 DATA "Mears", 67
100 DATA "Raho", 92
run
Syntax error in 10
Ok
10 DIM NAME$(4), GRADE(4)
```

13.11 An attempt was made to assign the employees' names and their hours worked to the indicated arrays; then, for those employees who worked over 40 hours, print their names and hours worked. The screen appeared as shown.

```
10 DIM EMPLOYEE$(4), HOURS(4)
20 FOR I = 1 TO 4
30    READ EMPLOYEE$(I), HOURS(I)
40 NEXT I
50 FOR I = 1 TO 4
60    IF HOUR(I) > 40 THEN PRINT EMPLOYEE$(I), HOURS(I)
70 NEXT I
80 DATA "Thomas", 23
90 DATA "Citizen", 52.2
100 DATA "Smith", 40
110 DATA "Jones", 45.5
run
Ok
```

Program Output. Problems 12–17.

Problems 12–17 use the program shown. Problem 12 requests you to assign the data to the array. This array is then processed by the problems that follow, and you are asked to show the output.

```
10 DIM SCORE(5)
20 FOR I = 1 TO 5
30    READ SCORE(I)
40 NEXT I
50 DATA -12.2, 6789, 1.234, 3, 55
60 END
```

13.12 After the program is run, number the following array and write in the exact array assignments.

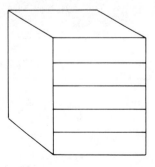

What is the program output when the following statements are added and the program is run?

13.13
```
55 PRINT SCORE(3), SCORE(2)
```

13.14
```
55 AVG = (SCORE(4) + SCORE(5)) / 2
58 PRINT "The average is" AVG
```

*13.15
```
55 ANSWER = SCORE(5) + 3 * SCORE(4) - 10
58 PRINT ANSWER
```

13.16
```
55 SCORES = -76
58 PRINT SCORE(5), SCORES
```

13.17
```
55 FOR K = 1 TO 5
56 PRINT SCORE(K);
58 NEXT K
```

Beginning Programs. Problems 18–27.
Write short BASIC programs to solve the requested problems.

13.18   Write a program to read the following values into an array called NUM-BERS:

```
9000 DATA 121, 476, 12, 374, 19, 28, 17, 18, 311, 42
```

Print the array in the order given. Then print the array in reverse order.

13.19   Develop a program to input N number of sales. Total the sales and calculate the average sale. Then calculate a bonus at 10% on all sales over the average. Print the above average sales and the bonus earned.

13.20   Develop a program to search the following DATA statements based on a user-entered car model. If the model is found, display the model (MODEL$), price (PRICE), and location on the car lot (LOCATION).

```
9000 DATA Camaro,   12500, 3
9010 DATA Celica,   15850, 1
9020 DATA Mustang,  13500, 2
9030 DATA BMW 390,  24000, 2
9040 DATA Maxima,   18500, 1
9050 DATA Audi,     21900, 3
9060 END
```

*13.21   Write a program to read the following product names into an array called PRODUCT$:

```
9000 DATA Chairs, Desks, Ashtrays, Pencils, Erasers,
          Staplers
9010 DATA Typewriter, Paper, Bookend, Calendar, Pad,
          Folders
```

Print the array in the order given. Then print the array in reverse order.

13.22   Write a program to read the following data into arrays COST and PRODUCT$. Then print the arrays in the order given.

```
9000 DATA   7.95, Staplers,    .39, Erasers
9010 DATA 139.95, Chairs,      .79, Pens
9020 DATA 379.95, Desks,      7.95, Staplers
9030 DATA  39.95, Calculators, 259, Monitor
```

13.23   Modify the program in Problem 22 to print the even array values (2nd, 4th, 6th, and 8th locations) by using FOR-NEXT statements.

* The answer to this problem is in Appendix E.

Problems 24 and 25 require that the arrays below be established with the indicated values.

PRODUCT$	QUANTITY	UNIT.PRICE
1 IBM Micro	1 3	1 4260
2 APPLE Micro	2 4	2 2300
3 Matrix Printer	3 6	3 750
4 Letter Printer	4 1	4 2800
5 Display Unit	5 2	5 385
6 Desk	6 2	6 525

13.24 Write a program using a FOR-NEXT loop to read values from DATA statements that will create the arrays shown. After reading all array values, print the arrays.

13.25 Write a program creating arrays called PRODUCT$, QUANTITY, TOTAL.COST and UNIT.PRICE. Assign the data to the appropriate array. TOTAL.COST is calculated by multiplying QUANTITY times UNIT .PRICE. Display the array values in the following format:

Product name	Quantity purchased	Unit price	Total cost
IBM Micro	3	$4,260	$12,780.00
- -	-	-	-
- -	-	-	-
- -	-	-	-
- -	-	-	-
- -	-	-	-

13.26 Write a program to read the following data into QUANTITY, PRICE, and PRODUCT$ arrays. Specify all arrays in a DIM statement.

```
9000    DATA    10,     139.95,     Chairs
9010    DATA    12,     379.95,     Desks
9020    DATA    36,        .79,     Ashtrays
9030    DATA    75,        .39,     Pencils
9040    DATA    50,        .29,     Erasers
9050    DATA   120,       7.95,     Staplers
```

Then calculate a TOTAL.COST array by storing the QUANTITY times the PRICE. After all calculations are performed, print the arrays according to the following format:

Product name	Quantity on hand	Unit price	Total price per product
-	-	-	-
-	-	-	-
-	-	-	-

13.27 Develop a program to enter 6 values via the keyboard into an array called SALE. Calculate the sales tax at 6% of the sale amount, and store the calculations in an array called SALE.TAX. Then calculate and store total sales (TOTAL.SALE) in an array as the sum of the sale plus sales tax.

After all values are entered, print the arrays according to the following format:

Sale	Sales tax	Total sale
-	-	-
-	-	-
-	-	-

Screen Design Problems. Problems 28–34.
Develop a BASIC program, paying particular attention to the design of the screen and the design of the printed output (when requested). General formats are shown for your consideration; they may be expanded on (improved) in your program.

13.28 Honest John's Used Cars needs a price analysis program. Develop a flow-chart and a program to input N number of sales (SALES), not to exceed 100, into the program. Calculate the sales tax (TAX) at 5% and develop the necessary calculations to print the analysis in the form shown below.

```
                    Honest John's Used Cars
                    Price Analysis Program
                          MM/DD/YY

Number of cars in analysis:                        X
Total value of inventory:                   $XX,XXX.XX
Average price of car:                        $X,XXX.XX
Highest priced car:                         $XX,XXX.XX
Total tax to be paid:                        $X,XXX.XX
```

Test your program by entering the following data:
4450, 5688, 7678, 13560, 2450, 3450.

The information below is required in Problems 29–32.

An inventory control system is needed for a college bookstore. Write a program to read the following data into STOCK.NO, PRICE, and BOOK$ arrays. Specify all arrays in a DIM statement. After the data is read into arrays, proceed with developing the program that will answer the problem.

```
8000 DATA 21, 43.95, BASIC Programming
8010 DATA 41, 19.50, The Family and You
8020 DATA 32, 46.50, Statistics is Fun
8030 DATA 12, 18.50, English as a First Language
8040 DATA 14, 19.00, Public Speaking
8050 DATA 55, 45.50, Psychology
8060 DATA 33, 58.50, Chemistry
```

*13.29 Develop a stock-check program that searches the STOCK.NO array based on a user entry of a stock number. If the item is in stock, display the PRICE and BOOK$ according to the general monitor format shown below. If an item is not in stock, display the message "Stock number not found."

* The answer to this problem is in Appendix E.

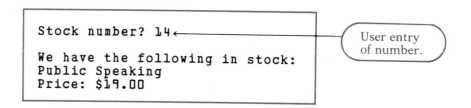

```
Stock number? 14 ◄───────────          ┌──────────────┐
                                        │ User entry   │
We have the following in stock:         │ of number.   │
Public Speaking                         └──────────────┘
Price: $19.00
```

13.30 Expand Problem 29 to include a printed confirmation that can be given to the student when an item is found in stock. A general format is shown below as a guide in designing your printed output.

```
      Tree Top College Bookstore                ┌──────────────┐
            MM/DD/YY ◄──────────────             │ Date entered on │
--------------------------------------          │ system start-up. │
We have the book  XXXXXX in stock.              └──────────────┘
The price of the book is:  $XX.XX.
--------------------------------------
Please place your order immediately.
```

13.31 Tree Top College Bookstore management needs a program to analyze the price of their books in inventory. Develop a program that can search the price array based on user entry of a target price. If a book is found that is within 10% of the target price, print the book's price and title.

Use the format shown as a guide in designing the printed output. If no books are found within 10% of the target price, print "No books in price range."

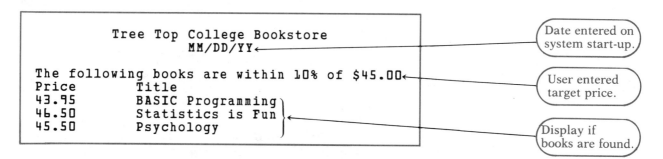

```
         Tree Top College Bookstore              ┌──────────────┐
               MM/DD/YY ◄──────                  │ Date entered on │
                                                 │ system start-up. │
The following books are within 10% of $45.00◄    └──────────────┘
Price         Title                              ┌──────────────┐
43.95         BASIC Programming                  │ User entered   │
46.50         Statistics is Fun                  │ target price.  │
45.50         Psychology                         └──────────────┘
                                                 ┌──────────────┐
                                                 │ Display if     │
                                                 │ books are found. │
                                                 └──────────────┘
```

13.32 Expand Problem 31 to include:
1. A means of looping the program until the user enters a code to end the loop. Note: Print the report only if books are found that are within 10% of the target price.
2. Calculating and printing an average price of the books found that 10% are within the target price range. Note: If books are not found, display "No books in price range," and do not print the report.
3. Have the program print an asterisk (*) next to the price for the highest-priced book for that price range. In the output shown in Problem 31, the asterisk would appear next to the price of $46.50.

Problems 33 and 34 require the data statements shown. Write a program using FOR-NEXT statements to read the DATA statements into arrays called ITEM and PRICE. After the data has been assigned to the arrays, compute the sales tax.

```
9000 DATA "Car wax"      ,  6.95
9010 DATA "Motor oil/case", 22.95
9020 DATA "Antifreeze"   ,  9.95
9030 DATA "Window cleaner",  2.55
9040 DATA "Brake fluid"  ,  5.25
```

*13.33   Develop a program to print the data as shown.

```
        Sales Tax Receipts Program.
     A 5% state sales tax is computed.

     Description        Selling    Sales
     of item            price      tax
     ---------------------------------------
     Car wax              6.95      0.35
     Motor oil/case      22.95      1.15
     Antifreeze           9.95      0.50
     Window cleaner       2.55      0.13
     Brake fluid          5.25      0.26
     ---------------------------------------
     Ok
```

13.34   Develop a sales tax receipts program that will permit the user to simulate receipts at various tax rates. Your program should display the data on a monitor (printed output is not needed) as shown. Note that the user entered a tax rate of 6% (.06), but this program can accept any decimal values.

```
     Sales Tax Receipts Program

     This programs simulates sales tax
     receipts at various tax rates.

     Sales tax is entered in decimal value.
     Enter 0 to end analysis.  What tax rate? .06

Description             Selling             Sales
of item                 price               tax
-----------------------------------------------------
Car wax                   6.95                0.42
Motor oil/case           22.95                1.38
Antifreeze                9.95                0.60
Window cleaner            2.55                0.15
Brake fluid               5.25                0.32
-----------------------------------------------------
Totals                   47.65                2.87

*** End of analysis.  Press any key to continue. ***
```

Other Problems. Problems 35–42.

Develop a BASIC program to solve each problem. Use a REM statement to identify the problem number, and clearly label all output.

The file "SUPPLIES.ASC" will be needed for Problems 35–37.

This file is organized as follows:

Product number	Location code	Quantity	Price	Description

* The answer to this problem is in Appendix E.

*13.35 Develop a program to read the "SUPPLIES.ASC" file into arrays. Then after the file is read, develop a printed report of the data in the arrays according to the format shown below.

Product number	Selling price	Product description
-	$X,XXX.XX	-
-	$X,XXX.XX	-
-	$X,XXX.XX	-

13.36 Modify the program developed in Problem 35 so that a material code can be entered via the keyboard. If the code entered matches the code in the array, display the selling price and product description. If the code entered is not in the array, display: "Code not found."

13.37 Modify the program developed in Problem 35 so that a product description can be entered via the keyboard. Use the first three characters of the entered description to compare with the first three characters of the array values. Display the selling price and full product description if a match is found. If not, display: "Product not found."

Hint: There will be several products matching the entered description. Display all such products.

Two ASCII files will be needed for Problems 38–40. The ASCII file called "STOCKNAM.ASC" is organized as follows:

Ticker symbol	Company name	Business and markets
--	--	--

The second file needed is the ASCII file called "STOCKS.ASC". This file is organized as follows:

Ticker symbol	1989		1990		Last sale	Earnings per share
	High	Low	High	Low		
--	--	--	--	--	--	--

13.38 Using the STOCKS.ASC file, write a program to identify:

1. the ticker symbol of the stock having the highest selling price in 1990
2. the ticker symbol of the stock having the lowest selling price in 1990

An array is not required to solve this problem.

13.39 Develop an information-retrieval system whereby a ticker symbol can be entered and, if it is found, display the company name, business and markets, and earnings per share. Develop this program by reading the STOCKS.ASC file into the appropriate arrays. Then read the STOCK-NAM.ASC file into another grouping of arrays. Then, based on a user-entered ticker symbol, display:

1. the ticker symbol
2. the company name (originally from the STOCKNAM.ASC file)

* The answer to this problem is in Appendix E.

3. the business and markets (originally from the STOCKNAM.ASC file)

4. the earnings per share (originally from the STOCKS.ASC file)

13.40 Develop an information-retrieval system whereby a target value for earnings per share can be entered. If the earnings per share are within 10% of the target, display the company name. Use a value of $4.50 to test your program.

Assume an inventory control has the information below. This will be needed by Problems 41 and 42.

Material code	Part number	Unit price	Quantity on hand
134	123	8.49	26
372	147	32.41	41
196	983	18.95	39
245	4993	2.16	832
871	271	3.26	16

13.41 Develop a flowchart and program using DIM statements to read the above from DATA statements into arrays called MATERIAL, PART, PRICE, and QUANTITY. Develop a flexible inquiry method whereby a search can be made and the information displayed if either the material code or the part number is known.

13.42 Using the inventory control data in Problem 41 write a program to read the data into arrays called MATERIAL, PART, PRICE, and QUANTITY. Have the program identify the highest unit price. Then print the unit price and its corresponding material code, part number, and quantity on hand.

Hint: Identify the array location of the highest-priced item.

14 MULTI-DIMENSION ARRAYS

Upon completion of this chapter you should be able to

- Create a table (a two-dimension array)
- Develop row and column totals
- Perform table searches
- Label a table such as

```
------------------------------------------------------------------------
                        Total Sales by Product by Week
PRODUCTS           Week #1    Week #2    Week #3    Week #4    Totals
------------------------------------------------------------------------
Pencils            $15.00     $20.00     $15.00     $10.00     $60.00
Staples            $48.00     $60.00     $25.00     $20.00    $153.00
Erasers            $10.00     $10.00     $35.00     $30.00     $85.00
Adding machines     $7.00      $5.00     $45.00     $40.00     $97.00
Typewriters        $18.00      $8.00     $55.00     $50.00    $131.00
Computers           $5.00      $5.00     $65.00     $60.00    $135.00
Weekly totals:    $103.00    $108.00    $240.00    $210.00    $661.00
------------------------------------------------------------------------
```

- Create three-dimension arrays
- Create multi-dimension arrays

A business report should be brief and easy to read. This can often be accomplished by displaying data in the row-and-column format of a table. A table organization of data is a natural evolution from the file cabinet arrangement of data already presented.

For example, the partial program shown below reads weekly sales for six products into an array called SALE1. The variable called ROW is used to index each location in the SALE1 array. Think of this single-dimension array as a church with six rows (pews, if you prefer). Data (people) are assigned to each row, beginning with the first row. Study the program and complete the array assignment that would occur when the program is executed.

```
10 REM Example of individual arrays
20 REM Reserve storage for SALE1
30 DIM SALE1(6)
40 FOR ROW = 1 TO 6
50     READ SALE1(ROW)
60 NEXT ROW
70 DATA 15, 48, 10, 7, 18, 5
```

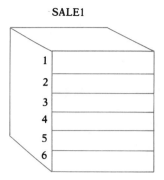

The array assignments from executing this partial program will be shown in a moment. Before leaving this topic, let's complete a few more assignments to develop an understanding of how data is stored in each row of a single-dimension array. Please do not skip over the following partial programs, as we are developing the conceptual framework that will enable us to understand how tables can be constructed.

In addition to the first week's sales figures, the partial program below reads the second week's sales into the array SALE2. Complete the array assignment that would occur when the following partial program is executed.

```
90 REM Reserve storage for SALE2
100 DIM SALE2(6)
110 FOR ROW = 1 TO 6
120     READ SALE2(ROW)
130 NEXT ROW
140 DATA 20, 60, 10, 5, 8, 5
```

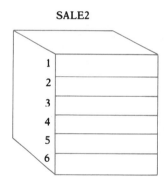

Complete the array assignment that would occur when the following partial program reads the third weekly sales into the SALE3 array.

```
160 REM Reserve storage for SALE3
170 DIM SALE3(6)
180 FOR ROW = 1 TO 6
190     READ SALE3(ROW)
200 NEXT ROW
210 DATA 15, 25, 35, 45, 55, 65
```

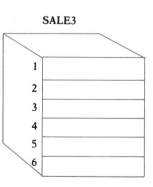

Finally, complete the array assignment that would occur when the following partial program reads the fourth week's sales into the SALE4 array.

```
230 REM Reserve storage for SALE4
240 DIM SALE4(6)
250 FOR ROW = 1 TO 6
260     READ SALE4(ROW)
270 NEXT ROW
280 DATA 10, 20, 30, 40, 50, 60
```

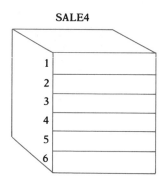

What we have accomplished so far is to create four arrays in memory called SALE1, SALE2, SALE3, and SALE4. Each array contains one dimension of data (rows). Hence, these are called single-dimension arrays. These partial programs have been combined into the single program shown in Figure 14.1. Notice that since this program only assigns data to arrays, no output is produced when the program is executed.

The rows in the various arrays are related to each other in that they contain product sales. All four arrays can be combined to form a table of sales data consisting of weekly sales by product. Because a table contains

```
10 REM Example of individual arrays
20 REM Reserve storage for SALE1
30 DIM SALE1(6)
40 FOR ROW = 1 TO 6
50     READ SALE1(ROW)
60 NEXT ROW
70 DATA 15, 48, 10, 7, 18, 5
80 '
90 REM Reserve storage for SALE2
100 DIM SALE2(6)
110 FOR ROW = 1 TO 6
120     READ SALE2(ROW)
130 NEXT ROW
140 DATA 20, 60, 10, 5, 8, 5
150 '
160 REM Reserve storage for SALE3
170 DIM SALE3(6)
180 FOR ROW = 1 TO 6
190     READ SALE3(ROW)
200 NEXT ROW
210 DATA 15, 25, 35, 45, 55, 65
220 '
230 REM Reserve storage for SALE4
240 DIM SALE4(6)
250 FOR ROW = 1 TO 6
260     READ SALE4(ROW)
270 NEXT ROW
280 DATA 10, 20, 30, 40, 50, 60
290 '
300 END
RUN
Ok
```

FIGURE 14.1 Example of individual arrays.

both rows of data (sales by product) and columns of data (sales by week), tables are processed as a two-dimension array.

The dimension statement needed to reserve storage in memory for an array called SALE consisting of six rows and four columns of data is written as **20 DIM SALE(6,4)**. This is interpreted as follows:

20	DIM	SALE	(6,	4)
Statement number	Reserve memory storage	Array name	Number of rows	Number of columns

Each column in the SALE table can be thought of as a separate one-dimension array. For example, the first column can be described as SALE (all rows, 1) that contains the same data as the SALE1 array. The relationship between the individual sales arrays by weeks and the table called SALE is shown in Figure 14.2.

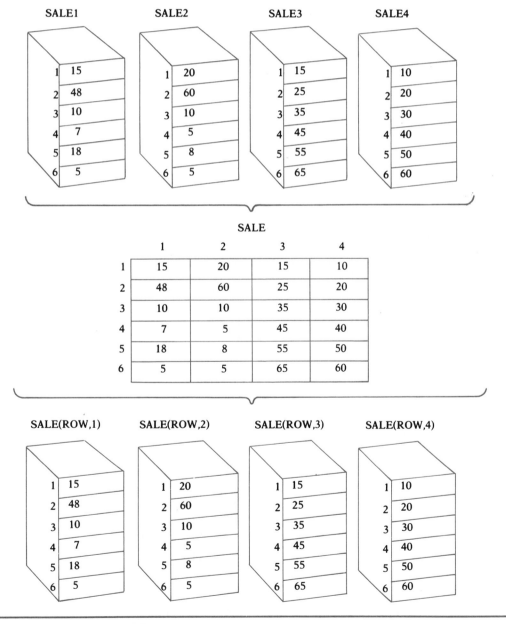

FIGURE 14.2 Constructing a SALE array

The two-dimension sales table shown in Figure 14.2 consists of six rows and four columns of data. The intersection of each row and column is a distinct location and can be identified by a row and column number. An example of the distinct locations in a table (a two-dimension array) is shown in Figure 14.3. Notice how the row values identify the side of the table, while column values identify the four locations across the table.

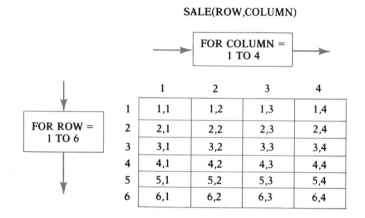

FIGURE 14.3   SALE table array locations

Two methods will be discussed to assign values to the SALE table shown in Figure 14.3. The first method consists of assigning each column (or each week, if you wish) of data before proceeding to the next column. The second method uses nested FOR-NEXT loops to assign array values.

Confused? Please do not be! All this will become clear in a moment. Statements that can be used to assign the data to the SALE array, beginning with the first column are shown below.

```
10 REM Creating a SALE table
20 REM Reserve storage for 6 rows & 4 columns
30 DIM SALE(6,4)
40 REM Assign 1st column
50 COLUMN = 1
60 FOR ROW = 1 TO 6
70    READ SALE(ROW,COLUMN)
80 NEXT ROW
90 DATA 15, 48, 10, 7, 18, 5
```

In this case, COLUMN is held constant at 1 while the values of ROW progress from 1 to 6. Statement **70 READ SALE(ROW,COLUMN)** is executed as follows:

SALE

15			
48			
10			
7			
18			
5			

READ SALE(1,1)
READ SALE(2,1)
READ SALE(3,1)
READ SALE(4,1)
READ SALE(5,1)
READ SALE(6,1)

This results in the array assignment shown above.

The program could be expanded to assign the second column of data to the SALE array. The statements to accomplish this are shown below.

```
110 REM Assign 2nd column
120 COLUMN = 2
130 FOR ROW = 1 TO 6
140      READ SALE(ROW,COLUMN)
150 NEXT ROW
160 DATA 20, 60, 10, 5, 8, 5
```

In this case, COLUMN is held constant at 2 while the values of ROW progress from 1 to 6. Statement `140 READ SALE(ROW,COLUMN)` is executed as follows:

SALE

15	20		
48	60		
10	10		
7	5		
18	8		
5	5		

```
READ SALE(1,2)
READ SALE(2,2)
READ SALE(3,2)
READ SALE(4,2)
READ SALE(5,2)
READ SALE(6,2)
```

Note that both the first and second columns now contain data. The following statements assign the third column of data in the SALE array:

```
180 REM Assign 3rd column
190 COLUMN = 3
200 FOR ROW = 1 TO 6
210      READ SALE(ROW,COLUMN)
220 NEXT ROW
230 DATA 15, 25, 35, 45, 55, 65
```

Then lastly, the following statements assign the fourth column of data in the SALE array:

```
250 REM Assign 4th column
260 COLUMN = 4
270 FOR ROW = 1 TO 6
280      READ SALE(ROW,COLUMN)
290 NEXT ROW
300 DATA 10, 20, 30, 40, 50, 60
```

The partial program statements have been combined into the single program shown in Figure 14.4, creating a SALE table. Notice that data is assigned to the array in memory and, since the program does not contain a PRINT statement, no output is produced. Program execution results in the SALE array containing the data shown in Figure 14.2.

```
10 REM Creating a SALE table
20 REM Reserve storage for 6 rows & 4 columns
30 DIM SALE(6,4)
40 REM Assign 1st column
50 COLUMN = 1
60 FOR ROW = 1 TO 6
70     READ SALE(ROW,COLUMN)
80 NEXT ROW
90 DATA 15, 48, 10, 7, 18, 5
100 '
110 REM Assign 2nd column
120 COLUMN = 2
130 FOR ROW = 1 TO 6
140     READ SALE(ROW,COLUMN)
150 NEXT ROW
160 DATA 20, 60, 10, 5, 8, 5
170 '
180 REM Assign 3rd column
190 COLUMN = 3
200 FOR ROW = 1 TO 6
210     READ SALE(ROW,COLUMN)
220 NEXT ROW
230 DATA 15, 25, 35, 45, 55, 65
240 '
250 REM Assign 4th column
260 COLUMN = 4
270 FOR ROW = 1 TO 6
280     READ SALE(ROW,COLUMN)
290 NEXT ROW
300 DATA 10, 20, 30, 40, 50, 60
310 '
320 END
RUN
Ok
```

FIGURE 14.4 Creating a SALE table

Although the programs shown in Figures 14.1 and 14.4 are similar, there are important differences. The program in Figure 14.4 uses a table format of data (a two-dimension array) to store data in row and column format. Notice that in statement 50 the value of column is 1, while row loops from 1 to 6. Then in statement 120 the value of column is 2, while row loops again. In statement 190 column is 3, while row loops again. Finally, in statement 260 column is 4 and again row loops from 1 to 6.

This is an ideal application for a nested FOR-NEXT loop. The program statements to accomplish this are:

```
50 FOR COLUMN = 1 TO 4
60 FOR ROW = 1 TO 6
70     READ SALE(ROW,COLUMN)
80     NEXT ROW
90 NEXT COLUMN
```

Notice that in this example, the first time through the loop, statement **50 FOR COLUMN = 1 TO 4** assigns the value of 1 to column. Statement **60**

FOR ROW = 1 TO 6 and its corresponding statement **80 NEXT ROW** result in the value of ROW progressing six times for every value of COLUMN. Statement **70 READ SALE(ROW,COLUMN)** is executed as follows:

```
READ SALE(1,1)
READ SALE(2,1)
READ SALE(3,1)
READ SALE(4,1)
READ SALE(5,1)
READ SALE(6,1)
```

That is, the first column of data is read into the SALE array. COLUMN increments to 2, and ROW goes from 1 to 6 resulting in the second column of data being read into the SALE array. This process repeats itself until all data is assigned to the array.

A program using nested FOR-NEXT loops to create a table is shown in Figure 14.5. Notice how the use of nested loops results in the same array assignments with less programming effort. The variable names of ROW and COLUMN are used for ease in interpreting the program. It would have been equally as logical to use variable names of I and J for indexing variables. Whatever is used, it is important to be sure data are entered in a logical and consistent format to minimize errors.

```
10 REM Creating a table with nested loops
20 '                                        Reserve storage
30 DIM SALE(6,4)
40 '                                        Nested loops
50 FOR COLUMN = 1 TO 4
60     FOR ROW = 1 TO 6
70         READ SALE(ROW,COLUMN)
80     NEXT ROW
90 NEXT COLUMN
100 '
9000 DATA 15, 48, 10,  7, 18,  5
9010 DATA 20, 60, 10,  5,  8,  5
9020 DATA 15, 25, 35, 45, 55, 65
9030 DATA 10, 20, 30, 40, 50, 60
9040 DATA
RUN
Ok
```

FIGURE 14.5 Creating a table

When the program shown in Figure 14.5 is executed, the SALE array shown in Figure 14.2 is created. No output is produced when the program is executed because no PRINT statements have been used. The program could be expanded to print the value in the second row, third column by addition of the statement **110 PRINT SALE(2,3)**. This would result in the value of 25 being displayed.

We could get fancy in displaying data by adding the following statements to our program:

```
110 ROW = 2
120 COLUMN = 3
130 PRINT SALE(ROW,COLUMN)
```

This would result in the value of SALE(2,3) being displayed, which again is 25. If desired, array values can be processed, perhaps to obtain a total of the fourth column (week). The statements to accomplish this are:

```
110 TOTAL = SALE(1,4) + SALE(2,4) + SALE(3,4) +
              SALE(4,4) + SALE(5,4) + SALE(6,4)
120 PRINT TOTAL
```

When executed this becomes:

```
110 TOTAL = 10 + 20 + 30 + 40 + 50 + 60
```

Statement 120 displays the value of the variable TOTAL which is 210. (Note: Don't just read about this process. Take a close look at the values stored in the SALE array shown in Figure 14.2.)

The sales data were read in column-by-column (week-by-week) because they were provided in that manner. If the data were provided in a different format, perhaps sales by product, four weeks at a time, then a different method of data entry would be used.

An example of changing the data entry format is shown in Figure 14.6. In this program, ROW is held constant in statement 30 for a particular product, while four COLUMNS of sales are entered. Note that the DATA statements have been rearranged to reflect a row-by-row entry of data. (This program does not produce an output.)

```
10 REM Entering sales row by row
20 '                                     Reserve storage
30 DIM SALE(6,4)
40 '                                     Read in values
50 FOR ROW = 1 TO 6
60     FOR COLUMN = 1 TO 4
70         READ SALE(ROW,COLUMN)
80     NEXT COLUMN
90 NEXT ROW
100 '
9000 DATA 15, 20, 15, 10
9010 DATA 48, 60, 25, 20
9020 DATA 10, 10, 35, 30
9030 DATA  7,  5, 45, 40
9040 DATA 18,  8, 55, 50
9050 DATA  5,  5, 65, 60
9060 END
```

FIGURE 14.6 Row-by-row data entry

It might be convenient to visualize this assignment of array values as similar to filling up rows in a church. The first row which can hold four columns (people), is filled up first. We then progress to the second row, fill it up with four columns of data, and so on.

PROCESSING TABLES

Now that we've mastered the technique of entering data into a table format, attention is directed to displaying the table in a logical, readable format. The program shown in Figure 14.7 reads data row by row into an

```
10 REM Displaying a table
20 '                                    Reserve storage
30 DIM SALE(6,4)
40 S$ = "$$####.##"                   ' Print string
50 '                                    Read in values
60 FOR ROW = 1 TO 6
70     FOR COLUMN = 1 TO 4
80         READ SALE(ROW,COLUMN)
90     NEXT COLUMN
100 NEXT ROW
110 '                                   Print heading
120 PRINT STRING$(40,"-")
130 PRINT TAB(10) "Product Sales Summary"
140 PRINT STRING$(40,"-")
150 '                                   Print data
160 FOR ROW = 1 TO 6
170     FOR COLUMN = 1 TO 4
180         PRINT USING S$; SALE(ROW,COLUMN);
190     NEXT COLUMN
200     PRINT
210 NEXT ROW
220 PRINT STRING$(40,"-")
230 '
9000 DATA 15, 20, 15, 10
9010 DATA 48, 60, 25, 20
9020 DATA 10, 10, 35, 30
9030 DATA  7,  5, 45, 40
9040 DATA 18,  8, 55, 50
9050 DATA  5,  5, 65, 60
9060 END
```

FIGURE 14.7 Program to display a table

array called SALE. A PRINT statement inside a nested FOR-NEXT loop results in the program output shown in Figure 14.8.

Program output shown in Figure 14.8 is virtually meaningless because it raises more questions than it answers. Look at the report title: "Product Sales Summary." What are the products? Why four groups of numbers? This output is not easy to understand and should not be used.

Instead of thinking of the table as six rows by four columns, do you prefer six PRODUCTS by four WEEKS? If so, the loops would become FOR PRODUCTS = 1 TO 6 and FOR WEEKS = 1 TO 4. Have it your way. Change the program, run it, and observe the output.

```
----------------------------------------
              Product Sales Summary
----------------------------------------
     $15.00    $20.00    $15.00    $10.00
     $48.00    $60.00    $25.00    $20.00
     $10.00    $10.00    $35.00    $30.00
      $7.00     $5.00    $45.00    $40.00
     $18.00     $8.00    $55.00    $50.00
      $5.00     $5.00    $65.00    $60.00
----------------------------------------
```

FIGURE 14.8 Program output in table format

```
10 REM Labeling a table
20 '                                          Reserve storage
30 DIM SALE(6,4), PRODUCT$(6)
40 S$ = "$$#####.##"  '                       PRINT USING string
50 '                                          Read products
60 FOR ROW = 1 TO 6
70      READ PRODUCT$(ROW)
80 NEXT ROW
90 '                                          Read in sales
100 FOR ROW = 1 TO 6
110     FOR COLUMN = 1 TO 4
120         READ SALE(ROW,COLUMN)
130     NEXT COLUMN
140 NEXT ROW
150 '                                         Print heading
160 PRINT STRING$(58,"-")
170 PRINT TAB(27) "Sales by Product by Week"
180 PRINT "PRODUCTS" TAB(22) "Week #1" "   Week #2" "   Week #3"
         "   Week #4"
190 PRINT STRING$(58,"-")
200 '                                         Print array
210 FOR ROW = 1 TO 6
220     PRINT PRODUCT$(ROW) TAB(18)
230     FOR COLUMN = 1 TO 4
240         PRINT USING S$; SALE(ROW,COLUMN);
250     NEXT COLUMN
260     PRINT
270 NEXT ROW
280 PRINT STRING$(58,"-")
290 '
9000 DATA "Pencils",          "Staples",      "Erasers"
9010 DATA "Adding machines", "Typewriters", "Computers"
9020 DATA 15, 20, 15, 10
9030 DATA 48, 60, 25, 20
9040 DATA 10, 10, 35, 30
9050 DATA  7,  5, 45, 40
9060 DATA 18,  8, 55, 50
9070 DATA  5,  5, 65, 60
9080 END
```

FIGURE 14.9 Labeling a table

```
------------------------------------------------------------
                         Sales by Product by Week
PRODUCTS               Week #1   Week #2   Week #3   Week #4
------------------------------------------------------------
Pencils                $15.00    $20.00    $15.00    $10.00
Staples                $48.00    $60.00    $25.00    $20.00
Erasers                $10.00    $10.00    $35.00    $30.00
Adding machines         $7.00     $5.00    $45.00    $40.00
Typewriters            $18.00     $8.00    $55.00    $50.00
Computers               $5.00     $5.00    $65.00    $60.00
------------------------------------------------------------
```

FIGURE 14.10 Labeling program output

Program output should be labeled so that the products can be understood and the weeks should be identified. The program listing shown in Figure 14.9 is used to obtain the labeled output shown in Figure 14.10. Notice that product names (PRODUCT$) are read into an array, which is then used to label the output. All that is needed to produce a professional business report is to incorporate row and column totals.

DEVELOPING ROW AND COLUMN TOTALS

Developing row and column totals for a table is similar to totaling a single-column array in that a FOR-NEXT loop is used. For example, suppose we want to develop a total for each product in our previously created SALE array.

A SALE array without assigned values is shown in Figure 14.11. An easy-to-understand way of obtaining a product total is to hold the ROW value constant while incrementing COLUMN totals. Unfortunately, for reasons to be seen in a moment, this method results in lengthy programs because the same statements will have to be repeated several times.

SALE(6,4)

FOR COLUMN = 1 TO 4

	1	2	3	4
ROW = 1 → 1	→	→	→	→
2				
3				
4				
5				
6				

FIGURE 14.11   Totaling the first row in a table

The following program statements total the values in the first row of the SALE array.

```
100 ROW = 1
110 TOTAL1 = 0
120 FOR COLUMN = 1 TO 4
130     TOTAL1 = TOTAL1 + SALE(ROW,COLUMN)
140 NEXT COLUMN
```

After totaling the first row and storing the total in TOTAL1, ROW can be set equal to 2, and a second total, TOTAL2, can be developed. The process could then be repeated for each of the six rows.

Another way of totaling is to store the row totals in an array called TOTAL.ROW. Nested FOR-NEXT loops can be used to develop row totals. Column totals can then be developed by holding COLUMN constant while incrementing the ROW variable. The total is then stored in an array called TOTAL.COLUMN.

A program using this approach is shown in Figure 14.12. Program output is shown in Figure 14.13.

There is a more efficient way of calculating row and column totals than shown in Figure 14.12. Increasing the SALE table from six rows and four columns to seven rows and five columns gives enough room to store

```
10  REM Totaling rows and columns
20  DIM SALE(6,4), PRODUCT$(6), TOTAL.ROW(6), TOTAL.COLUMN(4)
30  S$ = "$$####.##"                              ' Print string
40  '                                             Read in products
50  FOR COLUMN = 1 TO 6
60      READ PRODUCT$(COLUMN)
70  NEXT COLUMN
80  '                                             Read in sales
90  FOR ROW = 1 TO 6
100     FOR COLUMN = 1 TO 4
110         READ SALE(ROW,COLUMN)
120     NEXT COLUMN
130 NEXT ROW
140 '                                             Zero values
150 FOR ROW = 1 TO 6    : TOTAL.ROW(ROW) = 0         : NEXT ROW
160 FOR COLUMN = 1 TO 4 : TOTAL.COLUMN(COLUMN) = 0 : NEXT COLUMN
170 TOTAL.SALE = 0
180 '                                             Totals across
190 FOR ROW = 1 TO 6
200     FOR COLUMN = 1 TO 4
210         TOTAL.ROW(ROW) = TOTAL.ROW(ROW) + SALE(ROW,COLUMN)
220     NEXT COLUMN
230 NEXT ROW
240 '                                             Totals down
250 FOR COLUMN = 1 TO 4
260     FOR ROW = 1 TO 6
270         TOTAL.COLUMN(COLUMN) = TOTAL.COLUMN(COLUMN) +
            SALE(ROW,COLUMN)
280     NEXT ROW
290     TOTAL.SALE = TOTAL.SALE + TOTAL.COLUMN(COLUMN)
300 NEXT COLUMN
310 '                                             Print heading
320 CLS
330 PRINT STRING$(65,"-")
340 PRINT TAB(27) "Total Sales by Product by Week"
350 PRINT "PRODUCTS" TAB(21) "Week #1" " Week #2" " Week #3"
        " Week #4"        " Totals"
360 PRINT STRING$(65,"-")
370 '                                             Print output
380 FOR ROW = 1 TO 6
390     PRINT PRODUCT$(ROW) TAB(18)
400     FOR COLUMN = 1 TO 4
410         PRINT USING S$; SALE(ROW,COLUMN);
420     NEXT COLUMN
430     PRINT " "; : PRINT USING S$; TOTAL.ROW(ROW)
440 NEXT ROW
450 PRINT                                         ' Weekly totals
460 PRINT "Weekly totals:" TAB(18)
470 FOR COLUMN = 1 TO 4
480     PRINT USING S$; TOTAL.COLUMN(COLUMN);
490 NEXT COLUMN
500 PRINT TAB(56)
510 PRINT USING S$; TOTAL.SALE
520 PRINT STRING$(65,"-")
530 '
9000 DATA "Pencils",          "Staples",        "Erasers"
9010 DATA "Adding machines", "Typewriters", "Computers"
9020 DATA 15, 20, 15, 10
9030 DATA 48, 60, 25, 20
9040 DATA 10, 10, 35, 30
9050 DATA  7,  5, 45, 40
9060 DATA 18,  8, 55, 50
9070 DATA  5,  5, 65, 60
9080 END
```

FIGURE 14.12   Totaling table rows and columns

```
------------------------------------------------------------
                   Total Sales by Product by Week
PRODUCTS           Week #1  Week #2  Week #3  Week #4   Totals
------------------------------------------------------------
Pencils            $15.00   $20.00   $15.00   $10.00    $60.00
Staples            $48.00   $60.00   $25.00   $20.00   $153.00
Erasers            $10.00   $10.00   $35.00   $30.00    $85.00
Adding machines     $7.00    $5.00   $45.00   $40.00    $97.00
Typewriters        $18.00    $8.00   $55.00   $50.00   $131.00
Computers           $5.00    $5.00   $65.00   $60.00   $135.00

Weekly totals:    $103.00  $108.00  $240.00  $210.00   $661.00
------------------------------------------------------------
```

FIGURE 14.13   Totaling table rows and columns program output

the totals within the SALE table itself. This simplifies calculations and the table is easier to process.

The overview of this approach is shown in Figure 14.14. Notice that the sale data is still contained in the six-row and four-column format as before. However, storage of the row and column totals increases the overall array size to seven rows and five columns.

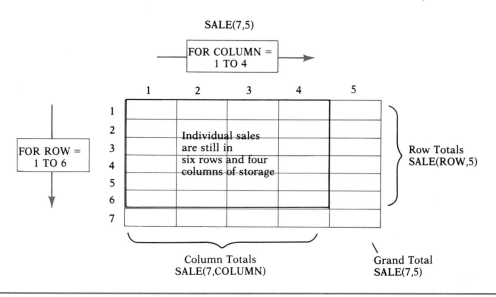

FIGURE 14.14   Table storage of row and column totals

The program shown in Figure 14.15 has been saved on the companion diskette as FIG14-15.BAS. This program can be loaded into memory by the command LOAD"FIG14-15". It will be easy to modify this program to answer many of the questions at the end of this chapter.

The program to store row and column totals is shown in Figure 14.15. The words "Weekly totals:" are included in the PRODUCT$ array to simplify formatting. (See DATA statement 9010.) Also notice how the totals are developed. Statements 180 through 230 are used to develop row totals. That is, for a given value of ROW, COLUMN goes from 1 to 4. Then after a row is totaled, this is added to SALE(7,5) to obtain a grand total in statement 220.

Storing the totals within the array results in a more efficient program. Program output is shown in the introduction to this chapter. The output is easy to read because it appears like a typical business report. Row totals

```
10 REM Storing totals within table
20 DIM SALE(7,5), PRODUCT$(7)
30 S$ = "$$#####.##"                                    ' Print string
40 '                                                    Read in products
50 FOR ROW = 1 TO 7
60     READ PRODUCT$(ROW)                               ' "Weekly totals" 7th
70 NEXT ROW
80 '                                                    Read in sales
90 FOR ROW = 1 TO 6
100     FOR COLUMN = 1 TO 4
110         READ SALE(ROW,COLUMN)
120     NEXT COLUMN
130 NEXT ROW
140 '                                                   Zero values
150 FOR ROW = 1 TO 7     : SALE(ROW,5) = 0    : NEXT ROW
160 FOR COLUMN = 1 TO 4 : SALE(7,COLUMN) = 0 : NEXT COLUMN
170 '                                                   Total across
180 FOR ROW = 1 TO 6
190     FOR COLUMN = 1 TO 4
200         SALE(ROW,5) = SALE(ROW,5) + SALE(ROW,COLUMN)
210     NEXT COLUMN
220     SALE(7,5) = SALE(7,5) + SALE(ROW,5)
230 NEXT ROW
240 '                                                   Total down
250 FOR COLUMN = 1 TO 4
260     FOR ROW = 1 TO 6
270         SALE(7,COLUMN) = SALE(7,COLUMN) + SALE(ROW,COLUMN)
280     NEXT ROW
290 NEXT COLUMN
300 '                                                   Print headings
310 CLS
320 PRINT STRING$(67,"-")
330 PRINT TAB(27) "Total Sales by Product by Week"
340 PRINT "PRODUCTS" TAB(22) "Week #1"    "  Week #2"
        "  Week #3"    "  Week #4"    "  Totals"
350 PRINT STRING$(67,"-")
360 '                                                   Print table
370 FOR ROW = 1 TO 7
380     PRINT PRODUCT$(ROW) TAB(18)
390     FOR COLUMN = 1 TO 5
400         PRINT USING S$; SALE(ROW,COLUMN);
410     NEXT COLUMN : PRINT
420 NEXT ROW
430 PRINT STRING$(67,"-")
440 '
9000 DATA "Pencils",         "Staples",      "Erasers"
9010 DATA "Adding machines", "Typewriters", "Computers",
          "Weekly totals:"
9020 DATA 15, 20, 15, 10
9030 DATA 48, 60, 25, 20
9040 DATA 10, 10, 35, 30
9050 DATA  7,  5, 45, 40
9060 DATA 18,  8, 55, 50
9070 DATA  5,  5, 65, 60
9080 END
```

FIGURE 14.15 Storing row and column totals within SALE table

are printed to the right of their respective rows. Column totals are printed below their respective columns.

The program shown in Figure 14.15 can be modified for a virtually unlimited number of applications. Such reports as sales analysis by units shipped, budget reports by account number, and expense reports can all be developed.

More than 80 columns of output are possible on many printers if a hard copy is desired. Substitute LPRINT for PRINT and experiment to determine the printer's capabilities.

TABLE SEARCHES

After data is entered into a two-dimension array, table searches and lookups can be performed. For example, suppose we were entering daily sales by salesperson into an array of three rows and five columns. This can be shown as follows:

| | **SALES** | | | | |
	Mon	Tue	Wed	Thu	Fri
Susan Smith	120	430	320	80	350
Tom Jones	50	330	110	180	525
Alice Hunt	100	220	650	80	125

An analysis program can be developed to identify average daily sales. An example of a program that utilizes a user-entered target value (called TARGET) to identify average sales is shown in Figure 14.16. Program output is shown in Figure 14.17.

```
10 REM Searching a Table
20 DIM SALE(3,5)
30 CLS
40 '                                          Read in sales
50 FOR ROW = 1 TO 3
60      FOR COLUMN = 1 TO 5
70          READ SALE(ROW,COLUMN)
80      NEXT COLUMN
90 NEXT ROW
100 '                                         User prompt
110 PRINT "Target sale [0 ends]";
120 INPUT TARGET
130 PRINT  '                                  Begin loop
140 WHILE TARGET
150 '                                         Search array
160     FOR ROW = 1 TO 3
170         FOR COLUMN = 1 TO 5
180             IF SALE(ROW,COLUMN) <= TARGET THEN 220
190 '                                         Display values
200             PRINT "There was a sale of" SALE(ROW,COLUMN);
210             PRINT "In ROW" ROW "and COLUMN" COLUMN
220         NEXT COLUMN
230     NEXT ROW
240     PRINT
250     PRINT "Target sale [0 ends]";
260     INPUT TARGET
270     PRINT
280 WEND
290 '
9000 DATA 120, 430, 320,  80, 350
9010 DATA  50, 330, 110, 180, 525
9020 DATA 100, 220, 650,  80, 125
9030 '
9040 PRINT "End of program."
9050 END
```

FIGURE 14.16 Searching a table

```
Target sale [0 ends]? 400

There was a sale of 430 In ROW 1 and COLUMN 2
There was a sale of 525 In ROW 2 and COLUMN 5
There was a sale of 650 In ROW 3 and COLUMN 3

Target sale [0 ends]? 500

There was a sale of 525 In ROW 2 and COLUMN 5
There was a sale of 650 In ROW 3 and COLUMN 3

Target sale [0 ends]? 600

There was a sale of 650 In ROW 3 and COLUMN 3

Target sale [0 ends]? 0

End of program.
Ok
```

FIGURE 14.17 Program output

The output shown is rather crude and primitive in that it does not identify the specific salesperson and day that the sale occurred. An example of a program that both searches a table based on a user-entered value and labels the program output is shown in Figure 14.18. Program output is shown in Figure 14.19.

THREE-DIMENSIONAL ARRAYS

Let's expand our example of the SALE array created by the program previously shown in Figure 14.6. The individual dollar sales for six products for each of four weeks could have been stored in a two-dimension array of the form SALE(6,4).

This array would appear as shown below where each row represents a different product and each column is a different week. The row and column intersection is a weekly sale for a particular product. For example, SALE(2,3) is the sale for the second product (whatever it may be) for the third week.

1,1	1,2	1,3	1,4
2,1	2,2	2,3	2,4
3,1	3,2	3,3	3,4
4,1	4,2	4,3	4,4
5,1	5,2	5,3	5,4
6,1	6,2	6,3	6,4

```
10 REM Searching a table & labeling output
20 DIM SALE(3,5), PEOPLE$(3), DAY$(5)
30 CLS
40 '                                        Read in sales
50 FOR ROW = 1 TO 3
60      FOR COLUMN = 1 TO 5
70           READ SALE(ROW,COLUMN)
80      NEXT COLUMN
90 NEXT ROW
100 '                                       Read in people
110 FOR ROW = 1 TO 3
120      READ PEOPLE$(ROW)
130 NEXT ROW
140 '                                       Read in days
150 FOR COLUMN = 1 TO 5
160      READ DAY$(COLUMN)
170 NEXT COLUMN
180 '                                       User prompt
190 PRINT "Target sale [0 ends]";
200 INPUT TARGET
210 PRINT
220 '                                       Begin loop
230 WHILE TARGET
240     FOR ROW = 1 TO 3                    ' Search array
250         FOR COLUMN = 1 TO 5
260             IF SALE(ROW,COLUMN) <= TARGET THEN 300
270 '                                       Display values
280             PRINT "There was a sale of" SALE(ROW,COLUMN);
290             PRINT "made by " PEOPLE$(ROW) " on " DAY$(COLUMN) "."
300         NEXT COLUMN
310     NEXT ROW
320     PRINT
330     PRINT "Target sale [0 ends]";
340     INPUT TARGET
350     PRINT
360 WEND
370 '
9000 DATA 120, 430, 320,  80, 350
9010 DATA  50, 330, 110, 180, 525
9020 DATA 100, 220, 650,  80, 125
9030 DATA "Susan Smith", "Tom Jones", "Alice Hunt"
9040 DATA "Monday", "Tuesday", "Wednesday", "Thursday", "Friday"
9050 '
9060 PRINT "End of program."
9070 END
```

FIGURE 14.18 Searching a table and labeling program output

Now suppose we wanted to keep track of the sales for each of our three people (A, B, and C) in the sales department. This could be accomplished by establishing (dimensioning) three different arrays. A dimension statement to establish three different two-dimension arrays called SALEA, SALEB, and SALEC is

10 DIM SALEA(6,4), SALEB(6,4), SALEC(6,4)

This reserves the following space in memory:

SALEA(6,4)   SALEB(6,4)   SALEC(6,4)

We could follow this line of logic by creating a nested FOR-NEXT loop for each person, reading values into the array, and proceeding as before. But what if we had several dozen people in our sales department? Obviously a more efficient way to approach the problem is needed.

A three-dimension array is a grouping of several two-dimension arrays. We group the previous arrays into a cube-like arrangement of data, with each person having his or her own row and column values. The first plane of the cube (the outermost rows and columns) contains the data for the first person. The second plane of the cube (the middle) contains the data for the second person, and the third plane contains the data for the third person.

This would appear as follows:

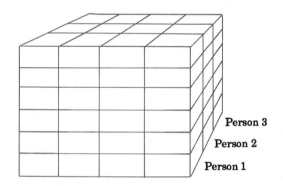

Person 3
Person 2
Person 1

```
Target sale [0 ends]? 400

There was a sale of 430 made by Susan Smith on Tuesday.
There was a sale of 525 made by Tom Jones on Friday.
There was a sale of 650 made by Alice Hunt on Wednesday.

Target sale [0 ends]? 500

There was a sale of 525 made by Tom Jones on Friday.
There was a sale of 650 made by Alice Hunt on Wednesday.

Target sale [0 ends]? 600

There was a sale of 650 made by Alice Hunt on Wednesday.

Target sale [0 ends]? 0

End of program.
```

FIGURE 14.19 Program output

As we discussed previously, each point in an array must have a distinct location which can be stated by a subscripted variable. In our array, the subscripted variable SALE(2,3,1) refers to the sales made by the second person for the third product in the first week. In order to develop a better understanding of how subscripts address a distinct location of a three-dimension array, let's take another look at nested loops.

The program shown in Figure 14.20 uses nested loops to index values for PERSON, ROW, and COLUMN. The process begins by initially setting PERSON equal to 1. Then ROW and COLUMN values are incremented as described previously. That is, for a given value of ROW, the innermost loop called COLUMN progresses the quickest, with values going from 1 through 4. After this loop is satisfied, ROW indexes to the next value, 2, and COLUMN indexes four times.

Data can be assigned to a three-dimension array of the form X(8,5,2) by assignment statements, INPUT statements, or READ/DATA statements. Array location values can be mathematically processed or used in IF-THEN statements as previously discussed. The only difference is that three subscripted variables must be specified to identify a specific array location. Caution must be exercised because the array size can quickly become excessively large. The X array is 8 times 5 times 2, or 80 memory locations, which is not very large. However, an array of size 100 by 100 by

```
10 REM    Nested FOR-NEXT loops
20 FOR PERSON = 1 TO 3
30        PRINT
40        PRINT "Salesperson # " PERSON
50        FOR ROW = 1 TO 3
60             FOR COLUMN = 1 TO 4
70                  PRINT PERSON ROW COLUMN "     ";
80             NEXT COLUMN
90             PRINT
100       NEXT ROW
110 NEXT PERSON
120 END
RUN

Salesperson #  1
  1  1  1      1  1  2      1  1  3      1  1  4
  1  2  1      1  2  2      1  2  3      1  2  4
  1  3  1      1  3  2      1  3  3      1  3  4

Salesperson #  2
  2  1  1      2  1  2      2  1  3      2  1  4
  2  2  1      2  2  2      2  2  3      2  2  4
  2  3  1      2  3  2      2  3  3      2  3  4

Salesperson #  3
  3  1  1      3  1  2      3  1  3      3  1  4
  3  2  1      3  2  2      3  2  3      3  2  4
  3  3  1      3  3  2      3  3  3      3  3  4
Ok
```

If the variables PERSON, ROW, and COLUMN are confusing in Figure 14.20, then try other variable names. For example, do you like the names PERSON, PRODUCT, and WEEK? Then have it your way. Change the program, run it, and observe the output.

FIGURE 14.20 Nested FOR-NEXT loops

100 would require one million memory locations, even if each data item were only one character long. This would far exceed the memory capacity of most microcomputers.

N-DIMENSION ARRAYS

The BASIC interpreter can handle very large, multi-dimension arrays. Assuming that sufficient memory exists, the maximum number of dimensions per array is 255, with up to 32,767 elements in each dimension. However, if you attempt to get fancy by utilizing arrays of greater than three dimensions for data storage, two problems will occur.

First, arrays of greater than three dimensions use up memory at an exceedingly high rate. For example, suppose we wanted to keep track of 50 different product sales for 52 weeks in the year for 40 different salespeople. This could be stored in an array SALE(50,52,40) which has 104,000 storage locations.

Now suppose we also want to keep track of the sales by each of the 50 states. A four-dimension array to accomplish this would be SALE(50,52,40,50). This requires an array of 5,200,000 storage locations, which would exceed the capacity of our micro as well as most large mainframe computers.

Second, arrays of greater than three dimensions often make the data structure too complex. Seemingly complex data requirements may not really require the use of a three-dimension, let alone a four-dimension, array.

For example, suppose we wanted to develop an inventory control program for car dealers that keeps track of 1000 used cars. Also, suppose that the system should be able to access up to 100 different car types, up to 50 different style types, up to 50 different color combinations, and by 100 different dealers. If a five-dimension array were constructed to store this data, 25 billion storage locations would be required (1000*100*50*50*100). As this is not practical, let's look at how the data can be coded to reduce storage requirements.

Car dealers have codes on just about anything you can imagine. Or, if necessary, coding could be developed for

CAR.TYPE	STYLE	COLOR	DEALER

Where:

CAR.TYPE	STYLE
1. FORD - Pinto	1. Four door
2. FORD - LTD	2. Hatchback
3. Corvette	.
.	.
.	.
.	.
100.	50.

COLOR	DEALER
1. Blue	1. Glendale Ford
2. Blue & White	2. Viewdale Pontiac
3. White	3. Downtown Motors
.	.
.	.
.	.
50.	100.

Our data then can be stored in the following four one-dimension arrays of size 1000: CAR.TYPE; STYLE; COLOR; DEALER. The requirement of 4000 memory storage locations is far more manageable.

SUMMARY

Congratulations! You now have the skills to develop meaningful, easy-to-read business reports. Using the companion diskette, select the tutorial on Tables. The screen should appear as shown below. Run this program several times so that you will be able to understand how data is stored and retrieved in a two-dimension array format.

```
BASIC Programming With the IBM PC

              Tables

                By
            Peter Mears
        (c) Copyright 1990
```

Summary of terms

Name	Example	Purpose
DIM	10 DIM SALE(4,5)	Reserves storage in memory for an array of four rows and five columns.
DIM	10 DIM SALE(8,5,2)	Reserves storage in memory for a three-dimension array.

PROBLEMS

True/False. Problems 1–4.

14.1 Tables are actually a two-dimension array.

14.2 A single value in an array may be retrieved without searching the whole array.

14.3 Using nested FOR-NEXT loops to create an array saves program space.

14.4 Either column or row totals may be calculated within FOR-NEXT loops.

Debugging Programs. Problems 5–8.
The following miniprograms contain one or more errors. Find and correct the error. Carefully study the corrected program in order to catch all errors that might occur.

*14.5 An attempt was made to read data into the ITEM$ array. The screen appeared as shown.

```
10 DIM ITEM$(4)
20 FOR ROW = 1 TO 4
30     READ  ITEM$(I)
40     PRINT ITEM$(I)
50 NEXT ROW
60 DATA "Pens-big", "Pencils-lead", "Clips-small, "Paper"
run
Pens-big
Pencils-lead
Syntax error in 60
Ok
60 DATA "Pens-big", "Pencils-lead", "Clips-small, "Paper"
```

14.6 After reading data into the TOOL$ and PRICE array, an attempt was made to display the first two array locations. The wrong data appeared on the screen as shown.

```
10 DIM TOOL$(4), PRICE(4)
20 FOR ROW = 1 TO 4
30     READ TOOL$(I), PRICE(I)
40 NEXT ROW
50 FOR ROW = 1 TO 2
60     PRINT TOOL$(I), PRICE(I)
70 NEXT ROW
80 DATA  "Hammer", 12.95
90 DATA  "Vise" , 34.95
100 DATA "Wrench",  4.95
110 DATA "Pliers",  8.95
run
Pliers          8.95
Pliers          8.95
Ok
```

14.7 An attempt was made to read data into the ITEM$ array. The screen appeared as shown.

```
10 DIM ITEM$(2,3)
20 FOR I = 1 TO 2
30     FOR J = 1 TO 4
40         READ ITEM$(I,J)
50     NEXT J
60 NEXT I
70 DATA "Blouses:", "White", "Red"   , "Blue"
80 DATA "Shirts:" , "Large", "Medium", "Small"
run
Subscript out of range in 40
Ok
```

14.8 An attempt was made to assign data to the ITEM$ and COST array. The screen appeared as shown. Note: This program contains more than one bug.

* The answer to this problem is in Appendix E.

```
10 DIM PRODUCT$(10,10), COST(10,10)
20 FOR I = 1 TO 2
30       FOR J = 1 TO 4
40             READ ITEM$(I,J)
50       NEXT J
60 NEXT I
70 FOR ROW = 1 TO 2
80       FOR COLUMN = 1 TO 3
90             READ COST(ROW,COLUMN)
100       NEXT COLUMN
110 NEXT ROW
120 DATA "White", "Red"   , "Blue"
130 DATA "Large", "Medium", "Small"
140 DATA 29.95 ,  24.95 , 19.95
150 DATA 34.95 ,  22.95 , 18.50
run
Out of DATA in 90
Ok
```

14.9   Identify the output that would occur when the program shown is executed.

```
10 REM Problem 14.9
20 DIM VEHICLE$(5,4)
30 FOR ROW = 1 TO 5
40       FOR COLUMN = 1 TO 4
50             READ VEHICLE$(ROW,COLUMN)
60       NEXT COLUMN
70 NEXT ROW
80 '                              Print in table format
90 PRINT TAB(6) "Honest Al's Pre-Owned Transportation"
100 PRINT "Type", "Year", "Mfg.", "Model"
110 FOR ROW = 1 TO 5
120       FOR COLUMN = 1 TO 4
130             PRINT VEHICLE$(ROW,COLUMN),
140       NEXT COLUMN
150       PRINT
160 NEXT ROW
170 '
180 DATA "Sport"   , "1991", "Chev"       , "Camaro"
190 DATA "Truck"   , "1990", "Ford"       , "Ranger"
200 DATA "Compact", "1990", "Volkswagen", "Scirocco"
210 DATA "Sedan"   , "1990", "Buick"      , "Century"
220 DATA "Camper"  , "1989", "GMC"        , "High Sierra"

run
```

```
Honest Al's Pre-Owned Transportation
```
} Identify
exact
output

Screen Design Problems. Problems 10–26.
Develop a BASIC program, paying particular attention to the design of the screen and the design of the printed output (when requested). General formats are shown for your consideration; they may be expanded on (improved) in your program.

14.10   Write a program to produce the output in the format shown. Note: Use the program shown in Problem 9 as a guide in developing your own program.

	Honest Al's Pre-Owned Transportation			
Type	**Year**	**Mfg.**	**Model**	**Cost**
Sport	1991	Chev	Camaro	$14,495
Truck	1990	Ford	Ranger	$13,000
Compact	1990	Volkswagen	Scirocco	$11,500
Sedan	1990	Buick	Century	$19,500
Camper	1989	GMC	High Sierra	$17,900

14.11 Develop a program to read the following data, calculate the indicated totals, and print the report (including labeling the report). Develop and store the totals within the same two-dimension array that contains the numeric data.

Big Sam, the Used Car Man
Cars Sold: Month ending MM/YY

	Week 1	Week 2	Week 3	Week 4	Total
Small	5	3	2	3	
Medium	3	4	1	5	
Large	7	9	12	10	
Total					

14.12 A candidate for the office of city mayor has conducted a pre-election poll of several voters. Each voter polled was identified as a male (1) or a female (2). Then they were asked if they would vote for our candidate, Honest John. Based on their response, they were assigned a number from 1 to 3 as follows:

1—Will vote for the candidate.
2—Will not vote for the candidate.
3—Undecided.

Develop a program to tally the results of this poll and to display the results in the following format:

Honest John for Mayor

Category	Males	Females	Total
For	XX	XX	XX
Against	XX	XX	XX
Undecided	XX	XX	XX
Total	XX	XX	XX

Use the DATA statements below to check your work. (The first DATA statement is coded for a female who has stated she will not vote for Honest John.)

```
9000 DATA 2, 2
9010 DATA 1, 3
9020 DATA 1, 1
9030 DATA 1, 2
9040 DATA 2, 3
9050 DATA 1, 1
9060 DATA 1, 1
9070 DATA 2, 2
9080 DATA 2, 2
```

14.13 Develop a program to show the distribution of grades in an Introduction to Programming class. The program should read in three test scores and a final exam score. Calculate the letter grade, then total and print the scores in the following format.

Introduction to Programming
Grade Distribution

Grades received	Test No. 1	Test No. 2	Final exam	Totals grades
A	—	—	—	—
B	—	—	—	—
C	—	—	—	—
D	—	—	—	—
F	—	—	—	—
Totals:	—	—	—	—

Grades are calculated as follows:

90–100	A
80–89	B
70–79	C
60–69	D
Below 60	F

The value of −99 ends the grades for each test. Twenty students took the first test, sixteen took the second test, and ten took the third test. Use the following DATA statements to check your work:

```
9000 DATA 78, 82, 90, 65, 87, 55, 38, 66, 93, 82
9010 DATA 67, 85, 86, 77, 80, 77, 61, 64, 78, 91, -99
9020 DATA 55, 83, 78, 50, 74, 89, 95, 99
9030 DATA 84, 88, 72, 78, 90,100, 88, 34, -99
9040 DATA 90, 88, 50, 58, 83, 92, 82, 90, 81, 80, -99
```

14.14 The DATA statements below have been prepared for each package size of "Super Breakfast" cereal. The figures represent weekly shipments of cases to each of four sales regions: New York, Atlanta, Dallas, and Los Angeles.

```
9900 DATA Large, Family, Economy, Giant
9910 DATA 325, 210, 119, 230
9920 DATA 310, 315, 220, 420
9930 DATA 440, 195, 360, 775
9940 DATA 550, 410, 445, 870
```

Develop a sales report according to the format below. Include totals by package size by region and label the report as shown.

Super Breakfast Cereal
Regional Sales Report
December, 1991

Package size	New York	Regions Atlanta	Dallas	L.A.
Large	—	—	—	—
Family	—	—	—	—
Economy	—	—	—	—
Giant	—	—	—	—
TOTALS	—	—	—	—

14.15   The following DATA statements have been prepared for each department of Ajax Hardware Store. The figures represent weekly sales for December. The first DATA statement contains sales figures for the houseware department for the four-week period. The second contains Lumber, the third Appliances, and the fourth the Garden department.

```
9900 DATA   87.20,   976.30,   412.75,   892.00
9910 DATA 1875.75,  1277.99,  1132.50,  1576.80
9920 DATA  650.24,   344.45,   545.50,   450.75
9930 DATA  225.50,   545.00,   445.75,   325.50
```

Develop a program to produce the output in the format shown below. Develop sales totals by department by week and label all output.

Ajax Hardware Store
Sales Report - December, 1991
Sales for Week Ending

Department	12/10	12/17	12/24	12/31	Total
Houseware	—	—	—	—	—
Lumber	—	—	—	—	—
Appliances	—	—	—	—	—
Garden	—	—	—	—	—
TOTALS	—	—	—	—	—

*14.16   The following is a summary of the number of inventory items by size and by type for a store selling fresh produce.

	Melons (crates)	Pears (boxes)	Cashews (pounds)	Corn (boxes)
Small	0	2	2	2
Medium	8	47	4	10
Large	14	52	83	98

The cost per item is as follows:

	Melons (crates)	Pears (boxes)	Cashews (pounds)	Corn (boxes)
Small	4.10	14.00	1.49	11.50
Medium	5.00	18.75	5.95	12.25
Large	8.95	21.50	7.95	13.10

Develop a BASIC program and the necessary DATA statements to read the data into arrays. Then calculate the inventory cost (number of items times cost per item). For example, two boxes of pears at a cost of $14.00 per box is $28.00. Complete the calculations and display the inventory cost analysis according to the format on the following page.

* The answer to this problem is in Appendix E.

Smith's Produce Store
Inventory Cost Analysis

	Melons (crates)	Pears (boxes)	Cashews (pounds)	Corn (boxes)	Totals
Small	—	28.00	—	—	—
Medium	—	—	—	—	—
Large	—	—	—	—	—
Totals	—	—	—	—	—

The following information is needed for Problems 17 and 18.

A sporting goods manufacturer makes foul-weather sailing jackets in the women's and men's product line. Each product line has three types of jackets: Regular, Heavy duty, and Thermal. The selling prices are as follows:

	Regular	Heavy duty	Thermal
Men	89.95	109.95	179.95
Women	69.95	94.50	169.95

The number sold last month was

	Regular	Heavy duty	Thermal
Men	100	76	54
Women	187	130	45

The manufacturing cost for each item is as follows:

	Regular	Heavy duty	Thermal
Men	29.95	54.45	69.70
Women	24.87	45.00	65.00

14.17   Develop a BASIC program to calculate and display total dollar value sold for each type of jacket in the product line. Develop and display subtotals of the dollar value sold by category. For example, Men's Regular = 89.95 × 100, or $8,995.

Sporting Goods Sales Report			
	Regular	Heavy duty	Thermal	Totals
---	---	---	---	---
Men	$8,995.00	$8,356.20	$9,717.30	$27,068.50
Women	$13,080.65	$12,285.00	$7,647.75	$33,013.40
Totals:	$22,075.65	$20,641.20	$17,365.05	$60,081.90

14.18   Compute a contribution-to-profit report that indicates the profitability of each item. This is computed as follows for men's Regular jackets: 100 (number sold) times (89.95 − 29.95) yields a contribution to profit of 100 × 60, or $6,000. This will then appear in the report as shown below. Develop a program to compute and display all figures in the report.

Contribution-to-profit report

	Regular	Heavy duty	Thermal	Totals
Men	$6,000	—	—	—
Women	—	—	—	—
Totals	—	—	—	—

14.19 A manufacturer of bicycles makes men's and women's bikes in three models: Economy, Touring, and Racing. The selling price for each type is

Model Type	Economy	Touring	Racing
28″	69.95	119.95	425.00
30″	79.95	139.95	450.00
32″	99.95	149.95	475.00

The number sold last month was

Model Type	Economy	Touring	Racing
28″	385	240	40
30″	590	100	80
32″	782	120	70

The manufacturing cost for each bicycle is

Model Type	Economy	Touring	Racing
28″	30.00	45.10	135.00
30″	32.50	48.95	165.00
32″	34.95	52.10	185.00

Develop a contribution-to-profit report, including subtotals by model and type of bicycle. (See Problem 18 for a description of preparing such a report.)

14.20 *The ASCII file called "BUDGET.ASC" will be needed for this problem.* This file is organized as shown below. Each DATA statement represents a department. The first statement is for the first department, the second for the second department, and so forth.

Pens	Tape	Staples	Paper	Typewriter
—	—	—	—	—

Read the DATA statements into a two-dimension array called BUDGET. Develop and display budget totals by department and by each of the five major supply accounts.

Use the following names in developing the output shown.

Department number	Department name
1	Production Control
2	Shipping
3	Marketing
4	Accounting
5	Quality Control
6	Engineering
7	Customer Relations
8	Typing Services
9	Personnel
10	Security
11	Plant Engineering
12	Mail Orders
13	Phone Orders

Program output should be in the following format:

	Department	Total supplies
Number	Name	budget
1	Production Control	$X,XXX.XX
—	——	$X,XXX.XX
—	——	$X,XXX.XX

Hint: Assume the file is organized by department. The first line is Department 1, Production Control. The second line is Department 2, Shipping, and so forth.

14.21 A clothing store maintains data on blouses offered for sale. The data is organized according to blouse size (SIZE) and type (TYPE). There are three sizes: small, medium, and large. There are four types: sleeveless, short sleeve, roll up, and long sleeve.

Selling price

	Small	Medium	Large
Sleeveless	9.95	9.95	10.25
Short Sleeve	10.50	10.50	11.75
Roll Up	11.25	11.50	12.95
Long Sleeve	13.25	12.50	15.95

Number of blouses

	Small	Medium	Large
Sleeveless	5	6	7
Short Sleeve	12	10	9
Roll Up	13	11	8
Long Sleeve	3	6	5

Write a program to read the data on selling price and number of units sold. Develop a sales analysis by multiplying the selling price times the units sold (store this product in an array called ANALYSIS). Then calculate the totals as indicated and print the last array in table format, including labels as shown below.

Sales analysis

	Small	Medium	Large	Total
Sleeveless	$49.75			
Short Sleeve				
Roll Up				
Long Sleeve				
Totals				

14.22 A profit analysis is needed by item sold. This requires the following data on cost/blouse:

Cost per blouse

	Small	Medium	Large
Sleeveless	5.50	5.50	5.50
Short Sleeve	5.75	5.75	5.75
Roll Up	6.25	6.25	6.25
Long Sleeve	7.10	7.50	8.25

Write a program to analyze the profit per blouse sold. The profit is calculated for each blouse as follows:

$$PROFIT = Number\ sold * (Price - Cost)$$

Print the profit analysis table, including totals in the format shown below. (See Problem 21 for number sold.)

Profit analysis

	Small	Medium	Large	Total
Sleeveless	$22.50			
Short Sleeve				
Roll Up				
Long Sleeve				
Totals				

14.23 An expense report is constructed according to the following format for the indicated salesperson.

Tom Citizen	MON	TUES	WED	THUR	FRI
Travel	24.62	42.10	00.00	00.00	12.10
Meals	18.90	6.00	00.00	00.00	26.25
Lodging	56.18	79.75	00.00	00.00	69.50
Misc.	2.55	8.12	00.00	00.00	4.30

Pete Smith	MON	TUES	WED	THUR	FRI
Travel	00.00	00.00	87.50	12.00	22.45
Meals	00.00	00.00	22.25	26.00	16.25
Lodging	00.00	00.00	52.30	79.00	89.25
Misc.	00.00	00.00	5.68	4.00	5.50

Read the preceding data from DATA statements, calculate totals, and print a Sales Expense Summary report according to the format below.

—Sales Expense Summary—

	MON	TUES	WED	THUR	FRI	TOTAL
Travel						
Meals						
Lodging						
Misc.						
TOTAL						

The ASCII file called "WAGES.ASC" will be needed for Problems 24–26.

The ASCII file is to be read into two arrays. The first array is a one-dimension array called E.NAMES$. The second array containing hours worked, hourly rate, and age is called ARRAY.DATA.

The "WAGES.ASC" file is organized as follows:

Employee name	Hours worked	Hourly rate	Age
—	—	—	—

14.24 After reading the arrays, print the arrays. Clearly label your printout.

14.25 Assume that the ASCII file was created by the personnel department at Ajax Department Stores. Develop a program to calculate the average hours worked in the time period. Then, for those employees having worked above the average, print out their names and the hours worked. The report should have the following format:

Ajax Department Stores
Personnel Department Analysis
Hours Worked Over Average
MM/DD/YY

Employee name	Hours worked
XX	XX

14.26 Develop a program to calculate the average hourly rate. Then, for those employees having an above-average hourly rate, print out their names and their hourly rate. Follow the general format shown in Problem 25, but change the titles to hourly rate.

Other Problems. Problems 27–35.
Develop a BASIC program to solve each problem. Use a REM statement to identify the problem number, and clearly label all output.

The following data is needed for Problems 27 and 28.

A clothing store keeps the following styles and sizes of short sleeve shirts in stock. Develop a program that enters the data into a two-dimension array from DATA statements. Their initial inventory by size and style is as follows:

	Cotton	Polyester	Blend	Oxford
Small	0	4	3	2
Medium	17	4	26	0
Large	12	19	3	8
X-Large	18	5	2	2

*14.27 Develop a program that shows the inventory on hand for a particular size and type. Clearly label this input and develop a logical means for ending this program in the event that multiple inquiries are made.

14.28 Develop a program that will permit the user to issue an amount from stock and reduce the amount in inventory. Do not permit a below-0 inventory condition to exist.

Problems 29 and 30 require that a two-dimension array be established containing the following data. This is the inventory of a used car lot, "Buy A Heap Cheap." Construct the necessary DATA statements to read the values into an array called CARS.

Number of Cars in Inventory By Week

Weeks	Week #1	Week #2	Week #3	Week #4
Model				
Trans Am	5	4	3	2
Corvette	2	0	7	5
Chev	2	4	8	4

14.29 Develop a small information-retrieval system that permits a search of the inventory based on a user-entered model. That is, the user will enter a model name such as "Trans Am." If the model is found, then print the average number of cars for that model that were in inventory during the four-week period. If the model is not found, print "Model not in inventory." Develop a logical means for stopping the search.

14.30 Develop a small information-retrieval system that calculates and displays the average number of cars in inventory based on a user-entered week. Compute only the average for the week specified. For example, if an average inventory were to be computed for week #1, the user would enter that week, and the average of 3 (5+2+2)/3 would be displayed.

14.31 A clothing store has found that sweaters are a highly profitable inventory item. The store maintains data on the sweaters in inventory by men's and women's styles in four sizes: small, medium, large, and extra large (x-large). There are three different fabrics for each size: cotton, wool, and blends.

* The answer to this problem is in Appendix E.

The sweaters inventory is shown below for each of three colors: tan, black, and brown. A sweater can be either men's or women's in one of four sizes and in one of three different colors.

Sweaters:	**Tan**			
	Small	Medium	Large	X-Large
Men	5	8	13	10
Women	10	13	7	3
Sweaters:	**Black**			
	Small	Medium	Large	X-Large
Men	8	14	12	11
Women	4	11	9	2
Sweaters:	**Brown**			
	Small	Medium	Large	X-Large
Men	0	4	2	6
Women	3	1	1	0

Read the data into a three-dimension array called SWEATER consisting of data stored by sex, size, and color (see below).

SWEATER Array (Sex by Size by Color)

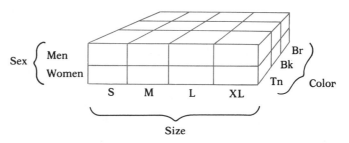

Develop the necessary totals to print a report according to the format shown below.

Sweaters inventory report by color

	Tan	Black	Brown	Totals
Men	XX	XX	XX	XX
Women	XX	XX	X	XX
Total	XX	XX	XX	XXX

Hint: It will be easier to solve this problem if a separate two-dimension array is constructed. This array can hold the various totals obtained from the data elements in the SWEATER array.

Problems 32 and 33 require the following data on five customers with four weekly sales figures.

	Weekly sales			
Customer	**#1**	**#2**	**#3**	**#4**
Susan Smith	12	80	5	90
John Jackson	5	90	30	20
Mary Jones	0	14	0	80
Pat Mears	18	70	40	30
Alfred Neuman	17	50	85	77

14.32 Develop a BASIC program and the necessary DATA statements to read the data into two arrays. The first array, CUSTOMER$, should contain the customer names. The second array, SALES, should contain the sales figures. Display the data as shown, including labeling the table.

Hint: Develop separate DATA statements and a separate array for the names.

14.33 Develop a program to calculate sales totals by week and by customer. Develop and print a grand total.

Problems 34 and 35 require the data below.
Ajax Cannery makes three types of canned peas: Regular, Large, and Giant size. Inventory is maintained on each size that is stored in cases in one of five warehouses. The current inventory, by type, for canned peas, for each warehouse is as follows (all figures in cases):

Type	\multicolumn{5}{c}{Warehouses}
	1	2	3	4	5
Regular	10	12	2	30	11
Large	2	4	5	70	20
Giant	40	60	11	1	90

14.34 Write a program to read the above numeric data into an array called HOUSE. Then develop a total inventory for each type, store the total in the HOUSE array, and display the array, including totals. For example, Regular has a total of 65 cases stored in the warehouses. (Do not worry about labeling the array.)

14.35 Write a program to read the previous numeric data into an array called HOUSE. Then develop a small information-retrieval system. This system should prompt the user to enter the type wanted (1 = Regular, 2 = Large, 3 = Giant) and the warehouse number. Then display the cases in inventory for that type and warehouse.

SORTING

Upon completion of this chapter you should be able to

- Sort sales figures
- Sort names in alphabetic order
- Rank an employee's sales compared to others
- Use the DOS SORT command

Sorting consists of arranging data in either numeric or alphabetic order. This helps to organize reports so that they are easy to read and so the reader can find the necessary information without having to search through the entire report.

Let's develop an understanding of how sorting is accomplished. Assume that the following array, SALE, is in memory. The array contains five values to be sorted from lowest to highest.

SALE

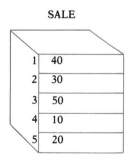

The partial flowchart shown in Figure 15.1 highlights the major aspects found in any sorting procedure. Values are compared, and if the condition is not satisfied, then an exchange of storage locations is made. A switch consists of trading storage locations: in this case, it moves the smaller value upward in the array. Let's go through the process step by step.

The process starts with the creation of a loop by the statement **FOR I = 1 TO 4**, which assigns the value 1 to the variable called I. The number of times through the loop that is created is one less than the array size. Let's use the FOR-NEXT loop to identify how the data in the array is processed.

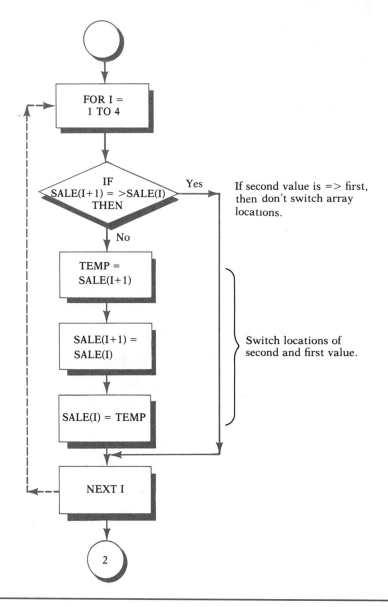

FIGURE 15.1 A beginning sorting procedure

FOR I = 1

During this first pass through the loop, the statement **IF SALE(I+1) =>
SALE(I)** becomes **IF SALE(2) => SALE(1)**. That is, the value stored in
the second array location (30) is being compared to the value stored in the
first array location (40).

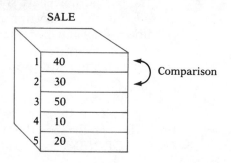

Since 30 is not equal to or greater than 40, control passes to the following statement, and the switching procedure begins. A temporary storage location (called TEMP) is assigned the value contained in the location SALE(2), which is 30. This is necessary so that the current value of 30 is not lost when SALE(2) is reassigned.

SALE(2) is now assigned the value of SALE(1) which is 40. At this point, memory storage locations exist for the SALE array and for the variable TEMP as shown in the next diagram. Note that SALE(1) and SALE(2) contain the same values, because the switching procedure is not yet complete.

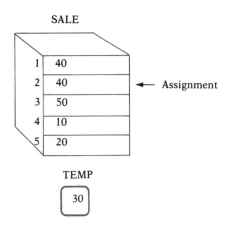

Now for the last statement in the switching procedure: **SALE(1) = TEMP**. This assigns the TEMP value (30) to the first array location. There is now a low-to-high arrangement of the first two locations of the SALE array, as shown in the next diagram. Technically, the TEMP variable still contains a value, but this is of no concern, because it is not used.

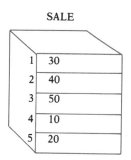

FOR I = 2

The second time through the loop, the statement **IF SALE(I+1) => SALE(I)** becomes **IF SALE(2+1) => SALE(2)**, which is the same as **IF SALE(3) => SALE(2)**. The value stored in the third array location is being compared to the value stored in the second location. Retrieving these values results in **IF 50 > 40 THEN**, which it is, so control passes to the statement **NEXT I**. No switch is made during this pass through the loop.

FOR I = 3

The third time through the loop, the comparison statement becomes **IF SALE(4) => SALE(3)**. This statement is executed as **IF 10 => 50**. Since it is not true, control passes to the following statement and the switching procedure is repeated. TEMP is assigned the value in SALE(4), which is 10; SALE(4) is assigned the value in SALE(3), which is 50; and, finally, SALE(3) is assigned the TEMP value, which is 10. The result is the following reassigned array:

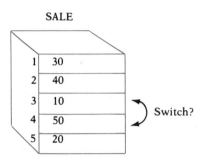

FOR I = 4

The fourth time through the loop, the comparison statement becomes **IF SALE(5)** (which is 20) is **=> SALE(4)** (which is 50), **THEN**. Since it is not true, the switching procedure is repeated, resulting in the following reassigned array:

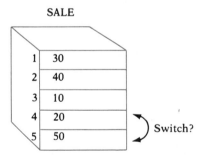

The partial sorting procedure has now been executed. The value of the variable I established in the FOR loop was used to check I+1 locations, but the array is still not in numeric order. Although the lowest value, 10, has moved up one location, the procedure will have to be executed several times before a low value can work its way to the top of the array.

This process by which values work their way to the top gives this procedure its popular name, *bubble sort*. The procedure will have to be repeated, if an exchange is made, so that the final array will be in the desired order. A partial flowchart for accomplishing this is shown in Figure 15.2. If the value of SWITCH is equal to 1, the procedure is repeated until a complete run-through has been made without changing any array positions. When a run-through has been made without any switching occurring, the **SWITCH = 1** statement will not have been executed and SWITCH will still equal 0. Then the test for the value of SWITCH at the

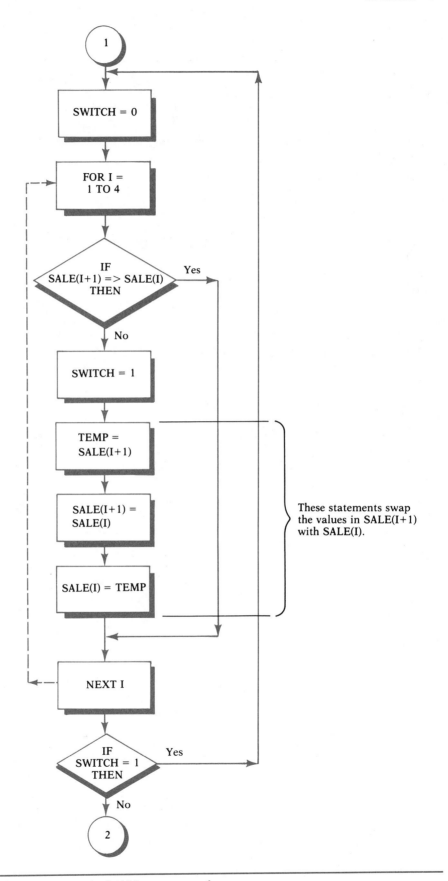

FIGURE 15.2 The bubble sort procedure

bottom of the flowchart will fail, and this portion of the program will be completed.

Strings can be sorted by substituting a string variable name for the previous numeric variable. The program shown in Figure 15.3 reads product names contained in DATA statements into an array. A bubble sort is then used to sort the product names (PRODUCT$) into alphabetic order.

```
10 REM Sorting strings
20 DIM PRODUCT$(5)
30 FOR I = 1 TO 5                          ' Read in products
40     READ PRODUCT$(I)
50 NEXT I
60 DATA Typewriter, Adding Machine, Stapler, Eraser, Pencil
70 '                                              Begin sort
80 SWITCH = 0
90 FOR I = 1 TO 4
100    IF PRODUCT$(I+1) >= PRODUCT$(I) THEN 150
110    SWITCH = 1
120    TEMP$  = PRODUCT$(I+1)
130    PRODUCT$(I+1) = PRODUCT$(I)
140    PRODUCT$(I)   = TEMP$
150 NEXT I
160 IF SWITCH = 1 THEN 80
170 '                                          Sort completed
180 PRINT "The products in alphabetic order are:"
190 FOR I = 1 TO 5                          ' Print products
200     PRINT TAB(10) PRODUCT$(I)
210 NEXT I
220 END
RUN
The products in alphabetic order are:
        Adding Machine
        Eraser
        Pencil
        Stapler
        Typewriter
Ok
```

FIGURE 15.3   Sorting strings

As shown in Figure 15.3, several changes have been made to the previous numeric variables to permit sorting strings. In this case, the array is denoted by a dollar sign and the temporary holding variable (TEMP$) has been changed to a string variable to prevent a type mismatch error from occurring.

Also, if uppercase and lowercase letters are used, each name must begin with an uppercase letter, or else an alphabetic order cannot be obtained. A modification of the sort program is shown in Figure 15.4 to demonstrate the error caused by mixing uppercase and lowercase letters. In this example, *eraser*, which begins with the lowercase letter *e*, appears at the end of the list.

The word *eraser* appears at the end of the sorting list not because of a program bug, but because of the way letters and numbers are processed. Remember: all letters, symbols, and even numbers are converted into

```
6Ø DATA Typewriter, Adding Machine, Stapler, eraser, Pencil
RUN
The products in alphabetic order are:
        Adding Machine
        Pencil
        Stapler
        Typewriter
        eraser
Ok
```

FIGURE 15.4 Sorting uppercase and lowercase letters

There are many different sorting routines. We are just centering attention on two common routines.

ASCII values by the computer. In a comparison, the ASCII value of the letters, and not the actual letters themselves, are sorted.

Capital letters have ASCII values ranging from 65 for *A* to 90 for *Z*. The ASCII values for lowercase letters range from 97 for *a* to 122 for *z*. Hence, a lowercase *a* (97) is larger than an uppercase *Z*. This results in the sorting sequence shown in Figure 15.4. (See the Appendix for complete ASCII codes.)

As can be seen in the modified program shown in Figure 15.5, blank spaces will affect the sorting sequence (statement 180 has also been changed from sorting products to show that names are sorted). The two names Smith, John, and Smith,John, are sorted differently because of the blank space between the names, which are otherwise identical. The entire name—not just the first letter—is automatically evaluated in the sort. The blank space has an ASCII value of 32, which is lower than the value of the letters. Therefore the name with the blank space appears first.

```
6Ø DATA "Smith, John",  "Smith,John",  "Smith",
        "Smith, Marty", "Smith, Mary"
RUN
The products in alphabetic order are:
        Smith
        Smith, John
        Smith, Marty
        Smith, Mary
        Smith,John
Ok
```

FIGURE 15.5 The effect of a blank space when sorting

SORTING MULTIPLE ARRAYS

It is often necessary to sort more than a single array of data. For example, suppose that arrays were created containing data on an employee's sales (SALE), names of the products sold (PRODUCT$), and the employee's name (E.NAME$). Any of these arrays can be selected for sorting but, for purposes of this example, the SALE array will be sorted.

The sorting procedure progresses as explained previously. However, when a value to be switched (swapped) has been identified, the swap is made for those locations in all arrays involved. This can be visualized as follows:

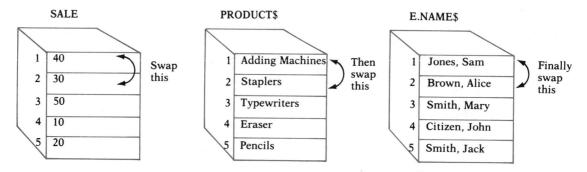

A special statement is provided in IBM BASIC called SWAP, which can be used to exchange the value of one variable for another. The general form of the SWAP statement which will simplify our sorting programs is

Statement
number   **SWAP**   variable1, variable2

The value of one variable can be swapped for the value of another variable as long as both variables are of the same type. That is, strings can be swapped for other strings, and numeric variables can be swapped for other numeric variables.

A program that sorts on the SALE array and then performs multiple swaps is shown in Figure 15.6. The swapping in the SALE, PRODUCT$, and E.NAME$ arrays is performed in statements 190, 200, and 210.

```
10 REM Multiple array sorting
20 DIM SALE(5), PRODUCT$(5), E.NAME$(5)
30 CLS
40 '                                        Read in arrays
50 FOR I = 1 TO 5 : READ SALE (I) : NEXT I
60 DATA 40, 30, 50, 10, 20
70 '
80 FOR I = 1 TO 5 : READ PRODUCT$(I) : NEXT I
90 DATA Adding Machine, Staplers, Typewriters, Erasers, Pencils
100 '
110 FOR I = 1 TO 5 : READ E.NAME$(I) : NEXT I
120 DATA "Jones, Sam", "Brown, Al", "Smith, Mary", "Citizen, John",
        "Smith, Jack"
130 '
140 '                                        Begin sort
150 SWITCH = 0
160 FOR I = 1 TO 4
170     IF SALE(I+1) >= SALE(I) THEN 220
180     SWITCH = 1
190     SWAP SALE(I),      SALE(I+1)
200     SWAP PRODUCT$(I), PRODUCT$(I+1)
210     SWAP E.NAME$(I),   E.NAME$(I+1)
220 NEXT I
230 IF SWITCH = 1 THEN 150
240 '                                        Sort completed
250 PRINT TAB(10) "Sort by dollar amount sold"
260 PRINT "Sale" TAB(10) "Products" TAB(30) "Salesperson"
270 PRINT STRING$(45, "-")
280 FOR I = 1 TO 5
290     PRINT SALE(I) TAB(10) PRODUCT$(I) TAB(30) E.NAME$(I)
300 NEXT I
310 END
```

FIGURE 15.6 Multiple array sorting

Note the difference between the DATA statements on line 90 and line 120 in the program shown in Figure 15.6. The quotation marks are required in line 120 because data elements contain commas. Program output is shown in Figure 15.7.

```
              Sort by dollar amount sold
    Sale      Products              Salesperson
    ------------------------------------------------
    10        Erasers               Citizen, John
    20        Pencils               Smith, Jack
    30        Staplers              Brown, Al
    40        Adding Machine        Jones, Sam
    50        Typewriters           Smith, Mary
```

FIGURE 15.7   Program output

Multiple array sorting using alphabetic (string) data is performed in a similar manner. The program listing shown in Figure 15.8 is a string sort by employee name. Again notice the swapping of storage locations in the SALE, PRODUCT$, and E.NAME$ arrays. Program output is shown in Figure 15.9.

```
10 REM Multiple array sort using a string array
20 DIM SALE(5), PRODUCT$(5), E.NAME$(5) : CLS
30 '                                     Read in arrays
40 FOR I = 1 TO 5 : READ SALE(I)       : NEXT I
50 DATA 40, 30, 50, 10, 20
60 '
70 FOR I = 1 TO 5 : READ PRODUCT$(I) : NEXT I
80 DATA Adding Machines, Staplers, Typewriters, Erasers, Pencils
90 '
100 FOR I = 1 TO 5 : READ E.NAME$(I)   : NEXT I
110 DATA "Jones, Sam","Brown, Al","Smith, Mary","Citizen, John",
          "Smith, Jack"
120 '                                   Begin sort
130 SWITCH = 0
140 FOR I = 1 TO 4
150     IF E.NAME$(I+1) > = E.NAME$(I) THEN 200
160     SWITCH = 1
170     SWAP SALE(I),     SALE(I+1)
180     SWAP PRODUCT$(I), PRODUCT$(I+1)
190     SWAP E.NAME$(I),  E.NAME$(I+1)
200 NEXT I
210 IF SWITCH = 1 THEN 130
220 '                                   Sort completed
230 PRINT TAB(15) "Sort by employee name"
240 PRINT "Employee name" TAB(20) "Product sold"
           TAB(45) "Dollars"
250 PRINT STRING$(50,"-")
260 FOR I = 1 TO 5
270    PRINT E.NAME$(I) TAB(20) PRODUCT$(I) TAB(46) SALE(I)
280 NEXT I
290 END
```

FIGURE 15.8   Multiple array sorting using string data

```
              Sort by employee name
    Employee name          Product sold          Dollars
    --------------------------------------------------------
    Brown, Al              Staplers                 30
    Citizen, John          Erasers                  10
    Jones, Sam             Adding Machines          40
    Smith, Jack            Pencils                  20
    Smith, Mary            Typewriters              50
    Ok
```

FIGURE 15.9 Program output—sorting by name

Do you want to freeze program output for a moment and then automatically continue? Change the loop size below to produce the delay desired:
```
100 FOR I = 1 TO 5000 :
NEXT I
```

RANKING DATA

The output shown in Figure 15.7 is rather short and consists only of the employees' names, products sold, and the dollar sales. Imagine a more elaborate report consisting of 40 or 50 employees' names and a multitude of products. Although the firm's sales are important and have a tremendous impact on profitability, employees are often more concerned with their own individual sales and how they compare with others'.

In other words, although sales reports are important, sales figures by themselves do not tell the whole story. If an employee achieved sales of $10,000 for a month, that might sound good. But if this ranked 40th in a group of 40 employees, you might wonder why this employee was the lowest in the group.

Ranking of key statistics such as sales adds meaning to the data. Rankings are not difficult to program, provided that the four steps in developing a ranking system are understood. The previous SALE and E.NAME$ arrays will be used to demonstrate the steps in ranking data.

Step 1. Enter SALE and E.NAME$ data into an array, resulting in

```
    SALE        E.NAME$
     40         Jones, Sam
     30         Brown, Al
     50         Smith, Mary
     10         Citizen, John
     20         Smith, Jack
```

Step 2. Sort by SALE.SWAP array locations, resulting in

```
    SALE        E.NAME$
     10         Citizen, John
     20         Smith, Jack
     30         Brown, Al
     40         Jones, Sam
     50         Smith, Mary
```

Step 3. Assign a RANK array. Leave other arrays unchanged.

```
    SALE   E.NAME$           RANK              RANK
     10    Citizen, John      1                 5
     20    Smith, Jack        2      Reverse    4
     30    Brown, Al          3      array      3
     40    Jones, Sam         4      order      2
     50    Smith, Mary        5                 1
```

When the RANK array is established, the highest SALE receives ranking 1, the next highest receives 2, and so forth. As SALE is sorted from lowest to highest value, ranking is the reverse of these values.

The program shown in Figure 15.10 has been saved on the companion diskette as FIG15-10. This can be loaded into memory by the command LOAD"FIG 15-10".

Step 4. Sort by E.NAME$. SWAP E.NAME$, SALE, and RANK arrays.

SALE	E.NAME$	RANK
30	Brown, Al	3
10	Citizen, John	5
40	Jones, Sam	2
20	Smith, Jack	4
50	Smith, Mary	1

```
10 REM Ranking sales data
20 DIM SALE(5), E.NAME$(5), RANK(5)
30 CLS '                                    Read arrays
40 FOR I = 1 TO 5 : READ SALE(I)     : NEXT I
50 DATA 40, 30, 50, 10, 20
60 '
70 FOR I = 1 TO 5 : READ E.NAME$(I) : NEXT I
80 DATA "Jones, Sam","Brown, Al","Smith, Mary","Citizen, John",
       "Smith, Jack"
90 '                                        Sales sort
100 SWITCH = 0
110 FOR I = 1 TO 4
120    IF SALE(I+1) >= SALE(I) THEN 160
130    SWITCH = 1
140    SWAP SALE(I),    SALE(I+1)
150    SWAP E.NAME$(I), E.NAME$(I+1)
160 NEXT I
170 IF SWITCH = 1 THEN 100
180 '                                        End sort
190 FOR I = 1 TO 5 : RANK(I) = 6-I : NEXT I '        Ranking
200 PRINT "Sorted by dollar sales:"
210 PRINT "Employee name" TAB(20) "Sales" TAB(36) "Ranking"
220 PRINT
230 FOR I = 1 TO 5
240    PRINT E.NAME$(I) TAB(20) SALE(I) TAB(36) "#" RANK(I)
250 NEXT I
260 '                                        Names sort
270 SWITCH = 0
280 FOR I = 1 TO 4
290    IF E.NAME$(I+1) >= E.NAME$(I) THEN 340
300    SWITCH= 1
310    SWAP SALE(I),    SALE(I+1)
320    SWAP RANK(I),    RANK(I+1)
330    SWAP E.NAME$(I), E.NAME$(I+1)
340 NEXT I
350 IF SWITCH = 1 THEN 270
360 '                                        End sort
370 PRINT : PRINT "Sort by employee name:"
380 PRINT "Employee name" TAB(20) "Sales" TAB(35) "Ranking"
390 PRINT
400 FOR I = 1 TO 5
410    PRINT E.NAME$(I) TAB(20) SALE(I) TAB(36) "#" RANK(I)
420 NEXT I
430 END
```

FIGURE 15.10 Program listing to rank sales data

A listing of a program that ranks sales by employee is shown in Figure 15.10. Program output is shown in Figure 15.11. Sales are first sorted from lowest to highest amounts. The rankings are shown in the upper half of Figure 15.11 as a guide to understanding the program. (Such rankings have little meaning and should be removed from commercial applications.)

The output shown in the lower half of Figure 15.11 is a sort by employee name, complete with each ranking. If your name was in this group, you would probably study the rankings very carefully.

```
Sorted by dollar sales:
Employee name          Sales              Ranking

Citizen, John          10                 # 5
Smith, Jack            20                 # 4
Brown, Al              30                 # 3
Jones, Sam             40                 # 2
Smith, Mary            50                 # 1

Sort by employee name:
Employee name          Sales              Ranking

Brown, Al              30                 # 3
Citizen, John          10                 # 5
Jones, Sam             40                 # 2
Smith, Jack            20                 # 4
Smith, Mary            50                 # 1
```

FIGURE 15.11   Program output

THE SHELL SORT

When executing the programs in this chapter, did you notice that the computer pauses for a moment before displaying output? This is because the bubble sort we've been using requires a lot of data to be manipulated for even the small applications used in the examples.

It takes about two minutes to sort, rank, and display 45 employee names, along with their sales. This is not an unreasonable delay, but a large sort of several thousand items would require hours if the bubble sort were used. Fortunately, there is a faster sort routine called the Shell sort.

The general rule of thumb for bubble sorting is that every tenfold increase in the number of data elements to be sorted requires a 70-fold increase in time using the bubble sort. On the other hand, the more efficient Shell sort only requires a 15-fold increase in time.

As can be seen in the listing of the Shell sort program shown in Figure 15.12, the sort essentially divides the arrays in half, then compares and swaps data. The appropriate statement lines will have to be changed from PRINT to LPRINT for paper output. Sample data is contained in statements 900 through 970.

Program output is shown in Figure 15.13 in condensed format. The data sorted from lowest to highest sales are shown on the left. The second

The Shell sort was introduced by D. L. Shell (thus the name) in 1959. This is a very useful sort. The program shown in Figure 15.12 has been saved on the companion diskette as FIG15-12. This can be loaded into memory by the command LOAD"FIG15-12". If large volumes of data are to be sorted, then shorten the variable names to speed up program execution.

```
10 REM Shell Sort - Ranking/Sorting
20 READ NUMBER                                  ' Data elements
30 DIM SALE(NUMBER), E.NAME$(NUMBER), RANK(NUMBER)
40 CLS                                          ' Read in arrays
50 FOR I = 1 TO NUMBER : READ SALE(I)    : NEXT I
60 FOR I = 1 TO NUMBER : READ E.NAME$(I) : NEXT I
70 '                                            Begin sales sort
80 D = NUMBER
90 D = INT (D / 2) : IF D = 0 THEN 200
100 C = NUMBER - D
110 X = 1
120 Y = X
130 Z = Y + D
140 IF SALE(Y)   =<    SALE(Z) THEN 180
150 SWAP SALE(Y),     SALE(Z)
160 SWAP E.NAME$(Y), E.NAME$(Z)
170 Y = Y - D : IF Y > 0 THEN 130
180 X = X + 1 : IF X > C THEN 90 ELSE 120
190 '                                           End sales sort
200 PRINT "The data sorted by sales:"
210 PRINT "Sales" TAB(12) "Employee name"
220 FOR I = 1 TO NUMBER
230     PRINT SALE(I) TAB(12) E.NAME$(I)
240 NEXT I
250 '                                           Rank
260 FOR I = 1 TO NUMBER : RANK(I) = NUMBER +1 -I : NEXT I
270 '                                           Begin name sort
280 D = NUMBER
290 D = INT (D / 2) : IF D = 0 THEN 410
300 C = NUMBER - D
310 X = 1
320 Y = X
330 Z = Y + D
340 IF E.NAME$(Y) =< E.NAME$(Z) THEN 390
350 SWAP SALE(Y),     SALE(Z)
360 SWAP RANK(Y),     RANK(Z)
370 SWAP E.NAME$(Y), E.NAME$(Z)
380 Y = Y - D : IF Y > 0 THEN 330
390 X = X + 1 : IF X > C THEN 290 ELSE 320
400 '                                           End name sort
410 PRINT "The ranked sales sorted by employee name:"
420 PRINT "Employee name" TAB(20) "Sales" TAB(36) "Ranking"
430 FOR I = 1 TO NUMBER
440     PRINT E.NAME$(I) TAB(20) SALE(I)  TAB(37) "#" RANK(I)
450 NEXT I
460 REM
900 DATA 45
910 DATA 1234.45, 12, 12345, 23, 34, 35, 67, 89, 90,
            12.3, 12, 123, 34, 56, 23
920 DATA 1111.11, 13, 23455, 33, 34, 45, 90, 88, 76,
            54.3, 22, 311, 77, 99, 22
930 DATA 1233.11, 43, 55555, 65, 78, 23, 89, 65, 55,
            34.1, 88, 343, 71, 29, 6
```

FIGURE 15.12 The Shell sort with sample data

```
 940 DATA "Mears, Pete"    , "Mears, Pat"     , "Mears, David"    ,
          "Citizen, John" , "Citizen, Alice", "Anyname, F. L."
 950 DATA "Jones"          , "Smith, Alice"   , "Smith, Jack A." ,
          "Smith, Sue S." , "Man, Hunted"    , "Citizen, Al"
 960 DATA "Johnson, P"     , "Johnson, Art"   , "Johnson, Pat"    ,
          "Brown"          , "Alexander, Hag", "Nixon, R."
 970 DATA "Eueing, J.R."   , "Smith, Mary"    , "Tipton, J.B"     ,
          "Deer, John"     , "Smith, Jack"    , "Smith, Sue"
 980 DATA "Anyname, First", "Anyname, Last"  , "Computer, Micro",
          "Alexander, Joy", "Test, Data"     , "Brown, B.J."
 990 DATA "Dandy, I. Am"   , "Citizen, Tim"   , "Pistol, Pete"    ,
          "Gonzolas, S."   , "Anybody, Tom"   , "Smith, A.A."
1000 DATA "Smith, Sue A.",  "Testing, Data",  "Name, Any"        ,
          "Name, Mine"     , "Son, No 3"      , "Son, No 1"
1010 DATA "Zip, Along"     , "Tipton, HJ"     , "End, Example"
1020 END
```

FIGURE 15.12 (*continued*)

The data sorted by sales:		The ranked sales sorted by employee name:		
Sales	Employee name	Employee name	Sales	Ranking
6	End, Example	Alexander, Hag	13	# 41
12	Mears, Pat	Alexander, Joy	77	# 18
12	Man, Hunted	Anybody, Tom	78	# 17
12.3	Smith, Sue S.	Anyname, F. L.	35	# 29
13	Alexander, Hag	Anyname, First	54.3	# 26
22	Anyname, Last	Anyname, Last	22	# 40
22	Brown, B.J.	Brown	1111.11	# 6
23	Smith, A.A.	Brown, B.J.	22	# 39
23	Johnson, Pat	Citizen, Al	123	# 9
23	Citizen, John	Citizen, Alice	34	# 31
29	Tipton, HJ	Citizen, John	23	# 36
33	Eueing, J.R.	Citizen, Tim	43	# 28
34	Johnson, P	Computer, Micro	311	# 8
34	Smith, Mary	Dandy, I. Am	1233.11	# 5
34	Citizen, Alice	Deer, John	90	# 12
34.1	Name, Mine	End, Example	6	# 45
35	Anyname, F. L.	Eueing, J.R.	33	# 34
43	Citizen, Tim	Gonzolas, S.	65	# 23
45	Tipton, J.B	Johnson, Art	56	# 24
54.3	Anyname, First	Johnson, P	34	# 33
55	Name, Any	Johnson, Pat	23	# 37
56	Johnson, Art	Jones	67	# 21
65	Gonzolas, S.	Man, Hunted	12	# 43
65	Testing, Data	Mears, David	12345	# 3
67	Jones	Mears, Pat	12	# 44
71	Zip, Along	Mears, Pete	1234.45	# 4
76	Smith, Sue	Name, Any	55	# 25
77	Alexander, Joy	Name, Mine	34.1	# 30
78	Anybody, Tom	Nixon, R.	23455	# 2
88	Son, No 3	Pistol, Pete	55555	# 1
88	Smith, Jack	Smith, A.A.	23	# 38
89	Smith, Sue A.	Smith, Alice	89	# 13
89	Smith, Alice	Smith, Jack	88	# 15
90	Deer, John	Smith, Jack A.	90	# 11
90	Smith, Jack A.	Smith, Mary	34	# 32
99	Test, Data	Smith, Sue	76	# 19
123	Citizen, Al	Smith, Sue A.	89	# 14
311	Computer, Micro	Smith, Sue S.	12.3	# 42
343	Son, No 1	Son, No 1	343	# 7
1111.11	Brown	Son, No 3	88	# 16
1233.11	Dandy, I. Am	Test, Data	99	# 10
1234.45	Mears, Pete	Testing, Data	65	# 22
12345	Mears, David	Tipton, HJ	29	# 35
23455	Nixon, R.	Tipton, J.B	45	# 27
55555	Pistol, Pete	Zip, Along	71	# 20

FIGURE 15.13 Shell sort–program output (condensed output)

portion of the program output following this sort shows the sales rankings by employee name. This output is shown beside the first output to conserve space. Notice how important rankings become to an individual employee when his or her name is buried in a long listing.

SORT—DOS 2.X STYLE

System master diskettes for DOS 2.1 and DOS 2.2 contain a SORT utility called SORT.EXE. This utility can be copied onto your working diskette, provided that your diskette is formatted in DOS 2.1 or higher. The examples that follow demonstrate how this program operates at the DOS level, using a demonstration file on the companion diskette called UN-SORT.SEQ.

With the companion diskette in drive A and with the computer at the DOS level, we can look at the contents of the companion diskette's file UNSORT.SEQ by using the TYPE command as follows:

```
A>TYPE UNSORT.SEQ
6
8
7
99
3
1
0
44
456
3
23
9
5
5
12
10
11
e
26
a
22
A
41
```

The general form of the SORT command is

SORT /R /+N <UNSORTED >SORTED

Where

/R is an optional parameter to reverse the output of the sort from high to low.

/N is an optional parameter to start the sort at column N. If no parameters are specified, the sort will be on column 1.

<UNSORTED > is the name of the file to be sorted. The < and > must be typed. There must be a blank space between the file name and the ending > symbol.

SORTED is the output file name. There is no blank space between the > and the file name.

Let's take a few examples. First, the command `SORT <UNSORT.SEQ >SORT.SEQ` would result in the following:

```
A>SORT <UNSORT.SEQ >SORT.SEQ
A>TYPE SORT.SEQ
0
1
10
11
12
22
23
26
3
3
41
44
456
5
5
6
7
8
9
99
A
a
e
```

The output is sorted beginning with the first column. A sort can also be specified starting on the second column as shown below. Notice that values in the first column are ignored.

```
A>SORT /+2 <UNSORT.SEQ >SORT.SEQ
A>TYPE SORT.SEQ
6
8
7
3
1
0
3
9
5
5
e
a
A
10
11
41
12
22
23
44
456
26
99
```

Try the SORT command for yourself and observe what happens. The companion diskette contains the UNSORT.SEQ file being discussed. Copy the file onto your diskette and see if you can get the results shown.

The SORT command is not particularly useful in sorting text files because of its sort-on-only-one-field feature. However, the command is useful in organizing your diskette directory.

Assume that the following occurred when the DIR command was given:

```
Volume in drive A has no label
Directory of A:\
COMMAND  COM     17792 10-20-83 12:00p
BASICA   COM     26112 10-20-83 12:00p
BACKUP   COM      3687 10-20-83 12:00p
SORT     EXE      1408 10-20-83 12:00p
EDLIN    COM      4608 10-20-83 12:00p
UNSORT   SEQ        77  1-01-80 12:03a
SORT     SEQ        76  1-01-80 12:11a
UNSORT   BAK        66  1-01-80 12:04a
SPREAD1            414  1-01-80 12:53a
DATA1    WKS       460  1-01-80 12:13a
DATA2    WKS       587  1-01-80 12:24a
DATA3    WKS       654  1-01-80 12:35a
DATA4    WKS       407  1-01-80 12:06a
SPREAD1A          414  1-01-80 12:03a
        14 File(s)    274432 bytes free
```

The command to sort this directory is **DIR ¦ SORT**.

The screen will then appear as shown below. The files %PIPE1 and %PIPE2 will disappear when DIR is retyped. These appeared because the SORT command causes the output of the directory command to be piped into the SORT filter.

```
    A>DIR ¦ SORT /+1

        16 Files(s)     273408 bytes free
    Directory of A:\
    Volume in drive A has no label
%PIPE1   $$$        0  1-01-80 12:00a
%PIPE2   $$$        0  1-01-80 12:00a
BACKUP   COM     3687 10-20-83 12:00p
BASICA   COM    26112 10-20-83 12:00p
COMMAND  COM    17792 10-20-83 12:00p
DATA1    WKS      460  1-01-80 12:13a
DATA2    WKS      587  1-01-80 12:24a
DATA3    WKS      654  1-01-80 12:35a
DATA4    WKS      407  1-01-80 12:06a
EDLIN    COM     4608 10-20-83 12:00p
SORT     EXE     1408 10-20-83 12:00p
SORT     SEQ       76  1-01-80 12:11a
SPREAD1           414  1-01-80 12:53a
SPREAD1A          414  1-01-80 12:03a
UNSORT   BAK       66  1-01-80 12:04a
UNSORT   SEQ       77  1-01-80 12:03a
```

The file size obtained by a DIR command starts in column 14. The directory can be sorted on the basis of the size of the file with the command **DIR ¦ SORT /+14**. This will produce the output shown on the following page. (It's bound to dazzle your friends.)

```
%PIPE1     $$$       0   1-01-80  12:01a
%PIPE2     $$$       0   1-01-80  12:01a
UNSORT     BAK      66   1-01-80  12:04a
SORT       SEQ      76   1-01-80  12:11a
UNSORT     SEQ      77   1-01-80  12:03a
DATA4      WKS     407   1-01-80  12:06a
SPREAD1A           414   1-01-80  12:03a
SPREAD1            414   1-01-80  12:53a
DATA1      WKS     460   1-01-80  12:13a
DATA2      WKS     587   1-01-80  12:24a
DATA3      WKS     654   1-01-80  12:35a
SORT       EXE    1408  10-20-83  12:00p
BACKUP     COM    3687  10-20-83  12:00p
EDLIN      COM    4608  10-20-83  12:00p
COMMAND    COM   17792  10-20-83  12:00p
BASICA     COM   26112  10-20-83  12:00p
```

SUMMARY

Do you want your business report to be read and understood? When appropriate, important data should be sorted and ranked according to the contribution made. If an employee's sale or unit quota is shown compared to other members of the group, then the report will be read with greater interest.

Using the companion diskette, select the tutorial on Sorting. Enter trial data to be sorted when requested. Observe the way uppercase versus lowercase letters are sorted. In addition to sorting data, reports can be made more readable not only by sorting their data, but also by presenting data in tabular format. This is discussed in the next chapter.

```
BASIC Programming With the IBM PC

                Sorting

                  By
              Peter Mears
         (c) Copyright 1990
```

PROBLEMS

True/False. Problems 1–5.

15.1 Sorting consists of arranging data in either numeric or alphabetic order.

15.2 Data is sorted by switching array locations of variables.

15.3 Bubble sort is a sorting method that moves values to the "top" of the array.

15.4 Ranking is helpful in comparing individual data with overall data.

15.5 The computer sorts data according to the ASCII code of each character in a variable (including blank spaces in a character string).

Screen Design Problems. Problems 6–15.
Develop a BASIC program, paying particular attention to the design of the screen and the design of the printed output (when requested). General formats

are shown for your consideration; they may be expanded on (improved) in your program.

The following information is needed in answering Problems 6–9.

Ajax automotive dealership had the following sales by employee on data statements.

```
9000 DATA "Smith, John"   , 28750
9010 DATA "Citizen, Susan", 12870
9020 DATA "Jones, John"    , 13214
9030 DATA "Worth, Alice"   , 49846
9040 DATA "Smith, Jack"    , 24876
9050 DATA "Brown, Al"      , 48750
9060 DATA "Smith, Mary"    , 42817
9070 DATA "Smith, JJ"      , 22750
```

*15.6 Sort the data alphabetically by employee name. Display the sorted array along with the sales figures and total sales in the format shown.

Ajax Automotive Dealership
Sales Analysis
mm/dd/yy

Employee name	Monthly sales
Brown, Al	$48,750
Citizen, Susan	$12,870
Jones, John	$13,214
Smith, JJ	$22,750
Smith, Jack	$24,876
Smith, John	$28,750
Smith, Mary	$42,817
Worth, Alice	$49,846
Total sales:	$243,873

15.7 Sort, rank, and display the data alphabetically by employee name. Then along with the name, display the monthly sales and the ranking of the sales. Print the output in the format shown.

Ajax Automotive Dealership
Sales Analysis
mm/dd/yy

Employee name	Monthly sales	Ranking in firm
Brown, Al	$48,750	# 2
Citizen, Susan	$12,870	# 8
Jones, John	$13,214	# 7
Smith, JJ	$22,750	# 6
Smith, Jack	$24,876	# 5
Smith, John	$28,750	# 4
Smith, Mary	$42,817	# 3
Worth, Alice	$49,846	# 1

* The answer to this problem is in Appendix E.

15.8 Modify the program developed in Problem 7 to print the highest sales (rank #1) along with the words "Top salesperson."

15.9 Develop a program to sort and display the data from highest to lowest ranking in the firm. Display the output as shown in Problem 7.

The ASCII file called "BUDGET.ASC" will be needed for Problems 10–12. This file is organized as follows:

Pens	Tape	Staples	Paper	Typewriter
--	--	--	--	--

15.10 Sort and display the file from highest to lowest budget for typewriter expenditures according to the format below.

Ajax Corporation
Typewriter Budget Analysis
Typewriter Budgets

	$XXX.XX
	$XXX.XX
	.
	.
	.
Total Budget	$XX,XXX.XX

15.11 Ajax Corporation needs a miscellaneous budget report that separates and totals the line item budgets for pens, tape, staples, and paper. (Each data-line is a line item budget.) Develop a total of these miscellaneous budget items and display the items from lowest to highest miscellaneous budget in the format shown below.

Ajax Corporation
Miscellaneous Budget Analysis
Line by Line Budget Totals

Pens	Tape	Staples	Paper	Total Misc.
150	100	400	540	1,190
100	100	100	1,000	1,300
.	.	.	.	.
.	.	.	.	.
Total Miscellaneous Budget				$XX,XXX

15.12 Develop a program that will read in student numbers (the identification number assigned by the school) and test scores from DATA statements. (You create the DATA statements.) Rank the students from highest to lowest scores. Print the words "A+ Student" next to the top 2 rankings. The display should be of the following format sorted by the student's number.

Introductory Programming
Student Grades

Student number	Test score	Ranking in class	Comments (if any)
XXX	XXX	XX	
XXX	XXX	XX	

The following information is needed for Problems 13 and 14.

Footwear Shoe Repair Company employs seven people. Management needs a program to rank the sales of the following seven employees:

Name	Sales
Citizen, J.	5000
Blair, S.	2200
Smith, T.	6350
Roberts, O.	1450
Seivers, L.	3300
Allen, R.	5100
Thomas, T.	4700

The sales report is to be of the following format sorted by last name:

Footwear Shoe Repair
Productivity Report
MM/DD/YY

Name	Sales	Ranking
XXXX	$XXXX.XX	
.	.	
.	.	
.	.	
XXXX	$XXXX.XX	

15.13 Develop a program to produce a report in the format just shown. Use an INPUT statement to enter the data given. Alphabetically sort and print the report by the employee's last name.

15.14 Develop a program to produce another report in the same format. Use a DATA statement to enter the data given. Print the report alphabetically, sorted by the employee's last name. Rank the sales from highest (#1 rank) to lowest sale.

15.15 Ajax Corporation has four people in their sales department: S. Smith, T. James, R. Mead, and J. Allison. A typical monthly sales report is shown below.

Ajax Sales Report
December, 1990
Sales for Week Ending

Salesperson	12/10	12/17	12/24	12/31	Total
S. Smith	$87.20	$976.30	$412.75	$892.00	$2368.25
T. James	$1875.75	$1277.99	$1132.50	$1576.80	$5863.04
R. Mead	$650.24	$344.45	$545.50	$450.75	$1990.94
J. Allison	$225.50	$545.00	$445.75	$325.50	$1541.75
Totals	$2838.69	$3143.74	$2536.50	$3245.05	$11763.98

Management wants a program that will prepare a sales report in the format shown. In addition, the program should develop a report, sorted by total monthly sales, from highest to lowest sales. That is, the top salesperson is T. James with monthly sales of $5863.04. This person and her sales should appear first. Print the sorted sales according to the same format.

Other Problems. Problems 16–25.
Develop a BASIC program to solve each problem. Use a REM statement to identify the problem number, and clearly label all output.

15.16 Develop a program to input five numbers into an array called SALES. Then sort and print the sorted array from lowest to highest value.

15.17 Develop a program to input six numbers into an array called NUMBERS. Then sort and print the sorted array from highest to lowest value.

15.18 Use the SORT program on the system master to sort your diskette files by file name.

The ASCII file called "SUPPLIES.ASC" will be needed for Problems 19–23. This file is organized as follows:

Product number	Location code	Quantity	Price	Description

15.19 Modify the Shell sort. Then sort and display the file from lowest to highest product number.

15.20 Modify the Shell sort. Then sort and display the file by item description.

15.21 Identify all items having a selling price over $100, and store these in an array. Then sort and display the file from highest to lowest price using a modified Shell sort.

*15.22 Develop a program that will permit a user to input up to 500 numbers into an array called ANALYSIS. Sort the array from lowest to highest value. Calculate the average value and print the sorted array. Identify the above average values by printing an asterisk (*) next to the value. Test your program by entering the following values: 12; 11; 15; 17, and 9.

15.23 Write a program that will sort a list of five last names and print the alphabetized list. Develop the program to read the names into an array called MY.NAMES$ from DATA statements that you develop.

A firm that sells office supplies has the following information on DATA statements regarding PRODUCT$, COST, and VENDOR$. Use these DATA statements in answering Problems 24 and 25.

9000	DATA	Typewriter	,	975	,	Speed King
9010	DATA	Electronic Stapler	,	39.95	,	Bang Away
9020	DATA	Electronic Calculator,		249.95	,	Nevada Co.
9030	DATA	Pear Micro & Drive	,	2125.95,		Pear Computing
9040	DATA	BMI Micro & Drive	,	3650.90,		BMI Corp.
9050	DATA	Desk Computer	,	495.90	,	Roll-Away Co.
9060	DATA	Desk-Plain	.	225.00	,	Roll-Away Co.

15.24 Sort and display the data by COST from least to most costly product. Then sort by PRODUCT$ and rank by cost.

15.25 Alphabetically sort and display the data by product, along with the vendor and the associated cost. Do not rank the cost.

* The answer to this problem is in Appendix E.

EXPANDING PROGRAMMING SKILLS

Upon completion of this chapter, you should be able to

- Use ON N GOTO statements
- Check for reasonableness of the data
- Use subroutines
- Use RND, INT, and CINT functions
- Use integer, single-, and double-precision numbers

THE ON N GOTO STATEMENT

The ON N GOTO statement is used to transfer control to one of several statement line numbers based on the value of N. The general form of the ON N GOTO statement is

Statement number   **ON N GOTO**   line#, line#, line#

Where: N is a numeric variable in the range of 0 to 255, line# is a statement line number

If the value of N is 3, then control is transferred to the third line number following the words ON N GOTO. If the value of N is 0 or greater than the number of line numbers in the list, control is not transferred and the program continues with the next statement.

This statement is particularly useful in creating menus. For example, the program shown in Figure 16.1 checks for a user response to the question: "Who was the first U.S. woman astronaut?" The value is entered into a variable called ANSWER, then ON N GOTO transfers control to print the appropriate response.

CHECKING FOR REASONABLENESS OF THE DATA

Remember the popular expression GIGO? Of course you do; it stands for "Garbage In, Garbage Out." In our example, what happens if a zero is entered? Or if a value greater than 4 is entered? Or if the user types a letter instead of a number? You know what happens: the program "bombs."

Data should be checked to determine if it is within a desired range before the program processes the data. It is simple enough to identify whether the data is in a desired range using an IF-THEN comparison.

345

However, if letters or symbols are entered into a numeric variable, an error message occurs before we've had a chance to check the data.

To prevent this from happening, the option selected should be entered into a string variable, then converted into a numeric value to determine reasonableness of the entry. And while we are going to this much trouble, let's do one more thing to improve our program. The menu shown in Figure 16.1 prompts the user with the words "Your choice". Doesn't it seem reasonable that users would simply type either a 1, 2, 3, or 4, and then do nothing? Why does the Enter key always have to be pressed?

Well it doesn't have to be typed. When a character is typed on the keyboard, it is entered into a keyboard buffer. Then the computer retrieves the character from the buffer into memory. If the INKEY$ statement is used to read a single character from the keyboard buffer, the Enter key does not have to be pressed after typing a letter or a number. That is, when the program encounters INKEY$, the computer retrieves a keystroke from the keyboard buffer and processes it. If the buffer is empty, the program automatically continues.

```
10 REM Testing input using INKEY$
20 CLS
30 WRONG = 0                                    ' Initalize counter
40 PRINT TAB(5) "Who was the first U.S. woman astronaut?"
50 PRINT
60 PRINT TAB(15) "1  Betsy Ross"
70 PRINT TAB(15) "2  Sally Fields"
80 PRINT TAB(15) "3  Joan Rivers"
90 PRINT TAB(15) "4  Sally Ride"
100 PRINT
110 PRINT TAB(5) "Your choice? ";
120 IF INKEY$ <> "" THEN 120                    ' Clears buffer
130 ANS$ = INKEY$ : IF ANS$ = "" THEN 130       ' Retrieves character
140 PRINT ANS$
150 ANSWER = VAL(ANS$)                          ' Converts to numeric
160 IF ANSWER => 1 AND ANSWER <= 4 THEN 200
170 BEEP
180 PRINT TAB(5) "Only type 1 - 4!" : GOTO 110
190                                             ' Transfer control
200 ON ANSWER GOTO 220, 260, 290, 340
210                                             ' Answer = 1
220 PRINT TAB(5) "No, she's the one who sewed the flag."
230 WRONG = WRONG + 1
240 GOTO 110
250                                             ' Answer = 2
260 PRINT TAB(5) "No, she's a movie star."
270 WRONG = WRONG + 1
280 GOTO 110
290                                             ' Answer = 3
300 PRINT TAB(5) "No, she's a TV comic."
310 WRONG = WRONG + 1
320 GOTO 110
330                                             ' Answer = 4
340 PRINT TAB(5) "Ah, yes!"
350 PRINT TAB(5) "Number of wrong answers:" WRONG
360 END
```

FIGURE 16.1   Using INKEY$ for data entry

The program shown in Figure 16.1 contains several new statements, so let's cover them before proceeding. Statement `120 IF INKEY$ <> ""` `THEN 120` clears the keyboard buffer before proceeding. Technically this statement is not needed, but it is included to eliminate problems that may occur from quickly pressing a key several times.

The first part of statement `130 ANS$ = INKEY$` retrieves a single character from the keyboard. The second part of the statement, `IF ANS$ =` `"" THEN 130`, loops control back to 130 until a key is pressed. Statement `150 ANSWER = VAL(ANS$)` converts the string to its numeric equivalent. Statements 160 through 180 check for data entry errors and prompt the user to reenter data if the data is not between 1 and 4.

Program output is shown in Figure 16.2. Notice that the letter *a* was accidently entered as an answer to a question. The program did not "bomb," but instead provided a prompt on how the data should be entered.

```
Who was the first U.S. woman astronaut?

            1   Betsy Ross
            2   Sally Fields
            3   Joan Rivers
            4   Sally Ride

Your choice? a
Only type 1 - 4!
Your choice? 3
No, she's a TV comic.
Your choice? 2
No, she's a movie star.
Your choice? 4
Ah, yes!
Number of wrong answers: 2
```

FIGURE 16.2 Program output

The INPUT$(1) statement can also be used to retrieve a single character from the keyboard buffer. This statement is a little simpler than INKEY$ for many applications. An example is shown in Figure 16.3. Program output is the same as previously shown.

SUBROUTINES

Subroutines are program segments (subprograms) within a larger program that do a specific task. They provide a means by which portions of a program can be used as often as desired, without repeating the same sequence of programming statements time and time again.

For example, suppose that a bakery that sells wedding cakes needs to quote prices quickly to potential customers, based on various cake diameters and thicknesses. Let's write a small program to accomplish this. There are three levels on the wedding cake: top, middle, and bottom. Each level is priced differently, based on the volume of cake mix involved in each

```
10 REM Testing data input using INPUT$(1)
20 CLS
30 WRONG = 0                                    ' Initialize counter
40 PRINT TAB(5) "Who was the first U.S. woman astronaut?"
50 PRINT
60 PRINT TAB(15) "1  Betsy Ross"
70 PRINT TAB(15) "2  Sally Fields"
80 PRINT TAB(15) "3  Joan Rivers"
90 PRINT TAB(15) "4  Sally Ride"
100 PRINT
110 PRINT TAB(5) "Your choice? ";
120 ANS$ = INPUT$(1)                            ' Retrieves character
130 PRINT ANS$
140 ANSWER = VAL(ANS$)                          ' Converts to numeric
150 IF ANSWER => 1 AND ANSWER <= 4 THEN 190
160 BEEP
170 PRINT TAB(5) "Only type 1 - 4!" : GOTO 110
180                                             ' Transfer control
190 ON ANSWER GOTO 210, 250, 280, 330
200                                             ' Answer = 1
210 PRINT TAB(5) "No, she's the one who sewed the flag."
220 WRONG = WRONG + 1
230 GOTO 110
240                                             ' Answer = 2
250 PRINT TAB(5) "No, she's a movie star."
260 WRONG = WRONG + 1
270 GOTO 110
280                                             ' Answer = 3
290 PRINT TAB(5) "No, she's a TV comic."
300 WRONG = WRONG + 1
310 GOTO 110
320                                             ' Answer = 4
330 PRINT TAB(5) "Ah, yes!"
340 PRINT TAB(5) "Number of wrong answers:" WRONG
350 END
```

FIGURE 16.3 Using INPUT$(1) for data entry

level of the cake. The volume of each level is calculated by the following formula:

$$CAKE.COST = 3.1416 * RADIUS^2 * THICK * COST$$

Where: RADIUS is one half the diameter (in inches). Because many customers do not understand RADIUS, we ask for the DIAMETER and then divide by 2 to obtain the radius. THICK is the thickness of the cake level (in inches); COST varies by level because the quality of the mix varies.

An example of a pricing program for our bakery is shown in Figure 16.4. Notice that the indented statements are repetitious.

Program output is shown in Figure 16.5. The desired diameter and thickness are entered for each level, and the cost is calculated. Take a very close look at this output, and notice the total. The sum of $80.58, $114.51, and $169.33 is $364.42, not $364.43. Can you imagine the customers' reaction to being overcharged when spending a small fortune on a wedding cake? This problem is due to the way numbers are internally stored and will be discussed in the next section.

```
10  REM   Note multiple sub-programs
20  CLS: S$ = "$$###.##"
30  COST = .95
40  PRINT "Top layer diameter, thickness";
50        REM   Calculating cake cost
60        INPUT DIAMETER, THICK
70        CAKE.COST = 3.1416 * (DIAMETER/2)^2 * THICK * COST
80        PRINT TAB(10); "This layer costs";:
90        PRINT USING S$; CAKE.COST
100 COST = .45 : TOTAL1 = CAKE.COST
110 PRINT "Middle layer diameter, thickness";
120       REM   Calculating cake cost
130       INPUT DIAMETER, THICK
140       CAKE.COST = 3.1416 * (DIAMETER/2)^2 * THICK * COST
150       PRINT TAB(10); "This layer costs";:
160       PRINT USING S$; CAKE.COST
170 COST = .22 : TOTAL2 = CAKE.COST
180 PRINT "Bottom layer diameter, thickness";
190       REM   Calculating cake cost
200       INPUT DIAMETER, THICK
210       CAKE.COST = 3.1416 * (DIAMETER/2)^2 * THICK * COST
220       PRINT TAB(10); "This layer costs";:
230       PRINT USING S$; CAKE.COST
240 GRANDTOTAL = TOTAL1 + TOTAL2 + CAKE.COST : PRINT
250 PRINT "The total cost of the wedding cake is";
260 PRINT USING S$; GRANDTOTAL
270 END
```

FIGURE 16.4 Program to calculate cost of each level in a wedding cake

```
Top layer diameter, thickness? 6,3
        This layer costs  $80.58
Middle layer diameter, thickness? 9,4
        This layer costs $114.51
Bottom layer diameter, thickness? 14,5
        This layer costs $169.33

The total cost of the wedding cake is $364.43
Ok
```

FIGURE 16.5 Program output

Take a close look at the repeating series of statements. First, notice statements 50–90:

```
50        REM   Calculating cake cost
60        INPUT DIAMETER, THICK
70        CAKE.COST = 3.1416 * (DIAMETER/2)^2 * THICK * COST
80        PRINT TAB(10); "This layer costs";:
90        PRINT USING S$; CAKE.COST
```

Then observe statements 120–160:

```
120       REM    Calculating cake cost
130       INPUT DIAMETER, THICK
140       CAKE.COST = 3.1416 * (DIAMETER/2)^2 * THICK * COST
150       PRINT TAB(10); "This layer costs";:
160       PRINT USING S$; CAKE.COST
```

Finally, notice statements 190–230:

```
190       REM    Calculating cake cost
200       INPUT DIAMETER, THICK
210       CAKE.COST = 3.1416 * (DIAMETER/2)^2 * THICK * COST
220       PRINT TAB(10); "This layer costs";:
230       PRINT USING S$; CAKE.COST
```

The statements are the same. When statements need to be repeated in a program, it is more efficient to use subroutines. The general form of a subroutine is

Statement   **GOSUB**   Statement
number   number

A RETURN statement is needed at the end of a subroutine to return control to the statement following the calling GOSUB. The general form of the RETURN statement is

Statement   **RETURN**
number

The program shown in Figure 16.6 uses a GOSUB and its corresponding RETURN statement to perform repetitive calculations. The GOSUB has been placed after the END statement to prevent the program from "accidentally" falling into the subroutine after performing the necessary calculations.

In the program shown in Figure 16.6 the GOSUB "calls" the subroutine, which begins in line 200. After executing the statements in the subroutine, the program returns control to the statement following the calling subroutine.

This process can be viewed as follows:

```
190                                    'GOSUB cake cost
200 INPUT DIAMETER, THICK
210 CAKE.COST = 3.1416 * (DIAMETER/2)^2 * THICK *
            COST
220 PRINT TAB(10) "This layer costs ";
230 PRINT USING S$; CAKE.COST
240 RETURN
```

The best way to learn about subroutines is to use them in your own programs.

```
10 REM   Note GOSUB's
20 CLS: S$ = "$$###.##"
30 PRINT "Top layer diameter, thickness";
40 COST = .95
50 GOSUB 200                                    ' GOSUB cake cost
60 TOTAL1 = CAKE.COST
70 PRINT "Middle layer diameter, thickness";
80 COST = .45
90 GOSUB 200                                    ' GOSUB cake cost
100 TOTAL2 = CAKE.COST
110 PRINT "Bottom layer diameter, thickness";
120 COST = .22
130 GOSUB 200                                   ' GOSUB cake cost
140 GRANDTOTAL = TOTAL1 + TOTAL2 + CAKE.COST
150 PRINT
160 PRINT "The total cost of the wedding cake is";
170 PRINT USING S$; GRANDTOTAL
180 END
190                                             ' GOSUB cake cost
200 INPUT DIAMETER, THICK
210 CAKE.COST = 3.1416 * (DIAMETER/2)^2 * THICK * COST
220 PRINT TAB(10); "This layer costs";
230 PRINT USING S$; CAKE.COST
240 RETURN
```

FIGURE 16.6   Using a GOSUB

Notice that placing repetitive statements in a GOSUB can simplify programming by eliminating the need to repeat the same series of statements several times. The subroutine GOSUB 200 is called in statements 50, 90, and 130. The statements in the subroutine are processed until statement **240 RETURN** is encountered. This transfers control to the statement following the statement that called the GOSUB.

GOSUBs permit programs to be developed in a modular format. That is, each of the logical processing modules can be identified and placed in a GOSUB. Then the main program can use a series of GOSUBs to call up the processing module needed.

An example of using modules in developing a program is shown in Figure 16.7. This is the program that produces the output previously shown at the beginning of Chapter 14. Notice how the main program consists of a series of GOSUBs that are used to perform the necessary computations.

There is a trick required to obtain the fancy statement numbering shown in Figure 16.7. The processing begins by carefully planning each program module before programming so that the program progresses logically from module to module. Then, simply type the statements into the computer without worrying about line numbering.

After the program is entered, use RENUM to number the statement lines in increments of 10. The screen will appear as shown after listing statements 10 through 110 for reference.

```
10 REM Using module
20 DIM SALE(7,5), PRODUCT$(7)                    ' Reserve storage
30 CLS
40 S$ = "$$#####.##"                             ' Print Using string
50 GOSUB 1000                                    ' Read products
60 GOSUB 2000                                    ' Read sales
70 GOSUB 3000                                    ' Total rows
80 GOSUB 4000                                    ' Total columns
90 GOSUB 5000                                    ' Print headings
100 GOSUB 6000                                   ' Print table
110 END
980 '
990 '
1000 FOR ROW = 1 TO 7                            ' Read products
1010     READ PRODUCT$(ROW)
1020 NEXT ROW
1030 DATA "Pencils"         , "Staples"     , "Erasers"
1040 DATA "Adding machines", "Typewriters", "Computers",
         "Weekly totals:"
1050 RETURN
1060 '
2000 FOR ROW = 1 TO 6                            ' Read sales
2010     FOR COLUMN = 1 TO 4
2020         READ SALE(ROW,COLUMN)
2030     NEXT COLUMN
2040 NEXT ROW
2050 DATA 15, 20, 15, 10
2060 DATA 48, 60, 25, 20
2070 DATA 10, 10, 35, 30
2080 DATA  7,  5, 45, 40
2090 DATA 18,  8, 55, 50
2100 DATA  5,  5, 65, 60
2110 '
3000 FOR ROW = 1 TO 6                             ' Total rows
3010     FOR COLUMN = 1 TO 4
3020         SALE(ROW,5) = SALE(ROW,5) + SALE(ROW,COLUMN)
3030     NEXT COLUMN
3040         SALE(7,5) = SALE(7,5) + SALE(ROW,5)
3050 NEXT ROW
3060 RETURN
3070 '
4000 FOR COLUMN = 1 TO 4                          ' Total columns
4010     FOR ROW = 1 TO 6
4020         SALE(7,COLUMN) = SALE(7,COLUMN) + SALE(ROW,COLUMN)
4030     NEXT ROW
4040 NEXT COLUMN
4050 RETURN
4060 '                                            ' Print heading
5000 PRINT TAB(27) "Total Sales by Product by Week"
5010 PRINT "PRODUCTS" TAB(22) "Week #1"    "   Week #2"
         "   Week #3"    "   Week #4"    "   Totals"
5020 RETURN
5030 '
6000 PRINT                                        ' Print table
6010 FOR ROW = 1 TO 7
6020     PRINT PRODUCT$(ROW) TAB(18)
6030         FOR COLUMN = 1 TO 5
6040             PRINT USING S$; SALE(ROW,COLUMN);
6050         NEXT COLUMN : PRINT
6060 NEXT ROW
6070 RETURN
```

FIGURE 16.7 Using GOSUBs to modularize programs

```
RENUM
Ok
LIST 10-110
10 REM Using module
20 DIM SALE(7,5), PRODUCT$(7)           ' Reserve storage
30 CLS
40 S$ = "$$#####.##"                    ' Print Using string
50 GOSUB 140                            ' Read products
60 GOSUB 210                            ' Read sales
70 GOSUB 330                            ' Total rows
80 GOSUB 410                            ' Total columns
90 GOSUB 480                            ' Print headings
100 GOSUB 520                           ' Print table
110 END
Ok
```

Now let's renumber our GOSUBs. Statement `50 GOSUB 140` is the first GOSUB. This is renumbered so that it begins at statement number 1000 by the command `RENUM 1000,140,10,` which means "renumber beginning at the new line number of 1000, starting at the old line number of 140, in increments of 10." The screen will appear as shown after listing statements 10 through 110 for reference.

```
RENUM 1000,140,10
Ok
LIST 10-110
10 REM Using module
20 DIM SALE(7,5), PRODUCT$(7)           ' Reserve storage
30 CLS
40 S$ = "$$#####.##"                    ' Print Using string
50 GOSUB 1000                           ' Read products
60 GOSUB 1070                           ' Read sales
70 GOSUB 1190                           ' Total rows
80 GOSUB 1270                           ' Total columns
90 GOSUB 1340                           ' Print headings
100 GOSUB 1380                          ' Print table
110 END
Ok
```

Now statement `60 GOSUB 1070` (the GOSUB that reads in sales) can be renumbered by the command `RENUM 2000,1070,10`. The screen will appear as shown after listing statements 10 through 110 for reference.

```
RENUM 2000,1070,10
Ok
LIST 10-110
10 REM Using module
20 DIM SALE(7,5), PRODUCT$(7)           ' Reserve storage
30 CLS
40 S$ = "$$#####.##"                    ' Print Using string
50 GOSUB 1000                           ' Read products
60 GOSUB 2000                           ' Read sales
70 GOSUB 2120                           ' Total rows
80 GOSUB 2200                           ' Total columns
90 GOSUB 2270                           ' Print headings
100 GOSUB 2310                          ' Print table
110 END
Ok
```

Then statement `70 GOSUB 1190` can be renumbered by the command `RENUM 3000,1190,10`. In a similar manner, the remaining statements can be renumbered to produce the logically numbered subroutines shown in Figure 16.7.

RANDOM NUMBERS (THE RND STATEMENT)

We have been using numbers in our programs without giving them much thought. It is now time that we take a closer look at numbers. First, we will look at how random numbers can be generated; then we will take a closer look at how numbers are stored.

The BASIC language provides many useful built-in programming functions. One of these is the RND function, which returns a random number between 0 and 1 useful for purposes such as simulation. Unfortunately, the same sequence of random numbers is returned each time a program using a RND statement is run unless the random number generator is "re-seeded."

A random number generator can be re-seeded by the RANDOMIZE (N) statement. N is any value between −32768 and 32767. If a value for N is omitted in the RANDOMIZE statement, program execution halts, and the user is asked for a value. This is awkward, and the message displayed ("Random Number Seed (−32768 to 32767)?") will confuse program users.

A beginning program to display five random numbers is shown in Figure 16.8. Notice that the RANDOMIZE statement seeds the random number generator, but at a constant number value. The same sequence of random numbers will be generated each time the program is run. Also notice that the statement PRINT RND is inside a FOR-NEXT loop, resulting in five values being displayed.

```
10 REM Example of RND and RANDOMIZE
20 RANDOMIZE(3)
30 FOR I = 1 TO 5
40     PRINT RND " ";
50 NEXT I
60 END
RUN
 .7655695      .3558607      .3742327      .1388798      .8231488
Ok
RUN
 .7655695      .3558607      .3742327      .1388798      .8231488
Ok
RUN
 .7655695      .3558607      .3742327      .1388798      .8231488
Ok
```

FIGURE 16.8 The RND and RANDOMIZE statements

THE INT FUNCTION

Random numbers are more useful as whole numbers. Two functions are useful in converting fractions (such as 20.5) to whole numbers: the INT function and the CINT function.

The INT function is of the form

Statement
number **PRINT INT(X)**

Where X is any number

The INT function returns the largest whole number value that is less than or equal to X. That is, the function always rounds down, never up. For example, **PRINT INT(3.8)** results in 3.

PRINT INT(-2.1) results in −3, which might seem confusing until you look at the following graph:

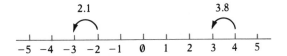

Rounding 3.8 down yields the smaller number of 3. Rounding −2.1 down yields the smaller number of −3 (remember that −3 is smaller than −2).

A program combining RND, INT, and RANDOMIZE is shown in Figure 16.9. The value of TIME$ provides a basis for the random number seed. As time changes, the seed value varies, resulting in a different group of random numbers. Also note that the range of the numbers produced is between 1 and 10.

```
10 REM  RND, INT and RANDOMIZE
20 T = VAL(RIGHT$(TIME$,2)) + 60*VAL(MID$(TIME$,4,2))
30 RANDOMIZE (T)
40 FOR I = 1 TO 8
50     X = RND *10
60     PRINT X, INT(X + 1)
70 NEXT I
80 END
RUN
 8.490503       9
 3.397932       4
 7.193102       8
 2.130223       3
 2.725964       3
 1.592428       2
 2.406975       3
 9.596512      10
Ok
RUN
 5.99325        6
 8.702191       9
 7.842821       8
 .4935652       1
 6.698437       7
 2.487509       3
 1.284233       2
 8.277238       9
Ok
```

FIGURE 16.9 Using the TIME$ function as a random seed value

The CINT function helps overcome this confusion by rounding the fractional portion of the number. The general form of the CINT function is

Statement
number   **PRINT CINT(X)**

Where X is any number between −32768 and 32767.

The CINT function converts X to an integer by rounding the fractional portion. For example, **PRINT CINT(3.8)** yields 4, and **PRINT CINT (−2.1)** yields −2. A program using RANDOMIZE, RND, and CINT is shown in Figure 16.10. RND produces a random number between 0 and 1. Statement 40 multiplies that number by 10 to obtain a range of randomly generated numbers between 0 and 10.

```
10  REM Generate RND numbers 0 - 10
20  T = VAL(RIGHT$(TIME$,2)) + 60 * VAL(MID$(TIME$,4,2))
30  RANDOMIZE (T)
40  FOR I = 1 TO 12
50      X = RND * 10
60      X = CINT (X)
70      PRINT X;
80  NEXT I
90  END
RUN
  3   9   2   8   9   5   9   7   0   0   2   3
Ok
RUN
 10   6   7   4   3   8   2   3   8   6   2   4
Ok
RUN
  2   1   4   3   5   3   9   2  10   0   9   3
Ok
```

FIGURE 16.10   Program to produce random numbers

INTERNAL DATA STORAGE OF NUMBERS

The computer internally stores data in either string or numeric format. We are familiar with strings, which can contain alphanumeric characters such as a street address and name. A dollar sign indicates the string variable: for example, STREET.ADDRESS$. Numbers are stored differently, in one of three forms: integer, single-precision, or double-precision.

Integer values are whole numbers in the range −32768 to +32767. Integers are whole numbers and do not contain a decimal value. A variable name to hold only an integer quantity is designated by the percent sign: for example, the integer variable ARRAY.LOCATION%.

Single-precision numbers are ordinary numbers with no special designation to identify the variable name. A single-precision variable (the variable we have been using so far, except for strings) contains seven or fewer digits of accuracy. As will be seen in a moment, this degree of accuracy is low enough to cause a problem in some special applications.

A variable can be declared a single-precision variable by using an exclamation mark after the variable name: for example, ANYVALUE!. If a variable is not declared, the computer assumes that it is a single-precision variable. Thus ANYVALUE (without the !) is a single-precision variable, the same as ANYVALUE!.

Although there is little need to declare single-precision variables other than to dazzle people with your programming skill, double-precision variables are a different matter. A double-precision variable contains a number with eight or more digits of accuracy. A variable can be declared to be double-precision by using the pound sign (#) at the end of the variable name. A double-precision number is stored internally with 17 digits of accuracy, which will handle many applications requiring very large (or very small) values.

In summary: ANYVALUE% is an integer (whole number); ANYVALUE and ANYVALUE! are single-precision numbers, and ANYVALUE# is a double-precision number. Double-precision numbers are often shown in exponential format.

EXPONENTIAL FORMAT

Exponential format, often called E format, is used for numbers greater than seven digits that are in the range of $2.9E-29$ to $1.7E+38$. As we will see in a moment, these are extremely small and large numbers. The computer automatically converts single-precision numbers to this format when the number is more than seven digits.

Let's look at an example of how the computer converts to E format. Suppose that the average cost of an employee, including pay, benefits, and overhead, is $22,137.42. If there are 1,000 employees in a firm, the labor cost for the firm is $22,137,420. As this number is more than seven digits, the computer converts the output to the exponential form of $2.213742E+07$, as shown in Figure 16.11. This number contains seven digits, which is the most that can be held with single-precision.

```
10 REM E (Exponential) Format
20 AVG.COST = 22137.42
30 NO.EMPLOYEES = 1000
40 LABOR.COST = AVG.COST * NO.EMPLOYEES
50 PRINT LABOR.COST
60 END
RUN
 2.213742E+07
Ok
```

FIGURE 16.11 Example of exponential format

The exponential format will not be difficult to understand once we become familiar with it. The E followed by a number means to move the decimal either to the right, if plus, or to the left, if negative. The example shown in Figure 16.11 can be read as "move the decimal seven positions to the right," which will yield the value we are familiar with as $22,137,420.

For example:

3.5E+02	is	350.
3.5E−02	is	.035
276.34E+03	is	276,340.
1.07E+08	is	107,000,000.
8.76E−04	is	.000876
34.6E+05	is	3,460,000.

The E format can be confusing to nonprogrammers attempting to read a computer output and should be avoided whenever possible. One way to avoid the E format is to employ the PRINT USING statement. This is shown in Figure 16.12, where LABOR.COST is displayed with a PRINT USING format that specifies the dollar sign, commas, and decimal point.

```
10 REM  PRINT USING on E numbers
20 AVG.COST = 22137.42
30 NO.EMPLOYEES = 1000
40 LABOR.COST = AVG.COST * NO.EMPLOYEES
50 S$ ="$$#########,.##"
60 PRINT USING S$; LABOR.COST
70 END
RUN
 $22,137,420.00
Ok
```

FIGURE 16.12 Controlling E format with PRINT USING

Another method of avoiding the exponential format is to use double-precision numbers. Double-precision numbers allow larger and smaller numbers to be displayed without resorting to the E format, and a higher degree of exactness is possible, although precision may still be a problem.

An example of double- versus single-precision numbers is shown in Figure 16.13. Notice that the E format did not appear in the double-precision variable.

```
10 REM Single versus Double-precision
20 AVG.COST       = 22137.42
30 NO.EMPLOYEES = 1000
40                                              ' Calculations
50 LABOR.COST    = AVG.COST * NO.EMPLOYEES
60 XLABOR.COST# = AVG.COST * NO.EMPLOYEES
70                                              ' Precision
80 PRINT "Single-precision" TAB(20) LABOR.COST
90 PRINT "Double-precision" TAB(20) XLABOR.COST#
100 END
RUN
Single-precision      2.213742E+07
Double-precision      22137420
Ok
```

FIGURE 16.13 Single- versus double-precision

A very practical problem can occur when an exact numeric answer is required of a large number. Even if double-precision numbers are used to achieve greater accuracy beyond seven digits, caution must still be exercised. As an example, examine the program shown in Figure 16.14, which is similar to the previous program except that the number of employees (NO.EMPLOYEES) has been increased to 1,111.

```
1Ø REM Single- versus Double-precision 2nd example
2Ø AVG.COST     = 22137.42
3Ø NO.EMPLOYEES = 1111
4Ø                                        ' Calculations
5Ø LABOR.COST    = AVG.COST * NO.EMPLOYEES
6Ø XLABOR.COST#  = AVG.COST * NO.EMPLOYEES
7Ø                                        ' Precision
8Ø PRINT "Single-precision" TAB(2Ø) LABOR.COST
9Ø PRINT "Double-precision" TAB(2Ø) XLABOR.COST#
1ØØ END
RUN
Single-precision     2.459468E+Ø7
Double-precision     24594674
Ok
```

FIGURE 16.14 Single- and double-precision errors

Output from the program shown in Figure 16.14 is not correct. When 1,111 is multiplied by the average cost per employee (AVG.COST) of $22,137.42, the answer should be $24,594,673.62. Before we proceed, let's double-check that answer:

$22,137.42 ×	1,000 =	$22,137,420.00
$22,137.42 ×	100 =	2,213,742.00
$22,137.42 ×	10 =	221,374.20
$22,137.42 ×	1 =	22,137.42
Totals	1,111	24,594,673.62

Now, take a closer look at the program output shown in Figure 16.14. The single-precision answer is off by $6.38 (too low) and the double-precision answer is off by $0.38 (too high).

The single-precision variable clearly does not have a high enough accuracy to be useful when dealing with large numbers. However, even the double-precision number is in error. The problem is due to the "least significant" digits in multiplying AVG.COST by NO.EMPLOYEES in statement 40. This $0.38 error is not a tremendous error, but to keep the Internal Revenue Service happy, let's see if we can't improve the accuracy of our cost figures by double-precisioning all variables.

A statement to define variables as double-precision so that the pound symbol will not have to be used throughout the program is the DEFDBL (define double) statement. A statement to double-precision variables beginning with a variable name letter of A through Z would be DEFDBL A–Z.

An example of a DEFDBL statement appears in the program shown in Figure 16.15. In this example, all variables from A through Z are double-

```
10 REM   Defining Double-precision variables
20 DEFDBL A-Z
30 S$ = "$$#########,.##"              ' Print Using string
40                                     ' Calculations
50 AVG.COST       = 22137.42
60 NO.EMPLOYEES = 1111
70 LABOR.COST     = AVG.COST * NO.EMPLOYEES
80                                     ' Precision vs Print Using
90 PRINT "Double-precision value:   " LABOR.COST
100 PRINT "The Print Using value:    ";
110 PRINT USING S$; LABOR.COST
120 END
RUN
Double-precision value:    24594673.53320313
The Print Using value:     $24,594,673.53
Ok
```

FIGURE 16.15   Using the DEFDBL statement

precision. Now look at the program output—we are only off by $0.09. It is strongly recommended that variables be double-precision if large numbers will be used.

PROGRAM GRAPHICS

Program graphics can be achieved by using a variety of symbols, lines, and boxes. Graphics created by the ASCII character set can be used on either of the two most common display systems: the IBM monochrome display with the parallel printer adapter or any type of monitor driven by the color/graphics monitor adapter.

The reports that have been produced so far have displayed data in a tabular format. In analyzing the reports, items had to be mentally compared with each other to determine if any relationship existed between the data elements. Sorting the data helped establish relationships, but nothing beats a visual display.

Character graphics are created by a careful selection of the appropriate ASCII code to produce the desired display. (See Appendix C, ASCII Codes.) You will have to experiment with your printer to determine if it can handle these symbols.

Let's go over a few of the fundamental displays. First, a bar chart can be developed by the following series of statements:

```
40   N = 15
50   FOR COLUMN = 1 TO N
60       PRINT CHR$(219);
70   NEXT COLUMN
RUN
████████████████
Ok
```

This is a rather cumbersome method and can be shortened by using the STRING$ statement shown below. The value of N determines how many times the CHR$(219) symbol will be repeated.

```
40 N = 15
50 PRINT STRING$(N,CHR$(219))
RUN
██████████████████
Ok
```

Boxes can be created by utilizing the following ASCII characters as previously shown in Chapter 9:

```
218        196        191
┌          ─          ┐         179
│                     │
└          ─          ┘
192        196        217
```

A subroutine which can be used to draw a box is shown below. Values for VTAB (vertical tab) and HTAB (horizontal tab) are required for the upper left-hand corner of the box. Also required are values for HLINE (the horizontal line across the top of the box) and VLINE (the vertical line down the side of the box).

```
9300 LOCATE VTAB,HTAB                              ' Draw Box
9310 PRINT CHR$(218) STRING$(HLINE,196) CHR$(191)
9320 FOR I = 1 TO VLINE -2
9330     LOCATE VTAB+I, HTAB          : PRINT CHR$(179)
9340     LOCATE VTAB+I, HTAB+HLINE+1 : PRINT CHR$(179)
9350 NEXT I
9360 LOCATE VTAB+VLINE-2, HTAB
9370 PRINT CHR$(192) STRING$(HLINE,196) CHR$(217)
9380 RETURN
```

Note: Type the subroutine shown and save it on your disk in ASCII format as "ENTERKEY.ASC". Then CHAIN MERGE the subroutine into your programs to add a professional look to the program output.

Let's put it all together. If you wanted to identify values quickly by time period or perhaps by product name, then a visual display of the data would be helpful. It should be simple enough to put a box around a screen, use STRING$ to print an N space bar, and then, presto—a graph. Simple, right?

Well, yes, it's true that printing graphics tends to be straightforward, but printing spaces can be a problem if we are not careful. Let's take a few general cases. First, a simplified bar chart will be constructed to show the number of traffic tickets issued by a small town on a day-by-day basis. Then two histograms will be presented. The first will consider the problem of scaling; the second will show student grades (perhaps of programming students?).

A SIMPLIFIED BAR CHART

A bar chart is often used to show relationships between data and time, such as sales by day or week, or—as in our case—number of traffic tickets issued by day.

We have to consider a few minor problems when graphing data. Although the screen is 24 lines by 80 characters, if a print is made in the 80th position, our graph will be disrupted, because the screen will "jump" as it attempts to wrap around to the next line. So, we will consider a meaningful print range to be from print positions 1 to 79.

The next problem is that we have been trained to graph data first on the X axis, then on the Y axis, while the general form of the LOCATE statement is the reverse:

Statement   **LOCATE** Line No., Position on line
number

That is, the Y axis is first, then the X axis.

```
10 REM Bar Chart for traffic tickets
20 '                                                    Reserve storage
30 DIM POSITION.LABLE$(7), LINE.LABLE$(5), TICKET(7)
40 '                                                    Merge box
50 CHAIN MERGE "ENTERKEY.ASC",70,ALL
60 '                                                    Draw box
70 CLS: HTAB=1: VTAB=1: HLINE=70: VLINE=23: GOSUB 9300
80 LOCATE 2,32: PRINT "Traffic Tickets"        ' Print heading
90 '                                                    Read days
100 FOR I = 1 TO 7
110     READ POSITION.LABLE$(I)
120 NEXT I
130 '                                                   Read range
140 FOR I = 1 TO 5
150     READ LINE.LABLE$(I)
160 NEXT I
170 '                                                   Read tickets
180 FOR I = 1 TO 7
190     READ TICKET(I)
200 NEXT I
210 '                                                   Print days
220 FOR I = 1 TO 7
230     LOCATE 20,10+I*6 : PRINT POSITION.LABLE$(I)
240 NEXT I
250 '                                                   Print ticket #
260 FOR I = 1 TO 5
270     LINE.NO = 21 - (I*3)
280     LOCATE LINE.NO,6: PRINT LINE.LABLE$(I)
290 NEXT I
300 '                                                   Print bars
310 FOR I = 1 TO 7
320     TOP = INT(.15 * TICKET(I) )
330     FOR PRINT.UP = 1 TO TOP
340         LINE.NO  = 20 - PRINT.UP
350         IF LINE.NO < 1 THEN LINE.NO = 1
360         LOCATE LINE.NO, 10+I*6+1 : PRINT CHR$(219);
370     NEXT PRINT.UP
380 NEXT I
390 '
9000 DATA Sun, Mon, Tue, Wed, Thu, Fri, Sat
9010 DATA 20-, 40-, 60-, 80-, 100
9020 DATA  10,  22,  35,  25,  40,  90, 50
9030 '                                                  Clear cursor
9040 LOCATE 23,1
9050 END
```

FIGURE 16.16 Simplified bar chart

This is not a major problem, but it is definitely something that we will have to keep in mind. One more point before proceeding: we will often be plotting "in reverse." We will often begin our plot on a lower line, perhaps 22,30, and plot up to 8,30. If you keep the following screen format in mind, you'll have no great problem in plotting.

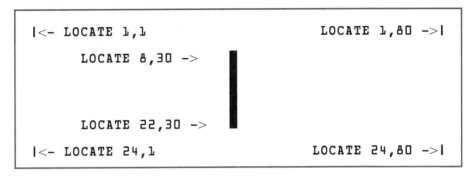

The program shown in Figure 16.16 produces a simplified bar chart. Note the use of the variable name POSITION.LABLE$, which is used to label the horizontal axis with the days of the week. The variable LINE.LABLE$ labels the vertical axis (the 24 lines on the screen) with the number of tickets issued. Statement 320 utilizes a scaling value of .15, which was determined through trial and error as being an accurate representation of the range of data. (More on this in the next program.) The "ENTERKEY-.ASC" program is not shown.

Program output is shown in Figure 16.17. Note that the output is in a relatively plain format that could be adapted to numerous applications.

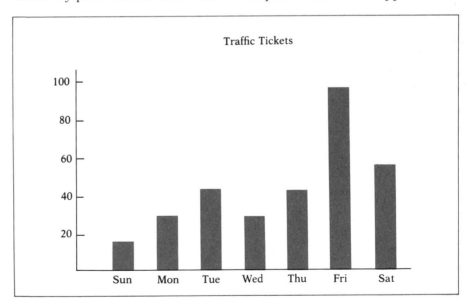

FIGURE 16.17 Program output

HISTOGRAM

The axes in the program output can be rotated so that the output is in the form of a horizontal bar graph called a histogram.

In addition to rotating the axes, let's consider an additional matter: scaling the data. A useful graphics program should be capable of handling data of any range and then developing a scale so that relationships can be shown within the confines of the standard screen.

A program that both scales and graphs the data is shown in Figure 16.18. Let's go over a few key statements in the program. After reading the sales value in statement **160 READ SALE(I)**, the lowest and highest values are calculated by the following statements:

```
170 IF SALE(I) < LOW  THEN LOW  = SALE(I)
180 IF SALE(I) > HIGH THEN HIGH = SALE(I)
```

Statement **220 PRINT.VALUE = 50/(HIGH - LOW)** is used to calculate the print increments. That is, we will be graphing from the lowest position up to the highest position, in increments that are often less than one. The N value in the PRINT STRING$ statement (statement 340) makes use of these print values in statement **320 N = INT(SALE(I) - LOW) * PRINT.VALUE**.

```
10 REM ASCII graphics characters
20 '                                            Reserve storage
30 DIM QUARTER$(4), SALE(4)
40 LOW = 9999 : HIGH = 0  '                     Set low & high
50 '                                            Merge box
60 CHAIN MERGE "ENTERKEY.ASC",80,ALL
70 '                                            Draw box
80 CLS: HTAB=1: VTAB=1: HLINE=75: VLINE=23: GOSUB 9300
90 LOCATE 2,25: PRINT "Quarterly Sales Analysis" '  Print heading
100 '                                           Read labels
110 FOR I = 1 TO 4
120     READ QUARTER$(I)
130 NEXT I
140 '                                           Read sales
150 FOR I = 1 TO 4
160     READ SALE(I)
170     IF SALE(I) < LOW  THEN LOW  = SALE(I)  '   Find lowest
180     IF SALE(I) > HIGH THEN HIGH = SALE(I)  '   Find highest
190 NEXT I
200 '                                           Calculate scale
210 N.STEPS = (HIGH - LOW)/10
220 PRINT.VALUE = 50/(HIGH-LOW)
230 LOCATE 20,20
240 '                                           Print scale
250 FOR I = 1 TO 10
260     PRINT LOW + INT((I-1)*N.STEPS)
270     LOCATE 20,20+I*5
280 NEXT I
290 '                                           Print output
300 FOR I = 1 TO 4
310     LOCATE I*4,8 : PRINT QUARTER$(I)   '     Print labels
320     N = INT(SALE(I) - LOW) * PRINT.VALUE
330     IF N < 1 THEN N = 1
340     LOCATE I*4,20 : PRINT STRING$(N,CHR$(219)) '  Print bar
350 NEXT I
360 '
9000 DATA Jan-Mar, Apr-Jun, Jul-Sep, Oct-Dec
9010 DATA     350,     400,     800,    1100
9020 '                                          Clear cursor
9030 LOCATE 23,1
9040 END
```

FIGURE 16.18   Product sales analysis

For example, suppose that sales are to be plotted on a graph that is 50 positions wide. Also suppose that the highest sale for the period is 1100 and the lowest 350. In order to show a meaningful graph, we would want to begin our plot at 350 so that relationships are visually compared to that lowest value.

The data range from 350 to 1100, for a total range of 750. The PRINT-.VALUE is calculated as 50/(range), which is 50/750, or .06667. That is, each dollar of sales receives .06667 of a print position. Let's check our work by identifying how the data would be displayed.

On a sale of 350, 350 − the lowest value (350) yields 0. Multiplying 0 times the PRINT.VALUE of .06667 yields 0 positions to be printed. Because we want to show that this data has not been forgotten, let's plot 1 position.

On a sale of 1100, 1100 − the lowest value (350) yields 750. Multiplying 750 times the PRINT.VALUE of .06667 yields 50 print positions. That is, the smallest value begins the display, and the largest value consumes the entire range of the display. Program output is shown in Figure 16.19.

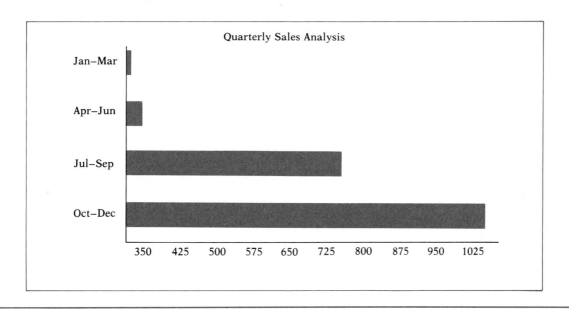

FIGURE 16.19   Program output

The program shown in Figure 16.20 totals grades within categories and then prints the grade distribution. I'll bet that if you were in this class, you would be interested in seeing the distribution of grades. Program output is shown in Figure 16.21.

```
10 REM Histogram
20 '                                           Reserve storage
30 DIM POSITION.LABEL$(4), LINE.LABEL$(5)
40 '                                           Merge box
50 CHAIN MERGE "ENTERKEY.ASC",70,ALL
60 '                                           Draw box
70 CLS: HTAB=1: VTAB=3: HLINE=60: VLINE=21: GOSUB 9300
80 LOCATE 4,25
90 COLOR 0,7 : PRINT " Grade Distribution " : COLOR 7,0
100 '                                          Read labels
110 FOR I = 1 TO 4
120     READ POSITION.LABEL$(I)
130 NEXT I
140 '                                          Grade range
150 FOR I = 1 TO 5
160     READ LINE.LABEL$(I)
170 NEXT I
180 '
190 READ GRADE   '                            Read grades
200 WHILE GRADE <> 9999 '                      Total grades
210    IF GRADE >= 90 THEN                  A = A + 1 : GOTO 260
220    IF GRADE >= 80 AND GRADE <= 89 THEN B = B + 1 : GOTO 260
230    IF GRADE >= 70 AND GRADE <= 79 THEN C = C + 1 : GOTO 260
240    IF GRADE >= 60 AND GRADE <= 69 THEN D = D + 1 : GOTO 260
250    F = F + 1
260    READ GRADE
270 WEND
280 '                                          Print labels
290 LOCATE 20,5: PRINT "Number:";
300 FOR I = 1 TO 4
310     LOCATE 20,9+I*10 : PRINT POSITION.LABEL$(I)
320 NEXT I
330 '                                          Print grid
340 FOR I = 1 TO 13
350     LOCATE 5+I,19 : PRINT CHR$(179)
360 NEXT I
370 LOCATE 5+I,19 : PRINT CHR$(192) STRING$(31,196)
380 '                                          Grade range
390 FOR I = 1 TO 5
400     LOCATE 3+I*3,5 : PRINT LINE.LABEL$(I)
410 NEXT I
420 '                                          # of grades
430 LOCATE  6,20 : PRINT STRING$(A,"*")
440 LOCATE  9,20 : PRINT STRING$(B,"*")
450 LOCATE 12,20 : PRINT STRING$(C,"*")
460 LOCATE 15,20 : PRINT STRING$(D,"*")
470 LOCATE 18,20 : PRINT STRING$(F,"*")
480 '
9000 DATA 0,   10, 20, 30
9010 DATA 90 -100, 80 -89, 70 -79, 60 -69, Below 60
9020 DATA 91,   92, 49, 59, 88, 74, 86, 88, 65, 74
9030 DATA 95,   94, 79, 59, 88, 74, 86, 88, 65, 74
9040 DATA 82,   76, 79, 95, 83, 88, 86, 78, 66, 69, 9999
9050 '                                         Clear cursor
9060 LOCATE 23,1
9070 END
```

FIGURE 16.20 Student grades

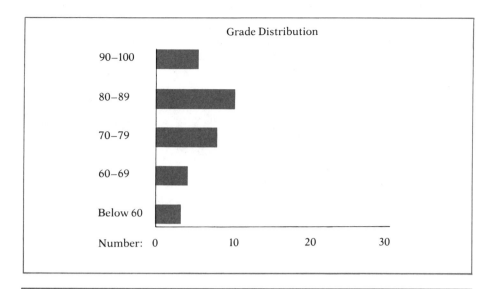

FIGURE 16.21   Program output

SUMMARY

Now that you understand subroutines, random numbers, the precision of numbers, and graphics using ASCII characters, you are well on your way to mastering the BASIC language. All that is left to "put it all together" is to develop a few techniques for handling errors. These will be discussed in the next chapter.

PROBLEMS

Beginning Programs. Problems 1–7.
Write short BASIC programs to solve the requested problems.

16.1   Renumber the DATA lines in the ASCII file "STOCKS.ASC" file beginning with line number 10100. Change this to 20000 and increment the line numbers by 20. Save the first 16 lines of the revised file and print the file at the DOS level.

16.2   Write a short program to print 22/7 in decimal form using single-precision and double-precision variables.

16.3   Write a program that accepts a string variable. Then develop an automatic centering routine to display the variable on the screen. Use the INT function to round values in centering.

16.4   Write a program to print 30 random numbers 1 through 100. Use the TIME$ function as a random number seed to develop a different number sequence each time the program is executed.

16.5   Write a program to simulate and display the outcome of tossing a coin 20 times. The output should be in terms of H for heads or T for tails.

16.6   Design a subroutine that will accept the current DATE$ and print out that date in a standard letter format. That is, the DATE$ function returns the date in the form of MM/DD/YY, such as 02-15-91. Convert this to February 15, 1991.

Test your program by assigning the DATE$ function various DATA statement values. Your program should demonstrate that the subroutine can handle all these values.

16.7 If two coins are tossed, the following outcomes are possible: two heads, two tails, or one of each. Write a program to simulate and display the outcome of 30 trials of tossing two coins per trial. The output should be a list of terms such as HH, TT, HT, or TH.

Screen Design Problems. Problems 8–17.
Develop a BASIC program, paying particular attention to the design of the screen and the design of the printed output (when requested). General formats are shown for your consideration; they may be expanded on (improved) in your program.
Problems 8 and 9 require the use of the ASCII file called "BUZZWORD.ASC".
This file is organized as follows:

	Language	Type	Jargon
File	--	--	--
Data	--	--	--
Variables	LANGUAGE\$	TYPE\$	JARGON\$

*16.8 Write a program to randomly generate six programming languages that a beginning student should learn. Each language selected is to be randomly generated, and duplicates must be avoided.

Random Number/Word Assignment Test Sample
The five different random numbers are:
8   10   7   4   6
The six different languages are:
ADA   FORTH   Machine   PL1   RPG

16.9 Write a program to randomly select one "buzzword" from each column using the indicated variable names. Then have the program display the following paragraph three times. The randomly selected buzzword is to appear in the underlined positions. Do not permit duplicate buzzwords.

```
The programming language LANGUAGE$ uses TYPE$
coding with JARGON$ for easy-to-understand
programs.
```

16.10 Write a program that will generate 200 random numbers between 1 and 100. Have your program display the necessary totals according to the following format:

Number range	Total occurrences
01–25	XX
26–50	XX
51–75	XX
76–100	XX

* The answer to this problem is in Appendix E.

16.11 Write a program to display the following five daily sales beginning with Monday: 200, 350, 500, 800, 575. Scale your output so that it can be displayed in the following format:

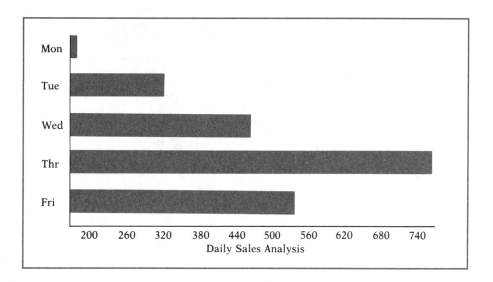

16.12 Big Springs county courthouse administers four driver's tests per day to people trying to obtain a driver's license. Write a program to produce the following output:

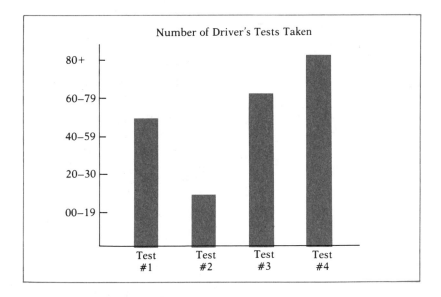

Use the following data for the number of people taking each test: 50; 22; 65, and 80. Hint: Attempt to obtain only a rough visual representation of these numbers. A scaling factor of .18 was used, but other factors are acceptable.

16.13 Develop a program to produce an output similar to that shown on the next page. This program is to accept student grades on DATA statements and count the students who had grades in the ranges indicated. For example, the following chart shows that 3 students had grades of below 60.

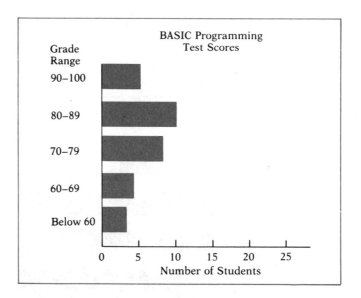

Use the following DATA statements to check your work.

```
9010 DATA 91, 92, 49, 59, 88, 74, 86, 88, 65, 74
9020 DATA 95, 94, 79, 59, 88, 74, 86, 88, 65, 74
9030 DATA 82, 76, 79, 95, 83, 88, 86, 78, 66, 69,
     9999
```

16.14 Develop a quiz program to test incoming freshmen on their knowledge of "world activities." Use ON N GOTO to capture their answers to the question shown below. Test for invalid (out of range) answers.

```
P. T. Barnum said:

1 What me worry?
2 A sucker is born every minute.
3 I don't get no respect.
4 Go ahead, make my day!
5 Be all that you can be!

Your selection?
```

The answers are

1 Alfred E. Neuman
2 Ah, yes. This is the answer.
3 Comedian Rodney Dangerfield
4 Clint Eastwood
5 No, but I think it's time you enlisted.

16.15 Develop a quiz program to test students on historical comments. Use an ON N GOTO statement to capture their answers to the question shown below. Test for invalid (out of range) answers.

```
Who said, ''Don't worry. I'm sure there are only
          a few of those Indians!''

a The Lone Ranger.
b Roy Rogers.
c Buck Rogers.
d General Custer.

Your selection?
```

The answers are

    a No, Tonto is his friend.
    b No, he was more interested in Dale Evans.
    c Boy are you on the wrong planet.
    d Yep! He sure was the bright one.

16.16 Develop a computerized game that generates a random number greater than 10, but less than 90. Store the number in a variable called GUESS.IT, then have the user attempt to guess the number. A sample run is shown below.

```
I'm thinking of a number between 10 and 90.
Try to guess it!

Your guess? 40
Too high. Guess again!

Your guess? 9
The number is > than 10 and < 90.

Your guess? 15
Too low. Guess again.

Your guess? 23
Correct! You guessed the number in 3 trials!
Play again (Y/N)? N
Ok
```

16.17 Develop a computerized game in which two Gremlins race from a starting line to a finish line. Both Gremlins are represented by the ASCII value of 001. These weird little creatures can do only the following:

    1 Nothing
    2 Move one step forward
    3 Move two steps forward
    4 Move one step backward

Generate a random number and use LOCATE to move the characters across the screen. Delay each move for a second.

The initial screen appears as follows:

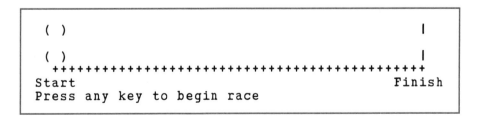

```
( )                                                      |
( )                                                      |
+++++++++++++++++++++++++++++++++++++++++++++++++++++
Start                                              Finish
Press any key to begin race
```

Other Problems. Problems 18–23.
Develop a BASIC program to solve each problem. Use a REM statement to identify the problem number, and clearly label all output.
The following information is needed for Problems 18 and 19.

Big Pizza, Inc., has developed statistics on the arrival of customers during Friday and Saturday evenings from 5 PM to 9 PM. The time between arrivals in minutes and the frequency of their occurrence are as follows:

Time between arrivals (minutes)	Frequency of occurrence
4	30%
5	50%
6	20%

16.18 Write a program to randomly determine how many customers Big Pizza Inc. can expect on a Friday evening. Simulate these arrivals four times.

16.19 Write a program to determine how many customers will arrive each hour on Friday between 5 PM and 9 PM. Simulate these arrivals six times.

16.20 Write a program to check the random numbers produced by the program shown in Figure 16.9. Generate 1000 random numbers and calculate how many times each of the numbers 1 through 10 occurred. How accurate are the random numbers when using the TIME$ function as a seed value?

Problems 21–23 require the following information to develop a computer program for "The Funky Chicken Game." There is to be a delay of a couple of seconds after generating a random number.

A chicken was being transported to market in a cage on the back of a pickup truck. Instinctively the chicken knew it had a short life ahead of it, so it pecked the cage open and leaped from the truck. Unfortunately it jumped when the truck was crossing a stream, and the chicken landed in the middle of a narrow bridge. The bridge crosses the small stream as shown.

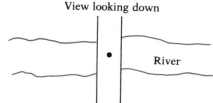

View looking down

River

If the chicken takes 5 steps to the right or left, it will fall off the bridge into the water. However, the chicken can walk off the bridge to safety in only 5 steps, forward or backward.

16.21 Develop the Funky Chicken Game assuming that the chicken can step only to the left or right. How many steps will it take before it falls off?

16.22 Develop the Funky Chicken Game assuming that the chicken can step to the left, right, or forward. How many steps will it take before it either falls off the bridge or reaches safety?

16.23 This funky chicken really has problems. Although it can step to the left, right, or forward, in 10 seconds an 18-wheel truck will come across the narrow bridge. Can the chicken make it to safety, or will it become "Chicken Patties?"

Plot the progress of the chicken (if any). Use the TIME$ function to display the remaining time. Use a half-second delay between plots.

17 PUTTING IT ALL TOGETHER

You have come a long way in programming, and only a few additional concepts are needed to put it all together. Upon completion of this chapter, you should be able to understand

- Word processing
- ERROR processing
- How to detect program bugs
- PC compatibles

WORD PROCESSING

Word processing consists of using the power of the computer to simplify making changes to text. The TIME\$ and DATE\$ functions will come in handy, as well as the VAL, LEN, RIGHT\$, LEFT\$, MID\$, and STRING\$ functions discussed in Chapter 7.

Word processing applications involve a lot of string processing. A general program to assure that a string is of a standard length (in this case 12) is shown in Figure 17.1. Notice that statement 60 adds a blank to X\$ until the string is 12 characters long. This is often called padding a string.

In addition to the LEN function, the INSTR function is useful in word processing programs. The INSTR function is used to search for the occurrence of one string within another string. The general format of the INSTR function is

Statement POSITION. = **INSTR** (BEGIN GIVEN SUB
number NUMBER .SEARCH, .STRING\$, .STRING\$)

Where:

POSITION.NUMBER is a numeric variable.

BEGIN.SEARCH is the optional position between 1 and 255 within the string where the search is to begin. If omitted, the search begins from the first position.

GIVEN.STRING\$ is the string being searched.

SUB.STRING\$ is the sub-string that you are searching for within GIVEN.STRING\$.

It is not as difficult to use the INSTR function as it appears. An example of using the INSTR function to find the occurrence of the sub-string called SUB.STRING\$ within the main string called GIVEN.STRING\$ is

```
10 REM    Example of a fixed string length
20 PRINT "Type a 12 character or less name";
30 INPUT X$
40 '
50 IF LEN(X$) > 12 THEN 60 ELSE 70
60 BEEP: PRINT "12 character maximum!": GOTO 20
70 IF LEN(X$) < 12 THEN X$ = X$ + " " : GOTO 70
80 '
90 COLOR 0,7: PRINT X$;: COLOR 7,0
100 END
```

FIGURE 17.1 Padding a string

shown in Figure 17.2. The string "All good men come to the aid of their country" was searched for the occurrence of the sub-string "good". This sub-string was found to begin in column 5.

String searches in a word processing application become more complicated. For example, the GIVEN.STRING$ shown in Figure 17.2 is changed in Figure 17.3. Notice that the program did not find the word "to" we were looking for, but instead found the sub-string starting in the word "together".

Several different approaches can be taken to solve this problem. One is to adjust the sub-string to include a leading and a trailing blank. This approach will not work when the word we're searching for is at the end of a line, where the following character is not a blank but an Enter symbol CHR$(13), nor if the word we're searching for is at the beginning of a line, where there is no leading blank. And, of course, it will not work if we are searching for a sub-string that is within a larger word.

One way around these problems is to find the sub-string, then give the user the option of substituting a different string value, as shown in Figure

```
10 REM Searching for a sub-string
20 GIVEN.STRING$ =  "All good men come to the aid of their country."
30 PRINT "123456789012345678901234567890123456789Ø"
40 PRINT GIVEN.STRING$
50 PRINT
60 PRINT "Let's search for a sub-string."
70 PRINT "Your sub-string";
80 INPUT SUB.STRING$
90 POSITION.NUMBER = INSTR(GIVEN.STRING$, SUB.STRING$)
100 IF POSITION.NUMBER = Ø THEN BEEP: PRINT "Not found":
       GOTO 120
110 PRINT "Your sub-string begins in column" POSITION.NUMBER
120 END
RUN
123456789012345678901234567890123456789Ø
All good men come to the aid of their country.

Let's search for a sub-string.
Your sub-string? good
Your sub-string begins in column 5
Ok
```

FIGURE 17.2 Searching for a sub-string

```
10 REM Finding an unwanted sub-string
20 GIVEN.STRING$ =  "All good men come together to aid their country."
30 PRINT "1234567890123456789012345678901234567890"
40 PRINT GIVEN.STRING$
50 PRINT
60 PRINT "Let's search for a sub-string."
70 PRINT "Your sub-string";
80 INPUT SUB.STRING$
90 POSITION.NUMBER = INSTR(GIVEN.STRING$, SUB.STRING$)
100 IF POSITION.NUMBER = 0 THEN BEEP: PRINT "Not found":
        GOTO 120
110 PRINT "Your sub-string begins in column" POSITION.NUMBER
120 END
RUN
1234567890123456789012345678901234567890
All good men come together to aid their country.

Let's search for a sub-string.
Your sub-string? to
Your sub-string begins in column 19
Ok
```

FIGURE 17.3 Finding an unwanted sub-string

17.4. The more difficult-to-understand portions of the program are statements 290 through 310 where the SUB.STRING$ is replaced by the string REPLACED$. (More on this point in a moment.)

The screen would appear as shown below when searching for the word "to" and replacing it with "xx". The first line of text is shown, where the decision was made to replace the "to" in "too" and in "togetherness" with "xx".

```
Search for? to
Replace with? xx




This is too much togetherness to expect results.
      ^   Replace Y/N?
```

The revised text in which a substitution was made whenever "to" was encountered is shown below. Notice that substitutions were performed for words at the beginning and end of the line and for the letters "to" occurring within a word.

```
Revised text:
This is xxo much xxgetherness xx expect results.
I'd rather be xxtally alone than have xx
auxxmatically continue with this group.  Have you
xxo had problems?  If so, xxmorrow is another day.
```

```
10 REM Finding and replacing strings
20 CLS
30 DIM TEXT$(4)
40 FOR I = 1 TO 4                                    ' Read into TEXT$
50     READ TEXT$(I)
60 NEXT I
70 '
80 PRINT "Search for";                               ' Set up sub-string
90 INPUT SUB.STRING$
100 STRING.LEN = LEN(SUB.STRING$)                    ' Establish length
110 PRINT "Replace with";                            ' Replacement string
120 INPUT REPLACED$
130 '
140 FOR I = 1 TO 4
150    POSITION = INSTR(TEXT$(I), SUB.STRING$)
160    WHILE POSITION                                ' Zero means true
170       LOCATE 10,1: PRINT SPACE$(159);            ' Clear lines
180       LOCATE 10,1: PRINT TEXT$(I)                ' Show line
190       LOCATE 11,POSITION                         ' Position cursor
200       PRINT "^   Replace Y/N?"
210       A$ = INPUT$(1)
220       IF A$ = "Y" OR A$ = "y" THEN 230 ELSE 300
230       LEFT.PART$  = LEFT$(TEXT$(I), POSITION -1) ' Left part of string
240                                                  ' Calculate right part
250       REJECT.LEN  = POSITION - 1  + STRING.LEN
260       KEEP.LEN    = LEN(TEXT$(I)) - REJECT.LEN
270       RIGHT.PART$ = RIGHT$(TEXT$(I), KEEP.LEN)
280                                                  ' Develop string
290       TEXT$(I)    = LEFT.PART$ + REPLACED$ + RIGHT.PART$
300       J = POSITION + STRING.LEN
310       POSITION = INSTR(J, TEXT$(I), SUB.STRING$)
320    WEND
330 NEXT I
340 '
350 PRINT "Revised text:"                            ' Display text
360 FOR I = 1 TO 4
370     PRINT TEXT$(I)
380 NEXT I
390 '
9000 DATA "This is too much togetherness to expect results."
9010 DATA "I'd rather be totally alone than have to"
9020 DATA "automatically continue with this group.  Have you"
9030 DATA "too had problems?  If so, tomorrow is another day."
9040 END
```

FIGURE 17.4 Finding and substituting strings

Now let's take a closer look at how this program finds and substitutes strings. The string we are searching for will be called SUB.STRING$. The desired replacement string is called REPLACED$. The given string, called TEXT$, is assigned the following string contained in the DATA statement:

```
This is too much togetherness to expect results.
```

```
123456789012345678901234567890123456789012345678
```

The process of finding and replacing strings begins with finding the sub-string. Then the left-hand portion of the main TEXT$ string up to the sub-string is stored in LEFT.PART$. Next, the text to the right of the sub-string is identified and stored in RIGHT.PART$. Finally, a new TEXT$ string is constructed by adding together LEFT.PART$ + REPLACED$ + RIGHT.PART$. Let's take a close look at the statements used to accomplish this.

In statement `310 POSITION = INSTR(J, TEXT$(I), SUB-.STRING$)` the search begins at the first column (J=1). The first occurrence of the sub-string "to" is found at position 9.

Statement `230 LEFT.PART$ = LEFT$(TEXT$(I), POSITION -1)` is used to identify the left part of the string "This is" and store it in LEFT.PART$ as follows:

```
LEFT.PART$
"This is"
```

```
This is too much togetherness to expect results.
```

```
12345678901234567890123456789012345678901234567 8
```
Position
Position -1

Calculating the right part of the string is tricky. The unwanted portion of the string is calculated in statement `290 REJECT.LEN = POSITION - 1 + STRING.LEN`. That is, the portion "This is " and then the string "to" is "rejected." This can be visualized as follows:

```
This is too much togetherness to expect results.
```

```
12345678901234567890123456789012345678901234567 8
```
Position -1
Reject.len

```
"This is to"                    String portion that will
                                be rejected.
```

Statement `260 KEEP.LEN = LEN(TEXT$(I) - REJECT.LEN)` calculates the length of the TEXT$ string (48) less the rejected length (10), yielding the keep length of 38. This can be viewed as follows when counting from the right:
String to keep:

```
        "o much togetherness to expect results."
         1234567890123456789012345678901234567 8
         |                                     |
This is too much togetherness to expect results.
12345678901234567890123456789012345678901234567 8
```

Statement `270 RIGHT.PART$ = RIGHT$(TEXT$(I), KEEP.LEN)` assigns "o much togetherness to expect results." to RIGHT.PART$. Finally, a revised TEXT$ string is developed in statement 290 by adding LEFT.PART$, REPLACED$, and RIGHT.PART$ together. The remainder of the statements in the program work as indicated.

PERSONALIZED FORM LETTERS

Have you ever received a letter from a national corporation that repeatedly mentioned your name within the letter? I'm sure you are wise enough to recognize that these firms mail out millions of letters and that they do not write a personal letter to each customer. Despite our understanding this point, it seems that firms specializing in sales promotions, particularly magazine sales, take particular delight in seeing if we "really believe" that they wrote us a personal letter.

One way that "personalized" form letters can be generated is shown in Figure 17.5. Notice that a single entry is made for the person's title, first name, last name, street address, city, state, and zip code. Yet by using the string processing functions, a personalized letter is created. Please note

```
10 REM A "personalized" form letter.
20 '                                        Read name & address
30 READ TITLE$,  F.NAME$, L.NAME$
40 READ ADDRESS$,  CITY$, STATE$, ZIP
50 '
60 WHILE TITLE$ <> "END"
70      CLS
80      PRINT "Dear " TITLE$ " " F.NAME$ " " L.NAME$ ":"
90      PRINT
100     PRINT "Thank you for recently shopping in our store "
                TITLE$ " " L.NAME$ "."
110     PRINT "Perhaps other members of the " L.NAME$
                " family would be interested"
120     PRINT "in receiving our charge cards.   "
                "Our firm deals with thousands"
130     PRINT "of people like youself that live in " CITY$ "."
140     PRINT
150     PRINT "So " F.NAME$;
160     PRINT ", please fill out the enclosed application and"
170     PRINT "we will send our charge card to your ";
180 '                                        Strip street No.
190     IF VAL(ADDRESS$) > 0 THEN 200 ELSE 240
200     S$        = STR$( VAL(ADDRESS$) )
210     X         = LEN(S$)
220     L.ADDRESS = LEN(ADDRESS$) - X
230     ADDRESS$  = RIGHT$(ADDRESS$,L.ADDRESS)
240     PRINT ADDRESS$ " address."
250 '                                        Print closing
260     PRINT : PRINT "Sincerely yours," : PRINT : PRINT
270     PRINT "John Jackson, Sales Manager"
280 '                                        Load next letter
290     IF INKEY$ <> "" THEN 290
300     LOCATE 24,1 :    PRINT "Load stationary & press any key.";
310     IF INKEY$ = ""  THEN 310
320 '
330     READ TITLE$,  F.NAME$, L.NAME$
340     READ ADDRESS$,  CITY$, STATE$, ZIP
350 WEND
360 '
9000 DATA Mr., Tom, Jones
9010 DATA 121 South Main, Louisville, KY, 40222
9020 DATA Ms., Alice, Smith
9030 DATA 1400 Broadway, New York, NY, 10010
9040 DATA END, 0, 0
9050 DATA 0,   0, 0, 0
9060 END
```

FIGURE 17.5 A personalized form letter

```
Dear Mr. Tom Jones:

Thank you for recently shopping in our store Mr. Jones.
Perhaps other members of the Jones family would be interested
in receiving our charge cards.  Our firm deals with thousands
of people like yourself that live in Louisville.

So Tom, please fill out the enclosed application and
we will send our charge card to your South Main address.

Sincerely yours,


John Jackson, Sales Manager




Load stationary & press any key.
```

FIGURE 17.6 Program output—partial

that this is a "thank you" letter sent to a customer. The customer is treated with respect and is not manipulated with false or misleading promises.

Partial program output is shown in Figure 17.6. In actual practice, PRINT would be changed to LPRINT so that program output would be on company letterhead. Notice statements 190 through 230 that process the ADDRESS$ string to remove the street number (if any). In statement 190 the VAL (value) of ADDRESS$ is assigned to the string S$ using the STR$ (string) function. The LEN (length) of S$ is subtracted from the LEN of ADDRESS$, yielding L.ADDRESS (the length of ADDRESS$ containing the street name). In statement 230, RIGHT$ removes the street number by reassigning the street name to ADDRESS$.

CONVERTING LOWERCASE TO UPPERCASE LETTERS

Letters can be converted from lowercase to uppercase by processing their ASCII values. Take a close look at the ASCII character codes contained in Appendix C. When 32 is subtracted from the ASCII value of a lowercase letter, the result is an uppercase letter.

a	097 − 32 = 065	A
b	096 − 32 = 064	B
c	095 − 32 = 063	C
.	.	.
.	.	.
.	.	.
z	122 − 32 = 090	Z

```
10 REM Converting lowercase to uppercase letters
20 CLS
30 LOCATE 5,1
40 PRINT "Type data and press Enter:"
50 A$ = INKEY$ : IF A$ = ""  THEN 50
60 IF A$ = CHR$(13) THEN 120 ELSE 80
70 '
80 AA$ = AA$ + A$
90 LOCATE 6,1: PRINT AA$
100 GOTO 50
110 '                                    Convert to upper case
120 FOR I  = 1 TO LEN(AA$)
130      X$ = MID$(AA$,I,1)
140      Y  = ASC(X$)
150 '                                    97-122 is lower case
160 '   IF Y => 97 AND Y <= 122 THEN N$ = N$ + CHR$(Y-32)
            ELSE N$ = N$ + X$
170 NEXT I
180 '
190 PRINT "Final string: " N$
200 END
```

FIGURE 17.7 Converting lowercase to uppercase letters

This technique can be used to convert lowercase to uppercase letters. The resulting string can be used to simplify finding a record in a file management system without having to worry about capitalization.

An example of converting cases is shown in Figure 17.7. The ASCII value of each character in the string AA$ is calculated, one at a time, and assigned to the variable Y. The key statement in this program is:

```
140 IF Y => 97 AND Y <= 122 THEN N$ = N$ +
         CHR$(Y-32) ELSE N$ = N$ + X$
```

Lowercase letters have an ASCII code between 097 and 122. When one is encountered, a value of 32 is subtracted to create the uppercase letter. The string N$ is then constructed of all uppercase letters. An example of converting to uppercase is shown in Figure 17.8.

```
Type data and press Enter:
Send to: 121 South Main, Apt. 4
Final string: SEND TO: 121 SOUTH MAIN, APT. 4
Ok
```

FIGURE 17.8 Program output

PROGRAM DETECTION OF ERRORS

If you have been working the problems in this book, you should be used to finding and correcting errors. When an error occurs, it is found and corrected. All is soon forgotten (unless it is a program bug) because, as programmers, we expect to make errors.

The user is different. A computer is a tool to assist in an application, and the program is used to instruct the computer in the steps needed to accomplish a task. Except for a few computer "hacks," adults normally do not enjoy running a program. The best that can be said is that many people will tolerate the exactness required by a program to accomplish an objective. Given this attitude (which I suspect is widely held), when an error is encountered, even if the user caused the error, there is little if any patience with it.

Although the term "user-friendly" has been abused by many commercial software firms, programs should be easy to use and as "forgiving" as possible. This permits users to concentrate on the problem at hand and to use the computer as a problem-solving tool.

Error messages have BASIC code numbers of 1 through 30 and 50 through 73. These codes can be used to find most common programming errors but, as we will see in a moment, are of little help in finding errors in logic.

The program shown in Figure 17.9 can be used to display error messages corresponding to a user-entered number. Statement `40 ERROR XERR` prints the message corresponding to the number of the error. This program is for demonstration purposes only, as the reserved word ERROR is normally used with an ON ERROR GOTO statement.

A complete listing of the BASIC error codes is shown in Figure 17.10.

The ON ERROR GOTO statement transfers control to a specific statement when a BASIC language error occurs. The general form of the ON ERROR GOTO statement is

Statement   **ON ERROR GOTO**   Statement
number   number

```
10 REM  Displaying error codes 1-30 & 50-72
20 PRINT "Error number";
30 INPUT XERR
40 ERROR XERR
RUN
Error number? 1
NEXT without FOR in 40
Ok
RUN
Error number? 3
RETURN without GOSUB in 40
Ok
RUN
Error number? 72
Disk Media Error in 40
Ok
RUN
Error number? 24
Device Timeout in 40
Ok
```

FIGURE 17.9 Displaying ERROR messages

Code	Explanation	Code	Explanation
1	NEXT without FOR	26	FOR without NEXT
2	Syntax error	27	Out of paper
3	RETURN without GOSUB	29	WHILE without WEND
4	Out of data	30	WEND without WHILE
5	Illegal function call	50	FIELD overflow
6	Overflow	51	Internal error
7	Out of memory	52	Bad file number
8	Undefined line number	53	File not found
9	Subscript out of range	54	Bad file mode
10	Duplicate definition	55	File already open
11	Division by zero	57	Device I/O error
12	Illegal direct	58	File already exists
13	Type mismatch	61	Disk full
14	Out of string space	62	Input past end
15	String too long	63	Bad record number
16	String formula too complex	64	Bad file name
		66	Direct statement to file
17	Can't continue	67	Too many files
18	Undefined user definition	68	Device unavailable
19	No RESUME	69	Communication buffer overflow
20	RESUME without error		
21	Unprintable error	70	Disk write protect
22	Missing operand	71	Disk not ready
23	Line buffer overflow	72	Disk media error
24	Device timeout	73	Advanced feature
25	Device fault	—	Unprintable error

FIGURE 17.10 BASIC error codes

When an error occurs, the ON ERROR GOTO statement transfers control to the specified statement number. Although the ON ERROR GOTO statement can be placed anywhere in the program, it frequently is placed as the first statement in the program.

The corresponding statement to permit program execution to resume after either correcting the error or alerting the user to take corrective action is

Statement   **RESUME**   Statement
number   number

After an error is trapped, the RESUME statement performs two functions. First, it resets the error trap so that new errors may be trapped. Second, program control is returned to the point where the error occurred. Unless the error is corrected before the RESUME statement is executed, the program may be placed in an infinite loop of logic.

An example of using an ON ERROR GOTO statement in a program is shown in Figure 17.11. This program calculates the square root of user-entered values. An error will occur if an attempt is made to take the square root of a negative number. The ON ERROR GOTO statement directs control to statement 90 to correct the condition.

The ON ERROR GOTO statement only traps for the occurrence of an error. It does not detect which error actually occurred. That is, our square root example actually traps for any BASIC error. If we wanted to be dis-

```
10 REM Test for an error
20 ON ERROR GOTO 1000
30 PRINT "Enter value for square root."
40 PRINT "Enter 999 to end program."
50 PRINT "Your value ";: INPUT X
60 WHILE X <> 999
70     ANS = SQR(X)
80       PRINT "The square roots of " X "are + and -" ANS
90       PRINT "Your value ";: INPUT X
100 WEND
110 PRINT "End of program"
120 END
130 '                                          ERROR message
1000 BEEP
1010 PRINT "You can't take a square root of a negative number!"
1020 PRINT "Press any key to continue."
1030 A$ = INPUT$(1)
1040 X = ABS(X)
1050 RESUME 60
1060 '
```

FIGURE 17.11   Using an ON ERROR GOTO statement

criminating, the ERR statement could be used to detect the specific BASIC error condition that occurred.

The ON ERROR GOTO statement is normally used to direct control to the ERR statement that tests for the specific error condition. Once the specific error is known, corrective action can be taken within the program or can be suggested to the program user.

The general form of the ERR statement is

Statement   **IF ERR =**   Error   **THEN - -**
number   number

```
10 REM  Note error processing
20 ON ERROR GOTO 1000
30 PRINT "Type name and press Enter";
40 INPUT EMPL.NAME$
50 LPRINT "Dear " EMPL.NAME$
60 END
70 '                                          ERROR message
1000 BEEP
1010 IF ERR = 24 OR ERR = 27 THEN 1020 ELSE 1070
1020 PRINT "Turn on printer.  Then"
1030 PRINT "Press any key to continue."
1040 A$ = INPUT$(1)
1050 RESUME
1060 '                                          Unknown error
1070 BEEP: PRINT "An unidentified error occurred."
1080 BEEP: PRINT "End of demonstration program."
1090 END
```

FIGURE 17.12   Trapping for an error

The RESUME statement is again used to permit program execution to begin automatically (resume) after the error condition is corrected.

A partial program using error trapping is shown in Figure 17.12. The error being detected is one that occurs frequently: the program is directing output to a printer, but the user may have forgotten to turn the printer on. To detect this condition, we are trapping for an ERR code of 24 (no printer) or 27 (out of paper or turned off).

One more point before leaving this subject of error trapping: the error statements may not work correctly on nonstandard computer equipment such as some printers. You will have to experiment to determine the suitability of these error-processing statements on your own computer.

THE TRON (TRACE ON) AND TROFF (TRACE OFF) COMMANDS

A programming language instructs the computer in the specific sequence required to solve a problem. If the logic is faulty, there is little the BASIC language, or any language, can do to correct it. However, a powerful technique for detection of programming errors is provided in BASIC: the TRON (trace on) and TROFF (trace off) commands to trace the sequence of program execution. The TRON command displays statement line numbers enclosed in square brackets. The TROFF command shuts off the TRON command. TRON and TROFF may also be used as program statements to trace portions of a program that contain a suspected error.

The general form of the commands is

TRON Turns tracing feature on. Command may be typed in full, or press function key F7 to start the trace.

```
10  REM Notice statement execution
20  FOR I = 1 TO 4
30      PRINT TAB(15) "Loop #" I "Note line numbers."
40  NEXT I
50  END
RUN
              Loop # 1 Note line numbers.
              Loop # 2 Note line numbers.
              Loop # 3 Note line numbers.
              Loop # 4 Note line numbers.
Ok
TRON
Ok
RUN
[10][20][30]  Loop # 1 Note line numbers.
[40][30]      Loop # 2 Note line numbers.
[40][30]      Loop # 3 Note line numbers.
[40][30]      Loop # 4 Note line numbers.
[40][50]
Ok
TROFF
Ok
```

FIGURE 17.13 Using TRON and TROFF

TROFF   Turns tracing off. Command may be typed, or press function key F8 to stop the trace.

The program shown in Figure 17.13 displays a PRINT message five times. Notice what occurs after the TRON is typed and the program is executed. Statement numbers are displayed each time a statement is executed.

ADVANCED DEBUGGING TECHNIQUES

There are two ways of viewing a program bug. The first views the bug as an annoying, nit-picking waste of time. If such an attitude is taken, little can be learned from your mistakes and you will be likely to continue to make errors. The second way is to take a positive approach when encountering a program error. If you try to determine why and how the error occurred, you will learn from your errors. I hope you take the second approach.

Let's examine an example of a program bug and use a step-by-step approach to identify the bug. The program shown in Figure 17.14 calculates a special tax levied for air pollution control. The tax is imposed by the local government on industrial property at the rate of ten mills per

```
10 REM  Do you see the bug?
20 DEFDBL A-L
30 S$ ="$$#######,.##"
40 TOTAL = 0
50 PRINT "Assessed Value" TAB(31) "Tax"
60 FOR M = 1 TO 4
70    READ ASSETS(M)
80    AIR.TAX = .001 * ASSETS(M)
90    PRINT USING S$;ASSETS(M);: PRINT SPC(10);
100     PRINT USING S$;AIR.TAX
110 TOTAL = TOTAL -  AIR.TAX
120 NEXT M
130 PRINT
140 PRINT "Total tax due:" TAB(25);
150 PRINT USING S$;TOTAL
160 DATA 1000000, 10000000, 40000000, 5000000
170 END
RUN
Assessed Value                Tax
 $1,000,000.00            $1,000.00
$10,000,000.00           $10,000.00
$40,000,000.00           $40,000.00
 $5,000,000.00            $5,000.00

Total tax due:           -$56,000.01
Ok
```

FIGURE 17.14   Example of a program bug

$100 of assessed value. For an assessed value of $10,000,000 of industrial property the tax would be calculated as follows:

$$\frac{\$10,000,000}{\$100} = \underbrace{100,000}_{\$100 \text{ units}} * \underbrace{10}_{\text{mills}} * \underbrace{.001}_{\text{value}}$$

This could be reduced to simply ASSETS * .001.

Do you see the program bug in Figure 17.14? The answer is negative, and we can identify by observation that the total must be a positive number. Also, the answer for total tax due contains an incorrect decimal value. Let's try to find the bug. First, we will trace the sequence of statement execution. Press function key F7 to turn the trace on, then run the program.

The results from tracing the output for the five loops is of no help in finding this bug. Look at the program shown in Figure 17.14 again. First, let's tackle the negative total. This is due to statement 110 containing a minus when we should be adding. Changing this to a plus will yield a positive total.

Now we still have the problem of the .01 value that showed up in the total. The best advice at this point is not to panic. Often the most difficult-to-find errors are the simple, subtle ones. Take a break and approach the problem later with a fresh mind.

Have you found the bug? It is in statement 20 where variables A–L were double-precisioned. The totaling variable (TOTAL) is not double-precision, which accounts for the rounding error. The correct program is shown in Figure 17.15, where all likely variables are double-precision by

Notice the two DEFDBL statements, A–L and T. These cannot be combined into one DEFDBL statement of A–T because of statement 60 FOR M = 1 TO 4. A type mismatch error would occur.

```
10 REM  Correct program.
20 DEFDBL A-L : DEFDBL T
30 S$ ="$$#######,.##"
40 TOTAL = 0
50 PRINT "Assessed Value" TAB(31) "Tax"
60 FOR M = 1 TO 4
70      READ ASSETS(M)
80      AIR.TAX = .001 * ASSETS(M)
90      PRINT USING S$;ASSETS(M);: PRINT SPC(10);
100     PRINT USING S$;AIR.TAX
110 TOTAL = TOTAL +   AIR.TAX
120 NEXT M
130 PRINT
140 PRINT "Total tax due:" TAB(25);
150 PRINT USING S$;TOTAL
160 DATA 1000000, 10000000, 40000000, 5000000
170 END
RUN
Assessed Value                   Tax
 $1,000,000.00               $1,000.00
$10,000,000.00              $10,000.00
$40,000,000.00              $40,000.00
 $5,000,000.00               $5,000.00

Total tax due:              $56,000.00
Ok
```

FIGURE 17.15 A personalized form letter

use of the # symbol. Technically, AIR.TAX does not have to be double-precision. Note also that if we were to double-precision all variables (A–Z), a type mismatch error would occur in statement 60, the FOR statement.

USE OF TEMPORARY PRINT STATEMENTS

Another technique that can aid in detecting program bugs is to insert temporary PRINT statements. These display program values so the error can be identified for correction.

An example of another hidden bug is shown in Figure 17.16. The program is simple enough, so let's verify the calculations first. We begin in statement 20 by reading a value of N, which in this case sets up a loop of four repetitions in statement `40 FOR I = 1 TO N`. Values are totaled, and an average is computed. Let's check the program: 10 plus 10 plus 15 plus 5 is 40; divided by 4 is 10. Yet the output shown is 8.

```
10 REM Another hidden bug
20 READ N    '                      N is the number of sales
30 TOTAL = 0
40 FOR I = 1 TO N   '               Loop N times
50     READ SALE
60     TOTAL = TOTAL + SALE   '      Develop a total
70 NEXT I
80 AVG = TOTAL/I '                   Compute the average
90 PRINT "The average sale is" AVG
100 DATA 4, 10, 10, 15, 5
110 END
RUN
The average sale is 8
Ok
```

FIGURE 17.16   Another program bug

Nothing unusual shows up on a trace analysis, nor does double-precision make any difference. We've already taken our break and reviewed the statements. But the bug still cannot be found. Our friends are beginning to run when we approach them, so we had better come up with a new technique to solve this problem.

The new technique consists of inserting temporary PRINT statements to display the value of variables used in the program. We can then trace through the program to determine if all values are reasonable. An example of likely PRINT statements as an aid in finding a program bug is shown in Figure 17.17. Program output is shown in Figure 17.18.

```
10  REM Another hidden bug
20  READ N '                              N is the number of sales
22  PRINT "** Value of N is" N
30  TOTAL = 0
32  PRINT "** Value of TOTAL is" TOTAL
40  FOR I = 1 TO N  '                     Loop N times
50      READ SALE
52  PRINT "** Value of SALE is" SALE
60      TOTAL = TOTAL + SALE  '           Develop a total
62  PRINT "** Value of TOTAL is" TOTAL
70  NEXT I
80  AVG = TOTAL/I  '                      Compute the average
82  PRINT "** Value of TOTAL is" TOTAL
84  PRINT "** Value of I is" I
90  PRINT "The average sale is" AVG
100 DATA 4, 10, 10, 15, 5
110 END
```

FIGURE 17.17   Using temporary PRINT statements to detect program bugs

```
RUN
** Value of N is 4
** Value of TOTAL is 0
** Value of SALE is 10
** Value of TOTAL is 10
** Value of SALE is 10
** Value of TOTAL is 20
** Value of SALE is 15
** Value of TOTAL is 35
** Value of SALE is 5
** Value of TOTAL is 40
** Value of TOTAL is 40
** Value of I is 5
The average sale is 8
Ok
```

FIGURE 17.18   Program output

Look at the output. We are only totaling four values, so how can the value of the variable I be 5? Ah, remember the way the loop variable works? The FOR-NEXT loop is exited when the value of the variable specified in the FOR statement exceeds the upper range of the loop. Revise statement 80 to read **80 AVG = TOTAL / N**. This is simple enough to correct, but perhaps it was not so easy to detect.

PC COMPATIBLES

The Apple microcomputer is credited with starting the micro revolution. Initially Apple was the only major producer, but, when the market for micros became large, IBM entered the field with their own micro called the PC (Personal Computer). Since IBM is a very large firm with tremendous financial strength, their entry into the market meant that the micro revolution was here to stay.

The IBM PC utilized the Microsoft Disk Operating System (called MS DOS). Vendors, particularly smaller vendors, who wanted to enter the market "riding on IBM's coat tails" called their PCs "compatibles," meaning that software developed for the IBM PC would run on their machines with little or no modification.

The list of vendors making PC compatibles is almost endless, among them Radio Shack (Tandy), Zenith, Hewlett-Packard, Epson, Canon, I.T. & T., A.T. & T., and Burroughs. By the time you read this book, even Apple Corporation itself will probably have developed a means for making themselves compatible with MS DOS. The question that arises is, What does compatible mean?

The issue of computer compatibility is a lot like compatibility with one's spouse. There are always differences that require at least some compromises. The major differences are obvious: the keyboard and the placement of the keys; the monitor's size, color, and clarity; the storage capacity of the diskette drive system; and the physical size of the machine.

The original IBM PCs were produced with 64K bytes of memory. The compatibles offered larger memory, but then IBM countered by offering 256K as standard. The original PCs were bulky and not designed to be portable, so several vendors developed portable PC compatible computers. Not to be outdone, IBM responded with their own PC portable.

At present, there are no clear-cut definitions of what makes a PC compatible with the IBM PC. However, there are several points that should be considered in the selection of a PC or PC compatible.

Compiled programs normally will run on PC compatibles, but it is always wise to run important programs before purchasing the desired computer. A particularly interesting condition exists regarding the BASIC language. Although the language syntax is virtually the same on all PC compatibles, to avoid infringing on IBM's and on Microsoft's copyrights, differences do exist. The most noticeable is that BASIC (the BASIC.COM and the BASICA.COM files) on the IBM PC will not normally load into memory on a PC compatible.

For example, the I.T. & T. micro's BASIC is called XBASIC.EXE. Although the language syntax is the same, the file is 52K bytes long, compared to approximately 28K bytes for IBM's DOS 2.1. Their XBASIC.EXE has to be loaded into memory on their PC compatible. Once accomplished, everything operates as intended. (This is because IBM has the bulk of their BASIC in ROM.)

Other PC compatibles such as the Hewlett-Packard have a $3\frac{1}{2}''$ diskette drive system versus the $5\frac{1}{4}''$ drive on the standard PC. This does not mean that both are not excellent computers; it's just that the word compatible means different things to different people.

Programs that address particular machine memory locations (outside of the BASIC language) may not run identically on all PC compatibles. This is particularly important with programs that read the status of special keys that may vary on some compatibles. It's best to check such software on a case-by-case basis before making a decision on using a particular microcomputer brand.

If the differences between the IBM PC and the compatible lines are not great, why are the PC compatibles so popular? Probably for the following reasons: price, specialized applications, quality, service, and personal preferences.

Despite what you might think from the advertisements, computers are expensive. Many of the PC compatibles offer price advantages that make them attractive. In addition, specialized applications such as portability, a touch screen, audio input or output, and faster processors can result in a compatible being an ideal choice.

Microcomputer repairs are best left to a professional. Because quality and service vary greatly, major consideration should be given to finding a local vendor who is willing to—and capable of—supporting the equipment you purchase.

The only way to answer the question of whether to buy an IBM PC, or a PC compatible is another question: Which is the best car: a Ford or a Chevrolet? If you select the Ford, there are just as many people who believe strongly in the Chevrolet. They are both high-quality products. Although most buyers do not want to admit it, the final purchase is often based on personal preferences.

When we address the issue of PC compatibles, we might even be looking at the wrong thing. The major issue is the computer system as a whole, not simply the hardware. You should run the software, and if it does what you want for your application, then find out if your local vendor will support the software through training you and updating the programs. If Yes, find out if the vendor will support the hardware. If still Yes, and if the system of software, hardware, and training is competitively priced, perhaps you should buy that computer that is running the software.

SUMMARY

Congratulations are in order. You have come a long way in developing an understanding of BASIC. You have expanded your programming skills by identifying and correcting an error once made. And you understand some of the issues involving the PC compatibles.

We are now going to begin a new and exciting portion of BASIC: file processing. The next chapter discusses the creation and use of sequential files. In practically no time at all, you will be handling files like a professional.

There are problems at the end of this chapter and there are cases in Appendix A. The problems reinforce the section on word processing. The cases are divided into the following five categories:

Accounting: Cases 1–5
Management: Cases 6–10
Marketing: Cases 11–15
Finance: Cases 16–19
File Processing: Cases 20–27

When developing programs for the cases in Appendix A, practice sound structured programming techniques. Document your programs with ample REMARK statements, and use error processing whenever practical.

PROBLEMS

Screen Design Problems. Problems 1–5.
Develop a BASIC program, paying particular attention to screen design.

17.1 The STOCKNAM.ASC file on the companion disk is needed for this problem. This file is organized as shown.

Ticker symbol	Company name	Business and markets
--	--	--

A program is needed that permits a search of the STOCKNAM.ASC file for either a ticker symbol, company name, or user-entered business and markets. Notice that the screen's title is highlighted and that there is a box around the search options.

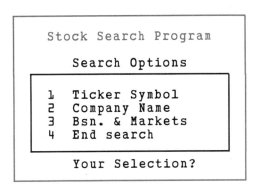

The screen would appear as shown after a search has been made for the ticker symbol "bud". Note: If a symbol called "buddie" was in a file, that would also have been displayed.

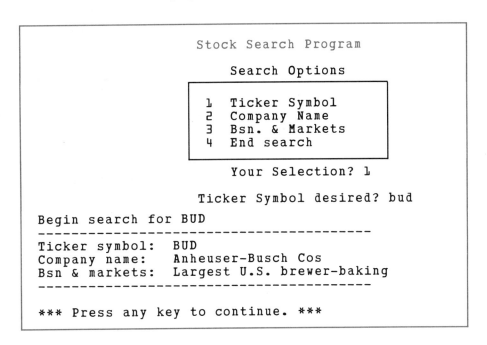

Problems 2–5 require the following information.

You have been assigned to a top-secret government agency, the 007 Group. This group uses spies to exchange secret coded messages of vital national importance. Selected "bits" of intelligence were gathered by people in the field section of the 007 Group, but the data is not complete. The only thing that is certain in all cases is that programmers developed the messages using ASCII codes.

*17.2 Our top agent managed to copy the below data on a cocktail napkin. Nothing is known about the message except that it looks like it is normal ASCII code for capital letters and blank spaces.

```
200 DATA 84, 72, 69, 32
210 DATA 87, 69, 69, 68, 83, 32
220 DATA 79, 70, 32
230 DATA 67, 82, 73, 77, 69, 32
240 DATA 66, 69, 65, 82, 32
250 DATA 66, 73, 84, 84, 69, 82, 32
260 DATA 70, 82, 85, 73, 84, 46
```

17.3 The number of coded messages received by the 007 Group has greatly increased, and it is taking too long to process the messages (see answer to Problem 2). The chief of security wants you to develop a 007 code program. He (or is it she? no one has ever seen the chief) left the following screen on your desk:

```
┌─────────────────────────────────────┐
│        007 Code Program             │
│  ┌───────────────────────────────┐  │
│  │ C    Code Line                │  │
│  │ O    Other [Help]             │  │
│  │ D    Decode Line              │  │
│  │ E    End Program              │  │
│  └───────────────────────────────┘  │
│        Your Selection?              │
└─────────────────────────────────────┘
```

Notice the inverse title and the program options within a selection box called "C O D E". This permits a user to enter a code line (a line to be coded) via the keyboard. The appropriate code is then developed and shown on the screen where it can be copied onto a message. The user can select a scrambling value by shifting the code −4 to +4 values.

The decode selection decodes a message based on user-entered ASCII values. An auto-decode option displays the lines based on a −4 to +4 shift in the ASCII values.

17.4 Use the program developed in Problem 3 to decipher the below message. The intelligence group reported something about shifting the ASCII code based on the number of children in the spy's family. It is not known how many children are in his family or whether the shift is plus or minus. However, he must have a small family because they all recently went on vacation together in a Volkswagen.

```
89 74 70 72 77 74 87 88 37
83 74 91 74 87 37
81 84 88 74 37
89 77 74 78 87 37
72 81 70 88 88 51
```

17.5 Use the program developed in Problem 3 to decipher the below message given to you by a senior agent.

```
87, 85, 71, 34
85, 67, 80, 70, 34
86, 81, 34
70, 71, 85, 86, 84, 81, 91, 34
86, 74, 71, 34
80, 71, 89, 34
86, 67, 80, 77, 48
```

* The answer to this question is in Appendix E.

Other Problems. Problems 6–11.
Develop a BASIC program to solve each problem. Clearly label all output.

Problems 6–8 require the use of the following DATA statements containing the names of presidents:

```
9000 DATA Dwight Eisenhower,    Ronald Reagan
9010 DATA Theodore Roosevelt,   Jimmy Carter
9020 DATA Abraham Lincoln,      Harry Truman
9030 DATA Grover Cleveland,     Ulysses Grant
9040 DATA Gerald Ford,          John Kennedy
9050 DATA Richard Nixon,        George Bush
```

17.6 Develop a program to search the data list for the occurrence of a user-entered character string. Display the president's first and last name in which the character string was found.

17.7 Develop a program to search the data list for the occurrence of a user-entered last name. The comparison should be made with uppercase letters. Display the president's first name in uppercase and lowercase letters when found.

17.8 Develop a program to count the occurrences of symbols entered via the keyboard. That is, the user should be permitted to enter any sequence of letters, such as the letters "O" or "o." The program should identify and count the occurrence of the letter(s) regardless of its case.

17.9 Develop a program to print a "personalized" form letter to three people of your choice.

17.10 Write a data entry subroutine that checks to see that no numbers have been included in a string entry. When a number is encountered, alert the user to reenter the string without including a number.

17.11 Write a data entry routine that both prompts the user to enter the following and checks to assure that such an entry is made. (Note: You might wish to save this routine for later use in file processing.)

   a. Enter a five-character product code in all caps.

   b. Enter a three-digit quantity with a minimum value of 1 and a maximum value of 299.

18 SEQUENTIAL FILES

After completing this chapter you should be able to

- Use OPEN, WRITE #, INPUT #, EOF, and CLOSE # statements
- Create and enter data into a sequential file
- Read from a sequential file
- Change data in a small sequential file
- Convert ASCII files to sequential files

If the volume of data to be processed by a program were not too large, we could continue to create DATA statements and save them in an ASCII file. The file could then be merged with our BASIC program to provide the necessary data for analysis.

This is a very clumsy method and, as the volume of data increases, several problems arise. First, DATA statements are cumbersome to use. Statement lines must begin with a statement number, and that number must not interfere with a line number in the program that will use the file. The word DATA has to be typed for each data line.

In addition, it is difficult to have a program create and store DATA statements for use by other programs. Finally, ASCII files are an inefficient storage medium because they contain a character-by-character representation of the data. This results in ASCII files being slow to load and save as well as requiring a lot of diskette storage space.

TWO ALTERNATIVES TO ASCII FILES

There are two major alternatives to ASCII files for processing large volumes of data: *sequential files* and *direct-access files*. In sequential files, records are processed one at a time, beginning with the first record and progressing throughout the file. In a direct-access, or *random-access*, file, a particular record can be retrieved directly without our having to begin with the first record in the file. We will first direct our attention to creating and processing sequential files.

A *record* within a file is a grouping of related data elements organized similarly to the way we previously organized DATA statement elements. For example, suppose that a BASIC program was created to read EMPLOYEE.NAME$ (employee name) and YEARS (years employed). The program and DATA statement (saved in ASCII format) could be viewed as follows:

```
--
--
70  READ EMPLOYEE.NAME$, YEARS          ⎰BASIC
                                        ⎱Program
--
--
9000  DATA  John Smith, 8               ⎰Data in
                                        ⎱ASCII file
```

Although we wanted only the data elements "John Smith" and "8", the ASCII file we had been using previously contains the statement number and the word DATA. A sequential file eliminates the need to save the statement number and the word DATA. In addition, the data elements are saved in a more efficient (compressed) mode than in the ASCII file, which saves in a character-by-character format.

CREATING A SINGLE-RECORD SEQUENTIAL FILE

Suppose that we wanted to create a sequential file composed of a single record containing an employee's name and years of service. As we have all along, we need a file name to store and retrieve this data. Remember that a file name should begin with a letter and may be from one to eight characters long. An optional three-character extension may be used.

A file is created by first *opening* it to accept program output. That is, the output from the program will be saved in the file. For example, in Figure 18.1 a file called EMPLOYEE is opened for output in statement 30. Then the program writes the value of the variables EMPLOYEE.NAME\$ and YEARS into the file in statement 60. The file is then closed in statement 70.

```
10 REM Creating a file: OPEN for OUTPUT
20 FILE$ = "A:EMPLOYEE"
30 OPEN FILE$ FOR OUTPUT AS #1
40 EMPLOYEE.NAME$ = "John Smith"
50 YEARS = 8
60 WRITE #1, EMPLOYEE.NAME$, YEARS
70 CLOSE #1
80 PRINT "File closed and saved."
90 END
RUN
File closed and saved.
Ok
```

FIGURE 18.1 Creating a file

Two data elements (called *fields*) were written into the sequential file created by Figure 18.1. The first is the employee's name, "John Smith", and the second is the years of employment, 8. This can be visualized as if the data were written on tape as follows:

"John Smith",8

Let's go over each statement in the program shown in Figure 18.1. Statement 10 is a REM statement that does not affect program execution. Statement 20 is a recommended shortcut statement to simplify file processing. This statement assigns the device code of A: for diskette drive A (B: is used for drive B) and the name of the file (EMPLOYEE) to the string variable called FILE$. The result is that, whenever FILE$ is used, the reference is to the EMPLOYEE file on drive A. Note that the colon must follow the identification of the device code. Specifying the device code avoids confusion but is not absolutely required. If the device code is not specified, BASIC defaults to the current diskette drive.

Statement 30 is interpreted as follows:

OPEN FILE$ FOR OUTPUT AS #1

OPEN A:EMPLOYEE This instructs the computer to create a file called EMPLOYEE on drive A and make it available for processing.

FOR OUTPUT AS #1 This instructs the computer to accept OUTPUT from the program into the file which will be referred to as #1.

The key words in statement 30 are OPEN and OUTPUT, which alert the computer that a file called EMPLOYEE is to be created (opened). When a file is opened for output, the file is made available for processing. If the file does not already exist, it is created. If the file exists, all data in the file is destroyed. Because the accidental opening for output of a file that already contains data will destroy the file contents, exercise caution when you open a file. Later in this chapter, APPEND will be used to avoid this danger.

Statements 40 and 50 assign the values "John Smith" and 8 to the variables EMPLOYEE.NAME$ and YEARS. Statement `60 WRITE #1, EMPLOYEE.NAME, YEARS` writes the values of the variables into the #1 file (the EMPLOYEE file).

Use of the WRITE# statement automatically inserts commas between statement items as they are written in the record. The separation by commas is necessary for the record to be read by other programs. String variables are enclosed in quotation marks and all values are separated by commas. In addition, a carriage return is inserted into the file after the last variable in the WRITE statement.

Statement 70 closes the file and frees the buffer (an internal computer workspace). Statement 80 displays the message "File closed and saved".

READING A SINGLE-RECORD FILE

A program to retrieve and display the single record previously saved in the EMPLOYEE file is shown in Figure 18.2.

As shown in Figure 18.2, statement 20 assigns the device code and file name "A:EMPLOYEE" to the string variable called FILE$. Statement 30 is interpreted as follows:

OPEN FILE$ FOR INPUT AS #1

OPEN A:EMPLOYEE This instructs the computer to go to disk drive A and make the file called EMPLOYEE available for processing.

FOR INPUT AS #1 This instructs the computer that the file called EMPLOYEE will be used as program input. That is, an INPUT statement will be used to assign the values contained in the file to program variables. This file will be referred to as #1.

```
10 REM Reading file: OPEN for INPUT (input into program)
20 FILE$ = "A:EMPLOYEE"
30 OPEN FILE$ FOR INPUT AS #1
40 INPUT #1, EMPLOYEE.NAME$, YEARS
50 PRINT "Data in the file " FILE$
60 PRINT EMPLOYEE.NAME$, YEARS
70 CLOSE #1
80 END
RUN
Data in the file A:EMPLOYEE
John Smith        8
Ok
```

FIGURE 18.2   Opening a file for program input

The term "#1 file" actually refers to a buffer associated with the file. Data is transferred to and from this buffer and to and from a named file. This speeds up disk operation.

Statement **40 INPUT #1 EMPLOYEE.NAME$, YEARS** instructs the computer to go to the #1 file, called EMPLOYEE. Data is to be input from the opened file into the variables EMPLOYEE.NAME$ and YEARS. The WRITE # statement inserts commas between statement items so that the items will be separated in the file. Statement 40 assigns the first data element in the record, up to the comma, to the variable EMPLOYEE.NAME$. The next data element is assigned to the variable YEARS. Statements 50 and 60 display data, and statement 70 closes the file.

CREATING A MULTIPLE-RECORD FILE

An example of a program to write multiple records into a file called PEOPLE is shown in Figure 18.3. A FOR-NEXT loop is created to read from DATA statements and to write onto the file. Note that the statements

```
10 REM Creating a multiple record file
20 FILE$ = "A:PEOPLE"
30 OPEN FILE$ FOR OUTPUT AS #1
40 FOR I = 1 TO 4
50     READ EMPLOYEE.NAME$, YEARS
60     WRITE #1, EMPLOYEE.NAME$, YEARS
70 NEXT I
80 CLOSE #1
90 '
900 DATA "John Smith", 8
910 DATA "Alice Doe", 12
920 DATA "George Washington", 21
930 DATA "Mary Worth", 2
940 '
950 PRINT "File " FILE$ " closed and saved."
960 END
RUN
File A:PEOPLE closed and saved.
Ok
```

FIGURE 18.3   Creating a multiple-record file

OPEN, WRITE, and CLOSE have not changed from the previous program that wrote a single record into a file.

READING A MULTIPLE-RECORD FILE

The program shown in Figure 18.4 can be used to input multiple records from a file called PEOPLE. Again, notice the use of the OPEN, INPUT, and CLOSE statements to enter records into a file called EMPLOYEE. (We'll discuss entering a varying amount of records in a moment.)

```
10 REM OPENing file for multiple record INPUT
20 FILE$ = "A:PEOPLE"
30 OPEN FILE$ FOR INPUT AS #1
40 PRINT "The " FILE$ " file contains employee names and years worked:"
50 FOR I = 1 TO 4
60     INPUT #1, EMPLOYEE.NAME$, YEARS
70     PRINT "Name: " EMPLOYEE.NAME$, "Years worked:" YEARS
80 NEXT I
90 CLOSE #1
100 END
RUN
The A:PEOPLE file contains employee names and years worked:
Name: John Smith           Years worked: 8
Name: Alice Doe            Years worked: 12
Name: George Washington    Years worked: 21
Name: Mary Worth           Years worked: 2
Ok
```

FIGURE 18.4 Reading a file: opening for multiple-record input

THE EOF (END-OF-FILE) FUNCTION

When reading multiple values from DATA statements, a trailer value was used to indicate the end of our data. This prevented us from reading more data than existed and avoided an "Out-of-Data" error message. A similar problem exists when using sequential files.

When writing onto a sequential file, BASIC indicates the end of the file (EOF) by writing a special character at the end of the file when the CLOSE statement is encountered. This character can be used like a trailer value when reading sequential files.

The EOF function is used to check for this special character, CHR$(26); when the EOF character is encountered, control is transferred to another statement. This permits a loop to be established that will read any number of records in a sequential file until the end-of-file marker is encountered.

The general form of the EOF function is

Statement   **IF EOF(N)**   **THEN**   Statement
number   number

Where (N) is the file number being checked. (1 if a single file.)

A particular procedure should be followed when using the EOF function. Begin by opening the file for input. Then check the file for EOF and, if it exists, close the file and end that portion of the program. If EOF does not exist, input and process the record. After processing the record, return, and again check for EOF. If EOF does not exist, repeatedly process a record, return, and check for EOF, until EOF is encountered. At that point, the file has been read and can be closed.

This procedure is shown in Figure 18.5, the steps required to read a sequential file. Notice that an EOF test is made to check for the existence of a record before the record is read (INPUT).

Step 1	Open the file for input. Read first record into buffer #N.
Step 2	Check for EOF. If it exists, go to step 6.
Step 3	Input the record. This transfers the contents of the buffer to the named fields. The next record is read into the buffer.
Step 4	Process the record.
Step 5	Go to step 2. Repeat steps 2, 3, and 4 until EOF is encountered.
Step 6	Close file and continue with program.

FIGURE 18.5   Detailed steps required to read a sequential file

The program shown in Figure 18.4 created a four-record sequential file called PEOPLE. Let's take a closer look at how those records are stored in the file so that we can develop a better understanding of how sequential file records are processed.

In step 1, the file is opened for input. This positions a file pointer at the first record in the file, as follows:

John Smith,8	Alice Doe,12	George Washington,21	Mary Worth,2

⇑
File
Pointer

In step 2, a check is made for the end of the file (EOF). No EOF is found (this is the first record) so proceed to the next step.

Step 3 inputs the first record into the variables EMPLOYEE.NAME$ and YEARS. The file pointer is then automatically indexed to the next record after completing an INPUT # statement.

After the first record has been read, the internal file pointer is now positioned on the second file record. The program is ready to read the second record but it is best that we process the assigned variables before proceeding. The file pointer is now pointing to the second record in the file, as follows:

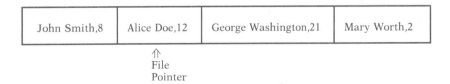

John Smith,8	Alice Doe,12	George Washington,21	Mary Worth,2

⇑
File
Pointer

In step 4, the first record is processed as previously shown in Figure 18.4. Then in step 5 program control passes back to step 2 where an EOF check is made. Since EOF is not present, step 3 is executed and the second record is read (INPUT). The file pointer is then indexed to the third record.

After processing the second record, control is passed back to step 2 where an EOF check is made. Since EOF is not present, the record is read and the file pointer is then indexed to the fourth record.

After repeating steps 2 through 5 to process the third and fourth records, the file pointer is positioned as follows:

| John Smith,8 | Alice Doe,12 | George Washington,21 | Mary Worth,2 |

⇑
File
Pointer

The file pointer is at the end of the file (actually at the end-of-file character, which is ASCII code 26). When an EOF check is made in step 2, control is transferred to close the file and complete that portion of the program.

An example of a program that follows these steps is shown in Figure 18.6.

```
10 REM EOF on multiple record INPUT
20 FILE$ = "A:PEOPLE"
30 OPEN FILE$ FOR INPUT AS #1
40 PRINT "The " FILE$ " file contains:"
50 IF EOF(1) THEN 110
60 INPUT #1, EMPLOYEE.NAME$, YEARS
70 PRINT "Name: " EMPLOYEE.NAME$, "Years worked:" YEARS
80 GOTO 50
90 '
100 CLOSE #1
110 PRINT "All " FILE$ " records processed."
120 END
RUN
The A:PEOPLE file contains:
Name: John Smith            Years worked: 8
Name: Alice Doe             Years worked: 12
Name: George Washington     Years worked: 21
Name: Mary Worth            Years worked: 2
All A:PEOPLE records processed.
Ok
```

FIGURE 18.6   Using the EOF statement

The program shown in Figure 18.6 can be changed to utilize a WHILE-WEND loop of logic. An EOF(1) value of −1 is returned when the end-of-file is reached. That is, when WHILE EOF is not equal to −1, records can be input. An example of this is shown in Figure 18.7. This is the preferred method because a GOTO is eliminated.

```
10 REM EOF on multiple record INPUT
20 FILE$ = "PEOPLE"
30 OPEN FILE$ FOR INPUT AS #1
40 PRINT "The " FILE$ " file contains:"
50 '                                          Begin Loop
60 WHILE EOF(1) <> -1
70     INPUT #1, EMPLOYEE.NAME$, YEARS
80     PRINT "Name: " EMPLOYEE.NAME$, "Years worked:" YEARS
90 WEND
100 CLOSE #1
110 '                                          End Loop
120 PRINT
130 PRINT "All records in the " FILE$ " file were processed."
140 END
RUN
The PEOPLE file contains:
Name: John Smith            Years worked: 8
Name: Alice Doe             Years worked: 12
Name: George Washington     Years worked: 21
Name: Mary Worth            Years worked: 2

All records in the PEOPLE file were processed.
Ok
```

FIGURE 18.7   Using a WHILE-WEND loop to input records

CHANGING RECORDS

Sequential files are called sequential because records are stored in one long sequence of data. The program shown in Figure 18.4, which wrote four records into the file called PEOPLE, wrote the records in the following format:

| John Smith,8 | Alice Doe,12 | George Washington,21 | Mary Worth,2 |

The first record "John Smith,8" is immediately followed by the second record, which is immediately followed by the third, and then the fourth. The computer designates the end of each record within the file by an end-of-record marker (the Enter symbol), so that the record can later be read from the file.

Changes to a record, particularly if the change results in a longer record, may "scramble" the remaining file records. For example, suppose we wanted to revise the first record to read "Johnny Robert Smith,10". As this is longer than the original record, the new record will "write over" the second record in the file, resulting in the following:

| Johnny Robert Smith,10 | 12 | George Washington,21 | Mary Worth,2 |

An error will occur when this file is read because the second record contains only one data element, not the two data elements that are specified in the INPUT # statement. Because records can be accidentally written over like this, caution must be exercised when changing files to correct errors or to update records.

There is yet another point to be considered when processing a sequential file. If a file is opened for input, data can be entered from the file into the program, but no revisions can be saved directly into the file while it is opened for input. You can write only into a file that has been opened for output.

Two ways of revising a sequential file are available; the first method is straightforward and suitable for processing small files. The second method, which is discussed in the next chapter, is a little more involved but can process sequential files of any size.

The first step in the quick, simple way to make changes to a record in a small file is to open the file for input. Then read the records into an array and, after all records are read, close the file. Make your changes to the data stored in the array. After all changes have been made, re-open the file for output, save the entire array (including the changes), and then close the updated file.

These steps to incorporate changes into a small file are shown in Figure 18.8. As the contents of the entire file must be in memory at one time, this method cannot be used to update large files.

Step 1	Open the file for input.
Step 2	Read the file into an array.
Step 3	Close the file.
Step 4	Make the necessary changes to the data stored in the array.
Step 5	Open the file for output.
Step 6	Save the entire array, including the changes.
Step 7	Close the file.

FIGURE 18.8 Steps required to update a small sequential file

An example of this technique is shown in Figure 18.9, in which the program reads the records contained in the PEOPLE file into arrays called EMP.ARRAY$ and YR.ARRAY. As exactly four records are in this example, a FOR-NEXT loop is used to simplify retrieval and subsequent storage of the records. After changes have been made, the arrays are saved to update the file. Note statement 80, which closes the file that was originally opened for input. The file is then re-opened for output in statement 360, and the arrays are written into the file.

Let's take a closer look at this program. Suppose that record #1 containing the name "John Smith" who worked 8 years was to be corrected to read "John R. Smith". Also suppose that only the name was to be changed and that the years worked are correct.

Execution of the program shown in Figure 18.9 is shown in Figure 18.10. The file revision program was just started, so type C to continue and press Enter. Then select the record to be changed, which is record #1. Type 1 and press Enter and the file record containing **"John Smith"**, **8** is displayed. Type the revised name "John R. Smith" and press Enter. The

```
10 REM Changing a file record
20 DIM EMP.ARRAY$(4), YR.ARRAY(4)
30 FILE$ = "A:PEOPLE"
40 OPEN FILE$ FOR INPUT AS #1                        ' Open PEOPLE
50 FOR I = 1 TO 4
60     INPUT #1, EMP.ARRAY$(I), YR.ARRAY(I)
70 NEXT I
80 CLOSE #1
90 CLS                                               ' Instructions
100 PRINT "After typing changes, press Enter."
110 PRINT "If no change, press Enter without retyping."
120 PRINT STRING$(43,"-")
130 PRINT "E to End or C to Continue.  Your choice? ";
140 A$ = INPUT$(1)
150 PRINT A$ : PRINT
160 IF A$ ="E" OR A$ = "e" THEN 380
162                                                  ' Select record
170 PRINT "Record # to be changed:  1, 2, 3, or 4? ";
190 RECORD$ = INPUT$(1)
200 PRINT RECORD$
210 IF RECORD$ ="E" OR RECORD$ = "e" THEN 380
220 N = VAL(RECORD$)
230 IF N > Ø AND N <= 4 THEN 270
240 BEEP
250 PRINT "Type 1 - 4, or E to End!" : GOTO 170
260                                                  ' Display record
270 PRINT "Record #" N " is " EMP.ARRAY$(N) YR.ARRAY(N)
280                                                  ' Revise name
290 PRINT "Revised name";
300 INPUT EMP$
310 IF EMP$ = "" THEN 330 ELSE EMP.ARRAY$(N) = EMP$
320                                                  ' Revise years
330 PRINT "Revised years";
340 INPUT YR$
350 IF YR$ = "" THEN 120 ELSE YR.ARRAY(N) = VAL(YR$)
360 GOTO 120
370 '
380 OPEN FILE$ FOR OUTPUT AS #1                      ' Save file
390 FOR I = 1 TO 4
400     WRITE #1, EMP.ARRAY$(I), YR.ARRAY(I)
410 NEXT I
420 CLOSE #1
430 PRINT : PRINT "File " FILE$ " is revised and saved."
440 END
```

FIGURE 18.9 Changing file records

The program shown in Figure 18.9 has been saved on the companion diskette as FIG18-9. This can be loaded into memory by the command LOAD"FIG18-9".

years worked are correct and do not have to be changed. Therefore, just press the Enter key again to go on to the next step in the program.

Also displayed are the changes to record #3. George Washington's years worked were recorded as 21 but should have been listed as 12. After making that change, type E to end the editing and save the updated data. The program shown in Figure 18.9 can be re-run to verify the changes that have been made in the PEOPLE file.

```
After typing changes, press Enter.
If no change, press Enter without retyping.
-------------------------------------------------
E to End or C to Continue.   Your choice? c

Record # to be changed:  1, 2, 3, or 4? 1
Record # 1  is John Smith 8
Revised name? John R. Smith
Revised years?
-------------------------------------------------
E to End or C to Continue.   Your choice? c

Record # to be changed:  1, 2, 3, or 4? 3
Record # 3  is George Washington 21
Revised name?
Revised years? 12
-------------------------------------------------
E to End or C to Continue.   Your choice? e


File A:PEOPLE is revised and saved.
Ok
```

FIGURE 18.10   Executing program to change records

APPENDING TO A FILE

Suppose that we wanted to expand the EMPLOYEE file by adding an additional record. The APPEND statement in the following form opens a file for output without destroying the data in the file:

50 OPEN FILE\$ FOR APPEND AS #1

This statement positions the file pointer so that output to the file will be placed at the end of existing data—that is, at the end of the file. The file is then treated the same as the OPEN for OUTPUT statement.

For example, the statement **50 OPEN FILE\$ FOR OUTPUT AS #1** results in the pointer's being positioned at the beginning of the first record in the file, as follows:

```
 _____
|      |       |       |       |       |
|      |       |       |       |       |
|_____|_____|_____|_____|_____|
⇑
File
Pointer
```

The statement **50 OPEN FILE\$ FOR APPEND AS #1** results in the pointer's being positioned at the end of the file. Output to the file will then be placed at the end of existing data.

```
 _____
|      |       |       |       |       |
|      |       |       |       |       |
|_____|_____|_____|_____|_____|
                                         ⇑
                                        File
                                        Pointer
```

```
10 REM Using APPEND to add a file record
20 FILE$ ="A:PEOPLE"
30 EMPLOYEE.NAME$ = "Alfred E. Neuman"
40 YEARS = 12
50 '                                      Positions pointer at end
60 OPEN FILE$ FOR APPEND AS #1
70 '                                      Write record in file
80 WRITE #1, EMPLOYEE.NAME$, YEARS
90 '                                      Close file
100 CLOSE #1
110 PRINT "The file " FILE$ " is appended and saved."
120 END
RUN
The file A:PEOPLE is appended and saved.
Ok
```

FIGURE 18.11   Using APPEND to add a file record

If a file is opened for append but the file does not exist, a file is created, the pointer is positioned at the beginning of the file, and the file is treated as though it had been opened for output. The purpose of the APPEND statement is to prevent accidental destruction of the data. A program using APPEND to add a name to the EMPLOYEE file is shown in Figure 18.11.

SUMMARY

This chapter directed attention to file processing. To simplify the statements using files, the diskette drive and file names were assigned to the string called FILE$ by an assignment statement such as **20 FILE$ = "A:EMPLOYEE"**.

In this example the string FILE$ refers to diskette drive A and to the file called EMPLOYEE. Other statements used in this chapter were

Opening a file for input
   30 OPEN FILE$ FOR INPUT AS #1
   This alerts the computer that data will be input into the program from the file and assigned to the variable. For example, the statement **FOR INPUT #1, A$** will result in data's being entered into the file designated as #1
Opening a file for output
   30 OPEN FILE$ FOR OUTPUT AS #1
   This alerts the computer to accept output from a program into a file. For example, the statement **40 WRITE #1 A$, HOURS** will write the value of A$ and HOURS into the file designated as #1.
Using APPEND to add to a file
   30 OPEN FILE$ FOR APPEND AS #1
   This opens a file for output and positions the file pointer so that output to the file will be placed at the end of existing data. If a file does not exist, one is created, and the pointer is positioned at the beginning of the file. The file is then treated the same way as by the OPEN for OUTPUT statement.

Closing a file
```
100 CLOSE #1
```
This closes the file and frees the buffer. A file cannot be opened or appended if the file is already open and has not been closed. CLOSE writes any incomplete blocks of records into the file and writes the end-of-file marker.

Summary of Terms

Name	Example	Purpose
	Assume that the following assignment has been made:	
OPEN	`20 FILE$ = "A:EMPLOYEE"`	
INPUT	`30 OPEN FILE$ FOR INPUT AS #1`	The EMPLOYEE file is opened and data will be input into the program from the file.
OPEN OUTPUT	`30 OPEN FILE$ FOR OUTPUT AS #1`	The EMPLOYEE file is opened and data will be output from the program into the file.
OPEN APPEND	`30 OPEN FILE$ FOR APPEND AS #1`	The EMPLOYEE file is opened and data will be output from the program into the file. Data will be added to the end of the file.
CLOSE	`200 CLOSE #1`	Closes the file.
EOF	`60 IF EOF(1) THEN 80`	When the end-of-file character is encountered, control is transferred to statement 80.
INPUT	`50 INPUT #1, EMPLOYEE$, YEARS`	Used after a file is opened to input (assign) values from file to variables specified.
WRITE	`50 WRITE #1, EMPLOYEE$, YEARS`	Used to write data into an opened file.

PROBLEMS

Partial Program Statements. Problems 1–8.
Write the BASIC statement that will accomplish the objective stated.
In Problems 1–6 write the BASIC statements that will accomplish the objective stated.

18.1 Open a file called EQUIP stored on a diskette in drive B for input into a program.
```
10 FILE$ = _____
20 _____
```

18.2 Open a file called RETURNS to be stored on a diskette in drive A to accept output from a program.
```
10 FILE$ = _____
20 _____
```

18.3 Open a file called ASSETS to accept output from a program. Open the file so that existing file data is not destroyed.
```
10 FILE$ = _____
20 _____
```

18.4 Write the values of variables ANYNAME$, HOURS, and RATE into a file previously opened for output as #1.
```
60 _____
```

18.5 Read values for variables EMPLOYEE$, DEPART.NUMBER, YEARS, and DEPENDENTS from a file previously opened for input as #1.
```
90 _____
```

18.6 Close a file previously opened as #1.

```
100 _____
```

Partial Programs. Problems 7 and 8.

18.7 The partial program below reads five records from a file called TRUCKS into an array. Complete the statements so the program will execute. Save the program, as we will be using it in a moment.

```
10 REM Problem 18.7
20 FILE$ = "A:
30 OPEN FILE$
40 FOR I = 1 TO
50     INPUT #1, MODEL$, YEAR
60     PRINT
70 NEXT I
80 CLOSE #1
90 PRINT
100 PRINT "File " FILE$ " read."
110 END
RUN
Dump truck      1987
Half ton        1983
18 Wheeler      1982
Four door       1986
Cement truck    1980

File A:TRUCKS read.
```

*18.8 Using the output of the program shown in Problem 7 as a guide, write a program to enter data into the file called TRUCKS.

Screen Design Problems. Problems 9–16.
The problems which follow require the use of ASCII files on the companion diskette. Each problem requires that two separate programs be developed.
The first program should read the ASCII file and save the data elements in a sequential file. Do not save the end-of-file record. The sequential file should have the same file name, but use the extension .SEQ in place of the former .ASC extension.
The second program (again note that this is a separate program) is to read the sequential file you created and display the data elements that are requested in the problem. Label all program output, and use the general format shown. Note: Some problems specifically call for a printed output. Others are simply a screen display in the format shown.

*18.9 The BUZZWORD.ASC file has the following format:

Language	Type	Jargon
--	--	--

The first program, which reads the ASCII file and saves the data elements in a sequential file called BUZZWORD.SEQ, writes to the file, not to the screen. This results in the rather limited screen output shown.

```
Writing records into sequential file BUZZWORD.SEQ
File BUZZWORD.SEQ created.
Ok
```

---

* The answer to this question is in Appendix E.

A second separate program reads the BUZZWORD.SEQ file and generates the output shown.

```
-----------------------------------------------------------------------
               Contents of BUZZWORD.SEQ sequential file:
    Language           Type                          Jargon
-----------------------------------------------------------------------
    Pascal      algorithm                   single entrance point
    FORTRAN     constant definition         user friendly variables
    BASIC       recursion technique         exponential formats
    PL1         semicolon and comma         control & function codes
    COBOL       alphanumeric variable       structured programming
    RPG         program subroutine          statement definition
    Machine     cryptic comment             random access files
    ADA         trig function               sequential access files
    C           assignment operator         decision statements
    FORTH       label declaration           auto loading
-----------------------------------------------------------------------
    File BUZZWORD.SEQ read.
    Ok
```

18.10 INCOME.ASC

This makes a nice WHILE-WEND loop to input a sequential file that has been opened for input. When an End-Of-File is reached, a −1 is returned.

```
WHILE EOF(1) <> -1
    INPUT #1, ----
WEND
```

Name	Age	Sex	Income
--	--	--	--

After creating a sequential file called INCOME.SEQ, create a second program that reads the sequential file and displays the records in the following format. (Consider Income to be the family income of students applying for financial support at Big State University. Note that an average family income is to be computed.)

Big State University
Student Assistant Aid Summary

Student	Family income
--	$XX,XXX.XX
--	$XX,XXX.XX
--	
Average Family Income:	$XX,XXX.XX

18.11 PRODUCTS.ASC

Product ID	Description	Cost	Retail price	Begin inven.	Qt. sold	Location code
XXX	XXXXXXXXXXXXX	$XXX.XX	$XXX.XX	XX	XX	X

After creating a sequential file called PRODUCTS.SEQ, create a second program to read the sequential file and print the items that sold over 20 units in the reporting period. Use the format shown below for your report.

J & J Wholesalers
Summary of Quantity Sold
Items Selling Over 20 Units

Product ID	Qt. sold	Location code
--	--	--

18.12 STOCKNAM.ASC

Ticker symbol	Company name	Business and markets
--	--	--

After creating a sequential file called STOCKNAM.SEQ, create a second program to read the file and display the ticker symbol, company name, business and markets for all stocks having a ticker symbol beginning with the letter B.

```
          Stocks, Ticker Symbol beginning with B
----------------------------------------------------------
Ticker    Company                   Business
Symbol    Name                      and Markets
----------------------------------------------------------
  --        --                        --
  --        --                        --
----------------------------------------------------------
File STOCKNAM.SEQ processed.  Symbols beginning with B.
```

18.13 STOCKS.ASC

Ticker symbol	1990 High	Low	1989 High	Low	Last sale	Earnings per share
--	--	--	--	--	--	--

After creating a sequential file called STOCKS.SEQ, create a second program to read the file and display the ticker symbol of stocks having an earnings per share greater than $5.00. Format the output as shown below.

Stock Analysis
Poor Folks' Investment Club
Stocks Earning Over $5.00/Share

Ticker symbol	Earnings per share
--	--

18.14 BUDGET.ASC

Pens	Tape	Staples	Paper	Typewriter
--	--	--	--	--

After creating a sequential file called BUDGET.SEQ, create a program to read the sequential file and print a summary of the supplies portion of the budget. Follow the format shown below.

Departmental Supplies Budget
Thomas County School System
Jefferson Middle School

Pens	Tape	Staples	Paper	Total
--	--	--	--	--

18.15   WAGES.ASC

Employee name	Hours worked	Hourly rate	Age
--	--	--	--

After creating the sequential file called WAGES.SEQ, create a program to read the file and display the data according to the format below.

Summary of Hours Worked
Save-A-Buck Department Stores

Employee name	Hours worked
--	--

18.16   SUPPLIES.ASC

Product number	Location code	Quantity	Price	Description
--	--	--	--	--

After creating the sequential file called SUPPLIES.SEQ, create a program to read the file and display the contents of the file according to the format below.

Inventory Summary
Items Priced Over $25.00

Product number	Price per item	Description of item
--	--	--

Other Problems. Problems 17–23.
Problems 17–19 require the demonstration of the TYPE command at the DOS level on the indicated ASCII files and on the indicated sequential files. The ASCII files are available on the companion diskette. Create the indicated sequential files if you have not already created them.

18.17 Use the TYPE command to display the contents of the BUZZWORD.ASC file and the sequential file you created called BUZZWORD.SEQ.

18.18 TYPE the contents of the BUDGET.ASC file and the sequential file you created called BUDGET.SEQ.

18.19 TYPE the contents of the WAGES.ASC file and the sequential file you created called WAGES.SEQ.

Problems 20 and 21 require use of the DATA statements below, which contain information on the TOOL.NAME$ and PRICE of various items in a hardware store.

```
900 DATA "Hammer",         12.95
910 DATA "Saw-Electric",   79.95
920 DATA "Screwdriver",     4.50
930 DATA "Drill-Electric", 39.95
940 DATA "Pliers",          7.95
950 DATA "Jack",           24.95
960 DATA "Sweeper",        89.95
970 DATA "END",                0
```

18.20 Develop a program to enter the data into a sequential file called TOOLS and store the file on diskette.

18.21 Develop a program to read the sequential TOOLS file created in Problem 20 into an array. Then, based on user input for a desired PRODUCT$, search the array for the TOOL.NAME$. If found, display the PRICE of the tool.

Problems 22 and 23 require two sequential files called STOCKNAM.SEQ and STOCKS.SEQ. Create these files from the corresponding ASCII files stored on the companion diskette. Do not read the data into arrays and do not assume the requested data exists in either file (see files created in Problems 12 and 13).

18.22 Develop a small information-retrieval system in which two files are searched. When the user enters a ticker symbol, display the corresponding company name (from the STOCKNAM.SEQ file) and display the company's earnings per share (from the STOCKS.SEQ file).

18.23 Develop a small information-retrieval system in which two files are searched. The user is to enter a target earnings per share. Search the STOCKS.SEQ file and, when a stock is encountered that exceeds this target, display the earnings per share and the company name. (The company name is in the STOCKNAM.SEQ file.)

PROCESSING SEQUENTIAL FILES

The previous chapter presented beginning statements for processing sequential files. This chapter expands file-processing skills by presenting additional programming statements.

Upon completion of this chapter, you should be able to

- Use mixed INPUT statements for prompts
- Use LINE INPUT statements
- Use PRINT # statements
- Use LINE INPUT # statements
- Copy a sequential file
- Update a large file

USING MIXED INPUT STATEMENTS

We have been using the INPUT statement in a traditional manner to assign values entered via the keyboard to program variables. PRINT statements were used to label each INPUT statement in order to reduce data-entry errors.

A typical program using an extensive amount of INPUT statements is shown in Figure 19.1. After the program is executed, the user is prompted to enter data for a person's name (PERSON.NAME$), then address (ADDRESS$), city (CITY$), state (STATE$), and finally the zip code (ZIP-CODE$).

In statements 30 through 70 shown in Figure 19.1, PRINT statements label all INPUT statements. Now that beginning programming skills have been mastered, let's take a shortcut by placing our message prompts within the INPUT statement. That is, data used to label an INPUT statement will be enclosed in parentheses following the word INPUT.

The general form of this mixed INPUT statement is

Statement			Variable
number	**INPUT**	"Message";	name

If a comma is used instead of the semicolon following the "Message" the ? prompt will not appear.

An example of a program using mixed INPUT statements is shown in Figure 19.2. Notice that the program is short and easy to read.

Figure 19.3 shows the entry of data into the program after it is executed. We will be using this logic in the programs that follow.

```
10 REM Using INPUT Statements
20 '                                          Data entry
30 PRINT "What is your name"    ;: INPUT PERSON.NAME$
40 PRINT "What is your address";: INPUT ADDRESS$
50 PRINT "What is your city"    ;: INPUT CITY$
60 PRINT "What is your state"   ;: INPUT STATE$
70 PRINT "What is your zipcode";: INPUT ZIPCODE
80 '                                          Is it OK?
90 PRINT "Do you want to change Y/N? ";
100 CHANGE$ = INPUT$(1)
110 PRINT CHANGE$
120 IF CHANGE$ = "Y" OR CHANGE$ = "y" THEN 130 ELSE 170
130 BEEP
140 PRINT "OK, let's try again."
150 PRINT : GOTO 30
160 '                                          Continue
170 REM    Any statements
```

FIGURE 19.1 Beginning program using INPUT statements

```
10 REM Using Mixed INPUT Statements
20 '                                          Data entry
30 INPUT "What is your name"    ; PERSON.NAME$
40 INPUT "What is your address"; ADDRESS$
50 INPUT "What is your city"    ; CITY$
60 INPUT "What is your state"   ; STATE$
70 INPUT "What is your zipcode"; ZIPCODE
80 '                                          Is it OK?
90 PRINT "Do you want to change Y/N? ";
100 CHANGE$ = INPUT$(1)
110 PRINT CHANGE$
120 IF CHANGE$ = "Y" OR CHANGE$ = "y" THEN 130 ELSE 170
130 BEEP
140 PRINT "OK, let's try again."
150 PRINT : GOTO 30
160 '                                          Continue
170 REM    Any statements
```

FIGURE 19.2 Using mixed INPUT statements

The data entry program shown in Figure 19.3 can be shortened to enter city and state on the same line. An example is shown in Figure 19.4, where the city and state are entered into the string variable CITY.STATE$.

Although entering multiple data elements on the same INPUT line will shorten your program, be careful! It is very easy for users to become confused when entering data. For example, execution of the program in Figure 19.4 is shown in Figure 19.5. Do you see what created the data entry error? Spend a moment looking at the figure and try to imagine the frustration of the user.

```
RUN
What is your name? Susan Citizen
What is your address? 121 Madison Avenue
What is your city? New York
What is your state? NY
What is your zipcode? 10010
Do you want to change Y/N? y
OK, let's try again.

What is your name? Susan Citizen
What is your address? 121 Madison Ave.
What is your city? New York
What is your state? NY
What is your zipcode? 10001
Do you want to change Y/N? n
Ok
```

FIGURE 19.3 Error prompts with mixed INPUT statements

```
10  REM Confusing INPUT Prompts
20  '                                        Data entry
30  INPUT "What is your name         "; PERSON.NAME$
40  INPUT "What is your address      "; ADDRESS$
50  INPUT "What is your city and state"; CITY.STATE$
60  INPUT "What is your zipcode       "; ZIPCODE
70  '                                        Is it OK?
80  PRINT "Do you want to change Y/N? ";
90  CHANGE$ = INPUT$(1)
100 PRINT CHANGE$
110 IF CHANGE$ = "Y" OR CHANGE$ = "y" THEN 120 ELSE 160
120 BEEP
130 PRINT "OK, let's try again."
140 PRINT : GOTO 30
150 '                                        Continue
160 REM    Any statements
```

FIGURE 19.4 Confusing data entry prompts

```
RUN
What is your name          ? Ms. Susan Citizen
What is your address       ? 121 Madison Ave.
What is your city and state? New York, NY
?Redo from start
What is your city and state?
```

FIGURE 19.5 Confusing data entry prompts resulting in data entry errors

The data entry error shown in Figure 19.5 was caused by the user entering a comma. As you know, a comma is used to separate data entries and, unless they are anticipated by the program, a data entry error will occur. Although the request to enter city and state may seem clear enough, people are accustomed to seeing a comma between the city and state. They will often enter that comma no matter how often the error message is repeated. If a condition occurs in which the entry of an unwanted comma is likely, the LINE INPUT statement should be used. (Don't forget that quotation marks can be placed around the entry to assign a comma to a string variable.)

THE LINE INPUT STATEMENT

The LINE INPUT statement is one way around the problem of unanticipated commas occurring in data entry. The LINE INPUT statement accepts an entire line, up to 254 characters including commas and quotation marks. The data entered in the line is assigned to a specified string variable. A LINE INPUT statement does not display a question prompt and, if the ? prompt is desired, it should be enclosed inside the quotation marks.

The general form of the LINE INPUT statement is

Statement number	**LINE INPUT**	"Message ";	String variable

The semicolon is required and a blank space inside the quotation marks makes program output easier to read. A string variable must be used with LINE INPUT.

A program using LINE INPUT is shown in Figure 19.6. Notice that the question mark is included inside the quotation marks in statements 30, 40, and 50.

If a program error is made after opening a file, the file is still open. And the computer will attempt to transfer data into the file, perhaps after you pressed Enter during the process of correcting the program. This can produce strange results. Again it is strongly recommended that you always work from a file backup copy.

```
10 REM LINE INPUT Statements
20 '                                              Data entry
30 LINE INPUT "What is your name?  "        ; PERSON.NAME$
40 LINE INPUT "What is your address?  "     ; ADDRESS$
50 LINE INPUT "What is your city and state?  "; CITY.STATE$
60 INPUT "What is your zipcode"             ; ZIPCODE
70 '                                              Is it OK?
80 PRINT "Do you want to change Y/N? ";
90 CHANGE$ = INPUT$(1)
100 PRINT CHANGE$
110 IF CHANGE$ = "Y" OR CHANGE$ = "y" THEN 120 ELSE 160
120 BEEP
130 PRINT "OK, let's try again."
140 PRINT : GOTO 30
150 '                                              Summary
160 PRINT
170 PRINT TAB(22) "- - -  SUMMARY  - - -"
180 PRINT "Name:"    TAB(22) PERSON.NAME$
190 PRINT "Address:" TAB(22) ADDRESS$
200 PRINT "City, state, Zip:" TAB(22) CITY.STATE$  TAB(40) ZIPCODE
210 END
```

FIGURE 19.6 Using the LINE INPUT statement

Figure 19.7 shows the entry of data into the program after it is executed. Notice how the LINE INPUT statements assign commas, colons, and quotation marks to the string variables for later use by the program.

```
RUN
What is your name?  Pete "Too Tall: jones
What is your address?  121 South Main St: Apt. 2b
What is your city and state?  Loisville, KY
What is your zipcode? 40203
Do you want to change Y/N? y
OK, let's try again.

What is your name?  Pete "Too Tall" Jones
What is your address?  121 South Main St. Apt. 2B
What is your city and state?  Louisville, KY
What is your zipcode? 40203
Do you want to change Y/N? n


                        - - -  SUMMARY   - - -
Name:                   Pete "Too Tall" Jones
Address:                121 South Main St. Apt. 2B
City, state, Zip:       Louisville, KY        40203
Ok
```

FIGURE 19.7   Program output from LINE INPUT statements

Before going on to a related statement, the LINE INPUT # statement, let's take a closer look at the difference between the WRITE # and PRINT # statements. To examine the difference, we will "trick" the computer. Previously, files were opened with BASIC statements such as the following:

```
20 FILE$ = "A:CUSTOMER"
30 OPEN FILE$ FOR OUTPUT AS #1
```

In addition to device codes of A: and B: for diskette drives A and B, there are device codes for the line printer and for the screen (monitor). The device code for the line printer is "LPT:" (the digit indicates the first line printer and must be specified). The device code for the screen is "SCRN:".

The effect of the WRITE # and PRINT # statements can be demonstrated by using the screen as an output device. As can be seen in Figure 19.8, the PRINT # statement outputs values without the comma being inserted. Also, quotation marks are not printed around variable names.

USING PRINT

An example of a program that reads multiple names and addresses into a sequential file is shown in Figure 19.9. The program will accept data entered via the keyboard and store the data in a sequential file called CUSTOMER. This program will be expanded later to check for data entry errors and to make it easier to update the file.

```
10 REM OPEN SCRN: for OUTPUT
20 FILE$ = "SCRN:"                              ' Assign Screen
30 OPEN FILE$ FOR OUTPUT AS #1                  ' Open Screen for output
40 EMPLOYEE.NAME$ = "John Smith"
50 YEARS = 8
60 '
70 PRINT "First WRITE # then PRINT # statement."
80 '
90  WRITE #1, EMPLOYEE.NAME$, YEARS             ' WRITE to screen
100 PRINT #1, EMPLOYEE.NAME$, YEARS             ' PRINT to screen
110 '
120 CLOSE #1
130 PRINT "Output to screen completed."
140 END
RUN
First WRITE # then PRINT # statement.
"John Smith",8
John Smith      8
Output to screen completed.
Ok
```

FIGURE 19.8 WRITE # versus PRINT # statements

```
10 REM Using PRINT# to create a file
20 FILE$ = "A:CUSTOMER"
30 OPEN FILE$ FOR OUTPUT AS #1
40                                              ' Data entry
50 LINE INPUT "Name?  "          ; PERSON.NAME$
60 LINE INPUT "Address?  "       ; ADDRESS$
70 LINE INPUT "City and state?  "; CITY.STATE$
80 INPUT "Zipcode"               ; ZIPCODE
90                                              ' Is it OK?
100 PRINT "Do you want to change Y/N? ";
110 CHANGE$ = INPUT$(1)
120 PRINT CHANGE$
130 IF CHANGE$ = "Y" OR CHANGE$ = "y" THEN 140 ELSE 180
140 BEEP
150 PRINT "OK, let's try again."
160 PRINT : GOTO 50
170                                             ' Summary
180 PRINT
190 PRINT TAB(22) "- - -    SUMMARY    - - -"
200 PRINT "Name:"     TAB(22) PERSON.NAME$
210 PRINT "Address:" TAB(22) ADDRESS$
220 PRINT "City, state, Zip:" TAB(22) CITY.STATE$  TAB(40) ZIPCODE
230                                             ' PRINT to file
240 PRINT #1, PERSON.NAME$
250 PRINT #1, ADDRESS$
260 PRINT #1, CITY.STATE$
270 PRINT #1, ZIPCODE
280 PRINT : PRINT "Add another record Y/N? ";
290 CHANGE$ = INPUT$(1)
300 PRINT CHANGE$
310 IF CHANGE$ = "Y" OR CHANGE$ = "y" THEN 50
320 CLOSE #1                                    ' CLOSE file
330 PRINT "File " FILE$ " closed and saved."
340 END
```

FIGURE 19.9 Using PRINT # to create a sequential file

When executing the program in Figure 19.9 sample data will be entered into the sequential file called CUSTOMER. As you can see in Figure 19.10, several errors were made in executing the program. However, guided by the user prompts and given an opportunity to reenter data, the user eventually entered the desired data. Answering N(No) to the question "Add another record?" closes and saves the file.

```
RUN
Name?  Pete "The wiz smith
Address?  121 South Main: Apt #12
City and state?  New York, NY   10012
Zipcode? 10012
Do you want to change Y/N? y
OK, let's try again.

Name?  Pete "The Wiz" Smith
Address?  121 South Main; Apt. #12
City and state?  New York, NY
Zipcode? 10012
Do you want to change Y/N? n


                      - - -   SUMMARY   - - -
Name:                 Pete "The Wiz" Smith
Address:              121 South Main; Apt. #12
City, state, Zip:     New York, NY          10012

Add another record Y/N? n
File A:CUSTOMER closed and saved.
Ok
```

FIGURE 19.10 Execution of program

USING THE LINE INPUT # STATEMENT

The LINE INPUT # statement reads an entire line from a file, including commas, and assigns it to a string variable. The LINE INPUT # is used to read what was previously written into the file by the PRINT # statement (just as INPUT # is used to read what was written by the WRITE # statement up to the Enter symbol at the end of the line).

A program using LINE INPUT # is shown in Figure 19.11. Statements 60 through 90 input a line from a sequential file into a specified string variable. This process continues until the end-of-file marker is reached.

COPYING A SEQUENTIAL FILE

Files can be copied at either the system (DOS) level or at the BASIC level. At the system level with the prompt A> displayed (or B> for drive B), the following command can be used to copy a file: `COPY PROGRAMA.BAS B:`.

This copies a program called PROGRAMA.BAS on the current drive (drive A) to drive B. If the file extension is present, it must be specified. A file created by another program could be copied in the same manner, such as `COPY ANYFILE B:` This command copies the file on the current drive to

```
10 REM LINE INPUT # to read a file
20 FILE$ = "A:CUSTOMER"
30 OPEN FILE$ FOR INPUT AS #1
40 '                                            INPUT from file
50 WHILE EOF(1) <> -1
60        LINE INPUT #1, PERSON.NAME$  : PRINT PERSON.NAME$
70        LINE INPUT #1, ADDRESS$      : PRINT ADDRESS$
80        LINE INPUT #1, CITY.STATE$   : PRINT CITY.STATE$;
90        LINE INPUT #1, ZIPCODE$      : PRINT ZIPCODE$
100 WEND
110 '                                            CLOSE file
120 CLOSE #1
130 PRINT
140 PRINT "End of " FILE$ " file."
150 END
```

FIGURE 19.11   Using the LINE INPUT # statement

drive B. (Refer to Chapter 5 for a complete discussion of copying files at the system level.)

File data can be difficult to reconstruct in the event that damage occurs, so it is wise to make a backup copy of such a file before changing the file. You can then make changes with the security of knowing that an old copy exists if something goes wrong.

An easy way to make a backup copy is to use the COPY command at the system level:

COPY ANYFILE ANYFILE.BAC A:

This copies ANYFILE on drive A and assigns the copy the name of ANYFILE.BAC, also on drive A. Whenever possible, label the backup file with an extension such as .BAC to indicate that the file is a backup of an original. This helps you keep track of numerous files on the same diskette.

Many software packages use .BAK to indicate a backup file. If you like .BAK, use it.

UPDATING A LARGE FILE

Do you remember the seven steps required to update a small sequential file? Fine, but just to refresh your memory, spend a moment and fill out the steps in the space below. The first step is to open the file for input. Now, complete steps 2 through 7.

Steps to Update a Small Sequential File

Step 1   Open the file for input
Step 2   _____
Step 3   _____
Step 4   _____
Step 5   _____
Step 6   _____
Step 7   _____

Check your answers with Figure 18.8, Steps Required to Update a Small Sequential File. These steps can be used to copy many sequential files but sooner or later a file will be encountered that is too large to fit in memory at one time. Our updating technique will not work then because it requires that everything be processed in a single large array.

You will recall that changes cannot be made to a file directly. A file opened for input cannot accept program output. The steps required to make changes to (update) lengthy files are shown in Figure 19.12. The trick is to open the primary file (the file you want to copy) for input and then open a temporary file for program output. Then read and process each record in the file one at a time. Begin by reading a record from the primary file, make whatever change is needed, and store the record in the temporary file. After copying all records from the primary file into the temporary file and making whatever changes are necessary, copy the contents of the temporary file back into the primary file.

Step 1	Open the original file for input.
Step 2	Open a temporary file for output.
Step 3	If EOF on input file, go to step 8.
Step 4	Read a record from primary (original) file.
Step 5	Make changes to record, if any.
Step 6	Save record, including changes, in temporary file.
Step 7	Go to step 3. Repeat sequence.
Step 8	Close files.
Step 9	Open the original file for output.
Step 10	Open the temporary file for input.
Step 11	Copy the temporary file back into the original file.
Step 12	Close files and kill the temporary file.

FIGURE 19.12 Steps required to change a large sequential file

```
10 REM      Copying/changing files
20 CLS    : PRINT "Current files:"
30 FILES : PRINT
40 '                                      Enter file name
50 LINE INPUT "File to be copied?   " ; FILE$
60 IF FILE$ = "" THEN 70 ELSE 90
70 BEEP  : PRINT "Enter a name" : GOTO 50
80 '                                      Set up files
90  OPEN FILE$  FOR INPUT  AS #1
100 OPEN "TEMP" FOR OUTPUT AS #2
110 '                                     Loop until EOF
120 WHILE EOF(1) <> -1
130     LINE INPUT #1, A$
140     PRINT A$, "     Change  Y/N? ";
150     CH$ = INPUT$(1): PRINT CH$
160     IF CH$ = "Y" OR CH$ ="y" THEN 170 ELSE 220
170     CLS
180     LOCATE 10,1 : PRINT "Revise & press Enter at end of line."
190     LOCATE 11,1 : PRINT A$
200     LOCATE 11,1 : LINE INPUT A$
210     PRINT
220     PRINT #2, A$
230 WEND
240 '
250 CLOSE #1, #2
260 KILL FILE$                            ' Be careful of this
270 NAME "TEMP" AS FILE$                  ' Update FILE$
280 PRINT "File "  FILE$ " updated."
290 END
```

FIGURE 19.13 Program to incorporate changes into a sequential file of any size

A program to incorporate changes into a sequential file of any size is shown in Figure 19.13. Several things should be noted about this program. First, a file of any size can be copied because only one record is loaded into memory at a time. Second, notice that statements 180–200 display a string and then accept revisions to the string at the same location. This saves having to retype the entire record and permits use of the program editor to make any revisions necessary. Also notice statement 260, which kills the original file. Then the TEMP file is renamed with the original file name, thus updating the original file.

The program shown in Figure 19.13 has been saved on the companion diskette as FIG19-13. This can be loaded into memory by the command LOAD"FIG19-13".

SUMMARY

The discussion so far has been devoted to processing sequential files. The next chapter discusses the creating and processing of random-access files.

It is very easy to damage a file, so be sure to copy the files from the companion diskette onto your working diskette before using them. In addition, why not back-up the backup? For example, after copying CH19SALE.SEQ onto your disk, try: COPY CH19SALE.SEQ CH19SALE.XXX. Then CH19SALE.XXX is your own back-up which can be renamed to CH19SALE.SEQ if something should go wrong.

PROBLEMS

Screen Design Problems. Problems 1–12.
Develop a BASIC program, paying particular attention to the design of the screen and the design of the printed output (when requested). General formats are shown for your consideration.

Problems 1–3 require use of sequential files stored on the companion diskette. These are sequential, not ASCII, files. Develop a program for each of the following problems to read and print the first three records in the file. Nothing is known about the format of the data in the files used in Problems 1–3.

*19.1 Develop a program to read the CH19SALE.SEQ sequential file and display the first three records as shown.

```
The first three records in the CH19SALE.SEQ file:
-------------------------------------------------
               111,12700,3
               107,49000,2
               125,1900,2
-------------------------------------------------
End of display.
```

19.2 Develop a program to read the CH19TRAN.SEQ sequential file and display the first three records as shown.

```
The first three records in the CH19TRAN.SEQ file:
-------------------------------------------------
          111,  2260, 1
          107,    50, 2
          111, 11175, 3
-------------------------------------------------
End of display.
```

* The answer to this problem is in Appendix E.

19.3 Develop a program to read the CH19ITEM.SEQ sequential file and display the first three records as shown.

```
The first three records in the CH19ITEM.SEQ file:
--------------------------------------------------------
        2006,"8 disk holders",85,20
        2004,"5 1/4 disk holders",135,40
        3000,"8-11 paper-cont.Rm",20,10
--------------------------------------------------------
End of display.
```

19.4 This problem requires that the "WAGES.ASC" file be converted to a sequential file called "WAGES.SEQ". If you have not already done so, convert the ASCII file to a sequential file. This file is organized as follows:

Employee name	Hours worked	Hourly rate	Age
--	--	--	--

Develop a program to read the WAGES.SEQ sequential file and display the first three records as shown.

```
The first three records in the WAGES.SEQ file:
------------------------------------------------------------
Employee                        Hours       Hourly      Age
Name                            Worked      Rate
------------------------------------------------------------
Alfred Loveland                 40.5        5.4         19
Betty Lowber                    39.23       6.1         22
Ruth Cox                        40          9.2         35
------------------------------------------------------------
End of display.
```

*19.5 Develop a program to read and incorporate changes into the WAGES.SEQ sequential file. (The format for this file is shown in Problem 4.) The records in the file are presented one at a time, and the user is asked if a change is desired. If a change is desired, then the fields are shown for revision. After revision, the next record is displayed. This continues until the end-of-file is reached. The revised file is then displayed.

The screen would appear as shown when Betty Lowber's age was changed from 22 to 53. After developing the program, make the following additional changes to the WAGES.SEQ file:
Ruth Cox worked 44 hours, not 40 hours.
Alfred Loveland was promoted; increase his hourly rate from $5.40 to $7.25.

* The answer to this problem is in Appendix E.

```
    Processing the WAGES.SEQ sequential file.
-----------------------------------------------
Employee                 Hours    Hourly    Age
Name                     Worked   Rate
-----------------------------------------------
Alfred Loveland          40.5     5.4       19    Change  Y/N? n
Betty Lowber             39.23    6.1       22    Change  Y/N? y

************************************************
Press Enter to continue, or space back and retype.
Employee name:
Betty Lowber
Hours Worked:
 39.23
Hourly rate:
 6.1
Age:
 53
Ruth Cox                 40       9.2       35    Change  Y/N?
```

19.6 The CH19ITEM.SEQ sequential file is an inventory file which has the following format:

Stock Number	Item Description	Minimum Quantity	Maximum Quantity

Develop a program to incorporate changes into the file.
Use the program and change:

Stock number 2004 should read "5¼ diskettes" not "5¼ disk holders".
The screen should appear as shown prior to making the change. Print the revised file.

```
    Processing the CH19ITEM    SEQ sequential file.
--------------------------------------------------------
Stock    Item                    Minimum   Maximum
Number   Description             Qt.       Qt.
--------------------------------------------------------
2006     8 disk holders          85        20    Change  Y/N? n
2004     5 1/4 disk holders      135       40    Change  Y/N?
```

19.7 Develop a general file processing program, so that any file can be selected for revision. (Note: As the fields are not known, they cannot be labeled.) Show each record within the file one at a time for possible revision. Display the revised file.

The initial selection screen, prior to showing the records for revision, would appear as shown. Note that diskette files are displayed by the program to aid in file selection. Unfortunately, the user did not spell the full name of the file, but the computer caught this error.

```
Current files:
A:\
COMMAND .COM         CH19SALE.SEQ         CH19TRAN.SEQ         CH19ITEM.SEQ
EMPSALE .SEQ         PAYDAY  .SEQ         CH19PAY .SEQ         UNSORT  .SEQ
WAGES   .SEQ         ANS19-5 .BAS         TEMP                 ANS19-6 .BAS
 309248 Bytes free

File to be Changed?  CH19TRAN
File not found.  Check spelling!
Current files:
A:\
COMMAND .COM         CH19SALE.SEQ         CH19TRAN.SEQ         CH19ITEM.SEQ
EMPSALE .SEQ         PAYDAY  .SEQ         CH19PAY .SEQ         UNSORT  .SEQ
WAGES   .SEQ         ANS19-5 .BAS         TEMP                 ANS19-6 .BAS
 309248 Bytes free

File to be Changed?  CH19TRAN.SEQ
```

Problem 8 requires that the "PRODUCTS.ASC" file be converted to a sequential file called "PRODUCTS.SEQ". If you have not already done so, convert the ASCII file to a sequential file.

Product ID	Description	Cost	Retail price	Begin inven.	Qt. sold	Location code
--	--	--	--	--	--	--

19.8 Management wants a report that would identify the profit to be made if the retail price were increased by 10% on all items and the same quantity were sold.

Prepare a report in the following format for all items in inventory:

Product ID	Description of item	Profit before increase (1)	Profit after increase (2)
--	--	$XXX.XX	$XXX.XX
--	--	$XXX.XX	$XXX.XX
Totals		$XX,XXX.XX	$XX,XXX.XX

(1) Profit = (Retail price − Cost) * Qt sold
(2) Profit = (Retail price * 1.1 − Cost) * Qt sold

Problems 9–11 require the sequential file called CH19PAY.SEQ stored on the companion diskette. This file is organized as follows:

Employee number	Employee name	Life insurance	Monthly salary	No. of depend.	Years service

19.9 Write a program to read the file and print out a summary report according to the following format.

```
        Big Rock County School System
        Employees with over 2 Years Service

        Employee                          Years
        name                              of service

              --                                --
              --                                --
```

19.10   Write a program to read a file and calculate how much it will cost the school system to give all employees a bonus of 10% of their monthly salary. Print the report according to the following format.

```
            Big Rock County School System
                Bonus Analysis Program

        Employee          Monthly         Computed
        name              salary          bonus

        Bill Smith        $1,500.00       $150.00
        John Citizen        $500.00        $50.00
            --                --              --
            --                --              --
            --                --              --

        Total salary for all employees:   $22,030.00
        Total bonus for all employees:     $2,203.00
```

19.11   The Superintendent of Big Rock County School System wants a report called SCHOOL.SRT that is sorted by employees' last names, containing all employees with more than 2 years of service. Develop and print the report in the format shown in Problem 10.

Hint: The file contains employees' first, then last names with a blank space between the first and last name. Display the first name, but do not sort on the first name.

19.12   Develop two mailing list programs that create and process a sequential file called MAILING. The first program is to have a menu screen with the options shown below.

```
        Mailing List Program
        a    Enter Record
        b    Revise/Delete Record
        c    Print Program
        d    Quit

        Your selection?
```

Selection a, Enter Record, should permit entry of the following: name, address, city/state, and zip code.

Selection b, Revise/Delete Record, should permit the records in the MAILING file to be revised and/or deleted to update the mailing file.

Selection c, Print Program, should execute a second program called MAILING.PRT. This program is to display the contents of the MAILING file in two-up format. That is, records are printed side-by-side to conserve space.

> Hint: Allow for any number of records to be processed by this print program.

19.13 Write a program to create a sequential file called MAGAZINE containing the titles of computer magazines. The screen should appear as shown below after the indicated titles are saved in the MAGAZINE file.

```
The following was read into a file called MAGAZINE:
----------------------------------------------------
  PC World          Softtalk          Byte Magazine
  Interface Age     Compute           PC Tech Journal
  Datamation        PC Week           PC Age
  Kilobaud          Tech Topics       PC Magazine
----------------------------------------------------
MAGAZINE file created and closed.
```

19.14 Develop a program to read the MAGAZINE file created in Problem 13. Sort and display the file as shown.

| Magazine Subscriptions: | |
Unsorted	Sorted
PC World	Byte Magazine
Softtalk	Compute
Byte Magazine	Datamation
Interface Age	Interface Age
Compute	Kilobaud
PC Tech Journal	PC Age
Datamation	PC Magazine
PC Week	PC Tech Journal
PC Age	PC Week
Kilobaud	PC World
Tech Topics	Softtalk
PC Magazine	Tech Topics

Title to be included in printed summary?

The program should have the capacity of printing the magazines beginning with a common title. The printout should appear as shown if the title "PC" was entered in response to the prompt "Title to be included in printed summary?"

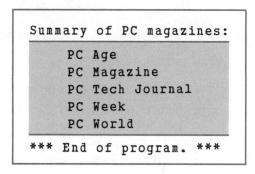

```
Summary of PC magazines:
    PC Age
    PC Magazine
    PC Tech Journal
    PC Week
    PC World
*** End of program. ***
```

Other Problems. Problems 15–24.

Develop a BASIC program to solve each problem. Clearly label all output.

Problems 15–19 require that a sequential file called INVENTRY.SEQ be first developed and saved on diskette. This file is to contain the following data.

Part number	Price per unit
107	8.75
347	19.95
554	5.45
627	4.95
243	1.98
722	.59
445	1.25
396	9.50

19.15 Write a program to create a sequential file called INVENTRY.SEQ containing the above data.

19.16 Write a program to retrieve and display the unit price of any item in the INVENTRY.SEQ file based on user entry of a part number. If the part number entered is not found, display the message "Part Number not in file".

19.17 Write a program to update the INVENTRY.SEQ file in the following ways. Incorporate the following price increases:

(a) Change the price per unit of part number 347 from 19.95 to 24.95.
(b) Change the price per unit of part number 243 from 1.98 to 2.45.
Add the following records:
(c) Part number 455 at a price per unit of 22.45.
(d) Part number 708 at a price per unit of 3.39.

Save the file, including all changes. Then print out the revised file.

19.18 Write a program to perform an automatic price increase of all items in the INVENTRY.SEQ file. That is, a percentage price increase will be entered by the user in decimal format (such as .10 for 10%), then all prices per unit on all records in the file are to be increased by that percent (in dollars-and-cents format). Save the revised file, then print out the revised file.

19.19 Write a program to sort the INVENTRY.SEQ file in ascending order by part number. Save the sorted file as SORTED.INV and display the sorted file.

The sequential file stored on the companion diskette called EMPSALE.SEQ will be needed for Problems 20–22. This sequential file is organized as follows:

Employee number	Sales in dollars	Sales code
--	--	--

The employee number is a three-digit number assigned to all salespeople. Each time a sale is made, the employee number, dollar sales, and sales code are recorded; hence the same employee number may appear several times in the file. Although the sales code is in the sequential file, it is not used in this problem.

19.20 Develop a program to display the sequential file EMPSALE.SEQ.

19.21 Develop a program to calculate the sales per salesperson based on a keyboard entry of an employee number. Use an employee number of 120 to check your work.

19.22 Write a program to sort the EMPSALE.SEQ file in ascending order by dollar sale. Save the sorted file as SALES.SRT consisting of the employee number and sales in dollars. (Do not save the sales code.) Display the sorted file.

Problems 23 and 24 require that the "PRODUCTS.ASC" file be converted to a sequential file called "PRODUCTS.SEQ". If you have not already done so, convert the ASCII file to a sequential file. The format for the "PRODUCTS.ASC" file is shown in Problem 8.

19.23 The sports equipment stored in location code 2 has increased in cost. Develop a program to increase the cost and the retail price of code 2 items by 10%. Save, then display the revised file (display code 2 items only) in a professional format.

   For example, one of the items with a location code of 2 is a Pro Super Exercycle. The cost is to be increased 10% from the current $90.50 to $99.55. The retail price is also to be increased 10% from $149.89 to $164.88. Display all values in dollars-and-cents format.

19.24 Management needs a detailed analysis of the sporting equipment in location codes 2 and 3. Develop a separate file called PRODUCTS.SRT containing the product identification, description, and retail price of all items that have a location code of 2 or 3. Sort and display the file from highest to lowest retail price.

20 RANDOM-ACCESS FILES

Upon completion of this chapter, you should be able to

- Change the BASICA parameters
- Use FIELD, LSET, PUT, and GET statements
- Store and retrieve string data
- Count file records
- Copy a random-access file
- Add, change, and delete a record

INTRODUCTION

As you remember, sequential files contain records stored in sequence, one after the other, on a diskette. In order to locate a desired record, a search is made beginning with the first record. The record is read and the key field is checked to determine if it is the desired record. If not, the next record is read and the key field is again checked. This time-consuming process is repeated until either the record is found or the end of the file is reached.

From a random-access file, a record can be retrieved directly without having to search other records. A penalty to be paid is that a little more care must be spent in creating the file. But once you are familiar with random-access files, they will be easy to use.

A file record is a logical grouping of data elements in a particular record within a file. For example, suppose that a car dealer wanted to create a customer file composed of car makes and the car owner's name. Each record within this file, which will be called CUSTOMER, will consist of two data elements: the car make (CAR$) and owner's name (OWNER$). This file could be constructed as a sequential file, but for this example, let's construct a random-access file.

Data is stored in a random-access file in a table-like arrangement consisting of rows and columns (fields) of elements. Each row in the table corresponds to a record in the file. The first row corresponds to the first record, the second row corresponds to the second record, and so forth. As this row number is the means by which the record is stored and retrieved, this will serve as our key field.

FILE RECORDS AND NUMBER OF FILES

In using random-access files, the length of the file record must be specified when the file is created. If the record length is not specified, the computer will assume that the maximum record length is 128 characters. Also, there is a maximum of three files that can be open at the same time.

Although the default parameters will suffice for most applications, you may wish to change the parameters, perhaps to accommodate a larger number of files. These parameters are changed at the system level before loading BASICA into memory.

A more complete form of the BASICA command to permit changing parameters is

$$\textbf{BASICA/F:} \quad \left\{ \begin{array}{c} \text{Number} \\ \text{of} \\ \text{files} \end{array} \right\} \quad \textbf{/S:} \quad \left\{ \begin{array}{c} \text{Buffer} \\ \text{size} \end{array} \right\}$$

Where:

/F: $\left\{ \begin{array}{c} \text{Number} \\ \text{of} \\ \text{files} \end{array} \right\}$ This establishes the maximum number of files (up to 15) that can be used. The system command **BASICA/F:6** permits up to six files to be open at the same time.

/S: $\left\{ \begin{array}{c} \text{Buffer} \\ \text{size} \end{array} \right\}$ This establishes the maximum record length (up to 32767) that can be used. The command **BASICA/F:6/S:200** permits six files to be open at a record length of 200.

RANDOM-ACCESS FILES

Although the computer can electronically process programming statements quickly, mechanical activities such as accessing a diskette are slow. To speed up file-processing activities, a temporary internal storage space called a buffer is created within the computer. Data coming from and going to a disk is stored in the buffer until the buffer is full. Then the data is transferred to the diskette.

CLOSE was previously specified at the end of a program using a sequential file to remove remaining data from the buffer and store it in the open file on diskette. Movement between the buffer and the diskette occurred automatically during program execution of a sequential file. However, data does not move "automatically" between the buffer and the disk when using random-access files.

Several steps have to be performed when creating a random-access file. First, the file has to be opened. Then fields have to be developed for the buffer that specify the length of the data elements within the record to be stored. Then the data to be stored has to be transferred from the program into the buffer. Now the important step: the data has to be transferred from the buffer to the diskette file for storage. Finally the file has to be closed.

Each of these steps is shown below:

Steps		Function
1	OPEN	Opens a random-access file and establishes a record length.
2	FIELD	Records are read from or written to a random-access file from a buffer. This buffer must be partitioned by the FIELD statement, which reserves character space in the buffer. The buffer can only hold string variables, and numeric values will first have to be converted to strings.

Steps		Function
3	LSET RSET	Although the FIELD statement reserves space for a string variable in the buffer, the statement does not transfer the data. LSET is used to left-justify and transfer a string variable from the program into the buffer. RSET transfers the string variable right-justified from the program into the buffer.
4	PUT	The PUT statement transfers the buffer contents to a random-access diskette file.
5	CLOSE	The CLOSE statement closes and saves the file contents.

CREATING A BEGINNING RANDOM-ACCESS FILE

In creating a random-access file, the record length has to be specified in the OPEN statement. The record length is in bytes (which we will call characters) and remains the same for all records in the file, regardless of the actual data stored in the record. For example, when DATA statements were created we had to know the READ statement variables so that each variable would have its own individual data element. The process of laying out a random-access record is similar but, in addition to knowing the variables to be read, we have to know the number of characters to reserve for each variable.

In a random-access record, each individual data element within the record must have a field reserved in the buffer. Once the fields and the size of the fields (number of characters) are identified, the record length is the sum of the record fields.

Let's go back to our problem of storing information about cars in a random-access file. The organization of data within the CUSTOMER file is as follows. Each row contains the data elements for a specific make of car and owner name.

1	Trans Am	Pete Mears
2	Pontiac LeMans	Tom Citizen
3	Corvette	Mary Worth
4	Buick	Alfred E. Neuman

Characters in field	12345678901234	1234567890123456
Program variables	F1.CAR$	F2.OWNER$

There will be two fields in this random-access file, one for the car make and the other for the owner's name. To make it easier to identify which variable goes with which field, variable names have been changed to indicate the field assignment. That is, the variable F1.CAR$ is associated with the first field, F1. F2.OWNER$ is associated with the second field, F2. More on this in a moment.

After identifying the number of fields that will be needed, you need to calculate the number of characters in each field. The largest element within the F1.CAR$ field is "Pontiac LeMans," which is 14 characters long. The largest element within the F2.OWNER$ field is "Alfred E. Neuman," which is 16 characters long. These lengths must be specified in the FIELD statement.

In actual practice, it is harder to identify the maximum length of a field than is indicated in this example. Files are often revised with new data so, to be safe, we should allow for the possibility of encountering a larger data element in the future. Instead of allowing for 14 characters in the F1.CAR$ field, perhaps we should allow for 18 or even 20 characters, so that longer data elements can be stored. For purposes of this example, however, we will allocate a maximum of 14 characters for the first field and a maximum of 16 characters for the second field. The length of the record is the sum of the two fields (14 + 16), which is 30 characters. This is stated in the OPEN statement.

OPEN

The random-access file CUSTOMER has to be opened to make it available for use by a program. This can be accomplished by using the following two statements:

```
10  FILE$ = "A:CUSTOMER"
20  OPEN FILE$ AS #1 LEN = 30
```

Statement 20 opens the file for random access. Each record in the file will have a length of 30 characters.

FIELD

The FIELD statement allocates buffer space for the string variable that will be written to the random access file. Field variables must be string variables and a FIELD statement cannot be executed until the file has been opened.

The general form of the FIELD statement is

Statement number	**FIELD** #	File number	,	First string length	,	**AS**	First string variable

In this example, the following FIELD statement would be used:

```
30 FIELD #1, 14 AS F1$, 16 AS F2$
```

Statement 30 reserves the first 14 characters of the buffer for the first string variable F1$. The second 16 characters of the buffer are reserved for the string variable F2$. The sum of the string lengths in the FIELD statement should equal the record length specified in the OPEN statement.

Only string variables can be used in the FIELD statement and the variables cannot be used elsewhere in the program in an INPUT statement or on the left side of an assignment statement. Doing so will disrupt internal computer pointers and an error will occur. This potential problem is avoided by selecting unique string variable names for the FIELD statement such as F1$ and F2$. That is, after F1$ and F2$ are specified in the FIELD statement, assignment statements will be used to assign F1.CAR$ = F1$ and F2.OWNER$ = F2$. Program statements will then process the variables F1.CAR$ and F2.OWNER$.

After reserving space in the buffer for the string variables F1$ and F2$, additional statements are needed to make the actual transfer of values from the program into the space that was reserved in the buffer. These are the LSET and RSET statements.

LSET AND RSET

LSET is used to left-justify and transfer a string variable from the program into the buffer. RSET transfers the string variable right-justified from the program to the buffer. In addition to transferring variables, blank spaces are added to the string when needed so that the string is of the length specified in the FIELD statement.

The LSET statement left-justifies the values within the string and adds blanks to the right so that the string is of the length specified in the FIELD statement. If the string is longer than specified, excess characters are eliminated from the right end of the string. As we usually want to left-justify rather than right-justify strings, LSET will be used in the examples.

The general form of LSET is

Statement number	**LSET**	Field statement string variable	=	String variable in program

In this example,

```
40   LSET   F1$ = F1.CAR$
50   LSET   F2$ = F2.OWNER$
```

The program shown in Figure 20.1 demonstrates how LSET changes string variables for storage in the buffer. Statement 30 opens the direct-access file called EXAMPLE of 15 characters in length. Statement 50 establishes fields of 5 characters in length for each of the string variables F1$, F2$, and F3$. Statements 70 through 90 assign and left-justify values to these variables. Notice how five positions are displayed as an output for each of these variables, even though the length of the character strings varied before the variables were left-set.

```
10 REM  Example of LSET
20 FILE$ = "A:EXAMPLE"
30 OPEN FILE$ AS #1 LEN = 15
40 '                                    Reserve space in buffer
50 FIELD #1, 5 AS F1$, 5 AS F2$, 5 AS F3$
60 '                                    Left justifies string
70 LSET  F1$ = "Abc"
80 LSET  F2$ = "Abcde"
90 LSET  F3$ = "Abcdefg"
100 '                                   Output demo
110 PRINT "This is how the characters are stored in buffer."
120 PRINT "The square brackets are for demonstration only."
130 '
140 PRINT TAB(5) "F1$" TAB(18) "F2$" TAB(28) "F3$"
150 PRINT "[" F1$ "]"  TAB(15) "[" F2$ "]" TAB(25) "[" F3$ "]"
160 CLOSE #1
170 END
RUN
This is how the characters are stored in buffer.
The square brackets are for demonstration only.
    F1$          F2$          F3$
[Abc  ]        [Abcde]    [Abcde]
Ok
```

FIGURE 20.1 Example of LSET

Let's take a closer look at the program output. The FIELD statement was used to specify that F1$, F2$, and F3$ are each five characters in length. LSET was used in statements 70 through 90 and produced the output shown below. The brackets are included so that spacing can be seen; they are not part of the string.

`70 LSET F1$ = "Abc"`	Two blanks are added, resulting in the string [Abc].
`80 LSET F2$ = "Abcde"`	Nothing is changed because the string is the length specified in the FIELD statement.
`90 LSET F3$ = "Abcdefg"`	The string is left-justified, and the first five characters [Abcde] are transferred to the buffer.

PUT

Once values have been transferred to the buffer, they can then be transferred from the buffer to a random-access record. The transfer is accomplished by the PUT statement.

The general form of the PUT statement is

Statement number	**PUT #**	File number	,	Record number

The PUT statement can be considered as creating the key field by which the random-access record can later be retrieved. If the record num-

```
10 REM Creating a random access file
20 FILE$ = "A:CUSTOMER"
30 OPEN FILE$ AS #1 LEN = 30
40 '                                    Reserve space in buffer
50 FIELD #1, 14 AS F1$, 16 AS F2$
60 '                                    READ and PUT records
70 FOR INDEX = 1 TO 4
80     READ F1.CAR$, F2.OWNER$
90     LSET F1$ = F1.CAR$
100    LSET F2$ = F2.OWNER$
110    PUT #1, INDEX
120 NEXT INDEX
130 '                                   CLOSE file
140 CLOSE #1
150 PRINT "File " FILE$ " created and closed."
160 '
9000 DATA Trans Am,      Pete Mears
9010 DATA Pontiac LeMans, Tom Citizen
9020 DATA Corvette,      Mary Worth
9030 DATA Buick,         Alfred E. Neuman
9040 END
RUN
File A:CUSTOMER created and closed.
Ok
```

FIGURE 20.2   Creating a beginning random-access file

ber is omitted in the PUT statement, the data in the buffer is transferred to the record immediately following the last record. That is, unless otherwise specified, the records established by the PUT statement will be in sequential order (1, 2, 3, 4, etc.) up to a maximum of 32767 records. The record number is very important because it is the only way the record can be retrieved.

A complete program to create a random-access file is shown in Figure 20.2. Processing is internal, so only the message that the file has been created appears on the screen. Statement **110 PUT #1, INDEX** specifies that the record number is the value of the variable INDEX. Because the value of the variable INDEX progresses sequentially, the statement could have just as logically been written as **110 PUT #1**.

The program shown in Figure 20.2 creates a random-access file called CUSTOMER and saves the file on diskette. This file is structured differently than a sequential file. Instead of records within the file being in one long sequence, the data is arranged in a file cabinet format consisting of a cabinet (called CUSTOMER) with four file drawers. Each file drawer is a separate and distinct record number (1, 2, 3, or 4) that identifies the drawer. Any file drawer (record) can be retrieved directly without having to process the drawers (records) preceding it.

A complete description of the CUSTOMER file created by the program shown in Figure 20.2 is shown in Figure 20.3. Notice that the total length of the random-access record is 30 characters. Further, the record consists of fields F1$ (length 14) and F2$ (length 16).

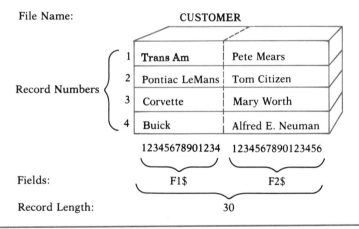

FIGURE 20.3 Arrangement of data in a random-access file

RETRIEVING A BEGINNING RANDOM-ACCESS FILE: THE GET STATEMENT

Note statements 170 and 180 in Figure 20.4. Technically these are not necessary and could be eliminated. FIELD statement variables cannot be used on the left side of an assignment, or in an INPUT, READ, or as an argument in MID$. Since we are not using the FIELD statement variables in this manner, the values of F1$ and F2$ could be displayed without reassignment.

After a random-access file has been created, a program is needed to retrieve the file and to "get" the desired record. The statement used to get a specific record in a random-access file is the GET statement.

The general form of the GET statement is

Statement number	**GET #**	File number	,	Record number

The GET statement is the opposite of the PUT statement. The PUT statement puts (places) data from the buffer into a random-access file record. On the other hand, the GET statement gets (retrieves) a record from the random-access file and places it in the buffer. For example, GET

#1,3 directs the program to go to file number 1, which has been previously opened as a random-access file. Record number 3 is obtained, placed in the buffer, and assigned to the string variables previously specified in the FIELD statement.

A program that retrieves a random-access file is shown in Figure 20.4. Statement **160 GET #1, RECORD** retrieves the record number from the first file (the CUSTOMER file that was specified as #1). There are two data elements in each record. The first element is assigned to the string variable specified in the FIELD statement (F1$) and the second element is assigned

```
10 REM Retrieving random access record
20 FILE$ = "A:CUSTOMER"
30 OPEN FILE$ AS #1 LEN = 30
40 '                                   Reserve buffer space
50 FIELD #1, 14 AS F1$, 16 AS F2$
60 '                                   User prompt
70 PRINT "Type record desired: 1,2,3,4.  E Ends program. ";
80 A$ = INPUT$(1)
90 PRINT A$
100 PRINT
110 IF A$ = "E" OR A$ = "e" THEN 230
120 RECORD = VAL(A$)
130 IF RECORD >= 1 AND RECORD <= 4 THEN 160 ELSE 140
140 BEEP : PRINT "Wrong entry!" : GOTO 70
150 '                                   GET selected record
160 GET #1, RECORD
170 F1.CAR$   = F1$                     ' Assign to string
180 F2.OWNER$ = F2$
190 PRINT "Record #" RECORD "contains " F1.CAR$;
200 PRINT " and " F2.OWNER$
210 GOTO 70
220 '                                   CLOSE file
230 CLOSE #1
240 PRINT "File " FILE$ " closed."
250 END
```

FIGURE 20.4 Retrieving a random-access file

```
RUN
Type record desired: 1,2,3,4.  E Ends program. 2

Record # 2 contains Pontiac LeMans and Tom Citizen
Type record desired: 1,2,3,4.  E Ends program. 4

Record # 4 contains Buick and Alfred E. Neuman
Type record desired: 1,2,3,4.  E Ends program. e

File A:CUSTOMER closed.
Ok
```

FIGURE 20.5 Program output

to the second string variable (F2$). Statements 170 and 180 assign these values to the string variables F1.CAR$ and F2.OWNER$. Program output is shown in Figure 20.5.

LOC FUNCTION

When working with random-access files, it is often necessary to know the record number used in the last GET or PUT statement. This is accomplished by the LOC function.

For example, the statement `100 PRINT LOC(1)` displays the last record number used in a GET or PUT statement associated with file number 1. If a GET or PUT has not been executed on the file specified, a value of zero will be returned. A program demonstrating this statement will be presented in a moment.

COUNTING RECORDS

Any unused random-access record is filled with null characters, CHR$(0). These null characters can be used to determine the number of the record in the file. A record in the file can be retrieved, and the field checked to determine if it contains all 0's. If not, the record is counted.

An example of this method of counting is shown in Figure 20.6. Note the use of STRING$ in statement 130. F1$ was established as containing 14 characters in the FIELD statement and then assigned to F1.CAR$. F1.CAR$ is checked to see if it contains 14 zeros, using STRING$(14,0). Finally, notice how the value of the last record used in a GET statement is displayed by the LOC function.

```
10 REM Counting records and the LOF function
20 FILE$ = "A:CUSTOMER"
30 OPEN FILE$ AS #1 LEN = 30
40 '                                    Reserve buffer space
50 FIELD #1, 14 AS F1$, 16 AS F2$
60 NRECORDS = 0
70 NRECORDS = NRECORDS + 1
80 '                                    GET a record
90 GET #1, NRECORDS
100 F1.CAR$   = F1$
110 F2.OWNER$ = F2$
120 '                                   Null string check
130 IF F1.CAR$ = STRING$(14,0) THEN 150 ELSE 70
140 '                                   Display count
150 PRINT "We counted" NRECORDS - 1 "records."
160 PRINT "The file contains" LOC(1) - 1 "records using LOC."
170 PRINT
180 '                                   CLOSE file
190 CLOSE #1
200 PRINT "File " FILE$ " closed."
210 END
```

FIGURE 20.6 Counting file records

The program shown in Figure 20.6 to count the number of records in a random-access file could be shortened to the subroutine shown below. NRECORDS is the number of records in the file.

At this point you should know how to do the following using string data with random-access files: create a file, display any record, and count the records in the file. If there is any confusion on these points, go back and make the programs shown in Figures 20.1 through 20.6 work as intended. We'll take a look at what is involved in changing a record, then we'll add a new record to the end of the file. Later, new records will be added to deleted positions within the file.

Avoid the LOF (length-of-file) function, which returns the number of characters in the file in units of 128. Care must be taken in adjusting this figure to determine the specific record count, particularly if the BASIC parameters are changed.

```
1000 N = 0                                        ' Counting GOSUB
1010 N = N + 1
1020 GET #1, N
1030 F1.REC$      = F1$
1040 IF F1.REC$ = STRING$(30,0) THEN 1050 ELSE 1010
1050 NRECORDS     = N - 1
1060 RETURN
```

As stated previously, a PUT statement retrieves a record from the buffer and saves it on a random-access file. This is accomplished by a statement of the form PUT #1, RECORD, where RECORD is the number of the file record to be added. Changing records in a random-access file produces an immediately updated master file. Simply assign values to variables, LSET the variables, and PUT the record into the file. The revised record is simply written over in place of the old record. (We will see an example of this in a moment.)

The technique for adding a record at the end of the file consists of counting the records and adding the new record to a position that is one greater than the number of records in the file. You know how to count records within a file, so it will not be difficult to add a new record to the end of a file.

Although changes and additions are a straightforward process, deleting a record can be tricky. Perhaps the easiest way to delete a record is to write a separate program that does not copy the record (leaves it behind) when copying the file. An example of deleting by not copying is shown in Figure 20.7. Notice how the field variable F1$ is defined as 30 characters, which is the former width of both F1$ and F2$.

Statements 80 and 230 are inserted to permit us to see what is happening and would be removed from commercial programs. Program output is shown in Figure 20.8. Notice that the program has been executed twice. The first time, record 2 was deleted. The second time the record did not appear and it was decided not to delete any additional records.

Although the program shown in Figure 20.8 can be used to delete a record, deleting a record from within a BASIC program that also performs other tasks is far more useful. Although a record cannot physically be removed from a file, we can "trick" the computer into thinking that the record is deleted. The technique consists of placing a code in a deleted record such as the word "DEL". Then, when adding to a random-access file, check all the records to determine if the code DEL exists. If DEL is found, we write the new record onto (over) the DEL code; otherwise, we add the new record to the end of the file.

Statements to delete a record are shown on the following page. Notice that the record is in fact still there but contains the code "DEL".

```
1200 PRINT "Record number to be deleted";
1210 RECORD$ = INPUT$(1)
1220 PRINT RECORD$
1230 N = VAL(RECORD$)
1240 IF N > 0 AND N <= NRECORDS THEN 1270 ELSE 1250
1250 BEEP
1260 PRINT "Enter a number between 1 -" NRECORDS: GOTO 1200
1270 LSET F1$ = "DEL"
1280 LSET F2$ = "DEL"
1290 PUT #1, N : GOTO 60
```

```
10  REM   Deleting a record
20  FILE1$ ="CUSTOMER"
30  FILE2$ = "TEMP"
40  OPEN FILE1$ AS #1 LEN = 30 : FIELD #1, 30 AS F1$
50  OPEN FILE2$ AS #2 LEN = 30 : FIELD #2, 30 AS F2$
60  GOSUB 1000                          ' Count records
70  NEW.REC = 0
80  PRINT "File " FILE1$ " contains" NRECORDS "records."
90  FOR I = 1 TO NRECORDS
100      GET #1, I
110      F1.REC$ = F1$
120      PRINT F1.REC$ "   Delete record #" I " Y/N? ";
130      A$ = INPUT$(1)
140      PRINT A$
150      IF A$ = "Y"  OR  A$ =  "y" THEN 250
160      IF A$ = "N"  OR  A$ =  "n" THEN 200 ELSE 170
170      BEEP : PRINT "Only type Y or N!"
180      GOTO 120
190  '                                         Record record
200      LSET F2$ = F1.REC$
210      NEW.REC  = NEW.REC + 1
220      PUT #2, NEW.REC
230      PRINT "File " FILE2$ " now contains " F2$
                 " as record #" NEW.REC
240      PRINT
250  NEXT I
260  '
270  CLOSE #1, #2
280  KILL FILE1$                        ' Be careful of this
290  NAME FILE2$ AS FILE1$              ' Now TEMP is CUSTOMER
300  PRINT FILE1$ " closed and updated."
310  END
320  '
1000 N = 0                              ' Counting GOSUB
1010 N = N + 1
1020 GET #1, N
1030 F1.REC$     = F1$
1040 IF F1.REC$ = STRING$(30,0) THEN 1050 ELSE 1010
1050 NRECORDS    =   N - 1
1060 RETURN
1070 END
```

FIGURE 20.7 A program to delete a record by not copying the record

```
RUN
File CUSTOMER contains 4 records.
Trans Am        Pete Mears           Delete record # 1   Y/N? n
File TEMP now contains Trans Am         Pete Mears         as record # 1

Pontiac LeMansTom Citizen           Delete record # 2   Y/N? y
Corvette        Mary Worth           Delete record # 3   Y/N? n
File TEMP now contains Corvette         Mary Worth         as record # 2

Buick           Alfred E. Neuman     Delete record # 4   Y/N? n
File TEMP now contains Buick            Alfred E. Neuman as record # 3

CUSTOMER closed and updated.
Ok
RUN
File CUSTOMER contains 3 records.
Trans Am        Pete Mears           Delete record # 1   Y/N? n
File TEMP now contains Trans Am         Pete Mears         as record # 1

Corvette        Mary Worth           Delete record # 2   Y/N? n
File TEMP now contains Corvette         Mary Worth         as record # 2

Buick           Alfred E. Neuman     Delete record # 3   Y/N? n
File TEMP now contains Buick            Alfred E. Neuman as record # 3

CUSTOMER closed and updated.
Ok
```

FIGURE 20.8 A program to delete a record—program output

Of course, now that the record has been deleted, we do not want it displayed when the file is printed. Statements for displaying "active" records are shown below. Notice that when "DEL" is encountered in F1.CAR$, the deleted record is not displayed.

```
1000 FOR I = 1 TO NRECORDS
1010     GET #1, I
1020     F1.CAR$ = F1$
1030     F2.OWNER$ = F2$
1040 '                                          Skip DEL records
1050     IF LEFT$(F1.CAR$,3) = "DEL" THEN 1070
1060     PRINT "Record #" I "contains " F1.CAR$ " and " F2.OWNER$
1070 NEXT I
```

A data entry subroutine is needed to assist in adding or revising records in our CUSTOMER file. We can then call the subroutine without having to repeat the same statements within the program. An example of statements to accomplish this is shown on the next page. After the subroutine has entered data and the variables F1$ and F2$ are LSET, the PUT statement can be used to enter values into the random-access file.

```
4000 LINE INPUT "Type car make "        ; F1.CAR$
4010 IF LEN(F1.CAR$) > 14 THEN BEEP   :
        PRINT "Limit of 14 characters - Re-enter." : GOTO 4000
4020 LINE INPUT "Type owner's name " ;F2.OWNER$
4030 IF LEN(F2.OWNER$) > 16 THEN BEEP:
        PRINT "Limit of 16 characters - Re-enter." : GOTO 4020
4040 LSET F1$ = F1.CAR$ : LSET F2$ = F2.OWNER$
4050 RETURN
```

Records can be added to the file after checking for the code "DEL". If this code is not found, all records are considered to be active and the new record is added to the end of the file. Statements to accomplish this are as follows:

```
700 FOR I = 1 TO NRECORDS
710     GET #1, I
720     F1.CAR$   = F1$
730     F2.OWNER$ = F2$
740     IF LEFT$(F1.CAR$,3) <> "DEL" THEN 780
750     GOSUB 4000
760     PUT #1, I
770     GOTO 60*
780 NEXT I
790 NRECORDS = I
800 GOSUB 4000
810 PUT #1, I : GOTO 60
```

* Where 60 is a menu or origin.

A program to process random access files is shown in Figure 20.9. This program can be used to revise, add, display, and delete records.

You may have noticed that the diskette drive responds differently when executing programs with random-access files. The drive will come on when the file is first opened but afterwards the drive may or may not be activated. This occurs because data is transferred between main memory and the diskette in blocks of 512 bytes (characters). This block is stored on the diskette in a sector. Since the programs we have been using often store less than a sector of 512 characters, the data remains in memory and is not frequently transferred to and from diskette storage.

```
10 REM Processing random access files
20 FILE$ = "A:CUSTOMER"
30 OPEN FILE$ AS #1 LEN = 30
40 FIELD #1, 14 AS F1$, 16 AS F2$
50 GOSUB 3000                                    ' Records count
60 CLS
70 PRINT "There are" NRECORDS "records in the " FILE$ " file."
80 PRINT  "1  Revise a record"
90 PRINT  "2  Add a record"
100 PRINT "3  Display records"
110 PRINT "4  Delete a record"
120 PRINT "5  Quit & save file"
130 PRINT "   Your choice? ";
140 CHOICE$ = INPUT$(1)                          ' Make choice
150 PRINT CHOICE$
160 N = VAL(CHOICE$)
170 IF N < 1 OR N > 5 THEN 180 ELSE 210
180 BEEP
190 PRINT "Only type 1 - 5" : GOTO 130
200 '                                            Directs control
210 ON N GOTO 500, 700, 1000, 1200, 7000
220 '
490 '                                            Revise record
500 PRINT "Record number to be revised? ";
510 RECORD$ = INPUT$(1)
520 PRINT RECORD$
530 N = VAL(RECORD$)
540 IF N > 0 AND N <= NRECORDS THEN 560 ELSE 550
550 PRINT "Enter a number between 1 -" NRECORDS : GOTO 500
560 GET #1, N
570 F1.CAR$ = F1$
580 IF LEFT$(F1.CAR$,3) = "DEL" THEN BEEP :
        PRINT "Deleted - select another record." : GOTO 500
590 GOSUB 4000
600 PUT #1, N : GOTO 60
610 '
690 '                                            Add-check for DEL
700 FOR I = 1 TO NRECORDS
710     GET #1, I
720     F1.CAR$   = F1$
730     F2.OWNER$ = F2$
740     IF LEFT$(F1.CAR$,3) <> "DEL" THEN 780
750     GOSUB 4000
760     PUT #1, I
770     GOTO 60
780 NEXT I
790 NRECORDS = I
800 GOSUB 4000
810 PUT #1, I : GOTO 60
820 '
990 '                                            Display records
1000 FOR I = 1 TO NRECORDS
1010     GET #1, I
1020     F1.CAR$ = F1$
```

FIGURE 20.9 Processing random-access files

```
1030       F2.OWNER$ = F2$
1040 '                                              Skip DEL records
1050       IF LEFT$(Fl.CAR$,3) = "DEL" THEN 1070
1060       PRINT "Record #" I "contains " Fl.CAR$ " and " F2.OWNER$
1070 NEXT I
1080 GOSUB 5000: GOTO 60
1090 '
1190 '                                              Delete record
1200 PRINT "Record number to be deleted";
1210 RECORD$ = INPUT$(1)
1220 PRINT RECORD$
1230 N = VAL(RECORD$)
1240 IF N > 0 AND N <= NRECORDS THEN 1270 ELSE 1250
1250 BEEP
1260 PRINT "Enter a number between 1 -" NRECORDS: GOTO 1200
1270 LSET Fl$ = "DEL"
1280 LSET F2$ = "DEL"
1290 PUT #1, N : GOTO 60
1300 '
1310 '
3000 N = 0                                          ' Count records
3010 N = N + 1
3020 GET #1, N
3030 Fl.CAR$    = Fl$
3040 IF Fl.CAR$ = STRING$(14,0) THEN 3050 ELSE 3010
3050 NRECORDS   = N - 1
3060 RETURN
3070 '
3990 '                                              Data Entry
4000 LINE INPUT "Type car make "      ; Fl.CAR$
4010 IF LEN(Fl.CAR$) > 14 THEN BEEP  :
         PRINT "Limit of 14 characters - Re-enter." : GOTO 4000
4020 LINE INPUT "Type owner's name " ;F2.OWNER$
4030 IF LEN(F2.OWNER$) > 16 THEN BEEP:
         PRINT "Limit of 16 characters - Re-enter." : GOTO 4020
4040 LSET Fl$ = Fl.CAR$ : LSET F2$ = F2.OWNER$
4050 RETURN
4060 '
5000 PRINT "Press any key to continue."            ' Stop display
5010 IF INKEY$ = "" THEN 5010
5020 RETURN
5030 '
7000 CLOSE #1
7010 PRINT "File " FILE$ " closed and saved."
7020 END
```

FIGURE 20.9 (*continued*)

SUMMARY

This chapter discussed creating, revising, adding, displaying, and deleting records consisting of string data in a random-access file. String data was stressed because random-access files store and retrieve only string data. Numeric data will be converted to string data for storage in the next chapter but the objective of this chapter is to develop fundamental proficiency in processing random-access files.

Although we can retrieve any file record, we have not developed a very useful procedure. That is, the first, second, third, or—for that matter—any record can be retrieved but we need to develop the ability to retrieve by another field. For example, instead of retrieving the third car, we need a method by which a record could be retrieved by the car's license plate code.

Attention is now directed to expanding our skills in processing random-access files. The next chapter discusses the conversion of numbers for random-access file storage and retrieval. In addition, a file index system will be created that will permit the development of a more useful random-access record-retrieval system.

PROBLEMS

Screen Design Problems. Problems 1–7.
Develop a BASIC program, paying particular attention to the design of the screen. General formats are shown for your consideration.

*20.1 Write a program to create a random-access file called "GRADES.RND" containing the student names and course grades shown.

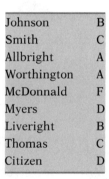

Johnson	B
Smith	C
Allbright	A
Worthington	A
McDonnald	F
Myers	D
Liveright	B
Thomas	C
Citizen	D

20.2 Write a program to retrieve, display, and change any record in the random-access file called "GRADES.RND" created in Problem 1. An example of the screen is shown. Notice that when a record is selected for changing (in this case record number 2), the student's name and grade are displayed before proceeding with the change.

* The answer to this problem is in Appendix E.

```
------------------------------
    Quick Change Grade Program
  Record      Student        Course
  Number      Name           Grade
------------------------------
    1          Johnson          B
    2          Smith            C
    3          Allbright        A
    4          Worthington      A
    5          McDonnald        F
    6          Myers            D
    7          Liveright        B
    8          Thomas           C
    9          Citizen          D
------------------------------
Record desired: 1-9. E Ends
2
Smith has a grade of C.
Change this Y/N?
Type student name Smythe
Type student grade B
```

20.3 Write a program to retrieve, display, change, delete, and add any record to the random-access file called "GRADES.RND" created in Problem 1. Develop your own screen.

20.4 Write a program to create a random-access file called "LICENSE.RND", using the following data on driver's license number (LICENSE$), state (STATE$), and driver's name (DRIVER.N$). Use a field width that exactly fits the data shown. This file is used in Problem 5.

K13B4	NY	Smith
XKEHOT	FL	Jones
MYCAR	CA	Citizens
LOVE1	KY	Jackson
HOWDY	GA	Thomas
BEAUTY2	GA	Neuman

20.5 Write a program to update the "LICENSE.RND" file created in Problem 4. Develop a screen following the general format shown.

```
There are 6 records in LICENSE.RND.

     Do you want to:
   1 Revise a record
   2 Add a record
   3 Display records
   4 Delete a record
   5 Quit & save file
     Your selection?
```

(a) Correct the spelling of driver's name in the second record from "Jones" to "Johnson."

(b) Delete the third record.

(c) Add a new record to the file as follows:

    NEWCAR   TN   Sampson

Problems 6 and 7 require the ASCII file stored on the companion diskette called "BUZZWORD.ASC". The data in this ASCII file is organized as follows:

File data			
	--	--	--
	--	--	--
Variables	LANGUAGE$	TYPE$	JARGON$
Field length	7	21	24

20.6 Write a program to convert this ASCII file into a random-access file called "BUZZWORD.RND". Do not copy the "LAST" record.

20.7 Write a program to count and display the number of records (NRECORDS) in the "BUZZWORD.RND" file. Then randomly generate a number between 1 and NRECORDS and display the corresponding record in the following format. (The randomly selected buzzwords appear in the underlined positions.)

```
The programming language LANGUAGE$ uses
TYPE$ coding with JARGON$ for easy to
understand programs.
```

Randomly select 3 records from the "BUZZWORD.RND" file and display the randomly generated messages in the preceding format. For example, if record number 5 were randomly selected, the following would be displayed:

```
The programming language COBOL uses alphanumeric
variable coding with structured programming for
easy to understand programs.
```

Other Problems. Problems 8 and 9.

Problems 8 and 9 require the use of the random-access file called "CUSTOMER.RND" stored on the companion diskette. This file consists of three fields of data: customer name (C.NAME$), street address (ADDRESS$), and city/state (CITY.STATE$). The "CUSTOMER.RND" file is organized as follows:

File data			
	--	--	--
	--	--	--
Variables	C.NAME$	ADDRESS$	CITY.STATE$
Field length	20	20	20

20.8 Write a program to display the records in the "CUSTOMER.RND" according to the format shown. Note that the program is also capable of displaying records requested by the user.

Random-Access Retrieval of the CUSTOMER.RND file.

Record number	Customer name	Customer address	City and state
1	Tom Jackson	121 South Main	Denver, CO
2	Jerry Jones	12 Main St., Apt 12B	Charlotte, NC
3	Susan Smith	111 Broadway	Portland, OR
4	Mean Joe Green	14 Western Way	Waco, TX
5	John Johns	132 Alp St.	Syracuse, NY
6	Joyce Citizen	12 Dixie Hwy.	Mobile, AL
7	Alice Myers	972 Jackson Ave.	St. Petersburg, FL
8	Susie Snowflake	78 Main St.	San Bernardino, CA
9	Tom Bigman	199 Iron Way	Youngstown, OH
10	Sharon Thomas	32 S. Mason	Wilmington, DE

Record to be displayed: 1 – 10 E Ends?

20.9 Write a program that can be used to update the CUSTOMER.RND file. The screen should appear as shown.

```
The CUSTOMER.RND file contains 10 records.

    1 Revise a record
    2 Add a record
    3 Display records
    4 Delete a record
    5 Quit & save file
      Your choice?
```

Use the program and make the following changes:

(a) Correct the address in the first record from 121 South Main to Apt. 21A South Main.

(b) Delete the fifth and eighth records.

(c) Add the following new customer to the file:

Tom Jackson, 123 West Broadway, New York, NY

21

Processing Random-Access Files

Upon completion of this chapter you should be able to

- Use numbers in random-access files
- Develop a random-access file index
- Use a file index to retrieve a record

USING NUMBERS IN RANDOM-ACCESS FILES

The random-access file programs have stressed string variables for one very important reason: random-access files can store and retrieve only strings. If numbers are to be stored, numeric values must first be converted to string values. There are special functions available to convert numeric to string data. These are the MKI$, MKS$, and MKD$ functions.

Which specific function should be used to convert numeric to string data depends on the type of numeric values being converted. Functions and examples demonstrating their applications follow. In these examples F1.ITEM% is an integer variable, F2.DOL! is a single-precision variable, and F3.PRICE# is a double-precision variable.

Function	Operation
F1$ = MKI$(F1.ITEM%)	This converts an integer variable (F1 .ITEM%) into the two-character string F1$.
F2$ = MKS$(F2.DOL!)	This converts the single-precision number F2.DOL! into a four-character string F2$. Be careful—when using dollars, values greater than 9.99 require 5 characters (the decimal counts as a character). Also, since variables are assumed to be single-precision, F2.DOL is the same as F2.DOL!
F3$ = MKD$(F3.PRICE#)	This converts the double-precision number F3.PRICE# into an eight-character string F3$.

If MK is thought of as an abbreviation for "MaKe," then these functions can be remembered by the following mnemonics:

Function	Operation
F1$ = MKI$(F1.ITEM%)	MaKe an Integer into a string$
F2$ = MKS$(F2.DOL!)	MaKe a Single-precision into a string$
F3$ = MKD$(F3.PRICE#)	MaKe a Double-precision into a string$

Numeric data that has been converted to string data can then be saved as a random-access record following the procedure previously discussed. An example of this conversion will be shown in a moment but remember that data read from a random-access file is string data. If numeric data is converted to string, it is no longer numeric data. If a program using a random-access file requires numeric data, the string data will have to be converted back into numeric values.

The conversion of string into numeric values is accomplished by the CVI, CVS, and CVD functions. The function to be used depends on the type of numeric values needed. A simple rule to follow is to use the function that "reverses" the previous function. For example, suppose that a double-precision number had been made into a string for random-access storage. When converting it back to a number, use the function that converts it to a double-precision number.

Function	Operation
F1.ITEM% = CVI(F1$)	This converts a two-character string (F1$) into an integer F1.ITEM%.
F2.DOL! = CVS(F2$)	This converts a four-character string (F2$) into a single-precision number F2.DOL!. This can be simplified to F2.DOL = CVS(F2$).
F3.PRICE# = CVD(F3$)	This converts an eight-character string (F3$) into a double-precision number F3.PRICE#.

These functions can be easily remembered by the following mnemonics:

CVI	Convert Variable–Integer
CVS	Convert Variable–Single-precision
CVD	Convert Variable–Double-precision

Let's use an example to demonstrate converting numeric to string data. Suppose we want to develop a random-access file containing the data shown below. Notice that the program variable F3.PRICE# is the price the buyer paid for the car and is a double-precision variable.

Record number	1st variable	2nd variable	3rd variable
1	Trans Am	Pete Mears	14105.43
2	Pontiac LeMans	Tom Citizen	12750.50
3	Corvette	Mary Worth	36895.00
4	Buick	Alfred E. Neuman	16789.00

Field Length:	14	16	8
Field Variables:	F1$	F2$	F3$
Program Variables:	F1.CAR$	F2.OWNER$	F3.PRICE#

Although the serious programmer should experiment with various numeric conversion functions, it would be best for beginners to use the MKD$ function. This function makes a double-precision into a string. Then use CVD to convert the string back into a double-precision value. Otherwise it is possible to become very confused. Also, do not forget to allow for a width of eight in the FIELD statement.

A program to create a random-access file called ANYOWNER containing data on F1.CAR$, F2.OWNER$, and F3.PRICE# is shown in Figure 21.1. Notice the conversion of the double-precision variable F3.PRICE# to

```
10 REM storing numeric data
20                                        ' Set up file
30 FILE$ ="ANYOWNER"
40 OPEN FILE$ AS #1 LEN = 38
50 FIELD #1, 14 AS F1$, 16 AS F2$, 8 AS F3$
60                                        ' Create file
70 FOR I = 1 TO 4
80      READ F1.CAR$, F2.OWNER$, F3.PRICE#
90      LSET F1$ = F1.CAR$
100     LSET F2$ = F2.OWNER$
110     LSET F3$ = MKD$(F3.PRICE#)        ' D-precision into string
120 PUT #1, I
130 NEXT I
140 '
150 CLOSE #1
160 PRINT "File " FILE$ " created and closed."
170 '
9000 DATA Trans Am,       Pete Mears,        14105.43
9010 DATA Pontiac LeMans, Tom Citizen,       12750.50
9020 DATA Corvette,       Mary Worth,        36895.00
9030 DATA Buick,          Alfred E. Neuman,  16789.00
9040 '
9050 END
RUN
File ANYOWNER created and closed.
Ok
```

FIGURE 21.1   Creating a random-access file: Converting numeric to string data

the string variable F3$ in statement 110. The FIELD width is eight charac-
ters so that a price up to 99999.99 can be accommodated (the decimal is
counted). It is often easier to use eight characters, even if the full field is
not required, and then later use the CVD function to convert the eight-
character string back into a double-precision number.

A program to read and display any record in the ANYOWNER file is
shown in Figure 21.2. Notice statement 210, in which the string variable
F3$ is converted back into the double-precision variable F3.PRICE# by
the CVD function.

Program output is shown in Figure 21.3. The third and second records
are retrieved from the random-access file and displayed. Notice that
F3.PRICE# is a double-precision number and is displayed with a PRINT
USING format.

Records within a random-access file can be added, deleted, and displayed following the program logic previously shown in Figure 20.9. Just
be sure to convert numeric to string data before storage and to convert the
necessary string data to numeric when required by the program. Attention
is now directed to developing a file index that will add greater flexibility in
record retrieval.

DEVELOPING A RANDOM-ACCESS FILE INDEX

The record number we have been using in our random-access files is
needed only for storage and retrieval and in most applications is of little, if
any, practical value. For example, if we wanted to store or retrieve records

```
10 REM Converting string to numeric data
20 '                                        Set up file
30 FILE$ = "ANYOWNER"
40 OPEN FILE$ AS #1 LEN = 38
50 FIELD #1, 14 AS F1$, 16 AS F2$, 8 AS F3$
60 '                                        User prompt
70 PRINT
80 PRINT "Record 1- 4 for display. E Ends.  Your choice? ";
90 A$ = INPUT$(1)
100 PRINT A$
110 IF A$  = "E" OR A$ = "e" THEN 300
120 RECORD = VAL(A$)
130 IF RECORD < 1 OR RECORD > 4 THEN 140 ELSE 180
140 BEEP
150 PRINT "Only type 1 - 4 or E to End!"
160 GOTO 70
170 '                                        Retrieve record
180 GET #1, RECORD
190 F1.CAR$   = F1$
200 F2.OWNER$ = F2$
210 F3.PRICE# = CVD(F3$) '                   Convert string
220 '                                        Display record
230 PRINT
240 PRINT "Record #" RECORD "contains " F1.CAR$;
250 PRINT ", " F2.OWNER$ " and " F3.PRICE#
260 PRINT "The price of the car is";
270 PRINT USING "$$######,.##";F3.PRICE#
280 GOTO 70
290 '                                        Close file
300 CLOSE #1
310 PRINT "File " FILE$ " closed."
320 END
```

FIGURE 21.2   Retrieving a random-access file: Converting string to numeric data

by car license number, a sequential numbering system (1, 2, 3, 4, etc.) could not be used. Nor could car serial numbers be used, even if they were all numeric. The reason for this is that random files are sequentially numbered, beginning with 1 and going up to a maximum number of 32767. If 30,000 random-access records were established to store and retrieve records, the file would be very inefficient if only a few of the locations actually contained any data.

To be practical, a random-access file needs an index that relates a unique record key to the sequential numbering system used in file storage and retrieval. The record key can be any value that uniquely identifies the record. Then an index (table) can be developed relating the record key to its assigned sequential number for storing and retrieving the random-access record.

For example, let's use the same variables as before: F1.CAR$, F2.OWNER$, and F3.PRICE#. Now let's add a new variable called LICENSE$, the function of which is to be able to retrieve the random-access record. The same record numbers (1, 2, 3, and 4) will be used but we will retrieve a record based on the value of LICENSE$.

```
RUN

Record 1- 4 for display. E Ends.  Your choice? 2

Record # 2 contains Pontiac LeMans, Tom Citizen      and  12750.5
The price of the car is  $12,750.50

Record 1- 4 for display. E Ends.  Your choice? 5
Only type 1 - 4 or E to End!

Record 1- 4 for display. E Ends.  Your choice? 1

Record # 1 contains Trans Am      , Pete Mears       and  14105.43
The price of the car is  $14,105.43

Record 1- 4 for display. E Ends.  Your choice? 1

Record # 1 contains Trans Am      , Pete Mears       and  14105.43
The price of the car is  $14,105.43

Record 1- 4 for display. E Ends.  Your choice? e
File ANYOWNER closed.
Ok
```

FIGURE 21.3   Program output

The technique is to relate the license plate to the record number. The record number is then used to retrieve the data in the random-access file. This process can be visualized as follows where the record number is the common element between the file index and the random-access file.

License plate	Record number	1st variable	2nd variable	3rd variable
96874DRM	1	Trans Am	Pete Mears	14105.43
1743	2	Pontiac LeMans	Tom Citizen	12750.50
M83110	3	Corvette	Mary Worth	36895.00
DEAR1	4	Buick	Alfred E. Neuman	16789.00

Data in   Data in the
File Index   Random-Access Record

What we need in order to store and retrieve records from this file by license plates is a program that will equate license plate identifications with record numbers. An example is shown in Figure 21.4, in which the license plate is the record key that uniquely identifies the record. The important word here is *uniquely*. This means that no two cars can have the same license plate—or the records cannot be retrieved independently. If duplicate license plate numbers do occur (perhaps from different states), then the record key will have to be expanded. (A simple solution might be to include a two-character state code.)

The program shown in Figure 21.4 reads license plate identifications (the record key) into the array LICENSE$. (We will later expand this

```
10 REM Creating a file index
20 DIM LICENSE$(4)
30 '                                        Read array
40 FOR I = 1 TO 4
50      READ LICENSE$(I)
60 NEXT I
70 '                                        User prompt
80 LINE INPUT "License wanted.  E Ends? " ; WANT.LICENSE$
90 IF WANT.LICENSE$ = "E" OR WANT.LICENSE$ = "e" THEN 200
100 '                                       Search
110 FOR RECORD = 1 TO 4
120      IF WANT.LICENSE$ = LICENSE$(RECORD) THEN 180
130 NEXT RECORD
140 '                                       Not found
150 BEEP : PRINT "License not found."
160 GOTO 80
170 '                                       Display record
180 PRINT "The record number is" RECORD
190 '
200 PRINT "End of program."
9000 DATA 96874DRM, 1743, M83110, DEAR1
9010 END
```

FIGURE 21.4   Relating record key with record number

example to read from a random-access file.) The user is asked for the license wanted (WANT.LICENSE$) in statement 80. Statement 120 then compares WANT.LICENSE$ to values in the LICENSE$ array. When a duplicate is identified, statement 180 prints the record number.

The major point of the program in Figure 21.4 is to relate a record key (license wanted) to a unique record number. This technique has numerous practical applications when developing a record-retrieval system. As shown in Figure 21.5, any record in the file can be retrieved by associating the record key with a record number.

Program output is shown in Figure 21.6. Notice that the first request is to find license number 1743. This is in the second position in the **READ** and **DATA** list (i.e., record number 2). Statement 220 retrieves this record from the ANYOWNER file previously created (see Figure 21.1). In a similar manner, the license for DEAR1 is retrieved and displayed.

```
10 REM Retrieval by index value
20 DIM LICENSE$(4)
30 '                                        Set up file
40 FILE$ = "ANYOWNER"
50 OPEN FILE$ AS #1 LEN = 38
60 FIELD #1, 14 AS F1$, 16 AS F2$, 8 AS F3$
70 '                                        Read array
80 FOR I = 1 TO 4
90     READ LICENSE$(I)
100 NEXT I
110 '                                       User prompt
120 PRINT
130 LINE INPUT "License wanted  E Ends? "; W.LICENSE$
140 IF W.LICENSE$ = "E" OR W.LICENSE$ = "e" THEN 340
150 '                                       Search
160 FOR RECORD = 1 TO 4
170     IF W.LICENSE$ = LICENSE$(RECORD) THEN 220
180 NEXT RECORD
190 BEEP : PRINT "License not found."
200 GOTO 120
210 '                                       Get record
220 GET #1, RECORD
230 F1.CAR$   = F1$
240 F2.OWNER$ = F2$
250 F3.PRICE# = CVD(F3$)                    ' Convert
260 '                                       Display record
270 PRINT
280 PRINT "Record #" RECORD "contains " F1.CAR$;
290 PRINT ", " F2.OWNER$ " and " F3.PRICE#
300 PRINT "The price of the car is";
310 PRINT USING "$$#####,.##"; F3.PRICE#
320 GOTO 120
330 '
340 CLOSE #1
350 PRINT "File " FILE$ " closed."
360 '
9000 DATA 96874DRM, 1743, M83110, DEAR1
9010 END
```

FIGURE 21.5 Relating a record key with a record number

```
RUN

License wanted  E Ends? 1743

Record # 2 contains Pontiac LeMans, Tom Citizen      and   12750.5
The price of the car is  $12,750.50

License wanted  E Ends? DEAR1

Record # 4 contains Buick            , Alfred E. Neuman and   16789
The price of the car is  $16,789.00

License wanted  E Ends? e
File ANYOWNER closed.
Ok
```

FIGURE 21.6 Program output

SUMMARY

Congratulations! You've come a long way in mastering the BASIC language. These last chapters on file processing have highlighted several major ideas for your consideration and undoubtedly there are many more ideas that should have been mentioned. But enough is enough!

Now it's your turn. Use the skill you have developed and create your own programs.

PROBLEMS

Screen Design Problems. Problems 1–6.
Develop a BASIC program, paying particular attention to the design of the screen. General formats are shown for your consideration.

21.1 Create the random-access file called ANYOWNER, using the program shown in Figure 21.1. This file will be used in Problem 2.

21.2 Create a car "updation" program that can be used to revise, add, display, or delete the records in the ANYOWNER file created in Problem 1. The screen should appear as shown.

```
                Car Updation Program
         File ANYOWNER contains 4 records.

          1 Revise a record
          2 Add a record
          3 Display records
          4 Delete a record
          5 Quit & save file
            Your choice?
```

Use this program to

(a) Delete record #2 on the Pontiac LeMans.
(b) Revise the price on record #4 from 16789 to the current price of $15,550.95.
(c) Add the following records:

| Cadillac | John Brown | 22595.00 |
| Jaguar | Don Jones | 12999.95 |

21.3 Create a random-access file called "PRODUCTS.RND" containing the following inventory data on part number, item description, quantity in stock, and unit cost. The actual file data should only consist of item description (ITEM$), quantity in stock (QUANTITY), and unit cost (COST). This file will be used in Problem 4.

1	Widgets	340	6.50
2	Gizmos	210	5.45
3	Things	12	15.95
4	What-its	5	1.50
5	Goop	20	2.50

Hint: It might be easier to read the file if you allow eight characters for QUANTITY and COST.

21.4 Create a product updation program that can be used to revise, add, display, or delete any record in the PRODUCTS.RND random-access file. (This file was created in Problem 3.) The screen should appear as shown.

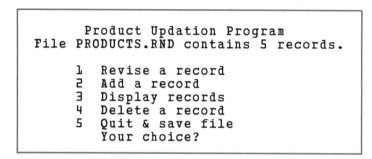

```
              Product Updation Program
        File PRODUCTS.RND contains 5 records.

             1   Revise a record
             2   Add a record
             3   Display records
             4   Delete a record
             5   Quit & save file
                 Your choice?
```

Use the program to

(a) Change the Gizmo price from 5.45 to 6.95.
(b) Delete the What-its record.
(c) Add the following to the file:

Don't-knows	12	21.45
Do-whats	3	1.49

Problems 5 and 6 require the use of the "CUSTOMER.RND" random-access file on the companion diskette. This file is organized as shown. A complete listing of the data in the file is shown in Problem 20.8.

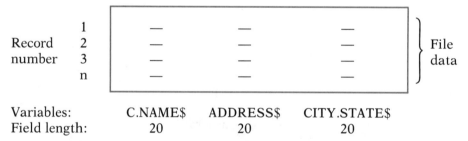

		C.NAME$	ADDRESS$	CITY.STATE$
Variables:		C.NAME$	ADDRESS$	CITY.STATE$
Field length:		20	20	20

Ajax Department Stores pride themselves on knowing each of their customers personally. When a customer calls up and gives his or her name, the firm wants to be able to enter the customer's last name into a computer. Have the program retrieve the "CUSTOMER.RND" random-access record containing the full name, address, city, and state. Then display the record.

The program you develop is based on a search of the last names contained in the index shown. When the last name is found, the record number is used to obtain the complete record from the CUSTOMER.RND file.

Index:	USER.NAME$
1	Jackson
2	Jones
3	Smith
4	Green
5	Johns
6	Citizen
7	Myers
8	Snowflake
9	Bigman
10	Thomas

Record
Number

21.5 Develop a customer-retrieval program following the format shown. Notice
that *Myer* was not found, but *Myers* was found and the 7th record was
displayed, containing his full name, address, city, and state.

```
        ┌─────────────────────────────────────┐
        │     Customer Retrieval Program      │
        └─────────────────────────────────────┘

        This program retrieves records from the CUSTOMER.RND
        file based on a customer's last name.

        Customer's last name.  E Ends program: Myer
        >>Name not found.<<

        Customer's last name.  E Ends program: Myers
        -----------------------------------------------
             *** Record # 7 contains: ***
Customer name:  Alice Myers lives at: 972 Jackson Ave.
City & state :  St. Petersburg, FL

        Customer's last name.  E Ends program e
        File CUSTOMER.RND closed.
```

21.6 Develop an advanced customer-retrieval program following the format shown. Notice that either the customer's last name or the city can be used to retrieve the complete record, which is accomplished by searching the appropriate indexes (you create the indexes).

```
          ┌─────────────────────────────────────┐
          │     Customer Retrieval Program      │
          └─────────────────────────────────────┘

    This program retrieves records from the CUSTOMER.RND file.

               ┌──────────────────────────┐
               │  Select:                 │
               │  L   Last name search    │
               │  C   City search         │
               │  E   Ends search         │
               └──────────────────────────┘

         Enter L, C, or E: l
         Customer's Last Name: Bigman
         ------------------------------------------------
              *** Record # 9 contains: ***
Customer name:  Tom Bigman lives at: 199 Iron Way
City & state :  Youngstown, OH

         Enter L, C, or E: c
         City: Youngstown
         ------------------------------------------------
              *** Record # 9 contains: ***
Customer name:  Tom Bigman lives at: 199 Iron Way
City & state :  Youngstown, OH

         Enter L, C, or E: e
         File CUSTOMER.RND closed.
```

A APPENDIX CASES

ACCOUNTING CASES 1–5

CASE 1: SUMMER'S HARDWARE

Summer's Hardware needs a statement of cost, profit, quantity, and sales for its major selling items—feed and seed. Mr. Summer has hired you to write a program that will calculate his price, profit, quantity, and sales accumulated during the month of November.

Program output should be in the format shown below. Notice that the price per unit of all goods is 30% above cost.

```
                      Summer's Hardware
                     Financial Statement
                   For the Month of November

                                    Cost     Price
        Consumer         Pounds     per      per      Total
        good             sold       unit     unit     sales

        Rabbit pellet      35      $3.10    $4.03    $141.05
        Homing meal        55      $5.10
        Grass seed        110      $10.50
        Cracked corn      250      $4.75
        Pig seed          210      $5.35
        Corn seed         800      $7.25
        Horse feed        200      $4.95
        Hog food          150      $6.95
        Dog food           75      $4.35
        Oats               95      $10.05
        Chick starter      50      $6.50

        Total pounds sold:            XXX
        Total sale:              $XX,XXX.XX
        Total cost:              $XX,XXX.XX
        Profit:                  $XX,XXX.XX
```

CASE 2: FARMER'S MACHINERY CORPORATION

The Farmer's Machinery Corporation sells machinery to local farmers on credit. This requires large sums of capital and, to encourage prompt payment, Farmer's Machinery has adopted a rebate policy. If their accounts are received on or before the due date, farmers are eligible for rebates. The rebate varies depending on a number of factors but ranges from 1 to 5 percent of the price of the product.

Prepare a report in the format shown below. The price of the product is the cost to the Farmer's Machinery Corporation, times the mark-up established for that item, rounded to the nearest dollar amount.

```
              Farmer's Machinery Corporation
                    Accounts Receivable
                       Monthly Report

Acc.  Price of  Date       Date      Rebate  Rebate
num.  product   received   due               (if any)

3745  $13,000   12/13/90   12/15/90  .05     $650
--    --        --         --        --      --
--    --        --         --        --      --

Total receipts =     $XX,XXX
Total rebates  =      $X,XXX
```

Use the following data in developing the report:

Account number	Date received	Date due	Cost of product	Mark-Up used	Rebate %
3745	12/13/90	12/15/90	10000	30%	5%
8172	01/02/91	12/30/90	20000	25%	2%
9241	03/12/91	04/22/91	5000	20%	4%
1158	05/02/91	04/20/91	4000	20%	4%
1677	05/02/91	05/02/91	30000	20%	1%
1251	06/02/91	06/01/91	18000	30%	3%
1557	08/18/91	08/20/91	4000	25%	2%

CASE 3: SPECIFIC ELECTRIC

Specific Electric has just purchased a wire-wrapping machine at a cost of $45,000. The machine will have a salvage value of $5,000 at the end of four years. The Accounting Department is to figure the depreciation annually on a straight line depreciation basis, which is figured on cost less salvage value divided by four years of useful life to the company.

Management desires a computer printout of the above data for its files along with the accumulated depreciation per year. The output should appear as follows:

```
                     Specific Electric
                   Depreciation Schedule

Beginning      Yearly          Ending      Accrued
cost           depreciation    cost        depreciation

$45,000        $11,250         $33,750     $11,250
$33,750        $11,250         $22,500     $22,500
$22,500        $11,250         $11,250     $33,750
$11,250        $11,250              $0     $45,000

Initial cost:      $11,250
Salvage value:      $5,000
Estimated life:    4 years
```

CASE 4: FIELDER INDUSTRIES

Fielder Industries employs several workers whose yearly gross incomes are listed below. You are to write a program to calculate each person's yearly federal tax, Social Security tax, state tax, and net income. Federal tax is computed as follows:

Total taxable income ($)	Tax (%)
0–2,500	No tax
2,501–5,000	2.5
5,001–10,000	5
10,001–25,000	10
25,001–50,000	25
Above 50,000	50

Social Security tax is 5% on the first $25,000 of income. There is no tax on additional income. State tax is 2% of the total income. The remaining income after taxes are subtracted is the net income.

You are to print his or her name, employee number, gross income, federal tax, Social Security tax, state tax, and net income. Also, print totals under appropriate headings, as well as the total taxes paid.

The required output is shown below.

			Fielder Industries			
		Yearly Statement of Earnings and Deductions				
Employee name	Emp. num.	Gross income	Federal tax	Social security	State tax	Net income
– –	–	$XX,XXX	$XX,XXX	$X,XXX	$XXX	$XX,XXX
– –	–	– –	– –	– –	– –	– –
– –	–	– –	– –	– –	– –	– –
Total		$XXX,XXX	$XX,XXX	$X,XXX	$X,XXX	$XX,XXX

Use the following data for this problem:

Name	Employee no.	Gross income
Pete Davis	48	$25,000
Liz Harris	22	18,000
Don Thomson	3	55,000
Harry Bliss	24	32,000
Frank Thompson	47	9,000
Susan Smith	51	2,400

CASE 5: ACME COMPANY

The Acme Company has recently offered the following profit-sharing plan to its employees. Each participant is allowed to contribute between one to ten percent of his or her gross biweekly salary to the plan. (Note that the deduction can be expressed only as a whole percent from one to ten percent.)

The profit-sharing plan stipulates that the company will match the employee's contribution at a rate of 50% on the first $10.00 biweekly deduction and 20% each additional dollar over the first $1000 deducted biweekly. John Boon, the plan administrator, has been asked to prepare a report with the following features:

1. Biweekly salary
2. Actual deduction amount
3. Company matching contribution
4. Total of all employee deduction amount
5. Total of all company matching contributions
6. The average employee deduction amount
7. The average company matching contribution

Write a program to generate a report with the above features. Use the following format for the output:

```
                    The Acme Company
                   Profit-Sharing Plan
───────────────────────────────────────────────────────────────────────
Employee    I.D.    Biweekly     Deduction    Deduction    Company
name        num.    salary       percent      amount       matching
───────────────────────────────────────────────────────────────────────
 - -        XXXX    $X,XXX.XX        X         $XXX.XX      $XX.XX
 - -        XXXX    $X,XXX.XX        X         $XXX.XX      $XX.XX

Total Deductions          $XXX.XX
Matching Contributions    $XXX.XX
Average Deduction          $XX.XX
Average Matching Amount    $XX.XX
───────────────────────────────────────────────────────────────────────
```

Use the following data for developing the output:

Name	I.D. no.	Annual salary	Deduction (%)
M. Board	2626	$48,750	6
D. Connor	1093	8,000	2
A. Decker	4026	12,000	5
S. Franklin	4671	17,875	6
F. Goodman	7174	21,120	7
L. Hatfield	1498	16,250	3
R. Jones	2470	29,250	4
J. Pike	4838	43,875	5
T. Swann	5718	40,625	6
T. Taylor	2753	16,500	2

MANAGEMENT CASES 6–10

CASE 6: HUMAN RESOURCES DEPARTMENT

The Human Resources Department of a state has a supervisory position that it needs to fill. The director of the department is conducting a survey to see who, within the department, is qualified for this promotion. The applicant must have a Master's degree, or a Bachelor's degree and two years' experience in accounting, or ten years' experience in accounting and no degree. Write a program, based upon the criteria, to help the director determine who is eligible for this position. The output format should be as follows:

```
┌─────────────────────────────────────────┐
│    Human Resources Department           │
│    Supervisory Position Survey          │
│   ─────────────────────────────────     │
│     Name              Status            │
│   ─────────────────────────────────     │
│                                         │
│      --                 --              │
│      --                 --              │
│      --                 --              │
│                   (Qualified or         │
│                    Not Qualified)       │
│   ─────────────────────────────────     │
└─────────────────────────────────────────┘
```

Use the following data for developing the output:

Name	Years employed	Degree	Accounting years experience
Kristen Jennings	2	Master's	1
Brad Carter	4	Bachelor's	5
Jeffrey Melvin	1	Bachelor's	3
Kimberly Cantwell	3	None	6
Brian Burke	2	Master's	2
Michael Wheeler	5	None	3
Gladys Vann	11	None	11
Donald Cartwright	7	Master's	7
Laura Moore	6	Bachelor's	6

CASE 7: WOODSIDE LOAN AGENCY

The manager of Woodside Loan Agency would like a report displaying the name, seniority, percent of errors, and total salary of his loan officers. The percent of errors is a statistic found by dividing the total number of errors made by the total number of cases handled by each officer. An error is considered to be any case where the loan officer fails to properly investigate the applicant before granting the loan. Since this statistic relates directly to job performance, it is one of the factors used to determine whether a loan officer deserves a bonus. The manager also considers seniority (years experience) because he feels a more experienced loan officer should make fewer mistakes. The guidelines that determine the amount of bonus are as follows:

If an employee has 2 or less years of service and less than 10% errors, then the bonus is $500.

or

If an employee has 5 or less years of service and less than 5% errors, then the bonus is $1,000.

or

If an employee has more than 5 years of service and less than 2% errors, then the bonus is $1,500.

The output format is as follows:

```
┌─────────────────────────────────────────────────────────┐
│                                                         │
│              Woodside Loan Agency                       │
│           Job Performance Comparison                    │
│                 Loan Officers                           │
│ ───────────────────────────────────────────────────    │
│ Employee  Years    %       Base     Bonus     Total     │
│ name      service  errors  salary   (if any)  salary    │
│ ───────────────────────────────────────────────────    │
│   - -       X      X.X     $XX,XXX   $X,XXX   $XX,XXX    │
│   - -       X      X.X     $XX,XXX   $X,XXX   $XX,XXX    │
│ ───────────────────────────────────────────────────    │
│                                                         │
└─────────────────────────────────────────────────────────┘
```

Use the following data in developing the output:

Employee name	Years service	Number of errors	Number of cases	Yearly salary
Bill Jones	2	10	120	$20,000
Ted Mack	1	8	100	20,000
Ruth Forth	4	12	250	25,000
Sue Wilkes	6	3	175	25,000
George Robuck	3	14	200	30,000
Phil Yanks	6	9	200	30,000

CASE 8: SOUTHERN HANDCRAFTS

Southern Handcrafts produces high-quality fabric items for use as decorative placemats, napkins, and tablecloths. The purchasing department needs to know the type of fabric and the cost per order. All orders have been produced previously, so the yards per piece is known as is the cost per yard of fabric. Marketing furnishes an estimate of the number of pieces that will be sold by item number.

The purchasing department requires a program with the format shown below. Notice that an option is available that permits program output to be sorted from lowest to highest cost per order to highlight which of the orders will be most expensive.

```
┌─────────────────────────────────────────────────────────┐
│                                                         │
│              Southern Handcrafts                        │
│            Fabric to Be Purchased                       │
│ ───────────────────────────────────────────────────    │
│ Fabric        Item    No. of   Yards/  Cost/   Cost/    │
│ description    number  pieces   piece   yard    order    │
│ ───────────────────────────────────────────────────    │
│   - -         XXXX    XX,XXX    X.XX    $X.XX  $XXX,XXX   │
│   - -         XXXX    XX,XXX    X.XX    $X.XX  $XXX,XXX   │
│ ───────────────────────────────────────────────────    │
│ Data sorted from lowest to highest order cost Y/N?      │
│                                                         │
└─────────────────────────────────────────────────────────┘
```

Use the following data for this problem:

Fabric description	Item number	Number of pieces	Yards per piece	Cost per yard
Cotton	1097	5,000	1.10	$3.43
Wool	1643	10,000	2.15	5.97
Denim	1154	7,500	1.50	2.03
Knit	7154	1,500	.90	4.28
Terry Cloth	2159	3,500	1.10	4.10
Suede	1298	1,200	1.40	6.40
Nylon	3881	200	.60	4.40
Polyester	1198	1,200	2.00	2.90

Note: Cost/Order is computed by:

Cost = (No. of Pieces) * (Yards per Piece) * (Cost per Yard)

CASE 9: WILLRUN INDUSTRIES

Willrun Industries needs a report that identifies how many weeks vacation are earned by each employee and the bonus that each employee is to receive. In determining the weeks of vacation and the bonus, the following criteria are used:

Grade level	Criteria used	Weeks and bonus
6	Bonus	$100
	Base Vacation	0 Wks.
	Employed over 1 yr. but less than 5 yrs.	1 Wk.
	Employed 5 or more yrs.	2 Wks.
7	Bonus	$300
	Base Vacation	1 Wk.
	Employed 2 or more yrs. but less than 5 yrs.	2 Wks.
	Employed 5 or more yrs.	3 Wks.
8	Bonus	$700
	Base Vacation	1 Wk.
	Employed 2 or more yrs. but less than 5 yrs.	2 Wks.
	Employed 5 or more yrs.	3 Wks.
9	Bonus	$1,100
	Base Vacation	2 Wks.
	Employed over 5 yrs. but less than 10 yrs.	3 Wks.
	Employed 10 or more yrs.	4 Wks.
10	Bonus	$1,300
	Base Vacation	3 Wks.
	Employed over 5 yrs. but less than 10 yrs.	4 Wks.
	Employed 10 or more yrs. but less than 15 yrs.	5 Wks.
	Employed 15 or more yrs.	6 Wks.

Employees are entitled to a bonus and base vacation (guaranteed vacation) depending on their labor grade-levels and years employed with the firm. For example, a grade-level 7 employee is guaranteed a 1-week vacation. However, if this person was employed by the firm for 3 years, he or she would be eligible for a total of two weeks.

Write a program that will produce a report in the following format:

```
┌──────────────────────────────────────────────────────────────┐
│                    Willrun Industries                          │
│                    Vacation Report                             │
│  ──────────────────────────────────────────────────────────   │
│  Employee      Grade      Years       Vacation      Bonus      │
│  name          level      employed    in weeks      award      │
│  ──────────────────────────────────────────────────────────   │
│    - -           X           X            X        $X,XXX       │
│    - -           X           X            X        $X,XXX       │
│  ──────────────────────────────────────────────────────────   │
└──────────────────────────────────────────────────────────────┘
```

Use the following data in developing the report:

Employee name	Grade level	Years employed
Nancy James	6	1
Jordan Moody	9	8
Tom Longman	7	5
Leroy Linman	10	6
William Richards	8	3
Karen Rich	10	10
Mary Tyler	9	7
Mary Moore	9	5
Charles Willis	6	4
Sam Winkler	7	6

CASE 10: ABC FABRICATION COMPANY

ABC Fabrication Company makes a product that must be processed through all four of its plant locations in order to become finished. Its management is concerned if any budget overruns have occurred in the month of October. Each individual product made is given a unique job code so that comparisons can be made between actual work units expended and budgeted work units. Given the data for this problem, write a program that will produce a production management report with the following format:

```
┌──────────────────────────────────────────────────────────────┐
│                  ABC Fabrication Company                       │
│               Actual vs. Budgeted Work Units                   │
│               Actual Work Units Expended by Plant              │
│  ──────────────────────────────────────────────────────────   │
│  Job code     Plant 1     Plant 2     Plant 3     Plant 4      │
│  ──────────────────────────────────────────────────────────   │
│    XXXX         XXX         XXX         XXX         XXX         │
│    XXXX         XXX         XXX         XXX         XXX         │
│  ──────────────────────────────────────────────────────────   │
└──────────────────────────────────────────────────────────────┘
```

Then display the total work units in the following format:

```
┌──────────────────────────────────────────────────────┐
│        Total Work Units Expended by Job              │
│  ──────────────────────────────────────────────────  │
│    Job code              Expended work units          │
│  ──────────────────────────────────────────────────  │
│      XXXX                      XXX                    │
│      XXXX                      XXX                    │
│  ──────────────────────────────────────────────────  │
└──────────────────────────────────────────────────────┘
```

Finally, display the budget overruns in the following format:

```
┌─────────────────────────────────────────────┐
│            Jobs with Budget Overruns          │
│      ───────────────────────────────────      │
│      Job code        # Overrun work units     │
│      ───────────────────────────────────      │
│        XXXX                   XXX             │
│        XXXX                   XXX             │
│      ───────────────────────────────────      │
└─────────────────────────────────────────────┘
```

Note: In the last section of this report include only the jobs that have overruns. Use the following data in developing the output:

Actual work units expended

Job code	Plant 1	Plant 2	Plant 3	Plant 4	Budgeted work units
7764	120	102	143	124	540
5376	136	80	201	46	450
5742	46	120	150	112	525
9237	86	122	40	140	400
7659	117	86	132	120	440

MARKETING CASES 11–15

CASE 11: BILL'S USED CARS

Bill's Used Cars needs a program to calculate the biweekly pay for their salespeople that is based on three factors: base pay, sales commission, and bonuses. A salesperson receives a base pay that is simply hours worked times hourly rate (overtime is not paid). Sales commission is 5% of the sales achieved during the two-week period.

Bonuses are based on the following scale. Nothing is paid if sales are $10,000 or less during the pay period. If sales are over $10,000, but less than or equal to $14,000, the bonus is $500. If sales are over $14,000, but less than or equal to $18,000, the bonus is $750. If sales are over $18,000, but less than or equal to $20,000, the bonus is $1,000. Finally, if sales are over $20,000 the bonus is $1,250.

Write a program according to the following format:

```
┌──────────────────────────────────────────────────────────────────┐
│                        Bill's Used Cars                            │
│                    Biweekly Payroll Report                         │
│      ────────────────────────────────────────────────────────     │
│      Employee   Regular    Sales      Bonus     Total              │
│      name       pay        comm.      pay       pay                │
│      ────────────────────────────────────────────────────────     │
│        - -      $XXX.XX    $X,XXX.XX  $X,XXX    $X,XXX.XX           │
│        - -      $XXX.XX    $X,XXX.XX  $X,XXX    $X,XXX.XX           │
│      ────────────────────────────────────────────────────────     │
└──────────────────────────────────────────────────────────────────┘
```

Use the following data in your program:

Employee name	Hours worked	Hourly rate	Sales achieved
Bill Lesser	80	3.80	$12,098
Sue Jones	72	3.50	28,501
Sam Smith	68	3.75	21,244
Connie Jeffries	38	4.25	14,210
Don Jackson	46	3.25	3,000
Pete Citizen	30	3.00	8,000
Mary Worth	80	4.00	11,250

CASE 12: CONSOLIDATED CORPORATION

Consolidated Corporation conducts a monthly sales analysis for its four major product categories: toys, hardware, housewares, and clothing. The format of the report is shown below. The program is to sort the products from highest to lowest total dollar value for the month.

```
                    Consolidated Corporation
                  Product Sales in October, 1990

Product     Week #1      Week #2      Week #3      Week #4       Totals

  - -      $XXXX.XX     $XXXX.XX     $XXXX.XX     $XXXX.XX      $XXXX.XX
  - -
  - -
  - -
Totals     $XXXX.XX     $XXXX.XX     $XXXX.XX     $XXXX.XX     $XXXXX.XX
```

Data for the report is as follows:

Product sold	Week #1	Week #2	Week #3	Week #4
Toys	88.70	512.22	212.75	552.00
Hardware	3875.75	1122.29	1237.57	1711.10
Housewares	353.23	841.41	115.50	650.65
Clothing	425.54	643.35	545.70	425.55

CASE 13: FIRST UNITED CHURCH

The members of First United Church have finished taking orders for the sale of their three types of Easter cards. First United desires a program that will produce a report displaying the dollar sales for each type of card sold by each person and the total dollar amount sold by each person, which will include a 3% delivery charge. Also, the report should indicate the total number of boxes sold for each type of card and a grand total of all sales, including the delivery charge. The output produced should appear as follows:

```
                    First United Church
                     Easter Card Sales

Name          Card X      Card Y      Card Z    Total sales

 - -            X           X           X         $XX.XX
 - -            X           X           X         $XX.XX

Total boxes of X sold is XX
Total boxes of Y sold is XX
Total boxes of Z sold is XX
Total sales including delivery charge is $XXX.XX
```

Use the following data to develop your output:

Name	Boxes of card X	Boxes of card Y	Boxes of card Z
Joe Smith	7	6	5
Felix Forte	4	4	4
Joe Brown	2	8	5
Pam Windgate	5	3	6
P. R. Ewing	6	7	3

Note that a box of Card X sells for $3.00; a box of Card Y sells for $6.50; a box of Card Z sells for $7.00.

CASE 14: ROLLER ALLEY

Mr. Smith owns Roller Alley skating rink. The rink has a capacity of 1500 people with open skating on Sundays, Wednesdays, Fridays, and Saturdays. Mondays, Tuesdays, and Thursdays are reserved for private parties. The fee for open skating is $2.75 per person plus 50¢ for skate rental. Private parties for a three-hour session are $100 plus skate rental of 50¢ per person. Mr. Smith would like to have a report of his total receipts for the week. Also, he would like to know the total number of paying customers and the amount of money made on skate rentals for the week.

The output of the program should be as follows:

```
                    Roller Alley
                Weekly Receipts Report

Day         Customers    Rentals      Admissions

 - -          XXX        $XXX.XX      $X,XXX.XX
 - -          XXX        $XXX.XX      $X,XXX.XX

Totals       X,XXX       $X,XXX.XX    $X,XXX.XX
Weekly receipts: $X,XXX.XX
```

Data to be used in the program is listed below:

	No. of customers	No. of skate rentals
Sunday	530	315
Monday	Private party	370
Tuesday	Private party	210
Wednesday	320	216
Thursday	Private party	187
Friday	760	440
Saturday	930	610

Note: Assume that the number of customers at a private party equals the number of skates rented.

CASE 15: JIM'S PIZZA INN

Jim's Pizza Inn has opened a chain of new stores in Indiana. Management wanted to examine the profit results of these stores compared to Jim's other stores in the area. In order to get data in a usable form, you have been asked to write a program that will generate the following reports for Jim's Pizza Inn:

1. A table of stores with monthly profits
2. A table of stores with three-month averages
3. A table of monthly averages for the region

Each of these three reports should be preceded by a heading indicating the purpose of the report.

The output should appear as follows:

```
                          Jim's Pizza Inn
                          Monthly Report
Store #         Mon. #1         Mon. #2         Mon. #3         Store avg.
XX              XX,XXX          XX,XXX          XX,XXX          $XX,XXX.XX
XX              XX,XXX          XX,XXX          XX,XXX          $XX,XXX.XX
Month Avg.      $XX,XXX.XX      $XX,XXX.XX      $XX,XXX.XX
```

Use the following data in developing the output:

	Profits		
44	$21,560	$18,743	$19,233
36	37,580	29,000	33,500
78	30,643	35,891	41,102
42	8,521	7,300	5,975
11	14,982	8,553	13,800

FINANCE CASES: 16–19

CASE 16: DECISION MANAGEMENT ANALYSIS, INC.

Decision Management Analysis, Inc. (DMA) is a company that publishes a monthly newsletter specializing in small business investments. The company evaluates each potential small business in three ways and, by its results, simply recommends whether or not to invest. A business is labeled GOOD if DMA has found it to be a satisfactory investment by its standards; otherwise the business is labeled POOR. The three ways in which DMA evaluates small businesses as being GOOD investments are net sales of more than $200,000 and a current ratio of greater than 2.5:1, a ratio of net sales to total assets of more than or equal to 1.5:1 and operating income of at least 10% of net sales, or total assets of more than $450,000 and a current ratio of over 2:1. All other businesses are rated as POOR investments. Given the data for this problem, write a program that will identify which companies are GOOD or POOR investments. The output should appear as follows:

```
┌─────────────────────────────────────────────┐
│        Decision Management Analysis          │
│                June Analysis                 │
│        ─────────────────────────────         │
│     Company              Recommendation      │
│     ─────────────────────────────────        │
│     - -                  (Good or Poor)      │
│     - -                  (Good or Poor)      │
│        ─────────────────────────────         │
└─────────────────────────────────────────────┘
```

Use the following data in developing the output:

Name of company	Net sales	Current assets	Current liabilities	Total assets	Operating income
Policy Place	$190,000	$79,000	$41,000	$125,000	$40,000
13 MI	$120,000	$80,000	$50,000	$100,000	$18,000
Quik Print	$241,000	$210,000	$97,000	$450,011	$22,000
Dad's Fix It	$127,000	$75,000	$75,000	$150,000	$30,000
Steno	$201,000	$103,500	$40,000	$290,000	$27,000
Grease Monkey	$199,100	$57,000	$24,000	$120,000	$20,950
Auto Office	$217,000	$107,200	$30,000	$190,000	$21,000

CASE 17: CARRINGTON, INC.

Carrington Inc. issues profit-sharing bonuses to their employees who qualify. The bonus is 5% of annual gross salary. To qualify, at least one of the following criteria must be met.

1. Employed for 4 or more years.
2. Employed for 2 or more years and receive an annual salary of at least $14,500.
3. Employed for 2 or more years and received a promotion within the last year.

Write a program that will produce a report in the following format:

```
                    Carrington, Inc.
                    Employee Analysis

   Employee     Yearly      Profit        Profit
   name         salary      sharing?      received

     - -        $XX,XXX     (Yes or No)    $XXX
     - -        $XX,XXX     (Yes or No)    $XXX
```

Use the following data in developing the output:

Name	Years employed	Annual gross salary	Promotion received within last year
Lesley Smith	4	$ 9,000	No
Sarah Mills	1	$12,000	Yes
Amy Baker	2	$11,000	No
Richard Carr	2	$10,000	Yes
Debi Dunn	3	$15,000	Yes

CASE 18: SMITH COMPANY

The Smith Company is planning to purchase a new milling machine at the first of the year. The company will adopt the depreciation method that gives the largest depreciation in the early years of the useful life of the machine. The purchasing manager needs a program that will calculate the depreciation for 1991 using the straight-line method, the sum-of-the-years-digits method, and the double-declining-balance method. The output should appear as follows:

```
                      Smith Company
        Milling Machine Project Cost:  $100,000
     Estimated Depreciation Expense Next Three Years
     ------------------------------------------------
     Straight Line:                  $54,000
     Sum of the Years Digits:        $72,000
     Double Declining Balance:       $78,400
     ------------------------------------------------
     The largest charge is   $78,400
```

Use the following data in developing the output:

Cost	$100,000
Estimated Life	5 years
Salvage Value	$10,000

CASE 19: VULETTA CONSTRUCTION COMPANY

The Vuletta Construction Company is a new company in the Valley Station area. Each month the company will deposit checks and cash from customers, and it will write checks to pay for supplies and other operating expenses. At the end of each month, the bank sends a statement of deposits and disbursements (checks written by Vuletta) as well as bank service charges and bad checks from customers (if any).

Write a program that will generate a report summarizing the month's transactions and reconciling the company's book balance with the bank's report of Vuletta's balance. Your program should read input data, total deposits, total disbursements, list bad checks, and show an end-of-the-month book balance. Then list the outstanding checks which, when subtracted from the book balance, will equal the bank's reported balance.

The output should appear as follows:

```
              Vuletta Construction Company
        Bank Statement and Monthly Cash Balance
                   Account # 10589
_____

Beginning Book Balance        $10,589.50
Deposits for the Month         $X,XXX.XX

Total Cash Accountability      $XX,XXX.XX

Less Bad Checks of
     -        - -                            $XXX.XX
     -        - -                            $XXX.XX
     -        - -                            $XXX.XX
Less Disbursements of                       $X,XXX.XX
Less Bank Service Charge of                    $X.XX

Plus Outstanding Checks of
     -        - -              $XXX.XX
     -        - -              $XXX.XX

Ending Bank Balance                         $XX,XXX.XX
_____
```

Use the following data in developing the output:

Deposit Data			
Deposit no.	**Customer**	**Amount deposited**	**Code**
250	Jim's Plumbing	$ 605.50	G
285	A & S Heating	1,050.37	G
310	David Supply Co.	235.65	C
150	Scotty's Builders	150.15	G
210	U-Cart Concrete	285.37	G
195	Jane's Bakery	75.00	C
330	Dixie Hi-Fi	100.95	C

Check Data			
Check no.	**Payable to**	**Amount of check**	**Outstanding or received**
150	A & S Heating	$650.37	Received
151	U-Cart Concrete	100.00	Outstanding
152	Dixie Hi-Fi	50.00	Received
153	Jane's Bakery	75.00	Received
154	Jim's Plumbing	100.00	Outstanding
155	Scotty's Builders	50.00	Received

Deposit data check code:
G—Good Check
C—Bad Check
Assume a service charge of $.30 per check written.

FILE PROCESSING CASES: 20–27

CASE 20: PODUNK SOCIAL CLUB

Five years ago, the city of Podunk, Kentucky started a community club primarily for senior citizens to use for meetings and social occasions. Last year, they initiated bingo games and club membership grew from a few people to the current active membership of four hundred. This growth in membership increased the funds in their treasury. They have purchased a microcomputer and have contacted you to develop a series of mailing list programs.

They want the following three programs:

I. A data entry program
II. A program to sort by ZIP code
III. A program to print the mailing list

I. The data entry program. The club's membership records are currently kept on three by five cards as follows:

```
Name:
Address:
City, State:
Zip Code:
```

The data entry program should limit the name, address, and city/state fields to 20 characters or less to accommodate the required mailing program. In addition, the ZIP code will be numeric characters. Develop a method so that the record, once typed, can be changed before it is saved. Of course, new and/or updated information will be entered into the file frequently.

II. The sort program. Postal regulations require that mail be sorted by ZIP code in order to receive an economical mailing rate. Develop a means of performing such a sort. Also, show the sorted records on the screen, one at a time, so that unwanted or duplicate records can be purged from the system. Save the revised file as MAILING.SRT.

III. The mailing list program. This program is to read the sorted file called MAILING.SRT and perform two functions. The first function is to print out a single record, properly positioned on a business envelope, as shown below. Stop after each record so that an envelope can be inserted in the printer.

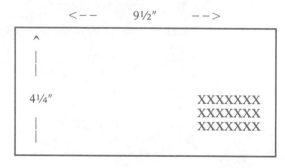

The program should have the capability of providing a membership summary in 3-up format. That is, the summary listing by ZIP code is to be spaced three records on the same line as shown below.

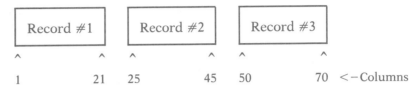

```
        Record #1          Record #2          Record #3

      ^           ^    ^           ^    ^           ^
      1          21   25          45   50          70  <—Columns
```

CASE 21: CASANOVA'S CASSEROLE

Casanova wants to computerize his "little black book," consisting of numerous distinguished countesses. Two major files are requested. The first file is to be called COUNTESS and contain the fields shown. Of particular interest is the Wine-liked field, which contains the countess's beverage preference—either a wine type or brand.

COUNTESS

Name last, first	Birthday mm/dd/yy	Phone No. [1]	Last gift [2]	Gift ideas	Dinner ideas [3]	Wine liked [4]	Songs liked

Notes:

1. Omit area code from phone number.
2. Last gift is used to assure gifts are not repeated in the following year.
3. Dinner ideas are items such as: likes candlelight, doesn't serve quiche, etc.
4. Wine liked is used to automatically search the Wine type and Brand fields in the BEVERAGE file to determine the bottles on hand.

The second file is called BEVERAGE. This is an inventory file of the wines available in Casanova's private wine cellar.

BEVERAGE

Wine type	Wine brand	Bottles on hand	Year capped	Quality/comments
Brandy	Napoleon	14	1815	Excellent
Burgundy	Thunderbird	3	1915	Cheap
Champagne	Jacques	32	1750	Sparkling
Cognac	Josephine	8	1810	Powerful
Creme de Menthe	Sir Walter	1	1910	Sweet, green
Creme de Menthe	Sir James	2	1905	Sweet, white
Rose	Don Pieron	10	1852	Excellent

Develop a BASIC program so that Casanova can enter the countess's last name. Then search the file and display the appropriate fields on the screen. The program should use the data in the Wine-liked field, to search automatically the BEVERAGE file to identify if the wine is listed in either the Wine-type or Brand fields. If found, display the bottles on hand.

The relationships between the fields in the COUNTESS file and the BEVERAGE file are as shown.

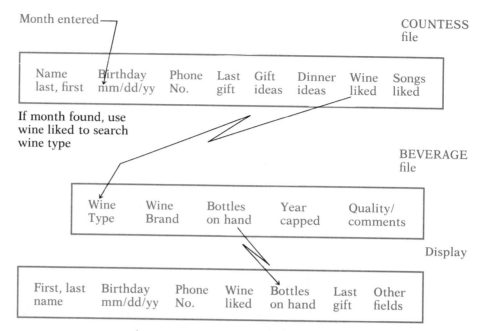

Casanova often has difficulties remembering the numerous last names in the COUNTESS file. Therefore, the program should be able to search the file, based on user entry of a month. Display all birthdays occurring in that month, along with the countess's last name, wine desired, and the bottles on hand (from the BEVERAGE file).

Develop your own data for the COUNTESS file. Then expand the data shown in the BEVERAGE file by entering five additional beverages of your choice. Develop support programs that permit data in either file to be changed.

Important Note: Lady Godiva has had many calls since her horseback ride, and she has a similar problem organizing her Prince Charming book. If you wish, change the COUNTESS file to PRINCE, and proceed with the problem.

CASE 22: AJAX DATA ENTRY SERVICE

Ajax Data Entry Service Company performs data entry activities (keypunching files) for small businesses in its immediate area. Work is received in batches of source documents containing a control number and a requested file name. Ajax prides itself on accuracy, so a great deal of attention is paid to correcting all errors in data entry.

A file is created when the batch of source documents is received and the work is typed (keypunched) into the file. After the file is completed, the work is verified by another operator. Verification is performed by re-keying the source documents into a program that compares this material with the data previously entered. Any changes detected are later entered into the file via a data correction program. This program not only makes the changes to the file but the program updates an exception report file as well. Finally, Ajax processes the exception report file that analyzes the changes made to the initial file.

Ajax has hired you to develop four data entry programs:

   I. The data entry program
  II. The data verification program
 III. The data correction program
 IV. The exception reporting program

All programs are to feature extensive error checking and must at least conform to the specified requirements. In addition, all programs are to be accompanied by a procedures manual that clearly tells the operator how the data is to be entered and what error checks are performed by the program.

I. The data entry program.   A data entry program is needed to create a file that will serve as input to other programs, such as a payroll program. The user will specify the file name, batch control identification, and the name of the data entry operator. Using the source documents, the employee's social security number and hours worked are then entered into a file.

The general form of the file is as follows. The batch number (Batch #) and operator name are the first line in the file. The social security number (SS. Number) and hours worked (Hours) are on succeeding lines.

```
Batch #, Operator name
SS.Number, Hours
   --          --
   --          --
   --          --
```

Where:

Batch #
: The batch control number—an alphanumeric code assigned to each batch.

Operator Name
: Name of the operator creating the file. This is to be on the same file line as the batch number.

SS.Number
: The employee's social security number, entered as a nine-digit number without dashes.

Hours
: The hours worked are entered in decimal format two digits to the left of the decimal (which is typed) and one digit to the right of the decimal. For example:

Hours Worked	Entered as
45	45.0
8	08.0
35.9	35.9

Particular care must be taken to ensure accuracy in the SS.Number and Hours fields. Ajax has signed a contract agreeing to a penalty of $100 per data entry error they created. Obviously, your program will be tested extensively to be sure that all combinations of errors are detected in these fields.

In addition to displaying the current diskette file names and prompting the user to enter a name, develop a method of error detection on the entry of a file name. If the file name entered is the same as an existing file, the user should be asked if they want to append the file or create a new file name. Naturally, all the programs should check for common errors, such as an open diskette door or the presence of a write protect tab.

Hint: If a file is opened for input that doesn't exist, an error code of 53 is produced.

II. The data verification program.   This program reads the file created by Program I. The file name, batch number, and operator name must appear on the screen at all times. However, the data being verified *does not* appear on the screen. The data is to be re-typed from the source document to verify that the original entry is correct.

When a keystroke made in verification varies from the original, the program should beep to alert the operator that a data verification error has occurred. The operator notes this on the source document for correction later by another operator using a data correction program.

III. The data correction program.   This program reads the file created by Program I. Any and all changes are to be permitted to the file. However, in addition to updating and saving the changed file, an exception report file is to be created. This exception report file called "TROUBLE" contains the following data:

> the batch number of the original file;
> the name of the operator who created the original file;
> the original file line (the record); and
> the revised (updated) file line.

IV. The exception reporting program.   This program reads and prints the "TROUBLE" exception file created by Program III. In addition to reporting the contents of the file, the program is to display:

> the number of revised lines and
> the time and date the report was created.

CASE 23: CRITTER CUTTERS

A new pet-grooming store, called Critter Cutters, keeps track of its four-legged clients. Currently, a three-by-five card is maintained on each client containing the following data:

```
Owner's Last Name:
Owner's First Name:
Title (Mr., Ms., Dr., etc.):
Street Address:
City, State, Zip Code:
Telephone Number:
Pet's Name:
Pet's Birthday:
Date of Last Visit:
Pet Code:
```

The Pet Code is assigned as follows:

Dogs		Cats		Other	
10	Mutt	20	Alley	30	Other pets
11	Poodle	21	Persian		
12	German Shepherd	22	Siamese		
13	Dachshund	23	Abyssinian		
14	Other breeds	24	Other breeds		

Critter Cutters is a very profitable little business in which they "trim the pet" and "clip the owners," so to speak. They want you to develop three file-management programs:

> **I.** A file updating program
> **II.** A critter recall program
> **III.** A birthday message program

I. The file updating program.   This program is used to establish the initial pet file called CRITTERS. The main menu for this program is shown below.

```
        Critter Cutter Program

                  By
             Your Name

        SET UP CRITTERS FILE

     1   Create New File
     2   Add Record to File
     3   Delete Record From File
     4   Run Recall Program
     5   Run Birthday Program

             Your Selection?
```

II. The critter recall program.   This program will be run during slack business periods to remind owners that it is time for their pets to visit Critter Cutters. The main menu for this program is shown below.

```
        Critter Recall Program

                  By
             Your Name

       DISPLAYS CRITTERS FILE

     1   Search on Owner's Name
     2   Search on Last Visit
     3   Run Birthday Program

             Your Selection?
```

Critter recalls are based on one of two options. Option 1 permits the entry of the owner's last name. A last name search is then conducted of the file. Of course, the last name is entered in upper- and lowercase letters but the search should be based on the program converting the name to uppercase letters.

The second option is a search based on user entry of a last visit. When the month entered is encountered, display the record.

III. A birthday message program.   Management of Critter Cutters has spent a lot of time discussing this program because it will be a unique marketing tool. Basically, the program should search out the month the pet was born, based on a user-entered month. When a birthday is found, print a personal birthday letter to the pet and send it in care of the pet's owner.

However, that is not the problem. Management wants to see the full capacity of the pet codes and has requested a demonstration of truly creative birthday messages, based on any one of the pet codes. That is, you are asked to select a pet code and, when it is encountered, develop the birthday message that, as the store owner said, "will bring tears to the eyes of the reader."

CASE 24: PET PEEVE

You are far enough along in your education to recognize the typical teaching/testing cycle. Topics are assigned, lectures are conducted, tests are given and graded. Then the tests are returned and the answers are explained. The teacher normally does not resent this cycle but many teachers have a "pet peeve."

This occurs after discussing the tests in class. Students not in attendance go to the teacher's office to find out their test scores. Excuses are given for why they were not in class. "I had to study for another test." "I knew the material." It is difficult for teachers to get their work completed due to these unnecessary interruptions.

Your assignment is to design a student grading system so that test grades can be posted on the office door. Two programs are needed. The first program is used to create a file called STUDENTS. This program establishes the students in the class and consists of the following data:

Social security number (9 digits)
Student last name   (10 characters)
Student first name   (10 characters)

The menu screen to produce this file is shown below. Students are not permitted to add or drop after the first test is given. Note that after the STUDENTS file is created and additions/deletions are made, it is sorted by social security number. The "Grade Program," option 5, is then used to enter and record grades.

```
            Student Grade Program

                    By
                Your Name

          SET UP STUDENTS FILE

        1  Create New File
        2  Add Record to File
        3  Delete Record From File
        4  Sort File
        5  Run Grades Program

           Your Selection?
```

The second program is the grade program that reads the STUDENTS file and creates a file called GRADES containing the contents of the STUDENTS file, as well as the grades received. Although this is a lengthy program, the menu screen is relatively simple as can be seen below.

```
            Student Grade Program

                    By
                Your Name

       GRADE ENTRY/PRINT PROGRAM

        1  Enter Scores
        2  Print Scores
        3  Exit to BASIC

           Your Selection?
```

Sub Menu Screen 1, Enter Scores.   In this screen, the user is prompted for the test number (1, 2, 3, 4, or final exam). The screen then shows the social security number, the name of the student, and the test scores to date. The instructor types the current test score (0 to 100) and presses Enter.

```
Social Security No.:
Last Name:
First Name:
Grades to date:
Test #1    Test #2    Test #3    Test #4    Final


Enter current test score:
```

On the first test, the GRADES file is created, based on the contents of the STUDENTS file. The STUDENTS file is not used again as the GRADES file contains all the needed data. After all scores are entered, the teacher is then asked if the GRADES file is to be updated.
Hint: Write the data into a TEMP file, then change into the GRADES file.

Sub Menu Screen 2, Print Scores.   This sub menu is used to print the test scores by social security number for all tests assigned. Test scores are entered after each test. The program computes the average score and the results are displayed in the format shown below. Then, after completion of the final exam, the letter grade in the course is computed and displayed.

Social security number	– – – Test #1	Test #2	Grades received Test #3	Test #4	– – – Final exam	Average score	Grade in course
xx	xx	xx	xx	xx	xx	xx	xx
.	.	.	.	.	.	.	.
.	.	.	.	.	.	.	.
xx	xx	xx	xx	xx	xx	xx	xx

Date Grades Prepared: mm/dd/yy

Technical Note: A zero is assigned for either a zero grade on a test or for a missed test. However, do not print a zero for a test not yet assigned. Just leave it blank.

The course grade is based on four regular tests of 100 points each. In addition, there is a 100-point final exam (counts double) for a total of 600 points in the course. Grades are assigned at the end of the term as follows:

Grade	Points achieved
A	540–600
B	480–539
C	420–479
D	360–419
F	Below 360

CASE 25: THIS CAR STOPS AT ALL GARAGE SALES

Ms. Sally Ann Beasley is one of the nicest persons you could ever hope to know. She has a nice, sincere personality and is liked by all who know her. However, she has one problem that is beginning to annoy her neighbors.

Sally cannot pass a garage sale without stopping and buying something. She doesn't spend a lot of money, but she is totally hooked on buying something at each garage sale in town. The problem is that Sally has a normal-sized house, with a normal-sized garage. The garage quickly fills up with her purchases. So what does Sally do once the garage is full?

She then has her own garage sale to sell her numerous miscellaneous items. This enables her to earn extra money, so that she can buy at even more garage sales, and the cycle repeats itself. Unfortunately her neighbors are complaining about the traffic because Sally is now having monthly sales.

Sally wants to make peace with her neighbors and needs your help. She feels that everyone must basically like garage sales because there are so many of them. If her neighbors made a little money by participating in her sales, then they wouldn't complain. She wants you to design a garage sale inventory system to keep track of all items received and sold by her.

Sally does not know exactly what programs she will need; she will rely on your judgment. However, she wants to enter all of the people in the neighborhood into a file called NEIGHBOR which contains the fields shown.

Neighbor code	Neighbor name	Phone number	Street address

Where: Neighbor code is a two-digit number uniquely identifying a neighbor.

All items received by the neighbors for sale are to be entered into a file called ITEM, which contains the fields shown. A price sticker is printed on a mailing label, one at a time as each item is received. This price sticker is then applied to the item to be sold.

ITEM file

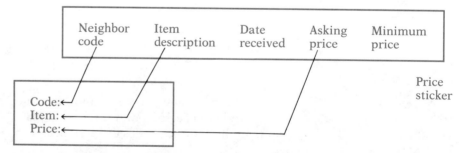

The night before the garage sale, Sally wants a printout of the ITEM file, sorted by neighbor code. This will permit rapid identification of a particular item if a customer wants a price lower than the sticker price.

CASE 26: DUSTY CORNER SURVEY

Two people are running for the elected position of mayor of the town of Dustville, Kansas. It is expected to be a close race with Honest John, a former minister, dominating the rural vote. On the other hand, Wyatt Earp, a former sheriff, has powerful downtown connections. Both people have been around for decades and are very well known in the community.

Dustville's local newspaper has developed the brief questionnaire shown below to survey the voters. These results will be tabulated and used in predicting the next mayor.

The Dusty Corner Voter Survey

Ask respondent

1 Are you a registered voter?   [1] Yes
                                  [2] No

2 Are you registered as a?   [1] Democrat
                                  [2] Republican
                                  [3] Other

3 Whom will you vote for?   [1] Honest John
                                  [2] Wyatt Earp
                                  [3] Other/Undecided

The newspaper's political science editor wants you to develop two programs:

I. The data entry program
II. The survey analysis program

I. The data entry program. The data entry program is used to enter the data from the survey forms into a file called ELECTION. The program must have the capability of allowing additional surveys to be added to the file when necessary. They are planning on taking a lot of surveys (probably a couple of thousand) and single-stroke data entry is to be used. All input is to be checked to ensure that it is within the desired range.

II. The survey analysis program. This program is to read the ELECTION file and tabulate the results. The political science editor believes that voters are crossing party lines in this election. The output format desired is shown below.

Survey Analysis of Registered Voters		
Democrats	Total	% Dem
for Honest John	xx	xx
for Wyatt Earp	xx	xx
Republicans	Total	% Rep
for Honest John	xx	xx
for Wyatt Earp	xx	xx

The total column is the number of registered voters in each category. The percent column represents the percentage for either the Democratic or the Republican voters. For example, suppose 10 Democrats vote for Honest John and 20 vote for Wyatt Earp. The percent of the people registered as Democrats for Honest John is calculated as follows:

Percent Democrat = 10 / (10 + 20); which is 10/30 or 33

(Express the percent as a number, not as a decimal.)

CASE 27: HONEY DO

A wise man once said that there are three stages in a marriage relationship. The first is the romance and a permanent relationship. The second is the growth stage where a family is raised. The third is the "honey do" stage.

This stage occurs when a spouse has so many chores to be performed that every other sentence seems to begin with "Honey, would you please do . . ." and then the chore. Eventually, this familiar honey-do message is met with a smile and quickly forgotten. The problem is that what is forgotten may be an important chore.

Your spouse has found out that you can develop BASIC programs to process sequential files. He/she wants you to create a program that will perform the functions as shown in the screen.

```
Honey Do Chores/Jobs Program

                By
            Your Name


 1   Add Job to File
 2   Record Completed Jobs
 3   Delete Job From File
 4   Job Status Report
 5   End Program

     Your Selection?
```

The selection of "Add Job to File" automatically creates a new HONEY.DO file or appends the file if it has already been created. Of particular concern is the selection "Job Status Report"; this lists the jobs to be completed. The program should be capable of producing a report according to the general format shown.

```
              Honey Do Job Status Report

Type J for Job listing, S to Stop and return to menu.
Or, type month 01 (Jan) - 12 (Dec) desired.

Your choice? j
-------------------------------------------------------------------
Job                   Beginning    Ending      Comments/
Description           Date         Date        Ideas
-------------------------------------------------------------------
Clean bedroom         11/02/90     11/02/90    Stall, delay, stall
Paint porch           01/01/91     10/02/91    Buy paint on sale
Clean windows         10/20/90     11/30/90    Hope for rain
Till garden           06/01/91     06/20/91    Rent tiller
Repair lawnmower      10/10/90     05/10/91    Get help!
-------------------------------------------------------------------

Press any key.
```

APPENDIX B
ASCII CODES

ASCII value	Character	ASCII value	Character	ASCII value	Character
000	(null)	035	#	070	F
001	☺	036	$	071	G
002	☻	037	%	072	H
003	♥	038	&	073	I
004	♦	039	'	074	J
005	♣	040	(	075	K
006	♠	041	)	076	L
007	(beep)	042	*	077	M
008	(backspace)	043	+	078	N
009	(tab)	044	,	079	O
010	(line feed)	045	-	080	P
011	(home)	046	.	081	Q
012	(form feed)	047	/	082	R
013	(carriage return)	048	0	083	S
014	♪	049	1	084	T
015	☼	050	2	085	U
016	►	051	3	086	V
017	◄	052	4	087	W
018	↕	053	5	088	X
019	‼	054	6	089	Y
020	¶	055	7	090	Z
021	§	056	8	091	[
022	▬	057	9	092	\
023	↨	058	:	093	]
024	↑	059	;	094	^
025	↓	060	<	095	—
026	→	061	=	096	`
027	←	062	>	097	a
028	(cursor right)	063	?	098	b
029	(cursor left)	064	@	099	c
030	(cursor up)	065	A	100	d
031	(cursor down)	066	B	101	e
032	(space)	067	C	102	f
033	!	068	D	103	g
034	"	069	E	104	h

ASCII value	Character	ASCII value	Character	ASCII value	Character
105	i	156	£	206	╬
106	j	157	¥	207	╧
107	k	158	Pt	208	╨
108	l	159	ƒ	209	╤
109	m	160	á	210	╥
110	n	161	í	211	╙
111	o	162	ó	212	╘
112	p	163	ú	213	╒
113	q	164	ñ	214	╓
114	r	165	Ñ	215	╫
115	s	166	ª	216	╪
116	t	167	º	217	┘
117	u	168	¿	218	┌
118	v	169	⌐	219	█
119	w	170	¬	220	▄
120	x	171	½	221	▌
121	y	172	¼	222	▐
122	z	173	¡	223	▀
123	{	174	«	224	α
124	¦	175	»	225	β
125	}	176	░	226	Γ
126	~	177	▒	227	π
127	⌂	178	▓	228	Σ
128	Ç	179	│	229	σ
129	ü	180	┤	230	μ
130	é	181	╡	231	τ
131	â	182	╢	232	Φ
132	ä	183	╖	233	θ
133	à	184	╕	234	Ω
134	å	185	╣	235	δ
135	ç	186	║	236	∞
136	ê	187	╗	237	$\varnothing$
137	ë	188	╝	238	$\in$
138	è	189	╜	239	$\cap$
139	ï	190	╛	240	$\equiv$
140	î	191	┐	241	$\pm$
141	ì	192	└	242	$\geq$
142	Ä	193	┴	243	$\leq$
143	Å	194	┬	244	⌠
144	É	195	├	245	⌡
145	æ	196	─	246	$\div$
146	Æ	197	┼	247	$\approx$
147	ô	198	╞	248	°
148	ö	199	╟	249	•
149	ò	200	╚	250	·
150	û	201	╔	251	$\sqrt{}$
151	ù	202	╩	252	ⁿ
152	ÿ	203	╦	253	²
153	Ö	204	╠	254	■
154	Ü	205	═	255	(blank 'FF')
155	¢				

APPENDIX
THE COMPANION
DISKETTE

This disk is for an IBM PC or compatible with 128K or more of memory, monochrome, or graphics monitor, dual-sided drive, and any PC DOS (2.X, or 3.X). This disk does not contain the BASIC language or the system files. These must be transferred from the PC DOS system disk (the system master) onto this disk. This process is performed at the DOS level. If A> is not displayed, restart the computer by holding down the Ctrl, Alt, and Del keys.

TRANSFERRING THE SYSTEM FILES AND BASIC LANGUAGE

This disk has been formatted using DOS 2.1 with space reserved on the disk for the system files. If DOS 2.1 will be used, then follow the steps below. If not, copy the disk onto a formatted disk as explained in the next section.

1. Insert the PC DOS disk in drive A (the drive on the left).
2. Insert the companion disk in drive B.
3. Type SYS B: This transfers the system files to the companion disk.
4. Type COPY COMMAND.COM B:
5. Type COPY BASICA.COM B: This transfers BASIC to the companion disk.
6. Remove the PC DOS disk and place the companion disk in drive A. Type START to execute the tutorials.

COPYING THE COMPANION DISK

1. Insert the PC DOS disk in drive A (the drive on the left).
2. Insert a blank disk in drive B.
3. Type FORMAT B:/S This formats the blank copy disk (often called a backup disk) and transfers the system files. After formatting, type
4. COPY COMMAND.COM B:
5. COPY BASICA.COM B: This transfers BASIC to the backup disk.
6. Remove the PC DOS disk and insert the companion disk in drive A.
7. Type COPY *.* B: This copies the programs onto the backup disk.
8. Store the original BASIC Programming With the IBM PC (the companion disk) in a safe place. Then place the backup disk in drive A.
9. Type START to execute the tutorials.

APPENDIX
COMPANION DISKETTE
FILE LISTING

This Appendix shows the first and last record in the files on the companion diskette.

BUZZWORD.ASC

Language	Type	Jargon
--	--	--

```
9000 DATA Pascal,   algorithm,              single entrance point
   :
9100 DATA LAST,     0,                      0
```

INCOME.ASC

Name	Age	Sex	Income
--	--	--	--

```
9000 DATA George Hunter,    31, m, 12000
   :
9999 DATA LAST,             0, 0,     0
```

SUPPLIES.ASC

Product number	Location code	Quantity	Price	Description
--	--	--	--	--

```
9000 DATA 700, 22, 225,     4.95, Disks-10 SS SD
   :
9270 DATA -999, 0,   0,        0, LAST
```

BUDGET.ASC

Pens	Tape	Staples	Paper	Typewriter
--	--	--	--	--

```
9000 DATA  370, 100,  110,  870,  400
   :
9900 DATA -999,   0,    0,    0,    0
```

PRODUCTS.ASC

Product I.D.	Description	Cost	Retail price	Begin inven.	Qt. sold	Location code
--	--	--	--	--	--	--

```
9000 DATA 003FU, Feugeot 27in mens 10sp #1,   94.34,158.95, 10,  3, 1
   :
9400 DATA  LAST, 0,                             0,    0,  0,  0, 0
```

WAGES.ASC

Employee name	Hours worked	Hourly rate	Age
--	--	--	--

```
9000 DATA Alfred Loveland,  40.50,  5.40, 19
   :
9150 DATA LAST,                0,     0,  0
```

`STOCKNAM.ASC`

Ticker symbol	Company name	Business and markets
--	--	--

```
12000 DATA ACV,    Alberto-Culver,    Hair care/beauty aid/boots
    :
12490 DATA GP,     Georgia-Pacific,   Plywood/lumber/paper/gyps'm
```

`STOCKNAM.ASC`

```
12500 DATA GET,    Getty Oil,         Major integrated oil concern
    :
13000 DATA LAST,   NULL,              NULL
```

`STOCKS.ASC`

Ticker symbol	1990 High	Low	1989 High	Low	Last sale	Earnings per share
--	--	--	--	--	--	--

```
10000 DATA ACV,    24.38,  10.88,  20.38,  13.75,  16.25,  1.02
    :
10490 DATA GP,     27.38,  13.38,  32.00,  22.50,  24.13,  0.41
```

`STOCKS.ASC`

```
10500 DATA GET,    65.00,  41.38,  73.38,  48.38,  71.38,  5.41
    :
11000 DATA LAST,       0,      0,      0,      0,      0,     0
```

`EMPSALE.SEQ`

Employee number	Sales in dollars	Sales code
--	--	--

```
140,1245.99,3
     :
107,11200,1
```

`CH19PAY.SEQ`

Employee number	Employee name	Life insurance	Monthly salary	No. of depend.	Years service

```
111,"Bill Smith",12000,1500,2,3
      :
172,"Sam Doe",2000,1525,5,7
```

APPENDIX
ANSWERS TO
SELECTED PROBLEMS

2.6 True. The last assignment to a variable name (i.e., the current assignment) is retained in memory.

2.13 These are correct statements. SUM is assigned the value of S, hence SUM contains the value of 27.

SUM

```
┌──────┐
│  27  │
└──────┘
```

2.21 Statement 30 should be 30 PRINT SALE

2.35 This is a correct statement. A variable can be a single letter (although it is not descriptive and therefore not recommended). A variable can also be assigned to a negative quantity.

2.49 Statement 20 should read 20 FIVE.PERCENT = .05

2.56 Statement 30 should read 30 SALE = 22.75

2.67
```
10 REM Problem 2.67
20 WEEKLY.PAY = 3.55 * 35
30 PRINT "The weekly pay is:"
40 PRINT WEEKLY.PAY
50 END
```

3.11 False! The space between TAB (20) will produce an error message.

3.21 Another day   another dollar. The extra spaces are due to the comma directing the output to PRINT zones.

	RATE	HOURS	PAY
3.28	4.35	10	43.5

3.32 Statement 30 should read 30 PRINT "The hours worked are:" HOURS .WORKED

3.36
```
20 PRINT TAB(17) "Student Enrollment"
```

3.41
```
100 PRINT USING "$####.##"; SOAP
110 PRINT USING "$####.##"; NAPKINS
120 PRINT USING "$####.##"; MEAT
```

3.45
```
40 PRINT USING "$$##.###";TAX
```

3.49 This is a correct BASIC statement, although the spelling is wrong (i.e., the program will execute correctly).

3.60 Closing quotation marks are missing before the semicolon in statement 30.

3.75
```
10 REM Problem 3.75
20 PRINT TAB(15) "Quick and Cheap Shop"
30 PRINT TAB(18) "Weekly Payroll"
40 PRINT
50 PRINT "Employee"    TAB(15) "Social Security"
   TAB(40) "Gross"
60 PRINT "Name"        TAB(15) "Number"
TAB(40) "Pay"
70 PRINT
80 PRINT "Mary Worth" TAB(15) "236-14-1856"
   TAB(40) "$235.75"
90 END
```

4.13 Simply retype the statement, using the same statement line number.

4.23 LOAD"ACCOUNT (i.e., the quotation mark is needed).

4.39 Two programs exist—the program in memory and the electronic duplicate saved on diskette called DEMO1.BAS.

4.44 Type BASICA to load the BASIC interpreter. Then remove the system diskette from drive A, insert your diskette in the drive, and type LOAD"CLOTHES to load the program into memory.

4.56
```
RUN
   75      ← The last statement 30 is used by the computer when
Ok            computing TOTAL.
```

4.64
```
 5 REM Problems 61-65
10 PAY = 40 + 5
20 PRINT PAY
30 END
OK
```

4.72 KILL "OHBOY2.BAS"

5.2 False. With the DOS System Master in drive A, the command to format a diskette in drive B is FORMAT B: (The colon is needed.)

5.22 The command that should have been typed is FORMAT B: The drive was not specified, and the computer is about to format the diskette in drive A.

5.37 Either type DELETE 45, or simply type 45 and press Enter.

5.41 Type SYSTEM, and press Enter.

5.44 10 REM Use of READ/DATA to prepare customer bill

6.13 30 DATA 55

6.23 20 READ ITEM$, PRICE, QUANTITY

6.25 60 PRINT TAB(20) PRODUCT$ TAB(32) SALE

6.28 MILES/GALLON = 20

6.47
```
10 REM Problem 6.47
20 READ STOCKHOLDER1$, STOCKHOLDER2$, STOCKHOLDER3$
30 READ SHARES.OWNED1, SHARES.OWNED2, SHARES.OWNED3
40 DATA "Will Free", "Karen Francis", "Brian Louis"
50 DATA 35, 14, 15
60 PRINT TAB(15) "Precious Metals Company"
70 PRINT TAB(16) "Stockholder Department"
80 PRINT TAB(14) "Outstanding Shares Report"
90 PRINT
100 PRINT TAB(14) STOCKHOLDER1$ " has" SHARES.OWNED1 "shares"
110 PRINT TAB(14) STOCKHOLDER2$ " has" SHARES.OWNED2 "shares"
120 PRINT TAB(14) STOCKHOLDER3$ " has" SHARES.OWNED3 "shares"
130 END
```

7.8 Statement 10 should be 10 PRINT "Today's date " DATE$ (i.e., DATE$ is a string).

7.15 Our car dealer is Glendale Ford.

7.23
```
30 PRINT "The current month is: " LEFT$(DATE$,2)
```

7.26 Five raised to the second power is 25, less 15 yields 10:
```
10
Ok
```

7.52
```
10 REM Problem 7.52
20 POTENTIAL = 1100 * (3.1416 * 4^2)
30 CUSTOMERS = POTENTIAL * .15
40 PRINT "The shopping center expects ";
50 PRINT USING "####"; CUSTOMERS;
60 PRINT " customers"
70 PRINT "out of ";
80 PRINT USING "#####"; POTENTIAL;
90 PRINT " potential buyers."
100 END
RUN
```
The shopping center expects 8294 customers out of 55292 potential buyers.

7.54
```
10 REM Problem 7.54
20 PRINT "Distance walked in miles";
30 INPUT X
40 FEET = X * 5200
50 PRINT X "miles =" FEET "feet."
60 END
RUN
```
Distance walked in miles? 2.3
 2.3 miles = 11960 feet.

8.15 The colon separates BASIC statements unless it is inside the quotation marks. There are at least two logical ways of rewriting this statement:
```
10 PRINT "Now is the time:  right now!"  or
10 PRINT "Now is the time"; : PRINT " right now!"
```

8.20
```
10 "Use of RENUM command
20 DOLLARS = 23.35
30 PRINT DOLLARS
40 END
```

8.26 3 shirts cost $29.14, including tax.

8.32
```
10 REM Problem 8.32
20 S$ = "$$###.##"
30 PRINT TAB(15) "Sam's Gravel Co."
40 PRINT
50 PRINT "Customer's name"; : INPUT CUSTOMER$
60 PRINT "Enter the tons purchased for each grade."
70 PRINT "Grade #1"; : INPUT G1
80 GRADE1 = 10.45 * G1
90 PRINT "Grade #2"; : INPUT G2
100 GRADE2 = 11.74 * G2
110 PRINT "Grade #3"; : INPUT G3
120 GRADE3 = 19.98 * G3
130 PRINT "Grade #4"; : INPUT G4
140 GRADE4 = 31.95 * G4
150 PRINT
160 PRINT "--------------------------------------------"
170 SUBTOTAL = GRADE1 + GRADE2 + GRADE3 + GRADE4
180 TAX = SUBTOTAL * .05
190 TOTAL = SUBTOTAL + TAX
200 REM
210 PRINT "Bill for:" TAB(19) CUSTOMER$
```

```
220 PRINT "Subtotal"  TAB(19); : PRINT USING S$; SUBTOTAL
230 PRINT "Tax"       TAB(19); : PRINT USING S$; TAX
240 PRINT "Total"     TAB(19); : PRINT USING S$; TOTAL
250 END
```

9.9 The TYPE command is a DOS command and is not recognized by BASIC. The contents of the file can be seen by loading and listing the file.

9.11 Enter a number between 1–255? 228
The ASCII character Σ has the value 228

9.17
```
10 REM Problem 9.17
20 CHAIN MERGE "BUZZWORD.ASC",30,ALL
30 READ LANGUAGE$, TYPE$, JARGON$
40 PRINT "Language" TAB(20) "Type" TAB(38) "Jargon"
50 PRINT LANGUAGE$  TAB(20) TYPE$  TAB(38) JARGON$
60 END
```

9.25
```
10 REM  Problem 9.25
20 CHAIN MERGE "SUPPLIES.ASC" ,30, ALL
30 CLS : PRINT
40 PRINT TAB(10) "Big Bubba's Supply Company"
50 PRINT "- - - - - - - - - - - - - - - - - - - -"
60 PRINT "Description" TAB(25) "Quantity" TAB(38) "Price"
80 READ PROD.NO, LOC.CODE, QUANTITY, PRICE, DESCRIPT$
90 PRINT DESCRIPT$ TAB(24) QUANTITY TAB(37);
92 PRINT USING "$$###.##";PRICE
100 PRINT "- - - - - - - - - - - - - - - - - - -"
110 END
```

10.11 Add a GOTO statement such as 22 GOTO 40

10.16
```
Stock # 2193 is less than 20
Stock # 2314 is less than 20
End of program
```

10.24
Sale	Tax	Total Sale
100	5	105
200	10	210
300	15	315

10.27
```
DATA 18875,18    Program output → Teen Ager
DATA 32750,47    Program output → Ok
DATA 26750,19    Program output → Ok
```

10.32
```
10 REM Problem 10.32     DATA Statements not shown.
20 CHAIN MERGE "INCOME.ASC",30,ALL
30 REM                   First data statement is analyzed.
40 READ EMP.NAME$, AGE, SEX$, INCOME
50 IF AGE <= 32 THEN 70
60 GOTO 80
70 PRINT EMP.NAME$, "Age is" AGE, "Income" INCOME
80 END
RUN
George Hunter Age is 31    Income 12000
```

10.39 See Chapter 11, Problem 11.37.

11.8 Add 42 READ WEIGHT, SEX$

Without a READ statement in the WHILE-WEND loop, only the values in the first DATA statement are assigned. Note: Even if this program is corrected, only "Ok" will appear when the program is executed because there is no value of WEIGHT in the indicated range.

```
        11.13  RUN
               Sale      Tax      Total Sale
               100        5       105
               200       10       210
               300       15       315
               Ok

        11.19  IF A = 4 THEN PRINT "A = 4" ELSE PRINT "A <> 4"

        11.25
```

```
10 REM Problem 11.25
20 PRINT "Enter sale amount";
30 INPUT SALE
40 IF SALE < 100 THEN PRINT "No free gift. " SALE "is less than $100."
               ELSE PRINT "Free gift. " SALE "is > or = $100."
50 END
RUN
Enter sale amount? 80
No free gift. 80 is less than $100.
Ok
RUN
Enter sale amount? 110
Free gift. 110 is > or = $100.
Ok
```

```
        11.29  10 REM Problem 11.29
               20 CHAIN MERGE"INCOME.ASC",30,ALL
               30 READ EMP.NAME$, AGE, SEX$, INCOME
               40 IF AGE > 21 THEN PRINT "Over 21 - " EMP.NAME$
                               ELSE PRINT "21 or under - " EMP.NAME$
               50 REM
               60 END
               RUN
               Over 21 - George Hunter
               Ok
```

11.37

```
10 REM Problem 11.37
20 CHAIN MERGE "PRODUCTS.ASC",30,ALL
30 CLS '                                       Enter target price
40 LOCATE 5,10: PRINT "Ajax Inventory Analysis Program"
50 LOCATE 7,10: PRINT "Target price -99 stops search";
60 INPUT TARGET.PRICE
70 IF    TARGET.PRICE= - 99 THEN 520
80 FLAG = 0
90 PRINT
100 PRINT "Description" TAB(35) "Retail" TAB(45) "Beginning"
110 PRINT "of product"  TAB(35) "price"  TAB(45) "inventory"
120 PRINT STRING$(53,"-")
130 READ PRODUCT$, DESCRIPT$, COST, RETAIL,
                  BEGIN.INV, QT.SOLD, AISLE.NO
140 '                                           Begin search
150 WHILE PRODUCT$ <> "LAST"
160     IF RETAIL > TARGET.PRICE THEN 170 ELSE 210
170     PRINT DESCRIPT$ TAB(34);
180     PRINT USING "$$###.##";RETAIL;
190     PRINT TAB(45) BEGIN.INV
200     FLAG = 1
210     READ PRODUCT$, DESCRIPT$, COST, RETAIL,
                  BEGIN.INV, QT.SOLD, AISLE.NO
220 WEND
230 '                                           End search
240 IF FLAG = 0 THEN PRINT "Product not found!"
250 RESTORE
260 PRINT "*** End of report ***"
270 PRINT
280 PRINT "Printed output Y/N";
290 INPUT ANSWER$
300 IF ANSWER$ = "Y" OR ANSWER$ = "y" THEN 320 ELSE 30
310 '                                           Begin print
320 LPRINT
330 LPRINT TAB(13) "Ajax Inventory Analysis Program"
340 LPRINT TAB(10) "Items with a retail price over";
350 LPRINT USING "$$###.##";TARGET.PRICE
360 LPRINT STRING$(53,"-")
370 LPRINT "Description" TAB(35) "Retail" TAB(45) "Beginning"
380 LPRINT "of product"  TAB(35) "price"  TAB(45) "inventory"
390 LPRINT STRING$(53,"-")
400 READ PRODUCT$, DESCRIPT$, COST, RETAIL,
                  BEGIN.INV, QT.SOLD, AISLE. NO
410 WHILE PRODUCT$ <> "LAST"
420     IF RETAIL > TARGET.PRICE THEN 430 ELSE 460
430     LPRINT DESCRIPT$ TAB(34);
440     LPRINT USING "$$###.##";RETAIL;
450     LPRINT TAB(45) BEGIN.INV
460     READ PRODUCT$, DESCRIPT$, COST, RETAIL,
                  BEGIN.INV, QT.SOLD, AISLE.NO
470 WEND
480 LPRINT
490 LPRINT "*** Report completed on " DATE$ " ***"
500 '
510 RESTORE:  GOTO 30
520 END
```

12.7 Statement 30 should read

```
30 NEXT INDEX
```
(i.e., not NEXT I).

12.19

```
10 REM Problem 12.19
20 S$ = "$$##.##"
30 PRINT TAB(24) "Jim's Bagel Delivery"
40 PRINT STRING$(60, "-")
50 PRINT "Customer" TAB(21) "Qt." TAB(30) "Selling" TAB(40) "Production"
                   TAB(55) "Jim's"
60 PRINT "name"       TAB(21) "sold"     TAB(30) "price"    TAB(40) "cost"
                   TAB(55) "profit"
70 PRINT STRING$(60, "-")
80  TOT.QTY  = 0  : TOT.COST   = 0
90 TOT.SALE =  0  : TOT.PROFIT = 0
100 READ CUSTOMER$, QTY
110 '
120 WHILE CUSTOMER$ <> "LAST"
130     PRICE       = QTY          * .5
140     COST        = QTY          * .3
150     PROFIT      = PRICE        - COST
160     TOT.QTY     = TOT.QTY      + QTY
170     TOT.SALE    = TOT.SALE     + PRICE
180     TOT.COST    = TOT.COST     + COST
190     TOT.PROFIT = TOT.PROFIT + PROFIT
200     PRINT CUSTOMER$ TAB(21) QTY TAB(28);
210     PRINT USING S$; PRICE;: PRINT TAB(38);
220     PRINT USING S$; COST; : PRINT TAB(53);
230     PRINT USING S$; PROFIT
240     READ CUSTOMER$, QTY
250 WEND
260 '
270 PRINT STRING$(60, "-")
280 PRINT "Totals:" TAB(20) TOT.QTY TAB(28);
290 PRINT USING S$; TOT.SALE;: PRINT TAB(38);
300 PRINT USING S$; TOT.COST;: PRINT TAB(53);
310 PRINT USING S$; TOT.PROFIT
320 '
9000 DATA Buck Smith   , 5, Bill Blaze,   2
9010 DATA Fred Herman  , 1, John Johnson, 2
9020 DATA LAST         , 0
9030 END
```

12.33
```
10 REM Problem 12.33
20 SOPH = 0
30 PRINT "Listing of Sophomores":
40 READ  S.NAME$, CLASS, HOURS
50 '                                        Begin loop
60 WHILE S.NAME$ <> "LAST"
70    IF CLASS <> 2 THEN 100
80     PRINT S.NAME$
90     SOPH = SOPH + 1
100    READ S.NAME$, CLASS, HOURS
110 WEND
120 '                                        End loop
130 PRINT STRING$(20, "-")
140 PRINT "Total sophomores:" SOPH
150 '                                        Data
9000 DATA John Dunlop   , 2,  40
9010 DATA Susan Smith   , 1,  28
9020 DATA John Jackson  , 2,  55
9030 DATA Pete Mears    , 4, 135
9040 DATA Alice Citizen, 2,  32
9050 DATA Mary Worth    , 2,  56
9060 DATA Susan Citizen, 3,  88
9070 DATA Alfred Neuman, 1,  15
9080 DATA LAST          , 0,   0
9090 END
```

```
RUN
Listing of Sophomores
John Dunlop
John Jackson
Alice Citizen
Mary Worth
--------------------
Total sophomores: 4
Ok
```

13.8 Values for CLOTHES\$, PRICE, and QUANTITY were never assigned to an array. Hence, QUANTITY(I) is zero. Add statement: 22 read CLOTHES\$(I), PRICE(I), QUANTITY(I)

Change statement 30 to the subscript I, not "1" as follows:

```
30 IF QUANTITY(I) > 4 THEN PRINT CLOTHES$(I), QUANTITY(I)
```

13.15
```
10 REM Problem 13.15
20 DIM SCORE(5)
30 FOR I = 1 TO 5
40 READ SCORE(I)
50 NEXT I
55 ANSWER = SCORE(5) + 3 * SCORE(4) - 10
58 PRINT ANSWER
60 DATA -12.2, 6789, 1.234, 3, 55
70 END

RUN
 54
Ok
```

13.21

```
10 REM Problem 13.21
20 DIM PRODUCT$(12)
30 '                                     Read array
40 FOR I = 1 TO 12
50     READ PRODUCT$(I)
60 NEXT I
70 '                                     Print in order
80 FOR I = 1 TO 12
90     PRINT PRODUCT$(I) "  ";
100 NEXT I
110 PRINT
120 '                                    Print reverse
130 FOR I = 12 TO 1 STEP -1
140     PRINT PRODUCT$(I) "   ";
150 NEXT I
160 '
9000 DATA Chairs, Desks, Ashtray, Pencils, Erasers, Staplers
9010 DATA Typewriter, Paper, Bookend, Calendar, Pad, Folders
9020 END

RUN
Chairs  Desks  Ashtray  Pencils  Erasers  Staplers  Typewriter  Paper
Bookend  Calendar  Pad  Folders
Folders   Pad   Calendar   Bookend   Paper   Typewriter   Staplers
Erasers   Pencils   Ashtray   Desks   Chairs
Ok
```

13.29
```
10 REM Problem 13.29
20 DIM STOCK.NO(10), PRICE(10), BOOK$(10)
30 FLAG = 0
40 FOR I = 1 TO 7
50     READ STOCK.NO(I), PRICE(I), BOOK$(I)
60 NEXT I
70 CLS
80 PRINT "Stock number";
90 INPUT X
100 FOR I = 1 TO 7
110    IF STOCK.NO(I) = X THEN 120 ELSE 180
120        FLAG = 1
130        PRINT
140        PRINT "We have the following in stock:"
150        PRINT BOOK$(I)
160        PRINT "Price: ";
170        PRINT USING "$$##.##";PRICE(I)
180 NEXT I
190 IF FLAG = 0 THEN PRINT "Stock number not found."
200 REM
8000 DATA 21, 42.95, BASIC Programming
8010 DATA 41,  9.50, The Family and You
8020 DATA 32, 46.50, Statistics is Fun
8030 DATA 12, 16.50, English as a First Language
8040 DATA 14, 19.00, Public Speaking
8050 DATA 55, 45.50, Psychology
8060 DATA 33, 58.50, Chemistry
8070 END
```

13.33
```
10 REM  Problem 13.33
20 DIM ITEM$(10), PRICE(10), TAX(10)
30 S$ = "###.##"
40 FOR I = 1 TO 5
50     READ ITEM$(I), PRICE(I)
60 NEXT I
70 CLS
80 PRINT
90 PRINT TAB(8) "Sales Tax Receipts Program."
100 PRINT TAB(5) "A 5% state sales tax is computed."
110 PRINT
120 PRINT "Description" TAB(26) "Selling" TAB(40) "Sale"
130 PRINT "of item"     TAB(26) "price"   TAB(40) "tax"
140 PRINT STRING$(43,"-")
150 FOR I = 1 TO 5
160     TAX(I) = PRICE(I) * .05
170     PRINT ITME$(I) TAB(25);
180     PRINT USING S$; PRICE(I);: PRINT TAB(38);
190     PRINT USING S$; TAX(I)
200 NEXT I
210 PRINT STRING$(43,"-")
220 '
9000 DATA "Car wax"        ,  6.95
9010 DATA "Motor oil/case", 22.95
9020 DATA "Antifreeze"     ,  9.95
9030 DATA "Window cleaner",  2.55
9040 DATA "Brake fluid"    ,  5.25
9050 END
```

13.35

```
10 REM Problem 13.35
20 DIM PROD(100), PRICE(100), DESC$(100)
30 CHAIN MERGE "SUPPLIES.ASC", 40, ALL
40 S$ = "$$####,.##"                              ' Print String
50 '                                                Counter
60 NUM = 0
70 NUM = NUM + 1
80 READ PROD(NUM), L.CODE, QT, PRICE(NUM), DESC$(NUM)
90 IF   PROD(NUM) = -999 THEN 110 ELSE 70          ' End of File
100 '
110 NUM = NUM - 1
120 '                                              Print Heading
130 LPRINT STRING$(50, "-")
140 LPRINT "Product" TAB(12) "Selling" TAB(25) "Product"
150 LPRINT "Number"  TAB(12) "Price"   TAB(25) "Description"
160 LPRINT STRING$(50, "-")
170 '                                              Print Data
180 FOR I = 1 TO NUM
190    LPRINT PROD(I)    TAB(10);
200    LPRINT USING S$; PRICE(I);
210    LPRINT TAB(25)    DESC$(I)
220 NEXT I
230 LPRINT STRING$(50, "-")
240 END
```

14.5   In statement 60, add a closing quotation to "Clips-Small".

14.16

```
10 REM Problem 14.16
20 DIM P.INV(4,5), PER.COST(3,4), COST(4,5), SIZE$(4)
30 CLS
40 '                                              Read labels
50 FOR ROW = 1 TO 4
60     READ SIZE$(ROW)
70 NEXT ROW
80 '                                              Read numbers
90 FOR ROW = 1 TO 3
100     FOR COL = 1 TO 4
110         READ P.INV(ROW,COL)
120     NEXT COL
130 NEXT ROW
140 '                                              Read cost
150 FOR ROW = 1 TO 3
160     FOR COL = 1 TO 4
170         READ PER.COST(ROW,COL)
180     NEXT COL
190 NEXT ROW
200 '                                              Compute cost
210 FOR ROW = 1 TO 3
220     FOR COL = 1 TO 4
230         COST(ROW,COL) = P.INV(ROW,COL) * PER.COST(ROW,COL)
240     NEXT COL
250 NEXT ROW
260 '                                              Zero totals
270 FOR ROW = 1 TO 4 : COST(ROW,5) = 0 : NEXT ROW
280 FOR COL = 1 TO 5 : COST(4,COL) = 0 : NEXT COL
290 '                                              Total across
300 FOR ROW = 1 TO 3
310     FOR COLUMN = 1 TO 4
320         COST(ROW,5) = COST(ROW,5) + COST(ROW,COLUMN)
330     NEXT COLUMN
340     COST(4,5) = COST(4,5) + COST(ROW,5)
350 NEXT ROW
360 '                                              Total down
370 FOR COL = 1 TO 4
```

14.16   continued

```
380       FOR ROW = 1 TO 3
390            COST(4,COL) = COST(4,COL) + COST(ROW,COL)
400       NEXT ROW
410 NEXT COL
420 '                                              Headings
430 PRINT TAB(23) "Smith's Produce Store"
440 PRINT TAB(22) "Inventory Cost Analysis"
450 PRINT TAB(14) "Melons" "       Pears" "         Cashews";
460 PRINT            "       Corn" "        Totals"
470 PRINT TAB(13) "(crates)"      "      (boxes)"
                   "        (Lbs)" "      (boxes)"
480 PRINT STRING$(70,"-")
490 '                                              Print #'s
500 FOR ROW = 1 TO 4
510     PRINT SIZE$(ROW) TAB(8);
520     FOR COL = 1 TO 5
530         PRINT USING "$$#######.##"; COST(ROW,COL);
540     NEXT COL : PRINT
550 NEXT ROW
560 PRINT STRING$(70,"-")
890     '                                          Data elements
900 DATA "Small", "Medium", "Large", "Totals"
910 '                                              Quantity
920 DATA        0,         2,         2,         2
930 DATA        8,        47,         4,        10
940 DATA       14,        52,        83,        98
950 '                                              Cost
960 DATA     4.10,     14.00,      1.49,     11.50
970 DATA     5.00,     18.75,      5.95,     12.25
980 DATA     8.95,     21.50,      7.95,     13.10
990 '
1000 PRINT "End of analysis."
1010 END
```

14.27

```
10 REM Problem 14.27
20 DIM SIZE$(4), TYPE$(4), SHIRT(4,4)                    Read in data
30 '
40 FOR I = 1 TO 4 : READ SIZE$(I) : NEXT I
50 FOR I = 1 TO 4 : READ TYPE$(I) : NEXT I
60 FOR ROW = 1 TO 4
70     FOR COLUMN = 1 TO 4
80         READ SHIRT(ROW,COLUMN)
90     NEXT COLUMN
100 NEXT ROW
110 '                                                    User prompts
120 PRINT                                              ' Shirt size
130 PRINT "Select shirt size by number.  -99 Ends"
140 FOR I = 1 TO 4
150     PRINT TAB(10) "#" I " " SIZE$(I)
160 NEXT I
170 PRINT "Your selection" ;: INPUT S
180 IF S = -99 THEN 970
190 IF S >= 1 AND S <= 4 THEN 230
200 BEEP : PRINT "Only type 1 - 4!"
210 GOTO 120
220 '                                                    Shirt type
230 PRINT "Select shirt type by number. "
240 FOR I = 1 TO 4
250     PRINT TAB(10) "#" I "   " TYPE$(I)
260 NEXT I
270 PRINT "Your selection" ;: INPUT T
280 IF T >= 1 and T <= 4 THEN 320
290 BEEP : PRINT "Only type 1 - 4!"
300 GOTO 230
310 '
320 PRINT STRING$(52, "-")
330 PRINT "The inventory for " SIZE$(S) " shirts made of ";
340 PRINT TYPE$(T) " is " SHIRT (S,T)
350 PRINT STRING$(52,"-")
360 GOTO 120
370 '
900 DATA "Small" , "Medium"    , "Large", "X-Large"
910 DATA "Cotton", "Polyester", "Blend", "Oxford"
920 DATA         0,         4,         3,      2
930 DATA        17,         4,        26,      0
940 DATA        12,        19,         3,      8
950 DATA        18,         5,         2,      2
960 '
970 PRINT "End of program."
980 END
```

14.27   Program output

```
Select shirt size by number. -99 Ends
        # 1 Small
        # 2 Medium
        # 3 Large
        # 4 X-Large
Your selection? 1
Select shirt type by number.
        # 1 Cotton
        # 2 Polyester
        # 3 Blend
        # 4 Oxford
Your selection? 2
-------------------------------
The inventory for Small shirts
made of Polyester is 4
-------------------------------

Select shirt size by number. -99 Ends
        # 1 Small
        # 2 Medium
        # 3 Large
        # 4 X-Large
Your selection?
```

15.6
```
10 REM Problem 15.6
20 DIM SALE(9), E.NAME$(9)
30 CLS
40 TOTAL = 0
50 FOR I = 1 TO 8
60     READ E.NAME$(I), SALE(I)
70 NEXT I
80 SWITCH = 0
90 FOR I = 1 TO 7
100     IF SALE(I+1) >= SALE(I) THEN 140
110        SWITCH = 1
120     SWAP SALE(I),    SALE(I+1)
130     SWAP E.NAME$(I), E.NAME$(I+1)
140 NEXT I
150 IF SWITCH  = 1 THEN 80
160 SWITCH = 0
170 FOR I = 1 TO 7
180     IF E.NAME$(I+1) >= E.NAME$(I) THEN 220
190        SWITCH= 1
200     SWAP SALE(I),    SALE(I+1)
210     SWAP E.NAME$(I), E.NAME$(I+1)
220 NEXT I
230 IF SWITCH = 1 THEN 160
240 REM
250 PRINT TAB(7) "Ajax Automotive Dealership"
260 PRINT TAB(13) "Sales Analysis"
270 PRINT TAB(16) "mm/dd/yy"
280 PRINT STRING$(38, "-")
290 PRINT "Employee" TAB(32) "Monthly"
300 PRINT "name"     TAB(32) "sales"
310 PRINT STRING$(38, "-")
320 FOR I = 1 TO 8
330     PRINT E.NAME$(I) TAB(30);
340     PRINT USING "$$######,."; SALE(I)
350     TOTAL = TOTAL + SALE(I)
360 NEXT I
370 PRINT TAB(32) STRING$(7, "-")
380 PRINT "Total sales:" TAB(30);
390 PRINT USING "$$######,.";TOTAL
```

15.6   continued

```
400 PRINT STRING$(38, "-")
410 END
9000 DATA "Smith, John"   , 28750
9010 DATA "Citizen, Susan", 12870
9020 DATA "Jones, John"   , 13214
9030 DATA "Worth, Alice"  , 49846
9040 DATA "Smith, Jack"   , 24876
9050 DATA "Brown, Al"     , 48750
9060 DATA "Smith, Mary"   , 42817
9070 DATA "Smith, JJ"     , 22750
```

15.22

```
10 REM Problem 15.22
20 DIM ANALYSIS(500)
30 PRINT "Program to sort, calculate average,"
40 PRINT "and identify above average values."
50 '                                          User prompt
60 PRINT "How many numbers to be analyzed (up to 500)";
70 INPUT N
80 '                                          Data entry
90 FOR I = 1 TO N
100     PRINT "#" I "Number" ;: INPUT ANALYSIS(I)
110 NEXT I
120 '                                          Begin sort
130 SWITCH = 0
140 FOR I = 1 TO N - 1
150     IF ANALYSIS(I + 1) >= ANALYSIS(I) THEN 180
160     SWITCH = 1
170     SWAP ANALYSIS(I+1), ANALYSIS(I)
180 NEXT I
190 IF SWITCH = 1 THEN 130
200 '                                          End sort
210 TOTAL = 0
220 FOR I = 1 TO N
230     TOTAL = TOTAL + ANALYSIS(I)
240 NEXT I
250 AVERAGE = TOTAL/N
260 '                                          Print array
270 PRINT "The" N "numbers in ascending numeric order are below."
280 PRINT "The average numeric value is" AVERAGE
290 PRINT "Above average values are indicated by *"
300 FOR I = 1 TO N
310     IF ANALYSIS(I) > AVERAGE THEN PRINT ANALYSIS(I) "*"
            ELSE PRINT ANALYSIS(I)
320 NEXT I
330 PRINT "End of analysis."
340 END
```

```
Program to sort, calculate average,
and identify above average values.
How many numbers to be analyzed (up to 500)? 5
# 1 Number? 12
# 2 Number? 11
# 3 Number? 15
# 4 Number? 17
# 5 Number? 9
The 5 numbers in ascending numeric order are
below.
The average numeric value is 12.8
Above average values are indicated by *
 9
 11
 12
 15 *
 17 *
End of analysis.
```

16.8

```
10 REM Problem 16.8
20 '                                         Reserve storage
30 DIM LANGUAGE$(20), TYPE$(20), JARGON$(20)
40 DIM RND.NO(6)
50 '                                         Chain ASCII file
60 CHAIN MERGE "BUZZWORD.ASC", 80, ALL
70 '                                         Assign arrays
80 CLS
90 FOR I = 1 TO 10
100     READ LANGUAGE$(I), TYPE$(I), JARGON$(I)
110 NEXT I
120 '                                         Begin RND #
130 T = VAL( RIGHT$(TIME$,2) ) + 60*VAL( MID$(TIME$,4,2) )
140 RANDOMIZE T
150 '                                         1st RND #
160 X = INT(RND * 10 + 1)
170 RND.NO(1) = X
180 '                                         Duplicates?
190 FOR I = 1 TO 5
200     X = INT(RND * 10 + 1)
210     FOR K = 2 TO I
220         IF RND.NO(K - 1) = X THEN 200
230     NEXT K
240 RND.NO(I) = X
250 NEXT I
260 '
270 PRINT STRING$(58,"-")
280 PRINT TAB(14) "Random Number/Word Assignment"
290 PRINT TAB(22) "Test Sample"
300 PRINT STRING$(58,"-")
310 PRINT "The five different random numbers are:"
320 PRINT
330 FOR I = 1 TO 5 : PRINT RND.NO(I), : NEXT I
340 '                                         Display
350 PRINT
360 PRINT "The five different languages are:"
370 FOR I = 1 TO 6
380     PRINT LANGUAGE$(RND.NO(I)),
390 NEXT I
400 PRINT: PRINT STRING$(58,"-")
410 END
```

17.2

```
10 REM Problem 17.2
20 READ A$                                    ' Assign A$
30 FOR I  = 1 TO LEN(A$)
40      X$ = MID$(A$,I,1)
50      PRINT ASC(X$);
60 NEXT I
70 PRINT
80 '                                          The message
90 DATA "THE WEEDS OF CRIME BEAR BITTER FRUIT."
100 '                                         Read
110 READ CODE                                 100 '
120 WHILE CODE                                ASCII code
130      PRINT CHR$(CODE);
140      READ CODE
150 WEND
160 PRINT
170 PRINT "Message completed."
180 '                                         THE
190 '
200 DATA 84, 72, 69, 32
210 '                                         WEEDS
220 DATA 87, 69, 69, 68, 83, 32
230 '                                         OF
240 DATA 79, 70, 32
250 '                                         CRIME
260 DATA 67, 82, 73, 77, 69, 32
270 '                                         BEAR
280 DATA 66, 69, 65, 82, 32
290 '                                         BITTER
300 DATA 66, 73, 84, 84, 69, 82, 32
310 '                                         FRUIT
320 DATA 70, 82, 85, 73, 84, 46
330 '                                         End of data
340 DATA 00
350 END
```

```
 84   72   69   32   87   69   69   68   83   32   79   70   32   67   82   73   77
 69   32   66   69   65   82   32   66   73   84   84   69   82   32   70   82   85
 73   84   46
THE WEEDS OF CRIME BEAR BITTER FRUIT.
Message completed.
```

18.8

```
10 REM Problem 18.8
20 FILE$ = "A:TRUCKS"
30 OPEN FILE$ FOR OUTPUT AS #1
40 FOR I = 1 TO 5
50      READ      MODEL$, YEAR
60      WRITE #1, MODEL$, YEAR
70 NEXT I
80 CLOSE #1
90 PRINT "File " FILE$ " created."
100 '
9000 DATA Dump truck,    1987
9010 DATA Half ton,      1983
9020 DATA 18 Wheeler,    1982
9030 DATA Four door,     1986
9040 DATA Cement truck,  1980
9050 END
```

18.9

```
10 REM Problem 18.9
20 CHAIN MERGE "BUZZWORD.ASC",30,ALL
30 READ LANGUAGE$, TYPE$, JARGON$
40 FILE$ = "BUZZWORD.SEQ"
50 OPEN FILE$ FOR OUTPUT AS #1
60 '
70 PRINT "Writing records into sequential file " FILE$
80 '                                             Begin loop
90 WHILE LANGUAGE$ <> "LAST"
100     WRITE #1, LANGUAGE$, TYPE$, JARGON$
110     READ     LANGUAGE$, TYPE$, JARGON$
120 WEND
130 CLOSE #1
140 '                                             End loop
150 PRINT "File " FILE$ " created."
160 END
```

18.9A

```
10 REM Problem 18.9A
20 FILE$ = "BUZZWORD.SEQ"
30 OPEN FILE$ FOR INPUT AS #1
40 '                                             Print Heading
50 PRINT STRING$(65,"-")
60 PRINT TAB(10) "Contents of " FILE$ " sequential file:"
70 PRINT "Language" TAB(19) "Type" TAB(49) "Jargon"
80 PRINT STRING$(65,"-")
90 '                                             Begin loop
100 WHILE EOF(1) <> -1
110     INPUT #1, LANGUAGE$, TYPE$, JARGON$
120     PRINT LANGUAGE$ TAB(12) TYPE$ TAB(42) JARGON$
130 WEND
140 CLOSE #1
150 '                                             End loop
160 PRINT STRING$(65,"-")
170 PRINT "File " FILE$ " read."
180 END
```

19.1

```
10 REM Problem 19.1
20 FILE$ = "CH19SALE.SEQ"
30 PRINT "The first three records in the " FILE$ " file:"
40 PRINT STRING$(49, "-")
50 OPEN FILE$ FOR INPUT AS #1
60 FOR I = 1 TO 3
70     IF EOF(1) THEN 110
80     LINE INPUT #1, A$
90     PRINT TAB(15) A$
100 NEXT I
110 CLOSE #1
120 PRINT STRING$(49, "-")
130 PRINT "End of display."
140 END
```

19.5

```
10 REM Problem 19.5
20 CLS
30 FILE$ = "WAGES.SEQ"
40 OPEN FILE$  FOR INPUT  AS #1                       ' Set up files
50 OPEN "TEMP" FOR OUTPUT AS #2
60 PRINT TAB(4) "Processing the " FILE$ " sequential file."
70 PRINT STRING$(47,"-")
80 PRINT "Employee" TAB(25) "Hours" TAB(35) "Hourly" TAB(45) "Age"
90 PRINT "Name"    TAB(25) "worked" TAB(35) "Rate"
100 PRINT STRING$(47,"-")
110 '                                          Check for EOF
120 WHILE EOF(1) <> -1
130    INPUT #1, E.NAME$, H.WORKED, H.RATE, AGE
140    PRINT E.NAME$ TAB(25) H.WORKED TAB(35) H.RATE TAB(45) AGE
              TAB(52) "Change  Y/N? ";
150    CH$ = INPUT$(1): PRINT CH$
160    IF CH$ = "Y" OR CH$ ="y" THEN 180 ELSE 360
170 '                                          Make changes
180    PRINT: PRINT STRING$(47, "*")
190    PRINT "Press Enter to continue, or space back and retype."
200    PRINT "Employee name:"
210        PRINT E.NAME$;
220        LINE INPUT A$
230        IF A$ = "" THEN 240 ELSE E.NAME$ = A$
240    PRINT "Hours Worked:"
250        PRINT H.WORKED;
260        LINE INPUT A$
270        IF A$ = "" THEN 280 ELSE H.WORKED = VAL(A$)
280    PRINT "Hourly rate:"
290        PRINT H.RATE;
300        LINE INPUT A$
310        IF A$ = "" THEN 320 ELSE H.RATE = VAL(A$)
320    PRINT "Age:"
330        PRINT AGE;
340        LINE INPUT A$
350        IF A$ = "" THEN 360 ELSE AGE = VAL(A$)
360    WRITE #2, E.NAME$, H.WORKED, H.RATE, AGE
370 WEND
380 '
390 CLOSE #1, #2
400 KILL FILE$                                ' Be careful of this
410 NAME "TEMP" AS FILE$                       ' Update FILE$
420 PRINT STRING$(47,"-")
430 '
440 PRINT "Display the revised " FILE$ " file Y/N";
450 INPUT ANS$
460 IF ANS$ = "Y" OR ANS$ = "y" THEN 480 ELSE 560
470 '
480 OPEN FILE$  FOR INPUT  AS #1                 ' Set up files
490 PRINT "Employee" TAB(25) "Hours"  TAB(35) "Hourly" TAB(45) "Age"
500 PRINT "Name"    TAB(25) "Worked" TAB(35) "Rate"
510 WHILE EOF <> -1
520    INPUT #1, E.NAME$, H.WORKED, H.RATE, AGE
530    PRINT E.NAME$ TAB(25) H.WORKED TAB(35) H.RATE TAB(45) AGE
540 WEND
550 CLOSE #1
560 PRINT "End of processing."
570 END
```

20.1

```
10 REM Problem 20.1
20 '                                    Set up file
30 FILE$ = "GRADES.RND"
40 OPEN FILE$ AS #1 LEN = 12
50 FIELD #1, 11 AS F1$, 1 AS F2$
60 '                                    Create file
70 FOR INDEX = 1 TO 9
80     READ F1.STUDENT$, F2.GRADE$
90     LSET F1$ = F1.STUDENT$
100    LSET F2$ = F2.GRADE$
110    PUT #1, INDEX
120 NEXT INDEX
130 '                                   Close file
140 CLOSE #1
150 PRINT "File " FILE$ " created and closed."
160 '
9000 DATA Johnson,        B
9010 DATA Smith,          C
9020 DATA Allbright,      A
9030 DATA Worthington,    A
9040 DATA McDonnald,      F
9050 DATA Myers,          D
9060 DATA Liveright,      B
9070 DATA Thomas,         C
9080 DATA Citizen,        D
9090 '
9100 END
```

INDEX